BALTIMORE

MATTHEW A. CRENSON

BALTIMORE

A Political History

Johns Hopkins University Press | Baltimore

© 2017 Johns Hopkins University Press
All rights reserved. Published 2017
Printed in the United States of America on acid-free paper
9 8 7 6 5 4 3 2 1

Johns Hopkins University Press
2715 North Charles Street
Baltimore, Maryland 21218-4363
www.press.jhu.edu

Library of Congress Cataloging-in-Publication Data

Names: Crenson, Matthew A., 1943– author.
Title: Baltimore : a political history / Matthew A. Crenson.
Other titles: A political history
Description: Baltimore : Johns Hopkins University Press, [2016] | Includes bibliographical
    references and index.
Identifiers: LCCN 2016025744| ISBN 9781421422060 (hardcover : alk. paper) |
    ISBN 9781421422077 (electronic) | ISBN 1421422069 (hardcover : alk. paper) |
    ISBN 1421422077 (electronic)
Subjects: LCSH: Baltimore (Md.)—History. | Baltimore (Md.)—Politics and government. |
    Baltimore (Md.)—Race relations.
Classification: LCC F189.B14 C74 2016 | DDC 975.2/6—dc23
LC record available at https://lccn.loc.gov/2016025744

A catalog record for this book is available from the British Library.

*Special discounts are available for bulk purchases of this book. For more information, please
contact Special Sales at 410-516-6936 or specialsales@press.jhu.edu.*

Johns Hopkins University Press uses environmentally friendly book materials, including
recycled text paper that is composed of at least 30 percent post-consumer waste, whenever
possible.

To Mac, Maxine, Gus, and Sam

CONTENTS

BALTIMORE

M Y PARENTS MOVED to Baltimore from the Bronx before I was born. I learned to talk from them. Their kind of talk marked me indelibly as a foreigner in Baltimore, where the local accent was practically a whole different language. This and my family connections in New York prevented me from becoming fully Baltimorean.

At age 20, I left for Chicago, where I soon began to have repeated dreams about various Baltimore street intersections. Much later, I learned what the dreams may have meant. Urban geographer Robert Sack writes that the sense of place usually lies below the level of conscious thought so long as you occupy your place. By remaining subconscious, it serves a practical purpose. Place-bound inhabitants can concentrate more fully on going about their business because they need not think much about where they are while going about. Sack adds, however, that the sense of place rises into consciousness once you leave your place or lose it.[1] That, apparently, is why my dreams of Baltimore emerged when I reached Chicago. I had discovered my sense of place.

The sense of place, of course, is not just a dream. Students of place-hood frequently describe it as "the personality of a location,"[2] and the connection between place and personality has deep roots. Just over a century ago, Edward Hungerford published *The Personality of American Cities*.[3] Hungerford spent most of his career riding and writing about railroads (including a two-volume history of the Baltimore & Ohio). His travels from town to town may have sharpened his perception of intercity differences, from which he composed distinct urban personalities. Hungerford never explained what it meant for cities to have personalities, but he was convinced that they did. The conviction persists among people who fill out online questionnaires to find the city whose personality best matches their own.[4]

Urban sociologists have attempted to identify the mechanisms by which cities acquire and maintain distinctive characters or traditions—approximations of Hungerford's urban personalities. Stated simply, they suggest that the past constrains the present. Past events and decisions foreclose some avenues of development and send cities down progressively narrower channels toward their current circumstances.[5]

History, in other words, endows places with personalities. Human geographer Yi-fu Tuan maintains that the ownership of a particular history distinguishes meaningful place from featureless space. Space, writes Tuan, is "that which allows movement." Place emerges when movement is suspended and we come to rest: "place is pause; each pause in movement makes it possible for location to be transformed into place."[6] Pause allows for the passage of time, and inhabiting a space over time endows it with a history, which transforms mere space or location into a distinctive place. A philosopher, Edward S. Casey, offers a different formulation. Our consciousness of place, he argues, precedes our awareness of space, and we experience a place not as a pause in movement but precisely by moving around in it. Our purposive movements carry us through a succession of places that leave their impressions on us even as we invest them with meaning and memory. This is approximately how we experience a city—as a connected succession of places. In Casey's rendition, "places gather." They "gather experiences and histories, even languages and thoughts."[7]

Still, for Casey and Tuan, the particularity of place remains peculiarly abstract. They are not unusual. Theorists of urbanism discuss the particularity of place without concentrating on any place in particular. The sense of place is essential to our experience of cities, but its particularity is an inconvenient distraction for any enterprise that seeks theoretical generalizations about cities or explanations of urban life at large. Recent movements in urban history, sociology, and political science have all tended to marginalize placehood.[8]

The particularity of local politics is all but dismissed. Restrictions imposed by state and federal governments constrain cities from above, as do the requirements that come with intergovernmental grants-in-aid. Variability among cities is further limited by their competition with one another for corporate and individual taxpayers, jobs, and capital investment. Significant deviations in tax rates, subsidies, and policies tend to diminish as cities jockey with one another to offer inducements to current and prospective residents that can match those available in other towns.[9]

In spite of these constraints on the variability of urban politics, it was the political particularities of Baltimore that became compelling for me after I woke from my dreams of its intersections and found myself in Chicago. Chicago showed that what I had barely noticed or understood about Baltimore was distinctive and meaningful. Racial struggle was harsh and aggressive in Chicago, but strangely subdued in Baltimore, even though African Americans made up a much larger portion of its population. As an undergraduate in Baltimore, I had written a research paper on neighborhood Democratic clubs. When I tried to do the same in Chicago, I was asked whether I had been cleared by city hall.

It was then—almost 50 years ago—that I began to collect material for this book about the political history of Baltimore, though at the time I had no idea that there would ever be a book. Local politics seemed especially expressive of the particularity of place. Political institutions provide an arena of engagement for the entire population of a town, and virtually every aspect of place and population is a potential candidate for the local political agenda—class, race, ethnicity, religion, recreation, location, water, fire, air, and garbage. While politics helps to define place, place is also essential to politics. It is the common ground for collective deliberation and cooperation, the "foundation for public life."[10]

My awareness of Baltimore's particularity advanced when I left Chicago to spend a year just across the Charles River from Boston, and then a year in Washington, DC. Once I returned to Baltimore, I noticed that local conversations frequently turned toward the puzzling hold that the town seemed to exercise over its residents—people like me. Still later, I looked for explicit indicators of Baltimore's distinctive status. Wikipedia, for example, provides a list of neighborhoods for almost every major city in the United States. Because neighborhood identities are imprecise, their enumeration is necessarily uncertain, as is Wikipedia. But Baltimore's status as an outlier is so pronounced that it overcomes imprecision. The size of Boston's population, for example, is not much different from Baltimore's. It has 105 neighborhoods. Milwaukee, Memphis, Denver, and Oklahoma City are also similar in size to Baltimore. According to Wikipedia, Milwaukee has 50 neighborhoods; Denver, 78; Memphis, 70; Oklahoma City, 25. Baltimore has 300. Even Chicago, the so-called City of Neighborhoods,[11] with three times the land area and four times the population of Baltimore, has only 245 neighborhoods.

Baltimore has often been described as "quirky"—usually by outsiders. Baltimoreans, who live with the quirks every day, are less likely to comment on them. In a Google experiment of questionable scientific status, I paired the word "quirky" with the names of 20 randomly chosen American cities in a search to find out whether Baltimore was linked with "quirky" more frequently than other towns. Baltimore finished second after New York, but not by much. At 2.84 million matches with "quirky," it was only 80,000 quirks (about 6 percent) shy of New York. Atlanta was next after Baltimore, with over 200,000 fewer "quirky" citations.[12] Baltimore's 300 neighborhoods may figure in its quirkiness by offering a multiplicity of arenas for the development of eccentricity. Or perhaps the quirkiness of Baltimoreans prevents them from living together in anything less than 300 neighborhoods.

New York's leadership in reports of quirkiness is hardly surprising. With more than 10 times the population of Baltimore, it has more to be quirky with and quirky about.[13] On a quirk per capita basis, Baltimore would clearly come out far ahead of New York. But since scarcely any two quirks are alike, it is impossible to say exactly what this measure means. It does suggest, however, that Baltimore is a highly unusual city, perhaps exceptional.

Baltimore's 300 neighborhoods and its millions of quirks are likely symptoms of urban underdevelopment. The centralizing tendencies that operate to consolidate institutions and cultures in other cities have remained relatively feeble in Baltimore—probably a sign that other cities have achieved concentrations of wealth and political power far greater than Baltimore's. Baltimore has had no Mayor Daley, Robert Moses, Tammany, or Boss Tweed; no Rockefellers, Wanamakers, Wrigleys, Mellons, or Marshall Fields; no Bill Gates.

It follows that one of the city's essential personality traits is a municipal inferiority complex. This extends even to the urban elite. In 2004, Mayor Martin O'Malley complained that "the culture of failure has crept into many circles of our city . . . I don't know whether it's attributable to the loss of manufacturing, or the drug epidemic . . . Some of Baltimore's leading citizens don't understand it, but they are often the leading spokespeople for that culture of failure."[14] By itself, of course, the "culture of failure" is hardly unique. Cleveland, Newark, and other victims of deindustrialization and disinvestment must harbor similar sentiments of civic self-deprecation. Baltimore, however, is notable for its embrace of failure.

Thirty years before Mayor O'Malley decried the culture of failure, Russell Baker, who grew up in Baltimore and began his journalistic career at the *Baltimore Sun*, described his hometown as the "city of losers." James Bready, one of Baker's colleagues on the newspaper, offered his own assessment of Baltimore's status: "Of the five big cities in the Eastern megalopolis . . . we are the smallest. We don't have as much history, we don't have as many ancestors, we don't have as much money. We are an innocent city. We never surrendered to the success dream. We are a city where people don't think they are very bright." He was not complaining. Baker notes that Bready seemed to enjoy his enumeration of Baltimore's shortcomings. Like him, Baker finds that there is something to be said for losers. Baltimoreans' experience of failure has made them generally tolerant of human failings, moral and otherwise. They recognize sin as an elemental constituent of the human condition. The result, says Baker, is that they are not given to moralistic crusades. Theirs is a "permissive" city,[15] where 300 quirky neighborhoods can coexist in relative peace.

As might be expected in a city of 300 neighborhoods, there are other views about Baltimore's response to its internal disjointedness. Stephen Hunter, a Baltimore resident and Pulitzer Prize–winning movie critic for the *Washington Post* (after 20 years of not winning a Pulitzer at the *Sun*), sees the city's cultural fragmentation as a source of trouble. "The first thing to understand about Baltimore," he writes, "is that hostility is somehow encoded into the Zeitgeist, like a rogue strain of DNA. It's not that there's no there there, as too many Washingtonians believe. Rather it's that there's too many theres there and they all hate one another." When William Manchester was a reporter in Baltimore during the 1950s, he wrote a novel that gave voice to similar hostility—*City of Anger*—in which a thinly disguised version of Baltimore is wracked by racial, class, and cultural resentments. Baltimore's anger may also flow from its status as the city of losers. "Think of Baltimore as the second brother," writes Stephen Hunter, "eternally resentful of the attention his older sibling was born into. Or think of it as a deposed prince virulently anguished over what could have been if something hadn't been stolen from him."[16]

Though it is difficult to imagine Baltimore as princely, there may be truth in both the hostile and tolerant versions of the city. In a town with as many subcultural niches as Baltimore, some may be tolerant and others hostile. For the same reason, David Simon (*Homicide* and *The Wire*), Barry Levinson (*Diner* and *Liberty Heights*), and John Waters (*Pink Flamingos* and *Hairspray*) have been able to spin wildly different stories about Baltimore. "We are writing about different Baltimores," says Simon, "and they are all credible in their own way." The production designer who has worked for all three filmmakers concurs. Different as they are, he says, every one of the disparate trio portrays "True Baltimore."[17]

"True Baltimore" is complicated. The city of 300 residential enclaves is also reported to have approximately 300 drug gangs, most with territories embracing only a few square blocks. Hostilities across this intricate cobweb of contested boundaries have helped to give the city of intimate urban villages one of the highest homicide rates in the country.[18]

"True Baltimore" is also resolutely parochial. "She is not cosmopolitan," wrote Edward Hungerford, "and she is proud of that."[19] As a border city, Baltimore has occupied the embattled front line in sectional hostilities. Its residents may have embraced parochialism to insulate themselves from the larger national conflicts that threatened to crush their city. But persistent provincialism may also help Baltimoreans to avoid discomfiting comparisons with places more successful or favorably endowed, and to turn their attentions inward so that they can accept their city as it is.

H. L. Mencken cultivated an appreciation of Baltimore's backwardness. He detested boosterism and railed against expensive ventures in urban development—skyscrapers, for example. "Wasting millions on such follies," he wrote in 1934, "is simply not Baltimorish. Every enterprise of the sort is a kind of confession that Baltimore is inferior to New York and should hump itself to catch up. No true Baltimorean believes that. He accepts the difference between a provincial capital and a national metropolis as natural and inevitable, and he sees no reason why any effort should be made to hide it. He lives in Baltimore because he prefers Baltimore. One of its greatest charms, in his eyes, is that it is not New York."[20]

No doubt, some Baltimoreans will point with pride to post-Mencken feats of downtown development, waterfront renaissance, and resulting triumphs of tourism as evidence that the city is no longer Mencken's provincial town. But John Waters sides with Mencken: "No one's making a movie about Harbor Place or the aquarium, and no one's going to. The extremes of Baltimore is why people like it, and it took a long time for the city to recognize that. When I grew up, Baltimore had an inferiority complex the way Cleveland and Pittsburgh still do, but once we embraced and exaggerated the things that we used to hide, then people felt good about the city." Baltimoreans, in other words, are proud of their inferiority complex. In an address at a local Chamber of Commerce dinner, Waters urged municipal leaders to abandon their promotional slogans and recognize the essential truth about Baltimore: "This is the strangest, coolest, most peculiar city in America." He suggested that the city's slogan should be "Come to Baltimore and be shocked!"[21] Of course, no city official has followed up on his suggestion. Nor are there many cities, however, where John Waters would be the keynote speaker at a Chamber of Commerce dinner.

Baltimore is not just different from other cities. Every city is different from every other city. Baltimore is eccentric. It may provide a unique vantage point from which to observe what other cities have in common. Its history also offers a moving picture of the process by which cities become different from one another and develop their own distinctive "personalities." But the attempt to generalize from Baltimore's experience to cities at large may obscure one of the town's essential features—its particularity.

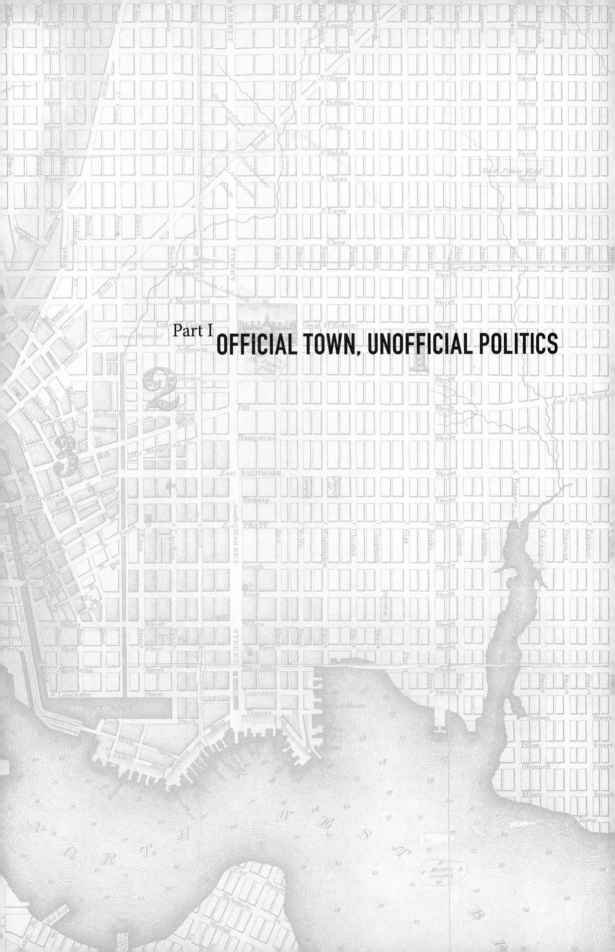

Part I **OFFICIAL TOWN, UNOFFICIAL POLITICS**

Chapter 1 **SETTLING**

BALTIMORE DID NOT BEGIN like other port cities on the East Coast. It was not planted on the continent by a band of transatlantic adventurers from the other side of the ocean. Instead, it drew most of its early residents, household by household, from colonists already settled in the New World.[1] The transatlantic adventurers usually had visions of the communities they wanted to create. Baltimore, by contrast, just happened.

The town was a late arrival. It emerged almost a century after the first British colonists landed in Maryland. The early settlers had little use for port cities. The Chesapeake Bay and its navigable estuaries gave most of them immediate access to shipping channels. Hardly any of the province's settlers lived far from a landing or harbor where British merchant ships and Maryland planters could trade goods. Some plantations had their own docks.[2]

The principal crop was tobacco. After drying, it was packed in hogsheads. Growers not fortunate enough to own waterfront property could hitch the huge barrels to teams of horses and haul them down "rolling roads" to landings, where they would meet British merchant ships with goods to exchange for tobacco. Even before Baltimore's official founding, ships sometimes anchored in deep water off North Point, about 16 miles east of the town, while locally owned sloops sailed back and forth from ship to shore, delivering goods and picking up tobacco from both sides of the Bay.[3] Across the Atlantic, in London, tobacco merchants provided credit and banking services for the planters of the Chesapeake. As long as the colony's population was concentrated in tidewater, the farmers had little need of a great port city to store and ship their crops, to sell them manufactured goods, or to bank and borrow.

Maryland was not hostile to cities. The provincial assembly passed 29 acts authorizing the founding of about 100 towns. Two of them were legislated into existence in 1683 not far from the eventual site of Baltimore, but neither seems to have attracted sufficient population to acquire a name. Many of these "towns" were actually tobacco inspection stations, designed to guarantee the quality of the product and maintain its price, and they had only a seasonal existence corresponding to the annual cycle of tobacco cultivation.[4]

By 1706, the legislature became concerned about the province's economic dependence on tobacco and sought to stimulate trade in other goods by designating a port of entry in each county. Three sections of Baltimore County vied for the distinction. To avoid offending any of the claimants, the assembly selected three ports, each on a different river. One of the sites, Whetstone Point (now Locust Point), was within sight of Baltimore Town's eventual location, but attracted little attention at the time. While politically expedient, the assembly's failure to settle on a single port for the county cannot have done much to concentrate population or economic activity. Six years later, however, one of Baltimore County's three ports—Joppa—was chosen as the site for the county courthouse.[5]

Joppa had few inhabitants until the courthouse went up. It was only then that the provincial assembly appointed town commissioners to lay out a 20-acre tract divided into 40 lots, which were "to be erected into a town." The assembly had recognized by this time that it could not will a town into existence by legislative fiat. To attract commercial activity, the assembly decreed that anyone who brought tobacco to Joppa to settle a debt would be allowed a 10 percent reduction in the amount owed. Tobacco and bills of exchange based on tobacco ("crop notes") served as currency in Maryland. Joppa became a favored destination for shipments of tobacco destined for London, and the town's prospects seemed to grow with each quarterly session of the court. It had little competition. Annapolis, the province's seat of government, was the only town of prominence. "As yet," wrote Baltimore historian J. Thomas Scharf, "no designation had been given to the significant settlement which had groped its way amid the creeks and marshes and under the hills of the northwestern branch of the Patapsco." In 1729, the assembly granted a charter naming those groped creeks, marshes, and hills Baltimore Town. Scharf's "significant settlement" had a population of 43.[6]

The political system that brought Baltimore Town into being was nearly feudal. Maryland was a proprietary colony, like Pennsylvania, but its charter was drawn up nearly half a century before its northern neighbor's. The Crown's grant of authority to the Lords Baltimore was modeled on the one that gave royal recognition to the Palatinate of Durham in the fourteenth century, but Durham's charter acknowledged rights and powers already in force centuries before. In a dispute about royal taxation in 1635, Durham's bishop claimed that the shire's privileged status predated the Norman Conquest, and an arbitration committee appointed by King Charles I affirmed that Durham was an "Auntientt Countie Palatyne."[7]

Henry VIII had asserted sovereignty over Durham, but the Palatinate remained a principality within his kingdom. The bishop of Durham occupied a "viceregal" office that retained the power to appoint a county sheriff, to take ownership of intestate land by right of escheat, and to establish courts, including courts of admiralty. Only a dozen years before the Lords Baltimore received their charter to govern Maryland, English legal opinion held that the bishop of Durham retained the right to create baronies.[8]

In theory, the Lords Baltimore held comparable powers. The Lord Proprietor both owned and governed Maryland. Taking up a "manor" under the terms offered by the Proprietor carried the authority to hold "courts baron" to punish minor offenses committed by one's tenants. But the attempt to exercise feudal authority in an era no longer medieval provoked a spirit of rebellion among the colonists, anticipating by more than a century the American uprising for independence.[9] The system had been designed for a settled, hierarchical society that rested on a population of submissive peasants. The footloose pioneers who had left their roots behind in England, Scotland, and Ireland were hardly so docile.[10]

Their willfulness came up against the concentrated authority of Maryland's proprietary government. Compared with the other colonies, writes Bernard Bailyn, Maryland seemed to have the makings of an "integrated, disciplined, and effective government." The Lords Proprietary were actively engaged in ruling their province; they controlled massive patronage resources in church, state, and real estate. But the very potency of proprietary power only provoked more insistent opposition. "Proprietary power," says Bailyn, "was prerogative power in its most extreme and obnoxious form: a land policy that was quasi-feudal, an executive jurisdiction that was 'Stuarchal,' and a cluster of social and economic privileges that seemed arbitrary and unnatural."[11] The result was chronic political turmoil.

Baltimore's town charter was as reactionary as the quasi-feudal government that issued it. The provincial assembly appointed seven town commissioners who would serve for life. The commissioners, not Baltimore's voters, were to choose replacements for departed colleagues.[12] The assembly authorized the commissioners to purchase 60 acres from the Carroll family (who had given advance approval to the legislation creating the town). The commissioners were then to have the land surveyed into 60 lots "and divided into convenient Streets, Lanes, and Allies." Finally, they were to sell the lots to prospective townsmen at 40 shillings apiece. The provincial assembly expected little more from the town's government. The commissioners were required to meet just once a year, and then only for the purpose of ensuring that the boundaries of the town's lots had "been kept up and preserved." There was little else for them to discuss. The provincial assembly had given them no authority to tax, legislate, or regulate.[13]

BALTIMORE DISCOVERED

The assembly had imposed an unelected government on Baltimore, and then gave it scarcely any authority to govern. At the time, no one seems to have recognized the troublesome potential in these arrangements. The simple exigencies of living together would create a need for government, but much of that need would have to be met by local improvisation outside the formal framework of public authority and occasionally in opposition to it. Public projects depended on private initiative. Early public works—a wharf, a bridge, a "market house"—were financed by lotteries or voluntary subscription, not by taxes.[14]

Such ad hoc measures may have been sufficient for a small town, and that was what Baltimore remained for at least a generation. More than a year after the town had been surveyed, the commissioners had sold only 17 of the 60 lots, and 11 purchasers forfeited title to their parcels of Baltimore because they failed to meet the requirement that they construct a house of at least 400 square feet on the property within 18 months of its purchase. Others never paid in full for the lots that they claimed. In 1747, the commissioners listed 25 lots of the original 60 for which the town had not received full payment. Asking purchasers for payment in full might have cooled the interest of potential settlers at a time when the commissioners' first priority was to increase their town's population.[15]

Baltimore Town was no boomtown. The settlement's site on the Northwest Branch of the Patapsco River was not the first choice of Baltimore's backers. They had preferred a location on Locust Point, a peninsula formed by the convergence of the Northwest and Middle Branches of the Patapsco. The Point stretched out opposite Baltimore Town on the south side of the Basin that would become Baltimore's harbor. The peninsula provided an abundance of waterfront sites for docks and warehouses. The provincial assembly had created one of its notional towns on the Point in 1706. But now the Point's owner was John Moale, who had found deposits of iron ore on his property and wanted no town to get in the way of his projected mining operations. Moale was also one of Baltimore County's representatives in the provincial assembly, where he saw to it that Baltimore Town would come to rest on someone else's real estate. With financial support from investors such as the Carroll and Dulany families, the Point became the base for the "Baltimore Company," which shipped tons of pig iron to England.[16]

The 60 acres on which the town finally settled offered little room for growth. On the north, a steep bluff blocked expansion. On the east were marshes and a river. On the west there was a deep gully. The site did not inspire great expectations.[17]

Two other settlements emerged nearby as potential rivals. Jones Town was a 10-acre village to the northeast, separated from Baltimore Town by a wide and rapidly flowing stream, the Jones Falls. The provincial assembly approved Jones Town's charter in 1732, "on the land where Edward Fell keeps store." Fell had arrived from Lancashire no later than 1726. He was a real estate speculator as well as a storekeeper. His brother, William, soon joined him. William was a ship carpenter and, while still a landowner and town commissioner in Jones Town, took up residence further south, on the Patapsco waterfront, east of the mouth of the Jones Falls. He opened a shipyard at "Copus Harbor," soon to be known as Fell's Point. His workers built sloops that carried passengers and cargoes around the Chesapeake. The water off the end of the Point was twice as deep as Baltimore Town's "Basin" and could accommodate ships of up to 500 tons' displacement, vessels of much deeper draft than Fell's sloops.[18] But Baltimore's hinterland would soon produce the cargoes to justify the construction of such large ships, and Fell's Point would grow into the third village on the Patapsco's Northwest Branch.

Baltimore Town prospered as tobacco prices fell and settlers moved west, along with the investment capital of the Carrolls and the Dulanys. Both families held warrants on extensive tracts west of Baltimore toward Frederick.[19] The land was not suitable for tobacco, and the German and Scots Irish immigrants who took up homesteads in Western Maryland knew nothing about tobacco cultivation. Instead they grew grain.[20]

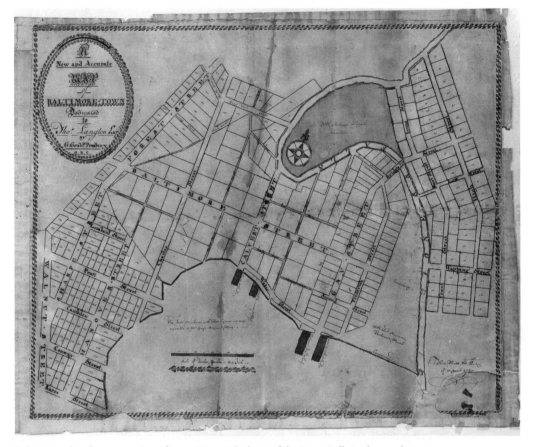

Baltimore after the annexation of Jones Town. The loop of the Jones Falls in the northeast flowed around a steep bluff about 50 feet high. The hill was later leveled, and the loop eliminated. The spacious lots at the center of the map made up the original Baltimore Town.

The first Baltimorean to grasp the commercial possibilities in the grain trade was a town physician, Dr. John Stevenson. He contracted with nearby farmers to purchase their wheat crops, then negotiated with ship owners to carry the grain to Ulster, from where he had emigrated; there, the cargoes were consigned to one of his old acquaintances for sale. According to William Eddis, a customs official in Maryland and a prolific letter writer, Stevenson's profits were so impressive that "Persons of a commercial and enterprising spirit emigrated from all quarters to this new and promising scene of industry."[21] Farmers in southern Pennsylvania west of the Susquehanna Valley found Baltimore a more accessible destination than Philadelphia. It saved them the ordeal of crossing the Susquehanna. Baltimore also lay miles closer to the grain-growing areas of the west than Joppa Town, the county seat, and it had a better harbor. By about 1745, a road connected Baltimore and the Monocacy Valley, near Frederick, extending the territory from which grain flowed into the town.

In the same year, the inhabitants of Baltimore Town and Jones Town joined in a petition to the provincial assembly calling attention to the towns' "contiguity" and asking that they "be reduced into one town by the name of "Baltimore Town." The two communities, of course, were still separated by the Jones Falls. A notable consideration in the case for merger was that the inhabitants had spanned their stream with "a good Bridge, which makes a very easy Communication between them, And proves greatly to the Service, not only of the said Towns, but travelers in general."[22]

Bridge building lay beyond the authority of the town commissioners, and nothing in their records suggests that they were responsible for the 70-foot span across the Falls. Some unnamed citizens must have financed the bridge or built it themselves. It was a product of private initiative undertaken to compensate for a deficiency in public authority. The motives need not have been public-spirited. The new bridge added considerably to the value of land at both ends. It carried a road that extended from Philadelphia through Baltimore to Georgetown on the north bank of the Potomac. Two years after the annexation of Jones Town, a wealthy merchant, Thomas Harrison, purchased 28 acres of marsh on either side of the bridge for £160 (sterling). The seller was a member of the Carroll family.[23] The legislature decreed "that the Bridge the inhabitants have built on the Branch that divided the said Towns, be for the future deemed a public Bridge, repaired and kept passable for Man, Horse, Cart, or Wagon, for the future at the Expense and charge of Baltimore County."[24]

The townspeople on the Patapsco made other requests in their petition to the assembly—needs that their town commissioners had been unable to fulfill. They petitioned the provincial legislature "that no Swine, Sheep, or Geese may be kept or raised in said Town unless they be well inclosed in Lott or Pen." The assembly concurred. Concerned about the accuracy and security of land records, the legislators also empowered the town commissioners to hire a clerk and to collect an annual tax of three pounds per household to pay the clerk's salary and the costs of surveying the expanded township. This modest enhancement of commissioners' powers was followed by an admonition. The legislature reminded the commissioners that funds from the sale of town lots could be expended only for "the Uses intended by the said original law for laying out the said town and in no other Manner."[25]

The assembly appointed a new set of seven commissioners to govern the newly consolidated settlement. At the beginning of 1748, the commissioners agreed to meet on the first Monday of each month, a more demanding schedule than the one followed by the commissioners of old Baltimore Town.[26] In 1747, the provincial assembly authorized Baltimore to annex an 18-acre tract between Jones Town and Baltimore Town, thus increasing the "contiguity" that had brought the communities together. The assembly approved further annexations in 1750 and 1765. The largest addition occurred in 1773 when the town absorbed 83 acres to the east and with it the village of Fell's Point. The three settlements north of the Patapsco had become one—with three disputatious neighborhoods.[27]

STRONG MARKETS, WEAK POLITICS

The town added territory more rapidly than people. Much of the new land was marshy and could not be occupied until it had been drained. A sketch of Baltimore drawn by a local resident in 1752 shows only 25 houses, one church, and two taverns, with a pair of small ships lying at anchor in the harbor. The town's population at the

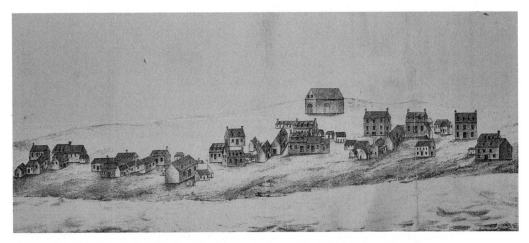

Baltimore Town in 1752. This sketch was made (from memory) by John Moale, owner of property on Whetstone Point, which seems to be the vantage point from which he made his drawing. *Courtesy Enoch Pratt Free Library, Cator Collection*

time is estimated at about 200. It grew rapidly as the market for Maryland's grain expanded beyond Britain to the Mediterranean, especially when European grain harvests failed. In the long run, however, the most reliable market for Baltimore's grain was in the Caribbean, where sugar had become the sovereign crop. It was so profitable that planters found it advantageous to import their slaves' food rather than divert land from sugarcane to food production.[28]

Baltimore's grain trade stimulated other businesses. The town's location on the fall line made it an ideal site for water-powered grist mills. It was more efficient to ship grain as flour or as baked biscuits and hardtack than to carry raw wheat. The flour mills, along with the biscuit and bread businesses, added jobs and profits to the town's economy. Baltimore wagon builders produced the vehicles that carried wheat and corn to Baltimore Town, and local shipyards built the vessels that carried these cargoes from Baltimore to foreign markets. As the town's hinterland expanded, many farmers and draymen would be unable to complete the round trip from farm to town in one day; local taverns provided them with overnight accommodations. When they set out for Baltimore, they had no way of knowing whether a ship would be waiting to receive their produce; an emerging merchant class provided warehouses to receive grain and maintained a supply of goods that farmers could purchase and carry home. The houses, inns, mills, bakeries, workshops, and warehouses needed for these activities all provided work for the construction trades.[29]

The grain trade transformed Maryland. The labor-intensive demands of tobacco cultivation tended to favor large plantations with slave or indentured labor. Grain was cultivated almost exclusively on family farms, with family or wage labor. And, while the tobacco trade had flourished without a port city, the grain trade created one. Larger tobacco plantations aimed at self-sufficiency. On the plantation where he grew up, George Mason recalled, "My father had among his slaves carpenters, coopers, sawyers, blacksmiths, tanners, curriers, shoemakers, spinners, weavers and knitters, and even a distiller." Smaller planters "contracted with itinerant workers or roughly skilled neighbors" to get the specialized goods or services that they needed to function or survive. The tendency toward self-sufficiency was especially pronounced when tobacco prices declined, as they did during the first third of the eighteenth century, and agricultural self-sufficiency was inimical to urbanization.[30]

By comparison with grain, tobacco was a low-volume crop. The same land area needed to produce 100,000 pounds of tobacco could produce 600,000 pounds of grain and generated a demand for shipping capacity several times that required for tobacco. The increased demand for ships enhanced the likelihood that a port would emerge where vessels could take on and unload cargoes and get needed repairs or maintenance. The same demand would support a shipbuilding industry and encourage Baltimoreans in the grain trade to become ship owners.

Most of the tobacco grown on Chesapeake farms and plantations went to a single destination—London—and London therefore became the focus of the tobacco trade. Its merchants financed the tobacco growers, its ships carried their crops, and its traders handled marketing and distribution. Grain, however, flowed from hundreds of small farms through Baltimore to a multiplicity of destinations in Europe, Britain, and the Caribbean, and so Baltimore became an entrepreneurial headquarters in the grain trade, managed by Baltimore's merchants and carried in Baltimore's ships. When the ships returned with manufactured goods from Europe or sugar, molasses, rum, and coffee from the Caribbean, they found a ready market among the farmers, bakers, millers, merchants, innkeepers, carpenters, and shipbuilders who were sustained by the grain trade. Tobacco made work for slaves and indentured servants, but they were not the kinds of consumers whose demand would sustain a lively two-way trade across the Atlantic.[31]

The Lords Baltimore took note of the profits being made in the town that bore their title. In 1746, the Lord Proprietor's secretary wrote to the governor of the province, praying to "learn again about reserved lands in and around cities and towns." The Penns, he said, had been farsighted enough to retain real estate in Philadelphia and its environs so that they could capture the rise in land prices that accompanied the growth of their town. But the secretary was concerned that Maryland's officials had not been "assiduous" in securing similar advantage for the Calvert family in the vicinity of Baltimore. The governor responded that the Calverts had never planned for towns, certainly not for Baltimore, whose growth and prosperity had been unplanned and unexpected. The lands on which the Proprietor now sought windfall profits had already been patented to private owners.[32]

The prospects for future growth—and the physical obstacles to expansion—prompted some Baltimoreans to manufacture new real estate. The law that merged Baltimore Town and Jones Town had empowered "any Person to make Land below the Banks of Baltimore Town and where the water usually flows." The legislature had decreed that whoever created new property by landfill owned that property. Local landowners took advantage of the opportunity "to improve into the water" and took up residence on a waterfront that they had refashioned.[33]

Town government saw no comparable expansion. The powers of Baltimore's commissioners grew modestly in 1747, when the provincial assembly empowered them to open new streets, hold two fairs a year, and deal with "nuisances." But it left the residents of the town in no doubt about their current and future political status. The assembly concluded with a declaration that nothing in its act should "be construed . . . to enable or capacitate the said Commissioners or Inhabitants of said Town, to elect or choose Delegates or Burgesses to set in the General Assembly of this Province as Representatives of the said Town. But it is hereby Enacted, That the Commissioners or the Inhabitants of the said Town shall not elect or choose any Delegate or Delegates, Burgess or Burgesses, to represent the said Town in any General Assembly of this Province."[34]

Baltimore would have no authoritative voice in Annapolis. It was a mere dependency of the provincial assembly. But the town commissioners made the most of the modest powers they had gained. Under the authority to deal with "nuisances" and the earlier statute regarding wayward swine, sheep, and geese, the commissioners contracted with one of their colleagues, William Fell, to build a fence of locust posts around Baltimore Town. The original plan requiring the animals to be fenced in had apparently proven unenforceable. There had been no one to enforce it. The commissioners decided instead to fence the animals out. Fell may not have been able to begin the task; he died soon after accepting the assignment. At their next meeting, the commissioners contracted with another of their colleagues to build a fence of "Oak Railes" around the former Jones Town. And, in 1750, they contracted with another commissioner to complete Fell's task of extending a fence around Baltimore. Financed with "Debts and arrearages" due to the town, the fence was designed to keep hogs, sheep, and geese from wandering along Baltimore's unpaved streets, turning them into odiferous mud wallows.[35]

The project failed for lack of public support. When the weather turned cold, Baltimoreans expropriated the fence posts for firewood. The commissioners took note of the theft and ordered their clerk to identify the culprits responsible for privatizing one of the few public works financed by local government. Among the suspects were Rev. Thomas Chase, rector of St. Paul's Church, and Dr. John Stevenson, the progenitor of Baltimore's prosperity.[36]

The commissioners decided to take legal action against the fence thieves by filing suit for damages, but dropped the case when they discovered that they were "not clothed with sufficient legal authority, and their inclosure was discontinued." The records do not specify the legal deficiency that prevented them from pursuing their suit, but the most likely problem was rooted in the town charter, which failed to designate Baltimore as a "body politic and corporate."[37] Since the town lacked legal personhood, the commissioners had no authority to initiate lawsuits on its behalf.[38] Above all, the affair of the fence posts reveals just how little authority the commissioners exercised over the town that they were supposed to govern. Baltimore would attempt repeatedly to regulate the wanderings of wayward swine, but for a century after the failure of the fence, porcine pedestrians would continue to walk the streets along with Baltimore's human beings.

COUNTY SEAT

Though politically underdeveloped, Baltimore continued to grow. Local annalist Thomas Griffith suggested that the town could thank the French and Indian War for its expansion. After General Braddock's defeat in the battle of the Monongahela in 1755, wrote Griffith, "the savages . . . got within eighty or ninety miles of the town, in parties of plunder and murder." By "preventing the extension of settlements westward," he claimed, the Indian raids caused many migrants to settle in Baltimore instead of moving further inland.[39] In the year of Braddock's defeat, the British expelled French settlers from Acadia, another episode in the global struggle between England and France. Like the Indian raids, the transformation of Acadia into Nova Scotia contributed to the growth of Baltimore. About 900 Acadians landed in Annapolis. They were distributed among several counties of the province, but none further west than Baltimore. Maryland's British authorities were apprehensive that if the Acadians settled as far west as Frederick, they might "find a means of communication with their compatriots in the French settlements on the Ohio River, and so prove to be dangerous guests."[40]

Just how many Acadian refugees became Baltimoreans, instead of Cajuns, remains uncertain, but they were sufficiently numerous to support a Roman Catholic chapel—the town's first—and the neighborhood where they settled, near today's Charles and Lombard Streets, was still known as "Frenchtown" more than 80 years after their arrival.[41]

Baltimore's growth accelerated. During each of the two decades from 1750 to 1770, the number of merchants in the town increased by 150 percent.[42] The general population grew even more rapidly. In 1774, just 22 years after John Moale sketched the scattered buildings that housed a village of 200, Baltimore had about 5,000 residents, and it would soon become the fastest growing city in the American colonies.[43]

Baltimore had displaced Joppa as county seat in 1768, but not without strife. Petitions to the legislature were printed as broadsides and crisscrossed Baltimore County, proclaiming the advantages and disadvantages that the two towns might offer to the county court and its clients. The pro-Baltimore sheets concentrated on Joppa's shortcomings. Its courthouse, according to one broadside, was rundown and "too small for transacting therein the Business of the County." The jail was alleged to be in bad shape as well, and not secure enough to hold prisoners, a "great Number of whom have escaped to the Loss and Vexation of Sheriffs and Suitors." Joppa itself was disparaged as a small and stagnant settlement located on a "low Penninsula the isthmus of which is so miry, as to be often nearly impassable, especially after high Tides or heavy Rains." The town also lacked the inns and taverns needed to accommodate the lawyers and litigants who attended court sessions, many of whom had to travel long distances to find lodgings, "whereby they are often exposed to the Danger of Catching Colds, Pleurisies, and other Disorders."[44]

The Joppans went beyond a mere rebuttal of such charges to disparage the moral character of the Baltimoreans. County elections had brought Baltimoreans to Joppa to cast their votes *viva voce*. It was on these occasions, according to the defenders of

Joppa, that the courthouse and jail were damaged. The buildings were "out of repair," according to one Joppa broadside, because of the "Interested Views of a part of the Inhabitants of said County in or near Baltemore Town who by Violence at a late and former Elections have torn and defaced the same with a design of Destroying the same and thereby paving a Way for a removal to Baltemore Town." The low motives of "a part of the Inhabitants" also tainted the whole. The Baltimoreans were "blinded by there Interest" and would drag "a great number of the most Antient and first settled Inhabitants" from their "distant habitations for the sole purpose of leaving some of there cash at Taverns" in Baltimore.[45]

The charges against the Baltimoreans were not groundless. In the election of 1752, at least one Baltimore candidate for the provincial assembly had appealed for support with so much rum punch that his partisans became disorderly. The sheriff suspended voting. By the time the election was over, there had been much fighting and two fatalities. The courthouse may well have been damaged. But the Baltimoreans' bad behavior did not keep the legislature from making their town the county seat and the site of a new courthouse.[46]

The new Baltimore County Courthouse, like earlier public works, was financed by voluntary subscription, not taxes.[47] It would stand prominently atop the high bluff that impeded the expansion of Baltimore to the north. A new county jail would be built nearby. At their meeting on June 30, 1768, the commissioners discussed the fund-raising campaign needed to pay for the buildings that would symbolize Baltimore's new status as county seat. They concluded their session by agreeing to meet weekly instead of monthly. They would gather every Monday evening at 6 o'clock "at Each Others houses by turns . . . and as Much oftener as may be necessary upon Notice given."[48]

INSTITUTIONS OF GOVERNMENT

The court that convened in Baltimore performed a variety of functions beyond adjudication. It levied taxes, oversaw the upkeep of roads and bridges, licensed taverns, maintained a standard set of weights and measures, and provided relief to the needy. The court's direct responsibility for poor relief ended in 1773, when the provincial assembly appointed trustees of the poor to oversee the construction and management of a county almshouse and workhouse. The site selected was northwest of the town, near the current intersection of Howard and Madison Streets. The almshouse was for those "disabled by sudden accidents, or otherwise totally unable to support themselves, and not merely the poor (who, in this country cannot suffer for a scarcity of bread or work)." The workhouse was to shelter—and discipline—"vagrants, beggars, vagabonds, and other offenders."[49]

The county court lacked the administrative capacity to manage the almshouse. It had only a clerk and a sheriff to carry out its will, which may explain why law enforcement relied heavily on citizen vigilance. For a variety of offenses, a citizen informant could claim half the fine imposed on a lawbreaker. "In a sense," writes Dennis Clark, "every citizen of the county was either actually or potentially a paid officer of the county." Their recruitment, he adds, was a judicial response to widespread lawbreaking and contempt for the law.[50]

As the province's established religion, the Anglican Church also had a governmental role. The vestry of St. Paul's Church in Baltimore was responsible (inexplicably) for nominating the local tobacco inspectors who were appointed by the governor. It also administered a tax on bachelors above the age of 25—an encouragement to matrimony. The church authorities bore special responsibility for punishing citizen immorality. Their domain embraced profanity, drunkenness, adultery, and fornication. To show that they meant business, the vestrymen erected a whipping post and stocks at the center of town.[51]

The circumstances of St. Paul's parish are likely to have complicated the exercise of ecclesiastical authority. Conflict between the church's first rector, Rev. William Tibbs, and its vestry began even before the parish had a church. The vestry accused the rector of being a common drunkard and charged him with neglect of his responsibilities to the parish—not because of his intoxication, but because he held another benefice in a parish some distance from Baltimore, near Joppa Town, and preferred to reside there. After making a futile appeal to the provincial governor, the vestry addressed Tibbs directly, asking him to send a curate to serve St. Paul's if he would not serve himself. He did so. But the curate, a convicted felon, proved unsuitable. The contention ended only with Tibbs's death in 1732. His successor lived just long enough to see the completion of the parish church, a modest building whose construction had taken eight years.[52]

St. Paul's next rector was preoccupied with his poverty. He was paid in tobacco, not coin, and since tobacco prices were falling, he found it difficult to make ends meet. He sent medicinal roots and surplus clothing to his brother in England. Their sale, he hoped, would augment his income.[53] He also speculated in town lots. When he died, in 1742, he held six of them, but he had not yet fully paid for his real estate investment and left his widow with a debt of £12.[54] But she was not destitute. Her husband's holy office was a material asset, and she would receive compensation from its next occupant. She and Rev. Thomas Chase agreed on a price for the position. Chase, however, fell behind in his payments and was imprisoned for debt. He was freed only because he could not perform his sacramental duties from a jail cell.[55]

Parson Chase's deliverance did not end his troubles. He and the Baltimore County sheriff were locked in a longstanding feud of obscure origins. Relations between the rector and the sheriff became so rancorous that when the two men encountered one another on the street, the sheriff knocked Chase to the ground.[56]

Taken together, the commissioners, the county court, and the vestry constituted the local government of Baltimore. They did not amount to much, and none of them were responsible to the town's voters. The provincial assembly addressed issues arising outside the purview of these institutions. Baltimore County elected two representatives in the assembly. Though its population was three times that of Annapolis, Baltimore Town had no representative of its own. Annapolis held two seats and, unlike Baltimore, was a self-governing municipality.[57]

Chapter 2 **GOVERNMENT IN THE STREETS**

Colonial Baltimore was politically stunted, and its impoverished public life set it apart from most other port cities in the colonies, where, as Gary Nash observes, "political life in general operated more vibrantly . . . than in the country because the urban communities required a greater degree of government, given their size and commercial character."[1] Baltimore was different. By the time it became a town, a provincial political establishment was already entrenched in Annapolis and was not inclined to grant sweeping powers to the upstart village on the Patapsco. Baltimore would be governed from Annapolis or improvise its own political arrangements.

In 1763, several dozen local merchants and tradesman formed a purely private association that would operate as though it were a local government. The Ancient and Honorable Mechanical Company of Baltimore could hardly have been ancient. It was mechanical because it enlisted many of the town's skilled craftsmen—"mechanics"—as well as its prominent merchants. Whether it was honorable was an open question. From 1763 to 1776, writes George McCreary, "members of the Company discharged nearly all the duties needed for the government of the town, its policing, magisterial function, and in addition, acted as firemen."[2]

The Mechanical Company opened the town's first schoolhouse and its first hospital. Since Baltimore had no post office, a member of the company received letters that came to the town and notified recipients by listing their names in a local newspaper. The recipients picked up their mail at his house. The company's members drilled regularly, the only organized force to defend Baltimore against attack. Quaker members of the company could not participate in the militia, but they volunteered for the town's night watch. The company also assumed responsibility for the regulation of public order and morality. Though it had no legal authority to do so, for example, it ordered the "ducking" of one John Brown in the horse pond "for ill-treating his good wife and industrious woman."[3]

The Mechanical Company was a new government—a government in the streets—which convened to remedy the obvious shortcomings of Baltimore's official political institutions. The company assumed responsibility for the maintenance of public order more than 20 years before the state legislature finally authorized the town's official government to hire its own constables and watchmen.[4] Since it was not an institution of government endowed with the authority to exercise legitimate coercion, the company often enforced its pronouncements through collective violence, like the dunking of John Brown.

Little more than two years after its founding, the Mechanical Company provided much of the membership base for Baltimore's Sons of Liberty, one of the organizations formed to protest the Stamp Act. The new organization had been born in the Mechanical Company's Lodge Hall at a special meeting of the organization in February 1766, the result of which was "the transformation of the Company into the Baltimore branch of the Sons of Liberty."[5] William Lux, a local merchant and member of the Mechanical Company, was the leading organizer of the Baltimore Sons. He had been corresponding with activists in New York, where the Sons of Liberty got their start, and with Stamp Act protesters in Virginia. In the protest against the stamp tax, Baltimore would become "the chief nexus between the southern colonies and headquarters in New York." Like other Baltimore traders, Lux refused to import British goods while the Stamp Act remained in force. He also informed his creditors in London that he would be unable to pay them until the Stamp Act was repealed. Such measures were designed to pressure British traders to lobby Parliament on behalf of the American colonists. But the embargo may have served other purposes. It helped local merchants to clear their shelves of unsold goods. And, since Maryland planters would have fewer opportunities for conspicuous consumption, they might accumulate sufficient funds to pay off their debts to local merchants.[6]

For Baltimore's mercantile community, the stamp tax was one more adversity following close behind low wheat prices in Europe and the rising debt to London's traders. Parliament aggravated these difficulties by approving the Currency Act of 1764, creating a currency shortage in the colonies by limiting their capacity to issue paper money. Bills of exchange served as a private currency by which merchants "sold" the debts that were owed them. But, in London, such bills traded at a discount because of the straitened state of the colonial economy.[7]

In concert with Samuel Chase of Annapolis, son of Thomas Chase, the unfortunate rector of St. Paul's, the Sons of Liberty spearheaded a movement to compel colonial officials to transact public business without stamped paper. Stamped paper was unavailable because the functionary responsible for issuing it had fled to New York in fear for his safety. The New York Sons of Liberty found him on Long Island, forced him to resign from his post, and earned a thank-you note from their Baltimore counterparts. The Baltimore Sons of Liberty were well represented at public meetings in Annapolis that finally pressured provincial officials to approve doing business without stamped paper, just days before news of the Stamp Act's repeal reached the provincial capital.[8]

TOWN VS. PROVINCE

The colony's next challenge to British authority would expose a fault line between the elites of Tidewater Maryland and the leadership of Baltimore. The Townshend Acts, approved by Parliament in 1767, imposed duties on paper, glass, paint, and tea. Popular sentiment from Massachusetts to Virginia supported the non-importation of British goods to protest the Townshend duties. The merchants of Baltimore were reluctant to go along. But after the commercial communities of Boston and Philadelphia fell into step with public opinion, pressure mounted for Baltimore's merchants to do the same.[9]

Baltimore's commercial community finally consented to a non-importation agreement in March 1769, a full year after Boston had initiated the movement.[10] At a meeting in Annapolis, representatives from all parts of the colony adopted a "Resolution of Non-Importation." The merchants of Baltimore helped to draft the agreement. It contained numerous exceptions allowing selected British goods to be landed in the town. The boycott never stirred the kind of fervor that had powered the movement against the Stamp Act, and its enforcement was remarkably lax.[11] The Stamp Act protest coincided with a downturn in the local economy that left many merchants and their customers in debt and hard-pressed. A suspension of trade provided them with the breathing space to retrench and regain their balance. The Townshend Acts, however, found Baltimore flush with commerce, and its merchants were in no mood to curtail trade.[12]

As in the case of the Stamp Act, Parliament repealed the Townshend Acts with the exception of the tax on tea, but the non-importation agreements remained in effect. Violations, however, became more frequent, and Baltimore's merchants broke ranks after hearing that Philadelphia had abandoned non-importation. Representatives of Baltimore's commercial class went to Annapolis to meet with delegates from other parts of the colony to propose the repeal of the non-importation agreement. They were received with open hostility: "the merchants and traders of Baltimore" were denounced for showing "a shameful Disregard . . . to the most Sacred Rights and Liberties of *America*" and endeavoring "to destroy the Union and Good Faith so necessary at this, and at all times, for the Safety and constitutional rights of these colonies."[13]

The rift was not entirely healed when the colonists staged their next confrontation with British authority—this one confined to Maryland. The dispute concerned the fees that the Lord Proprietor's officials could charge for performing their duties. As the population of the colony increased, the incomes of officials had grown fat. Delegates in the lower house of the provincial assembly insisted that the time had come for a fee reduction, but the upper house—a council appointed by the governor—included several officials who received fees, and the predictable result was deadlock. The governor prorogued the assembly and issued a proclamation authorizing a continuation of the current fee schedule.[14]

A pair of dueling essayists—"Antilon" and "First Citizen"—carried the ensuing controversy into the columns of the Annapolis weekly, the *Maryland Gazette*. They represented two of the wealthiest and most prominent families in the colony. Daniel Dulany (Antilon) was a member of the Governor's Council and provincial secretary. "First Citizen" was the young Charles Carroll of Carrollton, recently returned from several years of study in Britain and on the Continent. The debate between them began with an imagined dialogue, written by Dulany, in which "First Citizen" attacked the governor's fee-setting proclamation, and "Second Citizen," a wiser head, patiently defended the proclamation and exposed criticisms of it as groundless. Carroll surprised and enraged Dulany by assuming the identity of First Citizen, replacing Dulany's straw man with an independent and gifted debater.[15]

The rancorous newspaper duel went on from January to July 1773. Behind the exchange of invective, the antagonists were staking out the positions that would later be occupied by Tories and Revolutionaries. For Dulany, precedent was law, and the foremost precedent was the glorious settlement of 1688, which established the sovereignty of King-in-Parliament. Thereafter, the settled usages of judges, ministers, Parliament, and King supplied guidelines for policymakers of the future. By contrast, Carroll insisted on standards of political judgment independent of ongoing practice. "I would not have you confound Government," he wrote, "with the Officers of Government; they are things really distinct, and yet in your idea they seem to be one and the same."[16] First Citizen grounded his argument in the idea of a constitution—a government of laws, not men—that provided independent standards for evaluating the actions of public officials and distinguishing good precedent from bad. Carroll may also have had a more radical idea in mind. In 1763, while studying abroad, he had written to his father, "America is a growing country: in time it must and will be independent."[17]

Baltimoreans, at first, applauded Carroll's indictment of the proclamation and his contention that the fees unilaterally mandated by the governor were actually taxes that required the consent of the full legislature. In 1773, on the last day of balloting for Baltimore County's representatives in the provincial assembly, Baltimoreans assembled around the courthouse to celebrate the election of the new delegates. From the back of the crowd, a voice shouted, "No proclamation—hang—burn—and bury the proclamation." The celebration instantly became a demonstration. A mock proclamation was marched through the streets to the gallows, where it was destroyed. A few days later, Baltimore County's newly elected legislators published a letter praising First Citizen for his attack on the proclamation.[18]

In an odd turn of colonial politics, 106 residents of Baltimore Town, almost all of them merchants, signed a letter repudiating the one published by the county's legislative representatives. They also denounced the mock execution of the governor's fee-setting proclamation. "We are sorry to see any act of government treated with indecency, and in such a manner that can only inflame instead of healing, the animosities of the public." The members of the mob, they added, consisted of "the verie dregs of the earth."[19]

The Baltimore merchants did not fully explain why they opted out of the attack on the governor's proclamation. They may have had several reasons. One was their limited political experience in Maryland. Many were recent migrants attracted by the town's astonishing transformation from village to commercial emporium. Neither they nor their grandfathers had been parties to the more than a century of sparring between the gentry of Tidewater Maryland and the Lords Proprietary. Before Baltimore Town received its charter, Maryland colonists had risen in revolt three times against the Lords Baltimore. The third revolution followed the abdication of James II and accession of the Protestant monarchs William and Mary. In 1689, a faction composed of Protestant colonists took up arms against their Catholic overlord and, with little bloodshed, drove him from power. The Lords Baltimore would continue to hold property and collect quitrents in Maryland, but their political authority passed to the Crown. That was the goal of Maryland's early revolutionaries—not independence, but rule by King and Parliament.[20]

The rebel government made Anglicanism the colony's established religion, deprived Catholics of political and civil rights, and took possession of the offices and fees once monopolized by the Calvert family and its favorites. But the provincial assembly could not prevent the Calverts from returning to rule the colony in 1715. The fourth Lord Baltimore had renounced Catholicism and become an Anglican. That was sufficient to win the Crown's approval to reestablish proprietary rule in Maryland.[21]

Baltimore Town had played no part in the insurgency against the Lords Baltimore. The Calverts returned to power 14 years before the town received its charter. Perhaps Baltimoreans kept to the sidelines in the fee controversy with the Lord Proprietor because their political experience had not primed them for the fight.[22]

At least one historian suggests that the merchants condemned the mob that rose to protest the fee proclamation simply because it was not *their* mob. Notwithstanding the merchants' expression of distaste for riots, they were occasional rioters themselves. Only a month before the protest against the fee proclamation, about 100 of Baltimore's leading merchants and sea captains, faces blackened and disguised as sailors, had armed themselves with "Clubs and Staves" for a mob attack on customs officials who were trying to seize a merchant ship riding at anchor in the town's harbor. Failing to find the customs collector himself, they beat, then tarred and feathered, two of his assistants.[23] By contrast, the mob that rose against the fee proclamation had done violence only to a piece of paper.

PUBLIC MARKETS AND POLITICAL PATRONAGE

It remains unclear whether any of these popular tumults made an impression on Baltimore Town's commissioners. Gaps in their surviving records from 1754 to 1768 and from 1768 to 1776 conceal their reactions, if any, to the Stamp Act, the Townshend Acts, or the fee controversy. But there is evidence that the commissioners were busy with enterprises of their own, not revolutionary perhaps, but bound to bring change.[24] Baltimore was embarking on a venture in government-sponsored capitalism.

In 1751, the town commissioners had solicited voluntary contributions for the construction of a "market-house" at the current intersection of Baltimore and Gay Streets. The enterprise languished for more than 10 years before the market finally

Baltimore's first courthouse stood atop the bluff that overlooked the town, directly in the path of Calvert Street's northward extension. Baltimoreans, according to John Pendleton Kennedy, confronted an intractable question: "Was the street to give way to the Court House or the Court House to the streets?" The local stone mason, Leonard Harbaugh, fashioned a compromise. He excavated a trench beneath the courthouse, then constructed an arch through which Calvert Street could pass, leaving "the old Court-House quaintly seated upon its ponderous and solid bench of stone" (John Pendleton Kennedy, *At Home and Abroad: A Series of Essays* [1872], pp. 169–170).

materialized. The original subscriptions had to be augmented by the proceeds of a public lottery. The funds collected paid for the construction of a two-story building. The ground floor housed the market; upstairs was a large room where "public assemblies, dances, jugglery now and then, and other matters of public concern were held or exhibited." The building accommodated the sessions of the Baltimore County Court while its new courthouse was under construction.[25]

In leasing land for their public market and soliciting contributions from the project's "subscribers," the commissioners had traveled a bit beyond the law, and they acknowledged as much. When the subscribers made their pledges, they signed a document stating that "no Provision hath yet been made by Law or otherwise for Purchasing a Lott or Lotts, whereon to Build a Market House."[26] In fact, the commissioners had no business negotiating leases or purchasing property on behalf of Baltimore Town. Since the provincial assembly had not designated the town commissioners as a "body politic and corporate," they could not make contracts or sign leases.

The legislature took no official notice of Baltimore's effrontery until the town embarked on construction of a second market to replace the first. The new location was a marshy tract on the west bank of the Jones Falls. The commissioners first directed the owners of the property to drain it, and then leased it from them for eight pounds a year. The commissioners named the new establishment the Centre Market, but most Baltimoreans called it the Marsh Market. In 1765, the provincial assembly gave the enterprise its retroactive blessing. It decreed that the town commissioners could hold the site "for the Use and Benefit of the said Town in as full and ample manner *as if* the said Commissioners had been legally constituted as a Body Politick and corporate."[27]

The legislature proceeded to draw up regulations for operation of the public market. The county court would have the power to appoint a clerk for the market, who rented its stalls, maintained accurate weights and measures, and inspected provisions brought for sale. Goods deemed "unwholesome or unsound" were to be destroyed.[28] In 1773, perhaps in response to Baltimoreans with more markets on their minds, the assembly revisited the subject, but in much greater detail. It gave the town commissioners, rather than the county court, authority to appoint market clerks and to remove them "at their Pleasure and Discretion." The legislators went further in specifying a clerk's responsibilities. If "any Butcher or other person shall sell or offer for Sale any Meat within the said Market which shall be blown," the clerk was authorized "to seize all such Meat . . . and the same to Condemn to and for the use of the Prisoners confined in Baltimore County Jail." The practice seems to confirm charges that the jail was dangerously unhealthy. The assembly was unusually liberal in allowing the town commissioners to spend market revenues as they pleased. The market clerk was to expend all "Profits arising from . . . Rents and of all Fines and Forfeitures . . . according to the Directions of the Commissioners of the said Town."[29]

Baltimore's public markets were the physical expression of an urban political economy that extended beyond the market houses to the town at large. By an act of 1771, the provincial assembly authorized the town commissioners to exercise oversight of local commerce through a legion of new officers—inspectors of flour, corders of wood, weighers of hay, measurers of grain, gaugers of liquors, cullers of staves, and garblers of shingles. (In eighteenth-century English usage, garblers sorted rather than scrambled.) The regulations and regulators were a response to a perceived epidemic of short-weighting and shoddy goods.[30] They may also have contributed to emergence of the "free" market by building a foundation of trust among buyers in the quality and correct measure of goods offered by sellers.

Public markets enabled public officials to regulate prices and oversee the "merchantability" of goods. In Baltimore, the regulations extended to the docks from which lumber, flour, and "salted provisions" were shipped abroad. Like many other towns in the American colonies, Baltimore was a "commercial community." Its government was primarily concerned with the promotion and regulation of trade, not the delivery of public services. It carried on a municipal tradition extending back to Elizabethan England.[31]

Not all American towns were receptive to this tradition. In Boston, for example, the public market and its regulations were unwelcome infringements on freedom of commerce. In 1737, a mob attacked the town's three market houses, leveling one and sawing through the foundation of another. All three were closed. Five years later, the Boston town meeting reluctantly accepted the market that Peter Faneuil contributed to the community, but only on the understanding that it would not displace Boston's street peddlers and door-to-door provisioners. Baltimore was less resistant to regulated urban markets, perhaps because it had fewer street merchants, or because Baltimore had no institution like Boston's influential and officially recognized town meeting to organize opposition to regulated markets.[32]

BALTIMORE EMBRACES INDEPENDENCE

In Annapolis, the lower house of the provincial assembly continued to struggle not so much for self-rule as for English rule. After political reinstatement of the Proprietors in 1715, for example, one chronic point of contention between the assembly and the governor concerned the demand of the lower house to employ a colonial agent in London so that it could appeal over the heads of the Lords Baltimore and their governors to the King-in-Council.[33]

In Baltimore, the choice between kingly and lordly rule was joined by a third option—independence. The difference in revolutionary spirit between Baltimore and Annapolis may have had something do to with the contrasting economic regimes of tobacco and grain. Tobacco planters dominated the provincial assembly. Though Maryland tobacco found markets beyond Britain, the tobacco trade was conducted and financed almost exclusively through British merchants and carried in British ships. It fostered a colonial frame of mind. Baltimore's grain trade, on the other hand, was conducted by Baltimore merchants, usually in ships owned by Baltimoreans. The grain trade, in other words, was largely Baltimore's business and engendered a tendency toward independence. Of course, Baltimore continued to depend on imported British manufactured goods, which accounted for a sizeable trade deficit in the years leading up to the Revolution.[34] But debts owed to Britons provided revolutionaries with yet another incentive to sever the colony's connection with England.

Religion and ethnicity reinforced the economic tendencies that moved Baltimoreans toward independence. The town's leading merchants were disproportionately Scots Irish Presbyterians.[35] Behind them lay a history of deep animosity toward England and its Anglican establishment. According to James Webb, the "democracy of the Presbyterian Kirk, an ancient mistrust of higher authority, and a burning resentment of British hierarchy that had given them so much trouble in Ulster all fueled their interactions with other cultures from their first days in America." In 1775, the Anglican bishop of Londonderry wrote to the secretary of state for the colonies expressing anxiety about the mass migration of Scots Irish Presbyterians to the American "middle colonies." He was concerned not about Ireland's population loss but about the tumult that the Presbyterians were likely to raise in their new home.[36]

Indeed, this group provided backbone for the American Revolution, which Tories and Revolutionaries alike characterized as an uprising of Scots Irish Presbyterians. King George himself called it a "Presbyterian war," and a Hessian captain in his service agreed: "Call this war by whatever name you may, only call it not an American rebellion; it is nothing more or less than a Scotch Irish Presbyterian rebellion."[37] Scots Irish merchants such as Samuel Smith, the Purviance brothers, and Andrew Buchanan made up much of Baltimore's revolutionary elite.

One more stimulus to Baltimore's revolutionary impulse was its newspaper. During the colonial crises precipitated by the Stamp Act and the Townshend Acts, the town had no newspaper of its own. But in 1773, William Goddard and his sister Mary Katherine began publishing the *Maryland Journal and Baltimore Advertiser*. At the time of his relocation to Baltimore, Goddard was working to establish a colonial postal system, independent of the Crown Post, for distributing anti-British newspapers and correspondence. His *Maryland Journal* would keep Baltimore abreast of political developments in other colonies. Only four months after the paper began publication, it brought news of the Boston Tea Party to Baltimore.[38]

The newspaper gave the town a kind of consciousness, not just about revolutionary politics in Boston, but about life in Baltimore. An early issue of the journal carried a proposal for a library to be supported by subscription. As a channel of collective communication, the newspaper enhanced the feasibility of such enterprises. There was also an editorial by Goddard in which he urged a levy of one shilling a house to pay for street lamps, which were needed not just to keep the streets safe but "to enable us to explore our Habitations without encountering Quagmires and Masses of Mud and Filth." Goddard unlocked a torrent of complaints about the condition of the town's market and streets: "Butchers in our market exposing to sale the worst of carrion, and the best meat blown by their infectious breath . . . The stalls and blocks therein not cleaned or washed once a year . . . The passages about the market ancle deep in noisome filth!—Stagnant water in many of our streets, alone sufficient to produce diseases among us!—Hogs innumerable running at large, as ready to devour the innocent as to snatch the bread and butter from its hand!"[39] Goddard's paper gave Baltimore a voice.

Chapter 3 **REVOLUTION**

W HEN PARLIAMENT CLOSED the port of Boston after the Tea Party of 1773, appeals went out from Massachusetts seeking support for a new non-importation agreement directed against Britain. The appeal reached Baltimore by way of Philadelphia, though Samuel Adams also sent a copy directly to William Lux in Baltimore, with a request that it "be communicated as his wisdom shall dictate."[1] This time, Baltimore's merchants did not lag far behind Boston's in their response to British coercion. A committee of merchants forwarded Boston's plea for support to the "Gentlemen of Annapolis" and issued a broadside summoning all "Freeholders and Gentlemen of Baltimore County" to a meeting at the courthouse "to favor us with their Company and Advice." The Baltimoreans assembled just 18 days after Bostonians had held a meeting of their own.[2]

The public gathering at the courthouse acted on eight resolutions in support of Boston and in defiance of King and Parliament. Lux, who served as the meeting's clerk, recorded three dissents to the first resolution, which declared that every colony had a duty "to unite in the most effectual means to obtain a Repeal of the late Act of Parliament" closing Boston's port. Lux's minutes also show three dissents to a second measure, which stated that discontinuing trade with Britain "may be the means of preserving North America and her Liberties." Lux seems to have altered his report on the third resolution. It committed Baltimore County to join with other Maryland counties and American colonies in a boycott of British imports and a suspension of exports to Britain and the British West Indies. A notation of "Nine Persons" in dissent is scratched out and replaced by a report that the resolution passed "Unanimously."[3] The remaining five resolutions also passed unanimously because the dissenters were absent. They had been mobbed and beaten. One of them, "bloody and disheveled," staggered from the assembly and warned a temporarily absent ally not to return to the meeting.[4] Baltimore's tradition of government in the streets, formalized by the Mechanical Company and revolutionized by the Sons of Liberty, now served the cause of independence.

BALTIMORE AND THE CONTINENTAL CONGRESS

One of the resolutions passed unanimously at the riotous public meeting in 1774 endorsed the appointment of Maryland delegates to attend a general congress of all the colonies. Baltimore's freeholders thus became one of the first political assemblies to call for a continental congress.[5] The town also sent representatives to the provincial convention in Annapolis, which had all but displaced the institutions of proprietary government. Its most significant act was to order the formation of a state militia. Baltimore was the first jurisdiction in Maryland to organize such a company—the Baltimore Independent Cadets—which was commanded by Captain (later General) Mordecai Gist.[6] The Ancient and Honorable Mechanical Company would form its own unit, the Mechanical Volunteers, a year later. Its commanding officer, Captain James Cox, was the "most fashionable tailor in Baltimore town" and a writer of patriotic poems. He was killed at Germantown in General Washington's attempt to lift the British occupation of Philadelphia.[7]

Together with other Maryland troops, the Baltimoreans in Gist's command would cover George Washington's retreat from Long Island and across Brooklyn, suffering heavy casualties in the process. Gist commanded 200 men in the engagement. He and eight others survived.[8] Their firm defense would be commemorated in Maryland's identification as the Old Line State.

The general outrage provoked by Parliament's action against Boston inspired a mood of solidarity between Baltimore's leaders and the notables of Annapolis. Putting aside old disputes, Baltimore's Committee of Correspondence made a show of consulting with colleagues in Annapolis before convening a mass meeting in Baltimore to discuss responses to the Boston Port Act. The Baltimoreans looked forward, they said, to "harmonizing" with the leadership in Annapolis "and all our brethren, through the province, in the present crisis." Robert Alexander, a member of the Baltimore Committee of Correspondence, delivered his colleagues' harmonizing letter to Annapolis and reported that it had successfully overcome apprehensions in the provincial capital that Baltimore might be "lukewarm in the cause." The leaders in Annapolis may have had in mind Baltimore's reluctant support of the nonimportation agreement adopted in response to the Townshend Acts four years earlier. They were reassured by the Baltimoreans' forthright protest against the Boston Port Bill. The Annapolis committee responded with a pledge that it would "gladly harmonize with you in all possible measures."[9] Beneath the expressions of harmony, however, there was a sharp difference in revolutionary spirit between Baltimore and Annapolis.

CITY REBELS AND STATE TORIES

Self-described moderates identified Baltimore as the colony's hotbed of protest where "the most violent incendiaries resided."[10] The political mismatch between Baltimore and the rest of the colony may have made Maryland the unguided missile of the War for Independence. John Adams claimed that "Maryland is so eccentric a Colony—sometimes so hot, sometimes so high, then so low—that I know not what to say about it or expect from it . . . When they get agoing I expect some wild extravagant Flight or other from it. To be sure they must go beyond everybody else when they begin to go."[11] In the end, they did not go very far.

Elsewhere, the Revolution was not just a war of independence but a struggle to reshape American society by overthrowing a colonial aristocracy and advancing the claims of a solid middle class—but not in Maryland. "In that colony," writes Philip Crowl, "the masses of inarticulate citizens remained, on the whole, inarticulate." The colony's social elite led the Revolution and kept it from becoming too revolutionary.[12] As late as January 1776, the provincial convention was not ready for independence. On the contrary, it closed its session with a declaration of "affection for, and loyalty to, the house of Hanover." The convention's resolution held that Maryland's inhabitants were "connected with the British nation by ties of blood and interest, and . . . thoroughly convinced, that to be free subjects of the king of Great Britain . . . is to be the freest members of any civil society in the known world." Accordingly, they "never did, nor do entertain any views or desires of independency."[13]

Some Baltimoreans agreed. Robert Alexander, a member of both the provincial convention and the Baltimore Committee of Observation, expressed his support for the convention's views from Philadelphia, where he was about to begin his service as Baltimore's only member in Maryland's delegation to the Second Continental Congress. He was "much pleased" with the convention's sentiments: "they intirely coincide with my line of judgment & that Line of Conduct which I had determined to persue."[14] Alexander left Philadelphia and the Continental Congress six months later, without adding his signature to the Declaration of Independence. He later abandoned his public offices, his country, and his wife to join the British, and eventually moved to London. Maryland's moderates in Annapolis had done their best to keep the Revolution well in hand by entrusting it to conservatives like Alexander rather than his more radical colleagues in Baltimore.[15]

When the provincial convention announced its opposition to independence, two-thirds of Baltimore may have agreed. William Lux, an early advocate of separation from Britain, estimated that the town was "two to one against me." But some of those in favor of independence, like Lux, occupied strategic leadership positions in Baltimore. William's brother, George Lux, was both a proponent of independence and secretary of the town's Committee of Observation.[16] The committee's chairman, Samuel Purviance, was also ready for independence. Purviance's ability to mobilize Baltimore's merchants against British authority was obvious well before creation of the committee that he now headed.

In 1773, when the town's merchants and sea captains had resorted to mob violence to prevent customs officials from seizing a ship in Baltimore's harbor, they acted on behalf of Purviance. The ship's cargo was consigned to him. Customs officer Robert Moreton had prohibited unloading of the vessel on the suspicion that contraband goods were concealed beneath a shipment of salt. Purviance ignored the prohibition and ordered his men to unload the ship. Moreton returned to find not only that the cargo was being unloaded in violation of his instructions but that several casks of claret had appeared from beneath the salt. He ordered that the ship be seized. But then he saw "a number of people coming oft in Boats from the shore," and he decided to retreat. Several days later, a mob of merchants and ship captains beat, tarred, and feathered two of Moreton's assistants.[17]

In Baltimore, resentment against British authority was explosive, and Purviance seems to have been a leader of the Anglophobes. In April 1776, he would open a public rift between Baltimore and the semi-revolutionary elite in Annapolis that would move his town decisively toward independence from Britain. As chairman of Baltimore's Committee of Observation, he ordered the kidnapping of the proprietary governor, Robert Eden.

The capture of a Loyalist courier in Virginia had yielded letters addressed to Eden by the British colonial secretary, indicating that the governor had been providing information on the feasibility of landing British troops on the shores of the Chesapeake. The captured courier is described variously as a Pittsburgh or Baltimore merchant, Alexander Ross. His friend, congressional representative Robert Alexander, had attempted unsuccessfully to obtain a pass so that Ross could cross through the American lines to meet with Lord Dunmore, the royal governor of Virginia. Ross had risked the trip without a pass. The papers that were captured with him on his return journey were sent to General Charles Lee, commander of the Continental Army in the South. He forwarded the documents to Purviance and the Baltimore Committee of Observation, deliberately bypassing the Council of Safety in Annapolis because he regarded its members as "namby pambys." Purviance may have seemed sufficiently aggressive to act on Lee's urgent plea that Eden and his papers be taken into custody. Purviance sent copies of the documents to John Hancock, president of the Continental Congress, along with a cover letter accusing Maryland's Council of Safety of being "afraid to execute the Duties of their Stations" and being "timorous and inactive." Congress issued its own orders to seize Governor Eden.[18]

Purviance turned to Major Mordecai Gist, the highest ranking military officer in Baltimore, to recommend an officer to carry out the mission against the governor. On Gist's advice, Purviance sent a young captain of the militia, Samuel Smith, to apprehend Eden. Smith sailed to Annapolis with a detachment of militiamen, secured the port so that no ship could leave the harbor, and then presented a letter to the chairman of the Maryland Council of Safety explaining his mission. The council reacted with fury. Smith was its immediate target, but he was spared further reproach because he had merely been following orders, which the council countermanded.[19] It accepted Governor Eden's word that he would not attempt to flee Annapolis, and then turned its rage against Purviance for the part he played in slighting the council's authority and political reputation.[20]

The council called home Maryland's delegation to the Continental Congress and wrote to John Hancock complaining that Purviance's action endangered public order. The council, it claimed, had thwarted the governor's kidnapping in order to avert "immediate anarchy and convulsion." Purviance was formally censured by the Maryland convention. But only a month later, the convention ordered Governor Eden to leave Maryland. The colony thus took a further step toward independence.

Baltimore's merchants, unlike most of their colleagues in other commercial centers, had already committed themselves to the cause.[21]

REVOLUTIONARY SURVEILLANCE

Purviance may have seemed a threat to public order in Annapolis, but as chairman of the Baltimore Committee of Observation, he was a pillar of public authority. For the first time in its existence, Baltimore Town had its own elected government, albeit one with uncertain authority and few officers to carry out its edicts. It had been created under the authority of the Continental Congress, and Maryland's provincial convention gave it oversight of Baltimore County's Association of the Freemen of Maryland. The association formed in January 1775 at a meeting of Baltimore County's voters, who unanimously approved the appointment of 14 committees to oversee residents in each of the "hundreds" of Baltimore County. The committees were to solicit all freeholders in their districts to sign on as members of the Association of Freemen, signifying their willingness to stand in defense of American liberty. As a tangible token of support, each "associator" was to contribute financially to that defense. Able-bodied men were to be enrolled in militia companies. The committees were instructed that "the name of every person, who shall . . . refuse or decline to subscribe or contribute for purchase of arms and ammunition, be taken down and laid before the committee at the next meeting . . . together with the reasons of such refusal."[22]

Government authority had undergone an abrupt expansion in Baltimore. Under the embargo of British goods, Baltimore's Committee of Observation oversaw the cargoes entering and leaving the port. Now the committee was empowered to scrutinize the political conduct and loyalties of individual residents. The body's sweeping powers stood in sharp contrast to the sorry struggles of the town commissioners to regulate pigs.

The Committee of Observation was not a small or covert organization. Its membership included 29 representatives of Baltimore Town, along with another 38 elected from the "hundreds" of Baltimore County. It held its meetings in public. Since these meetings convened in Baltimore, the town's representatives probably attended more regularly than those from the rest of the county. The committee served as the judicial and executive arm of the Association of Freemen. The "non-associators," those who refused to sign, were required to pay fines, and their movements could be restricted. Non-associator Abram Evening, for example, wanted to collect all of his books and papers and transport them to a place well outside Baltimore so "that in case I cannot stay in such a violent place, they may be safe." Evening attempted "to go in the schooner to Cambridge, and two or three more places, to get the papers to send home." But he was not permitted to leave Baltimore unless he posted security of £350 to guarantee his return and promised that he would not communicate with officers of the Crown. He agreed to both conditions. But he was also required to pay his fine as a non-associator, which he refused to do as a matter of conscience. Evening was detained in Baltimore.[23]

Other subjects of the Committee of Observation's attention proved more malleable. Just one day after the general meeting that created the Association of Freemen, the committee took up the case of an Anglican clergyman, Rev. William Edmiston. An informant reported that Edmiston had publicly asserted "that all persons, who mustered, were guilty of treason; and that such of them as had taken the oath of allegiance, and took up arms, were guilty of perjury." Edmiston was called before the Committee of Observation, where he explained that no opinions were expressed "with greater warmth and intemperate zeal than those in politicks . . . which in cool moments of reflection men would disavow." For the future, Edmiston promised to avoid expressing any opinion at variance with the decisions of the revolutionary authorities. The committee dismissed him without punishment, but had his apology published in the *Maryland Journal*.[24]

In a similar case, ship's captain Richard Button of Fell's Point was accused of discouraging George Helms from joining the militia. Helms was a constable and had taken an oath of loyalty to the proprietary government. Button claimed that he had "no design to dissuade him from learning the military exercise." Like Rev. Edmiston, he promised not to oppose the resolutions of the Continental Congress or the provincial assembly, and apologized "if, by my conduct, I may have appeared inimical to the cause of American liberty."[25]

Public confession was one ritual that the Committee of Observation employed to disarm resistance to the Revolution.[26] In this respect, at least, Baltimore's revolution seems to have anticipated the "show trial" spectacles of twentieth-century revolutions in Russia and China.[27] But Baltimore County's new government had other responsibilities in addition to the regulation of political expression.

The committee routinely interviewed ships' captains to determine whether their cargoes fell under the proscriptions that barred British goods from the colonies. In March 1775, for example, the committee summoned Captain William Moat, master of the brig *Sally*, which had sailed from Bristol with 100 tons of salt. Appearing with him before the committee was Baltimore's entrepreneurial physician Dr. John Stevenson, the designated recipient of the *Sally*'s cargo. The captain testified (implausibly) that he had taken on the salt before December 12, 1774—the date on which the Maryland convention had voted to support the embargo on British goods proclaimed by the Continental Congress. Dr. Stevenson asked that he be given permission to land the salt, arguing that it was just ballast, not the kind of cargo that the Continental Congress intended to exclude. In fact, demand for salt was so strong that the committee had already posted a "recommended" price for the commodity, and it imposed price controls on salt in November 1775.[28] It was expensive ballast.

The committee rejected the arguments of both men and ruled that the salt could not be landed. A week later, the committee again required the presence of Captain Moat and Dr. Stevenson. Stevenson had sold the salt to purchasers outside Baltimore County under the impression that the committee's ruling did not extend beyond its boundaries. Stevenson must have recognized that he was in trouble. He offered to "return an Account of the Proceeds of the Salt, and the same will freely give for the Relief of the Poor of Boston; and that the remainder of the Salt now on board the said Brig, shall not be landed in any Part of America, between Nova-Scotia and Georgia." The committee voted to accept his apology.[29]

Three months later, Dr. Stevenson appeared once again before the committee, which had intercepted a letter addressed to him from Henry Lloyd, an agent for contractors who procured supplies for British troops in Boston. Lloyd's letter noted that a "stoppage of provisions from the Southern Governments" had made it necessary for him to "get supply by concealing from the publick eye the destination of provisions" shipped to His Majesty's army. He proposed that Stevenson load a ship with flour, ostensibly for the West Indies, and then divert it to the British troops in Boston. Lloyd also suggested third-party payment schemes that would mask Stevenson's involvement in supplying the British army, and he cautioned Stevenson to take care that his reply to the proposal not fall into the hands of the "provincials," who were apparently just as likely to violate the security of the postal system as the British had been. Presented with the letter at the committee hearing, Stevenson acknowledged that he recognized Lloyd's handwriting. In other words, he must have had previous correspondence with Lloyd. But Stevenson swore that he had never received the letter and that he would never execute any order "contrary to the Resolves of the Continental Congress or the Provincial Convention." The committee delivered no verdict concerning Stevenson, but found Lloyd "knowingly and willfully violated the Association of the American Congress."[30]

Dr. Stevenson managed to avoid such charges until June 1776. Committees of Observation throughout Maryland had been confiscating arms and ammunition from non-associators. Stevenson had written to the Council of Safety in Annapolis complaining that Baltimore's committee had confiscated two casks of gunpowder without compensation. But Stevenson's letter came to the attention of the Baltimore committee, which ruled that since Stevenson had neither signed as an associator nor enrolled for service in the militia, "he stands in the light of an enemy to America, and therefore it would be dangerous to trust so much powder in his hands."[31]

AMERICAN TERROR

Some of Baltimore's Tories were less subtle than Dr. Stevenson. In May 1775, the Committee of Observation considered the case of James Dalgleish, who had repeatedly declared that "as soon as the English troops land here, he will join them against the Americans." Dalgleish had already been called before the committee for announcing that the "King ought to be damned if he repealed the late oppressive Acts respecting America, and that said Acts were equitable." Dalgleish explained that he had made the incriminating statements while "much intoxicated with liquor" and assured the committee that "to disapprove of the resolves of the continental congress, or the proceedings of the publick was quite foreign to my sentiments when sober."[32] The committee adopted a new approach to deal with Dalgleish. It decided "to publish said Dalgleish to the world as an enemy of the liberties of Americans." The announcement provoked an immediate response. The *Maryland Journal* reported that as soon as Baltimoreans knew "that the Protection of the Committee was withdrawn from this imprudent Man," they regarded him as a "proper Object of their Resentment." Dalgliesh, "apprehending Danger from the People," fled Baltimore.[33]

The treatment of Dalgleish marked a new phase in Baltimore's rendition of the Revolution. A year later, the use of terror had become standard practice in Baltimore. The Whig Club, a new and secretive organization, proposed to deal with the "secret and disguised enemies, whom we have fostered in our bosoms" who were allied with "a cruel and foreign foe doing everything in their power to effect our destruction." The club claimed that it was merely acting to support the public authorities, whose best efforts might fail to apprehend "artful villains . . . and dignified Tories, under the cloak of moderation." The Whig Club did not specify how it would deal with these elusive traitors, but pledged that no one "shall be convicted . . . without being heard in his defence." Conviction required a two-thirds vote of the members, who were enjoined to "keep secret the proceedings of this Club."[34]

The Whig Club was more proletarian than earlier nongovernmental organizations in Baltimore. Militia membership had triggered political activism among laborers and tradesmen who had been too obscure to claim political standing. But, like the Mechanical Company, the Whig Club included prominent merchants and professionals. One of them was Robert Purviance, Samuel's brother and business partner.[35]

Soon, however, the Whig Club and the Committee of Observation seemed at odds with each other, at least in public. One of the club's more prominent targets was Baltimore County sheriff Robert Christie. The club's complaint against Christie was ceremonial. To solemnize the county's support of the Declaration of Independence, the Committee of Observation had planned a ceremony that would culminate with the county sheriff's reading of the Declaration from the courthouse steps. The committee informed Sheriff Christie about his role, and he had promised to perform his part in the pageant, but when the time came, he failed to appear.[36]

The sheriff soon received anonymous letters so threatening that he sought the protection of the Committee of Observation, claiming that he "had reason to be apprehensive of violence being offered to him . . . on account of his not attending to read the Declaration of Independence on Monday last." He feared that he might be forced to resign as sheriff. The committee expressed its "utter disapprobation of all threats or violence being offered to any persons whatever" and called on the town's citizens "to assist them in their endeavors to preserve the peace and good order of society, and to prevent all riots and tumults, and personal abuse and violence to individuals."[37]

Sheriff Christie had family and business connections that compounded the suspicions of disloyalty aroused by his failure to read the Declaration. A year earlier, a letter had been intercepted from James Christie, Jr. (a business partner and probably a cousin of the sheriff) addressed to another kinsman—Lieutenant Colonel Gabriel Christie of His Majesty's Sixtieth Regiment, stationed at Antigua. The letter complained about the "terrible confusion here with our politicks . . . and that, added to other things, makes me wish myself out of the Province . . . We have some violent fanatical spirits among us, who do every thing in their power to run things to the utmost extremity, and they are so far gone, that we moderate people are under the necessity of uniting for our defence, after being threatened with expulsion, loss of life, &c. for not acceding to what we deem treason and rebellion . . . A part of yours or any other Regiment, I believe, would keep us very quiet."[38] This was the portion of the incriminating letter entered in the committee's records. The full text did not appear until James Christie gave it to the *Maryland Journal* about a week later. It began with Christie's apology to his cousin in Antigua for not responding to earlier letters. He would have written sooner, he said, "had I not met with the greatest misfortune in the power of fate to inflict on me, in the loss of the wife of my soul, on the 15th of December last, that has almost put me out of my power to mind any thing for some time past, and all my fortitude is scarce sufficient to bear me up." His wife had died in childbirth, "and the dear little infant died a few days after its mother."[39] At the time of his alleged offense, in other words, Christie may have been too disabled by grief to conspire against the revolutionary authorities.

The Committee of Observation summoned James Christie to explain his incriminating letter, but he pleaded ill health and asked for a postponement until he was no longer bedridden. The committee sent a delegation to his house to inquire whether the letter to Gabriel Christie was indeed his. He admitted that it was, and again requested that any proceedings on the subject be postponed. But the committee refused his request and "immediately gave him notice" that the proceedings would proceed. He was represented by his kinsman, Sheriff Robert Christie.[40]

At the committee's next meeting, Sheriff Christie "declared that James Christie was very sorry for the letter he had wrote to Lieut. Colonel Christie, that he did not mean any harm by it." A delegation of committee members visited James Christie to inquire about those "moderate people . . . uniting for our defence" — a possible act of sedition. Christie responded that there had never been any association for mutual defense and the idea had been dropped because he and his friends believed "that no threats worth notice had been thrown against them."[41]

The Committee of Observation ruled that James Christie's crime was of "so dangerous and atrocious a nature" that it referred the case to the state's representatives in the Continental Congress. They also declared him "an enemy of this Country, and all persons are desired to break off all connections and intercourse with him." In the meantime, the committee placed a nine-man guard at his house; Christie was required to pay each of them five shillings for every 24 hours that they kept him under surveillance. The guards were removed only when five reputable citizens, including Sheriff Christie, guaranteed that he would not leave the province.[42] The Maryland congressional delegation referred Christie's case to the provincial convention, which fined Christie £500 and ordered that he "be expelled and banished from the Province forever."[43]

Sheriff Christie, who had repeatedly represented his kinsman before the Committee of Observation, remained behind in Baltimore, not only an object of suspicion, but a highly conspicuous officer of county government. The request that he read the Declaration of Independence from the courthouse steps may well have been a test of loyalty. The Committee of Observation's injunction against "riots and tumults" in July 1776 shielded him for a time, but as the Revolution moved from Declaration to bloody military engagements, animosity toward British sympathizers hardened.

In December, Sheriff Christie received another threatening letter. This one was signed "Legion," the Whig Club's code name. It warned Christie that unless he left Maryland "within six days your life shall be sacrificed by an injured people." Instead of turning again to the Committee of Observation, the sheriff met with some of the Whigs at a local tavern to plead for an extra day, but the club members seemed so close to violence that Sheriff Christie immediately fled to New York.[44] He left behind a list of the men he had confronted at the tavern. They included a member of the Committee of Observation, a Baltimore County delegate to the provincial convention, and several militia officers.[45]

As the Whig Club expanded its campaign of intimidation, the Council of Safety in Annapolis wrote to Samuel Purviance and his colleagues on the Committee of Observation, urging them to take action against the club before Baltimore was reduced to "anarchy and the end of all regular Government." There is no record of a committee response. Apparently, Purviance and his colleagues were less concerned about the club's rampages than were the moderates in Annapolis. By August 1776, the club was conducting full-scale military operations, with two artillery pieces and as many as 100 men, against the barricaded estate of Dr. Henry Stevenson, brother of the pioneering merchant and physician who had shown Baltimore a path to prosperity. Henry Stevenson was a pioneer of a different sort. He had introduced smallpox inoculation to Maryland and turned his estate, "Parnassus," into a hospital where patients could recover from the symptoms that followed "variolation"—an early method of immunization. It was here, in his mansion, that Stevenson, along with nine of his friends, was barricaded.[46]

An informant, merchant Cumberland Dugan, had accused Henry Stevenson of making uncomplimentary remarks about "all Congresses, Conventions, Councils of Safety, and Committees," and charged that he "also had been guilty of sundry other practices inimical to American liberty." The Committee of Observation summoned Dr. Stevenson to explain himself, but had to postpone the hearing because Dugan had left Baltimore on business before he could provide the particulars needed to back up his accusations. Stevenson never faced the committee. He managed to elude the forces that surrounded his estate and reached the British army in New York, where he became a military surgeon. At the end of the war, he turned down a permanent position as a medical officer, and in 1786 he returned to Baltimore, redeemed his estate (which had been confiscated by Maryland's revolutionary authorities), and reopened his smallpox hospital. He died in 1814 at the age of 93.[47]

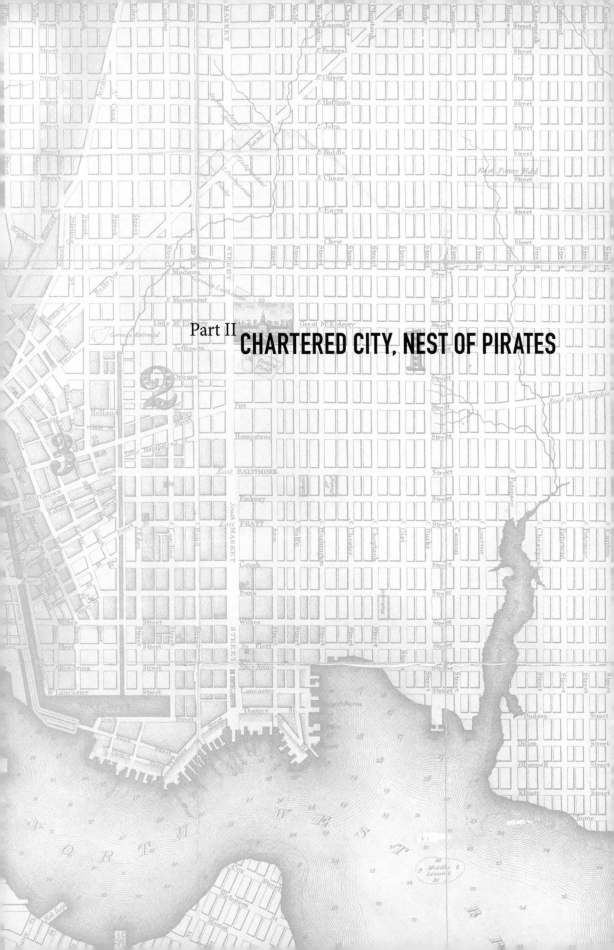

Part II
CHARTERED CITY, NEST OF PIRATES

Chapter 4

BALTIMORE AT WAR

N 1776, IT MUST HAVE SEEMED INCONCEIVABLE that Tories such as Henry Stevenson could ever live in peace with Baltimore's revolutionaries. In Baltimore and much of Maryland, Loyalists and Revolutionaries were engaged in something just short of civil war. The Loyalists were too numerous to imprison and not as easily intimidated as Rev. Edmiston or Captain Button. The Committee of Observation's authority may have seemed fearsome at first, but it lacked the muscle to enforce its revolutionary pronouncements. Defiant "non-associators" refused to pay the fines levied for their refusal to enroll in the Association of Freemen.

The Committee of Observation might have acted with greater efficacy if it had inherited a more efficacious political system. But Baltimore's unelected town commissioners had lacked the authority to govern even in relatively tranquil times. The Mechanical Company compensated for some of the limitations of township government, but its usefulness to the committee was limited. Many of its able-bodied members were away fighting the British, and those who remained in town could not provide a respectable alternative to the Whig Club because, like Robert Purviance, they were members of the Whig Club.

In November 1776, Samuel Purviance sent a letter to the Council of Safety in Annapolis concerning the circumstances that his committee faced in Baltimore Town and County. "We are sorry to inform you," he wrote, "that the spirit of opposition to the measures which have been adopted for our common safety, grows extreamly daring and outragious in this county, so that the officers appointed to carry into execution the Resolves of the convention dare not proceed without further assistance: And the militia threaten to lay down their arms unless the fines of non-enrollers who daily insult them are strictly collected."[1]

Captain James Bosley was one of the officers appointed by the Committee of Observation to collect the fines owed by non-associators. In November 1776, Bosley's duties took him to the farm of Vincent Trapnell outside Baltimore Town. According to Bosley, as soon as Trapnell caught sight of him, "he swore he would blow my brains out." Trapnell ran to his house to get his gun, but his wife stood in the doorway, and her "urging and begging" deterred him. Instead, Bosley testified, Trapnell "picked up a large stick swearing and cursing and with both hands struck my head. I fended it off as much as I could with a small cane I rode with." At this point, Bosley announced that he would leave the property and refer Trapnell's case to the Committee of Observation, but Trapnell chased him across his fields, throwing rocks and declaring that "he was fully determined to kill" Bosley. A neighbor opened a gate in Trapnell's fence so that Bosley could escape. At a safe distance, Bosley reined in his horse and repeated his warning that he would report Trapnell's defiance to the committee. Trapnell "answer'd the committee and I might kiss his arse and be damned, pulling his coat apart behind, for a parcel of roguish damn'd sons of bitches."[2]

In some quarters the committee got no respect, and its inability to discipline Tories seems to have reduced its ability to maintain the discipline of the militia. Samuel Baxter, one of Captain Bosley's colleagues as a collector of fines from non-associators, wrote to the Maryland Council of Safety requesting the assistance of the militia in carrying out his duties because "it cant be expected that any won man can manag such a set of toreys . . . they have all swore to kill me if I persist to distres them." If help were not forthcoming, "plees to let me now," he asked, "that I may resine my warent."[3]

In Baltimore Town itself, Loyalists and members of the Whig Club fought gun battles in the streets.[4] The local Committee of Observation did little to rein in the club, perhaps because it lacked the capacity to do so, or because the club performed essential political tasks, though by means inconsistent with the committee's civic respectability as a pillar of public order. The Council of Safety in Annapolis seems not to have understood this. On the same day that they responded to Samuel Baxter's plea for help, the council wrote to Baltimore's Committee of Observation complaining, once again, about the Whigs' use of threats to banish Baltimoreans of doubtful loyalty. This time the Whigs' target had been a member of a militia company "who is regularly inrolled and otherwise well behaved," yet the Whigs ordered him to leave town. The council's intent, it said, was "not to countenance Tories or disaffected persons, but we wish the peace of the State to be preserved, and that all offenders should be punished according to the law of the land."[5] The council members seemed unaware that they were presiding over a revolution in which the law of the land might occasionally cease to operate. The council's response to Baxter's request for militia support was no more helpful. The committee could do nothing, it wrote, because Baxter had provided "no proofs or depositions to lay a foundation for our proceeding."[6]

In January 1777, the Council of Safety wrote to the Baltimore committee on behalf of Melchior Keener, founding president of the Mechanical Company. Three soldiers from the company of Captain Nathaniel Smith, "and others who came without any authority or warrant," had searched and ransacked Keener's home "and committed divers irregularities." The council added that it took "for granted that the Whig Club had no hand in this riot." The council may have taken too much for granted. Captain Smith was a member of the Whig Club.[7] Complaints about the club's outrages continued to reach Annapolis. The Council of Safety dispatched a new letter to the Baltimore Committee of Observation complaining about the club's threat to public order. This time the complaint was backed up by three companies of militia. The committee responded that it was doing all it could. The militia companies, all commanded by Baltimoreans, refused to take action against the Whig Club. Most of the Whigs were members of the militia.[8]

The Whig Club may have miscalculated when it targeted the editor of the *Maryland Journal*. William Goddard was no Tory, but an article published in his newspaper over the name "Tom Tell-Truth" had offended the Whigs because it seemed to approve a peace proposal offered to the Americans by the British general William Howe. In fact, the piece was a derisive send-up of the general's offer. The Whig Club, apparently, did not appreciate irony, even though an article on the page opposite Tell-Truth's denounced the British peace offer. The Whigs demanded that Goddard reveal "Tom's" identity. Goddard refused. The club sent armed men to conduct Goddard to the club's meeting room at a local tavern, but the editor remained defiant. The club voted to banish him from Baltimore.[9]

Goddard left town after issuing a broadside naming 18 of the Whig Club members who had ordered his exile. He announced that he would petition the state legislature "for Protection against the Miscreants, who have been guilty of the flagitious Practices by which I am now suffering." The *Maryland Journal* continued to publish under the supervision of Goddard's sister and de facto coeditor, Mary Katherine. In Annapolis, Goddard presented a "memorial" to the Maryland Council of Safety demanding its legal protection and the censure of the Whig Club. The council referred the case to the state assembly. A committee of the assembly found that the "proceedings [of the Whig Club] are a manifest Violation of the Constitution, directly contrary to the Declaration of Rights." One of Goddard's advocates in the assembly was Samuel Chase, later a prominent Federalist politician and a justice of the US Supreme Court. Chase was also Tom Tell-Truth. With the assembly's assent, the governor issued a proclamation declaring that "bodies of men associating together . . . for the purpose of usurping any of the powers of government [are] . . . unlawful assemblies." The Whigs' attacks soon subsided, but the proclamation may have played a smaller role in this result than the fact that many of the militiamen in the club were called to active military service.[10]

CONGRESS COMES TO BALTIMORE

By the end of 1776, Philadelphia was under threat of British occupation, and the Continental Congress abandoned the city for Baltimore. It held its sessions in a tavern at the west end of Market Street.[11] John Adams enjoyed the sumptuous dinners at the country seats of Baltimore's merchants, but noted in his diary that the residents seemed too concerned with making money: "Landjobbers, speculators in land; little generosity to the public, little public spirit."[12]

Delegates also had criticisms of a more tangible nature. Oliver Wolcott of Connecticut wrote to his wife expressing the hope that Congress's time in Baltimore "might not be long for it is infinitely the most dirty Place I was ever in. No One can Walk about here but in Boots."[13] John Adams noted that "the Streets [are] the muddiest I ever saw. This is the dirtiest place in the World—our Salem, and Portsmouth are neat in Comparison." But Adams, at least, understood why Baltimore made such a poor appearance. "The Inhabitants are excusable because they had determined to pave the Streets before this War came on, since which they have laid the Project aside . . . This place is not incorporated. It is neither a City, Town, nor Burrough, so that they can do nothing with Authority."[14] Adams, of course, was mistaken about Baltimore's status as a town, but he may have had in mind the self-governing townships of Massachusetts that had an authority over local matters far exceeding Baltimore's.

The state assembly tried to minimize the muck with yet another act making it illegal for geese and pigs to wander the town's still unpaved streets. It also ordered some of the streets widened to accommodate increased wartime traffic.[15] But the persistently swampish condition of Baltimore's thoroughfares remained. The assembly in Annapolis lacked the capacity to make Baltimore presentable and denied Baltimore's government the power to do so itself.[16]

Apart from the mud, the chief congressional complaint about Baltimore was the cost of living. Benjamin Rush of Pennsylvania wrote to his wife that "every article of provision—cloathing and the common conveniences of life are 100 percent higher in this place than in Philadelphia." But Rush seems to have been particularly impressed with the rapidity of Baltimore's growth. "The town used to contain some 5000 inhabitants before the present war . . . It has for some years past vied with Philadelphia in commerce, and bids fair for being the most wealthy spot on the Continent."[17]

The member of Congress who felt most at home in the town was Samuel Adams, principal event planner for the Boston Tea Party. He was a master of politics in the streets and a supporter of William Goddard's American postal system. But in Samuel Purviance, Adams found a kindred spirit. To his wife, Elizabeth, Adams wrote that he was "exceedingly happy in an Acquaintance with Mr. Samuel Purviance a Merchant of this Place." He and Purviance had corresponded previously, "but I never saw him till I came here. He is a sensible, honest and friendly Man, warmly attached to the American cause, and has particularly endeard himself to me by his great Assiduity in procuring Relief in this part of the Continent for the Town of Boston at a Time when her Enemies would have starved her by an oppressive Port bill."[18]

Baltimore may have seemed a trial to members of the Continental Congress, but the congressional descent on Baltimore also created headaches for their hosts. Congress came to Baltimore with a retinue of civilian prisoners, Loyalists of sufficient importance to warrant congressional detention. Congress requested the local Committee of Observation to secure the prisoners "in a convenient room, under a guard . . . except the two Goodrich's, who are to be committed to Gaol."[19] The Goodriches were members of a notorious family of Virginia turncoats who discovered that they could make more money as provisioners and privateers for the British than by supplying gunpowder to the rebels. An unspecified number of North Carolinians later joined them in jail.[20]

A week after the Goodriches' imprisonment, Congress received a report "that the present situation of the Prisoners is very disagreeable and dangerous to their health, on account of the Prison being much out of repair." It responded with a resolution that "until the apartments in the Jail of Baltimore Town shall be repaired," the prisoners should be removed "to different rooms in the Court-House, or wherever else safely locked up and secured." Within only a week, an unspecified number of the congressional prisoners remaining in Baltimore's jail had escaped. Congress resolved "that the Committee of Observation for Baltimore County be requested to direct immediate and strict search for the Prisoners . . . and to offer a reward for apprehending and securing said Prisoners, and that said Committee make inquiry into the conduct of the Gaoler, or any other person suspected of permitting or assisting their escape."[21] Baltimore did not make a good impression.

THE WAR BUSINESS

Baltimoreans, however, were making a great deal of money. Some small portion of it may have come from overcharging members of Congress for food and accommodations. But the Revolutionary War itself provided Baltimoreans with their most lucrative business opportunities. The embargo on trade with Britain eliminated some of the usual paths to profit, and Congress narrowed them further when, to secure a food supply for the Continental Army, it imposed a general embargo on the export of flour, grains, rice, bread, pork, bacon, livestock, and other items. Though exceptions were later permitted for shipments among American states—and though merchants tried to create their own exceptions by smuggling—governmental and military customers were among the few significant clients remaining to Baltimore's commercial community.[22] The only alternative to the business of warfare was the trade in tobacco. Once the mainstay of Maryland's economy, tobacco was one of the few commodities for which the military and political authorities had no immediate use. Some merchants fell back on Maryland's old standby to sustain themselves.[23]

Feeding and equipping the Continental Army and Navy almost certainly yielded more profit than the tobacco trade. Baltimore became a major provisioner of the army, a depot for supplies of flour, iron, and salt, and premier shipbuilder for the navy.[24] The brothers Purviance became agents of Congress for "financial operations" essential to the revolutionary effort in the South.[25]

Baltimore merchants Abraham and Isaac Van Bibber did business for the new republic far from their Baltimore base. Abraham moved to St. Eustatius, an island in the Dutch Antilles, notable for having fired the first salute to the new American flag. Its renown was well earned. Along with a love of liberty, the island's merchants treasured the munitions business that came their way because of the American rebellion. Abraham's brother, Isaac, owned *The Hero of Baltimore*, an armed sloop that also carried cargoes—in other words, a privateer. In November 1776, the *Hero* captured an English brigantine just beyond the guns of St. Eustatius, entered the harbor with its prize, and left not long after, its hold full of gunpowder, cannons, blankets, and assorted munitions to carry back to Baltimore. Abraham probably arranged the shipment for Isaac. He also arranged others, with a marked mercantile ingenuity.

John Spear, a trader on the British island of Antigua, was the son of William Spear, a merchant of Baltimore and member of its Committee of Observation. Abraham Van Bibber served as middleman for a cargo of lumber and provisions from the elder Spear to the younger (patriotically forgoing the usual commission and sidestepping the embargo on exports to Britain or its possessions). In return, John Spear helped Van Bibber to assemble a cargo consisting of British manufactured goods, arms, and gunpowder to be shipped from Antigua through St. Eustatius to Baltimore.[26] The revolutionaries would use British munitions against British forces.

Abraham Van Bibber's work at St. Eustatius ended abruptly. In 1777, the commander of the British squadron in the West Indies registered a complaint with the governor of St. Eustatius, alleging that Van Bibber was directing the operations of American privateers. Though the charges were never proven, Van Bibber remained in custody until he managed to escape and return to Baltimore.[27] But Baltimore's trade with St. Eustatius would continue until the British invaded the island in 1781. In one 10-day period in January 1780, 18 of 22 ships clearing Baltimore harbor were headed for the Dutch island.[28]

Baltimore's shipbuilders stayed put in Baltimore, where they turned out both warships and merchant vessels. The first American cruisers were converted merchant ships, renamed the *Wasp* and the *Hornet*. They were fitted out and armed in Fell's Point shipyards and sailed under local officers with local crews. The *Hornet* was the first ship to fly the American flag. Its unfurling, on October 29, 1775, was accompanied by fifes and drums; a crowd gathered, and by evening the *Hornet* had signed up a full crew.[29] The Continental Congress had created the American navy only 16 days earlier, but had not yet authorized the construction of any warships. The *Hornet* and *Wasp* belonged to the navy of Maryland. Fell's Point also produced the first ship built expressly for the Continental Navy, the frigate *Virginia*, with 28 guns. As an agent of Congress, Samuel Purviance oversaw construction of the *Virginia* and secured the materials needed to build it.[30]

The Americans had no large ships that could match those of the British navy. Their vessels had to carry their cargoes through a British blockade and were therefore designed to be fast and maneuverable. If the fast vessels were armed, they could also overtake and capture slow-moving British cargo ships. Building ships for running blockades and privateering became a Baltimore specialty.

Baltimore shipyards built 248 vessels commissioned as commercial predators.[31] The vessels were early versions of the Baltimore clipper ships, though still known as "Virginia-built schooners." The ships' speed came at a cost. Not only was their cargo capacity limited, but they put their crews at greater risk than other ships of the time. The hull design, tall masts, heavy spars, and large sail area gave the clippers a disconcerting tendency to capsize bow-first and end-over-end when they ran before the wind. The weight of cannons increased this danger. By the early nineteenth century, sailors referred to such ships as "coffins." Oddly, the risk of capsizing remained even when the clippers lay at anchor. If they were caught between a tidal current in one direction and a strong wind in the other, the ships were in danger of going

To minimize weight, the clippers' hulls were not strongly reinforced by timbers or bulkheads.

The seafaring population of Fell's Point had more grievances against the British than most Baltimoreans. British commerce raiders and blockaders had already made victims of American ships and seamen before Baltimore started turning out privateers. For that reason, Robert Brugger suggests, the Point may have been a distinct stronghold of American patriotism,[33] which may have moved the Point's sailors to take chances that most British seamen would never tolerate. But if patriotism were not a sufficient motive to serve at sea, crew members' shares of the prizes captured by their fast ships might induce sailors to run risks posed by the flimsy hulls and capsizing tendencies of Baltimore clippers.

Privateering, shipbuilding, military procurement, and shipping all became vehicles of profit for Baltimoreans. The usual trade in tobacco and flour, though diminished, continued. In the Caribbean, flour was exchanged for arms, or for gold and silver that could be used to purchase arms.[34] Tobacco shipped across the Atlantic helped to establish the Revolution's credit with European governments.[35] The result was explosive growth. Craftsmen, manufacturers, entrepreneurs, and apprentices poured into Baltimore along with merchants, including six French commercial houses opened during or shortly after the war.[36] The population of Fell's Point alone doubled between 1771 and 1783, and the Point's slave population quadrupled, a reflection of the shipbuilders' dependence on slave labor. During the course of the war, the population of Baltimore as a whole increased by about 50 percent, from approximately 6,000 to 9,000.[37]

The wartime surge in wealth and population was due, in part, to Baltimore's being the only major American port to escape British depredations. Its position near the head of the Chesapeake Bay protected it from sea raids and, since any British invasion fleet would have to travel the length of the Bay before reaching Baltimore, the town would be alerted long before the British arrived at the Patapsco. Other cities were less fortunately situated. New York was occupied by the British for most of the war. The British were forced out of Boston, but were able to disrupt that town's shipping from their base at Halifax. Philadelphia, Newport, Charleston, and Savannah all experienced occupation at some point during the war. If their troop strength had been sufficient to hold Norfolk, the British might have been able to control both the Chesapeake and Baltimore. But instead of occupying Norfolk, they burned it.[38] All the better for Baltimore. The British had eliminated one of its commercial competitors. Johann Schoepf, a postwar visitor from Germany, observed that "the war, which elsewhere had an opposite effect, was favorable to the trade of Baltimore."[39]

TOWN IN PERIL

Baltimore did not completely avoid the shooting part of the Revolution. Its first scare came in March 1776, when a small British ship, the *Otter*, with 16 guns and 130 men, was sent up the Bay from Norfolk along with two armed tenders that could maneuver in shallow water. Its mission, apparently, was to neutralize the newly outfitted *Wasp* and *Hornet*. American pilot boats spotted the British force at the mouth of the Patuxent River and sailed up the Bay to alert Annapolis. The news led some residents of the provincial capital to move their families and portable possessions inland. As the *Otter* passed Annapolis, it was hailed by a man in a small boat. He was William Eddis, the letter-writing customs official, who carried a message from the proprietary governor, Robert Eden, asking what the *Otter*'s mission was. Its commander, Captain Matthew Squire, sent Eddis back to Annapolis with a disingenuous note in which he expressed regret that "the people of Annapolis should be under any Apprehensions from their Town being burnt . . . down; I must beg Leave to assure you Nothing of that Kind will happen from me; I am on a Cruise to procure fresh Provisions for the Kings Ships and . . . shall most readily pay the market Price." But Squire had already seized several American ships with their cargoes, and nothing was said about purchase at market price.[40]

A week after Captain Squire sent his note to Governor Eden, the Baltimore Committee of Observation interviewed Robert Brown, who had been captured by the *Otter* while crossing the Bay by boat. According to Brown, Captain Squire had announced that he intended to burn Baltimore.[41] The alarm prompted militia companies from as far away as Pennsylvania to march to the town's defense. A number of ships were sunk in the narrow channel leading to the Baltimore Basin. (These included vessels owned by Sheriff Robert Christie and Melchior Keener.)[42] A new ship, the *Defence*, was still being outfitted at Fell's Point. Its cannons arrived just days before the appearance of the *Otter* and were hastily mounted in preparation for the expected attack.[43]

The *Otter* ran aground off Bodkin Point at the mouth of the Patapsco. Captain Squire relied on a pilot from Virginia who was unfamiliar with the waters of the Upper Bay. Nor were his men in fighting trim. "Ague and fever" had begun to spread through the *Otter*'s crew even before the ship left Norfolk. Six of Squire's men died during passage up the Chesapeake. In Baltimore, hundreds of volunteers converged on Fell's Point to serve on the *Defence*—so many that several smaller schooners were called into service to carry surplus defenders out to meet the *Otter*. Squire had managed to refloat his ship, but went aground again just as the American flotilla came into view. Once refloated, the *Otter*, its tenders, and their captured American merchant ships retreated down the Bay, leaving behind one of their prizes—the *Molly*, a ship loaded with flour and grain that had run aground.[44]

Baltimore faced a more formidable invasion force in 1777, when a British fleet under the command of Vice-Admiral Richard Howe sailed down the Atlantic coast from New York and entered the Chesapeake. It consisted of transports for approximately 18,000 men, 300 cannons, and 1,000 cavalry horses. Twenty-five ships of the British navy escorted them. Baltimoreans prepared for an attack. A chain barred entry to the harbor. Behind it stood the frigate *Virginia* and the Maryland navy's *Defence*. The British sailed by without a shot. Their destination was the head of the Chesapeake, where they landed troops to march on Philadelphia.[45]

British operations in the Chesapeake never again extended as far north as Baltimore; Maryland and Virginia were relatively unscarred by the war, and their men and provisions helped to sustain the rebel forces.[46] General Henry Clinton, supported by Vice-Admiral Marriot Artbuthnot, planned another campaign in the Chesapeake in 1780, but news that a French fleet was sailing to the aid of the Americans led him to abandon his plans and divert his force to defend the British base of operations at New York. The British had long been apprehensive about French intervention on the side of the Americans. General Washington had consistently emphasized that the Revolution's success on land depended on a "decisive Naval superiority," which the Americans could not achieve on their own.[47]

The Chesapeake emerged as a critical arena in the war. General Cornwallis left his secure base in Charleston and took his army to Yorktown, where he was boxed in by French and American troops and French ships. The British failure to take control of the Bay was Baltimore's salvation. Baltimore's good fortune, and the misfortunes of other American ports, marked the beginning of its golden age as the fastest growing town in the United States and, briefly, its third largest city.

The town's political development, however, did not keep pace with its economic growth. Its political authorities were now elected, rather than appointed in Annapolis, but their exercise of authority was still restricted and largely unsupported by the powers-that-were in the colonial capital. Baltimore's circumstances were by-products of location and timing. Its location as the westernmost port on the East Coast made it a vital link between inland markets and Atlantic trade—especially the grain trade. This geographic advantage helped to power its economic expansion, but the town's timing was politically disadvantageous. It emerged after a colonial government had already taken root in Annapolis and denied Baltimore the capability to govern itself. The result was the underdevelopment of government institutions that might have kept order during the Revolution and provided more decorous accommodations for its residents and for members of the Continental Congress forced to abandon Philadelphia. Baltimore had to resort to unofficial political improvisation to meet essential needs for public order and safety.

Chapter 5

FROM TOWN TO CITY

T HE DECLARATION OF INDEPENDENCE posed two problems for Americans. One was obvious: waging war to transform the goal of independence into a political fact. The other was the need to fashion new systems of government for each of the independent states. The second task commands less attention today than it did among the revolutionaries themselves. State constitution making was one of their absorbing preoccupations. According to Gordon S. Wood, "Nothing in the years surrounding the Declaration of Independence—not the creation of the Articles of Confederation, not the military operations of the war, not the making of the French alliance—engaged the interests of Americans more than the formation of their separate state governments."[1] The Continental Congress stalled after the signing of the Declaration because so many delegates returned to their home states to design new institutions of government. The very idea that one could self-consciously write out a blueprint for government was one of the notions that made the Revolution revolutionary.

More than 10 years of debate about the rights of Americans and the powers of King, Parliament, and Lords Baltimore had primed Maryland's political class to enunciate the principles by which they would consent to be governed. Like four other colonies, Maryland began its constitution with a "Declaration of Rights," an innovation that anticipated the first 10 amendments of the US Constitution. Maryland's declaration began by stating: "All government originates from the people, is founded on compact only, and instituted for the good of the whole." It also established the people's right to participate in government through elections, which "ought to be free and frequent." But the declaration's "people" did not include everyone, not even all adult white males. The electorate consisted of "every man, having property in, and common interest with, and an attachment to the community."[2]

The connection between property and political status did not go unchallenged. Members of the state militia insisted that if they bore arms in the cause of their country, they should also carry the right to vote, no matter how small their property holdings. In 1776, a company of militiamen marched to a polling place in Annapolis and demanded the right to vote, even though the entire unit owned less than £40 in property.[3] Charles Carroll of Carrollton, once the radical thinker who gave life to "First Citizen," now saw only ruin in the populist turn of the Revolution. He wrote that "unless vigorously counteracted by all honest men, anarchy will follow as a certain consequence; injustice, rapine, and corruption in the seats of justice will prevail." Reducing the barriers to suffrage would only "throw all power into the hands of the very lowest of people," who would be manipulated by "evil and designing" political opportunists.[4] Carroll may have been a rebel, but he was no democrat.

He had helped to draft Maryland's revolutionary constitution of 1776—one of the least revolutionary in the former colonies. The terms of some elected officials were reduced. County sheriffs would be elected rather than appointed by the governor. Changes in property qualifications for voters were hardly revolutionary. To be a member of the electorate, a free male (including, until 1810, free black males) had to own at least 50 acres of land, or "visible property" worth at least £30. Pre-Revolutionary voters had needed £40 in property. This modest change moved some members of the state senate to threaten a boycott of the legislative session to prevent formation of a quorum, a move that they hoped would invalidate the new constitution. The senate's president persuaded them to relent because he feared that their protest would lead not to suspension of the constitution but to overthrow of the senate.[5]

The new constitution increased the number of eligible voters by only about 10 percent in most counties, and in no county did the men eligible to vote for the lower house of the legislature exceed 15 percent of the free white male population. Under the new constitution, voters did not directly elect the state senate. They voted for delegates to an electoral college, which elected the senators. The electors and members of the lower house had to hold at least £500 in real or personal property. Members of the senate and county sheriffs had to own property worth at least £1,000. The governor was to be chosen not by the voters but by joint ballot of both houses of the legislature, and he had to be worth at least £5,000.[6] In Maryland, men of middling means could vote, but they were allowed to elect only men of wealth.

For Baltimore, the most significant political consequence of Maryland's state-building exercise was that the town finally won representation in the lower house of the state legislature. Its two seats were far less than its population would warrant, and even these were given grudgingly. They were a temporary grant, "properly to be modified, or taken away" if the town suffered "a considerable decrease of the inhabitants."[7] The convention considered a resolution to increase Baltimore's representation to four delegates if the number of voters equaled or exceeded those of any county. But the measure was defeated by a vote of more than two to one.[8] Counties, no matter how sparsely populated, got four seats in the assembly. For more than 60 years, Baltimore would continue to elect only two.

The state constitution's guarantee of religious freedom extended only to Christians. But one of its more liberal provisions restored to Roman Catholics such as Charles Carroll the civil and political rights that had been taken away almost 90 years earlier. Carroll, however, was not much inclined to extend such rights to others. In 1779, as a member of the state senate, he sponsored a bill aimed at Baltimore that would make merchants ineligible to serve in the state's delegation to the Continental Congress. The bill passed.[9] Certain types of wealth were, apparently, not sufficiently respectable to earn their proprietors full membership in the political community.

FEDERALIST BOOMTOWN

By war's end, the town's 9,000 residents were sharing their crowded streets with a transient population of seamen, soldiers, traders, and other wanderers who greatly outnumbered the permanent residents. In 1782, one Baltimorean complained that, in addition to the local inhabitants, the town contained "10,000 swearing strangers and sea-farers."[10]

The strangers were evidence of the town's prosperity. Manufacturing had become a more prominent source of income during the Revolution. Industry expanded to fill the void that emerged when British goods disappeared from the market. Though the town continued to generate most of its wealth through commerce, local entrepreneurs added to the range of goods produced locally. A saddler branched out into making chairs and chaises; a printer went into bookbinding; a goldsmith hired a few clockmakers.[11]

In 1785, the members of the fledgling industrial sector organized the Association of Tradesmen and Manufacturers of Baltimore. Their immediate goal was to persuade the state assembly to enact a tariff on imported goods to protect them from the resurgence of British manufactures. In 1783, the legislature imposed a tariff on British goods, but only if carried by British ships. The purpose was not to protect domestic manufacturers but to retaliate against Britain for restrictions on American shipping to its possessions in the West Indies. Twice, the legislature failed to enact the protective tariff requested by the Association of Tradesmen and Manufacturers, and by 1787, the new industrialists had become ardent advocates of a federal constitution, hoping that a national congress might be more responsive to the interests of urban manufacturers than were the landed gentry who still dominated the state's legislature.[12]

While the legislature remained unmoved by the demands of Baltimore industry, lawmakers were adding to the complexity and disjointedness of Baltimore's government. The needs of the growing town demanded attention, but instead of expanding the powers of the town commissioners, the assembly created collections of "special commissioners" to perform limited functions with designated resources.

Special commissioners for street paving were appointed in 1782. Unlike the town commissioners, the special commissioners were designated a "body corporate and politic" with the power not only to file suits and impose fines but to levy taxes. In paving and grading the town's streets, the special commissioners were empowered to charge property owners a fee tied to their street frontage. They also collected taxes on four-wheeled carriages, riding horses, billiard tables, exhibitions, and theatrical performances, as well as fines for littering, chimney fires, or selling liquor without a license. The revenue thus accumulated paid for street paving, the hiring of street cleaners, the appointment of constables to enforce fines and collect assessments, and the wages of a treasurer to handle the money. A subsequent act of the legislature empowered the special commissioners to bring water to Baltimoreans by hiring contractors to dig wells and install neighborhood pumps. The expense was charged to the surrounding property owners.[13]

In a legislative afterthought, a year after appointment of the special commissioners, the General Assembly decreed that the commissioners should stand for election every five years. The original statute of 1782 provided that paving commissioners, like the town commissioners, should serve for life, but the civic order summoned up by the Declaration of Independence seemed to call for more democratic arrangements. The newly devised electoral process was restricted to residents with more than £30 in real property, who would choose nine electors (with property worth at least £500), who would then choose commissioners for paving and pumps, who had to meet the same £500 requirement as the electors. The special commissioners, unlike the town commissioners, were paid public officials. Three comptrollers were elected each year to fix their compensation. The assembly created another set of special commissioners as wardens of the port. They were to make a survey of the harbor and oversee its dredging and maintenance, and were required to have property worth £1,000.[14]

Eventually, the General Assembly got around to enhancing the powers of the town commissioners. In 1784, the legislature authorized the commissioners to hire as many watchmen as needed to patrol the streets at night. The members of the watch were "to apprehend all nightwalkers, malefactors, rogues, vagabonds, and disorderly persons, whom they find disturbing the peace, or shall have just cause to suspect of evil designs." The commissioners were granted the discretion to issue their own regulations for the watchmen "as the nature of the case may require." The members of the night watch were to be supervised by constables. Under the same statute, the commissioners were authorized to contract with "fit and proper persons to . . . put up and fix" as many streetlamps as seemed necessary and to hire lamplighters.[15]

Acknowledging the cost of watchmen, constables, lamps, and lamplighters, the General Assembly empowered the commissioners to levy a tax of one shilling and sixpence on each £100 in property to defray the expense. The assembly also removed the disparity between the special commissioners, who were paid, and the town commissioners, who were not. It directed the same comptrollers who fixed compensation for the special commissioners "to ascertain what allowance the said [town] commissioners shall be entitled to for the time involved in the several duties required by this act."[16]

While the General Assembly intervened to ensure that the town maintained its harbor, paved its streets, and preserved public order after dark, Baltimoreans were mobilizing to transform their city into a municipal corporation with expanded powers of self-government. An effort in 1782 and another in 1784 were defeated, allegedly by the town's "laboring classes." A writer in the *Maryland Journal* counseled his fellow citizens not to "be immediately hurried into [incorporation] by *those* who imagine they will be our rulers." They should consider whether "the lower class of people, and the extremities of the Town will not be loaded with heavy taxes while they gain very partial advantages."[17]

Critics of incorporation expected that Baltimore's propertied elite, which dominated town politics, would play an even grander role in exercising the enhanced powers of a municipality. But both the mercantile elite and the more humble mechanics were unhappy with the status quo. They wanted a more coherent and vigorous political authority, and they wanted to locate it anywhere but Annapolis. The mechanics and tradesmen wanted to empower a national government; the merchant elite preferred to expand local authority.

The merchants nevertheless joined the mechanics in support of the proposed US Constitution. Merchants might be wary of tariffs, but duties imposed uniformly across all American ports were preferable to tariffs imposed by Maryland alone.[18] Enhancing the powers of the national government also promised to advance mercantile interests by improving the nation's credit in foreign markets. The promiscuous issuance of paper currency by state governments made European financiers wary of investing in American debt. Maryland's debate about ratification, in fact, followed a two-year battle in the state assembly about a proposed "emission" of paper currency. The advocates of soft money generally became antifederalists.[19]

In most of Maryland, voters were indifferent to ratification. Statewide voter turnout to elect delegates to the state's constitutional convention was less than 25 percent, but in Baltimore turnout was well over 100 percent of eligible voters. Property qualifications and residency requirements were simply ignored by election judges. There were other irregularities, too. Violence punctuated the four days of balloting. Federalist mobs took possession of polling places until driven off by antifederalist mobs. The mobs were led by prominent citizens, sometimes by the candidates themselves. It was, writes Dennis Clark, a "pattern stemming from the time of the Stamp Act crisis and Revolution ... Violence in its various forms was an instrument readily wielded by the natural leadership of the community, that small group at the top of the socio-economic heap, for the furtherance of their own ends."[20]

Baltimore elected two solidly Federalist delegates to the state ratification convention, where they joined an overwhelming majority of likeminded representatives. Ratification was carried by a vote of 63 to 11. Baltimoreans were exultant. An estimated 3,000 merchants and mechanics paraded through the streets carrying signs and banners. Members of each trade marched together. The silversmiths and watchmakers carried a flag with the slogan, "No Importation and we shall live." The house carpenters bore a 13-story wooden tower with fluted pillars, arches, and pediments. In honor of Baltimore's commercial heritage, there was a miniature sailing ship on wheels, the "Ship Federalist." It would later be launched in the harbor, sailed to Mount Vernon, and presented as a gift to General Washington. The procession flowed around the west side of the town's harbor and climbed a steep hill south of the Basin that provided a sweeping view of the town. Federal Hill has carried the name ever since.[21]

BALTIMORE BECOMES MUNICIPAL

In 1790, Baltimore's population of 13,500 made it the fourth largest city in the United States. Under Maryland law, however, it was still just a town and a dependency of the state legislature, which spent much of its time managing Baltimore's affairs.[22] The town's legislative representatives exercised little influence in these deliberations; they were only two voices among more than 60 in the House of Delegates. But the townspeople had high aspirations—to make Baltimore the capital of the United States under the newly ratified Constitution. The town's geographic location at mid-republic seemed a decisive asset. The residents' hopes were so tangible that early in 1789, they arranged a loan to pay for the construction of the public buildings suitable to a national capital. Baltimore's partisans saw their town as the obvious seat of national government. As a commercial center, it would make Congress an "eyewitness to the operation of their commercial laws." "It is here that armies or fleets can be suddenly raised or recruited. It is here only that instant loans of money can be obtained to answer unexpected misfortunes, or great emergencies of state."[23] But the usual complaints about Baltimore's squalid appearance undermined its commercial qualifications as a capital city. A letter in the *Maryland Gazette* asked, "What would foreign ambassadors think . . . when they observed but few tolerable streets in all the metropolis, and even those disgraced by such a number of awkwardly-built, low, wooden cabins, the rest of the town being divided by irregular, narrow lanes?"[24]

Nevertheless, Baltimore remained a front-runner as national capital. Congressional support was almost evenly divided between Baltimore and another site on the Potomac between Conococheague Creek and the Eastern Branch (today, the Anacostia River). In the end, however, Baltimore's commercial prominence may actually have defeated its hopes. In a "large commercial community," it was argued, the business of governing the nation might be disrupted, by "the mixed character of the population and the many elements of discord which existed there." Congress might also be distracted from addressing national issues by the many local issues that arose in a busy port city. A motion to designate Baltimore the nation's capital failed in the House by a vote of 37 to 23.[25] The honor went to an imagined city on the Potomac, worse yet, a city that might compete with Baltimore for western trade. Baltimoreans blamed their state's congressional delegation for insufficient exertions on their behalf.[26]

Maryland had six congressional districts. Congressmen had to reside in the districts they represented, but Marylanders voted for the entire half-dozen in a statewide, at-large election. In 1790, angry Baltimoreans drew up their own slate of "Chesapeake" candidates in opposition to the "Potomac" ticket selected at a convention of county delegates. Baltimore's large population and its suspicious 99 percent turnout, together with votes from nearby counties, sent all six of its candidates to Congress. The town, wrote J. Thomas Scharf, "thereby took control of the politics of the State"—but only briefly. The legislature convened at the end of the year and voted to substitute district balloting for the statewide election of congressmen. Baltimore City and County would have only one congressional representative.[27]

Baltimore, deemed not good enough to be the nation's capital, once again became a dependency of the tobacco aristocracy. The accommodation that had united the town with the state's landed gentry in ratifying the Constitution now ruptured. Baltimore turned Jeffersonian and Republican, while state government remained Federalist. Unlike their counterparts in other cities, Baltimore's merchant elite did not succumb to the elitist appeals of Federalism. Baltimore had merchants, but no merchant aristocracy. "No such group existed in Baltimore," writes Frank Cassell. "The very newness of the city, the middle class origins of even the wealthiest merchants, and the opportunity for social and economic advancement available in the boom-town atmosphere prevailing up to the War of 1812 arrested the evolution of a self-conscious aristocracy."[28]

But the town's Jeffersonian unity was conditional. It stood as one against the gentry of Southern Maryland and the Eastern Shore. Baltimore Republicans turned against one another, however, over the issue of municipal incorporation. The more substantial citizens—mostly merchants—sought to consolidate their control of the town. In 1793, they renewed an earlier drive for municipal home rule and won legislative approval, but the vote had to be confirmed at the following session of the assembly, and by that time, the residents of Fell's Point had risen in vigorous opposition. They feared that a strong city government would tax them to dredge old Baltimore Town's Basin, negating the navigational advantages of the Point, where the water was twice as deep. The Mechanics' and Carpenters' Societies sided with them, and the artisans and shopkeepers of the Republican Society deserted the eminent merchants who led their organization to oppose municipal incorporation. The bill failed.[29] People of the city's outlying neighborhoods worried that they might get the short end of city benefits, but not of city taxes.[30]

The mercantile elite made another, more devious attempt at municipal incorporation in 1795. A town meeting produced a draft city charter, but the version that later surfaced in Annapolis differed sharply from the one presented to the public in Baltimore. The Annapolis version specified high property qualifications for office-holders and required indirect election for the mayor and the upper house of the city council. The stealth charter produced an immediate uproar in Baltimore, but the state assembly adopted it in 1796, perhaps because it promised conservative government immune to the radical tendencies that ran through the town's lower orders. The charter denied the city its own court system. Judicial authority would continue to lie with Baltimore County at large. But even limited municipal autonomy seemed preferable to the regime that required recourse to Annapolis for almost every local need. Two serious fires, a yellow fever epidemic, and a major flood increased local support for an "internal power" necessary to preserve "good order, health, and safety."[31]

Apprehensions about elitist government proved justified. Five of the city's eight wards were narrow slivers of real estate that carved up the mercantile residential areas close to the Basin. None held as many as 300 adult white males. The remaining three wards covered Fell's Point and the outlying areas of the city. Each held close to 600 adult white males, but got no more representation in the city council than the less populous mercantile wards. A special commission appointed by the governor had fixed the ward boundaries. As a concession to Fell's Point, its inhabitants were exempted from any taxes to deepen the Basin.[32]

The city's first mayor, James Calhoun, was a leading light of mercantile Baltimore and, like his five successors, a member of the Ancient and Honorable Mechanical Company that had served as Baltimore's unofficial government since 1763.[33]

The first branch (lower chamber) of the new bicameral Baltimore City Council consisted of two members elected from each of Baltimore's eight wards for a term of one year. Each man had to own taxable property worth at least $1,000. The second branch of the council included one representative from each ward who served for two years. Each member of the upper house had to own at least $2,000 in taxable property. The mayor also had to own at least $2,000 worth of assessed property. He and the members of the second branch were chosen by a board of eight electors, one from each ward, who had to meet the same property requirements as members of the council's first branch.[34]

The men elected to govern Baltimore had no trouble meeting the property qualifications. Between 1797 and 1815, the average wealth of members of the first branch was more than $6,000; for the second branch, more than $9,000. James Calhoun owned $12,600 in real estate and 11 slaves.[35]

In spite of the potential for political strife between the city's elitist government and its less prosperous inhabitants, Baltimore did not divide sharply along class lines. Its politics—even its riots—had been sustained by cross-class alliances at least as far back as the formation of the Mechanical Company. The continuation of this democratic tradition was partly the work of Baltimore's US congressman, Major General Samuel Smith, a wealthy merchant and revolutionary notable. Smith had fallen out with the Federalists, who had threatened to unseat him in the congressional election of 1796 because of his uneven support of President Washington. He had opposed ratification of the Jay Treaty with Britain, for example, because it did little to curb British harassment of American shipping, a vital concern of his fellow Baltimoreans. In response to the opposition of his former Federalist friends, he converted himself "from gentleman-politician to . . . a brass-knuckles, nuts-and-bolts politico." He did not abandon his friends among the city's elite, but he reached out for the support of the Baltimore Republican Society, the Carpenters' Society, and the Society of French Patriots. His military status gave him a base of support in Baltimore's militia companies.[36]

International conflict cemented the coalition that stood behind Smith. The European war precipitated by the French Revolution in 1793 had reawakened Baltimore's endemic Anglophobia—not just a holdover from the American Revolution, but a by-product of the city's ethno-religious composition. Many Baltimoreans were Britons, but they were Scots, Irish, and Scots Irish rather than English—Presbyterian, Methodist, Quaker, or Roman Catholic, rather than Anglican. None of these groups held much affection for the English, and the city's merchants were irate about the British seizure of American ships in the Caribbean, Baltimore's traditional trading region. Pro-French sentiment ran so strong that one local militia company called itself the Baltimore Sans Culottes. The port welcomed French warships and the prizes they captured.[37]

Congress soon decided, however, that the maritime insolence of the French was no less obnoxious than British seizures of American ships and impressment of American seamen. The Federalist Congress and the Adams administration steadily turned up the alarm concerning the French threat, both external and internal. The Baltimore Sans Culottes became the Baltimore Independent Blues. Congressman Smith resisted Francophobia. Though he supported some of the defense measures aimed at the French, he spoke out against the more repressive provisions of the Alien and Sedition Acts. His constituency of Acadian émigrés had been augmented by 1,500 French refugees from the Haitian revolution, carried to Baltimore in 1793 by a procession of more than 60 ships. The city's immigrant population in general would have been vulnerable to deportation under provisions of the Alien Act.[38]

In 1798, Smith fought the most difficult political campaign of his career. The Federalists began the attack months before the election, portraying Smith as unpatriotic, even Jacobin. The contest drew to a close, in the Baltimore manner, with mob violence. When a Federalist and a Republican parade crossed paths, Smith's supporters charged the Federalists and drove them from the streets. Some of his partisans broke into a private home to disrupt a Federalist meeting. Smith himself led a mob attack on a Federalist rally—not a new role for the congressman. More than 20 years earlier he had led an assault on the office of an unpopular newspaper editor.[39]

Smith won reelection, comfortably though not overwhelmingly. The *Federal Gazette* brushed off the violence: "Unfortunately, heated as the minds of the people were at the election, and as they ever will be in large cities where votes are taken *viva voce* and at but one poll, we can for the honor of Baltimore say but one house was assaulted, and that the contest terminated more peaceably than could reasonably have been expected."[40] The next state legislature mandated the creation of eight polling places in Baltimore, one in each ward, and in 1801, voice voting was abandoned for paper ballots.[41]

The city went for Jefferson by more than 75 percent in 1800. It was joined by the "Chesapeake" counties of central Maryland. This time, however, the formerly Federalist voters of Western Maryland shifted toward the Jeffersonians, too. The area's large German population took offense at the Alien Acts, and western sympathizers of the Whiskey Rebellion nursed an antifederalist grudge of their own.[42]

After the Census of 1800, Maryland's representation in the US House increased from six to nine seats. Baltimore County got two of them. Both went to Jeffersonian Republicans, as did a majority of the seats in the Maryland House of Delegates, whose members voted to elevate Samuel Smith to the US Senate. The General Assembly abolished all property qualifications for voters in elections for county sheriffs and state delegates. In 1805, Baltimore's two delegates, citing the city's population of 30,000, proposed that the city be granted an additional seat in the house. The two Baltimoreans cast the only yes votes.[43]

Chapter 6
"CALAMITIES PECULIARLY INCIDENT TO LARGE CITIES"

T HE MARYLAND LEGISLATURE might deny Baltimore the representation warranted by its size, but the newly incorporated city could
at last manage most of its own affairs without having to consult the
General Assembly about such details as the widening of streets or the
regulation of hogs. Still, the charter approved by the legislature failed
to grant some elementary powers to the city. It denied Baltimore the
power of eminent domain. It empowered Baltimore to tax the real and
personal property of its residents, but the legislature controlled the rate
of taxation.

The city used much of its revenue to pay a legion of public officials.
The procedure for appointing them was unusual. The second branch of
the city council nominated candidates for office, usually two for each
opening. The mayor selected the appointee from those put forward by
the council.[1] Some of the new public servants carried the same titles
as those who had served the old town but did not have the same functions. Five city commissioners were to take over the responsibilities of
the five special commissioners for street paving. In addition to the commissioners' existing duties for paving streets and installing pumps, the
new commissioners handled the contentious business of establishing
the boundaries of city lots.[2]

In other cases, job titles changed but the functions did not. An appointed harbor master, for example, took over the responsibilities previously assigned to the elected port wardens. One of his vital duties
was to direct the operation of the "mud machine," an ungainly wooden
contraption for dredging the city's shallow basin, which was always
silting up with runoff from the muddy and refuse-strewn streets and
the murky streams that flowed through them. The machine was a raft
or barge topped by a wheel big enough to accommodate a horse. The
wheel was connected to a string of scoops that scraped up muck from
the bottom of the harbor as the horse walked in the wheel. The spoil was
transferred to scows, and much of the foul sludge was dumped to create
a "City Block" east of Fell's Point.[3]

The mayor and council continued to regulate trades and transactions. They appointed inspectors of mahogany and ginseng to serve alongside the cullers, garblers, and gaugers who inspected goods sold in Baltimore's markets or shipped from its port. The regulatory regime of the commercial municipality encouraged interest-group politics. In 1797, for example, the corders of wood protested an ordinance requiring that all firewood be cut in four-foot lengths. The law, they argued, "prevented thousands of cords of wood already cut from being brought to market." Moreover, "any person acquainted with woodcutting cannot be unacquainted with the difficulty of chopping to an Exact Length." The council amended its firewood ordinance.[4]

The brick makers challenged the regulations governing the clay that they used, its tempering, and the size of their bricks. They filled three folio pages with double columns of signatures to protest not just the burdens imposed by these requirements but the inferior bricks that resulted from their enforcement. Brick making, they argued, was difficult work. A visitor to the brickyards "no doubt observed four black men for one white man, this is not owing to the wages, no labour in the City affords better wages than brickmakers give to their labourous, but merely because of the extream hard labor, if this could be lessened it would encourage poor white men and boys to come to the brickyard." The council repealed the brick ordinance.[5]

The lobbying activities of the woodcutters, brick makers, and other trades constituted only one arena of city politics. In the early nineteenth century, Baltimore, like many other cities, began to create a new regime that redefined the municipality as a provider of public services rather than a sponsor of markets and regulator of goods and trades. As the need for public services became more pressing, city officials began to regard the oversight of tradesmen and their products as a burdensome distraction. One official complained that too much of the city council's time was being spent "in digesting and preparing different inspection Ordinances." The ordinances occupied "not a little of the mayor's" time as well.[6] As the city's population grew, problems of public health, order, and safety became more acute. In its first session under the municipal charter, the council approved 64 ordinances, some quite lengthy, to address the hazards that arose in a dense, dirty, combustible town. Mayor Thorowgood Smith referred to these problems as "the calamities peculiarly incident to large Cities."[7]

At its next session, in 1798, the council created the office of city constable. Unlike the constables who supervised the night watch, the city constable was concerned exclusively with the enforcement of municipal ordinances, not state law. He was "to walk through the streets, lanes, and alleys of the City daily, with his mace in his hand, and give information to the Mayor or other magistrates of all nuisances within the City, and of all impediments in the streets, lanes and alleys." The constable was to report these violations of city ordinances, with the names of the offenders and witnesses, "to the end that prosecution may be commenced."[8]

The office of city constable was one token of a shift in Baltimore's government. The constable's jurisdiction was the entire city, and his responsibilities extended across the entire spectrum of municipal law and authority. Unlike the inspectors, gaugers, and graders who confined their surveillance to particular goods or trades, the constable represented an encompassing public sphere. Still, the constable only reported the violation of ordinances. He did not enforce them. But "calamities" of city life would energize the authority of Baltimore's government. The two most notable were epidemic disease and fiery conflagration.

PLAGUE

In the summer of 1800, an epidemic of yellow fever killed at least 1,200 Baltimoreans in just 65 days—more than 4 percent of the town's population. The city was already acquainted with the disease. In 1793, an outbreak of "American plague" in Philadelphia had prompted Maryland's governor to appoint a health committee for Baltimore. It consisted of two physicians: one responsible for preventing Philadelphia's epidemic from reaching Baltimore by water; the other, to prevent its entry by land. Enforcement of the embargo was strict. A visitor from Philadelphia reported that he had been stopped by a guard at the city's outskirts and refused entry. When the traveler asked for food, he was offered a piece of toasted cheese served at the end of a pitchfork.[9] Neither the precaution nor the quarantine was necessary. Yellow fever is spread by mosquitoes, not interpersonal contact, but quarantine continued, for a time, to be the principal measure to fight the disease.

Baltimore's municipal charter of 1796 empowered the new government to enact ordinances "necessary to preserve the health of the city" and to "prevent the introduction of contagious diseases within the city and within three miles of the same." Baltimore's officials put their new authority to use not long after the charter took effect. In 1797, the mayor and council approved an ordinance providing for the appointment of nine health commissioners and a physician to serve as health officer. The physician was to visit every ship that entered the port from April through November, and he could detain a vessel in quarantine for up to 20 days. The health commissioners were to convene monthly at the courthouse from May through November to "collect and receive every possible information of the healthiness" of the city, some of which was to come from the health officer. The commissioners were responsible for providing "persons laboring under infectious diseases" with "meats, drinks, bedding, and clothing," if they were not already provided for, and they were to remove such patients to a quarantine hospital at Hawkins Point or some other place at least three miles outside the city. The law indicated that Baltimoreans had learned something, but not enough, about yellow fever: "all ponds of stagnant water" and "all cellars and foundations . . . whose bottoms contain stagnant and putrid water" were to be "declared common nuisances, productive of offensive vapors and noxious exhalations, the causes of diseases, and ought to be regulated, restrained, and removed."[10]

An outbreak of yellow fever nevertheless struck Baltimore in late August 1797, concentrated in Fell's Point. Health officials established an encampment of tents and shanties on high ground so that the Point's residents could get away from the stagnant pond and marsh that lay between their neighborhood and the mouth of the Jones Falls.[11]

At the height of the contagion, the commissioners had to deal with unauthorized burials in potter's field, a cemetery for paupers located on the north side of today's Patterson Park. They gave the cemetery's official gravedigger, Edward Agnew, sole custody of the key to the burial ground and specified his fees and practices like those of any other regulated trade of the time. He was authorized to charge one dollar for an adult grave and 75 cents for the burial of a child, and he would be entitled to an additional dollar "if he attends with his carriage, to remove the corpse to the grave."[12]

In 1798, with financial support from the state, Baltimore established a public hospital "for the relief of indigent sick persons and for the reception and care of Lunaticks." A committee headed by the mayor chose the location for the hospital and supervised its construction. The site, at today's intersection of Broadway and Monument Street, is now occupied by the Johns Hopkins Hospital. The property had previously served as the location of a "retreat" for sick seamen and travelers.[13]

In 1799, the nine health commissioners notified the mayor and council "that having principally gone through the duties of our appointment for the late season [we] do now resign the same." The commissioners made no bones about the reason for their collective retirement. If the city wanted citizens to serve on any future health commission, "we would . . . propose the propriety . . . of being allowed a Salary as might in some measure compensate for the danger and time to which they are subjected."[14] A month later, the council assembled a new board of health; its members would receive two dollars for each day spent on their duties.[15]

In August 1800, the *Federal Gazette* published a "caution" for Baltimoreans. One of the paper's correspondents felt it "a duty I owe to the public (as the sickly season of the year is now approaching) to advise them to be particularly careful in their manner of living." Readers were warned to consume very little "animal food . . . and to drink lemonade" rather than other beverages. One week later, the paper carried a detailed description of the mosquito and advice about treating its bites, but failed to make the connection between the seasonal disease and the seasonal insect.[16]

On Fell's Point, the board of health found "inflammatory bilious fever"—yellow fever. It "made its first appearance along the water next to the cove . . . progressing gradually up Bond and Fleet streets, and thence spread . . . into other adjacent streets." The *Gazette* tried to minimize the bad news. It assured readers that no disease had spread west of the Jones Falls and reported that a healthful summer rain had halted the progress of the fever even on Fell's Point. The paper insisted that the disease was transmitted "entirely owing to our own local sources of filth, vegetable and animal putrefaction . . . and not to any imported or human contagion."[17]

The *Gazette*'s effort to avoid creating a panic was unsuccessful. The sickness spread. Local businesses suspended operations, and Baltimoreans who could afford to move elsewhere left the city. All but two health commissioners fled along with the other refugees. The city's hospital was still incomplete. It could accommodate only about 130 patients. A temporary camp of shanties housed the overflow.[18]

The two health commissioners who had remained at their posts—Adam Fonerden and Joseph Townsend—drew praise from Mayor James Calhoun and the city council for their "extraordinary exertions" and their "unwearied diligence." But a Fell's

Point physician who signed himself "Humanitas" complained that he had never seen either of the two health commissioners as he made the rounds of his neighborhood, and charged that "they kept themselves at home, and out of danger."[19]

"Humanitas" was Dr. James Smith, a medical gadfly, who had opened his home to yellow fever victims. His quarrel with the health commissioners extended beyond nonfeasance to incompetence. The members of the board of health, he charged, were "men inadequate to the task . . . without information, without talents, ignorant, illiberal, insincere." He later presented a comprehensive plan for a new board of health that would have a president and secretary who were respected physicians and include three "resident physicians."[20] The existing board of health had no medical professionals. Adam Fonerden was a shoe merchant, and Joseph Townsend dealt in dry goods, ranging from pots and pans to schoolbooks and textiles.

The sad case of Polly Elliott may have done more to mobilize sentiment against the health commissioners than Dr. Smith's professional criticism. Polly was an orphan who had been taken in by a Baltimore family. She was too sick to accompany them when they fled the epidemic, so they left her in the city. She staggered through the streets until a local grocer gave her shelter in his storehouse. A stonecutter, William McCormick, learned of her plight and approached health commissioner Joseph Townsend to get Polly admitted to the still-incomplete city hospital. Townsend refused to accept her without a physician's certificate affirming that she had yellow fever. With some difficulty, McCormick obtained the document. Townsend approved her admission to the hospital, but declined to provide her with transportation there. McCormick attempted to leave Polly in Townsend's custody, but the commissioner insisted that he take the girl with him. As McCormick recounted the episode, Townsend followed him to the door "and taking the child by the shoulders put her, again, out into the street!!" McCormick was unable to find any stage driver willing to carry the sick child. Stopping frequently for rest and water, McCormick walked her the long mile to the hospital, where Polly died a few days later.[21]

Polly Elliot's case produced a tempest in the columns of the *Federal Gazette*. Denunciations of heartless health commissioners provoked testy responses from the commissioners themselves and their allies in the medical profession. In January, the *Gazette*'s editors called a halt. The dispute, they noted, had "become extremely lengthy and personal, and . . . so uninteresting to a great portion of . . . readers and irksome to the editors" that they asked the combatants "to find some other vehicle for the dissemination of their pieces."[22] Besides, the yellow fever season was long past.

PUBLIC INVESTMENTS IN PUBLIC HEALTH

During its next session, in 1801, the city council approved a comprehensive health ordinance providing for five health commissioners, two from the east and three from the west side of the Jones Falls. They were to divide the city into five districts, and each commissioner was to be responsible for one district. They did not have to be physicians, but they were expected to be much more watchful than their predecessors. During the "sickly season" from April through October, they were to meet weekly rather than monthly. The law "invited and requested" Baltimore's practicing physicians to assist the commissioners "with their counsel and advice in all matters that relate to the preservation of the health of the inhabitants."[23]

The new law extended the health commissioners' authority and responsibility. Unlike their predecessors, the commissioners of 1801 had "full power and authority to enter upon any lots, grounds or possessions of any person or persons . . . and inspect the same as far as it respects the health of the city." They were also responsible for "removing all offensive substances and nuisances," and they could command the assistance of constables and the superintendents of streets, who were "to obey without delay all orders of the said Commissioners of Health." The most telling difference between the old and new commissioners was their compensation. The new health commissioners received an annual salary of $400. The job was no longer a two-dollar-a-day sideline for dealers in dry goods or shoes.[24]

The yellow fever epidemic of 1800 made a lasting impression on Baltimore's government. In August 1802, at the height of the fever season, Mayor Calhoun wrote that there was "no duty more incumbent on the City Commissioners at this particular season than attention to the repairs of paved streets where they are sunk so low as to retain stagnant water."[25] Another sign of the city's heightened concern about public health was a new quarantine hospital, the Lazaretto, which replaced the Hawkins Point quarantine station. It could accommodate people and cargoes on ships suspected of carrying contagious diseases. The Lazaretto stood on the east side of the entrance to the harbor, just across from Whetstone Point and Fort McHenry.[26]

The city hospital for the indigent sick and insane provided seasonal accommodations for the victims of yellow fever, but apparently fell short in its care of the mentally ill. In 1807, Mayor Thorowgood Smith complained that too many "maniacs . . . have appeared in our streets to the dread of some and the annoyance of many of our fellow citizens." Though caring for the mentally ill had been one of its original responsibilities, the hospital had been "very badly constructed for that purpose." Among other things, it lacked a fence or wall to keep the inmates from wandering away. Smith urged the city council to appropriate the funds "required to make the indispensable alterations in the building."[27]

The council could not bring itself to spend the money. The hospital stood almost empty. An agreement with the local customs collector to care for sick and injured seamen ended in 1807. In February 1808, the board of health reported that the hospital had only two inmates; they were both private patients of the superintendent, whose expenses were not charged to the city. The board concluded "that the City hospital is at present no expense to the City: but it is equally true, that it is of no public utility."[28] This was the situation in February, of course. When the "sickly season" arrived with the spring, the patient population might increase sharply.

It was in early spring that two local physicians—Drs. Colin MacKenzie and James Smyth—offered to "take in Charge & Support such an Institution" as the mayor had proposed for the care of the mentally ill. MacKenzie was familiar with the hospital, having served as its attending physician.[29]

The ordinance formalizing the new arrangements for Baltimore's hospital stopped well short of complete privatization. The municipality controlled admissions to the institution. MacKenzie and Smyth had to accept "Maniacs and diseased persons of every description . . . that may be placed under their care, or sent to the said Hospital by the Commissioners of Health or other persons authorized by the Corporation." The hospital would receive 50 cents a day for each of these patients, less if the patient population exceeded 30. The city retained the right to revoke the lease on six months' notice. Unlike most lessees, Smyth and MacKenzie paid no rent. But they were to "use their best endeavours to obtain from the Legislature of the State of Maryland a sum of Money or a Law authorizing a Lottery to raise a sum for erecting additional buildings and improvements on the said Grounds."[30]

MacKenzie and Smyth seem to have developed the hospital according to the city's rather complicated plan. The state provided much of the money needed to build the kind of asylum that Mayor Smith wanted. The city later promised that, if the physicians completed the new asylum building before their 15-year lease expired, the lease would be extended by another 10 years. The state later provided more money to expand the facility, and finally, after paying Baltimore a sum equal to its investment, Maryland took control of the hospital.[31]

BURNING QUESTIONS

Until the middle of the nineteenth century, most cities relied on volunteer fire companies. The Mechanical Company formed the first of Baltimore's firefighting units in 1763 and sponsored a lottery to raise money for the purchase of two fire engines, hand-powered water pumps on wheels to be pulled through the streets by the company's volunteers and fed with water by buckets. But the lottery failed to raise sufficient funds for the engines, and the firefighters had to make do with water buckets alone for six more years—then made the unlikely purchase of an engine from a Dutch sea captain who happened to have one on board his ship. The engine was named "The Dutchman."[32] Returning Revolutionary War veterans formed the Union Fire Company, the town's second, in 1781. Its engine, also a hand-powered suction pumper, was called "Tick-Tack," perhaps because of the sound it made. The Union Company's firehouse was on Baltimore's west side; the Mechanical was further east. After the Union came the Friendship, the Deptford (on Fell's Point), the Commercial (formed by local merchants), the Liberty, the Vigilant, the New Market (near Lexington Market), and the Independent, whose firehouse at Gay and Ensor Streets is still in use as the city's fire museum.[33]

Weeks before Baltimoreans were to vote on municipal incorporation, in 1796, a fire broke out on Light Street. The flames consumed a furniture factory, several homes, two schools, and a Methodist meeting house where a funeral was under way. A nearby hotel was saved only because one of the guests suggested that wet blankets be spread on its roof. All six of the city's fire companies worked to prevent the spread of the fire. In the end, several unharmed structures had to be pulled down to check the flames.[34]

The Light Street conflagration transformed Baltimore's arrangements for coping with fire. A town meeting appointed a committee to suggest "such measures as may appear best calculated . . . for the preservation of the town from fire and other calamities." In a report submitted two weeks later, the committee recommended a voluntary night patrol of citizens in each of eight districts to report fires in their earliest stages. It urged that the street commissioners "cause to be established immediately a competent number of large, good pumps in each street" along with "deep and spacious wells." The committee requested that representatives from all of the town's fire companies meet to "digest some system that may tend to insure a uniform government of companies in time of fire," so that they would be prepared to work together at fires too big for one company to handle.[35]

The new municipal government also took up the issue of fire prevention. It was not a new concern. As early as 1748, local householders could be fined for "any Chimney found blazing out at the top," and each household with a chimney had to have a ladder that reached its rooftop.[36] In 1798, the mayor and council adopted an ordinance to reduce the likelihood of chimney fires. They appointed three superintendents of chimney sweeps, one for the east side of Jones Falls, and two who divided the territory on the west. In return for posting bond of $100 and an annual $50 licensing fee, each superintendent gained a monopoly of chimney sweeping in his district and became sole employer for all of the neighborhood boys who worked as sweeps. Occupants of buildings with chimneys were required to purchase the superintendent's services at least once every four weeks. Residents who failed to do so would have to pay the superintendent's fee each day until they had their chimneys cleaned, and the city could fine them up to five dollars.[37]

The regulation of chimney sweeps occupied an intermediate stage between the commercial city of regulated markets and the modern, service-providing municipality that succeeded it. The city authorities had organized chimney sweeping as a regulated trade. The superintendents were licensed entrepreneurs. The city prescribed their fee schedule—8 cents for a one-story chimney, 12½ cents for two stories, 15 cents for three, and 18 cents to sweep four or more stories. The municipality also monitored the results of the sweeps' work. If a blaze erupted from a chimney swept during the previous 30 days, the superintendent might have to pay a $10 fine.[38] But chimney sweeping was a service, not a product, and its benefits were not restricted to the household that gathered around the hearth of a swept chimney. A chimney "blazing out at the top" was a menace not only to the occupants of that dwelling but to every building in the vicinity. Chimney sweeping was a *public* service, and that was why Baltimoreans had to be compelled to pay for it. The household bore the full cost, but the benefits were shared with a larger public.

The superintendents of chimney sweeps were soon required to perform other public services. They were to determine whether the residents of their districts complied with an earlier law requiring each household to hang two leather buckets near the front door. In the absence of fire hydrants and piped water under pressure, buckets filled at the neighborhood pump remained the principal tools in case of fire. The superintendents were also empowered to inspect stove pipes and report those that were "dangerous or defective" to the mayor.[39] Later still, the superintendents acquired responsibilities that had nothing to do with chimneys. In 1810, for example,

The superintendents of sweeps were both private entrepreneurs and public servants.

FIRE AND WATER

Baltimore continued to rely on part-time, volunteer firefighters, but the amateurs were now backed by a system of full-time vigilance and citywide coordination, and they received annual subsidies from city government to pay for firehouses, equipment, and maintenance. But the firemen continued to operate with their primitive engines fed by bucket brigades from neighborhood pumps, not water mains and fire hydrants.

Shortly after Baltimore became a municipal corporation, the city council formed a committee to "consider the difficulties of introducing pure . . . water into the City." The committee evidently went well beyond mere consideration. Its report, issued in 1799, urged the mayor to "preserve and safely keep all the timber and materials that have been provided for the completion of the said undertaking." An expert adviser had confirmed that the plan to draw water from the Jones Falls was feasible, but the committee was stymied by a legal deficiency. Lacking the power of eminent domain, the city could not lay water pipes on private property without owners' consent, which some of them refused to give.[41]

The committee urged Mayor Calhoun to ask the General Assembly to grant the municipality the power to condemn property needed to supply the city with water, while paying compensation to its owners. Months later, the mayor reported that he had "made application to the General Assembly" to grant Baltimore the power of eminent domain, "but the Legislature was pleased to postpone consideration of the subject."[42]

In 1803, Mayor Calhoun once again cited the deficiencies of the city's water supply and proposed that the city council consider the possibility of forming a private water company to remedy the city's water shortage.[43] The council responded with an ordinance providing for the appointment of commissioners to "ascertain the force & quantity of water which issues from any sources . . . or streams within ten miles of the city." The commissioners, together with the mayor, were to consider the "practicability" of drawing water from these sources and across "the tracts . . . thro' which this water may be conducted to this city."[44]

The commissioners surveyed privately owned springs and estimated the gallons per minute produced by each of these "fountains." But they stopped short of "endeavoring to estimate the expense of purchasing & conveying the water into the city"—information clearly requested in the ordinance creating the commission. The commissioners concluded that "to discharge this part of their duty was impossible" because "so many persons" owned the water sources or the land through which the water would have to pass on its way to Baltimore. The obstacle, once again, was the city's inability to secure property by eminent domain, which the commissioners saw as "indispensably necessary, if it should be the wish and decision of the City Council, to water the city from the springs in its vicinity." It was up to the council to judge "the propriety of obtaining a law from the State" that would enable the city to take this real estate "upon equitable terms" of sale.[45]

Mayor Calhoun, like the commissioners, assigned the council responsibility for "introducing a copious and permanent supply of water into the city." The council promptly returned responsibility to the mayor, authorizing him to accept proposals "by an individual or company" for bringing the "copious and permanent supply of water" to Baltimore. As on earlier occasions when public authority faltered, the citizens took matters into their own hands. Baltimoreans gathered at a public meeting "to devise some scheme to relieve the city from the unpleasant dilemma in which it was placed." The scheme was a joint stock company in the water business. Local notables served on its board of directors. Samuel Smith was its chairman. On May 1, 1804, they began receiving subscriptions for stock in the Baltimore Water Company.[46]

At first, sales were slow, a disappointment to the directors, but no surprise to the *Federal Gazette*, which observed that every "enterprise of this kind, in a city so devoid of public spirit as ours, must depend upon a few." After a handful of notables, including Charles Carroll, made exemplary purchases, the stock took off, and a multitude of small stockholders helped to finance "the watering of the city." But the state legislature once again proved an obstacle. For obscure reasons, the General Assembly seemed unwilling to grant the firm a charter of incorporation. The city council issued a charter of its own and the permission to lay pipes in city streets, provided that the streets were promptly returned to good condition.[47]

The council also considered the possibility that the city might purchase the Water Company, but concluded that it would be difficult to negotiate a sale with the company's 500 stockholders. Besides, the council's committee judged that "the great object of watering the City is full as likely to be effected by the present Water Company . . . as it can possibly be by the [municipal] Corporation with its present means."[48]

In fact, the Water Company demonstrated the shortcomings of private enterprise in the water business. The company extended its service to those streets where residents were willing and able to pay for the delivery of water to their homes. As late as 1825, when Baltimore's population was between 60,000 and 80,000, only 1,640 households paid the annual $10 fee for running water.[49] Much of Baltimore continued to draw its water from neighborhood pumps. The city's marshy situation meant that the water table was close to ground level. The pumps drew water contaminated by drainage from the town's gutters and privies.[50]

The Water Company drew water from a mill race on the Jones Falls to fill a hilltop reservoir at the intersection of Franklin and Cathedral Streets, near the site now occupied by the Central Branch of the Enoch Pratt Free Library. Gravity was supposed to carry water from this elevated storage pond through pipes and under the streets of Baltimore.[51]

The city had evidence that clean water reduced death rates. A local entrepreneur, George Waddell, had been collecting fresh water in "puncheons and pipes" from springs on the city's outskirts and carrying it in his cart to "subscribers" in Baltimore. He reported that during a six-month period in 1805, "in the most unfavorable part of the year, only *two* deaths . . . occurred out of Two Hundred and Sixteen Sub-scribers; and what is still more surprising, both of these two were aged and infirm."[52]

City officials might have paid more attention to Waddell's evidence if they had been chiefly interested in securing a supply of clean drinking water. But their top priority was securing enough water to protect Baltimore against the threat of fire. Drinking water, according to Sherry Olson, "was a secondary matter, for conve-nience and for defraying the costs of the fire-protection system." The joint commit-tee of the city council overseeing the water supply seems to have been principally concerned about the purchase, placement, and repair of fire plugs.[53]

In the end, George Waddell may have had some influence on the council. While the council turned to a private company to make the capital investment for the city's water system, it proposed to augment Baltimore's water resources by exploit-ing natural springs. In 1808, it authorized the mayor to purchase five parcels of land on Calvert Street containing several small springs. One of these was converted into a municipal showpiece. Surrounded by Doric columns and topped with a classic dome, the "City Spring" became the focus of a downtown park. Its popularity led to purchase of still other springs. Although the city employed "keepers" to see that its springs stayed clean, the spread of pavement and buildings reduced the land area open to rainfall—a source of the springs' fresh water—and the encroachment of privies made citizens justifiably suspicious about the purity of spring water.[54]

PUBLIC SERVICE, PRIVATE GOVERNMENT

Fires and epidemics propelled Baltimore's government into the business of provid-ing essential public services to its residents, but it did so without much expansion of the public domain. The city depended on volunteer fire companies that relied, in turn, on water provided by a private corporation. The superintendents of sweeps, who functioned as agents of fire prevention, were private entrepreneurs licensed by the municipality. Although the threat of yellow fever had moved the mayor and council to increase the powers and pay of the city's health commissioners, the city's supposedly public hospital was under private management.

Baltimore was not entirely distinctive in this. New York and Boston relied on private water companies and volunteer fire companies. Like them, Baltimore was, in some respects, a "private city"—a public enterprise dedicated not to delivering pub-lic services but to supporting its residents' pursuit of private prosperity. "Privatism," according to Sam Bass Warner, was the dominant motif of urban political culture in America. Warner's classic study of Philadelphia shows how this preoccupation with individual independence and prosperity undermined public initiatives and left the city ill-prepared to meet its twentieth-century problems.[55]

At least one historian, however, suggests that urban privatism was not so prev-alent as Warner claims. E. Digby Baltzell acknowledges that it was characteristic of Philadelphia, but it was much less powerful in Boston.[56] More generally, some wide-spread features of urban political economy seem out of joint with Warner's culture of privatism. The public markets of Baltimore and other cities during the eighteenth and nineteenth centuries certainly created opportunities for private profit, but the markets also stood at the center of a far-reaching regime of government regulation that covered goods, trades, and transactions both inside and outside the markets.[57] Against Warner's account of the private city, one must place William J. Novak's case for the "well-regulated society" in which municipal authority encroached on many matters seen today as decidedly private.[58] Baltimore lived in both worlds. On the one hand, it had regulations for brick makers, butchers, and lumber and mahogany merchants; health commissioners empowered to enter private property and command the removal of nuisances; and a night watch authorized to apprehend nightwalkers and people suspected of "evil designs." On the other hand, it had volunteer fire companies, a privately managed city hospital, and private entrepreneurs who provided public goods such as fire prevention and water.

Some relatively consistent patterns emerge from this complex interaction of public authority and private institutions. In general, Baltimoreans seemed to avoid large-scale, long-term public investments. The town turned its public hospital over to private management precisely to avoid making the capital investments necessary for the institution's operation. The municipality settled on a private water company for the same reason. Even the authorities' decisions about the purposes of a water system focused on the immediate need for water to extinguish fires rather than its less proximate role in preventing disease.

The city was prepared to pave and to install pumps. These investments were made in incremental installments—street by street and block by block—and the costs were borne by the property owners who benefited most immediately from these improvements. In fact, they frequently indicated their willingness to cover these costs by petitioning the street commissioners for paving or pumps. In a sense, the special commissioners "privatized" the financing of these public improvements by relying on user fees to pay for them. Even more private were the fire-prevention efforts of the superintendents of sweeps. They paid the city to practice their trade and supported themselves and their chimney sweeps with income from their clients. In general, the city made public investments to meet immediate perils posed by conflagration and epidemic disease. More distant objectives were left to private finance and initiative.

The town's powder magazine was a token of its willingness to exercise public authority and expend public funds in the face of immediate, explosive danger. Citizens were allowed to keep only two quarter casks of gunpowder in their homes or shops, stored in at least four separate tin canisters. Anything above that amount had to be deposited in the city's powder magazine, at a storage cost of 12 cents per barrel per month. The location and construction of the magazine and measures against the possibility of its explosion were subjects of vital concern to the mayor and council. They paid particular attention to the duties of the magazine's superintendent and the extent to which his public responsibilities restricted his private pursuits. He would forfeit his position if he were to take out "any license for the sale of any wine or spirituous liquors or any tavern license or a license for any kind of entertainment or amusement or shall sell or cause to be sold any Cider Beer or berry meed."[59]

The original plans for the powder magazine had even prescribed the superintendent's place of residence. He was to live in a brick house within the brick wall that surrounded the magazine. The superintendent expressed reservations about the housing arrangement. He did not mention the possibility of an explosion but noted instead that the site did not have an adequate supply of water, which made the place "an unhealthy situation to live on." He suggested that the city save itself the cost of building his house and allow him to rent another nearby "in an eligible location, near a good Well of Water, and sufficiently convenient to the Magazine." The mayor and council apparently approved the modification of their plans.[60]

Baltimore's residents and political leaders were prepared to spend public funds to manage the clear and present dangers posed by urban contagion and combustibility, but they resisted investments for public purposes with payoffs further in the future. Perhaps the most pointed expression of this temperament applied to government itself. Its officials met in rented rooms, and when the city council approved an ordinance to build a city hall, Baltimoreans—especially those living in Fell's Point and the former Jones Town—rose up to condemn this. A petition accompanied by yards of signatures denounced the project. The signers declared that there was "no present necessity for such a public building." Four days later, the council allowed that "it might be inexpedient at this time to go to the expense of purchasing a piece of ground and erecting a city hall thereon." Two weeks later, it passed an ordinance to postpone construction of a city hall for three years.[61] In fact, Baltimore would not have a city hall until the 1830s, and it was not even a new building, but a second-hand museum.

"Present necessity" was the driving force in Baltimore's public decisions. In a town with a short-term history, short-term calculations were the only kind that counted. Between 1790 and 1800, Baltimore's population grew by more than 96 percent; by 1810 it had added another 75 percent. In a city where nothing stood still for very long, plans for a faraway future seemed unrealistic. Baltimore was a boomtown on the make. A majority of its residents were not natives of the city. As they had little past in common, they could imagine little collective future.

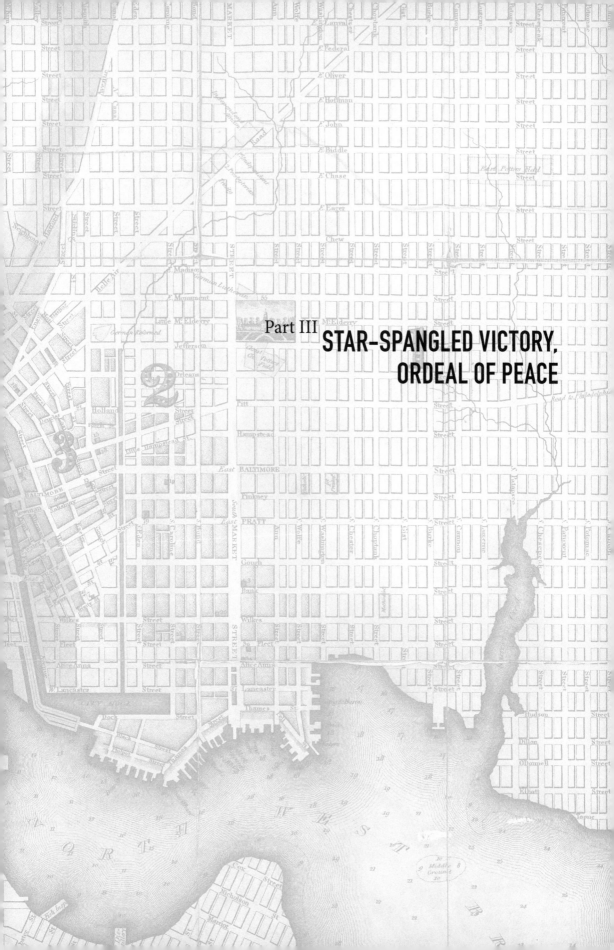

Part III **STAR-SPANGLED VICTORY,
ORDEAL OF PEACE**

Chapter 7

TRIAL BY COMBAT

BOOMTOWN BALTIMORE EXPANDED so rapidly that it had little time to plan beyond the present. There was no accurate map of the city. In 1784, the legislature had authorized the town commissioners to "make a correct survey of the city." The project was never completed, though one of the surveyors hired to do the job produced a fragment that covered Fell's Point, the Basin, and parts of the Jones Falls. It was one of a patchwork of maps that covered successive additions to the town. Their disjointedness reflected the situation on the ground. The "streets, lanes, and alleys" of the additions had been laid out with little regard to the existing street system of Baltimore, and Baltimore failed to correct such mismatches. In 1792, the legislature stepped in to authorize the extension of some city streets to the west, because all the traffic from that direction on its way to the Centre Market, or "Marsh Market," converged on one thoroughfare—Market (now Baltimore) Street—described as "often so crowded with cars, waggons, and drays that there is not sufficient room for the inhabitants to pass and repass to and from said market."[1]

The city could not see itself clearly, and it expanded blindly until it encountered some snag, like the one on Baltimore Street. A few commercially produced maps of Baltimore were available in the 1790s, but as Richard Fox points out, they were "not connected with any authorized surveying or planning system" and therefore of "little value for resolving property disputes and of no assistance for city planning." But once framed, the commercial maps could hang with other works of art that adorned the walls of the town's parlors and drawing rooms. Shortly after the city received its municipal charter in 1796, the mayor directed the street commissioners to produce a general survey of Baltimore, but the commissioners were preoccupied with the more immediate tasks of adjudicating disputes about property lines or hiring contractors to install water pumps and pave streets. They never got around to the survey. Finally, in 1812, the city council approved a contract with Thomas Poppleton, an Englishman and a stranger to the city, to produce a "Correct

Plat of the City as it is at present improved" for a sum not exceeding $1,000, a sum soon exceeded.[2]

Poppleton was selected by the board of city commissioners and the mayor, but the decision was not unanimous. One commissioner, Henry Stauffer, campaigned strenuously for another candidate—Jehu Bouldin, a local surveyor who had conducted at least 63 surveys in and around Baltimore City, many for the commissioners themselves. He started his company in 1790, but his family had been in the surveying business since the mid-seventeenth century. He underbid the competition by $50, confident that his familiarity with the area would enable him to complete the project more cheaply than out-of-town competitors.[3]

Richard Fox suggests that Bouldin lost the job to Poppleton because the ordinance calling for the survey specified that it be conducted by "an experienced and skillful artist."[4] Bouldin may have been a solid surveyor, but he was no artist. Poppleton submitted a work sample tinted with watercolors and decorated with tiny depictions of local landmarks and buildings. The council wanted a work of art, like the maps that already hung in Baltimore homes, but a work of art that was also drawn to scale, with details down to the boundaries of lots.

MAPPING POLITICS

Trouble between Poppleton and the commissioners developed almost immediately. A document submitted by Poppleton outlined the procedures that he would follow. Someone—perhaps a commissioner or a clerk—scratched out every provision but one. It said that the commissioners, with the approval of the mayor, "are at liberty at any moment—or in any stage of the Business to stop the proceedings."[5]

Poppleton's first test came a few days after his appointment. He was summoned to meet the commissioners between Charles and Light Streets to establish the boundary between two lots—but not just any lots. One of them belonged to former mayor James Calhoun; the other, to a city councilman, James Carey. Poppleton was to use a compass to locate the corner of Light and Camden Streets, which the commissioners had marked with a wooden peg eight years earlier. Poppleton missed the peg by 11 feet, 5 inches. According to the surveyor, the problem was the compass, which was not a reliable surveying instrument. The meeting moved to Charles Street, where Poppleton was unable to find a property line. The ordeal went on for the better part of three days. The commissioners finally "found the Locations so questionable as to Inaccuracies that they could not find themselves at liberty in Conscience to confirm the same." Poppleton sent a note to the board declining to serve as a "*private* Surveyor" for the city. He had signed on to conduct a general survey of the city, not to resolve disputes about property lines.[6]

Poppleton next wrote to the mayor suggesting that the task assigned him by the commissioners had been contrived to portray him as professionally incompetent. But he charged that the test of his abilities had been rigged because he was not allowed to use his own surveying practices "founded on an improved & scientific method now in general use in civic & military surveying in Europe." He proposed that the mayor "allot a section of the City as the trial." He would map the area, and when he was finished, the council could judge the results.[7]

Mayor Edward Johnson called the city council into special session to address "the difficulties which have occurred in attempting to carry into effect the law authorizing . . . a survey of the city." The mayor pointed out that Poppleton's surveying practices differed from those specified in law and required "a special reference to the wisdom & decision of the City Council." He added that "however anxious we may be to encourage an artist of superior talents," the essential consideration was whether the project could "be made to serve a useful & valuable purpose."[8]

The city's attempt to form a clear picture of itself dissolved in conflict. According to the mayor, "Such a contrariety in the sentiments of the board existed as to the proper mode of effecting the views and wishes of the city council as to render it impossible to proceed." In the meantime, someone had apparently taken up Poppleton's offer to show what he could do on a part of the city. Relying on "the patronage of a few individuals," the mayor reported, Poppleton "commenced the undertaking and has sent me a specimen of the work for your inspection."[9]

A joint committee of the council attempted to resolve the "contrariety" that impeded the survey. Its report, which repeatedly referred to Poppleton as "the Artist," was a one-sided vindication of the English surveyor. The committee implied that the commissioners' hostility toward Poppleton erupted because the surveyor found errors in some of the board's old "establishments." The committee attributed such mistakes to the commissioners' employment of different surveyors using different instruments instead of relying on one man operating "in the best manner the latest improvements in surveying admit." That man, they concluded, should be Poppleton. Extending his expertise to the entire city would achieve an accuracy and consistency not previously attained. The committee drafted an ordinance requiring the board of city commissioners to provide Poppleton with all the data that he needed for his survey of the city. The commissioners, however, would no longer supervise his work, which he was to perform under the direction of the mayor. When he was done, his map of the city would be reviewed not by the commissioners but by "three Persons to be appointed by the Mayor."[10]

The proposed ordinance was defeated. The commissioners then asked the mayor to approve their decision to replace Poppleton with Jehu Bouldin. Poppleton's refusal to work on anything but the "general Survey" seems to have been the chief justification for their decision. They argued that making "establishments" to clarify disputed property lines was essential to the larger project of mapping the city as a whole. The original contract had not required Poppleton to make such "private" surveys, but commissioners subsequently drafted a "Stipulation of Contract" that added this duty to Poppleton's responsibilities.[11]

Poppleton, however, was still in the game. In July 1812, he wrote to the board of assessors (appointed and overseen by the commissioners) to inform it that he had completed a survey of a portion of the city soon to be affected by the opening of a new street. It may well have been the work he had done "under the patronage of a few individuals" while the council considered his contract. Poppleton offered to provide this survey to the assessors at almost no cost if they would retain him to make "a general Plan of the *whole district*." But the assessors did not hire him for the larger survey. Poppleton surrendered. He wrote to the board claiming that "it is therefore your Body Gentlemen who have declined entering into the engagement, which consequently falls to the ground."[12]

Baltimore's failure to produce a map of itself in 1812 was symptomatic of the city's chronic incapacity to conceive of itself as a whole, rather than a collection of "streets, lanes, and alleys." Under the city charter, the mayor appointed the board of city commissioners, but he seems to have exercised almost no control over it. The city council was clearly divided about Poppleton's work, and though Commissioner Stauffer may have swayed his colleagues to fire Poppleton, there was plentiful "contrariety" among the commissioners themselves.

ANGLO-ANIMOSITIES

Baltimore abruptly abandoned its disputatious attempts at mapmaking in order to make war. For many Baltimoreans, the hostilities could not come soon enough. In 1807, the USS *Chesapeake* had sailed out of the Gosport shipyard near Norfolk, Virginia, its guns still not mounted. The British frigate *Leopard* intercepted it. A messenger from the *Leopard* demanded that a party from the English ship be permitted to board the *Chesapeake* to search for British deserters. The *Chesapeake*'s commander refused. The *Leopard* fired a broadside into the American ship, killing three seamen and wounding others. The *Chesapeake* struck its colors. The *Leopard*'s commander refused the *Chesapeake*'s surrender. He had three men removed from the *Chesapeake*, leaving the ship to limp back to Norfolk with its dead.[13]

Baltimore's merchants called a town meeting that resolved to support whatever actions President Jefferson took in response to the outrage.[14] Other meetings in other towns registered similar sentiments. And there would be further provocations. Baltimore's merchants, seamen, and ship owners had sailed into the middle of the Napoleonic Wars.

The Jefferson administration had been determined not to antagonize the combatants. But Senator Samuel Smith was willing to risk their enmity on behalf of his city's merchants. He recast a bill to protect American shipping against Morocco's Barbary Pirates into a measure requiring naval protection of American merchant ships against any nation—meaning Britain in particular. The administration also attempted to curb American trade with Haiti to avoid offending the French, who were trying to win back their former colony. Baltimore merchants resented the threat to their trade with the new nation, and Smith spoke up for them.[15]

Two years later, however, Smith was a leading advocate of Jefferson's trade embargo that kept Baltimore's ships in port. The embargo came at a time when it added little to the burdens borne by the city's mercantile class. French privateers and British warships were devastating the town's merchant fleet. Senator Smith's own firm suffered serious losses. He argued that total cessation of American commerce would starve French and British Caribbean colonies and force both nations to treat American shipping more respectfully.[16]

Baltimore's Republican merchants initially welcomed the embargo. They continued to support it even when it failed to alter British and French policies.[17] There was much talk of turning to manufacturing as a substitute for diminished trade. William Patterson, a local merchant whose 12 ships lay idle in port, wrote to a New York newspaper inviting any persons with knowledge of cotton or woolen manufactures to turn their expertise to practical account in Baltimore.[18] The enthusiasm for manufactures helped to sustain local support of the embargo. But enthusiasm was not actuality. Though a few factories appeared in and around the city, the embargo brought only small steps toward its industrial future.[19]

As the city's economy declined, support for the embargo faded, but animosity toward Britain thrived. An English journeyman shoemaker expressed views partial to his homeland. A mob tarred and feathered him, then hauled him in a cart from the center of the city to the tip of Fell's Point and back. Some members of the mob were arrested and sentenced to fines and imprisonment. All were pardoned. In 1809, some British seamen jumped ship in Annapolis and traveled to Baltimore, where they were arrested at the request of the English consul. Amid public clamor, the court released them on a writ of habeas corpus.[20] Hostility toward Britain was soon blunted by the attacks of French privateers on American ships—all the more galling since Baltimore shipyards had outfitted some of the French commerce raiders.[21]

In 1812, one month before Congress declared war on Britain, exasperated Baltimoreans were ready to fight, and not especially particular about the choice of an adversary. Delegates elected in a town meeting sent a resolution to President Madison urging that the country go to war with Britain or France or both, with a slight preference for Britain.[22] As soon as war was declared, local merchants lined up for the letters of marque that authorized them to arm their ships and operate as privateers. Within six months, 42 privateers had sailed from Baltimore. By war's end, Baltimore had sent out more privateers than any other US port. About a fifth of the city's population had investments or livelihoods in legal piracy.[23] Other cities avoided association with privateers because they recognized that it invited British attack. The *New Bedford Mercury* advised against welcoming privateers to its town's port: "Let them fit and refit at that *Sodom* of our country, called Baltimore."[24]

URBAN WARFARE

Baltimore's most immediate act of war, however, was another riot—the most deadly so far.[25] The spark was an editorial attack on the American declaration of war against Britain, written by Alexander C. Hanson, Federalist publisher of the Baltimore *Federal Republican*. Hanson's paper denounced the war: "'*Thou hast done a deed whereat valor will weep.*' Without funds, without taxes, without an army, navy, or adequate fortifications . . . our rulers have promulgated a war against the clear and decided sentiments of a vast majority of the nation."[26]

A crowd destroyed the paper's press and demolished its office building. The first fatality occurred when a member of the mob, tearing out a window, fell from an upper story. Mayor Johnson wandered ineffectually through the mob, addressing the rioters one by one, trying to dissuade them from further violence.[27] Hanson fled, but continued to publish his paper from Georgetown, stoking the fury that had triggered the original attack. In the meantime, mobs sought out others suspected of English sympathies. One tradesman whose shop sign included the words "from London" fled the city, and rioters demolished several ships at Fell's Point thought to be carrying provisions to Britain or its allies.[28] None of these acts of destruction exceeded the limits implicit in earlier riots. But the mob took on a life of its own. It reassembled almost every night for more than a month, roaming the streets and attacking targets that sparked its members' racial, class, ethnic, and religious animosities.[29]

Hanson slipped back into Baltimore, determined to take a stand against the city's pro-war Republicans and convinced that the mob would disintegrate if met with the stern response that the Republican city government had been unwilling to adopt. Hanson and as many as 30 well-armed allies occupied a building on Charles Street, converting it into a combined fortress and distribution center for his paper. The next issue of the *Federal Republican* carried an attack on municipal officials for their failure to contain the rioters. The paper's masthead stated that it was published at "No. 45 So. Charles St.," inviting an attack on the building where Hanson and his friends waited, armed and barricaded.[30]

A rock-throwing mob gathered outside the building as night fell. Hanson's force responded by firing blank cartridges or warning shots. The mob scattered, but only temporarily. When it reconvened, the confrontation escalated into an exchange of real gunfire. One of the Federalists in the house was wounded, and two members of the mob were killed. The rioters positioned a cannon in front of the house. General John Stricker, the city's militia commander, called out a squadron of cavalry. He and the mayor persuaded the barricaded Federalists that their best hope of survival was to allow the troops to escort them to the city jail. On the following day, General Stricker called out a force of nearly 1,000 men to protect the jail from a rumored mob attack. Fewer than 50 soldiers reported, almost all of them Federalists. Stricker dismissed them, since they were not numerous enough to protect the jail, and their known political affiliation might only inflame the antifederalist mob. Mayor Johnson tried to block the entrance to the jail, but was swept aside. The rioters stormed in and killed General James Lingan, an aged veteran of the Revolution, and beat eight other Federalists unconscious with clubs. Among the wounded was Henry ("Light-Horse Harry") Lee, father of Robert E. Lee. The elder Lee later published an account of the riot, hinting that local civil and military officials were cooperating or conniving with the rioters. He was one of those left in a pile on the street, where the injured were repeatedly stabbed. Members of the mob poured hot candle wax into victims' eyes. Some survived only by pretending they were dead; others, by mingling with the mob. Some of those who played dead were rescued by physicians who claimed that they needed the "cadavers" for instruction or experimentation.[31]

Even at the time, there were those—such as the eulogist at General Lingan's funeral—who believed that the riot opened a new and ominous stage in public conduct. The actions of the Baltimore mob had prompted protest meetings far from Baltimore, and in the elections three months later, reaction to the riot helped Federalists take a majority of the Maryland House of Delegates, the governorship, and one seat in the US Senate. Alexander Hanson was elected to the House of Representatives. The riot, wrote Scharf, "left a stigma on the city, which bore for a long time the name of 'mobtown.' "[32]

TWILIGHT'S LAST GLEAMING

Baltimore had come through the Revolution virtually untouched. In the War of 1812, it stood in the thick of the fighting. In 1814, English troops and ships arrived outside Baltimore, fresh from their rout of the American militia at Bladensburg and their unopposed entry into Washington, where they burned the Capitol, the White House, and other public buildings. Baltimore, with its warehouses and merchant ships, would make an even richer prize, and there was a score to settle. The city's privateers had captured or sunk about 500 British ships since the start of the war. The British also knew that several American warships were under construction in Baltimore. The most significant was the *Java*, important not just because it carried 60 guns but because it was to be commanded by America's naval hero of Lake Erie, Oliver Hazard Perry.[33] Waiting for them in Baltimore was Samuel Smith, a Revolutionary veteran who was now a major general in command of a militia division.[34]

Francis Scott Key would never have been able to proclaim that "our flag was still there" had it not been for an extraordinary mobilization of Baltimore's civilians to make their city defensible. The town was unprepared because the threat seemed remote. Even Samuel Smith assumed that most of the war would be fought at sea. A local regiment had been sent off to support the American invasion of Canada. At the end of 1812, the British had declared a blockade of the Delaware and Chesapeake Bays, but it was only when British ships entered the Chesapeake and dropped anchor at Hampton Roads in February 1813 that Baltimore's peril became tangible. In fact, the threat may have been less than it seemed. The British ships carried insufficient troops to occupy any cities, only a raiding party intended to create enough panic on the Chesapeake to induce the Americans to divert their forces from the invasion of Canada.[35]

As a military venture, the enterprise was sensible enough, but its political consequences worked against British interests. The presence of an enemy fleet in the Chesapeake engendered a sense of threat that aroused Baltimoreans to improve the defenses of their city. It also lent urgency to their pleas for assistance in Washington and Annapolis. By itself, however, the atmosphere of alarm would have accomplished little without Major General Samuel Smith, US senator, who had the political sensibilities and connections to exploit it.

Had the British attacked Baltimore in 1813, they would probably have destroyed the city. Fort McHenry, at the tip of Whetstone Point, guarded the entrance to Baltimore's harbor. It was held by 52 officers and men, and critical elements of its defenses had deteriorated since its construction in the 1790s. The earthworks and artillery batteries that would have faced an invading fleet had washed away. There were at

Major General Samuel Smith

least 60 cannons in the fort, but most were scattered on the ground, not yet mounted on gun carriages, and the carriages had yet to be built—a project that required tons of seasoned oak or mahogany and skilled carpenters. If a British fleet got past Fort McHenry, Baltimore could be leveled by naval bombardment.[36]

The Northwest Branch of the Patapsco converges with Back River as it enters the Patapsco's main channel to form a peninsula, North Point. The Point reaches out to the shipping lane in the Chesapeake, where merchantmen once anchored to unload their cargoes into lighters. The deep water that accommodated these merchant ships also served the 74-gun ships of the line that were the most intimidating vessels in the British fleet. The end of the Point, 16 miles east of Baltimore, provided the British with a place to land troops under the protection of their naval guns. A day's march up the Point would place British forces in position to attack Baltimore from the east. Samuel Smith recognized the threat. He paid Jehu Bouldin $20 for the surveyor's map of North Point.[37]

The proximity of the British aroused concern, which Smith exploited to get attention in Washington and Annapolis. A month after the enemy fleet entered the Chesapeake, Smith took Governor Levin Winder on an inspection tour of the city's defenses. Winder authorized Smith "to take the earliest opportunity of making the necessary arrangement of the militia for the defense of the Port of Baltimore." The order was ambiguous. It did not clearly call Smith or his militia to mobilize in the active service of the state. But Smith used it to seize the greatest possible discretion. Even before Winder had returned to Annapolis, Smith wrote to Secretary of War Armstrong demanding reinforcements for Fort McHenry. He noted that the proximity of the British fleet had "caused apprehension for the safety of this important City and has induced Governor Winder (now here) to issue an order directed to me to 'make the necessary arrangements for the defence of the Port of Baltimore.'" Winder had actually ordered Smith to prepare the *militia* for the defense of Baltimore. By omitting this detail, Smith conveyed the impression that he had been placed in overall command of Baltimore's defenses, including Fort McHenry and its garrison.[38]

It is doubtful whether an ordinary major general could have carried off this arrogation of authority so deftly. But Smith was a practiced politician, and his militiamen were a substantial part of his political base. Their loyalty reinforced his military authority. As a US senator, Smith also had influence in Washington. He was chairman of the Senate's Committee on Naval Affairs and a member of the Military Affairs Committee. When he pled Baltimore's case for money or munitions before the secretaries of the army or navy, he got a respectful hearing.[39]

The federal authorities, however, had little to offer. Alexander Hanson had not been far wrong in charging that the government had started its war "without funds, or taxes, without an army, navy, or adequate fortifications." Baltimore would have to provide for itself. Above all, it needed funds to fortify the city and to equip and pay troops to defend it. In this respect, Smith the businessman was in a position to be useful. A successful merchant, he sat on the boards of two local banks and held stock in several others.[40]

Smith drew his influence from his institutional connections, but his power was personal rather than institutional. Baltimore's public institutions had never commanded much authority in any case. They had been unable to reach agreement on how to map the city, and their officers stood by helplessly as fellow citizens turned homicidal in the riot of 1812.[41] Baltimore's leaders could not reliably command their own people. Smith could—partly because of the cause to which he summoned them and partly because he was Samuel Smith.

Chapter 8

BALTIMORE TRIUMPHANT

MAJOR GENERAL SMITH COMMANDED the Maryland militia's Third Division, embracing four brigades of uneven quality. Two of them consisted of men from the rural counties west of Baltimore. Smith made no use of these in the defense of his city against the British. The better prepared of the two remaining brigades was the Third, commanded by Brigadier General John Stricker and made up of men from Baltimore City. Its 4,500 members were prepared to mobilize for the defense of the city with only an hour's notice—if they chose to respond to the summons. The men of the Eleventh Brigade, commanded by Brigadier General Tobias Stansbury, were drawn from parts of Baltimore County outside the city, and while they were not as well prepared to fight as the Third, Smith decided that they would improve with training.

Neither the state nor the federal government had officially called up the militia in response to the British threat, and the soldiers could not be paid for service. But militiamen were obliged to mobilize without pay for short periods of duty each year. Smith called a different regiment to active duty every week for training and preparation. Cavalry units patrolled both shores of the Patapsco to familiarize themselves with the terrain, and artillery companies trained on Fort McHenry's big guns.[1]

The fort's garrison consisted of regular army troops commanded by Major Lloyd Beall. As a regular army officer, he was not obliged to obey the commands of a militia officer, even a major general. Smith worried that the fort might be vulnerable to a night attack and wanted to station some of his men there. Beall refused to allow them to remain in the fort after nightfall. His soldiers were living there with their families, and the barracks were needed for wives and children. There was no room for the militia. Smith could not afford to object too vehemently. Beall controlled funds needed to improve the defenses of the fort, and Smith cooperated with him in the effort. Work gangs composed of both militiamen and civilians rebuilt the two batteries that once faced the entrance to Baltimore's harbor, and a team of carpenters built gun carriages for the cannons that lay unmounted. Army Secretary John Armstrong ordered Beall to turn over to Smith 500 unused weapons stored at the fort.[2]

Work went forward on other fortifications as well. The eastern approaches to Baltimore were not protected against a possible British land attack made from North Point. Civilian laborers were conscripted to construct trenches and earthworks at Hampstead Hill, just east of the city (in today's Patterson Park), as a last-ditch defensive line against a British land attack. The city was divided into four districts, and work crews from each district were to show up at the construction site one day in four. Those expected to serve as laborers were white men exempt from militia service and free black men, who were excluded from bearing arms as members of the militia. In addition, Baltimore slave owners were required to send their slaves to work on the defenses. Wheelbarrows, pick axes, shovels, and lumber were also conscripted.[3]

While General Smith prepared for the defense of Baltimore, the British fleet moved slowly up the Chesapeake, conducting raids on shore as they went. It gained little from these attacks, except to demonstrate to communities on the Bay that their government was incapable of defending them. Their larger purpose—consistent with the burning of Washington the following year—was "to bring the Republican government into such disrepute and scorn that it would have to make peace on British terms, or yield to a revolution favorable to British interests." The raids, however, only seemed to stoke Americans' hatred of the British. Even some British officers objected to the conduct of their troops. After a raid on Hampton, Virginia, Captain Sir Charles Napier complained that his superior officer "ought to have hanged several villains at Little Hampton; had he so done, the Americans would not have complained; but every horror was committed with impunity, rape, murder, pillage; and not a man punished!"[4]

AD HOC GOVERNMENT

On April 13, 1813, after several weeks of raids and destruction, the British fleet moved from the mouth of the Potomac toward Annapolis and Baltimore. On the same day, Baltimore's mayor and city council voted to create a Committee of Public Supply. Its job was to serve as General Smith's "purchasing agent"—to raise the money needed to arm, equip, and pay the soldiers under his command. Mayor Edward Johnson was the only elected official on the committee. One of its other members was Smith's business partner, James A. Buchanan. The mayor and council immediately appropriated $20,000 for the use of the committee. General Smith had sent his aide, Major Isaac McKim, to meet with Armstrong to convey Smith's request that the secretary call up part of the Maryland militia to meet the threat of British attack on Baltimore. Armstrong was not persuaded that the British fleet carried sufficient troops to make such an attack. He was probably right. But he sent Major McKim back to Smith with a letter promising to request that Governor Winder provide 2,000 of the state's militiamen for the defense of Baltimore. Since the request was made in the name of the federal government, the federal government would be responsible for paying and provisioning these troops. Until the "drafted" militiamen were assembled and prepared for their duties, 2,000 soldiers from Smith's division would stand in for the new troops.[5]

The Committee of Public Supply soon decided that it needed much more than the $20,000 appropriated by the city government. Instead of turning to the city council, the committee asked Baltimoreans to convene at the customary polling places, where the voters of each ward were to select four of their neighbors to attend a meeting in the city council chambers. The assembled representatives unanimously recommended that the mayor call the council into session to pass an ordinance "authorizing the borrowing of whatever sum of money may be required for the defence of the City of Baltimore not exceeding $500,000." The city's leaders undoubtedly hoped that authorities in Washington and Annapolis would reimburse them for expenditures made in defense of state and nation. But they were not certain and allowed that "a part may not be reimbursed by the General or State Governments." If the city was left burdened with war debt, it was "but just and reasonable that all the property in the City" should be taxed to pay for Baltimore's defense. Three of the assembled delegates drafted a petition to be circulated in the city, then submitted to the city council, and finally presented to the General Assembly with a request for "a Law to authorize the laying of a tax on all property aforesaid."[6]

Mayor Johnson called the city council into session and explained that the Committee of Public Supply, "well knowing the restricted powers vested in you by your charter," had convened a representative body—an ersatz city council—to recommend that the city incur up to half a million dollars in municipal debt to underwrite the defense of the city. "The monied institutions of our City," the mayor reported, "with a liberality highly honorable to them have offered to loan any reasonable amount that the present exigency may require upon receiving such guarantee as for its reimbursement as we are able to give."[7]

The "monied institutions" of Baltimore agreed to finance the city's defense on the understanding that the mayor and council would petition the General Assembly for a significant extension of the municipality's taxing authority. The condition promised something for everyone. It gave the banks a source of revenue to secure their loans; the state acquired a means to immunize itself against the war debts of Baltimore; and Baltimore would gain a substantial addition to the taxing authority it exercised under the charter granted by the General Assembly.

The General Assembly declined to play its assigned role in this arrangement, but the need to concoct such a scheme demonstrates the limitations of Baltimore's municipal charter. Its restrictions led the council to cede authority for the defense of the city to the Committee of Public Supply instead of assuming the responsibility itself. It was clearly the reason for creating a shadow city council to endorse an extraordinary loan from the city's banks—and to propose an extraordinary increase in the city's taxing powers to generate the revenue needed to cover the debt. The pattern was familiar. Given the shortcomings of official institutions, Baltimore created unofficial institutions outside the limitations imposed by the city charter and state law.

ORGANIZING FOR DEFENSE

While the municipality attempted to stretch its powers to meet the British threat, Samuel Smith faced a challenge to his position. The 2,000 militia troops "drafted" into service at the request of the secretary of war needed a commander. Governor Winder nominated a Baltimorean, Brigadier General Henry Miller, a regular army officer. Like the governor, Miller was a Federalist, and he was a close friend of Secretary Armstrong, who approved Miller's nomination. When he did, it was no longer clear which general was in charge in Baltimore. Miller tried to get the Committee of Public Supply to acknowledge his authority, but its members responded with a pledge of support for Samuel Smith. Miller and Smith appealed to Armstrong to settle the question of command. Armstrong decided that Miller should be in charge unless Smith could show that Governor Winder had called him to active service before Miller's appointment. Smith dispatched Major McKim on another political mission: to get the governor to confirm that Smith had been called to active duty in March, when the governor had asked him to make arrangements for the militia's defense of Baltimore. Winder hesitated, but decided in favor of Smith, even though none of his orders had explicitly called Smith to active duty.[8] To do otherwise might well have sparked a rebellion in Baltimore's militia, Smith's loyal political base, and would have gone against the clearly expressed wishes of the Committee of Public Supply, whose work was essential to Baltimore's defense. Miller would command the "drafted" militia, but Smith would exercise overall command.

Just as Smith's command solidified, the British fleet sailed past the Patapsco and headed for the Upper Bay. The local militia was demobilized, and Smith became a commander without troops. But the British presence had created the sense of urgency he needed to mobilize his forces and prepare the city's defenses. In addition to the earthworks on Hampstead Hill and the rebuilding of Fort McHenry, Smith had ordered the construction of a battery at the Lazaretto and two other sites that would prove useful in case any British ships or barges tried to circumvent the fort by approaching Baltimore on the Middle Branch, or "Ferry" Branch, of the Patapsco. A row of hulks had been anchored next to Fort McHenry. In the event of a British attempt to get past the fort, the hulks could be sunk to block the channel. Booms made of ships' masts would block other creeks and inlets that might get British ships or barges within cannon range of Baltimore. Smith had also obtained arms for his troops. When the British made their first appearance in the Bay, one-third of Smith's Third Brigade had no weapons. The 500 muskets from Fort McHenry and another 1,500 provided by Armstrong helped to remedy the deficiency.[9]

Smith organized a warning system to alert Baltimore's defenders to the approach of the British fleet. The commander of the only navy gunboat defending the harbor established a lookout post at the end of North Point. A string of guard boats between the Point and the city would relay the lookout's flag signals to Smith and his forces in Baltimore. North Point itself was defended by a detachment of Baltimore City troops encamped at Bear Creek. The force was instructed to slow down a British offensive on North Point and withdraw toward the defensive works on Hampstead

Hill.[10] When the British came back, they would find Baltimore much better prepared than on their first encounter.

TAKING COMMAND

In June 1813, General Smith became Senator Smith. Leaving General Stricker in charge in Baltimore, he went to Washington. His assignments on the Naval Affairs and Military Affairs Committees gave him frequent opportunities to meet with the secretaries of the army and the navy. Not surprisingly, he used these encounters to lobby strenuously on behalf of Baltimore's needs. He even brought the Committee of Public Supply to Washington to add volume to his requests. But the federal government had given the city about as much as it was going to get. Armstrong agreed to consider reimbursing some of the supply committee's expenses, provided some additional muskets for the Maryland militia, and replaced Fort McHenry's uncooperative commander, Major Beall, with Major George Armistead. But he refused to order a further mobilization of the Maryland militia, which would have made the federal government responsible for pay and provisions.[11]

A British flotilla had meanwhile been leveling towns at the head of the Chesapeake. When it had finished bombarding, looting, and burning buildings and docks in Frenchtown and Havre de Grace,[12] it sailed down the Bay to rendezvous with a British squadron at the mouth of the Chesapeake. This united fleet began to move north, now carrying reinforcements, including more than 2,500 new troops. Napoleon's defeat and exile to Elba meant that Britain could now transfer soldiers and ships from its European war to fight its American war.[13]

Smith was back in Baltimore by mid-July. By August 1, the British fleet neared Annapolis, and Secretary Armstrong supported General Smith's decision to mobilize part of the militia. About 15 warships approached Baltimore a week later, but withdrew without attacking. The British summer offensive concentrated instead on the Eastern Shore and left Baltimore unmolested. But the alarm—and the ability to charge the federal government for the troops' pay and provisions—gave Smith the opportunity to put Baltimore County's Eleventh Brigade through the same sort of training he had given the city's Third Brigade earlier in the year. The following summer, regiments drawn from the Eleventh Brigade were among the few units that gave a good account of themselves at the disastrous battle of Bladensburg.[14]

One day before the defeat at Bladensburg, Baltimore formed a larger citizen committee to replace the Committee of Public Supply. The Committee of Vigilance and Safety was elected by wards. It met almost daily and functioned as the city's de facto wartime government.[15]

As Baltimore drew itself together for what seemed the certainty of a British assault, General Smith found his authority under attack once again. The War Department had divided the country into 10 military districts and appointed a regular army officer to command each of them. Maryland, together with the District of Columbia and part of northern Virginia, made up the tenth district, under the command of Brigadier General William H. Winder, the nephew of Maryland's governor. General Winder was a native of the Eastern Shore who had moved to Baltimore in

1807 to begin a successful law practice. He had served as a captain and company commander under Samuel Smith in the Maryland militia. At the start of the war he had volunteered for duty as a regular officer and was commissioned as a lieutenant colonel in command of a regiment that participated in the campaign against Canada. Shortly after being promoted to brigadier general, Winder was captured, and he remained a prisoner of war for a year. But he was not idle. Under parole, he traveled between Montreal and Washington to negotiate a prisoner exchange. He was one of its beneficiaries.[16]

Winder's negotiations brought him into contact with President Madison and Secretary of State James Monroe, and, though he was a Federalist, he won appointment as district commander in charge of the defense of Washington. Secretary Armstrong had opposed the appointment, and subsequently did little to support Winder's efforts to protect the capital. There were reasons for choosing Winder, however, that had nothing to do with his capabilities as a commander. The defense of Washington would require energetic support from the citizens and militia of Maryland. Maryland was sharply divided concerning the war, a division evident in Baltimore's riot of 1812 and the state's response to it. Entrusting the capital's defense to the Federalist nephew of Maryland's Federalist governor could mobilize those Marylanders most likely to harbor doubts about the conflict with Britain and rally them to support the defense of Washington and its Democratic-Republican administration.[17]

Samuel Smith wasted no time in trying to establish his status in relation to General Winder. He wrote to Governor Winder, noting the practice that militia officers, no matter what their rank, were subordinate to regular army officers unless the militia officers had been called into the service of the United States. Smith asked the governor for instructions. The governor temporized. Smith wrote to Armstrong, asking to be granted the power to call militia troops into federal service as he had the previous summer. A positive response would clearly demonstrate that Smith was in the service of the federal government. Armstrong never replied.[18]

Brigadier General Winder also wrote to Armstrong, expressing "astonishment" that Smith "still conceives himself in command and persists to exercise it." Winder suggested that Smith's pretensions to command could be stifled if the secretary promoted Winder from brigadier to major general. Armstrong sent Winder an evasive response and ordered him to return to Washington with his troops, apparently to guard against attack by a British force that had captured Alexandria. Armstrong's role in the defeat at Bladensburg cost him his job soon after President Madison returned to Washington. He was replaced as secretary of war by James Monroe, who would simultaneously head the Department of State.[19]

General Winder's humiliating defeat at Bladensburg may have damaged his military status, but in his eyes, at least, it had nothing to do with his status as commander in Baltimore. A day after the Bladensburg rout, however, the Committee of Vigilance and Safety received a petition delivered personally by Brigadier General John Stricker, commander of Baltimore's Third Brigade; Major George Armistead, commander of Fort McHenry; Admiral Oliver Hazard Perry, in Baltimore to take command of a new ship; and Master-Commandant Robert T. Spence of the US

Navy. They asked that Major General Samuel Smith assume overall command of the forces defending Baltimore. Immediately after receiving the petition, the committee sent a delegation to ask General Smith if he was willing to accept command. His response came so quickly that he may have been waiting nearby. He said that he would accept command, if Governor Winder approved his appointment. For the governor, there remained no choice. To force his nephew on the military forces of Baltimore against the will of their commanders might have created another disaster like the one that left Washington open to British incendiaries. Governor Winder's problem was that Smith remained a militia major general, outranked by regular army Brigadier General Winder. The governor retrieved a mobilization order issued by President Madison more than a year before, which called for one major general from Maryland. The governor designated Smith, not his nephew, as that major general. As Ralph Robinson points out, "Baltimore had selected the man it wanted to assume the defense of the city." The enemy was preparing to attack. This was no time to squabble about military rank and status.[20] Smith was in charge, and Baltimore was ready.

PERILOUS FIGHT

The British were uncertain. Their commander, Major General Robert Ross, was at first persuaded by his aides that an assault on Baltimore would be unwise. The burning of Washington surely alerted the forces in Baltimore to the imminence of attack, and the shallowness of the Patapsco would handicap the fleet in providing support to Ross's troops once they landed. Though victorious at Bladensburg, the British soldiers were in poor condition, not only from the stress of battle but from months of life aboard crowded ships and long marches in the heat of August. Admiral George Cockburn argued for the offensive. Baltimore's ships, warehouses, and naval stores made the city too tempting to pass up, and its privateers made it a target of revenge. The vulnerability of Washington reinforced reports on the lack of protection for Baltimore's harbor. Unfavorable winds also detained the British fleet in the Chesapeake, "thus requiring something to do until the weather cleared."[21]

British hesitation allowed Baltimoreans more time to prepare, and the proximity of the enemy intensified their efforts at defense. In a letter to her brother in New York, a young woman in Baltimore wrote, "White and black are all at work together. You'll see a master and his slave digging side by side. There is no distinction whatsoever." General Smith's 11-year-old nephew disappeared from home during the uproar. He was found digging trenches on Hampstead Hill. Other citizens needed inducements to mobilize. The Committee of Vigilance and Safety paid a dollar a day, provisions, and liquor to each of 150 men hired to build earthworks on North Point.[22] The British threat brought Baltimore's public to life, as nothing else in the city's politically inhibited history had done. Its mobilization extended to free blacks and slaves.

When the British attack came, it was almost exactly the assault that Samuel Smith anticipated. A British fleet assembled off North Point, and on September 12, 1814, a force of 3,270 men disembarked under the protection of their ships' cannons, the

A VIEW of the BOMBARDMENT of Fort McHenry, near Baltimore, by the British fleet taken from the Observatory where the Commander of Admiral Cochrane & Cockburn, on the morning of the 13 of Sep.r 1814 which lasted 24 hours, & thrown from 1500 to 1800 shells in the Night attempted to land by forcing a passage up the ferry branch but were repulsed with great loss.

The bombardment of Fort McHenry

most powerful being the 74-gun *Royal Oak*. They had not marched far from their landing place when they encountered gunfire. It was during this initial skirmish that the British commander, Major General Robert Ross, was killed. By some accounts, his death demoralized the British forces and left their command to a less confident officer, Colonel Arthur Brooke, who did not press the attack as Ross might have. But Ross himself had been uncertain about attacking Baltimore, and the defenses of the city would probably have defeated the British no matter who was in command. Observing the American lines at Hampstead Hill, Lieutenant G. R. Gleig concluded that an attack was feasible only with naval support, but the British fleet—checked by Fort McHenry's artillery—was out of range. A council of war convened by Colonel Brooke "decided that all idea of storming the enemy's lines should be given up." The British returned to their ships.[23]

An American military surgeon, James McCulloh, received permission to cross the British lines to treat the American wounded on North Point. "The reason the British did not attack our trenches," he wrote, "was that they considered the position too strong & the hill being slippery in consequence of the heavy rain." But the decision had not been unanimous. "Some officers told me that Admiral Cockburn wished to storm our lines & that the seamen had volunteered for the purpose, but Gen [*sic*] Brooke would not acquiesce in this arrangement." The rough treatment that the British encountered on North Point may also have figured in their decision to break off the offensive. McCulloh reported that he had "passed over the ground where the British had met the most serious opposition"—where General Ross had been killed—"I think I saw at least 300 killed & wounded on my view with the red uniform."[24]

The British were not finished. They planned a night attack on the Middle (Ferry) Branch of the Patapsco. General Smith had ordered the placement of two artillery batteries on the Middle Branch to counter just such a maneuver. They opened up in the dark on the British barges and their oarsmen and forced them to turn back— with more casualties.[25]

General Smith had given a new dimension of meaning to the maxim that war is the continuation of politics by other means. Smith's political influence and military skill had given Baltimore the capacity to wage war against its British attackers and to defeat them. But Baltimore's struggles were not over. Its next mission was to get either the federal government or the State of Maryland or both to reimburse its expenditures for defense.

GIVING PROOF

Not long after the British forces gave up on Baltimore, the Committee of Vigilance and Safety sent three of its members to Washington to "wait upon the President of the United States and the heads of Departments." Since the British were still lurking in the neighborhood, the defense of both cities was a prominent subject of discussion, but money was clearly a pressing concern. According to the Baltimore delegation's report, President Madison assured them that Baltimore's expenditures for fortifications "which can be brought under the appropriation laws would be immediately paid," and that costs not covered by existing appropriations "would be included in an equitable arrangement . . . and that the Government was disposed to be liberal." In a subsequent meeting, the secretary of war told the visitors from Baltimore that he had already informed General Smith that the federal government would cover "the bomb-proof fortification in the Fort and other works." Armstrong (not yet dismissed) echoed the president's assurance that the government would be "liberal" in reimbursing other expenditures, but it could not provide ready cash; "the City would have to advance the money."[26]

A month later, Treasury Secretary A. J. Dallas deposited $30,000 in a Baltimore bank, a first installment in the federal government's reimbursement for the city's expenditures.[27] When the deposit was made, however, the city was still spending its own money to perfect its defenses. The British might return, and expenses were still mounting from their last visit. The Baltimore City Hospital was caring for 26 sick and wounded combatants. Property owners wanted the city to pay for the damage done by fortifications and entrenchments, and ship owners whose vessels had been sunk to block the harbor channel expected compensation.[28]

The city needed much more than $30,000 to cover its costs. The state government offered no help, and years after the retreat of the British, Baltimore would still be wheedling the federal government to compensate the city for its contribution to national defense. The initial obstacle was the War Department's contention that it had "never recognized the authority under which the principal part of the amount asked for had been paid." By 1818, the persuasive exertions of senator and major general

Smith finally induced the secretary of war to take responsibility for some of these expenses. The War Department's accountant, however, insisted that the secretary's approval carried no weight unless Baltimore could produce documents attesting to the expenditures. The department also wanted to know what happened to durable goods, such as artillery pieces, for which it was to pay.[29]

The strict accounting required by the federal government after the war ended was a far cry from its handling of military expenditures when still threatened with invasion, when General Smith had been assured that under the threat of British invasion, "we may venture expenditures which till then would be indiscreet." Baltimore's spending was "very proper under the circumstances. You are making yourselves ready."[30]

Now, however, the government wanted ledgers and receipts and the equipment mentioned in them. Top city officials and leading members of the Committee of Vigilance and Safety set off in search of vouchers, receipts, account books, and artillery pieces.[31] A critical item of evidence in justifying the city's reimbursement was General Smith's orderly book for 1813, which recorded many of the expenditures that he had authorized for Baltimore's defense. The book and a substantial trove of other documents turned up in a trunk stored in the mayor's office, and some artillery pieces were found, unaccountably, at a riding academy.[32]

At the end of 1820, Baltimore still awaited a final accounting from the federal government. A Treasury Department official acknowledged that documents provided by the city had validated some of its claims, but he added that many others remained unsubstantiated because the city had not yet been able to "perfect the vouchers." Some months later, the Treasury Department agreed that the federal government still owed Baltimore a bit more than $33,000, but immediately added that the department's limited funds would not permit full payment. The city would get only $18,273. The sum fell far short of Baltimore's expectations. Early in its negotiations with the federal government, the Committee of Vigilance and Safety had anticipated that Washington might not have the cash to meet its claims. In correspondence with Secretary of War James Monroe, the committee relayed an offer from Baltimore banks to lend the federal government as much as $613,000 to repay the town for its military expenditures in 1813 and 1814. The banks, of course, expected to profit from the loan. For every $80 advanced to the US Treasury, they expected to be repaid $100.[33]

The proposal may have been a tactical error. In effect, the city was offering to finance its own reimbursement—with something extra for its leading bankers. Baltimore's government might be strapped, but the city seemed far from destitute, and the banks that now offered to finance Baltimore's reimbursement were presumably the same ones that originally made the loans that paid for the city's defense. Now they would collect interest twice—once on the original loans to the city, and again on the money that the federal government would use to reimburse the city. The proposal seemed another instance of the mercenary grasp for which Baltimore was well known. The federal government declined to borrow in Baltimore.

The banks, in fact, were approaching ruin, and by the time Baltimore received its pittance from the federal government, several of them had already collapsed. The downturn in the city's economy had begun with the end of the Napoleonic Wars, as Britain reimposed mercantilist restrictions on trade with its colonies in the Western Hemisphere. In the meantime, manufactured goods from England and Germany flooded the city, driving down the prices for locally made products. Trade in western agricultural produce suffered from falling prices and the devaluation of currency issued by "country" banks. When the Bank of the United States tried to rein in the surfeit of banknotes and bank loans, Baltimore plunged into the Panic of 1819 along with the rest of the nation—only more so.[34]

The panic was nationwide, but the shady practices of Baltimore's merchants and bankers added a local component to the national distress. Some members of the city's mercantile community, for example, found it impossible to give up the habit of privateering simply because America was at peace. Local traders invested heavily in privateers supposedly sponsored by Latin American revolutionaries; in fact, the ships sailed out of Baltimore. Congress began to crack down on the maritime desperadoes in 1817, and civil suits filed by Spanish and Portuguese ship owners imposed heavy losses on Baltimore's investors in piracy and fed the larger panic.[35]

Bank shenanigans further undermined the city's prosperity. Several mercantile firms took effective control of the local branch of the Bank of the United States and used its assets to finance their speculative ventures without providing any collateral for the "loans" they made to themselves. One of the central figures in the scandal was Samuel Smith's business partner, James A. Buchanan. A congressional investigation and the dismissal of the president of the Bank of the United States helped to bring the Baltimore irregularities to light. The new president demanded that the Baltimore branch settle up its accounts in specie, forcing the branch to call in loans to other banks. One after another, they collapsed, and the Baltimore branch itself went down in May 1819. In June, the national panic arrived and merged with its local antecedent. The conduct of the city's leading merchants and the ensuing financial failures led John Quincy Adams to observe of Baltimore "that there is not a city in the Union which has had so much apparent prosperity, or within which there has been such complication of profligacy."[36]

In the Adams family's home state, the national panic had also disrupted the standing order. The organic unity of Boston—still a town and not yet an incorporated city—had begun to break down, and its Federalist regime was forced to adjust to the heterogeneity of a growing community.[37] Baltimore, by contrast, had not yet become a fully unified urban community. From 1790 to 1820, its population more than quadrupled. Most of its residents came from someplace else. It was an unsettled settlement where everything seemed to be in motion. Notwithstanding its municipal charter, it was still subject to the authority of a state legislature in everything from tax rates to the opening of new streets and flood control in the Jones Falls valley. Its representation in Annapolis was far less than its population would warrant, and its requests of the General Assembly frequently met with hostility.

RED GLARE

The federal government recognized at least some responsibility for supporting the defense of Baltimore. The Maryland legislature provided nothing and had even denied the city the authority to tax itself to cover the costs of fortification and mobilization. Baltimore's resentment against the General Assembly had begun to harden at least a year before the British bombs burst over Fort McHenry. In the *Baltimore Patriot*, a column signed "Pericles" denounced the legislature for denying Baltimore's "respectful petition" that "simply asked leave for the citizens, to tax themselves for their own defense . . . the privilege of self defense was denied to the city of Baltimore, by the House of Delegates, every federalist voting against it." There was no justification for "a vote so disgraceful and perfidious."[38]

The tension between city and state grew more pronounced. The animosity centered at first on the "precincts"—urbanized extensions of Baltimore that spread outside the city boundaries. In 1809, the General Assembly, acting in response to petitioners living in the "Western Precincts," appointed three commissioners "to grade and Level the several streets, squares, Lanes and alleys and to Establish the Corners and fix the boundaries thereof." The precinct commissioners, in other words, functioned much like the street commissioners of Baltimore. In 1811, a similar board of commissioners was created for the "Eastern Precincts."[39]

The growing population just outside the city line could no longer get by with unpaved streets and hazy property lines. In an earlier time, Baltimore and the precincts might simply have petitioned the General Assembly to annex these suburban areas to the city. But Baltimore City paid for a variety of services beyond street paving, for which it collected a variety of taxes.[40] The residents of the precincts were not ready for the full range of urban services or the taxes that financed them. Baltimore County's government also had an interest in preventing, or at least postponing, annexation of the precincts to the city. The "precincters" accounted for about a third of the county's population, and their property represented over 40 percent of the county's assessed valuation.[41]

City authorities had long argued that these properties derived "all their high value from their proximity to the commercial parts [of the city], to the markets, to the navigation &c., and consequently ought in justice to contribute to the maintenance and support of these important objects."[42] At the end of 1816, the city sent an annexation petition to Annapolis. It omitted any mention of taxes, but emphasized the need of the city and the precincts to achieve consistency in street alignments and grades. In 1817, the General Assembly voted to consolidate the precincts with the city. But it ruled that the city could not tax undeveloped real estate in the precincts, and it defined undeveloped land as any tract with less than five houses per acre, thus excluding approximately 80 percent of the precincts from the city's tax rolls.[43]

Niles' Weekly Register cited an even more objectionable feature of the annexation, under which "the *city* acquires a population of 16 or 17,000 souls, and still has only two seats in the house of delegates—a *fortieth* part of the power of legislation, and a *fifth*, if not a *fourth*, of all white persons in the whole state." "Of the political motives that led to this procedure," the *Register* added, "it does not belong to this work to say anything."[44] At the time, the motives were obvious. Voters in the precincts, like those in the city, were lopsidedly Republicans of the Jeffersonian variety. Transferring the "precincters" from Baltimore County to Baltimore City increased the likelihood that Federalists would win all four of the county's seats in the General Assembly. At the same time, it accentuated the underrepresentation of Baltimore.[45]

Annexation provoked protests from both city and precincts. An anonymous pamphleteer from the precincts cited as precedent the consolidation of Baltimore Town and Jones Town in 1745, when annexation was achieved "on the *joint petition* of the *inhabitants* of *both towns*." From the time of this first annexation, "the *principle* of *consent* of the *owners of property*, to *any incorporation*, with the town, has been invariably observed."[46] In adding the precincts to Baltimore, the General Assembly had substituted legislative fiat for consent of the residents.

STRENGTH IN WEAKNESS

The city's political leaders had apparently failed to anticipate the way in which the General Assembly would impose annexation. But their response was unhurried. Weeks after the legislature approved annexation, a group of petitioners led by John Eager Howard urged the city council to "suspend taking measures to carry the said act into execution" until the next session of the assembly, when Baltimore could obtain "such relief as they are entitled to claim and expect." Howard was one of the town's most prominent citizens—a colonel in the Continental Army during the Revolution and a former governor, US senator, and congressman. Howard was also a Federalist, like the state legislators who had approved the conditions for annexation, but Baltimore's politicians did not take shelter behind him to support his assault on the action of his fellow partisans in Annapolis. Instead, they deferred to their legal counsel, John Purviance, who told them it was "the bounden duty of the Mayor and City Council to proceed to pass the necessary Ordinances and regulations to carry into effect the late Act of the Assembly for Enlarging the bounds of the City."[47]

The council's first step against the annexation statute did not come until mid-October 1817, when it passed a resolution creating a joint committee of its two branches "to draw up a respectful petition . . . to be presented to the Legislature of Maryland," asking for an amendment to the state constitution "by which the number of its delegates may be increased." The petition was not ready until December. It was respectful and impassioned, and went on for almost eight closely written pages. Its central point echoed the complaint of the *Niles' Weekly Register*, with slightly different arithmetic: "how is a participation in Legislation any Security of Liberty, or indeed of any advantage to those, who notwithstanding they constitute a *Seventh* part of the whole population of the State, have only the Voice and influence of a *Fortieth*?"[48]

Instead of marshalling all of their political force behind the demand for more representation, however, the mayor and city council tossed a mixed bag of petitions at the legislature. A rather cheeky "memorial" offered to provide free buildings for the use of state officials if the legislature moved the "seat of government" from Annapolis to Baltimore. The proposal may have originated with Mayor George Stiles, who heard that some legislators might prefer to govern the state from his city. He added that he knew of "no reason why we would want to have them here, except that . . . if they knew us better, they would be less hostile."[49]

Another request asked the General Assembly to authorize Baltimore to increase its property tax to provide "for the support of the Poor of the city."[50] Still another "memorial" presented a disjointed assortment of proposals. It asked that the districts used for conducting state elections within the city be reconciled with the wards used in municipal elections. Without transition, it asked the "sanction and authority of the General Assembly" to carry out flood control projects on the Jones Falls. It continued with a request for authority to offer greater compensation to property owners affected by the extension of Pratt Street across the city—one of the measures to reduce Baltimore's east-west traffic jams. Finally, it suggested that "an enlargement of the power & duties of the Judges of the City Court would have a beneficial influence on security & peace of the city."[51]

This grab bag of requests may have been designed to show the General Assembly what favors it might grant to quiet Baltimore's complaints about underrepresentation—at least for the present. The legislature's longstanding refusal to grant Baltimore more delegates must have left the city's leaders with little hope that their new petition would succeed. The politicians seemed to be using their hopeless appeal for additional legislative representation as a bargaining device, suggesting how the General Assembly might compensate for the expected rebuff by agreeing to other items on the city's laundry list of requests.

While there is no direct evidence that this was their purpose, the impression is reinforced by the fact that the council sent a committee to Annapolis to observe the legislative session and to negotiate on the city's behalf. The committee's lengthy report began by noting that the proposal to grant Baltimore four delegates instead of two "lost by a considerable majority." As might have been expected, the proposal to move the state capital from Annapolis to Baltimore was also rejected.[52] A resolution introduced during the discussion of this measure reflected a legislative perspective on the city. An Annapolis delegate urged that the capital not be moved to Baltimore "where great outrages have frequently occurred, and where mobs the most furious are raised with unparalleled facility, such that might, and very probably would retard and infringe the freedom necessary and essential in legislation, and might cause the enactment of measures destructive of the interest of the more thinly populated parts of the state . . . to the baneful injury of society and corruption of good morals."[53]

On other matters the city succeeded. As requested, the legislature approved a bill to facilitate the extension of Pratt Street; it added approval to extend two other streets as well and gave the city full authority to make improvements along the Jones Falls. The assembly also accepted the city's suggestion that state election districts should correspond to the city's wards, and it enacted a formula for increasing the number of wards in proportion to the city's population. The city won approval of its request to increase the authority of city judges. Most important, the legislature granted Baltimore full power to collect property taxes "to such amount as shall be thought necessary for public or city purposes." Almost as significant was the legislature's decision to authorize Baltimore to borrow up to $1 million and to grant the city the power of eminent domain. By the end of the legislative session, as Gary Browne observes, Baltimore had gained "a greater measure of autonomy than the city had ever known."[54]

Baltimore was still far from full municipal autonomy. It would continue to suffer the interference of the General Assembly, where the city's voice was grossly underrepresented and scarcely heeded. But the ever-changing boomtown had begun to develop a sense of itself. It was the city that stood up to British imperialism. It had become heroic, if only briefly. It had demanded its due from the federal government to cover the costs of its defense. (Since Washington's response left it deep in debt, it also seems to have acquired the habit of operating on borrowed money.) Finally, though the city and the precincts had initially differed on the desirability of annexation, they stood together in their opposition to the state legislature's highhandedness. The legislature's repeated slights, in fact, may have helped to unify the city at large.

There were other signs of increasing urban awareness. In 1819, the city put up its first street signs "affixed to the corner house of each and every street, lane, and alley." And in 1822, it again contracted with Thomas Poppleton to make a map of the recently expanded city and a plan for its further expansion. This time, he completed the assignment. Baltimore could see itself and glimpse a possible future.

Chapter 9 **PUBLIC DEBT AND INTERNAL IMPROVEMENTS**

EDWARD JOHNSON, who had preceded George Stiles as mayor of Baltimore, also succeeded him. Johnson was a physician and owner of one of the city's largest breweries, but politics was his principal occupation. The office to which he returned in 1819 was more powerful than the one he had left in 1816. While Johnson was sidelined, the Maryland General Assembly had changed the city charter to give the mayor, rather than the second branch of the city council, the authority to nominate city officials. The mayor also gained the authority to dismiss them. The measure was one of those passed during the session that began with the representation controversy, and, like other changes approved at the same session, it seemed a positive gain for Baltimore. The council members who monitored the legislative session commented favorably on the change in the appointment process, even though it augmented mayoral authority.[1]

Mayor Johnson was allied with Samuel Smith. Smith had come close to financial ruin as a result of the 1819 Panic, but he still had a political following. A rival faction led by John Montgomery, former congressman and Maryland attorney general, contested Smith's control of the city, and Montgomery won the mayor's office in 1820. For six years, Montgomery and Johnson took turns as mayor. They were evenly matched. *Niles' Weekly Register* declared the municipal election of 1822 "one of the most severe electioneering contests that we have known." Johnson won by only 48 votes out of more than 7,000.[2]

The Smith-Johnson faction drew much of its support from maritime Baltimore—Fell's Point, the wards east of the Jones Falls, and those nearest to the Basin. Montgomery's strength came from the westward and inland parts of the city, where prosperity depended on overland trade from the country's interior and, later, on the profits of textile mills. Mayoral elections became more complex in 1824, when homebuilder and carpenter Jacob Small ran against both Johnson and Montgomery. Though Montgomery won, the defeated forces formed an alliance that solidified behind Small in the election of 1826 and gave him an overwhelming victory.[3]

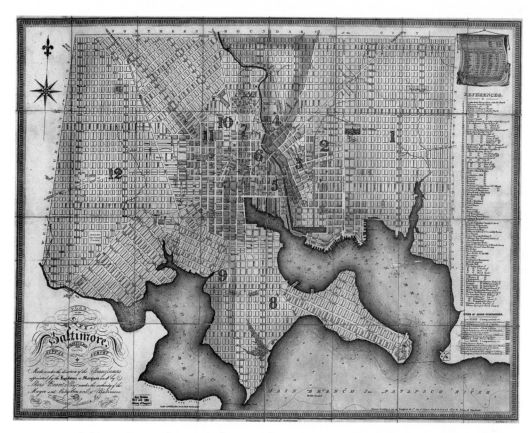

Baltimore in 1822, showing the location of wards

Small was the first mayor of Baltimore who might have qualified as a tradesman or "mechanic." His elevation was followed by the emergence of Jacksonian Democrats as a force in both local and national politics. Small and his political patron, Samuel Smith, recast themselves as champions of Baltimore's "workingmen" and linked local issues to the Jacksonian creed unfolding in national politics.

PUBLIC ENTERPRISE

Baltimore was building a public vision of itself, the political counterpart of Poppleton's map. This emerged, in part, as a defensive response to external threats. Baltimore's location—west of New York, Philadelphia, and Boston—gave the city a locational advantage that grew in value as the population drifted farther away from the Atlantic. The completion of the National Road in 1818 provided Baltimore with a connection to the Ohio River. Canals, however, threatened to cancel out Baltimore's privileged geographic position. Geography was still decisive, but now the crucial distances were vertical rather than horizontal. Baltimore might be nearer than New York to the "waters of the West," but the elevation it had to overcome to reach them was almost five times that achieved by the locks on the Erie Canal. The Chesapeake and Ohio Canal brought the challenge even closer to home. In effect, the C&O enabled the merchants of Georgetown to bypass the Great Falls of the Potomac and send their goods along a navigable waterway that used the Potomac Valley as a path through the Alleghenies and far to the west. The C&O would exceed Baltimore's inland reach on the south as the Erie Canal did to the north.[4]

For a time, Baltimore's political and commercial elites became preoccupied with canals of their own design. One of the most ambitious proposals came in 1820 from Robert Mills, architect of the city's Washington Monument. In his "Treatise on Inland Navigation," Mills proposed a canal that would link the Potomac with the Susquehanna and then give Baltimore access to both by means of a branch canal. The state legislature advanced another possibility. To soften Baltimore's opposition to the C&O Canal, it proposed a "cross-cut" branch of the C&O—called the Maryland Canal—that would extend from Georgetown to Baltimore. A further possibility, discussed at public meetings in 1823 and 1824, envisioned a "stillwater" canal that would run northeast along the edge of the Chesapeake as far as Havre de Grace, cutting across the necks of land that extended into the Bay, to the mouth of the Susquehanna, from which it could reach Port Deposit several miles upriver. It would allow the shallow-draft boats that rode down the Susquehanna a protected channel all the way to Baltimore.[5]

The extravagant canal system proposed by Robert Mills was prohibitively expensive—and unworkable. But distinct political factions lined up behind the two remaining alternatives. Sometime-mayor Edward Johnson, backed by Senator Samuel Smith, led the proponents of the Susquehanna Canal, which would enter Baltimore from the east. Its backers were concentrated in the eastern wards, where Johnson and Smith generally ran strong. John Montgomery's faction supported the "cross-cut" canal from the C&O to Baltimore. It would enter the city from the west, and its advocates were concentrated in the western and northwestern wards, where the project was likely to stimulate development and the voters tended to support Montgomery. A third faction, backing future mayor Jacob Small, consisted of property-owning tradesmen worried about the taxes needed to finance expensive canal projects.[6]

Though weak on results, canal politics helped to transform Baltimore. During the era of mercantile prosperity before 1815, Baltimoreans had engaged in trade singly or in small partnerships, though larger groups of investors sometimes shared the risks of chancy ventures such as privateering. But the internal improvements needed to maintain Baltimore's economy in the era of canal building were large-scale, collective enterprises—as much political as economic ventures—and government was an essential participant.

The theorist of this new political economy was Baltimore lawyer Daniel Raymond. His *Thoughts on Political Economy*, published in 1820, is regarded as the first major treatise on economic theory printed in the United States.[7] Raymond wanted to explain what contributed to the wealth of nations, and his views on the subject differed sharply from Adam Smith's. Smith, according to Raymond, failed to distinguish national wealth from individual wealth. Individual wealth, Raymond argued, was the "possession of property, for the use of which, the owner can obtain a quantity of the necessaries and comforts of life." Private wealth, in other words, was the capacity to support oneself without labor. "Talents and skills" might be a means to acquire individual wealth, but they did not constitute wealth, because the people blessed with such endowments had to exercise them to support themselves. They had to labor, and a "man who is obliged to labor for the necessities and comforts of life cannot be called wealthy."[8] The wealthy performed no labor beyond collecting rents or clipping coupons.

National wealth was different. It was not simply the aggregation of a country's individual wealth. Labor was essential to national wealth. National wealth was "a capacity or ability to acquire, by labour, the necessities and comforts of life." The wealth-producing capacity of industrious citizens could be enhanced by "improvements in the arts and sciences, and in agriculture, if [a nation's] lands are in a higher state of cultivation, if its roads, bridges, canals, mills, buildings, and improvements are in a greater state of perfection than those of another nation." Economic equality also contributed to national wealth because it enabled all citizens to participate in their nation's prosperity and gave them an incentive to contribute to economic growth. Slavery was inimical to the wealth of nations because it excluded slaves from the enjoyment of the nation's good fortune and also encouraged sloth among slave owners.[9]

Raymond offered an alternative to economic individualism. He envisioned a market in which wealth resulted from collective action to produce collective goods. The idea was essential to his argument for collectively generated internal improvements that magnified the productive power of industrious citizens. The work of building these improvements was "effective" labor as opposed to the "productive" labor of the nation's workers. Effective labor, he argued, made productive labor more productive. Raymond was also a proto-Keynesian who, unlike many of his contemporaries, recognized that an excess of production over consumption represented not an accumulation of profit or wealth but an economic problem. In fact, Raymond argued, it was just such an underconsumption crisis that explained the extended economic slump experienced by his city and nation: the "distress" arose "from the circumstance, that consumption has not equalled production."[10]

BOOMTOWN GONE BUST

Raymond extended his analysis from the nation as a whole to regions and states,[11] and he might as well have been writing about his own city, Baltimore. The local economy lay in a prolonged state of stagnation. Municipal debt grew as revenues lagged. In 1819, before the full force of the national panic had hit, Mayor Johnson reported to the city council that "it evidently appears that there are ample funds *if they can be collected*, to pay the just demands against the City."[12] His emphasized caveat about collecting was serious. When Johnson's rival John Montgomery was mayor, the city's collector died before completing the tax collections for 1820; there were also significant tax arrearages remaining from 1819 and 1818. Montgomery asked the city council to authorize him to borrow $15,000 to meet immediate expenses and suggested the wisdom of having more than one collector, not just because the city might need a spare, but because the city's taxes were "too heavy to be collected in the

same year they are levied." An additional collector might help to reduce arrearages.[13]
His suggestion was apparently ignored.

Baltimore was sliding more deeply into debt. In 1818, a year before the panic, the council's Committee on Ways and Means issued a report on municipal finances. It pegged the city's debt at a little over $212,000 — about $4 million in today's dollars — far less than today's municipal debt. But in 1818, the amount was larger than the entire city budget. Over a third of this amount was "military debt," money that Baltimore hoped to wring from the federal government to cover city expenditures for defense in the War of 1812. The effort to extract these funds from Washington would go on for decades. The remainder of the debt consisted of short-term notes issued in anticipation of revenue and city "stocks" carrying 5 or 6 percent interest. (Today they would be called municipal bonds.) The committee estimated that expenditures for 1818 would exceed $180,000, but revenues would fall short of this amount by $50,000, increasing the city's debt by almost one-fourth. The committee expressed no alarm about this, but promised another report on a municipal "sinking fund" to retire the city's debt.[14]

The council voted to contribute $6,000 a year to this fund. The cashiers of three local banks would serve as the fund's unpaid commissioners. They would use the fund to purchase city stocks from the citizens or banks that held them, but only if they were offered for sale at par value or below. (There was no point in buying back municipal debt at a price higher than the amount owed.) The commissioners would add the purchased stocks to the sinking fund, and the city would continue to make interest payments on these certificates in the hope that the fund would grow large enough to erase the city's debt. Money extracted from the federal government to pay the city's "military debt" would also go to the sinking fund.[15]

In practice, the fund may have encouraged the city to go even deeper into debt. According to the Committee on Ways and Means, one of the sinking fund's virtues was that it would "have a powerful tendency to keep up the price & credit of the Stock, which is all important for enabling the City to borrow."[16] If the price of the stock remained high, of course, the commissioners of the sinking fund would rarely be able to purchase shares below par and reduce outstanding debt, but the reliable marketability of the stock would facilitate borrowing and the growth of city obligations.

The sinking fund was aptly named. Less than a year after its creation, municipal debt approached $400,000, an increase largely due to the cost of various "improvements": new bridges, new streets, land purchased for a new market house, expansion of an existing market, and a new powder magazine.[17] The sinking fund itself added to Baltimore's fiscal distress. The annual $6,000 payment and the interest charges on city stock held by the fund enlarged the municipal deficit. In 1819, just a year after creation of the fund, an ordinance passed by the first branch of the council called for suspension of all payments to the sinking fund and their diversion into the city treasury, where they could be used "to meet appropriations in the same manner as any other city or public money." The second branch defeated the measure, but by

1821, Mayor Montgomery and a committee of the council again proposed to dissolve the sinking fund and use the proceeds for "extinguishment" of Baltimore's growing debt, which had risen to more than $450,000. The proposal became a fixture of local fiscal politics, introduced almost annually.[18]

The General Assembly, where Baltimore had recently won additional autonomy in taxing and borrowing, now posed another threat to the town's fiscal stability. In 1822, John Pendleton Kennedy, one of the city's two representatives in the house of delegates, sent an ominous report suggesting that the legislative session would be "marked by more than one act of unequivocal hostility to our city." Kennedy, a young lawyer with literary as well as political ambitions, thought that the assembly was "characterized in a greater degree by a disposition to subject us to the convenience of the counties than I have ever known it before." His particular concern was the rumored preparation of a bill that would transfer Baltimore's auction tax and its receipts to the state treasury. The loss would be significant. In 1820, the auction tax accounted for almost 11 percent of municipal revenue, but before the Panic of 1819, it had yielded 30 to 40 percent.[19] The city council was sufficiently alarmed to authorize the mayor to "select such gentlemen of the City" as he thought appropriate to travel to Annapolis in an effort to secure the auction tax against legislative pilfering.[20]

In Annapolis, however, the debate veered, improbably, toward the issue of "internal improvements." One of the earliest improvements underwritten by the federal government was the National Road, begun at Cumberland, Maryland, in 1813 and completed to Wheeling on the Ohio River in 1818. Various private turnpikes extended from Cumberland eastward to Baltimore and other seaboard cities. In 1821, a delegate from Washington County introduced a resolution that renounced the state's claim to the city's auction tax, provided that Baltimore would purchase the private turnpike extending from Baltimore to Boonsboro or the road from Hagerstown to Cumberland and make them toll-free roads. Both Boonsboro and Hagerstown were located in Washington County. The delegate acknowledged Baltimore's financial "embarrassments" but argued that using funds generated by the auction tax to purchase the turnpikes would "ultimately return [those funds] into her own coffers."[21] Like those who wanted the state to expropriate the city's auction tax, the Washington County delegate sought to exploit Baltimore's declining but still sizeable revenues to advance his own constituency's interests.

A delegate from the Eastern Shore complained that the resolution was calculated to prevent the assembly from voting on the auction tax at the current session, since it would take months for Baltimore to arrange the purchase of the turnpikes. Baltimore's two delegates frankly acknowledged that this was precisely their reason for supporting the proposal. John Pendleton Kennedy noted that the resolution advanced by his colleague from Washington County might induce Baltimore to accept a compromise to keep its auction duties. Baltimore, said Kennedy, was burdened by debt and "suffering under a taxation tenfold heavier than that felt by any other portion of the state." But Kennedy announced that he would nevertheless vote in favor of the resolution because it would postpone the legislature's consideration of the auction bill until the following year. Baltimore, he added, was a "great patron of internal improvements" and would embrace the purchase of the toll roads, as well as other projects, if its circumstances were more prosperous.[22]

The resolution to create toll-free roads was overwhelmingly defeated, but the auction bill did not pass either. Baltimore's financial circumstances, however, continued to deteriorate. In his annual message for 1822, Mayor Montgomery cited the city's heavy debt and emphasized the need for public thrift—"no other than the ordinary expenses of the City are deemed necessary." Surplus revenue, if any, should be "applied to the discharge of so much of the city debt or a reduction of the rate of taxes may be made as the Council may consider expedient." But little more than a month after delivering this lecture, Montgomery returned to the council for approval to borrow $15,000 in anticipation of city revenue. The second branch refused him. Ten days later, however, both branches approved his request to borrow up to $20,000.[23]

The city's growing debt may have had some role in Mayor Montgomery's defeat in the hard-fought mayoral campaign of 1822. One of ex-mayor Johnson's partisans claimed (inaccurately) that the city owed only $15,000 when Johnson left office in 1820 but was burdened with over $400,000 in debt at the end of Montgomery's term. So many other claims, charges, insults, and countercharges were fired off during the campaign that it is impossible to determine how much weight the issue of municipal indebtedness carried in the election's outcome. Montgomery was also attacked for neglecting to pay his dues in the Hibernian Society (the Irish defaulter was actually another John Montgomery). Johnson was accused of being "indolent." His friends referred to his exertions—as both mayor and physician—in the "fever of 1819." Montgomery was described as "an aristocratical man . . . who rather thinks of gratifying personal feuds and partialities than public benefit." Another citizen claimed that Montgomery was "the poor man's friend." Johnson's supporters countered that their candidate was not only the poor man's friend but "the widow's hope" and "the orphan's benefactor."[24]

In his first annual message after being returned to office in 1822, Mayor Johnson chose to compare the city's current financial condition not with the previous year's but with its status on November 1, 1820—weeks after he had lost the office to John Montgomery. His figures showed that city debt had increased by over 40 percent while his opponent was mayor. Municipal debt may not have been the election's decisive issue, but Johnson clearly made it an issue after he took office.[25]

Johnson's strictures against municipal expenditure were even more severe than Montgomery's. According to Johnson, "the particular condition of the city will not admit of any expenditures . . . that the immediate welfare of its inhabitants does not imperiously demand." The mayor cautioned the members of the council to "give their most serious consideration whether we are in a situation to attempt anything new." He was willing to make only two exceptions to his injunctions against new spending: when money was needed to preserve "the Health of the City" or "our navigation and harbor." Outside those priorities, he hoped that he and the council would be "united in a fixed and determined resolution not to increase the amount of our debt." Only weeks later, the council granted the presidents of its two branches and the mayor the joint authority to issue up to $80,000 in city stock at 6 percent interest, money apparently needed to meet the city's operating expenses.[26]

THE CANAL CRAZE

There was another odd departure from Mayor Johnson's regime of austerity. In spite of his reluctance "to attempt anything new," he left undisturbed a $50,000 appropriation for improving navigation on the lower Susquehanna River, where swift currents and navigational obstacles interfered with upstream shipping. Heavy-timbered, shallow-draft "arks" and rafts made the one-way trip downriver and were broken up for lumber when they completed the journey. As early as 1801, work had begun on a nine-mile canal parallel to the river so that boats could move upstream past the worst of the rapids. Its engineer was Benjamin Latrobe, architect of the US Capitol and founder of an illustrious line of Baltimoreans. The first Susquehanna Canal was not successful. It was too small to accommodate the larger craft descending the Susquehanna, and it had been excavated with a curved bed not suited to accommodate flat-bottomed canal boats. But Baltimoreans had not abandoned the canal that might tap the trade of the Susquehanna Valley, drawing it away from Philadelphia. If successful, the project might remedy the "Stagnation of our Commerce," which Mayor Johnson blamed for the decline of municipal revenue.[27]

The Susquehanna venture also seemed to provide the city with its only hope of responding to the threat of a "Potomac" canal that might negate Baltimore's locational advantage for trade with the West. The Potomac proposal was all the more aggravating because, if the General Assembly embraced it, Baltimore might have to bear a substantial share of the project's cost. Mayor Johnson wrote to the city council, noting that an act to reincorporate the Potomac Canal Company was being considered in Annapolis, and he urged "the adoption on your part of the most prompt & efficient measures to defeat this project."[28]

Four members of the city council dutifully traveled to Annapolis to defend the interests of Baltimore. They found that the latest version of the Potomac Canal bill provided for an enterprise supported entirely by private funds. Baltimore, in other words, would not be compelled to contribute. Consideration of the bill had also been delayed until the next session of the assembly (when it was defeated). But the extended discussion of the Potomac Canal and the difficulties that it faced seems to have put Baltimore's four councilmen in a canal-building frame of mind. They returned to Baltimore with a report that covered not only the fate of the Potomac Canal Company but an ambitious proposal for a canal that would carry freight from Baltimore to "our mighty river Susquehanna" at a point above the rapids that interfered with navigation. A canal "from this beautiful river to Baltimore, taken out above all the obstructions on the river would be from 60 to 70 miles (one third the length of the Potomac Canal) without crossing or perforating a single mountain." The General Assembly "at the instance of our delegates" had already appointed commissioners to consider the feasibility of such a canal, as well as another proposed canal that would link Baltimore with one to be built in the Potomac Valley.[29]

The councilmen had been sent to Annapolis to kill one costly canal but returned with proposals for two others. They gave only passing attention to the reduced state of their city's treasury and commerce, but confidently trusted "that in proportion to the extent of our depression and inactivity, will be the renewed vigor and awakened spirit with which the people and the government will unite in this great work." They were not alone. Mayor Montgomery had chaired a public meeting to discuss the Susquehanna Canal project in April 1822, and soon afterward, Baltimoreans were making voluntary donations to finance an engineering survey for the enterprise. One local visionary claimed that a further Susquehanna Canal should also be dug from the headwaters of the river in Lake Otsego to Lake Erie, thus making it possible that "a man may *walk in the water* from Baltimore to Quebec."[30] Though this dreamer may have held odd ideas concerning the use of canals, the prospect of canal digging seems to have lifted Baltimore's political and business classes from somber preoccupations with debt and decline to grand schemes for what J. Thomas Scharf called "a fresh start in the race of prosperity."[31]

The Maryland Canal Commission appointed to examine the prospects for a Susquehanna waterway did nothing to dim Baltimoreans' enthusiasm for their canal-to-be. The commissioners mapped what they regarded as a technically feasible route, with the assistance of officers on loan from the army's topographical engineers. Thomas Poppleton helped to plan the "leveling" of the route, and Jehu Bouldin surveyed it. The canal would leave the Susquehanna just above the Conewago Falls in Pennsylvania and run along the west bank of the river to Havre de Grace in Maryland, a distance of more than 56 miles, at an estimated cost of about $1.8 million. If the canal ended at Havre de Grace, canal boats' cargoes would have to be transferred to other vessels. The narrow, shallow-draft canal boats could not manage the currents, tides, and swells of the Chesapeake Bay—and the mules and horses that pulled them would have to swim. The Susquehanna "arks" had to shift their cargoes to other boats once they reached the Bay, and their experience suggested that the business of transferring freight to bay vessels might delay its arrival in Baltimore by as much as five days. The stopover could be avoided by cutting another leg of the canal southwest from Havre de Grace to enter Baltimore's harbor, not far from Fell's Point. The distance would be something over 36 miles and add $1.4 million to the cost. This leg of the canal would cut more than 30 miles from the journey because the boats would not have to sail down the Chesapeake to the mouth of the Patapsco and then up the river to Baltimore. This, and the ability of canal boats to make the trip without any transshipment of cargoes, might save as much as eight days on the trip from Havre de Grace to Baltimore.[32]

The commissioners were especially sanguine about the wealth that would flow to Baltimore by means of the Susquehanna Canal. Some of that wealth, they recognized, would come to Baltimore at the expense of Philadelphia. But the bounty of "Susquehanna country" embraced much more than the wealth of Philadelphia. The region's population was "considered as among the most active, vigorous, and productive of any within our union," and beneath its soil, the report claimed, were immense deposits of iron ore and coal.[33]

The commissioners concluded with a plea that the canal of their dreams should not be abandoned to the meanness of private enterprise. The Erie Canal, they emphasized, "progressed under the direction, and has been the work of a free people." It was a state project. The Susquehanna venture should also move forward under public auspices. "But, if by any misdirected notions, the grand work of opening a canal from Baltimore to Conewago, should be fashioned into the shape of a joint stock company, and thrown into the market, among money dealers and speculators, to be gambled for, by having its vast merits noised and bruited abroad, until immense sums have been filched from some and squandered by others, and all without effect, we should calculate on beholding the effort terminate in an abortion and then on its dropping into oblivion."[34] The feeble accomplishments of the Potomac Canal Company, chartered in 1784,[35] may have contributed to this prejudice against the use of private capital for public improvements. The privately financed corporation was formed by Maryland and Virginia to improve navigation on the Potomac as far upriver as possible and to build a canal from that point to Cumberland. But the company accomplished little, and an investigation of its status conducted in 1821 found it insolvent and incapable of completing the project assigned to it.[36]

Not long after publication of the Maryland Canal Commission's report, a town meeting assembled in the rotunda under the dome of the new Exchange Building in Baltimore, designed by Benjamin Latrobe. The citizens in attendance were asked whether the city should give priority to the Susquehanna Canal or to another canal that would connect Baltimore, by way of the Potomac, with the Ohio River. Robert Goodloe Harper, a former congressman and US senator, made the case for a newly conceived Chesapeake and Ohio Canal. This had succeeded the long-stalled Potomac Company plan, and Harper argued for a lateral branch of the C&O that would reach Baltimore and carry its trade on the C&O, through Pittsburgh, to the Ohio River. He argued that the arks and rafts of the Susquehanna had already given Baltimore unrivaled control of the downriver trade; building a canal alongside the Susquehanna would bring no great gain for the city. Robert Winchester, one of the commissioners who had recommended the Susquehanna route, countered that it would give Baltimore access to "the fairest portion of the United States," not the frontier West, but a region already populated, developed, and prosperous. By a large majority, the assembled citizens declared themselves in favor of the Susquehanna option.[37]

A joint stock company, the Susquehanna and Tidewater Canal Company, eventually undertook the project. The work faltered in the face of unexpectedly high costs—about $80,000 a mile, more than twice the commission's estimate. The Maryland legislature had to be persuaded to subsidize the venture; the Pennsylvania legislature refused at first to grant a right of way to a canal that challenged the commercial prosperity of Philadelphia. Construction would not begin until 1835. The canal was completed in 1840, but without the extension from Havre de Grace to Baltimore. The canal company was insolvent by 1842.[38]

INSTITUTIONALIZING INDEBTEDNESS

It took only an imaginary canal to reanimate Baltimore's commercial aspirations. In fact, the imaginary canal inspired larger hopes than the actual, disappointing canal could possibly have sustained. A more general enthusiasm about internal improvements of all kinds held out hope that municipal indebtedness and commercial stagnation might end and that Baltimore might once again become the boomtown of the eastern seaboard. These expectations were not fully realized. Internal improvements may have energized commerce, but they led Baltimore's government to higher levels of indebtedness than it had ever risked in the days when the city's health, harbor, and water supply were its primary concerns.[39]

Baltimore refashioned itself for a new era of public expenditure. In 1826, the commissioners of the sinking fund were replaced by three commissioners of finance, consisting of the mayor and the presidents of the city council's two branches. The principal goal of the sinking fund had been to retire the city's debt, but the primary mission of the new commissioners was to manage the debt. The commissioners of finance were to receive an annual appropriation of $27,000, along with any proceeds generated by the sale of city-owned real estate. They were to use these funds to cover the costs of debt service. Only if a surplus remained after these obligations had been met were the commissioners authorized to purchase city stock from private investors and thereby reduce outstanding public debt. Even the money for debt service might be held up by the mayor, who was instructed to release funds to the commissioners "in such payments and at such times as the Treasury shall best admit."[40]

Baltimore's "fresh start in the race for prosperity" would be sustained by deficit spending, but local canal promoters looked to the state, as well as the city, for construction funds. In 1825, a Maryland Convention on Internal Improvements assembled in Baltimore. Its purpose was to reach some consensus about the competing canal projects being promoted in different parts of the state and to identify those with the strongest claims to state support.[41]

The quest for consensus was messy. A delegate from Allegany County wanted a canal from Baltimore to Allegany County. A representative for Harford County promoted the Susquehanna Canal, which would pass through Harford County. They agreed that the C&O Canal would facilitate trade between America's East Coast and the West, but this very fact "invested the proposed . . . canal with a national character" and made the venture a suitable project for "the energies and funds of the government of the United States." The federal government should finance the C&O, in other words, and Maryland should invest in an Allegany canal—or the Susquehanna Canal. Samuel Ellicott, a Baltimore City delegate, agreed that the C&O should be a federal project, but Maryland should underwrite a connection between the C&O and Baltimore, while simultaneously engineering a grander version of his city's favorite canal along the Susquehanna.[42]

A delegate from Allegany County, reaching for consensus, integrated all of these proposals along with others in a grandiose extravaganza of engineered waterways that would create a "continuous line of interior canal navigation . . . from Lake Erie to the Ohio, from the Ohio to the Potomac, from the Potomac to the Patapsco, from the Patapsco to Havre de Grace, on the Chesapeake Bay, from the Chesapeake Bay to the Delaware Bay, from the Delaware to the Hudson and thence by the Buzzard and Barnstable canal through to Boston."[43]

Toward the close of the proceedings, John Pendleton Kennedy delivered an admonition against entrusting the canal projects to private enterprise. He echoed the warning of the Susquehanna Canal Commission two years earlier, but was even more harshly skeptical about corporate capitalism. In making the case for the C&O Canal, Kennedy cited the need for "a security that the canal to be constructed, shall be managed with reference to the national convenience; and for the people's good." "Under such a conviction," he continued, "this convention do utterly reprobate the idea of risking so grand an enterprise upon the feeble means of an incorporated company . . . drawn together by the lure of gain."[44]

For Kennedy, at least, the "market revolution" elicited profound reservations about private enterprise, and he was not alone. Daniel Raymond's critique of economic individualism reflected a similar skepticism. But Kennedy's warnings were omitted from the report of the Internal Improvements Commission. A private corporation, supported in part by public funds, undertook construction of the C&O Canal. The arrangement reflected the General Assembly's longstanding preference "to run the state without the need for direct taxation" by financing its operations with "income derived from state investment in corporations chartered by the state legislature."[45] The canal company exhausted its capital far short of Pittsburgh and the Ohio River. Almost 25 years of planning and construction carried it only as far as Cumberland, where it stopped.[46] The Baltimore City Council was decidedly cool toward proposals to extend the canal beyond Cumberland. The estimated cost of the extension was $2.5 million and would add to the state's already considerable debt. But the council insisted that, if the state extended the C&O to the Ohio, it should also provide for the construction of the Maryland Canal from Washington to Baltimore.

General Simon Bernard, former aide-de-camp to Napoleon, was now an officer of the army's board of engineers. His study of the proposed Maryland Canal pronounced it impossibly expensive, and he reached the same conclusion concerning Baltimore's Susquehanna project. According to Scharf, "our people may be said to have sat down, like the Israelites of old by the waters of Babylon and wept."[47]

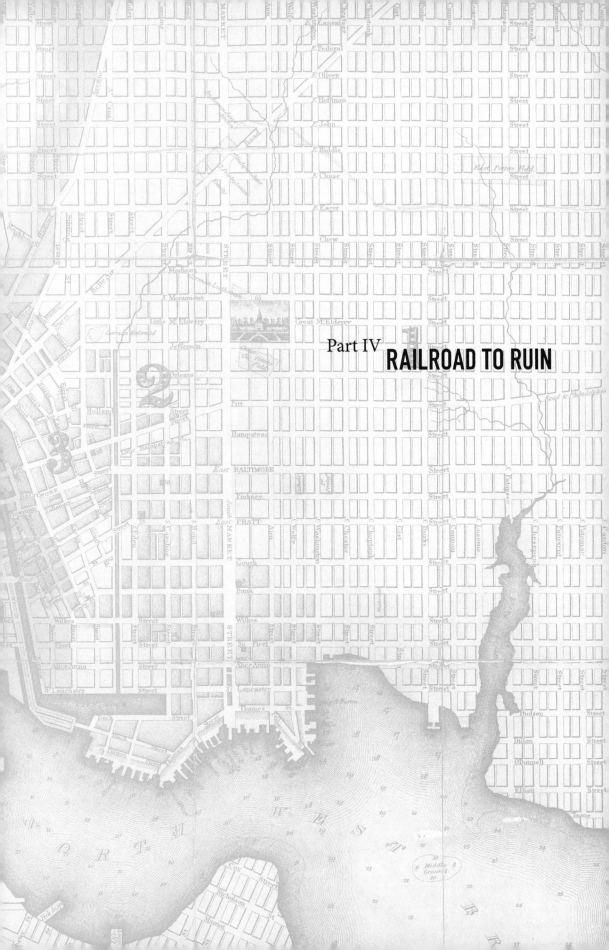

Part IV **RAILROAD TO RUIN**

Chapter 10 # WORKING ON THE RAILROAD

A S THEY DREAMED OF CANALS, Baltimore's entrepreneurs worked with steam. Mayor George Stiles had been a pioneer in the field. He introduced a small rotary steam engine at least as early as 1814, and later demonstrated its efficacy by using it to power one of the city's first steamboats and a gristmill for corn.[1] In 1813, a steam-powered flour mill was built on a wharf, where it could receive raw wheat at one end and transfer flour directly to the hold of a ship at the other. A steam-powered sawmill began operation at about the same time, and a steam-driven textile mill began operation in 1814. By 1826, the mayor and city council were soliciting proposals to replace the harbor's horse-powered mud machine with a steam-powered dredge.[2]

The city may have lost the canal race, but it stood at the cutting edge of antebellum invention. While its businessmen found new uses for steam engines, in 1817, Baltimore became the first American city to light its streets with gas. Delegates to the Internal Improvements Commission of 1825 mentioned "rail roads" as an alternative to canals and turnpikes, and the commission's final report called on the legislature to create a board of public works to consider, among other things, "what canals and rail roads are practicable." The Maryland General Assembly did create a board of public works at its next session, in 1826, but the legislation mentioned only roads and canals, not railroads.[3]

The subject came up again less than a year later when "sundry citizens of Baltimore" gathered "for the purpose of devising the Most Efficient Means of Improving the Intercourse between that City and the Western States." From the outset, the assembled Baltimoreans seem to have known what their conclusions would be. During their first sessions, "Various documents and statements, illustrating the efficiency of Rail Roads, for conveying of articles of heavy carriage, at a small expense, were produced and examined." The evidence seemed convincing that the railroad was a superior mode of transportation "over Turnpike roads or Canals." But to achieve an even higher degree of certainty (and prestige) for this view, the "sundry citizens" submitted their documents and statements to a committee of seven prominent Baltimoreans, who were to examine the collected materials, together with "any other facts or experiments as they may be able to collect," and then recommend a course of action.[4]

The committee did not abandon canal building, but its priorities were obvious. Its report recommended a canal from Baltimore "intersecting the contemplated Chesapeake and Ohio Canal within the District of Columbia, and . . . A DIRECT RAIL ROAD FROM BALTIMORE TO SOME ELIGIBLE POINT UPON THE OHIO RIVER." The "sundry citizens" resolved that "immediate application be made to the legislature of Maryland, for an act incorporating a joint stock company, to be styled 'The Baltimore and Ohio Rail Way Company.' "[5]

The committee members numbered only about two dozen, but they included some of the most influential members of Baltimore's business elite. They convened at the home of George Brown, son of investment banker Alexander Brown; the younger Brown would become a director and first treasurer of the B&O. Philip E. Thomas, a local hardware merchant before he became president of the Merchants' Bank, was chairman of the committee that reported to the sundry Baltimoreans; he would become the first president of the B&O. His brother, Evan Thomas, traveled to England to observe the Stockton and Darlington Railway and came back with decidedly positive impressions. Steam locomotives hauled coal hoppers over the tracks from inland mines in the north of England to the seaport of Stockton. The road soon added passenger service. William Brown, George's older brother, had been Alexander Brown and Sons' agent in Britain since 1809. His letters home added to local enthusiasm about the potential of railroads and steam engines.[6]

John McMahon was one of the youngest participants in the meetings at Brown's house, and the only elected officeholder in attendance—serving his second term in the Maryland House of Delegates. He was also an attorney, and the job of drafting the new railroad's corporate charter fell to him. The B&O venture commanded such ready support that the General Assembly approved its incorporation only days after McMahon finished writing the charter. The legislature authorized the B&O to issue $3 million in stock at $100 a share. It reserved 10,000 shares for the State of Maryland and 5,000 for Baltimore City.[7]

On March 20, 1827, the B&O opened its books to subscribers. On the same day, the city council authorized the mayor to subscribe for $500,000 in B&O shares on behalf of the municipality. The city appointed two directors to the B&O's board— the presidents of the first and second branches of the city council.[8]

At its inception, the B&O was not simply a private, profitmaking corporation. Governments—state and local—subscribed half of its initial stock offering. The General Assembly granted the company a tax exemption and claimed the right to set its rates. In short, the railroad was a venture in state capitalism. After Baltimore and Maryland had taken ownership of half the company, the residents of Baltimore rushed to purchase the shares that remained. By the time the company closed its books on March 31, 1828, local residents had signed up for 36,788 shares, more than twice the allocation for private subscribers, so these had to be doled out in fractional shares. About 22,000 Baltimoreans—more than a quarter of the city's population—purchased stock in the railroad. The B&O was not only a quasi-public corporation; it was a community enterprise. Its primary purpose was not to turn a profit but to restore Baltimore's advantageous connection with the territory beyond the Alleghenies. The city's government and citizens would later provide most of the financing for another railroad: the Baltimore and Susquehanna.[9] The two imaginary canals conceived to link Baltimore to the Potomac and Susquehanna Valleys would be replaced by a pair of real railroads.

Imagined canals had awakened a spirit of public enterprise in Baltimore. The railroad gave that spirit a tangible vehicle. The B&O project was a unifying focus of public endeavor, and it had majestic scope. Its grandeur commanded awe as far away as Massachusetts, where the *Berkshire Star* declared that "Pyramids . . . palaces and all the mere pomp of man sink to insignificance before such a work as this . . . a single city has set foot on an enterprise . . . worthy of an empire."[10]

The symbolic start of the B&O's journey was a ceremony on July 4, 1828, when 90-year-old Charles Carroll of Carrollton, after prayer and oratory, sank a spade into the ground near the corner of Pratt and Amity Streets, where the railroad would lay its "first stone." (The railroad initially used granite ties on its 13-mile leg from Baltimore to Ellicott's Mills and on most of its tracks in the city.) On the same day, President John Quincy Adams was engaged in a similar ritual in Georgetown, the starting point for the Chesapeake and Ohio Canal. The president's execution of the ceremony ran into trouble. His spade hit a stump or a tree root just under the surface, and it required several attempts for him to produce a quantity of dirt worthy of the occasion.[11]

The B&O Railroad and C&O Canal were obvious competitors. The managers of the C&O made an early decision to challenge the B&O in court before their company had to face the railroad in the market. The legal struggle turned on Point of Rocks, where the Potomac Valley narrowed, and the level ground available for construction on the Maryland side of the river seemed insufficient to accommodate both a canal and a railroad. The B&O's attorney was John H. B. Latrobe, son of the architect Benjamin Latrobe, who was assisted by the aristocracy of the American bar, including Daniel Webster, William Wirt (future US attorney general), Roger B. Taney (future chief justice of the US Supreme Court), and Reverdy Johnson (future US attorney general and senator). Neither the C&O nor the B&O had reached Point of Rocks by the time the C&O Canal Company filed suit in Frederick. By January 1832, the dispute reached the Maryland Court of Appeals, which delivered a decision granting the Canal Company exclusive construction rights on the left, or Maryland, bank of the Potomac. The majority opinion rested on the contention that the C&O Canal had inherited the rights set out in the charter of the defunct Potomac Company. Since those grants were made in 1784, the canal's claim took priority over the B&O's.[12]

The dispute migrated to the General Assembly, which had financial stakes in both railroad and canal. It imposed a compromise. The B&O's double-track line would become single-track at Point of Rocks so that it would take up only a 20-foot strip of the riverside terrace. The C&O would dig its channel in the 40 or 50 feet remaining.

When the railroad reached Harper's Ferry, the B&O would have to abandon the Maryland side of the Potomac and cross the river by bridge. The work of finding and surveying a feasible route beyond Harper's Ferry was assigned to Benjamin Latrobe, Jr., John's brother. Benjamin also designed the bridge at Harper's Ferry.[13] These inconveniences did not prevent the railroad from reaching Cumberland in 1842, eight years before the canal had been dug that far, and unlike the C&O, the B&O continued beyond Cumberland to the Ohio River.

CORPORATE CULTURE

Mayor Jacob Small celebrated the progress of the railroad. Baltimore's government and its citizens, he said, were "deeply concerned, both as regards their immediate interest in the stock of the company, and [about] the effects which this splendid scheme of internal improvements, if it is successfully accomplished, will not fail to produce in the future prosperity of our City."[14] But for all the celebration, there was an undercurrent of uneasiness, at least on the city's side, about its partnership with the B&O.

The first curious note in the relationship between city and railroad was a resolution introduced in the second branch of the city council in February 1828, little more than a month after the mayor's celebratory remarks. It authorized him to dispose of the city's shares in the B&O whenever it seemed advantageous to do so. The stock was selling well above par, and the resolution held that the city's installment payments on its $500,000 stake in the railroad imposed an undue burden on taxpayers. The sale of the city's B&O shares could provide the funds needed to cover the cost of shares subscribed for but still to be purchased.[15]

The measure did not pass, but it was followed by others suggesting a lack of transparency in the relationship between the city government and the corporation it had helped to create. City officials participated directly in the railroad's governance. The mayor represented the city at the B&O stockholder meetings; the presidents of the city council's two branches held seats on the railroad's 14-person board of directors. But their participation in corporate governance did not give them access to the railroad's plans on matters vital to Baltimore. The mayor and council were concerned in particular about the route that the railroad would take through the city and the location of its "depot or depots."

Solomon Etting, president of the first branch of the council, suggested that the railroad call a meeting of its board of directors to decide "the *Point* at which it *shall enter the City*—and also upon the *direction* of its continuance *through the City*, to its point of termination or general depot."[16] The directors met and approved a resolution instructing the engineers to plot the best course from Point of Rocks on the Potomac to Baltimore's city limits and "terminate at a point calculated to distribute the trade throughout the Town as now improved." Etting wrote to Mayor Small expressing "regret that this resolution leaves undefined the point at which the Rail Road will enter the City, or the point at which it shall terminate within the City."[17]

If the B&O planned to locate as close as possible to tidewater, it would choose a point on the Patapsco at the mouth of its Northwest Branch and south of Baltimore, from which the railroad could have followed the Patapsco westward toward the Potomac. Etting and other city officials were concerned that this would lead to intense commercial and industrial development several miles south of the city limits, and they were not about to invest $500,000 of their constituents' taxes to promote a competing commercial center.[18]

The city was pursuing another strategy designed to lock the railroad's terminal facilities into place within the limits of Baltimore. In March 1828, the B&O had placed a newspaper advertisement announcing that it was interested in acquiring "suitable grounds, or sites for depots, or points of stoppage . . . at any place within or near the city of Baltimore." Mayor Small sent a clipping of the notice to the city council, adding that "the City is in possession of a large property East of the Jones Falls . . . which might suit the views of the Company."[19] The property, at Fell's Point, was the "City Block," created by the municipal mud machines out of spoil dredged from the bottom of the harbor. At first, the council was disposed to sell the real estate to the railroad, but the sale was converted into a donation, apparently with the hope that the gift of free land would make the city irresistible as the site for the railroad's terminal facilities. The council authorized the mayor "to convey to the Baltimore and Ohio Rail road company certain property &c" without any pecuniary consideration.[20]

The city did not complete the property transfer until 1832, but the gift of real estate seems to have satisfied the needs of both parties. The land provided the B&O with "direct communication between the railway and the shipping in the harbor,"[21] and the railroad's foothold in Baltimore reassured local officials that the city would be able to capture commercial and industrial development stimulated by the railroad terminal. The B&O was already building a depot on the west side of the city on a 10-acre tract of Mount Clare, a Carroll family estate, also donated to the railroad. In time, the B&O would build its shops and a roundhouse here. And at Locust Point, across the harbor from its Fell's Point depot, it would lay down a gigantic railyard with towering grain elevators and spindly coal piers that would carry gondolas high enough to tip their contents into the holds of ships.

INVESTING IN UNKNOWNS

The B&O's negotiations with the city had given the municipal corporation its first experience of dealing with a big business corporation. Public officials, accustomed to handling the concrete grievances of individual citizens, now engaged in complex, corporation-to-corporation transactions. The municipal and railroad corporations were like nations conducting diplomatic relations rather than officials dealing with clients. The B&O introduced a new impersonality into Baltimore's politics, a development soon to be accentuated by the institutionalization of political parties and elaboration of ideologies during the Jacksonian era. Both were political abstractions from the personal. But it was not just corporate impersonality that complicated communications between municipal and business corporations. Even if the B&O had tried to be completely clear about its plans, it could not offer straightforward answers to all of Baltimore's questions.

Railroad technology was in its infancy, and railroads were among the first large-scale industries in the United States. Basic questions about equipment and organization remained unsettled. What should rails look like? At first, they were just iron straps fastened directly to granite or wooden ties; later, the iron straps were fastened to wooden stringers secured to the ties. The ends of the iron straps, however, tended to curl upward and break loose from the stringers when subjected to heavy loads. These loose rails were called "snakeheads," perhaps because they were so deadly. A loose snakehead could derail an engine or erupt through the floor of a passenger car to maim and kill its occupants. Snakeheads became a problem when the B&O shifted from horsepower to heavy steam engines, a transition not completed until 1836. Even after 1836, a municipal ordinance required horse-drawn trains within the city limits, and an agreement with the C&O required the B&O to use horsepower in the narrow pass from Point of Rocks to Harper's Ferry. (Steam locomotives frightened the horses and mules that pulled the canal boats.)[22]

Even a horse-powered railroad seemed a remarkable improvement in transportation to passengers of the 1830s. During the first phase of its construction, the B&O offered public officials and prominent Baltimoreans junkets by passenger car from Pratt Street to the Carrollton Viaduct, a bridge that still carries railroad tracks across the Gwynn's Falls in far southwest Baltimore. The *Baltimore American* marveled that a single horse could pull a carriage occupied by "twenty-four ladies and gentlemen . . . at the extraordinary rate of *fifteen miles an hour!*"[23]

Though Peter Cooper's *Tom Thumb* is supposed to have lost its famous race with a gray mare, Cooper persuaded at least some of the B&O directors that steam locomotion was feasible on the railroad's westward path to the Alleghenies. Cooper had a tangible stake riding on the outcome of the race, but not on the locomotive itself. He had come to Baltimore from New York and, with two partners, purchased 3,000 acres on the waterfront just east of the city. It had once been the property of a Baltimore sea captain engaged in the China trade. He called his estate Canton, the name that the area carries today. Cooper was convinced that the operations of the B&O would send the area's land prices soaring. He became a director of the Canton Company, which presided over conversion of the captain's estate into one of the country's earliest industrial parks—10,000 acres on which the corporation hoped to see the construction of "wharves, ships, workshops, factories, stores, dwellings, and such other buildings and improvements as may be deemed necessary, ornamental, and convenient." When the grading and draining of Cooper's land turned up iron ore deposits, he converted his real estate investment into an industrial venture. Trading much of his land for stock in the Canton Company, Cooper retained enough waterfront real estate to accommodate the furnaces and forges of the new Canton Iron Works, poised to sell iron rails to the B&O.[24]

The success of Cooper's ironworks and the value of his shares in the Canton Company depended on the success of the railroad, and the fortunes of the B&O, he thought, hinged on the decisive advantages of steam power. But the B&O directors were skeptical about the use of steam locomotives, even though the engines had proven themselves in England. The route from Baltimore to the Potomac River had

A replica of the *Atlantic*, the second locomotive built by Phineas Davis for the Baltimore and Ohio Railroad in 1832. The B&O built 20 other locomotives based on Davis's design.

to follow the winding bed of the Patapsco, then the turns of the Potomac, and after that there were mountains to be circumvented. Settled opinion held that steam locomotives could not handle tight curves. On the 13-mile run from Baltimore to Ellicott's Mills, Cooper showed that his *Tom Thumb*—though admittedly a very small steam engine—could negotiate curves. Early in 1831, the railroad's directors offered a prize of $4,000 for the best four-wheeled locomotive of three-and-a-half tons, more than three times the weight of *Tom Thumb*. Phineas Davis, a former watchmaker from Pennsylvania, won the competition and went on to build several other locomotives for the B&O. Davis's career as an engine builder was cut short in 1835 when he was killed in the derailment of his prize-winning locomotive.[25]

Some of the B&O's most vital innovations were administrative rather than mechanical. The railroad was a multistate corporation operating on an unprecedented scale. It opened the age of big business and managerial capitalism. The corporation's counsel, John H. B. Latrobe, weighed in on crucial matters of administrative structure. He acknowledged that the company's president could not possibly exercise personal supervision over the railroad's extensive operations, but he rejected a proposal to appoint an assistant president because it would "amount to dividing between two persons the duties which are performed in other enterprises by one." Latrobe wanted the company to be led by a "single mind." Instead of appointing an assistant president, he proposed to organize the company into three divisions, all of which would report directly to the president. Two of these divisions would consist of subdivisions. Under the chief engineer, for example, there would be a superintendent responsible for surveying the route and acquiring land for the right of way; a superintendent of construction, responsible for laying the track, building the bridges, and boring the tunnels; and a superintendent of machinery, in charge of building locomotives and rolling stock. After the road reached Cumberland and prepared for its final surge toward the Ohio River, the company developed an even more elaborate structure.[26] Its annual reports were regarded as textbooks for the railroads that followed. In 1835, the *American Railroad Journal* named the B&O the "Rail Road University of the United States." It enabled its successors to save time and money that might have been wasted on technological and organizational dead-ends.[27]

Uncertainties about technology and organization translated into doubtful estimates of time and cost. Building the railroad from Baltimore to Wheeling took more than 25 years and millions of dollars more than expected. Some of that time was spent in the B&O's legal skirmish with the C&O Canal Company. The agreement under which the two corporations shared the Potomac Valley right-of-way west from Point of Rocks required the B&O to stop laying track past Harper's Ferry until the C&O had reached Cumberland. The railroad survived the halt because, by reaching Harper's Ferry, it was also able to make a connection with the Winchester and Potomac Railroad, which brought the B&O freight and passengers from the length of the Shenandoah Valley. It also used the hiatus to build a branch line from Baltimore to Washington. Together with its short branch line to Frederick, completed in 1831, these links enabled the railroad to generate revenue even while it made no progress toward its intended destination at the "western waters."[28]

Just to reach Harper's Ferry, however, the B&O needed an accelerated infusion of cash. In 1833, it persuaded the Maryland legislature and the City of Baltimore to step up the schedule of installment payments on their stock subscriptions. In 1836, the General Assembly released the B&O from its obligation to stand still while the C&O burrowed toward Cumberland. But the railroad could not proceed until Baltimore added a subscription of $3 million to its original stake of $500,000. The state agreed to provide another $3 million, in three annual installments. The B&O borrowed additional money to cover cost overruns on the line to Harper's Ferry, and extensive repairs were needed along the existing line because the rails dated to the railroad's "experimental" phase and had not been built to stand up to heavy traffic and the weight of locomotives and rolling stock.[29]

DEBTS BEFORE DIVIDENDS

The task confronting the founders of the Baltimore and Susquehanna Railroad seemed less daunting than the B&O's project. Though the Susquehanna line would have to cross high ground between the valleys of the Patapsco and the Susquehanna, no mountain ranges separated the railroad's city from its river. But it encountered a political obstacle in the Pennsylvania state legislature, whose members were understandably reluctant to charter a railroad that threatened to divert commerce from Philadelphia to Baltimore.[30]

In 1828, the Maryland General Assembly authorized Baltimore to purchase as many as 2,000 shares of the Baltimore and Susquehanna, with a par value of $50 per share; an equal amount was reserved for the State of Maryland. The city council was more wary about making this investment than it had been for the B&O. A committee recommended that the city hold back its money until the Baltimore and Susquehanna had received a charter to operate in Pennsylvania,[31] but the arrangement finally adopted would have the city pay only $2,000 toward its subscription of $100,000—one dollar on each $50 share. Nothing more would be advanced until the railroad demonstrated that "individuals and private corporations" had submitted subscriptions for stock amounting to $250,000 and that each purchaser had advanced at least as much cash per share as Baltimore.[32]

In return for its stake in the railroad, Baltimore could appoint one of its councilmen as a director of the company. The appointment may have given the city a voice in running the railroad, but it also created an advocate for the railroad in the city council. From his first report, in 1830, Councilman John Diffenderffer reassured his colleagues in city government that all was well with the railroad, even though it remained unclear whether private stock subscriptions had reached the $250,000 minimum necessary to unlock further payments from the city.[33]

When George Winchester, president of the Baltimore and Susquehanna, finally informed the mayor and council that his company had met the $250,000 requirement, he had something further to ask of the city. The railroad's directors wanted the council to "advance the credit of the city" as security for their company's debts. This financial vote of confidence "would give the company the Stability that would insure the accomplishment of its great object—the Salvation of the most important branch of trade now left to the city." This and "perhaps one small installment more" would "put in operation the first division of the road from the city to the lime stone region" north of Baltimore. The railroad's capacity to carry bulk cargoes would significantly reduce the cost of materials such as limestone, lime, and marble. Together with passenger traffic and the carriage of freight "to and from the various mills and factories upon the Jones' Falls," the marble and limestone trade would, Winchester claimed, enable the railroad to generate annual revenue of $25,000 without having to cross the still impenetrable legal barrier that kept the company from entering Pennsylvania.[34]

Winchester also hinted that he was having trouble getting the state government to back his railroad and that the city's support might "insure to us a subscription on the part of the state for the amount reserved for her use." But there was good news from Pennsylvania, where information from "authentic sources" indicated that "all opposition to the passage of the charter . . . will be withdrawn at the next session." In fact, four years would go by before Pennsylvania granted the Baltimore and Susquehanna the right to operate north of the Maryland line, and even then the company could not extend its tracks to its original objective on the Susquehanna River, only to the town of York. A Pennsylvania-based railway would provide a link to the river and to the web of canals and rails that stretched north and west from Philadelphia, but the Susquehanna line would not get guaranteed and permanent access to this branch until 1837, seven years after Winchester's hopeful report.[35]

Councilman Diffenderffer remained stalwartly optimistic about the railroad's prospects. Even if York were to be the end of the line, he said, "the wealth and population" of the area "would of themselves justify the construction of a railroad thereto and its extensive commercial relations with Baltimore and the fertility of the surrounding districts would induce an ample revenue to such a work." The possibility of a connection to the Susquehanna Valley opened up possibilities more promising than those that lay beyond the Alleghenies to the west. The western trade had once given Baltimore prosperity. "To retain its secure possession," wrote Diffenderffer, "has been the object of her anxious care and her most earnest endeavors and for that object millions have been expended; but as yet in vain."[36] Diffenderffer did not mention the B&O by name, but the implication was clear: the Baltimore and Susquehanna might offer a more proximate and reliable return for the city than the other railroad.

Some city council members may have shared Diffenderffer's hopes for the Susquehanna line. Four months after receiving his report, in April 1835, the council agreed to offer security for any interest payments that the Baltimore and Susquehanna owed to the State of Maryland.[37] The city tied its fortunes even more firmly to those of the railroad two years later, when the company exhausted its resources with one-third of the line from Baltimore to York still incomplete. The city added another $600,000 to its original investment of $100,000. The commissioners of finance issued still more city stock to cover the payment. A year after that, in 1838, the railroad once again ran out of money. Baltimore provided a loan of $150,000, together with a promise to pay an additional $100,000 to the railroad when it completed the line to York. Yet another issue of city stock covered the loan. In return, the city gained three additional council members to serve with John Diffenderffer on the railroad's board of directors.[38]

Railroads had once seemed to offer the city a new route to municipal solvency, but an 1836 report of the city council's Committee on Ways and Means explained how they had placed Baltimore on a fiscal treadmill. The commissioners of finance received an annual appropriation of $27,000 to cover debt service and reduction, but loans and stock purchases for railroads added so much to municipal borrowing that the entire sum went for interest payments. According to the committee, "The amounts of the demands of the Rail Road companies, and the period at which the City would derive a profit from her subscriptions to these companies being uncertain, it became impossible to limit the payment of interest and redemption of the City Debt at any given sum."[39]

The city debt exceeded $1 million in 1836 (equivalent to $21.5 million today), on which its annual interest payment was almost $54,000 ($1.26 million). Baltimore had gotten on the train and could not disembark without losing its substantial "subscriptions" and any prospect of a golden return on investment that would erase debt and taxes.

Chapter 11 **CORPORATE CHALLENGE TO EQUALITY AND AN EDUCATIONAL RESPONSE**

RAILROADS, AS ALFRED CHANDLER OBSERVED, were "pioneers in the management of modern business enterprise." They faced unprecedented problems of coordination and control. The swift, safe, and reliable transportation of goods and passengers over relatively long distances required carefully scheduled, multisite operations; continuing maintenance of locomotives, rolling stock, rails, and roadbed; and "brand new types of internal administrative procedures and accounting and statistical controls." Accounting and statistics were the means by which "an administrative command of middle and top executives" managed and monitored the day-to-day operations of their railroads. As a result, writes Chandler, the "operational requirements of the railroads demanded the creation of the first administrative hierarchies in American business."[1]

The railroad embodied a new order of inequality. The directors and principal executives of the Baltimore and Ohio Railroad worked many ranks above the men who prepared the right-of-way and laid the rails. Many of these laborers were recent immigrants from Ireland, not directly employed by the corporation, but supervised and paid by contractors, with whom they frequently had disputes about pay and employment. The trackmen's working conditions were conducive to radical protest. Matthew Mason observes that they "often lived and worked in remote and sparsely populated country, associating with few people besides their fellow railroad men. They toiled in gangs which could number in the hundreds, much larger work groups than in other antebellum industries besides canal work."[2]

The concentration and isolation of the trackmen created the conditions for intensification of grievances and organization of protest. Occasions for conflict multiplied because the contractors' profits depended on getting the greatest possible effort from their workers for the lowest possible pay. The work was also dangerous, even deadly. Riots and protests radiated along the B&O right-of-way from Baltimore to the west and down the branch line to Washington. The uprisings were serious enough to warrant mobilization of the militia. In one outbreak, the railroad carried a combined force of deputy sheriffs, bailiffs, and militia more than 26 miles from Baltimore toward Washington to arrest rioters suspected of destroying a section of track when a defaulting contractor failed to pay them.[3]

The expansion and industrialization of Baltimore's economy both created and depended upon an expanding class of menial laborers, no longer linked to an older, artisan tradition as apprentices or journeymen aspiring to become masters of their own workshops.[4] But there was little evidence of class animosity or class consciousness. Even among the Irish trackmen on the B&O, hostilities broke out not just between labor and management but also among Connaught men, Corkonians, and the "Fardowns" from County Longford. Regional loyalties originating in Ireland often took precedence over class identity in America.[5]

In Baltimore, the struggling wage laborers were no doubt treated as inferiors by their betters, but they were also regarded as possible candidates for elevation into the respectable classes. In 1818, the first of several banks went into business as special depositories for workingmen. Encouraging habits of thrift and industry among common laborers might lift them into the bourgeoisie. The votes of workingmen helped to elect the "mechanic" Jacob Small as mayor, and his victory may have persuaded them that democracy afforded paths of advancement beyond their present stations. But the most important and costly initiative taken to salvage the egalitarianism of the remembered republic was public education.[6]

SCHOOLS AND DEMOCRACY

Charity schools for children of the poor had operated in Baltimore since the eighteenth century. Many were sponsored by churches. But free schools were designed to serve poor children, not all children. In 1824, citizens in some of the town's 12 wards held meetings to discuss the possibility of a public school system that would bring together children of all classes. Delegates selected from each ward formed a citywide committee on public education, which met for the first time in January 1825 and soon produced a petition urging the General Assembly to authorize establishment of a "uniform, cheap, and excellent" system of public education in Baltimore like those already operating in Philadelphia, New York, and Boston. In 1826, the house of delegates passed a bill empowering Baltimore's mayor and city council to establish public schools in the city. The town's sole representative in the state senate was uncertain how to vote on the measure and wrote to Mayor Montgomery for guidance.[7]

His uncertainty was understandable. Public schooling was a controversial proposition that would agitate the city's politics. The legislature authorized the city to impose something close to a progressive income tax to support public education. It urged city government to have "a due regard . . . for the actual wealth of the persons" who were to pay school taxes, and taxable income would include "all profits of industry, salary, hire, rents, annuities, the revenues of property held in trust for minors," unless specifically exempted from taxation.[8] Wealthy Baltimoreans grumbled about the burdens they would bear to educate other people's children. Critics also worried that some religious denomination might capture the school system and use it to indoctrinate children in its own faith. Still others attacked the apparent collectivism of a scheme that aimed at "amalgamating . . . society into one mass, or, the harmonizing of the general community." Advocates of the public schools countered that this was just what the city needed: in the "*Public Schools* there is the most perfect republicanism, for here the rich and the poor literally meet together."[9] The schools would not only educate pupils but expose them to a common political culture that would reanimate republican spirit and unify society in the face of widening class divisions.

The proposals for public schools met determined opposition. The first branch of the city council appointed a committee to decide whether it should support the measure. Its report recommended that Baltimore's representatives in the state legislature be instructed to oppose the bill under consideration. The committee's chairman, William Krebs, dissented from this conclusion. In the meeting of the first branch, Krebs introduced a perverse amendment that would strike out the word "oppose" and instruct the legislators instead to "procure" a system of public education for the city. The amendment passed by a vote of 14 to 10, but the second branch rejected this attempt to create a city school system.[10] The negative result was denounced by "Citizens of Baltimore" in the columns of the *Baltimore Patriot*. The council, they argued, had "listened to the voice of such of your *rich* men as are not willing to be taxed in proportion to their wealth. They have listened to the voice of men who wish to keep the common people in ignorance . . . They have not hearkened to your call for *public schools*, in which the son of the rich man, and the son of the poor man are educated together."[11]

In an earlier time, Baltimoreans might have called a town meeting to vote on public schools, but with its population on the way from 60,000 to 80,000, Baltimore was too big for such meetings and could solicit citizen opinion only through ballot questions in regular elections or at partial town meetings in individual wards. In a city of Baltimore's size, even voting had become problematic. Election judges in each of the 12 wards might once have recognized the citizens who presented themselves at the polls as eligible voters, but now many of the people who showed up to vote were strangers. To guard against electoral fraud, the state legislature had authorized Baltimore to introduce a system of voter registration. Though this legislation passed in 1821, the mayor and council did not address the subject until 1823, and disagreements between the council's first and second branches delayed its resolution. The controversy about voter registration was still unsettled when the public school debate erupted, and the two controversies got snarled up in one another.

In 1810, the state legislature had eliminated all property qualifications for voting in federal and state elections for free white males (Free black males, no matter what their wealth, were disenfranchised by the same statute.) The state law did not cover Baltimore's municipal elections, but property qualifications were apparently dropped in these contests, even though the city had adopted no ordinance on the subject. Enforcing different requirements for state and municipal contests was inconvenient. The new debate about voter registration in Baltimore afforded the advocates of property requirements an opportunity to reinstate such qualifications for municipal elections.[12] A committee of the city council drafted a bill that required the mayor to provide election judges with lists of tax-paying Baltimoreans. It proposed that only "persons assessed . . . for City taxes would be considered and taken by said Judges as registered according to the provisions of this ordinance"[13]

In the first branch, the opponents of a property requirement sought to undermine the measure by requiring any ordinance on voter registration to be submitted to the voters, presumably including those who had been informally qualified to vote when the state abolished property tests in 1810. The measure succeeded in the first branch of the council by a narrow margin, but was rejected in the second branch.[14]

The stalemate on voter registration now joined the stalemate on public education. The citywide committee that drew up the original proposal for a public school system early in 1825 may have unintentionally linked the two issues. Although it prescribed several eligibility criteria for pupils enrolling in public schools, one of these standards allowed children to attend if their fathers were registered voters, defined as taxable inhabitants.[15] The relationship between voting and ownership of taxable property thus became a focus of debate within the controversy about schooling. Proponents of public education argued that suffrage restrictions were designed to disenfranchise supporters of common schools who owned no taxable property and to exclude their children from such schools. In the *Baltimore Gazette*, "A Citizen" disputed this contention but also made the case for municipal voting restrictions: "the corporation of the City of Baltimore" was a private institution much like a bank or a turnpike in which the privilege of voting belonged only to those subscribers "who are the holders of its stock and are affected by its various fluctuations and liable to make good on its losses." The nation and its states were bodies politic, and their citizens had a democratic right to vote, no matter what their stake in the economy, but in the municipal corporation of Baltimore, the privilege of voting was merely "a municipal regulation growing out of the very nature of the institution and belonging only to those who are interested and contributed toward its support." It was a perspective that may have been grounded in the old commercial community that operated markets and regulated trades, goods, and transactions. In case this corporate perspective on the city failed to persuade, "Citizen" assured his readers that most Baltimoreans, including the advocates of public schools, were taxpayers. The proposed restriction on suffrage would not prevent most white males from voting.[16]

The advocates of public education remained unconvinced. As security against electoral fraud, they conceded, voter registration was "deservedly popular," but it was "blended with several other propositions calculated in their nature to overthrow the success of Public Schools" because they would "place large property holders in the Councils of the city, whose feelings and interests are alike hostile to a broad and equitable establishment for Public Education."[17]

Those who insisted on property requirements for voting did indeed seem solidly aligned with those opposed to public education. When the city council's first branch approved a public school resolution in September 1826, every one of the 10 members who voted against it had previously supported a property requirement for voters.[18] The proponents of public education had originally argued that common schools would help to bridge the class divisions that were pulling Baltimoreans apart. As a political issue, however, public education precipitated an eruption of class politics that dominated the 1826 municipal election in which the public school referendum appeared on the ballot.[19]

The school and suffrage controversies served as mechanisms for sorting out candidates and voters in an era of no-party politics. Maryland's Federalist party had virtually vanished. The state's peculiar procedure for choosing state senators through an electoral college meant that all 15 senators were either Federalists or Republicans. The party that controlled a majority of the electors could fill every senate seat. In 1821, the Federalists had lost control of the electors, and having already forfeited the governorship and the house of delegates, they soon became one of the lost tribes of Maryland politics. Without a Federalist opposition to unite them, the Republican organization had begun to fragment. But a realignment was under way.[20]

ARISTOCRATS FOR OLD HICKORY

In Baltimore, some of the dispossessed Federalists would find a new home in the party of Andrew Jackson. Though he won a plurality of the electoral votes in 1824, Jackson needed a majority to take the presidency. Under the Constitution, the selection of the president fell to the House of Representatives, where each state delegation cast one vote. The House made John Quincy Adams chief executive. In 1826, while Baltimoreans fulminated about schooling and voting, residents in 10 of the city's 12 wards held meetings to express their support for Andrew Jackson and their hostility to the Washington establishment that had denied him the presidency. Earlier meetings had denounced the Congressional Caucus for its presumptuous arrogation of the power to nominate presidential candidates. Party conventions had emerged as the preferred mode of nominating candidates for both state and local offices.[21]

Baltimore voters, like those in the rest of the state, were an electorate in motion. Many came to rest with the Jacksonians. One of the most unlikely of these converts was Robert Goodloe Harper. A Princeton graduate, he had grown up on his family's North Carolina plantation, with a workforce that included at least a dozen slaves. Harper studied law in South Carolina and, after opening a practice in Charleston, won election to the House of Representatives for three terms. Though he had been a youthful advocate of egalitarianism, his political principles underwent profound alteration in response to the violent consequences of the French Revolution and the slave rebellion in Haiti. Harper became a staunch Federalist and a congressional champion of the Alien and Sedition Acts. The Jeffersonian "revolution" of 1800 led him to retire, temporarily, from politics. He moved to Baltimore, where he married the daughter of Charles Carroll of Carrollton. His service as defense counsel in the impeachment trial of rock-hard Federalist and US Supreme Court justice Samuel Chase made him a distinguished figure of the Baltimore bar. As Carroll's son-in-law and luminary of the city's legal profession, he was the town's nearest approximation to an aristocrat, next to Carroll himself. Maryland's legislature elected him to the US Senate in 1816, but he resigned a year later to attend to his law practice. When fellow Carolinian John C. Calhoun abandoned his presidential aspirations to join the Jacksonians, Harper followed suit. He issued a pamphlet to explain his decision.[22]

Though known for his public and courtroom orations as well as his essays on politics, Harper presented himself, unconvincingly, as a "plain man, having no pretensions to literary acquirements, the graces of style, or diplomatic learning." (He wrote the pamphlet under a pseudonym.) Those acquirements, graces, and learning were precisely the attainments he attributed to John Quincy Adams, only to dismiss them as accomplishments of little help to a president. What was most needed, he argued, was "judgment prudence discernment firmness and decision"—precisely the qualities of character that he claimed for Andrew Jackson, traits that the general had put to good use when he confronted the British at New Orleans. Jackson's other great virtue, according to Harper, was his lack of political experience. Jackson "was not a member of the cabinet, has held few or no offices under the government, and has very little connexion with power." Political inexperience was an advantage because it meant that Jackson was untainted by the intrigues of cabinet politicians scheming to succeed the president.[23] It also meant that Old Hickory did not keep company with the Republican forces that had overwhelmed Harper's fellow Federalists and taken title to Washington.

Harper died shortly after publication of his pamphlet and never saw his hero elevated to the presidency. Other Baltimoreans converged in support of Jackson from a variety of political starting points. Roger B. Taney, one of Maryland's most eminent Federalists, wrote to a friend about his support for Jackson shortly after moving his law practice from Frederick to Baltimore in 1824. Like Harper, Taney was "sick of all Secretary candidates" and was drawn to Jackson by the general's political independence and the hope that he might enter the White House unbound to any section, faction, or any "combination of mercenary presses, or local interests."[24] Taney would become Jackson's secretary of the treasury and later his nominee as chief justice of the Supreme Court. Even the ancient Charles Carroll of Carrollton, who had once denounced democracy as a form of anarchy, joined the Jacksonians.[25]

John Pendleton Kennedy ran as a Jacksonian congressional candidate in 1826, promising that if the presidential election were again to wind up in the House of Representatives, he would pledge his vote for Jackson. Kennedy lost, probably because of an unpopular vote on canal legislation while in the Maryland General Assembly. (His critics in Baltimore called him John "Potomac" Kennedy.)[26] Ten years later, when he finally succeeded in getting elected to Congress, it would be as an anti-Jacksonian Whig. Samuel Smith came to Jackson by way of William H. Crawford, one of the "Secretary candidates" for the presidency. Crawford had headed the Treasury Department under James Monroe. He and Smith had served together in Congress, and Smith attached himself to the faction promoting Crawford's presidential prospects as early as 1818. When Crawford's candidacy collapsed, Smith migrated to the Jacksonians. It was Smith, according to Gary Browne, who introduced "the Jacksonian-party machine into local elections." His control of federal patronage provided the "machine" with essential political resources. He earned his spoils not because of longstanding loyalty to Jackson but because, as chair of the

John Pendleton Kennedy—novelist, congressman, Navy secretary. He also designed an iron bridge that could withstand floods on the Jones Falls.

Senate Finance Committee, he was a valuable ally in the administration's war with the Bank of the United States.[27]

Local issues such as public schooling and voter registration may have been obscured by the reshuffling of factions into the grand realignment that set Jacksonian Democrats against Whigs, but these local matters were moved toward resolution by the same tide of egalitarian rhetoric that announced the Jacksonian consensus. William Krebs, the determined advocate of public education, served alongside Roger B. Taney as a delegate on the Jackson General Convention of Baltimore.[28] Local personages and local issues fell in with national alignments.

ELECTORAL AND EDUCATIONAL DEMOCRACY

It took the Baltimore City Council almost a year to act on the state legislation of 1826 that empowered the city to create a public school system. In the meantime, the General Assembly had approved legislation authorizing local school systems to apply for state financial support.[29] Though Baltimore was eligible for state education funds, it was in no hurry to open schools. Several months passed before the council approved the appointment of six school commissioners to supervise six schools, not yet built, and a superintendent to a make a weekly inspection of each nonexistent one of them. In April 1829, the council approved an ordinance creating "one or more schools on the Monitorial Plan." But it had yet to designate any specific tax to support the schools. The school commissioners finally forced the council's hand by renting rooms, hiring teachers, and opening three schools in the fall of 1829. Early the next year, the council finally levied a tax of 12½ cents per $100.00 of assessed property for public education. State aid was initially less than $1,000 a year.[30]

The city also arrived at a temporary resolution of the voter registration issue. In 1829, it extended the franchise to free white males without any property qualifications, the same eligibility standard set out by the General Assembly for state and federal elections. But the new law raised other barriers to voting. After an initial registration period of 17 days, the annual enrollment of voters was limited to three days in October, between 3:00 and 6:00 p.m.[31]

In the Tenth Ward, a meeting of "Mechanics, Labourers, and Poor People generally" convened to demand the "equal rights, and equal political and civil privileges" that the government guaranteed "to every man high and low, rich and poor." As soon as the mechanics and laborers adjourned, another protest meeting convened in the same hall. It made a more direct attack on the "law for the Registry of Voters as a prelude to an infringement on the right of suffrage." The participants adopted a resolution demanding the resignations of the two "commissioners of registry" appointed for the Tenth Ward. One of them, William K. Mitchell, responded while the meeting was still in progress. He was proud, he said, "of the opportunity that is afforded . . . me to give an evidence of my ready deference to the will of the people." He resigned on the spot. He had served as chairman of the preceding protest meeting.[32]

A week later, "a numerous and respectable assemblage of citizens" expressed their opposition to the ordinance and elected a committee to issue a public statement explaining why they regarded the registration law as "a restriction of the inestimable right of suffrage." They objected in particular to the severely limited time that voter rolls would be open to new registrants. The "shortness of the daily session and the multiplicity of the applicants" would mean long waiting lines for would-be voters "who must abandon the dearest privilege of freemen or forego the probable emoluments of several hours of labour." The statement also challenged the need for a board of registrars to ensure the integrity of the electoral process. Under the legislation, voters could challenge the eligibility of other voters. If the people were "competent to self government, they are also competent to guard the institutions which uphold it."[33]

At the beginning of 1830, in his annual message to the city council, Mayor Small declared that the "Ordinance to provide for the Registering [of] all the Qualified voters of the City of Baltimore passed at the last annual session of the City Council has been tested at the late election . . . and has been found inefficient in its provisions. This matter is respectfully submitted to the wisdom of the City Council." The council thought it wise to repeal the registration ordinance.[34] Baltimore presumably reverted to its usual slapdash voting methods.

It was more difficult to get into the public schools than onto the voter rolls. Households could enroll their children by paying one dollar a year for schooling. The fee could be waived for orphans or children from very poor families, but seldom was. Public school advocates wanted to maintain the difference between charity schools and public schools. In practice, however, only a small fraction of the city's parents could improve their offspring through public education. With only six schools, the system could accommodate no more than 700 students in a population of more than 80,000 children and adults.

The public schools managed to handle even this small enrollment only by treating instruction as an exercise in mass communication. The ordinance creating Baltimore's public schools had required that they adopt the "Monitorial Plan" of instruction. As originally conceived by British educator Joseph Lancaster, the monitorial method was devised for the education of children of the poor in schools with little revenue, few teachers, and many pupils. Older students were designated as monitors to hear small groups of young students recite their lessons in arithmetic and spelling, while a senior teacher, through an elaborate system of hand signals, conducted an instructional symphony that coordinated recitation and study across the various groups of learners. In Baltimore, the monitorial system broke down. When children got old enough to be monitors, they were also old enough to leave school and go to work, which is what their parents often wanted them to do. The monitorial method was generally abandoned in favor of simultaneous recitation: a mass chorus of pupils chanting their multiplication tables or spelling words in unison.[35]

Baltimore's public schools were financially starved. At the end of 1832, for example, the school commissioners reported a total annual expenditure (including construction costs) of $16,416—about $443,000 today, or approximately $692 per pupil in today's dollars. Perhaps because they had never known anything better, the commissioners hoped they could run a successful educational enterprise on the funds at hand. In Baltimore, they proclaimed, public education was a "great experiment . . . to determine whether economy of expenditure and efficiency of instruction could not be combined in the same institution." By the end of 1831, the commissioners were ready to pronounce that the experiment had "completely succeeded." Their measure of success was enrollment: "Three months of successful operation at the school on Aisquith Street under the care of Mr. Coffin has placed the matter beyond reasonable doubt. This school was calculated to accommodate 400 children. There are at this moment 390 attending." The number of applications for admission received each week had not diminished since the school opened three months earlier. "The male school under Mr. Willigman and the female school under Miss McConkey on Eutaw Street" were "under similar favor." Mr. Coffin and Mr. Willigman were paid $600 for the year ($15,600 in today's dollars); Miss McConkey received $200.[36]

A year later, some of the most successful schools had encountered setbacks. The school on Aisquith Street had "been very seriously defaced in its exterior." Even more seriously, Mr. Coffin had lost almost half his enrollment. He claimed that almost all of the scholars withdrawn had "been taken from this school to be placed in business." The pupils who remained were presumably those too young for "business" or whose family circumstances allowed them to get by without the income generated by child labor. The school commissioners seized on the presence of these children as another sign of success, "that men of liberal minds and in affluent circumstances are found in full proportion amongst the patrons of our system."[37]

Chapter 12
ROAD HOGS

STREET-WANDERING SWINE had been an abiding annoyance for Baltimore's public authorities since the 1730s, when the town commissioners unsuccessfully attempted, first, to fence the hogs in, and then to fence them out. In 1812, the mayor and city council sought to meet the problem with an ordinance that declared open season on hogs. Any resident could legally kill or "seize, take and dispose of, for their own use, all swine" caught roaming the streets, lanes, or alleys of the city. The municipal authorities periodically placed notices in local newspapers to remind Baltimoreans that they could hunt for pork on the city streets. Later, in 1816, the city imposed a fine of two dollars per hog per day on owners of street pigs, but the ordinance did not specify how the ownership of stray hogs might be established.[1]

The situation grew more complicated when Baltimoreans realized there was something to be said for wayward swine. The hogs would consume almost any sort of garbage, and during the warm months of summer, when offal in the streets became awful, pigs performed a valued public service. An ordinance of 1821 made it lawful for hogs to roam at large from May 1 to November 1, but only within the limits of direct taxation, where hog hunting would be prohibited. In those parts of the Eastern and Western Precincts still exempt from city taxation, hog hunters could lawfully pursue their quarry year round.[2]

In November, swine restrictions applied once again across the city, and the city bailiffs began the annual hog roundup. The swine caught in their dragnet were taken to one of the city's public markets to be auctioned off to the highest bidder. By 1828, Mayor Jacob Small pronounced the system a failure: "Three or four bailiffs accompany a covered cart, driver, and four persons, who seize swine under the protection of the Bailiffs, and convey them to the market . . . Persons (frequently females) follow the Carts and become the purchasers of those they think proper to claim, at from 5 to 100 cents each, and from the clamour they create, no person will bid against them, to this there would be no objection, provided they would keep them out of the street, but the next time the

Carts take the circuit, the same swine are again found." Small suggested an alternative to the stray-pig auction. Instead of selling swine to the highest bidder, the city could donate the hogs to the trustees of the city-county almshouse.[3]

This arrangement would feed poorhouse inmates at the expense of poor people in town. The hogs that roamed the streets usually belonged to impoverished Baltimoreans who had insufficient real estate to accommodate pigsties. They economized on pig feed by sending their swine into the streets of Baltimore to find food. One council member observed that the "several ordinances . . . for preventing swine from going at large within the limits of direct taxation have been found to operate severely on the poorer classes of the community." He introduced a proposal that all such ordinances should be repealed, but failed to persuade a majority of his colleagues to go along. A local physician had recommended that poor families purchase piglets in the early spring and let them forage on the city's streets during the seven months of mild weather. A street pig could provide a household with as much as 300 pounds of meat through the winter.[4] The city's November pig roundup would deprive these families of their hogs just when the pigs were ready for slaughter and consumption.

An 1828 ordinance provided the mayor with a $200 appropriation to pay for the apprehension of stray swine during the cold months. The city handed the captives over to the almshouse. The hogs' warm weather exemption was extended from April 1 to December 1 by an ordinance of 1831 and confirmed in 1838.[5] By 1842, Mayor Samuel Brady declared that the "Hog Law is a nullity; but two hundred dollars are appropriated annually to take up the Swine running at large within direct taxation. As soon as that sum is expended (a fact of which the owners of hogs become very soon apprized) every hog is set at large again."[6]

STREET FIGHTS

The management of wandering swine was just one expression of a more general concern about the municipality's capacity to control and maintain its public thoroughfares. One mayor after another used his annual message to complain about the state of the streets. In 1834, for example, Mayor Jesse Hunt noted "the roughness of many of our principal streets." Repairs, he said, had been made up to the limit of the appropriation for that purpose, but many of the streets were in such "miserable condition" that mere repairs were pointless; "nothing short of an entire new pavement will effectually remedy the evil."[7] The complaint was commonplace. So was the request to place "flag stones" at street crossings so that pedestrians might walk on them instead of stepping into the murky effluent that oozed down city streets during and after a rain. On the positive side, the money the city earned by selling the harvest of manure collected by its street scrapers more than offset the cost of paying them at 75 cents a day.[8]

Other sources of pedestrian annoyance were "assemblages of unruly boys" who caused "great inconvenience to peaceable citizens in every part of the city, especially at the corners of streets, where young men assemble, particularly on the Sabbath day, and give offence to females passing them." The young men not only gave offence but carried concealed weapons, which they sometimes used to stab one another.[9]

The crossing at Liberty and West Baltimore Streets provided flagstones so that pedestrians could avoid stepping in the odorous ooze that flowed down many of the town's thoroughfares.

While the municipality contended for control of the streets with footloose swine and juvenile delinquents, it also had to struggle with chartered corporations. The city allowed the Baltimore Water Company to sink its mains beneath the streets on the condition that the company return the paving to its original condition after the excavations. This responsibility was so frequently disregarded that the city commissioners prepared a printed form to notify the Water Company of the locations where it was supposed to undo the damage left in its wake.[10] The negligence was all the more annoying because the company was not providing sufficient water to the town's fire plugs when it was most needed. In 1835, Mayor Hunt acknowledged that the "want of an abundant supply of water has upon some occasions rendered the invaluable services of our Fire Companies less effectual than they would otherwise have been." The city had considered purchasing the Water Company to remedy the problem, but Hunt worried that Baltimore's "large stock debt"—arising principally from its railroad investments—made such additional investments infeasible.[11]

Railroads posed the most serious threat to the city's control of the streets. City officials had gone out of their way to ensure that the B&O would locate its terminals within the limits of Baltimore. A necessary consequence was that the railroad would have to run its tracks down city streets. In 1840, when the Philadelphia and Trenton Railroad had attempted to extend its right-of-way along Front Street in Philadelphia, the Irish immigrants of Kensington had rioted and attacked the railroad workers.[12] Baltimoreans were in no position to do the same. Their city officials had committed half a million dollars of municipal revenue—the people's taxes—to the B&O and would later pledge millions more. Thousands of the city's residents had invested in the company. Baltimoreans were nevertheless sharply divided about sharing their streets with railroads. The city government regularly sided with the railroads in the face of citizen protests. Officials claimed that they were protecting not only the city's investment but its future prosperity.

The B&O's starting point in Baltimore was the "first stone" on West Pratt Street, where Charles Carroll had planted a spade in the ground on July 4, 1828. Nearby were the roundhouses and shops of the railroad's Mount Clare depot, the site of today's B&O Railroad Museum. From this yard, the railroad's "main stem" would extend northeast, then east along Pratt Street, across town to Fell's Point, where it turned south to reach the nine-acre parcel of waterfront land created out of harbor sludge. The B&O president, Philip Thomas, noted that the company's tracks would be "running parallel with the entire water front of the city, communicating with all the wharves, and intersecting all the principal streets which extend northwardly and southwardly." For much of this distance, the Pratt Street line would parallel another track on Camden Street, one block to the south, so that the railroad would be able to run trains in both directions simultaneously.[13]

The city imposed conditions on the railroads' use of the streets. An 1831 ordinance prohibited the use of steam locomotives in the city. Only "animal power" could propel the trains. If at any time the council determined that trains constituted an obstruction on a street, it could require the company to take up its rails and return the street to its original condition.[14] B&O president Philip Thomas assured city officials that "there will be less interruption and danger from the passing of railway cars along the Streets than from the passing of Drays now commonly in use."[15]

CORPORATIONS IN THE STREETS

The city ordinance that authorized the B&O to build its railway down the middle of Pratt Street also allowed branch lines to be laid down by local businesses whose owners wanted to make connections with the main stem.[16] The branches were arteries of city prosperity, and Baltimoreans in outlying neighborhoods wanted access to the commercial concentration arising from the B&O's waterfront operations. Residents of Northwest Baltimore unsuccessfully petitioned the city for permission to build their own tracks from the intersection of Presstman Street and Pennsylvania Avenue to the railroad's main stem.[17]

Baltimoreans in immediate contact with the railroad did not always appreciate its advantages. As the B&O extended its line along the waterfront, the *Patriot* carried a letter "To The Citizens Of Baltimore" from "a number of . . . fellow citizens interested in the prosperity of Pratt Street." The fellow citizens declared that the railroad was "fraught with immense mischief to a great portion of the city, particularly to persons owning property on Pratt Street." The practice of backing up carts and wagons to load or unload goods at Pratt Street businesses had to stop because the wagons would block the tracks. The railroad cars would pass "so near the stores and dwellings that they will keep the whole neighborhood continually under alarm, danger and excitement." The wells from which the neighborhood pumps drew water lay under the tracks; there was no way to open and clean them out. The "main pipes" of the Water Company also ran under the center of the street; any effort to repair them would halt all train traffic. The rails also constituted a "frightful barrier" between the two sides of the street, and parents would "labor under constant apprehensions for their children, they will hesitate to send them on errands, or to school, across the street." The citizens reminded *Patriot* readers "that the original motive for the enterprize was, not to build up a corporation for the exclusive benefit of particular interests, but to raise the City from a state of deep depression to which its business had sunk."[18]

While the B&O extended its tracks across Baltimore from west to east, the Baltimore and Susquehanna prepared to enter the city from the north. On its way south to the harbor, the railroad was required by the council to build a branch westward to a parcel of land between Madison and Biddle Streets, once occupied by the city-county almshouse and still owned by the city. Like other property owners, the city sought to exploit rail access to enhance the value of its real estate. The Baltimore and Susquehanna had less bargaining power with the city than did the B&O. It still lacked legal access to its intended destination in Pennsylvania. It was also heavily dependent on the city's stock subscription and the security that Baltimore had pledged to guarantee the company's interest payments to the state. For once, the city seems to have taken advantage of a railroad. It required the company to use one acre of the almshouse site for construction of a depot, a possible benefit for northwest Baltimoreans cut off from the B&O's main stem. The rest of the property would be parceled out into lots. A special board of assessors decided how much the value of the land would increase because of the planned rail depot. The unoccupied land would pass to the school commissioners, who were to sell it; the proceeds would help to support Baltimore's underfunded attempt at public education.[19] After this diversion in the cause of learning, the railroad traveled east and crossed the Jones Falls on a "Costly Viaduct," then turned south to the waterfront—all on or across city streets—to the same Fell's Point plot originally donated to the B&O. The B&O, in the meantime, had decided to move its depot a short distance to the east and requested permission to extend its tracks for several blocks along four streets in this already congested area.[20]

A third railroad sought to enter the city from the east. The Baltimore and Port Deposit (soon to become part of the Philadelphia, Wilmington, and Baltimore Railroad) proposed to operate on an unusual and possibly unworkable business plan. It presented itself as the "perfect Winter line" for passengers traveling south from Boston, New York, and Philadelphia to Washington during the season when the steamboats were "shut up by the Ice" and the "Stage road" from Philadelphia to Baltimore became impassable. The profitability of its seasonal business depended on minimizing its own capital investments by renting track and depot space in Baltimore from the B&O. The two companies concluded an agreement by which the B&O would accommodate the Port Deposit line for $2,500 annually.[21]

The agreement became controversial when the city council instructed its eight representatives on the B&O board of directors to vote against it. (Since the city's investment in the company had increased, its representation on the B&O board had grown as well.) Six of the eight city directors rebelled. Their 18-page manifesto suggested that the city council was opposed to the shared-depot agreement because it would deprive local merchants of access to potential customers who would otherwise have disembarked in Baltimore to shuttle between separate Port Deposit and B&O stations. More precisely, the opponents of a single depot held that if "Southern and Western Traders" had to travel through the city from one station to the other, they might "trade more extensively with our Citizens."[22]

Like John Diffenderffer, the councilmen on the B&O board of directors had become advocates for the railroad they were directing, which would gain $2,500 in annual rent under the agreement, at little or no cost to itself. They argued, in opposition to their colleagues on the council, that any additional cost or inconvenience imposed on travelers through Baltimore would actually hurt the city's trade. But the most striking feature of their argument was their dismissive assessment of their own city. Baltimore could not afford to inconvenience traders or travelers—it had nothing to offer but the speediest possible passage through town. In the directors' view, there was "nothing in our past history, or in our present population, trade, or accumulation of Capital, to authorize the conclusion that Baltimore is unrivaled—on the contrary, is not the comparative tardiness of our progress in trade and in wealth, a constant theme of reproach in the newspapers, founded on the allegation, that the public spirit of Philadelphia, and of New York, their Canals, Railways, Steamboats, and Packets, facilitate the freest system of internal and external communication, are the sole causes of their relative superiority in trade and riches."[23] Baltimoreans repeatedly chastised one another for a deficiency of "public spirit."

The controversy about the Port Deposit Railroad became moot when it merged with the Philadelphia, Wilmington, and Baltimore line—a company with its own depot at the President Street Station in Fell's Point and its own stretch of track extending east along Fleet Street and across the city line to the industrial precincts of Canton.[24]

RAILROAD RUCKUS AND RESOLUTION

As the length of the railroad tracks grew, so did complaints about them. A correspondent of the *Baltimore Gazette*, "Civis," expressed concerns about the railroad's interference with street drainage. Civis was not alone. In 1835, the city council's Joint Committee on Rail Roads had considered complaints about flooding on Pratt Street. The problem arose at intersections where the B&O tracks crossed gutters. The company had devised small iron bridges to carry its rails across these channels, but in heavy rains trash would collect around and under the bridges, causing water "to overflow the whole street to the great inconvenience of the public." The garbage that collected under the rails was "seldom or never cleaned out by a flow of water, consequently the stench arising from it in hot weather is a great grievance to the neighbourhood." Winter storms created problems of their own. The snow pushed off the tracks on Pratt Street created a solid barrier on the sidewalk that made "many of the houses on the street inaccessible to wheel carriages for several days." The Committee on Rail Roads concluded that the B&O tracks constituted an obstruction on Pratt Street, and under the terms of the ordinance authorizing construction of the railroad, the rails would have to go. Tearing up the tracks on Pratt Street, of course, would deprive many rail sidings of access to the main stem. Both branches of the city council dissented from the committee's report.[25]

The committee report also drew opposition outside the council. More than 200 persons and business firms endorsed a petition declaring that the B&O tracks did not constitute an obstruction on Pratt Street and, noting the railroad's contribution to local prosperity, asked the mayor and council for an ordinance making the "railways . . . permanent and not liable to be removed or their location changed except for the purpose of repairing or improving, and adding to their usefulness."[26] Uncertainty about the staying power of the railroad's main stem could undermine the value of its stock, to which the city and its residents were major subscribers.

The council referred the petitions not to the Committee on Rail Roads, which had already betrayed its odd animosity to railroads, but to an ad hoc select committee. The majority on the select committee deferred ruling on whether the railroad constituted an obstruction on Pratt Street in order to raise questions about the city's legal authority to order the removal of railroad tracks. The "General System" for approving branch lines required that the owners of more than half the street frontage along the proposed track endorse its construction. The property owners who sponsored the siding had to bear a portion of its cost. According to the select committee, these payments gave the property owners a "vested interest which no present action of the Council can impair." If the council ordered the removal of the main stem on Pratt Street, it would violate "the well known principle which make[s] . . . Laws impairing the obligations of Contract Unconstitutional." The committee reasoned that since the value of the branch lines depended on their connections with the main stem, the city's right "to order the removal of the main stem Ceased as fully . . . as though the ordinance reserving said right had been expressly repealed."[27]

An indignant dissent to the select committee's report was submitted by a minority of one. James Peregoy was a councilman from the Twelfth Ward, a sparsely populated district extending to the western frontiers of the city, the same region whose residents had petitioned the council for a rail connection to the B&O tracks on the waterfront. Peregoy denounced the surrender of the streets to the railroad as a "monstrous impropriety." Granting legal permanence to the tracks would require the city to surrender one of the powers granted in its charter—its authority over the city's streets. Peregoy insisted that "the legislative authority of the Mayor and City Council over the streets, must forever remain unimpaired." He went on to question the B&O's contribution to municipal prosperity. The railroad, he said, operated "most injuriously to the town. The immense amount of produce formerly brought hither in wagons, was diffused throughout the City, giving ample employment to draymen, porters, and others, who, though toiling in a humble sphere constituted the foundation of a great and opulent community." These "labourious poor" made a contribution to the city's prosperity just as worthy as the railroad's. In fact, Peregoy maintained, the B&O was engaged in a "ruinous competition with the labouring classes for the internal transformation of the City." If the railroad prevailed, Baltimore would become a "mere point of transit, where nothing will remain for the consumption of a rapidly decreasing population."[28]

A further appeal came to the council from carters, hackney drivers, and draymen required to pay license fees for the right to use city streets. They complained of being "greatly hindered in their enjoyment of this right by the introduction of the

Baltimore and Ohio Rail Road . . . and especially by its extension along several of the
most frequented thoroughfares, which are completely blocked up by long trains of
cars standing or moving on them." The relief requested was removal of the railroad
tracks from city streets. The Joint Committee on Rail Roads found these complaints
to be "well founded," and it expressed "peculiar" gratification that by granting their
request, "we are presented with an opportunity of relieving one of our main avenues
of a Rail Track, which we were assured by the projectors should occasion not the
slightest interruption to the general travel in the street." While acknowledging the
property rights of the railroad, the committee added that it also had a duty "to take
the same care that those who depend for their support on their daily labours should
be protected in their employments."[29] Their jobs were their property.

The conclusion of the Committee on Rail Roads was startling. It proposed "terminating the Baltimore and Ohio Rail Road at a distance from tide water on the
West and the Susquehanna Rail Road at a distance from tide water to the East. Then
will the labouring classes find employment in carrying the trade thro' your streets
to the different parts of town." When the growth of trade required urban expansion,
"then will the labour of your mechanics be called in" to enlarge the city's "accommodations in the East and in the West." Competition between the two sides of town
would "regulate the price of unimproved property, and the whole community will
thrive."[30]

In the face of contradictory petitions and reports, the city council came down
solidly on the side of the railroads. It resolved "that the General Welfare of the
Citizens and the especial advantage of the property of the City . . . require that
the said rail ways should *no longer* be considered temporary and liable to be removed."[31] The resolution did not silence citizens' complaints about tracks in the
streets. In 1837, a petition reached the council expressing "*surprise* and *uneasiness*"
at the attempt "on the part of some of your honorable body, to divest it of legislative
authority over certain streets of this city, as regards the rail ways of the Baltimore
and Ohio Rail Road Company." The petitioners wanted representatives "whose
fortunes and feelings are identified with theirs," not "agents of a moneyed corporation, which may hereafter belong to strangers, and whose immediate object is its
own pecuniary advantage."[32]

The select committee refashioned its argument to answer this new petition. Those
who demanded that the council remove the B&O tracks from city streets mistakenly
conveyed "the impression that the Mayor and City Council have the absolute control
over the streets of Baltimore." But the paramount "power to shut up or close any of
those High way[s], whether they be called roads or streets, is a Sovereign power,
vested where all Sovereign powers are vested" — in the state legislature.[33] As a mere
corporation, a creature of the state, Baltimore could not claim "sovereign" power.

The sovereignty of states (and railroads) over municipalities has since been en-
shrined in American law. In 1868, Chief Justice John Foster Dillon of the Iowa Supreme Court resolved a dispute between the town of Clinton and the Cedar Rapids
and Missouri River Railroad. Iowa's state legislature had authorized the railroad to
extend its tracks through Clinton to complete a rail connection between Council

Bluffs and Cedar Rapids. The Clinton City Council immediately objected to the railroad's intrusion and obtained an injunction against the company in the district court. But Justice Dillon and the state's supreme court overturned the injunction, reasoning that the enactment by the legislature superseded the provision of Clinton's charter that gave the city control over its streets. It was the legislature, after all, that granted Clinton its charter and its control of the streets. It had done so in the service of a public interest—not just of Clinton's public, but the public in general. Acting on behalf of that same interest, the legislature had provided the railroad with all the power and permission it needed to extend its tracks down Clinton's streets.[34]

The "Dillon Rule" entered American jurisprudence as a principle (occasionally contested) establishing the near-absolute supremacy of state over municipal governments. In a sense, the Baltimore City Council's deference to the General Assembly in the case of city streets and their occupation by railroads simply recognized that principle. Of course, the Dillon Rule lay 30 years in the future, and instead of being compelled to observe the principle by a court or state legislature, the council simply imposed its anticipation of the rule on itself.

Chapter 13 **POLICING THE DISORDERLY CITY**

ALTIMORE'S PUBLIC AUTHORITIES might cede control of the streets to railroads or the state legislature, but they were vigilant in defending those streets against public disorder. In 1835, Hezekiah Niles noted the "lofty reputation" the city had earned "by twenty-three years of *happy obedience to the law*—Baltimore having been, from the war riots of 1812, remarkable for the peaceable demeanor of its inhabitants, and the safety and security, and perfect quiet, of all its population." A year earlier, a correspondent of the *Baltimore Patriot* had "entertained the opinion, that there was no city in the union, of equal magnitude, so well guarded at night, or where there were so few robberies committed." The guardians of the night were Baltimore's watchmen.[1] In 1834, the *Patriot* reported that the city had been "infested by a gang of wretches" who "reduced house-breaking to a science." But the "Mayor, with his characteristic promptness . . . devised and executed plans for the arrest of these night prowlers, and by the vigilance of the watchmen (who deserve great credit for their exertions) has succeeded in securing seven of the villains."[2]

A watchman's responsibilities extended to street lighting as well as the preservation of order, and the work was exhausting. In 1828, Mayor Jacob Small outlined the watchmen's duties in an effort to win them a pay increase. The watchman, he wrote, was "required to appear in the watch house at half past 8 Oclock; at the hour of 9, he is on his post, and take[s] his rounds to cry the hour, which duty he continues to perform until 6 o'clock in the morning, when he again returns to the watch house where he is detained with prisoners, &c. and is seldom discharged until after sunrise at which time he returns home for the necessary nourishment, after which he proceeds to clean and trim the lamps, which consumes at least one fourth of the day; in the evening he has his lamps to light; from which ro[u]tine of duty it is evident that he has no time for rest, except the interval [between] the trimming and the lighting of the lamps; thus it appears this man's whole time is exacted for the sum [of] about 75½ cents per 24 hours; in addition, he runs the risk of being beaten and wounded."[3]

In the night, between the lighting and trimming of the lamps, the watchman performed the traditional responsibilities for dealing with "nightwalkers, malefactors, rogues," and those suspected of "evil designs."[4] He was also supposed to give the alarm on the outbreak of fires "as well as to prevent any burglaries, robberies, outrages, or disorders, and to apprehend any suspected persons, who in such times of confusion, may be feloniously carrying off the goods and effects of others." The city appointed constables to oversee the watchmen, and as the number of watchmen expanded along with the population of the city, captains and lieutenants were employed to provide additional supervision. Until 1826, the watchmen and supervisory officers answered to a board of three police commissioners; in that year, the city "police" became a direct responsibility of the mayor.[5]

Mayor Small was the first to exercise this authority, but his power did not extend to the compensation of the watchmen, and his effort to raise their pay was not immediately successful. He concentrated instead on restructuring the forces of public order to achieve greater coordination. In addition to the watchmen, for example, the city also employed bailiffs. Small wanted to bring the two, disconnected categories of lawmen into alignment to provide the city with something near to round-the-clock policing. At first, the city made the bailiffs responsible for enforcement of city ordinances, and it augmented their meager salaries (just over $60 a year) with half of all the fines collected as a result of the violations they brought to the attention of the courts. By 1823, the city's public markets had become bases of operation for the bailiffs; they were to aid the clerks "in preserving order therein." Mayor Small gave the bailiffs specific responsibility for dealing with violations of the many "ordinances relating to the markets" and the goods sold in them. The mayor also expected the bailiffs to assume a larger role in the prosecution of market violations, so that the market masters would be less frequently distracted by "attending the trial of cases before the Justices of the Peace." But Small's chief objective was "to strengthen the city police, in making the bailiffs auxiliaries of the watch." In particular, the bailiffs were to walk the watchmen's beats during the early evening, before the watchmen came on duty. The plan would not only extend the hours when the city was under the protection of lawmen but also "detect watchmen who are not at their posts and doing their duty" on time.[6]

The mayor issued his new directive to the bailiffs and the night watch in February 1826. By the end of the year, Baltimoreans perceived an improvement in public order. The *Baltimore Gazette* reported that it had "been requested by several citizens to notice, and we do so with pleasure, the good effects which have resulted from the exertions of the Mayor and the city officers under his direction, in preserving quiet and good order during Christmas day and the day preceding." The holiday season had been a time of revelry and fireworks when boys and young men took their celebrations into the streets. The "gratifying quiet which the citizens have experienced on the present occasion, is the best evidence of what may be effected by a vigilant Police."[7]

Mayor Small may have appreciated the burdens under which the watchmen labored, but he was not averse to increasing them. In regulations issued at the start of 1829, he repeated the usual injunctions about nightwalkers, malefactors, and persons with evil designs, but he added that when any "orderly" citizen "decently requested" it, the watchman was obliged to escort that person to any destination within the watch district. He was also expected to "examine all doors and windows, every round through the night; and if found open, give immediate information to the owner thereof." Finally, it was the explicit "duty of the Watchman to disperse all unlawful assemblages of negroes, wherever they may be collected within the limits of the city." Two years later, he reminded them of this duty. The streets, he complained, were "swarming with hords of colored persons and boys, who prowl about the streets, take possession of the foot-ways, annoy persons passing, particularly those who occupy the premises before which they assemble . . . this class of persons must be dispersed by the Watchman at and after *ten o'clock*."[8]

In 1832, Small campaigned for the mayor's office on the National Republican ticket, running against Jacksonian Democrat Jesse Hunt. Like Small, Hunt could qualify as a "mechanic," though a very prosperous one. He was a saddler who employed 20 workmen. Hunt won decisively.[9] He was the first mayor to be elected by popular vote rather than an electoral college. Small apparently left him with a solid, if underpaid, "police department." After a year in office, Hunt discussed the city's arrangements for preserving public order in his annual message. He found that the "Night Watch as a part of this system, is efficient and well-organized," but the bailiffs were badly underpaid. The budget provided an annual total of only $715 to pay the salaries of all 24 of them. The city council took no action, and Hunt repeated his plea on behalf of the bailiffs in his annual message of 1835.[10]

This time, the council responded with an ordinance that transferred most of the bailiffs' duties to 12 lieutenants of the watch—one for each of the city's wards. In addition to their responsibilities for the night watch, the dozen officers were to assume the duties that the bailiffs performed at the city's four public markets. They were required to live in the wards to which they were assigned, and each lieutenant was to have "a conspicuous sign attached to his house with his name and office inscribed thereon." For his duties on the night watch, the city would pay each lieutenant $20 a month, and for his responsibilities in the city's markets, $220 a year.[11]

Baltimore had evolved beyond the unpoliced boomtown where the majority enforced its will by collective violence. The city seemed to have left behind the deadly mayhem of 1812 that had made Baltimore "mobtown." But the city's peaceful interlude of well-regulated respectability would end less than six months after Mayor Hunt signed the ordinance empowering the lieutenants of the watch.

THE LAWLESS ELITE

Mayor Hunt's undoing resulted from a combination of elements for which Baltimore was already well known: bank fraud and mob violence. The bank was one of Baltimore's oldest, the Bank of Maryland, chartered in 1790. It seems to have been a senescent institution until it was taken over in 1831 by a genial Quaker entrepreneur,

Evan Poultney. He had previously run a "discount house" that traded in the currency issued by banks. Poultney's ambition soon ran beyond trading in banknotes to issuing them, and he acquired the Bank of Maryland, in part, for the purpose of printing his own money. The bank's capacity to issue notes depended on the value of its deposits. Poultney attracted depositors by offering 5 percent interest on all accounts. Banks of the time usually offered interest only for large or long-term deposits. Poultney's innovation produced a 20-fold increase in deposits and attracted the savings of modest shopkeepers and tradesmen. He used the increase in cash to back a threefold increase in the bank's issue of currency.[12]

Poultney recruited some prominent Baltimoreans to share ownership of the bank. Reverdy Johnson was an influential attorney who had served in the General Assembly. He persuaded Maryland officials to deposit $335,000 of state funds in Baltimore banks; Poultney's institution got $50,000. David Perrine was clerk of the Orphans Court; its jurisdiction covered wills, estates, and inheritance. Perrine transferred all of the funds in the court's custody to the Bank of Maryland. Johnson, Perrine, and three other prominent Baltimoreans borrowed money from the bank to buy its stock. Poultney and the five other owners controlled 900 of the bank's 1,000 shares, but Poultney was the only publicly identified owner. He and the five secret owners formed an investment "club."[13]

The combined lobbying efforts of Johnson and another bank stockholder, Hugh McElderry, secured a charter from the state legislature for a new firm, the General Insurance Company. They and the three other secret directors of the Bank of Maryland borrowed more of the bank's funds to purchase shares in the insurance company. The insurance firm might yield substantial profits in the long run, but in the meantime its shares could be used as security to obtain more loans. The Bank of Maryland bought $500,000 in Tennessee State bonds on credit, with the hope that the bonds could be sold quickly for cash while the bank gradually retired the loan used to buy them with profits from the insurance company. In an effort to secure wider circulation of its notes, the bank established branches as far away as Little Rock, Louisville, New Orleans, and Cincinnati. The branches were run by members of the bank club and provided them with additional opportunities to make loans to themselves. The club's next large acquisition was a 6,000-share stake in the Union Bank, a Baltimore institution rumored to be in line for a sizeable injection of federal funds when Andrew Jackson's prosecution of the war against the Bank of the United States led to removal of its government deposits and their redistribution to the administration's "pet banks." Roger B. Taney, who had just become Jackson's secretary of the treasury, was friendly with several of the bank club members and may have tipped them off about the Union Bank's impending good fortune. One of these friends was Bank of Maryland director John Glenn, who bought Union Bank stock on his own account, offering as security the half million dollars in Tennessee State bonds, which had yet to be paid for. He then distributed the Union Bank's shares among his clandestine partners at the Bank of Maryland.[14]

The club's stake in the Union Bank brought its president, Thomas Ellicott, into the orbit of the conspiracy. Ellicott was a respected member of Baltimore's financial elite, known for his probity. In the town's last bank scandal, in 1819, Congress had called on him to serve as chairman of a committee that investigated the complex dealings that had brought down the local branch of the Bank of the United States. Secretary Taney now consulted him on the plan to redistribute federal deposits from the US bank to state-chartered banks.[15] Since his own bank would benefit from the transfer of government funds, Ellicott's role as an adviser to Taney seems to have been a conflict of interest—a notion that may not have been current in the age of Jackson.

Ellicott's involvement in the affairs of the Bank of Maryland began at a time when the bank and its secret owners were hard-pressed. The club's extensive acquisitions had left them and the bank short of liquid funds. Secretary Taney channeled additional federal deposits through Ellicott's bank to the Bank of Maryland, an arrangement apparently devised to obscure Taney's partiality to his Baltimore friends and their shaky financial institution. It was at about this time that the document recording the creation of the bank club was destroyed, and Evan Poultney bought back the bank shares held by its secret members. But club members continued to control the bank's branches from which they drew more loans, and their General Insurance Company withdrew $200,000 from the vault in Baltimore. The Bank of the United States may have aggravated the troubles of the Bank of Maryland. The US bank curbed its lending in order to accumulate the reserves that would be needed if the Jackson administration withdrew its federal deposits. The resulting curtailment of credit reverberated through Baltimore's financial institutions, including the Bank of Maryland.[16]

Poultney was left with his bank and its secret debtors. In March 1834, the bank closed. Poultney placed a reassuring notice in the local newspapers explaining that the sudden suspension of business was designed to minimize losses to depositors and creditors. "My confident opinion," he wrote, "is that the Bank is able to pay all its obligations, but to obviate any difficulty whatever and to satisfy the holders of the notes and special certificates of the Bank, I hereby pledge my whole private estate . . . to redeem any deficiency that the means of the Bank may, by any possibility, be unable to redeem." The bank's cashier published a guardedly optimistic statement at the same time. Another measure that may have shored up public confidence in the institution was the appointment of Thomas Ellicott to serve as trustee to oversee consolidation of the bank's assets and discharge of its obligations.[17]

Prominent among the bank's debtors were the former members of the club, who had borrowed heavily from the bank and its branches, as had their General Insurance Company. Encouraging reports about the bank's ability to make good on its obligations no longer served their interests. If the bank's creditors and depositors expected that they could soon collect all or most of what they were owed, they would be unwilling to sell their credits in the bank to third parties at a discount. If, on the other hand, depositors and creditors believed that the Bank of Maryland's assets fell far short of what they were due and that its affairs would remain unsettled for a long time, they might be willing to sell their credits at a deep discount. The members of the club could then buy up credits at 50 or 25 cents on the dollar, use them to pay off their debts to the bank at face value, and make a respectable profit in the process.[18]

The members of the club embarked on a campaign to discredit Poultney and his account of the bank's financial condition. In time, they also turned on Ellicott, who seemed determined to reach a prompt settlement of the bank's affairs. His former involvement in the business of the bank led a committee of creditors to recommend that two additional trustees should be appointed to oversee both the bank and Ellicott. One of the new trustees was John B. Morris, a former president of the Bank of Maryland whom Poultney had displaced when he took control of the bank in 1831. Morris could not be counted among Poultney's friends. The other trustee was Richard W. Gill, who had once served as Baltimore's agent in Washington to recover its war debt from the federal government. Now he was a close associate of Reverdy Johnson. Without opening the books to public scrutiny, Morris and Gill wasted little time in producing a report that exaggerated the Bank of Maryland's financial liabilities. Ellicott refused to take part in the charade.[19]

The two attorneys who had originally selected Ellicott as trustee and served as his legal advisers now resigned. They chose as their replacements John V. L. McMahon, who had drafted the B&O's charter, and club member Reverdy Johnson. Johnson's first piece of legal advice was that the bank's debtors must be permitted to pay off what they owed using credits on the bank "without regard to the period at which such debtors may have become proprietors of such notes, certificates, or accounts or the value they may have paid for them." In other words, members of the club could now purchase the accounts of bank depositors at a fraction of face value and use these credits at full value to retire their obligations to the bank. By one estimate, the club's secret members covered their indebtedness and made an additional $450,000.[20]

The machinations required to achieve this result were complex and risky, and they required the conspirators to achieve two essential objectives: to sustain the impression that the Bank of Maryland was unable to meet its financial obligations and to discredit Poultney and Ellicott, who claimed otherwise. In its final episodes, this fiduciary stage play moved to the courts, where Poultney and Ellicott were charged with committing the frauds that brought down the Bank of Maryland. The prosecutor was assistant attorney general Richard W. Gill, and the foreman of the grand jury that handed down the indictments was Hugh McElderry, one of the secret members of the club. Thomas Ellicott's half-brother, Evan, also belonged to the club, so the two found themselves on opposite sides in the bank controversy. It was not their first clash. They had previously fought over the distribution of their father's estate. In Baltimore, a tight little tangle of men dominated the practice of law and the business of finance, and they surfaced repeatedly in one encounter after another. Thomas Ellicott and Poultney themselves had more in common than their status as defendants. Ellicott was married to Poultney's sister, and his Union Bank had provided Poultney with the loan that enabled him to take control of the Bank of Maryland. Transfer of their trials to Harford County might have provided a means to escape Baltimore's incestuous coterie of capitalists and attorneys. But Reverdy Johnson showed up to lead the prosecution.[21]

RETURN TO MOBTOWN

Baltimore's earlier bank crisis, in 1819, had direct and serious consequences for a relatively narrow stratum of traders, merchants, and bondholders, though its indirect effects touched many more. The Bank of Maryland, however, had attracted depositors from a broad spectrum of the city's residents because of its offer to pay interest on all accounts. Its closing imposed a hardship on thousands of Baltimore households, including many of modest circumstances. As a result, there was a sizeable and attentive audience for the flood of accusations and denials that ran on for more than a year after the bank failed.

Robert Shalhope suggests that the political culture of the time may have intensified the audience reaction to these spectacles. The Jacksonian attack on the Bank of the United States helped to create a diffuse animosity against banks in general, and the era's renewed emphasis on popular sovereignty fed the sense of outrage that ensued when privileges bestowed by government—corporate charters, for example—were used to take advantage of people without privilege. Though politicians of all stripes committed themselves to the sovereignty of the people, they held different views of what it meant. There was the popular sovereignty of free elections and representative democracy, protected by the Constitution and the rule of law. But there was also the popular sovereignty of direct action. The Constitution could not enforce itself. There were occasions when popular mobilization was the only way to achieve justice.[22]

The long afterlife of the Bank of Maryland, with its public disputes, lawsuits, and prosecutions, seemed to open a widening gap between the principles of justice and the processes of law. While judges and trustees blocked a public examination of the bank's books, its depositors waited for more than a year to find out whether any of their money would be returned to them. Reverdy Johnson and the no longer secret members of the bank club tried the patience of less prominent Baltimoreans with their delaying tactics. While the club members profited from the delay, their standing in public opinion declined. Evan Poultney gave a good account of himself in pamphlets and letters in the Baltimore press. Correspondents calling themselves "Honesty" and "Junius" weighed in on his behalf. Poultney made an especially strong case for himself where it counted most—on the witness stand—and won an acquittal in 1836.[23] At least a year before Poultney's vindication in the courts, however, public opinion was flowing in his favor and against Reverdy Johnson.

A crowd gathered on the evening of August 6, 1835, in Monument Square, not far from the Battle Monument, the memorial to Baltimoreans who fell defending their city in 1814. Only a few days earlier, a new pamphlet written by Johnson and John Glenn had appeared, followed by a response from Poultney.[24] Johnson's mansion was one of the grand residences on the square, and several hundred Baltimoreans assembled in front of it. Between 9 and 10 p.m., young boys began to throw stones at the house, breaking a few windows. At about this time, Mayor Jesse Hunt took up a position in front of the house, accompanied by a squad of watchmen. The mayor spoke in support of law and order. Several bystanders intervened to stop the boys from throwing stones, and the crowd dispersed.[25]

Mayor Hunt, unsure that peace would last, called a public meeting at the Merchants' Exchange for the following afternoon. The respectable Baltimoreans who assembled there approved a series of resolutions in favor of law and order. Near the end of the session, but before the other resolutions could be voted on, a member of the assembly rose to add a further declaration proposing that the trustees of the Bank of Maryland might serve the goal of public order by resigning and opening the books of the bank to its creditors. The resolution earned loud applause and unanimous approval,[26] and it may have lent legitimacy to mob action.

That night, a crowd of thousands collected in front of the Johnson mansion. Some pried up paving stones and hurled them at the house. Mayor Hunt, accompanied by watchmen, bailiffs, the county sheriff, and supportive citizens, mounted the steps of a nearby hotel in another attempt to talk the crowd into peacefulness, but he had trouble holding the mob's attention. He called on two of the prominent citizens in attendance to assist him. These men were the attorneys for the bank's creditors, and they had been arguing before a state court that the institution should be required to open its books. At first the crowd was attentive, but grew boisterous again when it became evident that the attorneys were unlikely to win their case anytime soon, if ever. The presiding judge had fallen ill, and another judge in Harford County, who was hearing the cases against Evan Poultney and Thomas Ellicott, had impounded the bank's records. The mayor, assisted by bailiffs and members of the watch, managed to force his way through the crowd to take up a position between the mob and Johnson's mansion. They were met with a shower of brickbats. For the first time, Mayor Hunt resorted to force. Together with the bailiffs and members of the watch, he attempted to penetrate the crowd to arrest the assailants. Most eluded apprehension. The crowd dispersed in its own good time, but not until almost all the front windows of Johnson's house had been broken.[27]

Mayor Hunt called another meeting for August 8. About 200 of the town's leading citizens attended. This time, the adoption of resolutions took second place to the organization of defense. The participants agreed on the formation of a citizen guard consisting of about 50 men from each ward, but they argued about whether the members of this guard should carry firearms. Mayor Hunt, concerned that the use of lethal weapons might infuriate the mob, urged instead that the volunteers should be armed only with wooden clubs, and his view prevailed. A mounted force of about 100 men would compose a mobile "flying battalion," ready to move quickly from one trouble spot to another.[28]

That evening went badly. The first sign of trouble was that so few volunteers showed up to defend the peace of the city. Preserving the peace, on this occasion, was indistinguishable from protecting Reverdy Johnson's mansion—a mission that commanded almost no support among the city's workingmen. Those who did turn out, armed with wooden batons, took up posts blocking the streets that entered Monument Square. The crowd that accumulated on the square's periphery ridiculed them as "Mayor Hunt's rolling pin brigade." The mounted "flying battalion," numbering only a few dozen, was stationed in the middle of the square. A mixed crowd of rioters bent on destruction and spectators seeking a spectacle surged up Calvert

Street toward the square, compelling the undermanned rolling pin brigade to give ground. The flying battalion galloped to the weak point and charged into the mob, indiscriminately riding down both troublemakers and trouble-watchers. Their action may have caused at least some spectators to become rioters. The horsemen were pelted with rocks and debris. Some were seriously injured, and one—toppled from his saddle—was nearly run through with his own sword, until bystanders intervened to keep the confrontation from escalating beyond violent to deadly. The mounted men pressed the mayor to let them break out their firearms. Mayor Hunt hesitated. Nearby was Nicholas Brice, judge of the city's criminal court. He gave his sanction to the use of guns. The horsemen armed themselves and subsequently fired into the crowd in Monument Square, killing at least five. The forces of public order were responsible for the only known fatalities of the Baltimore Bank Riot.[29]

On Charles Street, north of Monument Square, a man beating a drum collected a mob in front of John Glenn's house. Glenn had recently moved there from a smaller residence. Like several other members of the club, his involvement in the affairs of the Bank of Maryland had led to the purchase of upscale residential property. The flying battalion galloped to the scene to confront a mob of 2,000 to 3,000 people. Only a few hundred of them seemed determined to demolish Glenn's house. By the time the horsemen arrived, the mob had already taken possession of the building and thrown its furnishings onto the street, where they were set on fire. The flying battalion was again met with a shower of rocks and sticks. Several riders were severely injured, and the battalion fired into the crowd several times. Some early accounts of the riot claimed that as many as 22 were killed here, but the official count for the entire uprising was five dead and about 20 wounded.[30]

Injuries and fatalities seemed only to strengthen the mob. The flying battalion retreated to the relative safety of Monument Square. Mayor Hunt, who had earlier rejected suggestions that he call out the militia, now decided that his citizen guard needed military support. But no more than 20 men responded to the call-up. In effect, Baltimore's militia companies had sided with the mob. The streets belonged to the rioters. They completed the destruction of Johnson's house, burned his law books, and consumed the contents of his wine cellar. They removed a gilded eagle from the building and, instead of adding it to the flames, set it ceremoniously on the Battle Monument. Then the rioters turned on others implicated in the machinations of the bank club, and still others who had been conspicuous in the city's ineffectual efforts to restore order. Rioters, marching in military formation, set off to Hugh McElderry's house on Calvert Street. Another contingent attacked the home of bank trustee John B. Morris, burned his furniture in the street, and drank up another wine collection.[31] Then it was Mayor Hunt's turn; after his house had been sacked, the rioters went to work on Evan Ellicott's. At Evan Poultney's house, the mob hesitated. Poultney, unlike the mob's other targets, had not fled the city, and he came out to meet the rioters, announcing that he would offer them no resistance if they tried to enter his house, but, he added, his home was pledged, like everything else he owned, to reimburse the depositors and other creditors of the Bank of Maryland. A voice from the mob reportedly shouted, "No! No! We have nought to do with honest men!" A cheer went up from the crowd. Someone cleaned up the mud that the rioters had tracked onto Poultney's front steps, and the mob moved on.[32]

William E. Bartlett, a Quaker merchant from the Eastern Shore, was in Baltimore at the time of the riot; he followed the crowds and recorded their operations in a letter to a friend in Montgomery County. Like other eyewitnesses, he noticed that the actively violent members of the mob were often a small minority, but that many more bystanders looked on in acquiescence. At Glenn's house, for example, the vandals continued their work for a full day after the first attack on the property. Bartlett observed them "picking at Glenn's House till 6 P.M." when they knocked off. "Now what think thee? These twenty persons carried on their unlawful game in the presence of from 2000 to five Thousand persons, who witnessed it and not one word of objection was raised!" At Johnson's house he found another minority of activists performing their destructive work before an audience of bystanders: "5000 Persons stood looking on men and boys, some of them . . . not over ten years of age, hauling and pulling all parts of the house."[33]

Late on Saturday, August 9, after his unsuccessful attempt to rouse the militia, Mayor Hunt issued a statement announcing that "the resort to deadly weapons" was "AGAINST MY JUDGMENT AND ADVICE, and was unfortunately taken." The notice was posted throughout the city. The mayor had effectively disavowed responsibility for the actions of his own citizen guard. Some of the guard's leaders left town for their own safety, and those who remained were no longer inclined to endanger themselves in the defense of public order. Mayor Hunt recognized his mistake the following day and sent out another message to correct the impression "that the use of firearms was entirely unauthorized by any competent power." But it was too late. The civil government of the town had evaporated. Rioters held in the jail were released. "On Sunday," recorded Niles' Weekly Register, "the people, without a head, had nothing to do but fear and tremble. No one felt himself safe—as everything was given up. Anarchy prevailed. The law and its officers were away!"[34]

Mayor Hunt resigned. Anthony Miltenberger, the president of the city council's first branch, briefly replaced him, as the city charter required. Remnants of the mob were still wandering the streets before dawn on August 11. After daylight, the venerable Samuel Smith rode through those streets in his carriage, which flew an American flag. He had been called from his country estate, Montebello, to a meeting of prominent and anxious citizens at the Merchants' Exchange, near his townhouse, and he promptly took control of the proceedings. He led the participants on a march to Howard's Park on the northern fringe of the city, where the Washington Monument towered over the greenery. According to William Bartlett, "deliverance was at hand! Our brave and worthy Citizen Genl. Samuel Smith was here. He rallied some of the Blood royals. They carried the Star Spangled Banner waiving over their heads, marched through the streets and thus collected a pretty considerable band."[35]

By some accounts, several thousand Baltimoreans had fallen in behind Smith and his notables. When they reached the monument, there was some talk of adopting resolutions. General Smith reportedly cut off the discussion: "Resolutions? I tell you what kind of resolutions suited a mob during the Revolutionary War. They were Powder and Ball. These are the kind we now want." Smith, having led several mobs himself, could presumably speak with authority on the subject. Dispensing with democratic procedure, the general ordered those in attendance to hold meetings in their wards, where they were to sign up volunteers to assist in the restoration of public order. The new citizen guards were then to report to the mayor's office at 6 o'clock to receive arms and ammunition. From there, the volunteers were dispatched to patrol those areas of the city where the rioters had been most active.[36]

This time, there was no shortage of volunteers. In the Third Ward, they assembled in the public school on Aisquith Street and elected Jacob Deems captain. He reported that he and his 56 men, if "furnished with arms & accoutrements," were prepared to "co-opperate with our fellow citizens in maintaining the peace and preservation of our city." Forty-four men of the Fourth Ward convened in the engine house of the neighborhood's fire company, where they formed "an association to be called the 4th Ward City Guards." Its men stood ready to confront the mob that was "convulsing the good order of the society." The city's volunteer fire companies also offered their services. Their chief marshal informed acting mayor Miltenberger that he had established a headquarters in one of the city's watch houses and that "any orders from Headquarters to the Firemen shall be promptly obeyed." The militia's obedience had improved. When once again called to service, militiamen responded in large numbers. Their commander was Samuel Smith's son, Major General Samuel Spear Smith. He put his division on parade in Monument Square in the early evening of August 11. Six days later, Mayor Miltenberger expressed the city's gratitude for their efforts and informed the younger Smith that the "happy restoration of tranquility" made the further service of his men unnecessary.[37]

The mob had diminished but was not destroyed. It retreated to the suburbs and to parts of the city not patrolled by the new crop of volunteers, and its anger veered off toward targets remote from the Bank of Maryland and the men who stole from its depositors. There were reports of the "demolition of some small wooden tenements occupied by free Negroes, as dwellings or as schools, and the breaking [of] the windows of one of their houses of worship." A suburban "house of ill fame" was set afire. It was the mob's last assault.[38]

CONTEXT AND CONSEQUENCES

The riot had cost Baltimore an elected mayor, and now it needed a new one. Local Jacksonians convinced Jesse Hunt to run for the office from which he had recently resigned. But the majority rallied behind Samuel Smith, the man credited with ending the uprising that Hunt had been unable to manage. Smith's critics painted him as the candidate of the "lordly aristocrats of the land." But Smith, at least, was a popular lordly aristocrat. In the face of defeat, Hunt abandoned his candidacy four days before the election. The city's Jacksonians put forward a carpenter, Moses Davis, as Hunt's replacement. A political unknown, Davis had little to recommend him but his humble origins and his relative youth, which set him apart from his 83-year-old opponent. "As to age," Davis wrote, "I am beyond the green days of youthful simplicity, nor am I so far advanced as to require the Slipper and the Cane." But Davis may have had other infirmities. Newspaper reports suggested that he was a heavy drinker. Smith defeated Davis by more than three to one, but turnout had dropped sharply. The previous mayoral election, in 1834, had generated a total vote of almost 10,000; in 1835, only 6,801 Baltimoreans cast ballots for mayor. Perhaps the drop in participation reflected Baltimoreans' disappointment with the city that produced the bank club and the riot.[39]

The vote, though small, still counted as a victory for Smith, who could now add the title "mayor" after major general, congressman, and senator. His most immediate task was to oversee the arrest and imprisonment of Baltimoreans suspected of participation in the riot. When order returned, only a dozen accused rioters were being held in the city-county jail. They were soon joined by many more. Some were committed on the testimony of respectable citizens who claimed to have witnessed acts of violence. Robert Shalhope suggests that the respectability of these witnesses often carried more weight with the authorities than the credibility of their testimony. On such testimony, hundreds of young Baltimoreans were imprisoned. Other suspected rioters were caught in possession of items stolen from the homes destroyed. Patrick McClasky, Patrick McNeilly, and Joseph Whelan, for example, were found carrying law books from Reverdy Johnson's library, and two of Johnson's mattresses. The grand jury indicted only 28 of the many arrested and imprisoned.[40]

Joseph Walters was the first man to be convicted on a riot-related offense. His accuser was Charles Tensfield, who had been a volunteer in the flying battalion. He was the man who had fallen from his horse in Monument Square. Walters, he claimed, was the person who threatened to run him through with his own sword. The defendant was fined $100 and sentenced to six months in jail. On his release, he was to post a bond of $500 as security for keeping the peace. The *Baltimore Gazette* carried reports of 28 "mob cases" in addition to Walters's. Juries acquitted 16 of the accused; another was found guilty, but the jury recommended a pardon.[41]

The Baltimore Bank Riot was one outburst among many during the era of Andrew Jackson. By one count, there were 147 riots in 1835 alone, 109 of them occurring between July and October. In early September, Hezekiah Niles noted that he had "cut out and laid aside more than *five hundred* articles, relating to the various *excitements* now acting on the people of the United States, public and private! *Society seems everywhere unhinged*, and the demon of 'blood and slaughter' has been let loose upon us!"[42] Rioters in different cities lashed out at different targets, but civil disorder was so widespread that observers of the general tumult understandably looked for some common denominator that animated the various mobs. Historians have continued the search. Rapid urbanization, they suggest, surely contributed to the disorder. But the growth of cities is a multifarious phenomenon, and it remains to specify just what aspects of urban growth created the conditions for civil disorder. The concentration of population in cities clearly created the critical mass of people who provided the raw material for riots, but city life was also associated with the "overall disorganization of social and moral systems in Jacksonian America." Immigration and rapid urbanization, says Michael Feldberg, undermined the influence of traditional mainstays of order—parental authority, the apprenticeship system, deference to one's betters—and contributed to social disorganization.[43]

In the Baltimore Bank Riot, however, there was little evidence of disorganization. It was an oddly orderly disorder. The mob's operations may not have been planned in advance, but they were less than spontaneous. Weeks before the riot began, handbills appeared that demanded the "bank robbers" be tarred and feathered. Anticipating trouble, most members of the bank club left town just before the riot. The mob, once it got down to the business of settling accounts with the club, was discriminating in its choice of targets. The rioters spared not only Poultney's house but also McElderry's new home. Its construction had just been completed, and the builder told the mob that he had not yet handed the keys to McElderry. If the building were damaged, the costs would fall to him, not the prospective owner. The mob moved on. At Evan Ellicott's house, a neighbor told the mob that the house actually belonged to an elderly widow. The crowd deferred its destruction until a delegation made certain that there were no women in the building. As in its other depredations, the mob limited its destruction to Ellicott's furnishings, which it piled in the street to be burned. Setting fire to the house itself might have endangered surrounding structures. The mob considered burning a lumberyard belonging to McElderry, but by majority vote decided against it because of the possibility that the conflagration might spread to adjacent properties.[44] The rioters killed no one. They directed their violence against inanimate objects, and they injured people only when attacked by the citizen guard. The crowd's restraint is all the more remarkable because many of them must have been intoxicated. John B. Morris's cellar reportedly contained 171 dozen bottles of wine; John Glenn's, between 3,500 and 4,000 bottles, a "pipe of Madeira, and other liquors."[45]

In spite of appearances, riots are not necessarily anarchic explosions. As instances of collective action, they usually presuppose a degree of collective organization. In the urban riots of the Jacksonian era, as Michael Feldberg points out, violence was orchestrated by new institutions such as street gangs and volunteer fire companies.[46] But the discipline and discrimination of Baltimore's mob may also have originated in the singular circumstances that provoked it. The looting of the Bank of Maryland by its shareholders was not just a symbol of some more diffuse grievance but a clearly identifiable offense. The local press had identified specific culprits as the guilty parties, and Baltimoreans had 17 months, from the closing of the bank to the outbreak of the riot, in which to consider the harm done and the possibilities for retribution. The accused rioters brought to trial in Baltimore seem to have been members of local networks. They were not, as Reverdy Johnson claimed, "the dregs and refuse of society," but, according to David Grimsted, were "young men, employed and moderately respectable . . . and susceptible to the attraction of peer group activity."[47]

The political culture of the Jacksonian era undoubtedly set the stage for the riots of the period. The ideology of popular sovereignty lent legitimacy to the mob's vision of justice, and its extralegal means of enforcing it. But the mob's anger may have had more complex origins. The political exaltation of the common people was not matched by social or economic elevation. In fact, as Edward Pessen pointed out, the Jacksonian "age of egalitarianism appears to have been an age of increasing social rigidity." The inequality of wealth was increasing, and the "overwhelming majority of wealthy persons appears to have been descended of parents and families who combined affluence with high social status."[48] The riot was a violent expression of egalitarian anger against a corrupt economic elite.

RECKONING

In the end, the Baltimore riot would fail to exact retribution from the wealthy men who had looted the bank accounts of the city's mechanics and workingmen. The prominent owners of property damaged in the riot petitioned the General Assembly to compel the City of Baltimore to indemnify them for losses suffered at the hands of the mob. Those with the biggest claims included two of the men who had robbed the Bank of Maryland's depositors and one, bankruptcy trustee John B. Morris, who had delayed settling its affairs. The assembly extracted the indemnity from Baltimore by means seemingly contrived to stifle any vestige of civic pride. After repeated attempts, the legislature had finally expropriated Baltimore's auction tax in 1827, but as a sop to the city, it had agreed to return $20,000 of its proceeds to Baltimore each year, on the condition that these funds be used only for maintenance of its harbor. The legislature now diverted $100,000 of these payments to the privileged victims of the riot. Reverdy Johnson and John Glenn collected more than three-quarters of the total. John James Audubon got $120. Six sets of prints from Audubon's *Birds of America* had been destroyed along with the furnishings belonging to Morris. The dilatory bankruptcy trustee had not yet paid the artist for them.[49]

The legislature's case against Baltimore held that a riot could have been anticipated in the days leading up to the disorders and that the city had failed to take sufficiently vigorous steps to prevent it. The mayor and council held that city authorities had "exercised all the powers and authority with which they were invested . . . to quell the riots." The failure of these efforts, according to the council's resolution, may have resulted from errors in judgment, but not from an insufficient determination to keep the peace and protect property. Besides, requiring Baltimore to pay an indemnity for damages suffered by Johnson and his friends would indiscriminately penalize all of the city's residents, including "those who took no part in the riots, and those too who risked their property and their lives in endeavoring to quell the disturbance." And finally, local authorities had called up the state militia—a step that state officials themselves might have taken—but the response was insufficient. The state bore some responsibility for the damage wreaked by the rioters.[50]

The first branch of the city council denounced the indemnification statute as "unjust and unconstitutional and consequently an infringement on the rights of the people of this city and as such should be resisted by all constitutional and lawful means." The branch also offered an explanation for the assembly's attack on Baltimore: "this unrighteous and unconstitutional law has been passed, if passed at all, by means of the rotten borough system which exists in this state whereby the representatives of a small minority are enabled to tyrannize over and oppress the many, in violation of every principle of justice and propriety and in opposition to every thing like republicanism and equal rights." A joint committee of both branches of the council, with the approval of Mayor Smith, took the unusual step of hiring a trio of prominent attorneys to argue the city's case before the legislature. They resolved to challenge not just the indemnity law but the General Assembly's earlier statute by which the state made off with Baltimore's auction tax.[51]

The legislature did not yield on either issue. But it was not immovable. While the indemnity issue simmered, another dispute, at least as contentious, erupted to threaten the authority of the General Assembly. Southern Maryland and the Eastern Shore still enjoyed the representation allocated to them under the state constitution of 1776, but the populations of these areas had stagnated, while Baltimore and the counties of Central and Western Maryland experienced high rates of growth. A civil crisis more potent than the bank riot took fire in 1836, when an insurgent "convention" of representatives from the western counties and Baltimore met in the city to demand a reallocation of representation in the state legislature. It closed with a threat. If the General Assembly failed to take steps toward the calling of a constitutional convention within the first 40 days of its session, the insurgents would reassemble to consider "the adoption of such *ulterior* measures, as may then be deemed expedient, just, and proper." The legislature instructed a select committee to consider whether a conspiracy against the state constitution amounted to high treason.[52]

Tension grew when the Democratic senatorial electors refused to meet with their Whig counterparts to vote a state senate into office. Given that the governor was elected by the two houses of the General Assembly under the 1776 constitution, the result was paralysis. Representatives of "Old Maryland" finally proposed a compromise. They agreed that the governor and the state senate should be elected by popular vote and that the western counties, along with Baltimore City, should get a modest increase of representation in Annapolis. Baltimore's representation in the house of delegates increased from two seats to four.[53] The city now had the same number of delegates as the state's counties, but its population was still grossly underrepresented.

Baltimore had fallen behind its urban competitors in other states, and its efforts to catch up by financing railroads burdened the city with debt that impaired its capacity to provide Baltimoreans with basic public services. As Baltimore's first big corporation, the railroad also presaged a new and wider range of inequality in the city's economy and politics. The looting of deposits in the Bank of Maryland by a wealthy, privileged elite and their ability to evade legal consequences were a perverse expression of the new inequality. The riot of 1835 was the response of the unprivileged.

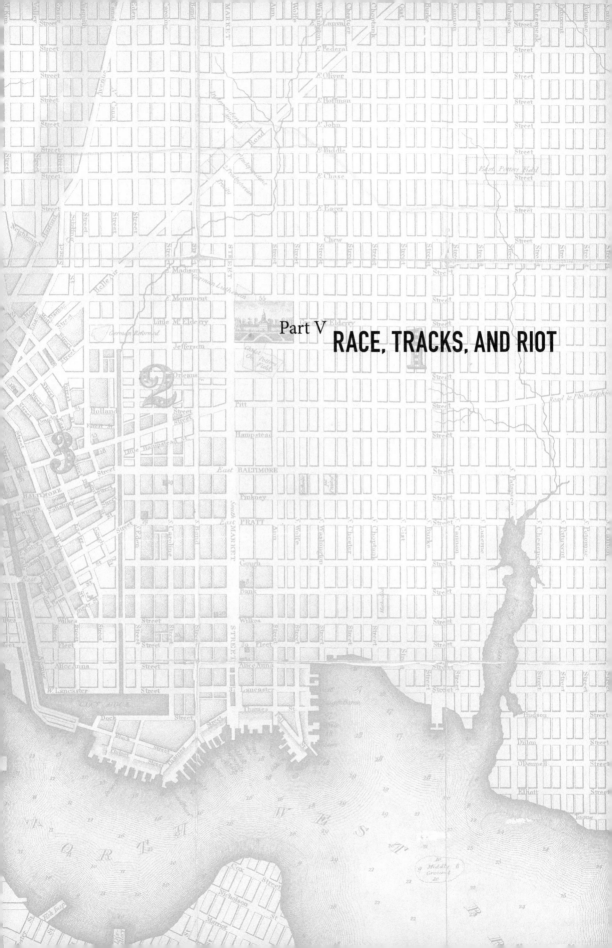

Part V RACE, TRACKS, AND RIOT

Chapter 14

RACIAL BORDERS

J AMES SILK BUCKINGHAM stopped off in Baltimore for about a
month in 1838. Buckingham was a prominent British journalist and
social reformer who had just retired from the House of Commons.
He was also a world traveler who wrote extensively about his journeys.
This trip, his second in North America, would provide him with the
material for a two-volume narrative of his year-long tour: *America: Historical, Statistic, and Descriptive.*[1]

Buckingham seems to have enjoyed his time in Baltimore. He pronounced the city "unusually favorable in every point of view." But from
some points of view, the city struck him as a curiosity. "It is worthy of
remark," he wrote, "that in all our intercourse with the people of Baltimore, and we were continually out in society, we heard less about slaves
and slavery than in any town we had yet visited." Other discoveries
about Baltimore seemed even more surprising. "It seemed remarkable
to us, and was not less agreeable than unexpected, that we should meet,
in the populous capital of a slave-state, more toleration on the subject
of slavery, and a more general sympathy with its removal, than with a
larger number of those residing in the free state and populous city of
New-York."[2]

By Buckingham's account, in other words, Baltimoreans seldom
spoke of slavery, but when the subject came up, it did not provoke much
strife. The limited and subdued character of discussions of this delicate
topic may have been suited to the city's position on the frontier between
slave and free states. But other border towns were not notable for moderation in matters of race. St. Louis mobs destroyed the printing presses
of abolitionist editor Elijah Lovejoy on three occasions, until he decided
to move across the Mississippi River to Alton, Illinois, another border
town, but in the supposed safety of a free state. An Alton mob killed him
while he was trying to defend a fourth press.

Noisy abolitionists could run into trouble in Baltimore as well, but
not such deadly trouble as Lovejoy's. William Lloyd Garrison came to
Baltimore in 1829 to help Quaker abolitionist Benjamin Lundy with the

publication of his newspaper, the *Genius of Universal Emancipation*. Lundy, according to Harriet Beecher Stowe, was "a quiet, persistent, drab-clothed, meek old man," and his abolitionist newspaper roused little opposition in Baltimore because "everybody was good-naturedly sure" that what it said was of no practical consequence. When Lundy left town for about six months, leaving Garrison in charge of his paper, trouble began not long afterward. Garrison later conceded that he "wasn't of much help" to Lundy, "for he had been all for gradual emancipation . . . I became convinced that immediate abolition was the doctrine to be preached, and I scattered his subscribers like pigeons."[3]

Garrison attracted official attention after writing an article about a New England ship owner, Francis Todd. One of Todd's ships, the *Francis*, had picked up a cargo of 75 slaves in Baltimore for shipment to Louisiana. Though the domestic trade was legal, Garrison argued that it would have been no worse for Todd "to fit out piratical cruisers or to engage in the foreign slave trade, than to pursue a similar trade along our coasts." Such "men who have the wickedness to participate therein," he continued, ". . . should be SENTENCED TO SOLITARY CONFINEMENT FOR LIFE. *They are the enemies of their own species—highway robbers and murderers.*" Then he sent a copy of the article to Todd. The ship owner filed a $5,000 libel suit against him, and the State of Maryland prosecuted Garrison for criminal libel. He was found guilty and fined $30, which he refused to pay, and was sentenced to six months in jail. Imprisonment, however, proved no great hardship for Garrison. He took his meals with the warden's family and was not confined to his cell, and wrote sonnets on its walls. He used his seclusion to compose three lectures on slavery, a number of public letters, and a dramatic account of his trial. Though its healthfulness and internal arrangements had been troublesome, it must have been a fine-looking jail. James Buckingham had pronounced it one of Baltimore's "public buildings that may be spoken of with praise." Of course, "being encompassed with high walls," it could be appreciated only from "one of the commanding eminences in other parts of town."[4] Garrison had the privilege of seeing it up close.

Arthur Tappan, a prosperous New York abolitionist, paid Garrison's fine and secured his release after only seven weeks of imprisonment. By the time Todd's civil suit for libel came to trial, Garrison had removed himself from the jurisdiction of the Maryland courts, and he avoided paying the $1,000 judgment handed down in favor of the ship owner. Given Baltimore's well-established record of dealing harshly with unpopular newspaper editors, its relatively gentle treatment of Garrison was not standard practice, and it is worthy of note that the court awarded Todd only $1,000, not the $5,000 he originally claimed.

Like Elijah Lovejoy, abolitionists in other border towns did not fare as well as Garrison. Cassius Marcellus Clay of Kentucky was converted to abolitionism when he attended a lecture by Garrison at Yale in 1832, while Garrison was on the lam from the libel judgment in Maryland. Clay returned to Lexington, where he began publishing an abolitionist newspaper. He made a habit of carrying a Bowie knife at all times. The knife helped him to survive two assassination attempts. In 1843, he used it against an assailant who had shot him in the chest. In 1849, six assailants beat, stabbed, and attempted to shoot him. He killed one with his Bowie knife and drove off the others. In 1845, a mob broke into his newspaper office and expropriated his printing press, but instead of destroying it, they shipped it across the Ohio River to Cincinnati. Perhaps they had heard about the knife.

The geographic ambivalence of border towns did not routinely create an atmosphere of moderation on issues of race. Their location at the boundary between slavery and freedom might just as easily have placed them on the front lines of the irrepressible conflict. If Baltimore succeeded in repressing, or at least gentling, this raw sectional animosity, its geographic location as the northernmost southern city (or the southernmost northern city) cannot, by itself, provide a complete explanation. Perhaps Baltimore's connection with the West did as much to mute the town's deliberations about race as its position between North and South. The western grain trade, the foundation of the city's prosperity, linked Baltimore to a region where slavery was relatively unimportant. Slaves were part of Maryland's tidewater tobacco economy. Some Baltimore-owned ships carried tobacco to England, but the city had no substantial economic stake in the slave-based culture of tobacco growers.[5]

The town's geographic affinities and economic interests distanced Baltimoreans from plantation slavery. But some Baltimoreans owned slaves, and others engaged in the slave trade. The US Constitution had made the importation of slaves illegal after 1808, but the prohibition served as a stimulus to domestic commerce in human beings. The demand for slaves in Maryland was declining, but there was a strong market for slaves in New Orleans. Baltimore attracted merchants who purchased slaves in the city and its surrounding counties and shipped them to the Deep South, where they were needed to cultivate sugar, cotton, and rice. The business had its critics. In 1827, abolitionist editor Benjamin Lundy attacked the city's leading slave dealer, Austin Woolfolk, as a "monster in human shape." Woolfolk encountered the editor on the street, knocked him to the ground, and tried to strangle him, until bystanders intervened. Woolfolk was charged and found guilty of assault, for which he was fined one dollar.[6]

There was a kind of symmetry — admittedly imprecise and scarcely just — between the limited penalties imposed on William Lloyd Garrison and Austin Woolfolk. They suggest a community doing its best to avoid making a fuss about slavery. Though its geographic position between North and South with an economy oriented toward the West may explain its ambivalence, Baltimoreans' reticence concerning slavery may have had as much to do with *who* they were as where they were.

When James Silk Buckingham was "out in society" in Baltimore, he encountered the diverse members of the city's merchant class. It consisted of emigrants from Southern Maryland and the Eastern Shore, who owned slaves or took slavery for granted, as well as businessmen who traded in slaves. In addition to these there were prominent Quaker millers, merchants, and bankers such as Philip and Evan Thomas, Thomas and Evan Ellicott, Evan Poultney, and Johns Hopkins.[7] Some of the Quakers' ancestors were Puritans who settled in Maryland under the Act of Toleration passed by the provincial assembly in 1649 (and repealed five years later), and later joined the Society of Friends. Later still, Quaker businessmen were attracted to Baltimore from neighboring Pennsylvania by the town's rapid growth and prosperity. During the Revolution, more Quaker merchants left Philadelphia, where the British occupation had become an inconvenience to commerce. Some relocated in Baltimore. Their sons and grandsons made or inherited fortunes.

Abolitionist Quakers and proslavery patricians coexisted within Baltimore's economic and social elite in what was still a relatively small city. They socialized with one another and, perhaps more important, did business with one another. For Baltimoreans "out in society," there was one subject suitable only for subdued conversation or none at all. Baltimore's location just south of the Mason-Dixon Line undoubtedly made a difference for its residents' responses to the issues of slavery and race, but border cities, almost by definition, are complicated places, and Baltimore's experience of the "middle ground" was not the same as that of St. Louis or Lexington.

In Baltimore, slavery itself represented a compromise with freedom. The local conditions of servitude allowed considerably more autonomy to slaves than they could exercise on the tobacco plantations of Southern Maryland. In Baltimore, for example, "term slavery" was relatively common. It was a variant on indentured servitude. About 20 percent of all slaves sold in the town were term slaves, who usually reached manumission after 8 to 12 years' service. Term bondage did not represent a gesture to conscience on the part of slave owners. After slaves had served out their terms, their former owners often purchased new slaves. Term slavery was a practical expedient. Term slaves were less expensive than lifetime slaves, and they were thought to be more willing workers. They were also less likely to run away than slaves who could look forward only to a lifetime as chattel, and running away was a practical option for Baltimore slaves.[8]

In another departure from plantation slavery, some of Baltimore's masters hired out their slaves to manufacturers and shipyards and expropriated their pay as profit. Frederick Douglass worked under such an arrangement as a ship caulker in Fell's Point. He was expected to find work on his own and turn his wages over to his owner at the end of each week. Though he had more freedom than he might have had as a field hand, he did not enjoy his independence. "I endured all the evils of being a slave," he wrote, "and yet suffered all the care and anxiety of a responsible freeman." Some of his anxieties may have resulted from the animosity and violence that black workers suffered at the hands of their white competitors in the labor market. Douglass was able to put aside enough of his earnings to finance his escape.[9]

Some owners permitted their slaves to save enough from their earnings to purchase their freedom. Once free, former slaves often bought and freed family members still in bondage.[10] According to Christopher Phillips, term slavery, self-purchase, and practices such as "living out," under which slaves resided away from their masters, all revealed "more than fleeting glimpses of a developing autonomy already begun during enslavement."[11] Douglass had glimpsed it almost as soon as he arrived in Baltimore from the Eastern Shore plantation where he had spent his childhood: "A city slave is almost a free citizen, in Baltimore, compared with a slave on Col. Lloyd's plantation. He is much better fed and clothed, is less dejected in his appearance, and enjoys privileges altogether unknown to the whip-driven slave on the plantation."[12]

Douglass reasoned that slavery "dislikes a dense population in which there is a majority of non-slaveholders." Acts of cruelty and marks of violence would be heard or seen by neighbors, some of whom, including Baltimore's Quakers, might regard them as wordless arguments for abolition. But in Baltimore, Quakers toned down their abolitionism much as masters toned down slavery. In 1789, the city's Quakers had joined some emancipationist Methodists to form the Maryland Society for the Abolition of Slavery. But in 1800, the society disbanded. In 1807, an attempt to revive the organization failed when some of the town's most prominent Quakers declined to take part. In 1816, however, the abolitionists regrouped to form the Protection Society. Its purpose was not to free slaves but to prevent free black people from falling into the hands of slavers.[13] In private, its members might harbor abolitionist principles, but in public at least they adjusted their objectives to accommodate local circumstances. Conflict avoidance has been an enduring motif in Baltimore's engagement with slavery and race.

AFRICAN AVOIDANCE

The Protection Society provided antislavery Baltimoreans with a platform for opposing slavery that posed no immediate threat to slave owners or dealers. They soon created another, more substantial vehicle that served the same purpose. When James Buckingham came to Baltimore in 1838, the city was at the center of the African colonization movement, whose advocates proposed to ease conflict about slavery by reexporting African Americans to Africa. The American Colonization Society was founded in 1816 at a meeting led by Henry Clay in the chamber of the US House of Representatives, and Baltimoreans had been among the organization's earliest and most earnest supporters.

In 1817, Baltimore attorney Robert Goodloe Harper, still in his Federalist phase and serving in the US Senate, issued a public letter outlining a rationale for colonization. Harper's lengthy statement was printed, widely circulated, and became a manifesto for the emergent colonization movement in Baltimore and elsewhere. Although he was a member of the Protection Society, whose purpose was to ensure that free black people remained free, Harper's justification of the colonization project emphasized its usefulness in reducing the presence of free black people in American society. Colonization, he said, would "confer a benefit on ourselves, by ridding us of a population for the most part useless, and too often vicious and mischievous. These persons are condemned to a state of hopeless inferiority and degradation." In America, Harper thought, to be both black and free was a personal tragedy with collective consequences that would become a social affliction. "You may manumit a slave," wrote Harper, "but you cannot make him a white man." The mark of his former, degraded status was indelible, and he could never escape it. He could never penetrate the "barrier between him and the whites . . . between him and the free class." Losing all hope of advancement, the free black person also lost the desire to rise. "The debasement which was at first compulsory, has now become habitual and voluntary . . . He looks forward to no distinction, aims at no excellence, and makes no effort beyond the supply of his daily wants . . . The authority of the master being removed, and its place not being supplied by moral restraints or incitements, he lives in idleness and probably in vice, and obtains a precarious course by begging and theft."[14]

Harper's disparagement of free blacks was not unusual, even among white Baltimoreans who opposed slavery. Antislavery proto-economist Daniel Raymond thought that manumitted slaves, though industrious before their emancipation, "become vagabonds, and one half of them perhaps, get into the penitentiary" once they were freed. Hezekiah Niles observed that "free blacks among us are less honest and correct, less industrious and not so much to be depended on . . . as the well-treated slaves."[15]

Harper claimed that "free people of colour" not only were "a nuisance and a burden" to themselves but also "contribute greatly to the corruption of slaves . . . by rendering them discontented and disobedient." Unable to enter white society, free blacks remained members of the same class as the unfree, who envied the idleness of their emancipated acquaintances and grew resentful of their masters' authority.[16]

For white Baltimoreans, the problems presented by free people of color were a particular concern because Baltimore, since 1810, had held the largest concentration of free black people in the United States. By 1830, Baltimore's population of about 80,000 included 14,000 free black people, almost four times the number of slaves in the city. By 1860, before President Lincoln had emancipated a single slave, 92 percent of all African Americans in Baltimore were free.[17] From its inception, the American Colonization Society had embraced the goal of enabling free blacks to leave America for Africa.[18] The organization's cause appealed to those who thought, like Robert Harper, that free black people had no proper place in American society. In Africa, they would no longer be inferior misfits. "They would become proprietors of land, master mechanics, ship-owners, navigators and merchants, and by degrees schoolmasters, justices of the peace, militia officers, ministers of religion, judges and legislators."[19]

Beyond its usefulness in reducing the population of free blacks, Harper saw a larger promise in the colonization movement. "It tends," he wrote, " and may powerfully tend to rid us gradually and entirely in the United States of slaves and slavery: a great moral and political evil, of increasing virulence and extent, from which much mischief is now felt, and very great calamity in future is justly apprehended."[20] The calamity that Harper apprehended, apparently, was not the Civil War but a slave insurrection like the one in Haiti, which, a generation earlier, had helped to make him a Federalist. Such "terrible convulsions in civil society" might yet lie far in the future. But, in Harper's view, slavery also did more immediate damage. It was bad for white people.

A casual survey of the country, Harper suggested, demonstrated that prosperity and growth were concentrated in regions that relied on free labor; stagnation and decline, in the slave states. This was so partly because slaves labored for their masters rather than themselves and therefore worked as little as possible. In slave society, white people were idlers too. They "insensibly associate the ideas of labour and of slavery, and are almost irresistibly led to consider labour as a degradation." In slave society, indolence was a habit shared by both races.[21]

According to Harper, the liberation of slaves depended on the departure of their free sisters and brothers. Once America's free black residents migrated to Africa and established a colony there, the settlement could serve as a destination for newly emancipated slaves. Its existence might increase the frequency of manumission, "for many persons who are now restrained from manumitting their slaves, by the conviction that they would generally become a nuisance if manumitted in the country, would gladly give them freedom if they could be sent to a place where they might enjoy it, usefully to themselves and to society."[22] Colonization would therefore lead to the gradual decline of slavery.

Robert Harper became a life member of the American Colonization Society and a founder of its Maryland auxiliary. It was Harper's suggestion that led the society to name its African colony Liberia, from the Latin *liber*, meaning "freeman." Harper also enlisted a diligent apprentice in the enterprise. John H. B. Latrobe, future attorney for the B&O, studied law in Harper's office for more than two years and listened to him speak at length on his two favorite subjects: internal improvements and African colonization. Harper's projected canal from Baltimore to the C&O came to nothing, but colonization took hold, and Latrobe became one of its most ardent advocates. He suggested naming Liberia's capital city after President Monroe, whose liberal interpretation of the Slave Trade Act of 1817 enabled the federal government to give financial support to the American Colonization Society's settlement in Liberia. The law authorized the president to provide for captives rescued from slave ships by resettling them in Africa.[23]

Like Baltimore itself, the colonization movement was full of compromises about race and slavery. It could accommodate both pro- and antislavery sentiments. To the defenders of slavery, the movement offered a solution for the problem posed by the coexistence of free and unfree blacks in the same society. Colonization would remove free black people to the continent where they belonged, where they could flourish as full citizens of their own nation, but too far away to encourage resentment and disobedience among their brothers and sisters who remained behind in America and in slavery. On the other hand, for many whites with antislavery sentiments, colonization promised to remove one of the difficulties posed by emancipation. America could liberate its slaves without the inconvenience of having to live with them after they were free.[24]

Colonization promised social and political equality for black people, but not in the United States. In Africa, free black people could achieve equality among themselves, while whites preserved it for their own part in America. The population of Africa, though not part of the colonization movement, also stood to gain. America's black emigrants, having been exposed to the elevating influence of Anglo-American civilization, would contribute to the civilization and Christianization of Africans even more inferior than they.[25]

The enterprise foundered on one immovable obstacle. The vast majority of African Americans—slave and free—were generations removed from Africa and had no interest in going back. For them, America was birthplace and home, however unwelcoming, and Africa seemed alien, dangerous, and backward by comparison. The colonization scheme also embodied a distinctly unfavorable assessment of African American rights and capabilities. It held that free blacks in the United States could never hope to become citizens with the same rights as white Americans. Not surprisingly, abolitionists condemned the colonizers. William Lloyd Garrison mounted an extended assault on the movement.[26]

FALSE START

After Robert Harper's death in 1825, John Latrobe became the principal worker for the colonization movement in Maryland. Since he was only 22 years old, he depended on men older and more prominent than himself to serve as the leaders of the Maryland auxiliary. One of these was Eli Ayres, a physician who had acted as agent for the American Colonization Society in negotiating the purchase of the site where Liberia's capital city would rise. Ayres also sought to reinvigorate the colonization movement in the United States. Its local auxiliaries, according to Latrobe, consisted "of elderly gentlemen whose respectability gave a countenance to whatever they set their name to." Ayres wanted to create local executive committees made up of "active, zealous, young men—*working* men—who brought to the task assigned a portion of enthusiasm." He organized an executive committee for the colonization society's auxiliary in Baltimore. In addition to Latrobe and Ayres, it included Charles Harper, the son of Robert Harper.[27]

Latrobe and the younger Harper set out to overcome black resistance to colonization. They decided that "an address from the people of Liberia to the colored people of this country might do some good here." After receiving the statement from Monrovia and circulating it "as extensively as we could," the next task was to "get up an address from the colored people of Baltimore to their brethren . . . and we waited upon the clergymen of the Methodist church to aid us in providing a place of meeting." Harper and Latrobe were invited to make the case for colonization to a black congregation at a Methodist church on Fish (now Saratoga) Street. They arrived to find that "the meeting was not full by any means." Harper delivered an address "to expound the subject to the good people." Latrobe followed with a motion that the address be adopted by the meeting. The congregation endorsed it without objection.[28]

The next morning, Harper and Latrobe discovered that they had been at the wrong church—a congregation of "radical" Methodists. If they wanted solid black support for colonization, they would have to persuade the "orthodox folks" who attended the Sharp Street Methodist Church. Organized in 1787, it was the oldest black congregation in Baltimore. When Latrobe and Harper arrived at Sharp Street, the sanctuary was full, "and our colored friends were stowed like herrings in a barrel—men, women, and children all flocked to hear about Africa." The two advocates of colonization delivered the same speeches they had made at the Fish Street church. Latrobe later recalled that "an intelligent whitewasher, black as the ace of spades," rose to deliver a response, "and a most excellent speech he made." He did not object to colonization itself, but insisted that African Americans had to be educated and prepared before they departed for Africa. After his response, according to Latrobe, "one or two colored men manifested an inclination to speak, but the chairman seemed to think that quite enough had been said . . . and put the question whether the address just read should be adopted. He only took the *ayes*, but did not call for the *nays*." The "presiding clergyman" declared that the address had been adopted, "gave out a hymn, and dismissed the congregated people . . . rather peremptorily with a prayer." When Latrobe "remarked to [the clergyman], upon his prompt proceedings, he said that if he had let one talk, a dozen would have followed, and nobody's opinions would have been altered."[29]

Harper and Latrobe also attempted to mobilize a white constituency for colonization. In 1827, they organized a meeting of colonization supporters in Baltimore that resolved to establish as many chapters as possible across the state. They recruited Charles Carroll of Carrollton to serve as the president of the organization. Other officers included Philip E. Thomas, Hezekiah Niles, Roger B. Taney, Solomon Etting, and General Samuel Smith—all Baltimoreans. The two young organizers also solicited funds for the American Colonization Society, and in 1827, the state legislature agreed to make an annual appropriation of $1,000 for the colonization of free black Marylanders.[30]

The General Assembly terminated its grant because, by the end of 1828, the American Colonization Society had been able to transport only 12 black Marylanders to Liberia. The results for African Americans overall were no more impressive. By 1827, after 10 years of effort, the colonization society had conveyed a total of only 802 colonists to Liberia, and some of these were recaptured from slave ships by the US Navy.[31]

BALTIMORE SECEDES

By 1831, the Maryland Colonization Society was sufficiently dissatisfied with the performance of its parent society to consider steps toward independence. At first, the issue was money. The Maryland chapter, while willing to provide financial support to the national organization, wanted to become something more than a conduit carrying the state's contributions to the society in Washington. The chapter wanted to control funds of its own. The members aspired not merely to support the colonization movement but to organize their own parties of emigrants to Liberia. That was why they needed money. The managers of the national organization conceded the point, provided that the Maryland organization would pay $20 for every African American transported from Maryland to Liberia, to cover the cost of settling them after they landed.[32]

A dispute ensued about this "tax." Marylanders, after all, had been among the most generous contributors to the colony's purchase. They also contributed to the operating expenses of the national organization. Now they were to be assessed an additional charge for colonists transported to Liberia at their expense. A committee of the state society also argued that the $20 charge for each emigrant was excessive and that the actual expense for settling emigrants was only $2.75 per person. The controversy forced the cancellation of Maryland's first, independently organized party of free black emigrants in June 1831. In the fall, another contingent of free black people was collected to leave for Liberia. Eli Ayres, who had been appointed agent of the Maryland Colonization Society, assembled them in a six-week sweep through the counties northeast of Baltimore and down the Eastern Shore. The party numbered only 31. Ayres had been stymied on the Eastern Shore by rumors that he was a Georgia slave dealer using the emigration scheme to ensnare free black people for a return to slavery in the Deep South. But this time, at least, the ship sailed.[33]

The dispute with the parent society in Washington exposed differences between the state and national organizations that extended beyond organizational finances to the issue of slavery itself. The Baltimoreans who were negotiating with the national board of managers complained that one of "the greatest difficulties now presented to the Parent Board at Washington, is to reconcile the discordant views entertained on the Subject of colonization by the friends of it. The New Englander considers it in one point of view & is impelled by one notion: — the N Carolinian looks at it quite differently and acts from opposite feelings." The Baltimore committee suggested that by trying to conciliate the two wings of the colonization movement, the national organization became "an object of suspicion" to both. If the various state societies were allowed to pursue their own views, this "sectional jealousy which is now daily exhibiting itself to impede the progress of the Society, would at once cease to exist."[34]

The discordant "sectional jealousies" concerning race and slavery produced disputes of precisely the sort that Baltimoreans sought to avoid. They were poised between the New Englanders and the North Carolinians and were likely to turn against one another in the debate about the proper course of the colonization movement — whether it was to preserve slavery by deporting free blacks or to diminish slavery by providing a place of exile for manumitted slaves. The Baltimoreans could distance themselves from these tensions by organizing their own parties of emigration to Liberia, open to both free blacks and manumitted slaves. This liberality preserved a convenient ambiguity about the aims of the colonization movement, a way to sidestep the sectional jealousies that disturbed the national society.

The Maryland Colonization Society made its first move toward independence in 1831, when it applied for a corporate charter from the state legislature. The group had chosen an opportune moment to launch its own African colonization program. In 1831, a Virginia slave, Nat Turner, had led an insurrection of slaves and free blacks in which as many as 55 white people may have been murdered. For many whites, African colonization now became a mission of life-and-death importance.[35]

The Maryland General Assembly embraced colonization as state policy. In March 1832, the legislature not only granted the colonization society its charter but directed the governor to appoint three members of the society as a board of managers "whose duty it shall be to remove from the state of Maryland, the people of color now free, and such as shall hereafter become so, to the colony of Liberia," or to any other place so long as it was out of state. Every court clerk in Maryland who received a deed of manumission and every register of wills who recorded a bequest that freed slaves was required to notify the board of managers of the names and ages of these former slaves within five days or face a $10 fine. The board of managers was to take custody of the manumitted slaves and deliver them to either the Maryland or the American Colonization Society. The ex-slaves were then to be readied for transportation to Liberia. If former slaves rejected that option, the board of managers was to transport them to places of their own choosing outside Maryland. If recalcitrant ex-slaves refused that option as well, the managers were to notify the county sheriff, who was to place these supposedly free black persons under arrest and deposit them somewhere outside the boundaries of Maryland. Manumitted slaves could avoid this outcome in two ways. They could renounce their freedom and continue to live as slaves, or they could obtain annual permits from a county court to remain free "if the said courts be satisfied by respectable testimony that such slave or slaves so manumitted, deserve such permission on account of their extraordinary good conduct and character."[36]

To finance the departure of free black people, the legislature was ready to pay the board of managers—and the Maryland Colonization Society—as much as $20,000 in 1832, and up to $200,000 over the next 20 years. The legislature directed that the state borrow the money needed to finance the enterprise, and it imposed a special levy to pay off the debt.[37]

Little more than a month after the General Assembly made the Maryland Colonization Society an instrument of the state's racial policy, the society's board of managers issued an "address" to the people of Maryland. It observed that the mandate the board had received from the state legislature "purports to effect the free people of color alone," but the state's colonization society operated "upon the entire colored population, slave and free; and, if followed up . . . the spirit of the age and the experience of the state warrant the belief that it will . . . entitle Maryland to be ranked among the free states of the Union." Robert Goodloe Harper's vision continued to guide the society, but it was also guided by the enduring political necessity of charting a path between the supporters of slavery and its opponents. Its purpose was to demonstrate "the ability of a slave holding state to free itself from slavery by its own resources, in its own way, and without the ill-timed and injudicious interference of others in [its] internal concerns."[38] Colonization was not abolition, but it was not a defense of slavery either.

The contentious proceedings at the annual meeting of the American Colonization Society in 1833 imperiled the political balance that Baltimore's board of managers was struggling to maintain. Latrobe explained that for many years, the Maryland auxiliary had relied on the national society as "the expounder of the principles of Colonization . . . At the last annual meeting, however, . . . circumstances exhibited themselves, which demanded from the State Society a different course in relation to the *principles*." It had become apparent that "Colonization had two sets of friends, who supported it from motives diametrically opposed to each other. The north looked to Colonization as the means of *extirpating* slavery. The south as the means of *perpetuating* it." "The Colonization Society," wrote Latrobe, "had attempted to conciliate for years, between these parties, and so long as it would keep the question of *principle* from being publicly mooted, it was partially successful. But the explosion came at last. The discussions of the last winter in Washington led, as a necessary consequence, to the fair and distinct development of opposing parties."[39]

Less than a month after that fractious meeting, banker Thomas Ellicott, a member of the Maryland society's board of managers, offered a resolution deploring "the existence of division and discord in the board of managers of the American Colonization Society. The dispute threatened the "great and philanthropic objects" of the movement that had invested so much in the creation of a colony on the African coast. Ellicott added, however, that the Maryland board of managers was "nevertheless of the opinion that it is neither politic nor expedient, nor within the limits of their chartered powers . . . to interfere in the disputes which may arise out of conflicting principles in that Board." William G. Read, also a board member of the Maryland society, offered another resolution, urging that the "benevolent tendencies of the enterprise ought to be left to disclose themselves in all their various aspects, and that it is the duty of every well wisher to the cause to cooperate strenuously in promoting our immediate object of planting on the shores of Africa a free and happy colony without introducing new topics of discussion which might tend to distract our counsels and paralyze our exertions."[40] The board tabled both resolutions, declaring in effect that it would take no position on taking no position.

At the board's next meeting in April 1833, John Latrobe offered another resolution announcing that the success of colonization in Maryland depended upon "the facilities afforded for the transportation and reception of emigrants on the coast of Africa which can only be secured . . . by the establishment of a settlement in Africa where there will be no restraint upon emigration beyond the control of the State Society." Latrobe proposed that the Maryland Colonization Society purchase a site at Cape Palmas on the African coast, south of Monrovia. His proposal was not new. He had been promoting the acquisition of Cape Palmas by the American Colonization Society at least as early as 1829, but the organization had taken no action.[41] Now, however, the purchase acquired new significance. It would allow Maryland's organization to operate independently of its parent society, not only in transporting emigrants to Africa, but also in providing them with a separate place to live once they got there. In taking this step, the Maryland society would insulate itself more completely from the controversies that shook the national organization and threatened the unity of its Baltimore-based subsidiary. Other branches of the American Colonization Society could depart from the quarrels in Washington and retreat northward or southward to the comparative unanimity of their home states. But the divisions that erupted in the national organization were essentially the same as the ones that might provoke open conflict among the Baltimoreans who ran the Maryland Colonization Society. They were precisely the issues that James Buckingham's hosts refrained from discussing when they were "out in society."

Though they did not reject Latrobe's proposal, the board of managers hesitated. Latrobe made a persuasive case for Cape Palmas, but he had never seen the place (and never would). Its reported advantages justified the "Society in taking further steps for its more particular exploration and purchase."[42] There was also the matter of money. Even the injection of state funds would not enable the organization to

purchase, establish, and staff its own African colony. But the society's new independence afforded it an opportunity to enlarge its territory for fundraising. Since
the organization's explicit, though very long-term, objective was the "extirpation"
of slavery, it could appeal for support to friends of colonization in the North, where
there were few African Americans to be exported to Africa, but many philanthropic
white people with antislavery inclinations. The Maryland society hired an agent to
collect contributions "North of the Potomac," in addition to their local agent who
concentrated on organization building, fundraising, and recruitment of emigrants
within the state. When it took its first steps toward independence in 1831, the society
also enhanced its fundraising prospects in Maryland. The *Baltimore Gazette* commented that the organization's "plan of appropriating the funds raised in the State,
to the use of the State in the removal of its own emigrants" made it "more than ever
the interest of the people of Maryland, to contribute to its resources."[43]

After assuring themselves that their purchase of a colony in Africa would not
endanger their state financing, the Maryland Colonization Society's managers voted
to acquire Cape Palmas, renaming it "Maryland in Africa." While it lasted, it was a
relatively successful enterprise. Emigrants who were unhappy with life in Monrovia
frequently moved to "Maryland" because it was well-run by comparison, and getting
there was not as difficult as returning to the United States.[44]

COLONIZATION AND THE COLOR LINE

Colonization provided a basis for consensus about slavery and race among prominent white Baltimoreans, but it opened new schisms among the city's free black
people. For its time, the free black community of Baltimore was both large and
well-organized. Its population had achieved the critical mass needed to sustain a variety of independent black institutions. Black churches were the first to emerge, and
some of them sponsored their own schools; there were no public schools for black
children until 1867. After the churches and schools came social, business, charitable,
and cultural organizations that transformed the city's African American population
"from a formless aggregate of transients . . . to a society that coalesced around the
affirmation of racial distinctions." This mosaic of African American organizations
was undoubtedly an asset to black Baltimore. It was a source of identity along with
psychological and social support, and it "provided an essential undergirding for the
development of a unique urban culture and cohesive community in Baltimore."[45]

This collective asset, however, was also a liability. Organization meant division.
African Americans joined different churches, different denominations, different organizations that produced rival leaders with disparate constituencies and divergent
interests. Sometimes the burden of maintaining unity was too much to bear, even
within a single organization. One of the earliest rifts split the Sharp Street Methodist Church, where John Latrobe and Charles Harper had delivered their appeal
on behalf of colonization. Eleven years before their visit, the church's pastor, Daniel Coker, and a minority of his congregation had seceded to form a new church.
The issue was race. The Sharp Street church was part of a denomination governed
by whites. Rev. Coker and his followers wanted to be free of the white hierarchy.

Rev. Daniel Coker, a portrait probably painted by African American artist Joshua Johnson around 1805, when Coker was 25 years old. Three years earlier, while living in New York, Coker was ordained as a deacon in the Methodist Episcopal Church. In 1816, he became one of the founders of the African Methodist Episcopal denomination. Four years later, he was one of the first black Baltimoreans to accept the invitation of the American Colonization Society to set sail for Africa, where he settled in Liberia and later relocated to Sierra Leone.

They founded Bethel Church, which would soon join a new, black denomination to become Bethel African Methodist Episcopal Church. Bethel was the radical "Fish Street church" to which Latrobe and Harper had addressed their first appeal for colonization.[46]

Its founding was one of the initial steps in a long series that contributed to disengagement of Baltimore's free black community from the city's white population. This estrangement may have become more pronounced after 1831, when the white response to Nat Turner's Rebellion intensified the pressure to ship black people to Africa and imposed new restrictions on free black people who remained in Baltimore. The state had attempted to prevent free African Americans from entering Maryland as early as 1807, but policies of exclusion became increasingly harsh after 1831. Free black people who entered the state were permitted to remain for only 10 days. Those who stayed longer could be fined $50 for each week they remained beyond 10 days. Any free black person who left the state for more than 30 days was considered a nonresident and, on return, was subject to the same 10-day limit, followed by the fine of $50 a week. Subsequent legislation made it illegal for free black people to enter the state at all, except as servants with their masters. First offenders were to be fined $20; a second offense carried a fine of $500. Offenders unable to pay would be sold as slaves. In Baltimore it was difficult to enforce these restrictions. The city's free black population was so large that outsiders could escape detection for up to a year, and the state courts held that penalties for remaining in the state illegally had to be imposed within 12 months of the offense.[47]

Other restrictions imposed in the aftermath of the Nat Turner scare limited the right of assembly for African Americans. A state law of 1831 prohibited black religious services unless conducted or authorized by a white clergyman, who had to be present at the service from beginning to end. An exception was made for Baltimore's numerous free black people and their numerous churches. They could hold their own services up to 10 p.m. with the written permission of a licensed white preacher. Meetings of African Americans for nonreligious purposes were forbidden by a later statute, but another exception was made for Baltimore, at the request of some of its white citizens, who argued that the law prevented the functioning of black charitable societies organized to assist destitute members of the race. In Baltimore, free blacks certified to be of good character, and who paid annual taxes of at least five dollars, could form such organizations, but only with the written permission of the mayor, which had to be renewed annually. The mayor was also empowered to send observers to oversee the meetings of these groups.[48] There is no indication that any mayor actually did so.

By the late 1830s, it had become customary for black Baltimoreans who wanted to hold social functions to petition the mayor for permission. The requests were usually accompanied by letters of recommendation from white citizens. In 1838, for example, white acquaintances intervened with the mayor so that a "Mrs. Ross" and her "very quiet family" could hold a Christmas Eve party. John Miller, "a very discreet genteel colored man," carried a letter to the mayor's office urging that he be allowed to hold a "Ball" in Long Alley. For black Baltimoreans, even oyster suppers called for mayoral approval. Those who needed to be out on the streets after 10 p.m. because their jobs required them to work late also needed mayoral permission and found whites to support their requests.[49]

By comparison with the rest of Maryland, however, Baltimore seems to have responded permissively to African American efforts at independent organization and socializing. A few of the requests written by white Baltimoreans in support of black social gatherings refer to the prospective black hosts—perhaps surprisingly—as good or worthy "citizens." The term implies an autonomous political status, but of course, free African Americans were considerably less than citizens in practice. They could not vote or hold office. White acquiescence to freedom of association among free blacks was not an acknowledgment of their equal citizenship, but an acceptance of black separation and the existence of a distinct African American community.

The racial divergence did not come all at once. The emigration of black Methodists from Sharp Street to Bethel and other AME churches was slow, and some black Methodists never left the denomination that they shared with whites. Black Methodists sorted themselves into three groups: those who continued to worship with whites (but only from the rear pews), those who joined all-black congregations under Methodist Episcopal governance, and those who belonged to AME churches.[50]

Black Methodist divergence was only one of the divisions that impeded black Baltimore's achievement of unity. According to Christopher Phillips, the city's free black community was less "fractious" than the one in Philadelphia, but black Baltimoreans were sharply divided on African colonization.[51]

Daniel Coker seems to have been an early storm center within Baltimore's black community. At one point, he was expelled from his AME church on the basis of charges never disclosed. He was soon reinstated, but his position had been undermined, and he faced difficulty in restoring his personal finances. In addition to these problems, Coker found himself an unwilling partisan in bitter conflict between his Bethel church and his former Sharp Street church. Convinced that the battle was weakening both congregations, Coker decided, in 1820, to accept the invitation of the American Colonization Society to sail on its first ship to Liberia so that he could "leave all these divisions behind in America" and return to the land of his ancestors. On his trip from Baltimore to New York, where he was to board ship for Africa, Coker made several speeches in support of colonization before large audiences of African Americans. He continued to propagandize for colonization from Liberia, where he became not only the pastor of another AME church but a ship owner and coastal trader, a leader of the American colony, and eventually a combatant in still more controversies.[52]

William Watkins was one of Coker's students at the Sharp Street school when Coker was its principal teacher. Watkins became a teacher in the school at just about the time that Coker embarked for Africa, and he later established an independent school of his own.[53] Watkins expressed strong opposition to the colonization movement promoted by John Latrobe and Charles Harper. The "address" they had presented at the Sharp Street and Bethel churches appeared in Baltimore newspapers as a "Memorial of the Free People of Colour," signed not by Latrobe and Harper, who were its authors, but by the chairs and secretaries of the meetings convened at the two black churches.[54]

Watkins responded as "A Coloured Baltimorean" in the abolitionist *Genius of Universal Emancipation*, challenging the memorial's authenticity as a statement of black support for colonization. In fact, he argued, most of "our coloured brethren" had been "not a little surprised to see a memorial . . . containing sentiments so repugnant to their well known opinions." To support his contention that few free black people wanted to leave for Africa, Watkins noted that a recent ship departing Baltimore for Liberia carried only 10 emigrants from the largest population of free black people in the country.[55]

Watkins next published an indictment of the American Colonization Society itself. Behind the fog of ambivalence about slavery that sustained the precarious unity of Baltimore's colonization movement, Watkins found hypocrisy. It seemed "very strange" to him "that those benevolent men should feel so much for the condition of the free coloured people, and, at the same time, cannot sympathize in the least degree, with those whose condition appeals so much louder to their humanity and benevolence—Nor is this all: we are apprized that some of the *most distinguished* of that society are themselves SLAVEHOLDERS!" Members of the colonization society expressed deep concern for "poor, degraded Africa." Their remedy for the sorry continent was to dispatch free black Americans as agents of civilization—the same free black people condemned in the speeches of colonization advocates as "of all classes of the population of this country, the most vicious; who, being contaminated ourselves extend our vices to all around us, to the slaves and to the whites." These were "to be the pioneers of this great work of regeneration and reform. Fine materials indeed to accomplish so glorious a work!"[56]

Having deflated the colonization movement's disingenuous claims to benevolence, "A Coloured Baltimorean" next appealed to the material and emotional interests of free black people themselves. "Why should we abandon our firesides and everything associated with the dear name of *home*—undergo the fatigues of a perilous voyage, and expose ourselves, our wives, and our little ones to the deleterious influences of an uncongenial sun, for the enjoyment of a liberty divested of its usual accompaniments, surrounded with circumstances which diminish its intrinsic value?" It was better, he wrote, to "die in Maryland under the pressure of unrighteous and cruel laws than be driven, like cattle, to the pestilential clime of Liberia."[57]

In 1831, as secretary of a meeting of Baltimore's free black people, Watkins— under his own name—recorded a series of resolutions adopted in opposition to colonization. But along with these there was one that acknowledged the division that colonization had produced among the city's free black people: "We are deeply sensible that many of our warm and sincere friends have espoused the colonization system, from the purest motives—and that we sincerely regret their efforts to ameliorate our conditions are not more in accordance with our wishes."[58]

Not all black endorsements of colonization were engineered by white partisans of the cause. In 1835, Watkins would find himself standing in opposition to acknowledged leaders of black Baltimore, including the pastor of his own church. Three black ministers issued a statement, claiming to speak for the city's free African Americans, in which they declared the sympathy of their community for the cause of colonization. Watkins challenged their claim to speak for Baltimore's black population, since they had not called a single meeting to find out exactly what sentiments black Baltimoreans held on the subject. He stood in opposition not just to respected leaders of the black community but to his own professional colleagues. A year earlier he had become a preacher at the Sharp Street church. Writing to William Lloyd Garrison, whose abolitionist newspaper had provided Watkins with a public, if anonymous, voice, he claimed that the black ministers had threatened him with a coat of tar and feathers and that a meeting had been called in Baltimore County to consider what means might succeed in putting an end to his advocacy of abolition and his attacks on colonization. Though Garrison had published many of Watkins's previous letters in the *Liberator*, Watkins asked him not to print this one. For the moment, at least, he had been silenced. After 1835, Watkins's letters to Garrison became infrequent.[59]

Watkins's dispute with the black ministers carried implications that extended beyond the issue of colonization. In Baltimore's black community, whose members were divided by denomination, church, and social status, it was not clear whether anyone could speak for the race as a whole on any issue. The colonization movement, moreover, posed special difficulties for its black critics. It was not just that the movement had many genuine sympathizers among black Baltimoreans. In Baltimore, at least, the colonization movement was a vehicle that prominent whites employed to sidestep hard questions about slavery and racial equality. For black Baltimoreans, it was no easy matter to mobilize against ambivalence and evasion, even though they might conceal hypocrisy. Moreover, the town's free African Americans facilitated white evasion. As they withdrew further into their own, separate community, they made it easier for whites to avoid the explicit consideration of relations between the races.

William Watkins made a final assault on the black clergy in 1837, complaining of the "incompetency of the colored ministry, in general, to supply the intellectual wants of the colored population of our country."[60] It was one of his last outbursts in print. After 1838, not much more is heard from him. By 1844, he was no longer listed as a Methodist preacher. In that year, he was overwhelmed by the conviction that the end of the world was imminent, and he joined a millenarian movement whose purpose was to prepare for doomsday. Perhaps he had found it impossible to live in the world as it was. Finally, like Daniel Coker before him, he found that the only escape from the internal strains of black Baltimore was emigration. He left, not for Africa, but for Canada.

Chapter 15

BETWEEN MOBS AND CORPORATIONS

CONGRESSMAN, SENATOR, MAYOR, and major general Samuel Smith died on April 22, 1839. He was 87 years old. He had been out riding in his carriage that morning. When he returned, he lay down on a couch to rest and never woke up. His funeral procession began three days later at his townhouse on Exchange Place. It moved north on Gay Street to Baltimore Street and turned west. In the lead was a sizeable detachment of cavalry, followed by several infantry regiments and then companies of artillery with their horses, caissons, and guns. Two open carriages followed the troops. The first carried the president of the United States, the secretary of state, the governor of Maryland, and the city's mayor. In the second carriage were the secretaries of the treasury and navy and the US attorney general. The hearse followed, drawn by four white horses and flanked by mounted dragoons. Many more carriages came behind, containing dozens of urban notables. The city guard of Baltimore, whose members Smith had mobilized to put down the bank riot of 1835, marched behind the carriages, without their firearms. Then came a pedestrian procession including the members of the Baltimore City Council, other city officials, judges, members of the bar, professors of the University of Maryland, officers of the army and navy, members of the state legislature, and foreign consuls. When the cortege turned onto Baltimore Street, it was joined by all of the city's fire companies in their resplendent uniforms. Behind them, thousands of citizens fell in for the march to the cemetery on Green Street on the city's west side, where Smith was buried.[1]

Only a year earlier, Samuel Smith had been the city's mayor. Now he was gone, and so was the Baltimore that made him. His stately departure was one more sign that Baltimore had arrived. The attendance of President Van Buren and his cabinet members could be regarded as a sign of respect, not just for Major General Smith, but also for Baltimore. The Census of 1840 would show that the town's population had surpassed 100,000. Baltimore had also become a focus of national politics. It was the location of choice for political party conventions, which had inaugurated a new era in national democracy by seizing the authority to nominate presidential candidates from the congressional caucuses. Smith would probably have approved.

The democratization of local politics carried carpenters and saddle makers to the top ranks of political leadership. But they presided over a political system that had fallen under the domination of corporations engaged in "internal improvements" by which the city's leaders hoped to maintain its competitive position in the emerging national economy. As Gary Browne points out, the "personal and private elitism" of Samuel Smith's Baltimore gave way before an "impersonal elitism" of corporations and institutions.[2]

THE DOWNSIDE OF INTERNAL IMPROVEMENTS

The new limits on urban democracy were not inherent in cities themselves but by-products of urban history. The members of the Baltimore City Council's Joint Committee on Internal Improvements had experienced that history at first hand, and little more than a month before Samuel Smith's last carriage ride in 1839, the committee issued a long and unusually reflective report on the troubles it had seen.

Ironically, the new strictures on urban politics followed from success in overcoming the limits of geography. So long as horses and wagons remained the principal vehicles of commercial transportation, Baltimore's geography was its destiny. According to the Committee on Internal Improvements, Baltimore had the "natural advantages of [a] geographical frontier, with reference to foreign commerce and the internal trade of the country." This intermediate position between the western mountains and Atlantic shipping transformed Baltimore from "the condition of a small hamlet" into one of the nation's leading cities. "Long before political economy was known as a science," the committee observed, "the fact was well understood that the growth and prosperity of a marine Emporium depended upon the extent of her internal trade. Allow this to be diverted into other channels, and Baltimore will relapse into the condition from which it sprang."[3] Progress had made the relapse more likely: "The mountains were at first only crossed by the adventurous trader on horse back . . . In a short while, new roads were cut—Turnpikes followed—canals were projected—Steam over came the impetus of ascending currents, and Rail Roads have been invented, which transport man from place to place with a celerity that would have been regarded only at the commencement of this century, as the prognostic of some moon struck dreamer. In fine a new era has burst upon us. Baltimore to maintain the advantages of her natural frontier must . . . resort to all the judicious improvements of the age that are calculated to overcome time & space."[4]

Even the most judicious improvements were freighted with uncertainty and would not "fully realize the expectations of this community or of those by whom they were projected." Even more uncertain were the costs of the projected canals and railroads. The corporations overseeing these projects had "in every instance, after a short lapse of time, been constrained to apply to the State or city for necessary aid." The state and local governments would meet these requests by purchasing shares of stock, often by issuing stock of their own—increasing the burden of public debt to finance privately run railways and canals. But corporations' initial requests for more support "only proved to be an entering wedge for another" and another, until the city and state together held more than $7.5 million in debt for unfinished projects, a capital investment that could only be listed "under the head of 'Unproductive.'"[5]

The investment of Baltimore and Maryland amounted to more than $180 million in current dollars. But the sum was hypothetical. The city had pledged to purchase $3.5 million more in B&O stock, but it had not yet paid for the shares. And, in the aftermath of the Panic of 1837, it would not have been able to float an issue of city stock to cover its stake in the railroad. Its certificates would have to be discounted so heavily that they would have added more to the city's debt than it actually owed to the B&O. For a time, the commissioners of finance met the city's obligations to the railroad by borrowing from Baltimore banks instead of issuing city stock. To reassure the banks, city authorities levied a tax generating enough revenue to meet the first year's interest payment.[6]

The B&O had troubles of its own. The cost of extending the rails from Harper's Ferry toward Cumberland had already exhausted the company's capital, and the tracks that led back toward Baltimore needed expensive repairs. They had not stood up well under the weight of heavy steam locomotives. The company's directors at first decided to demand that its subscribers pay installments on their outstanding balances of $2.50 per share each month from August 1838 through March 1839. Its most important subscribers were unlikely to be able to make these payments. Maryland's financial condition may have been even more fragile than Baltimore's. In London, Maryland state bonds were heavily discounted, and there were few buyers even at the reduced price.[7]

In the autumn of 1839, the B&O directors hit upon a scheme to compensate for the shaky credit of the debt-burdened municipality that helped to underwrite construction of the railroad. With the approval of the Maryland General Assembly, the company began to issue its own currency—called "stock orders" or "railroad notes"—in denominations as small as two and three dollars (later reduced to bills worth as little as 12 cents). The notes were backed by the city stock that the railroad already held, but they insulated the B&O from the depreciation of those municipal bonds. The stock orders were pegged at the full value of the city notes, not their current market value. The company used them as "scrip" to pay for land, labor, and materials. The workers, suppliers, and landowners who received the stock orders could use them to pay Baltimore City taxes or present them to the city for redemption. They would receive an equivalent amount of city stock at par value plus 6 percent interest.[8]

In effect, the stock orders made Baltimore a financial subsidiary of the B&O. The city council's Joint Committee on Ways and Means was clearly uneasy about the entire arrangement, and at the end of 1841, the committee addressed an inquiry to a city attorney, asking for his written opinion on a series of legal questions. The core question was whether the city, by agreeing to redeem the railroad's stock orders, would give them the status of its own municipal bonds. In other words, had the city empowered the B&O to issue city stock?[9]

Contractors and workers initially accepted the stock orders in payment for supplies and services. The suspension of specie payments occasioned by the Panic of 1837 made the railroad notes an essential medium of exchange and prolonged their circulation. To secure the status of stock orders as currency, the city council petitioned the General Assembly to enact a law making it a felony to steal B&O notes or to obtain them under false pretenses.[10] In other words, they held value just like real money. But no amount of official recognition could save the stock orders from their fate. They were doomed to depreciate because they were backed by city bonds that traded at much less than face value.

The stock orders also undermined the city's credit. Mayor Samuel Brady may have been the first city official to criticize the railroad on this score. In his first annual message to the council in 1841, Brady blamed the B&O's stock orders for having "brought a vast amount of city stock . . . directly into the market, and by this means held as if at auction." By flooding the market with its railroad notes, the B&O had undermined the value of the city stock on which the notes were based. The resulting depreciation of city bonds produced a drag on the value of any new bonds that the city intended to issue. According to the mayor, it had become "impossible to sell the stock of the city except at a loss of fifteen to twenty per cent." Brady worried that the city's notes might become "unsaleable" if the B&O continued to issue the stock orders. The mayor "felt great anxiety to avoid this result" and recommended that the city use any revenue surplus to retire its debt to the railroad. It also made sense for the city to redeem the notes and withdraw them from circulation. Brady claimed that this would stabilize the value of the stock orders and the city bonds to which they were tied.[11]

The city council refused to make the sacrifices needed to buy up the stock orders and pay down the city's railroad debt. Instead, it passed a "Currency Bill" that ordered the city register to continue paying 6 percent interest on the B&O's stock orders. Mayor Brady vetoed the ordinance, but his veto was overridden in both branches of the council. Brady announced his resignation. Obviously unprepared for the mayor's reaction, the council reversed its override of his veto; Brady reversed his resignation and proceeded with his plan to withdraw about $250,000 in railroad notes from circulation.[12] Two months later, Brady resigned again, this time for good. "It is not necessary," he wrote, "for me to state the cause that has influenced me to take this course at this time."[13]

Stock orders continued to circulate in the city, but they were being discounted at 12 to 14 percent. And in his annual message at the beginning of 1842, Maryland's governor, William Grason, denounced the B&O for using the scrip "to dispose of city stock . . . at its par value; and to transfer to the holders of their certificates the risk and loss, which they were not willing to encounter themselves of selling it in the market." The railroad had shifted this risk to laborers, tradesmen, shopkeepers, and suppliers. By March 1842, the stock orders were discounted in Baltimore at more than 25 percent.[14]

Two pieces of legislation adopted by the Maryland General Assembly aggravated the currency crisis. The first prohibited any organization not chartered as a bank from issuing currency. The measure was clearly aimed at the B&O's stock orders, and they were soon trading at a 50 percent discount. The second act required all banks to resume specie payments or forfeit their charters. The banks responded by curtailing their issues of paper currency that could be redeemed for hard money. The reduction in the money supply triggered a wave of bankruptcies, and invalidation of the B&O's stock orders imposed severe losses on workers and suppliers who had accepted the railroad notes.[15]

While Baltimore endured the Panic of 1842, the railroad extended its tracks to Cumberland and met the eastern terminus of the National Road that led to the Ohio River. The road's traffic fed freight to the B&O, and the coalfields in the region contributed more tonnage and revenue, but the expenses incurred in reaching Cumberland made it impossible to pay any dividends in 1842. There were only the faintest hints of a brighter future. In 1841, for example, the railroad had delivered to the city its biggest dividend to date—$60,000—an annual return of only 1.7 percent on the city's investment. Baltimore immediately gave the money back to the B&O to cover its stock subscription. In return, the B&O handed over to the city the remaining difficulties created by their stock orders. Baltimore borrowed another $500,000 to redeem the last of the $1.5 million in notes issued by the railroad.[16]

DEBT AND DISORDER

After serving as mayor, Jesse Hunt had returned to municipal service in an appointive capacity as the city register. He was responsible for keeping the city's accounts and overseeing expenditures. Though he no longer had to face mobs, his job still had its difficulties. In July 1840, he had written with regret to Mayor Sheppard C. Leakin concerning the "embarrassed condition of the City Treasury." Until July, Hunt had held out hope that taxes not yet collected from 1839, together with those paid in 1840, would permit the city to meet its obligations. In fact, Baltimore's total revenue of about $130,000 was not even sufficient to cover the interest on the city's stock debt (mostly for internal improvements). Further payments would come due at the start of August, and the city was already $7,300 behind in paying its bills.[17]

At the beginning of November, on the same day the newly elected mayor, Samuel A. Brady, was sworn in, Hunt sent him another letter about the city's "financial embarrassment." He mentioned his earlier "communication to the ex-Mayor . . . in reference to which no action was taken." The register stressed the urgency of the situation: "It appears impossible to meet the required payments unless additional means are provided." Mayor Brady may have been too distracted to deal with the city's financial embarrassments, not only because he had held office for less than a day, but because it was a day that ended with a riot. It coincided with the presidential election in which President Van Buren was defeated by William Henry Harrison. Van Buren had carried the city by 31 votes, but Harrison carried the state. The local Whigs had gathered in front of the office of their party's newspaper, the *Baltimore Patriot*, to celebrate or to get the latest election results. Ex-mayor Leakin was there with his fellow partisans. The outbreak of violence occurred when a fire company attempted to drag its engine through the crowd and return to its station. In fact, the alarm that called them out in the first place may have been a signal for the assembly of a mob. The trouble began with "a regular brickbatting," and then some shots may have been fired. Mayor Brady arrived with a cohort of watchmen, as the violence was subsiding, to address the combatants, urging them to return to their homes. They apparently complied, but ex-mayor Leakin had been seriously injured. The *Patriot* and the *Baltimore Sun* would prolong controversy for several more days in a dispute about the *Sun*'s report that shots had been fired from the *Patriot*'s offices.[18]

The city's financial embarrassment lasted much longer. The debt that Baltimore had incurred to finance railroads and canals and the depletion of its revenues by interest payments left little money for such basic government responsibilities as the maintenance of public order. In his annual message delivered at the start of 1840, Mayor Leakin had noted with satisfaction that the city's tranquility had been interrupted by only a single riot during the preceding year, and on that occasion the outbreak of collective violence had been "quelled without serious consequence," demonstrating "the alacrity, promptitude and firmness, with which the City Guard, volunteer corps, police officers and citizens generally resist attempts to disturb the peace." But Leakin followed up his confident assessment by noting that "the City Watch, upon which the repose of our citizens and the safety of our property so much depends" had not been expanded "in ratio of our population, or the rapidly extending dimensions of our city." He recommended an increase in the size of the force, which was too small "to afford sufficient protection to all sections of the city."

The *Sun* agreed. It contended that "the number of police officers should be doubled at least, and we hope the authorities will become convinced of this fact before our city is disgraced many times more by riot and disorder. — We have no cause to complain of the efficiency of the police generally, but there is not enough of them." More police, of course, would mean more spending, but Mayor Leakin argued that "inasmuch as it would be disbursed for the protection of the persons and property of our citizens, it would be judicious economy."[19]

The single outbreak of disorder that Leakin mentioned in his annual message was a notable one. It had occurred after a mentally unstable nun fled a Carmelite convent. Her pleas for help drew a crowd and roused or confirmed dark suspicions about what went on inside such Roman Catholic institutions. The suspicions may have fed on the sensational (and fabricated) *Awful Disclosures of Maria Monk*, published three years earlier, which claimed to reveal the sordid and deadly secrets of a convent in Montreal. But a mob need not have read the book before assaulting a convent. Two years before the appearance of *Maria Monk*, a Protestant mob had attacked and burned an Ursuline convent just outside Boston. The assault began, like Baltimore's, with a runaway nun.[20]

Though Mayor Leakin portrayed Baltimore's convent riot as a singular interruption of urban tranquility, it was an early episode in a siege of violence that gripped the city for over a decade, much of it spawned by the anti-Catholic Know-Nothings. The city's most riotous years coincided with a sustained period of heavy annual losses on Baltimore's investments in railroads and canals.[21] Municipal debt was not the source of disorder, but it surely impaired the city's capacity to suppress violence.

Volunteer forces such as the city guard or the militia might deserve all the praise that Leakin gave them for helping to put down the convent riot. But it could take critical hours to assemble these forces, allowing a street fight to grow into a murderous riot.[22]

The city council, nevertheless, found it inexpedient to comply with the mayor's request for additional watchmen. The Joint Committee on Police reported that "in the existing state of the city finances no appropriation can be properly made for the compensation of the officers proposed to be appointed."[23]

The B&O's financial demands on the city continued unabated. Early in 1842, the railroad's president, Louis McLane, wrote to the chairman of the council's Joint Committee on Ways and Means to announce that the company would "unavoidably require in current bankable money" several installment payments on the city's stock subscription, along with back payments, to reimburse the railroad for money it had borrowed over the last two months "in aid of the City Commissioners of Finance, and to meet deficiencies in their payment." When the city fell behind in its payments, apparently, the B&O had been taking out loans on the city's behalf and charging them to the commissioners of finance. McLane wanted at least $140,000 over the next eight months, and he wanted the first installment — $30,000 — in three days. If the railroad failed to receive the payment, it would take out additional loans "in aid of the City Commissioners."[24]

McLane's request was followed by a series of contradictory demands for payment until, in April 1842, he finally decided that the "sum of $200,000 between this and next November, perhaps less, would probably be sufficient to put the road in full operation."[25]

UNRULY BOYS AND RIOTOUS MEN

Once the B&O reached Cumberland, its demands for Baltimore's money temporarily subsided. The city remained in debt for borrowing money to finance a variety of "internal improvements." A council resolution noted that the city's support of the B&O had "caused the heavy imposition of burthens on the people for the purpose of paying interest on said stock," but the city and its citizens had "as yet received but little benefit for said work on account of the great expense of said company."[26]

The city not only failed to benefit; it suffered from a shortage of funds to pay for essential municipal services. Repeated recommendations for expansion of the night watch were rejected as "inexpedient" because of the city's straitened circumstances.[27] Two additional watchmen were hired in 1840 when, under state law, Baltimore was reapportioned into 14 rather than 12 wards to accommodate an expanded electorate.[28] Each night, a population of more than 102,000 entrusted its safety to 26 officers. During the day, the number dropped to 14. Though Boston's population was smaller than Baltimore's, it had a night watch of 100 men.[29]

Aside from the occasional outbreak of collective violence, Baltimore also had to cope with everyday criminality. The *Sun* complained of "infestations" of burglars. So did Mayor James O. Law. In his first annual message at the beginning of 1844, he urged the city council to expand the night watch or to create a "double set" of watchmen, "one set to be on duty every other night." Though the number of watchmen on the streets would not increase under this arrangement, the men who patrolled the city would not be "worn down by fatigue" from the previous night's exertions, and the arrangement might make it possible to employ "young active and respectable mechanics" who would not be able to serve as watchmen every night. The council's only step to curb the wave of burglaries was one that required no additional expenditure: the night watchmen were instructed to abandon the custom of crying the hour. The practice was not just a public service for residents without clocks; it was supposed to reassure citizens that a peace officer was at hand and to signal the watch lieutenants that their men were not sleeping on the job. But it also told alert burglars when and where to strike.[30]

The mayoralty was the first political office to which James Law was elected, but his career had carried him through most of the civic institutions that sustained the political life of antebellum Baltimore. He began as a member of the city's mercantile community and soon became the president of a volunteer fire company—the Independent. He was a longtime member of the local militia and would combine his duties as mayor with those of a regimental commander. He was a Whig, like a majority of the city council elected with him, and after retiring from elective office, he became a supervisory flour inspector.[31]

Almost exactly a year before his election, Law had served as foreman of a grand jury whose report urged the city courts, their constables, and the city police to cooperate in an effort to restore order to Baltimore's streets. It was not Law's first public appearance as a champion of public peace. In 1841, his fire company had collided with another, the Vigilant, at the intersection of Baltimore and Gay Streets. In the riot that ensued, the *Sun* singled him out for credit as one of a handful of firemen who "exercised all the powers they possessed to quell the disturbance . . . Capt. James O. Law, president of the Independent Company . . . acted in a most determined manner, and for his pains, had his coat nearly torn from his back."[32]

Law's first message to the council in 1844 conveyed an optimistic assessment of the city's financial condition. Baltimore, he wrote, had endured the "monetary trials" occasioned by the panics of 1837 and 1842, demonstrating that even "in her former embarrassed situation," the city was "able to meet all her liabilities with promptitude and dispatch." The previous year had left the city with a budget surplus of more than $80,000. It had paid the final installment on its stock subscription to the B&O, and the day was "not remote when the city" would "reap the benefit of her vast outlay in the prosecution of this great work."[33]

The mayor may have thought that a positive spin on municipal finances would overcome the city council's resistance to making needed expenditures. And, in Law's view, the expenditures most needed were those designed to preserve public order. More annoying than the burglars were the "collections of unruly boys at the corners of the streets." The *Sun* agreed: "The citizens of Baltimore are more pestered by ungovernable, mischievous, wicked boys, than the people of any other city in the United States." The newspaper's concern was echoed by Baltimoreans in their petitions to the mayor. A resident of Lloyd Street complained that "our privacy [is] broken in upon, and our property endangered by crowds of white boys & young men with songs, cursings, fightings, blasphemies" that made "the street a bedlam, from about sun set to ten or eleven at night." Another Baltimorean wrote to the mayor asking that he instruct "the Police and watchmen of this ward . . . to disperse from these corners the youths who assemble nightly to the great injury of our business and the annoyance of the neighbourhood by their vulgar songs, obscene language and the striking of coloured persons taking off their caps and hats and keeping them."[34]

Controlling juvenile disorder was not simply a problem for the police. There was also the problem of what do with the delinquents once they had been arrested. The city jail was hardly a fit place for them. Its design did not allow much segregation among its inmates. The building's deficiencies had been a subject of common complaint for years when, in 1843, a local grand jury took official notice of the issue. If space were available, juveniles convicted of crimes were placed with imprisoned debtors "or in other rooms where persons are confined for light offenses." But a subsequent inquiry conducted by a committee of the city council found that "juvenile delinquents—whose faults are frivolous—often growing out of the mischiefous tricks of youth" were being "placed in rooms where old and hardened offenders are permitted to corrupt their morals." Lacking the money to build a new jail or to modify the existing structure, the committee could only urge that the jail visitors be "earnestly requested to take into consideration the present inconvenient arrangement of the Balt. City & County Jail & to employ all means in their power to remedy the same." Private citizens had been trying to raise the funds to build a separate institution for juvenile criminals since at least 1830, when the General Assembly had issued a corporate charter for a projected "house of refuge." Jesse Hunt and John H. B. Latrobe were members of its board.[35] But the fundraising effort stalled. The city council approved a resolution authorizing trustees of the almshouse to build the house of refuge on the poorhouse grounds, but the grant of authority was unaccompanied by any money, and construction of the juvenile institution would not begin until 1851, on a site southwest of the city.[36]

In the meantime, the city's urchins and delinquents found a source of diversion in Baltimore's volunteer fire companies. The firefighters had been lionized in the local press throughout the 1830s, but the volunteer companies were difficult to control. The rivalries among them often turned fires into occasions for street fights and riots. At first, the "fire riots" were blamed not on the firefighters themselves but on ruffians who collected at the scenes of fires, or delinquent gangs that attached themselves to fire companies—the Gumballs, the Screwbolts, the Cock Robins, and the Neversweats. But eventually it became impossible to overlook the riotous conduct of the firefighters themselves. Soon they needed no fires to bring them into combat with one another. A false alarm might be the signal for companies to charge out of their engine houses to do battle with one another, or it could be a ploy used by one company to lure another into an ambush. The fighting became so routine that the *Sun* concluded a report on the fires of one September evening with the observation that "there were the usual amount of riots among the firemen."[37]

LAW AND ORDER

A city council ordinance of 1841 had aimed to bring the volunteer firefighters under control. It empowered the mayor to cut off city appropriations to any company "the members of which shall . . . be engaged in fighting or rioting at fires." Mayor Brady clearly drew no satisfaction from the exercise of this authority. Firefighters were not just voters; they were organized voters. To the presidents of Baltimore's volunteer companies, Brady wrote that, though no groups "render more invaluable services to the Community," and "none more readily receive or deserve universal approbation," he (reluctantly) had to invoke "an obligation still stronger" than the one owed to firefighters—his responsibility for "the maintenance of peace and good order within the limits of the City." A few ruffians among the volunteers had "subjected the whole body of firemen to the charge of gross improper conduct." So serious had the problem become that "the Council felt the necessity of passing strong remedial Laws—and imposed upon the Mayor the duty of seeing them executed."[38]

In fact, the council's resolution had merely charged the fire companies to draw up their own rules of conduct and impose discipline upon the members who violated them. But self-regulation proved insufficient, and the problems posed by rowdy firefighters were still serious enough to demand the attention of Mayor James Law in 1844. As a fire company president of long standing, Law brought credibility to the task. To prevent false alarms from being used to bring out battling fire companies, he proposed the creation of a "General Central Alarm Bell, to which all other alarm bells shall be subordinate." It would be guarded, day and night, by a city watchman. No fire company enlisting minors would be eligible for municipal appropriations. No company could receive support from the city unless it empowered its president to strike from the rolls any member deemed to have acted "in a manner unbecoming a Fireman." Damage to any apparatus caused by an altercation between two or more fire companies would have to be repaired at a company's—not the city's—expense.[39]

The council approved most of Mayor Law's recommendations. It also empowered him to impose any additional regulations upon fire companies that, in his judgment, might help to prevent street fights among their members.[40] But the council stopped short of creating a central fire alarm guarded by a watchman. That would have required an expenditure of city funds. So would the mayor's recommendation for a general increase in the number of watchmen. The council did not explicitly reject this increase. The Joint Committee on Police suggested that an expansion of the night watch might help to reduce the frequency of "nocturnal robberies," and the council forwarded to the mayor two citizen petitions requesting additional watchmen, along with its disingenuous assurance that under "existing ordinances the Mayor has full power & authority to employ as many watchmen as he deems necessary."[41] The mayor, however, did not have the authority to pay as many officers as he deemed necessary.

Mayor Law nevertheless hired 14 additional watchmen. He instructed them to stay on the move, challenging everyone they met at an "unseasonable hour" of the night. In the first month that the new watchmen were on the job, he reported, there were no successful burglaries, and three burglary suspects were arrested. The mayor claimed that he had hired the additional watchmen on the expectation that the council would appropriate the funds to pay them. It did not. The second branch refused the appropriation. The mayor professed surprise and disappointment at the council's failure to provide funds for additional day and night police on Sundays, when the town's "unruly boys" were at their worst. Law concluded that he would be "compelled to withdraw those I have employed." Addressing the council, he declared that "upon you the joint responsibility must rest for whatever destruction and loss of property may ensue."[42]

A succession of one-term mayors in the 1840s tried to reassure the city council that the municipality had the means to secure the safety and health of Baltimore's residents. A succession of city councils refused to authorize expenditures for these purposes. Thaddeus Thomas, a nineteenth-century commentator on Baltimore's municipal government, suggested that this deadlock may have followed from the democratization of city government. After 1833, the mayor and the members of the city council's second branch were chosen by popular vote rather than an electoral college. Perhaps the direct election of these officials increased their wariness about expenditures that might raise their constituents' taxes. "A summary of some of the chief ordinances of this period," wrote Thomas, "will show the variability and the confusion of functions due to the lack of a true principle of administration."[43]

The city council's guiding principle, however, seems to have been a determination to avoid spending money. While rejecting increased expenditures, the council also attempted to reduce municipal outlays. Most of the duties assigned to the city's health commissioners were transferred to the street commissioners, who took over responsibility for removing "nuisances" and pools of standing water. The superintendents of streets and pumps lost their jobs and responsibilities to the bailiffs or "day police," and the council decided that the city could dispense with the deputy high constable. Subsequent modifications of these modifications produced the "variability and confusion of functions" mentioned by Thomas.[44]

The council pressed on in its mission to reduce city expenditures. It rejected a request from the volunteer fire companies for a special appropriation, not because the funds were unneeded, but because the council's Committee on Fire Companies did not "feel themselves justifiable in recommending any thing that will increase the many burdens now hanging over the corporation." A newly created Committee on Retrenchment recommended an across-the-board 20 percent reduction in municipal salaries, though the council rejected it.[45] The council did increase disability pay for members of the night watch injured in the course of duty; they could receive full pay (up from half pay) for as much as two months off the job. But the city's legislators ignored the watchmen's petition for an increase in pay while they were on the job.[46]

The council also turned its back on citizen demands for more public schools. In 1845, northwest Baltimoreans asked for construction of a school in their part of the city and even offered to provide the lot on which to build it. At the same time, northeast Baltimoreans complained that they had no school. Enrollment in the existing public schools had grown to almost 3,500, an increase of more than 25 percent over the preceding year. In addition to its 17 primary schools (nine for boys and eight for girls), there were also three high schools. A Central High School for males had been in operation for more than five years, and the school commissioners had recently added Eastern and Western Female High Schools. The young women needed two facilities rather than one to reduce the distance to their schools because "females are more delicate than males, and cannot attend school at a remote distance, especially in inclement weather." Faced with overcrowding at some of its existing schools and the demands for more schools, the commissioners declared that they deeply felt "the importance of having Schools established in all sections of our beloved city," but they could not meet the need within their existing appropriation.[47]

The school commissioners backed the neighborhood requests with pleas of their own. A special committee of the city council was appointed to respond to them. Its report conceded that "it would be desirable (if it were at the disposal of the Board) to erect new schools" for the two neighborhoods requesting them. It suggested, however, that other sections of the city might be just as needful as these. But the committee did not make any systematic survey of the need for new schools—"for these reasons: After some reflection, they have concluded it would be impolitic & inexpedient to ask from the Council, for this year, a further appropriation . . . for the purposes of education." The committee members were apparently unmoved by the school commissioners' prediction that those deprived of schooling would "idle their time away in our public streets, many of them contracting those seeds of vice & immorality which the mind is so susceptible of receiving at that tender age." In time, some of these unschooled children would no doubt join the legions of "unruly boys" and young men who posed a nightly threat to public order. But the commissioners would have to make do with the revenue generated by the existing school tax of 5 cents for every $100.00 of assessed valuation. The council's committee calculated that the revenues already available, together with railroad bonds held by the school commissioners, would finance the creation of one additional primary school for girls.[48]

Baltimore faced enormous debt. Signs of this daunting burden were plainly evident in the city's tax rates. Though it collected only 5 cents per $100.00 for schools in 1845, the city levied a tax of 31 cents to cover interest on debt incurred to finance internal improvements. At more than $360,000, the interest payment was the single largest item in the municipal budget. Total expenditures for the schools amounted to only a bit over $45,000; for "watching and lighting" the city, $47,000. Another 25 cents per $100.00 of assessed valuation was needed to cover the city's share of state debt, most of it for internal improvements.[49] And there was more to come. The B&O still had to make the push from Cumberland to the Ohio River. The Baltimore and Susquehanna line had yet to pay a dividend and was struggling to find a profitable set of linkages with the railroads, rivers, and canals of Pennsylvania. The city's $380,000 stake in the Susquehanna Tidewater Canal had already been written off. Mayor Law doubted whether "the city will ever receive any benefit from her investment in this work, or at least, the period will be very remote."[50]

Baltimore made large and questionable investments in its future prosperity at the expense of its current capacity to maintain public order, public health, and public education. Somewhere beyond this regime of frugality, the city's officials envisioned a fanciful future in which Baltimore's willingness to forego dividends would enable the B&O to reach the Ohio River without requiring the municipality to incur additional debt, and would "remunerate the City for a temporary surrender of interest, double her capital, and ultimately reduce her taxes, and incalculably augment her trade, and the value of every description of her property."[51]

Until that golden age arrived, however, the city would continue to scrimp on essential expenditures to underwrite its investments in long-term prosperity. In 1848, for example, the mayor and the Committee of Visitors of the city-county jail concurred in the judgment that the existing structure was "wholly inadequate." They recommended the construction of a new jail, or at least significant additions to the existing building. Not only were juvenile offenders being held with adult criminals, but witnesses detained for pending trials were confined with convicted felons. The city council's jail committee dismissed these complaints "owing to the distressed condition of the City treasury" and recommended that no jail improvements should be undertaken until the state legislature had compelled Baltimore County to pay its share of the costs.[52] In the meantime, the city would suffer grievous costs of its own.

BREAKING POINT

In November 1850, shortly after taking office, Mayor John H. T. Jerome called an extraordinary session of the Baltimore City Council to take action against the "fearful increase of crime, disorder, and bloodshed during the past few weeks." Jerome asked the council's support in "devising and adopting . . . such measures and means as will effectually restore and permanently maintain the public peace, and give to all good citizens assured protection for their *persons* and *lives* from the murderous assaults and lawless depredations of that ruthless band of Ruffians, Rowdies, and midnight assassins, who have long infested the city, filling it with terror and lamentation."[53]

Jerome cannot have taken the council's cooperation for granted. He was a Whig, and the council majority was now Democratic. Until his election as mayor, he had not even been a prominent Whig. Orphaned at the age of 5 years and raised by grandparents, he had "been compelled of necessity," he said, "to struggle on and build up for myself, without any hereditary means or money, a character and a position in life that I am grateful to know commands the respect and confidence of the community."[54]

He was a grocer who operated from a stand at Lexington and Paca Streets, just outside the Lexington Market. He did not cater to the city's elite. Jerome advertised his location as "the OLD CHEAP CORNER," where patrons got discounts for paying in cash. Until his election as mayor, his political career had been dismal. A year before his victory in the mayoral election, he had sought the Whig nomination for a seat in the house of delegates. The Whig convention gave him just six votes and last place among its contenders for the legislature. Jerome had achieved his only previous electoral victories as a member of the Independent Order of Odd Fellows, a fraternal organization founded in Baltimore in 1819. In 1850, he was voted grand master of the organization's Maryland chapter; after several years, as president of the Odd Fellows' temperance organization—the Crystal Fount Society. Jerome acknowledged that he was a "humble and obscure person . . . suddenly brought before the people for their suffrages." His speech accepting the Whig nomination for mayor was a kind of autobiography by which he introduced himself to an electorate that knew him only from the advertisements for his grocery stand.[55]

Only a week before the mayoral election, Baltimore had given a substantial majority to the Democratic candidate for governor. But the Democrats had fallen to fighting with one another over the party's choice of a mayoral candidate at its August convention, where J. Mabury Turner, an East Baltimore butcher, won a majority of the votes. The partisans of John Watkins, a West Baltimore bricklayer, refused to accept their party's choice and marched out of the convention to contest the election as "Reubenites," choosing to name themselves, for obscure reasons, after one of the 10 lost tribes of Israel. Their political inclinations were only slightly less obscure. Reubenite street processions in the weeks preceding the election denounced the Democratic candidate Mabury Turner, a member of the Hibernian Society, as a fawning friend of Irish and German immigrants. Their organizational base seems to have been the New Market Fire Company, of which Watkins was a member.[56]

The conflict between the Reubenites and the regular Democrats apparently accounted for much of the violence that occurred during the 1850 municipal election. In the tavern that served as the Eleventh Ward's polling place, Reubenites were suspected as the attackers who had beaten and shot Francis Lafferty. Another man was struck on the head with a club and severely injured. A police officer trying to keep order was knocked to the floor "having been overpowered by superior numbers." In the tough Ninth Ward on the waterfront, Washington Goodrich, who had a long record as a brawler, attacked Patrick Donegan. "Goodrich adopted his usual mode of fighting," according to the *Sun*, "by seizing Donegan's finger with his teeth, and biting it almost in twain." At the polling place in the Fourth Ward, just east of the Ninth, Officer Gorton "labored hard to preserve the peace" and "received a severe wound near the eye" for his efforts. The Reubenites deserted their party and threw their votes to the Whigs, giving Whig candidate John Jerome 52 percent of the 20,000 votes cast.[57]

It was hardly a popular mandate, yet Jerome advanced a more sweeping program for maintaining public order than any of his predecessors and convinced the council to make its most substantial additions so far to the city's embryonic police force. Two murders had abruptly focused the city's anxiety on its long slide toward violence. The first occurred just days after Jerome's election. Edmund Mitchell, president of the Vigilant Fire Company since 1846, had been shot and killed as he was about to enter a "public house" to celebrate Jerome's victory. The mayor, the governor, and the Vigilant Company all offered rewards for anyone who would identify his killer. Several suspects were arrested, but no one was ever indicted for the crime. The *Sun* reported that at least 1,000 people marched in Mitchell's funeral procession, including Mayor Elijah Stansbury, who was flanked by mayor-elect Jerome and defeated mayoral candidate Turner. Clergy of three different denominations—Presbyterian, Methodist, and Baptist—officiated in the obsequies.[58]

Fire company presidents were local celebrities in mid-nineteenth-century Baltimore, and Mitchell's murder may have sensitized Baltimoreans to subsequent incidents of disorder and violent death. Another homicide, less than a month after Mitchell's killing, again captured the public's attention. The victim was James Michael, a young man who happened to be standing on a corner outside the hall where the New Market volunteer fire company was holding its annual ball. Men with muskets were stationed outside the door to ensure the safety of those who attended. There were apprehensions that the Stingers, a local gang hostile to the New Market Company, would launch an attack on the organization's annual celebration. The watchmen on duty in the area later testified that many of the men gathered in the vicinity of the dance hall were carrying guns, but the officers apparently made no attempts to disarm them. The watchmen themselves carried no weapons save their "spontoons" (the Baltimore term for an officer's nightstick, later modified as "espantoon" and "battoon"). One watchman stood by as a group of about 15 armed men arrived at an intersection near the ballroom. One of them fired a shot at a group gathered on a corner, and several more then fired as well. James Michael fell and soon died. The *Sun* condemned the "outrageous conduct of a gang of desperadoes, whose lawlessness . . . plunged an amiable young man into a premature grave."[59]

The murders of Mitchell and Michael were the only specific crimes that Mayor Jerome mentioned in his message to the special session of the city council, though he might have cited many others committed during the recent election. He focused instead on the more general environment in which the killings had occurred, one in which multitudes of "men and even boys five years of age and upwards are in the constant habit of carrying deadly weapons concealed about their persons, and used by them with heartless indifference." There was also "the alarming extent and increase of the intemperate use of intoxicating liquors," and Jerome complained further that the courts were too lenient in imposing penalties on convicted criminals. But the mayor was peculiarly preoccupied with the effect of poor street lighting. Jerome insisted that a "burning lamp throwing a strong, clear light in front of any dwelling, store or shop, during the night, is a better and more certain protection against midnight marauders and felons than the presence and patrolling of the most vigilant watchman."[60]

The watchmen themselves drew Jerome's attention partly because they were responsible for cleaning and maintaining the streetlamps, tasks that had to be performed in daylight when the lights had been extinguished. Jerome recommended that a team of lamplighters should be hired to relieve the patrolmen of this duty, which in any case, according to the mayor, the watchmen performed badly. In fact, the mayor was no more satisfied with the watchmen's effectiveness as patrolmen than as lamp tenders. He charged that some of them rarely left their watch boxes and slept while they were supposed to be patrolling. He went further. He dismissed several watchmen for neglecting their duties or for sheer incompetence. Previous mayors had consistently praised the "efficiency" of the watchmen.[61] To acknowledge that they were anything less might have undercut mayoral requests for hiring more of them.

Jerome, however, combined his plea for more watchmen with a plan for the comprehensive reorganization of the arrangements for policing Baltimore. He accompanied his request for 100 new officers with a curious scheme in which only half the force would patrol the streets in the manner of the watchmen. The other half were to be plainclothesmen; the officer might "stand at a corner or lurk in an alley or by-place, or . . . secrete himself from observation in some ambush or covert for whole nights and days in succession for the purpose of detecting and arresting criminals and violators of the law." Jerome also pledged to eliminate the watch boxes where officers could sleep or avoid unpleasant weather.[62]

The city council did not grant Jerome everything that he wanted. But it authorized him to add 40 men to the night watch. The new officers were to be drawn from the bailiffs who patrolled the streets as part-time watchmen on Sundays, when rowdies and ruffians had the leisure to make trouble. The council also passed an ordinance authorizing the mayor to appoint 34 additional bailiffs. Another resolution instructed the committee on police and jail to prepare a plan "for the complete reorganization of the police and watch force of the city."[63]

The reorganization plan never materialized, but Jerome was apparently satisfied. He congratulated the council on its "judicious action" in expanding the city's police force. The mayor had assigned the officers to two shifts. One reported at sunrise; the other, at 9 p.m. The high constable was effectively the city's police chief, though he also commanded one of the four police districts into which Jerome divided the city. In 1852, the mayor organized the "boat police" to patrol the harbor, watching out for thefts from docks and vessels.[64]

Baltimore's government was still deep in debt and would sink deeper still.[65] During 1851, the city ran a deficit of almost $75,000. But it was no longer preoccupied with cheese-paring economies. Mayor Jerome had initiated an era of municipal activism in which the council was sometimes a willing partner. It authorized Jerome to negotiate a new contract with the Baltimore Gas Light Company that would help him realize his plan to reduce crime by illuminating the city. At the mayor's suggestion, the council approved a plan to accumulate the sum of $50,000 for building a new jail or improving the old one. Jerome also noted the longstanding insufficiency of the local water supply and recommended that the city should either buy out the Baltimore Water Company or build a waterworks of its own. The council did not immediately respond to this proposal, but the municipality would take over the Water Company a year after Jerome left office. His proposal that the city should purchase land for public parks would also be carried out by a later administration, but Jerome managed to secure the top of Federal Hill for the city and provided for grassy open spaces in several city squares.[66]

The city no longer lived for the far-off day when the B&O would reach the "western waters" and bring wealth to Baltimore. The railroad had announced that it would reach Wheeling on the Ohio River within the next year, and the wealth of the West was expected to flow into Baltimore. The city could address its current deficiencies and hardships because it had finally begun to live in the present.

Chapter 16

PIGS AND POLITICIANS

I N 1851, BALTIMORE CITY became fully independent of Baltimore
County. Its new status was, in part, the result of a state constitutional convention summoned to replace the constitution under which
Maryland had labored since 1776. Southern Maryland and the Eastern
Shore—"Old Maryland"—clung desperately to their disproportionate
representation under the state's old constitution. The adjustments to
that constitution in 1836 had quieted the demand for reform, but only
temporarily.[1] The underrepresentation of Baltimore and the counties
of Central and Western Maryland had hardly been erased, and the in-
equities grew more pronounced as their populations continued to expand during the 1840s. State taxes aggravated the grievances of both
the underrepresented and overrepresented constituencies. The state's
$16 million debt, incurred largely for internal improvements, weighed
heavily on its citizens and set off tax protests that sometimes edged into
violence.[2] Many favored constitutional reforms that would restrict the
legislature's authority to issue bonds and run up deficits. By the time
of the state's constitutional convention of 1850, a sea change in party
politics was further unsettling Maryland. In Baltimore, the Democrats
remained divided between regulars and Reubenites. Now the Whigs
were on the rocks.

In national politics, the Whigs were undone not just by the epochal
issue of slavery but by the prosaic politics of patronage. Whig president Zachary Taylor could nominate as many Whig officeholders as he
liked, but they had to be confirmed by the Senate's Democratic majority.
To win approval for the Whig nominees, therefore, Whig members of
Congress had to win the support of Democratic senators. The need for
cross-party cooperation on patronage compounded intraparty animosities on the issue of slavery that tended to make northern and southern
Whigs the enemies of one another and the allies of northern or southern
Democrats.[3]

Although the constitutional controversy in Maryland seemed a matter of adjusting representation to reflect population, it had as much to

do with slavery as with apportionment. Maryland's slaves were concentrated in the southern part of the state and on the Eastern Shore—both Whig strongholds. In Central and Western Maryland, where the state's population was increasingly concentrated, free black people were becoming more numerous and slaves less so. The defenders of slave property felt threatened, in particular, by Baltimore. The city was by no means a nest of abolitionists, but its investment capital and economic interests did not ride on the preservation of slavery, and it did not seem a trustworthy defender of the institution. A Baltimore delegate to the constitutional convention of 1850 tried to calm the anxieties of the state's slave owners by introducing a provision that would forbid the legislature from ordering any changes in the relationship between master and slave. The constitutional guarantee was not good enough for the slave owners of Southern Maryland. Constitutions could change.[4]

The convention itself was a lesson in the fragility of constitutions. The constitution of 1776 did not provide for the calling of constitutional conventions. It specified that the General Assembly could approve amendments to the state constitution by majority vote at two consecutive sessions of the legislature. Though the procedure was alleged to have produced a "shapeless mass of unintelligible and contradictory provisions," it was the only one explicitly sanctioned by law. But advocates of a convention argued that their preferred procedure—popular referendum—was not explicitly prohibited by law and that the state's Declaration of Rights gave Maryland's people the power to change their government. The most compelling argument in favor of calling a constitutional convention may have been the one voiced by Maryland's governor in his annual address of 1850. If the legislature ignored the demands for constitutional reform reverberating from the most populous sections of the state, "the sanction of the legislature would not much longer be invoked."[5]

Baltimore gained little from the constitution approved in 1851. It provided that seats in the house of delegates were to be apportioned according to population—but not for Baltimore. No matter how large its population, the city's delegation in the house could not exceed the most populous county's representation by more than four delegates. This meant that the city would gain five seats in the house, giving Baltimore only half of the representation it would have been entitled to on the basis of population. One-fourth of Maryland's people lived in Baltimore, but the city would hold only one-eighth of the seats in the house.[6]

Separation of the city from Baltimore County was first proposed by the General Assembly in 1850 as a concession to the county, which had become a decidedly junior partner in the institutions it still shared with the city—the courthouse, the jail, and the almshouse. The legislature authorized residents of the county to elect a commission to resolve such issues as the location of the new county seat. The commission, however, had been unable to reach agreement on anything—even the county's separation from the city. The resolution of this question then passed to the state constitutional convention, which, in the meantime, had convened in Annapolis. The delegates, as part of a larger scheme to reduce the cost and complexity of the state's judiciary, redesigned the state's judicial districts so as to place the city and county courts in separate jurisdictions, and thus eliminated any reason for the city and county to share a courthouse and a jail. In 1853, the General Assembly advanced the separation by authorizing the voters of Baltimore County to decide on the location of the new county seat and the construction of buildings to house its criminals, paupers, and judges. In Baltimore, where each jail cell housed 12 to 14 prisoners, the city had begun to accumulate funds for a new jail in 1851, but disputes about its location delayed construction until 1856.[7]

In principle, at least, the city's separation from Baltimore County endowed it with a distinctive status. Since it no longer lay within the jurisdiction of any county, Baltimore became a municipality that also bore the responsibilities of a county. Formally, the city had achieved a greater degree of functional autonomy than most of the towns that sprouted up as the nation's population moved west, where governing was usually conducted by a plurality of overlapping public institutions—municipal, county, and special district governments.[8] Baltimore's institutional arrangements concentrated public business under the authority of a single government and seemed to lead to greater-than-average political integration. In practice, the city still struggled to pull itself together. The underrepresentation of Baltimore in the General Assembly facilitated legislative interference in the city's business. State lawmakers would eventually extract major responsibilities of urban government from the city and place them under the jurisdiction of the state.

SWINE

Baltimore's new political autonomy and increased representation in the state legislature seemed fitting counterparts for Mayor John H. T. Jerome's municipal activism, but old concerns remained. The town's enduring preoccupation with "swine going at large" continued. In 1851, a petition reached the Baltimore City Council requesting that hogs be prohibited from wandering the streets. It was referred to the Committee on Health, which was reluctant to adopt any such restrictions because of the hogs' supposed contribution to public sanitation "under the present imperfect operation of our garbage law system." The committee confessed that it was unable to agree whether wandering swine should be treated as public servants or public nuisances. Given "such a contrariety of opinion" among its members, there was "no hope of their being able to frame any resolution differing materially from the present ordinances." The committee asked to be "discharged from further consideration of the subject," and it was.

A year later, however, a majority of the city council arrived at a sterner position on swine. It sent the mayor a proposed ordinance prohibiting Baltimoreans from keeping hogs in "any sty or yard, or elsewhere on their premises." The bill also provided that "no hog will be suffered to run at large" in the city. Those portions of the "precincts" still exempt from direct taxation would be exempt from the ordinance.[9] Mayor Jerome applauded the council's determination to keep swine out of the "streets, lanes, and alleys" of the city. But he vetoed the bill because, he claimed, it would have had exactly the opposite of its intended effect. If city residents could no longer keep hogs on their own premises, was "it not reasonable to infer that the streets, lanes, and alleys of the city must necessarily be made *hog pens at large*?"

Of course, the law proposed by the council also made it illegal for pigs to roam the streets, but the exemption for hogs from areas not subject to direct taxation complicated enforcement of this prohibition. Since these pigs were exempt from regulation, they would be free to wander the city's streets, lanes, and alleys, "and as a necessary consequence," the mayor argued, "hogs owned by parties within direct taxation will enjoy the same privileges." There was no way for the agents of law enforcement to distinguish between taxable and nontaxable pigs. The mayor also took issue with the bill's blanket exemption for "butchers, packers, or drovers." The members of this privileged class could keep hundreds of hogs in pens or let them run free.[10]

The council made a new attempt at a hog law. It approved an ordinance making it illegal to bring any hogs into the city except for sale or slaughter, and those entering would have to depart, in one way or the other, within 10 days. Pig owners and their pigs would be subject to the law even if residents of districts exempt from direct taxation.[11]

Mayor Jerome was satisfied with the new bill. Many Baltimoreans were not. As soon as the council convened for its next session at the start of 1853, it received petitions, some signed by hundreds of citizens, taking issue with the hog law. Almost 120 residents of the Eighteenth Ward complained that, in the absence of swine to consume garbage, refuse was collecting in the streets "creating a nausea which in our opinion will contribute much to the unhealthfulness of the city. And we believe there can be no better plan desired to dispose of such Offal and Slops than to keep Swine to consume it."[12] Another petition asserted that the hog law was "very oppressive upon the poor, who, but for the privilege of keeping Hogs, would be deprived of putting up their pork in the fall." The petition acknowledged "the argument of some" that the full cost of raising a hog might be greater than buying an annual supply of pork each fall. But Baltimore's poor, "when their wages is but seventy-five cents a day," could save "twenty-five or fifty cents out of their stinty wage per week to buy feed for their Hogs, when they cannot raise forty or fifty dollars on one time to buy their pork in the fall." Allowing pigs to forage in the streets, of course, saved their owners the burden of buying feed out of their "stinty" wages. The petition closed with the familiar claim that roaming swine were "a great means of keeping streets or more especially alleys clean." It asked that the law be repealed.[13]

The public reaction to the hog law clearly shook the members of the city council. On being referred one the first petitions, the Committee on Health recommended repeal of the previous year's ordinance and adoption of a substitute that would transfer the unpopular work of hog regulation from the city council to the mayor. Residents could keep swine in pens or let them run at large if they obtained permits from the mayor. In the council's second branch, the bill was rejected. Days later, a member of the first branch introduced a bill that would allow pigs the freedom of the city between the beginning of May and the end of October, and hog proprietors could confine their pigs during the rest of the year in "stye or yard," but if "the filth and stench thereof" should be "offensive to, or annoyed any neighbor or person," a notification would come from the Department of Health, followed by a daily fine until the filth and stench were no longer cause for complaint. This bill was tabled.

A third proposal combined features of the two others. It required pig permits from the mayor and prohibited stench and filth offensive to neighbors. It too was tabled.[14]

As the petitions continued to come in, members of the council continued to backpedal. One bill would return to the status quo ante: hogs could wander at will from the end of May to the beginning of October, and citizens could keep them penned in—without filth or stench—for the rest of the year. Another proposal allowed residents to keep hogs that were inoffensive to neighbors, but wandering hogs were to be apprehended by police officers and delivered to the almshouse for the sustenance of its inmates. To encourage the officers to tangle with wayward swine, the mayor was directed to pay them 50 cents per pig. A variant included the customary warm-weather privileges for swine in the streets, with the injunction against stench and filth in sties or pens, but directed that roaming *"boar* hogs," immense creatures with tusks, would be "forfeited to the city." It did not indicate who was to apprehend the boars or mention any special compensation for this service. In the second branch, this measure was approved after being read and tabled three times and amended to increase the fine for "stench and filth" from one to five dollars. It won approval in the first branch after being read and tabled twice, but a week after its passage, the first branch moved to reconsider the ordinance, and tabled it again.[15]

The *Baltimore Sun* expressed contempt for these proposals to amend or repeal the hog law, especially when their sponsors on the council claimed that wandering swine were essential to public sanitation. The *Sun* argued otherwise. When public-sanitation pigs were allowed to patrol the city, they only encouraged "total disregard of the ordinance prohibiting the deposit of garbage and offal in the streets!" Reliance on scavenging hogs made humans sloppy. The hog ordinance, claimed the *Sun*, had been operating effectively, and the experience of swine-free streets demonstrated that the city's health and cleanliness had not suffered.[16] There was no need for further discussion.

But it went on. The city council continued to consider modification of the hog law for at least two more years. Judging by the frequency with which the subject came up, it must have been one of the members' principal concerns. Many of the proposals made exceptions to the prohibition against keeping penned hogs in Baltimore. Others attempted to upend the ordinance as a whole. In 1854, the city council's first branch repealed the hog law, but there is no record that the second branch went along. In at least two other instances, both branches concurred in their efforts to roll back the ordinance, but were blocked by mayoral vetoes.[17]

Other cities had pig problems of their own. In fact, the use of street swine as agents of public sanitation (and winter sustenance for the poor) was common in American towns. European visitors regarded the wandering hogs as a distinctive and colorful feature of American urban life in the mid-nineteenth century—even charming. A Norwegian traveler of 1847 reported that he had not "found any city or town where I have not seen these lovable animals wandering about peacefully in huge herds." But for many Americans, street pigs ceased to be serviceable or lovable, and the utilitarian case for granting them the freedom of the streets lost its persuasiveness. Efforts to eliminate the pigs were sometimes vigorous and uncompromising. In New York, early efforts to round up street pigs persisted in the face of "hog riots" by poor residents who relied on the animals to feed their families. And when swine were suspected as the source of a cholera epidemic in 1849, the city's police, often in the face of violent resistance from hog owners, "flushed five to six thousand pigs out of cellars and garrets and drove an estimated twenty thousand swine north to the upper wards." Subsequent pig round-ups purged lower Manhattan of swine and banished the animals to the semirural regions north of 86th Street.[18]

PIG TALES OF TWO CITIES

By comparison with New York, Baltimore's political authorities seemed hesitant and indecisive. The politics of pigs revealed not just official diffidence concerning hogs but the municipality's limited capacity to control its streets and deal with the conflicting interests of lower-class hog proprietors and more prosperous Baltimoreans averse to sharing the streets with swine. New York handled these matters more resolutely. The contrast reflects, once again, the distinctive circumstances that inhibited Baltimore's political development. The two cities had emerged and evolved in utterly different political environments. New York City was a functioning polity before New York State came into existence. In fact, the city was the seat of state government until the capital moved to Albany in 1797, and the Albany authorities continued to respect the city's municipal autonomy for some years thereafter.[19] Baltimore, on the other hand, had operated under the shadow of the political authorities in Annapolis since its founding. State officials restricted the city's legal powers and interfered in its internal operations. The state legislature, for example, had created the areas "not subject to direct taxation" that complicated Baltimore's regulation of street swine.

The Baltimore City Council's years of dithering about the hog law in the face of public protests suggest an unusual diffidence on the part of public authorities about exercising their authority over the voters who elected them. Of course, New York's Democratic politicians also had to cater to their voters, and New York's municipal institutions were hardly models of efficiency. Their disjointedness meant that the city was governed by a plurality of governments that often acted independently of one another.[20] But New York had Tammany Hall, and behind Tammany was a wealth of patronage, all of which served to organize and discipline the municipal rank and file while imposing some measure of order on the fractious fragments of city government.

Baltimore's party organizations were ephemeral creatures that came to life—often disjointedly—only during election campaigns. But, as Gary Browne observes, parties "played a negligible role compared to ward interests in the City Council voting on important issues."[21]

Baltimoreans were accustomed to the limited capacities of their city government. They compensated for its deficiencies through civic institutions such as the Mechanical Company and periodic assemblies outside the courthouse or at the Merchants' Exchange. But along with the political limitations imposed on Baltimore by the state legislature and aggravated by evanescent party organizations, there were crippling handicaps acquired in the city's struggle to maintain its prosperity. Baltimore financed its investments in railroads and canals by going deep into debt. By 1853, the city had issued more than $5.5 million in interest-bearing municipal "stock." It had made itself liable for another $2 million as guarantor of loans taken out by railroads, and it had incurred more than half a million dollars in "floating debt" to pay for such amenities as Mayor Jerome's public square atop Federal Hill and to finance the construction of a new jail.[22] The resulting tax burden became sharply controversial within the city council's Committee on Ways and Means. To avoid increasing the levy to cover quarterly interest payments, a minority of the committee proposed selling some of the city's B&O stock to pay the interest on money the city had borrowed to buy the stock in the first place. Failing that, the city would have to borrow more money at interest to pay the interest on money already borrowed. But a majority of the committee and the council held fast to the debt, the stock, and the hope that both would soon carry Baltimore to a new golden age.[23]

Like Baltimore and Maryland, New York had gone into debt to finance internal improvements designed to stimulate economic growth, though the State of New York, rather than the city, seems to have been the principal borrower for such projects as the Erie Canal. Populous New York City, of course, would have to finance the lion's share of state debt. But Baltimore residents must have borne a burden more crushing than New Yorkers carried. By the early 1840s, Maryland's debt exceeded $15 million. Though New York State's, at almost $22 million, was higher, the per capita burden for New Yorkers was just a little more than one-fourth of what Marylanders had to carry. At more than $32 for each resident, Maryland's per capita state debt was the third highest in the country—so high that the state eventually defaulted.[24] Baltimoreans had the added interest payments made by the city to finance the railroads and canals that were to restore local prosperity. The city's property tax rate was higher than in most of the nation's big cities—10 times higher than in New York.[25]

There was one more critical difference between New York's and Baltimore's investments in internal improvements: New York's investments generally paid off. Baltimore's were not so productive. The city's hopes began to fade even before the B&O had made its fateful rendezvous with the Ohio River. A delegate to the state constitutional convention in 1850 invited his fellow representatives to look back to the days of high optimism concerning internal improvements when "every man dreamed he was about to reach a new El Dorado. Taxation was to exist no longer—public debt was to become an obsolete idea."[26] But even after discarding these delusions, Baltimoreans may have been shaken by the disappointments that lay ahead. When the B&O finally reached the "western waters" in 1853, Baltimore's first return on its investment was an industrial recession. Once the railroad reached its destination, its demand for the locomotives, rolling stock, rails, and other equipment manufactured in Baltimore suddenly dropped. Supplying the B&O with iron rails, in fact, probably never created as much business as some Baltimoreans had hoped. The company imported most of its rails from Britain. Much of the repair work needed for the completed railroad would be diverted from Baltimore to new shops at Martinsburg and Wheeling.[27]

While it waited for its train to come in, Baltimore had taken its dividends from the B&O not in cash but in more B&O stock. Once the railroad reached the Ohio River, the city council apparently expected that the city would receive cash dividends that could be used to meet the enormous interest payments and retire the debt incurred for internal improvements. In 1854, some members of the council charged that the railroad had made "incorrect" statements in its annual report. The city's representatives on the railroad's board of directors were asked to ascertain "what revenue was earned by said company during their last fiscal year w[h]ich was applicable to the purposes of a dividend and if such dividend was earned why it was not paid to the city."[28] The council had already considered selling the "dividend stock" it had received and using the proceeds to cover its interest payments, but only if it received at least $70 per share. (Almost 25 years earlier, the city had paid $100 a share for the B&O stock.) The city apparently failed to get $70. Once again, it borrowed money to pay interest on money already borrowed.[29]

The B&O was profitable, though burdened by debt incurred for its unexpectedly heavy construction costs, and would eventually pay its dividends in cash. But after reaching the Ohio River in 1853, the company requested and received yet another loan from Baltimore—this one for $5 million—to meet its most pressing debts and to pay for needed improvements, including double-tracking the line from Cumberland to Wheeling so that it could run trains in both directions at the same time. Baltimore financed this loan, like others, by floating a loan of its own.[30] B&O revenues consistently exceeded operating expenses, and it would flourish during and after the Civil War, but its profits piled up under the shadow of a looming, long-term liability that would eventually lead to suspension of dividend payments and, before the century was over, bankruptcy.

Baltimore had also begun to accumulate new expenses and debts in anticipation of the urban prosperity that the B&O was supposed to yield. The new spirit of municipal enterprise that germinated under Mayor Jerome increased city expenditures and borrowing. There was the "floating debt" incurred to pay for municipal improvements proposed by the mayor. Acting on Jerome's concern about the lighting of city streets, the city now had bigger gas bills. After decades of grumbling about the inadequate water supply, the city bought the Baltimore Water Company in 1854 and, in the process, added another $1.35 million of municipal debt.[31]

The expansion of Baltimore's police force initiated by Jerome continued, but slowly and unevenly. In 1853, when the council approved an ordinance "to provide for the City of Baltimore an efficient Police system," Jerome's successor, Mayor John Smith Hollins, vetoed the measure, claiming that it would be "less efficient and much more costly than the present watch and police system."[32]

By 1855, the city employed about 135 officers to protect a population approaching 200,000, and the conditions of police work had apparently changed. In 1852, a council resolution had asked the Committee on Police and Jail to consider the advisability of arming members of the day police and night watch with revolvers. The committee concluded that the police needed guns. Its members were "compelled to admit that the spirit of riot & disorder prevails in our city at the present time, to an extent heretofore unknown & that it is constantly on the increase, & unless met by the strong arm of the law, no one will be safe either in person or property." The committee asserted "that one means of meeting those who are disposed to riot & disorder is to place the city officers in a position that they may fearlessly meet all who are engaged in any riot & the fact of an officer being armed will in most cases materially aid them in the discharge of their duty without resort to the use of the weapons carried by them." The committee acknowledged that there might be "some danger in thus arming the police," but held the hope that by hiring officers of "good moral character," there would be no danger in giving them guns. The first branch of the council, it seems, was unconvinced; it rejected the committee's recommendation,[33] and for several more years, Baltimore's peace officers continued to walk their rounds armed only with their wooden espantoons. But the city they patrolled was increasingly troubled by conflicts reflecting ethnic, racial, and political inequalities.

Chapter 17
KNOW-NOTHINGS

N 1854, BALTIMOREANS BROKE OUT of the two-party system to elect a Know-Nothing government. Mayor Samuel Hinks and a majority of the city council belonged to secret lodges of the American Party. Hinks won even though he had never held public office, announced his candidacy only two weeks before the election, and did almost no public campaigning. Like his party, his election was an underground affair. Even the convention that nominated him was held in secret, and his victory shocked the Democrats for whom Baltimore had been a rare and reliable stronghold in a state that usually went for Whig presidential candidates. Know-Nothings later swept the state elections, and in 1856, the party elected four of the state's six congressmen. Maryland was the only state to give its electoral votes to Know-Nothing presidential candidate Millard Fillmore. He won a larger percentage of votes in Baltimore than in any of the counties. By 1858, the city was "a political barony controlled by the Know-Nothings."[1]

In Baltimore, the ground had been prepared for the Know-Nothings by a short-lived American Republican Party, whose members declared their animosity toward foreigners in general. Its convention in 1845 nominated candidates for local and state offices, but won few converts and went underground.[2]

The inciting spark for the reemergence of nativist sentiment, now intensified by anti-Catholic hostility, was a piece of legislation introduced in the Maryland General Assembly in 1852. The bill was sponsored by Baltimore Democrat Martin Kerney, a prolific author of school textbooks, who chaired the house of delegates' Education Committee. Its most incendiary provision came near the end of the 70-page bill. It provided that "whenever any white child or children . . . shall be taught gratuitously or at the same rates as the pupils in the Public Schools, in any Orphan Asylum, School, or Academy . . . it shall be the duty of the School Commissioners of the City of Baltimore and the Trustees of the School Districts of the several counties to pay . . . such sum for the education of each child taught."[3] The bill was an ancestor of today's school voucher proposals. And it was explosively controversial because it would have authorized the payment of public funds to parochial schools. The debate in the legislature spread to the Baltimore City Council when the local archbishop petitioned its members to grant a portion of the school budget to Roman Catholic schools. The response inside the council and out was vituperative and only intensified when Maryland Catholics asked that their Douay Bible be substituted for the King James version in the public schools.[4]

Other states went Know-Nothing too. By the mid-1850s, the American Party had elected nine governors, 70 members of the US House of Representatives, and majorities in 12 state legislatures. In the South, the biggest cities—Baltimore, New Orleans, and St. Louis—were all centers of Know-Nothing strength.[5] The sudden eruption of the new party was most obviously a reaction to foreign immigration. During the 1850s, nearly 100,000 foreigners entered Baltimore. Many of them stayed only long enough to find transportation further inland, but by 1860, one in four of the city's 212,000 residents had been born in Europe. Yet it was the character as well as the volume of immigration that may have been decisive for igniting nativist animosities. Through the 1840s, most of the foreigners arriving were Germans, but at the end of the decade, Irish immigration rose abruptly as a result of the potato famine. Most came from rural Ireland; they lacked literacy and the skills suited to an urban economy. To native-born Protestants, the immigrants' supposed obedience to the Roman pope made them a threat to the autonomy and democracy of the United States.[6]

Even the Germans did not escape the nativist attack. Many of them had arrived in Baltimore after the failure of the European revolutions of 1848, and they expected to return to Germany as soon as political conditions allowed. They resolutely resisted Americanization, and some ex-revolutionaries advanced proposals so radical that they outraged many Americans.[7]

Apart from the rancorous nativism that energized them, the Know-Nothings also capitalized on voters' estrangement from the old parties. Like many other Americans, Baltimoreans disliked the contention generated by warring Whigs and Democrats. John Pendleton Kennedy longed for the deference and civility of political life in a younger, smaller Baltimore. The party organizations formed in the 1830s, he thought, had mobilized "the profoundly ignorant, the vicious and dissolute, the frequenters of tippling houses, the idle, the unthrifty, the fraudulent debtors, the decayed and brokendown workmen, the outlawed and cast off members of society under bar for incorrigible faults." Kennedy, a Scotch-Irish Presbyterian, was drawn to the Know-Nothings, but never formally joined the party.

He became a secret member of the secret party. In a letter marked "confidential and private," he wrote that the "American party, of which I have been from its first public development, a member in every thing but the form of initiation, is, I think, destined to the consummation of great good to the nation." He publicly supported Millard Fillmore's Know-Nothing bid for the presidency in 1856. (Kennedy had served in the Fillmore administration as secretary of the navy.) But Kennedy's advocacy was ostensibly nonpartisan support from a political independent. In fact, he was a Know-Nothing operative: "I would not have hesitated to enroll myself amongst its members if it had not been that in consultation with some of the most influential members in New York it had been thought advisable that I should not do so." Fillmore's candidacy, he was told, would be regarded more favorably if promoted by someone outside the Know-Nothing ranks. "In short, they thought that I could do more for the cause outside of the order than in it."[8]

Kennedy clearly viewed the Know-Nothing candidates and officeholders as an improvement on the Whig and Democratic hacks they had displaced. They were, he wrote, "Young men new in our politics . . . very worthy men I understand, and much above the average of our former delegates." Because they were young, however, they were also inexperienced, and Kennedy judged some of them as undeserving of public office: "Every man now is fit for every place, and I hear men talked of for Senator who have never rendered any recognized service to the state or have any political antecedents known to anybody." One of them was his younger brother Anthony, who became a Know-Nothing member of the legislature and then a US senator. John regarded his brother's elevation not as a credit to the party but as "the strangest freak of fortune." "He is a pleasant, careless, light hearted fellow who never thought a thought, read a book, or troubled his head with a serious application to any grave purpose." Anthony, according to his older brother, "knows nothing of history, diplomacy, political concerns, national law or any one subject that a Senator might [be] expected to know."[9] He was the perfect Know-Nothing.

The Know-Nothing party appealed to antipartisan sentiment by pretending not to be a party. It was a movement dedicated to principle, not an organization in pursuit of public offices. The "Maine Law" temperance movement had opened the way toward nonparty politics in 1853, when it offered to back local candidates of any party who would support prohibition. Alcohol and immigration were closely linked in the rhetoric of the Maine Law enthusiasts. Irish whiskey and German beer fests, they claimed, contributed to Baltimore's crime and moral turpitude.[10] The temperance crusaders served as an opening act for the Know-Nothings.

Nationally, the Know-Nothing movement disintegrated when the slavery issue trumped the immigration issue. Northern delegates walked out of the American Party convention in 1856, and the party's national council dissolved in 1857, advising its adherents to adopt structures and policies "best suited" to local circumstances.[11] In most states, the party simply collapsed; in Maryland, the Know-Nothings soldiered on. Their cause, however, had evolved. The vehement anti-Catholicism of the party subsided. It had always been a bit awkward; Maryland's founders and first families were Roman Catholics. Some of the party's Maryland lodges dropped Catholicism as a bar to membership. A Baltimore delegate to the National Council of the American Party in 1855 tried to persuade the body that native-born Roman Catholics should be permitted to join the party. His proposal was overwhelmingly rejected. But, in Baltimore at least, Protestant nativism was replaced by a fervent devotion to the preservation of the Union.[12]

In 1855, a Know-Nothing congressman from Baltimore contended on the House floor that his party pointed the way to the nation's salvation. It had sidetracked the slavery debate that was destroying the old parties and, unlike them, had become a truly national party, "knowing no North, no South, no East, no West." For Baltimoreans, Know-Nothingism was the solvent of sectionalism, a party ready "to stand by the Union as it is and the Constitution as it is." By 1859, another of the party's congressmen from Baltimore was arguing for formation of a new party, "an opposition that rejecting all dangerous and useless dogmas, all questions of vain and irritating differences between sections and people will array itself firmly up on the platform of the constitution and win by its moderation, its good sense, its high conservatism, its unquestioned nationality, the good and true men of all parties and sections." His fellow partisan, Senator Anthony Kennedy, joined in the call for a party to succeed the Know-Nothings, a "union organization" that would insist on the preservation of the Constitution and the Union and "exclude the slavery question."[13]

Many Baltimoreans desperately wanted to extract themselves from the imminent collision between North and South on the issue of slavery. Baltimore congressman and premier Know-Nothing orator Henry Winter Davis embodied his city's position on the subject. Though a slave owner, his misgivings about the peculiar institution moved him to offer his slaves their freedom—but only if they would move to Liberia. Davis shared Baltimoreans' longstanding preference for saying as little as possible about slavery, at least in public. "The way to settle the slavery question," he said, "is to be silent on it."[14]

THE KNOW-NOTHING MUNICIPALITY

Baltimore's Know-Nothing government did nothing to limit the political rights of immigrants or papal loyalists. Once Baltimore's Know-Nothings "finally possessed the power they had been seeking . . . they stoutly refused to use it for nativist purposes." Nativism, as William Evitts observed, was "suited for agitation, not action."[15] Once the party ceased to be a movement and became a government, its concerns differed hardly at all from the enduring preoccupations of the city's mayors and councils.

First came railroads. In December 1854, Samuel Hinks began his term as mayor by calling the city council into special session to choose Baltimore's representatives for a meeting of the directors of the newly formed Northern Central Railroad. The Northern Central had absorbed the Baltimore and Susquehanna Railroad, in which the city held a substantial interest. The new company had also taken over several other roads and had finally offered Baltimore the chance to succeed in its longstanding quest to secure a direct rail connection to the Susquehanna Valley. The Northern Central reached even farther. It could carry Baltimore's commerce through Harrisburg and another 55 miles north to Sunbury, Pennsylvania, where it could make rail connections with Buffalo and Lake Erie. In their enthusiasm for the project, the members of the city council voted to transfer to the Northern Central the city's entire stake in the Baltimore and Susquehanna—stock, interest, and unpaid debt. Mayor Hinks's predecessor, John Smith Hollins, had vetoed the proposition as overly generous, but the council had overridden his objection.[16]

The city turned over $950,000 in Baltimore and Susquehanna stock to the new railroad and relinquished the city's claim to unpaid interest on its investment. By the time the Know-Nothings seized control of the municipality at the end of 1854, there was reason to regret this decision. The Northern Central announced sharp increases in its rates for freight and passengers, "very seriously interfering with & retarding the business of the City by driving freight & passengers to other routes." The mayor and council sent a resolution to the railroad's directors to register their objections, which appear to have been ignored. While the rate increases angered city officials, they created a buzz in the market that drove up the price of the company's stock. The *Baltimore Sun* commended the Northern Central for its "wise and practical determination—that is not to work for nothing." The directors "revised their toll sheet so as to increase their rates to the standard set by the late Railroad Conventions."[17] In a later age, the Northern Central might have been charged with price fixing, but in the 1850s, it was simply doing business as usual.

Baltimore's unhappy experience with the Northern Central did not sour the city on financing railroads. It agreed to provide a loan guarantee to the Pittsburgh and Connellsville road, which made its connection with the B&O at Cumberland. The city had a similar agreement with the Northwest Virginia Railroad. The line met the B&O at Grafton and carried its traffic to the Ohio River at Parkersburg, expanding the B&O's reach toward western markets. Together, the two B&O feeder roads represented another $3 million liability for Baltimore.[18]

A second concern was the city's water supply. Having bought out the Baltimore Water Company, the city now became responsible for overcoming the deficiencies that had induced the municipality to purchase the waterworks in the first place. The town's citizens were impatient. A petition signed by more than 1,300 Baltimoreans complained about "the long delay on the part of the city authorities to obey the people of Baltimore to introduce an additional supply of Water into the city." The petitioners complained that the municipality's inaction had "exposed a large part of the city to the risk of conflagration, and continues to impede the growth and prosperity of the city."[19] In the special session of the city council called by Mayor Hinks after his inauguration, the first ordinance approved would create a new agency— the water board—charged with the management and maintenance "of the dams, reservoirs, mains, pipe-yard, and property" of the waterworks. It was a formidable establishment consisting of "foremen, mechanics, keepers, watchers, laborers, and other persons," including a treasurer, a bookkeeper, and two collectors to oversee the receipt and disposition of "water rents."[20] The water board promptly submitted a request that the city sell $98,000 in municipal stock to finance the purchase of land and water rights needed to increase Baltimore's water supply.[21]

Another ongoing project that the Know-Nothings embraced was the construction of a new jail. The council formed a committee to select a site and solicit proposals from building contractors.[22] The only city ordinance that may have reflected the distinctive ideological inclinations of the Know-Nothings had to do with "the encouragement of the Volunteer Corps in the City of Baltimore." The law provided subsidies to local militia companies on the condition that they parade in full regalia on days specified for patriotic celebration.[23] Patriotic display was a natural indulgence for nativists, but it was not their paramount concern.

KNOW-NOTHING PUBLIC ORDER

Like many of their predecessors, the Know-Nothings were concerned to prevent crime and public disorder, even though some of the party's adherents were known for their ferocity as street fighters. Not long after the election of Mayor Hinks, the city council made two attempts to overhaul the city's night watch and day police by consolidating them under the authority of a chief of police. Disagreements within the council prevented both bills from reaching the mayor's desk.[24] But a new urgency about law and order marked the administration of Hinks's successor, Thomas Swann. Swann had been president of the B&O Railroad. He won the mayor's office as a Know-Nothing by defeating the president of the Northern Central Railroad, a Democrat.

The election itself may have helped to intensify fears of collective violence and mob rule. Baltimoreans were already acquainted with the coincidence of voting and violence. But the public disorders that surrounded the municipal and presidential elections of 1856 exceeded anything in the city's experience. Both parties were backed by street-fighting forces made up of fire companies and their allied gangs. The New Market Fire Company sided with the Democrats, who were also supported by the Calithumpians, the Pioneers, and the Empire Club. The Know-Nothings relied on the Mount Vernon Fire Company, the Plug Uglies, the Rip Raps, and a variety of smaller gangs—the Blood Tubs, Rough Skins, Black Snakes, Tigers, Decaturs, Little Fellows, and Ranters.[25]

The Rip Raps opened the election season by attacking the Seventeenth Ward Democratic headquarters on Federal Hill. There were two fatalities and 22 seriously injured, some of them nonparticipants struck by stray bullets. On October 5, Democratic partisans triggered a riot by tearing down a Know-Nothing banner. They held off the Know-Nothings by barricading a house and defending it with firearms and a small artillery piece.[26]

As the election drew near, the *Sun* published a lengthy editorial headed "Riot." It begged voters to cast their ballots in peace. Elections conducted by fraud and violence threatened the preservation of the Union just as much as did the slavery question or "the Pope of Rome himself." "Of late," the *Sun* observed, "we have recorded frequent riots in our city, and it is beyond doubt that they have been of a political complexion." The preelection disturbances, the *Sun* predicted, were a portent of the severe violence likely to occur on the day of the election itself. "And if we consent . . . to such violence, intimidation, or any other demonstrative means by which legal votes can be excluded from, or illegal votes admitted into the ballot-box, we are guilty of moral treason to the republic."[27]

The political street fighters were beyond persuasion. In a postelection report, the *Sun* claimed that the "Municipal Election in this city yesterday was accompanied by a most unusual amount of violence and disorder—more perhaps than ever before on such an occasion." The Rip Raps and the Plug Uglies had engaged the New Market Fire Department in a pitched battle in and around the Lexington Market, lasting two to three hours, "unchecked and unheeded, apparently, by any efficient show of police force."[28]

In the Irish, Democratic Eighth Ward, Know-Nothing voters were driven from the polling place. Know-Nothings of the Seventh Ward launched a counterattack on the Eighth Ward Democrats. The two forces clashed near the intersection of Calvert and Monument Streets, and the battle flowed up and down the slope of Monument Street, with the Washington Monument towering high in the background. Combatants fired at one another from behind tree boxes and marble doorsteps. According to the *Sun*, at least two were mortally wounded.[29]

Violence swirled around each of the city's 20 polling places, one in each ward. The Know-Nothings generally got the best of the fighting. The party's paper ballots were "striped" and easy to recognize. Election judges received them from behind wooden counters or windows that could easily be blocked by a few strong men. Voters who approached the polls with ballots lacking the correct stripe risked beating or worse. The Know-Nothings' characteristic weapon, the shoemaker's awl, became a party symbol in Baltimore. Its image was displayed on banners. Easily concealed, an awl could inflict nasty puncture wounds. Occasionally, however, conflicts to control the polls expanded into quasi-military engagements, with organized volleys of gunfire and small artillery pieces.[30]

According to the *Sun*, in the First, Second, Third, Fourth, and Fifth Wards, "we heard of nothing more than the usual fighting." In the Fourth, the "usual fighting" included an attack on a voter who "received a severe cut across the top of his head with a pistol, and was shot at three times while making his escape." He was apparently unable to cast his ballot. Elsewhere, the election turned deadly. "A man named either Andy or Charles Brown was shot through the chest near Paca Street and was brought down through the Lexington Market by four men, one having hold of each hand and foot, while the unfortunate victim's face lay toward the ground. He was taken into the apothecary shop of Mr. Smith . . . where, lying gasping upon the floor he breathed out his life." The *Sun* estimated that the election had cost four killed outright and five or six wounded, "whose cases are pronounced hopeless."[31]

Know-Nothing electoral violence was another indication that anti-Catholic nativism had ceased to be the party's driving force—even among the rank and file. If nativist sentiment had continued to animate the street fighters, they might have attacked convents, churches, or the meetings of the local Hibernian Society. But they concentrated on polling places. Their principal concern was to win control of public offices and political patronage.[32]

The disturbances surrounding the October municipal election aroused widespread apprehensions about violence in the November elections for president and state offices. A committee of prominent citizens petitioned outgoing Mayor Hinks to convene a special session of the city council to adopt measures "to preserve the peace of the city, especially on the day of the Presidential election." Hinks replied that such precautions were "inexpedient" because he had no information "to justify me in anticipating a recurrence of the scenes which recently disgraced the city." In any case, he was confident that the arrangements already made "as to the civil and military force" would "quell any disturbance that may arise."[33] Hinks ordered a division of the local militia to assemble at its armories on election day, but later withdrew the order. Governor T. Watkins Ligon, a Democrat, came to the city just before the election to offer the state's assistance in keeping order. His offer was dismissed.[34]

Mayor Hinks called "special meetings of the city police captains to inform them that the services of their men would be required for special duty on election day." The police seem to have made an earnest effort to preserve public order, but they were generally ineffective. The presidential election generated even more carnage than the local election. In a reprise of the October riots, a mob from the Know-Nothing Seventh Ward, "armed with muskets and every description of small arms," attacked the Democratic Eighth Ward's polling place. Twenty-five armed police officers were dispatched to restore order, but "found themselves utterly unable to cope with either party of rioters." The battle soon spread to the Sixth Ward, where the election judges "refused to receive a vote until order was restored."[35]

Fighting erupted at the Belair Market in Old Town (formerly Jones Town). The chief constable, his deputy, and a police sergeant rushed to the scene and confiscated two muskets and a "swivel"—a small artillery piece—but were unable to restore order even when reinforced by additional police officers. The Belair Market engagement resulted in 10 or 11 fatalities. At an apothecary shop nearby, 12 of the wounded were laid out on the floor.[36]

Many of the wounded and a few of the dead appear to have been noncombatants—a 12-year-old girl shot while entering her house, a 15-year old boy returning from work, a man "aged about sixty years and an excellent citizen" whose jaw was shattered. A justice of the peace was hit on the back of the head by a brick. One of the fallen was reported to have "died of fright" that brought on a heart attack.[37]

A precise casualty count is impossible. The *Sun* offered a terse summary: "Killed, 5; wounded, supposedly mortally, 15; wounded, 53—total 113." Assuming that the mortally wounded fulfilled expectations, the death toll of 20 is probably close to accurate, but recent accounts of the November riot estimate the number of wounded at about 250.[38] The election riots of 1856 cost close to 30 lives and at least 300 other casualties. Fillmore carried Baltimore by more than 7,000 votes.

FIXING THE POLICE

Six days after the presidential election, Mayor Swann delivered his inaugural address. He did not mention the election riots. He did acknowledge that government was responsible for the "quiet and good order of a city." And, without mentioning Mayor Hinks by name, he seemed to endorse his predecessor's decision not to use troops against the rioters: "A resort to military interference . . . is not only irritating to the people, but in direct hostility and theory of our free institutions." It might also backfire by inciting more violence.[39]

Little more than a week later, Swann summoned the city council into special session and wasted no time in addressing the city's failure to preserve public order. "It cannot be disguised that for some time past a spirit of lawlessness has prevailed to a large extent in our city, and that the power of the corporation is at this time wholly inadequate to its suppression." The remedy was to create "a proper system of police." The value of the system was "not to be estimated by dollars or cents," and the "burthen of taxation" should not be a consideration. He urged the council to make "the establishment of an efficient police" its first order of business.[40]

The year before Swann's election, Know-Nothing councilman Charles Krafft, a member of the Joint Committee on Police and Jail, asked that his committee be instructed "to convene from time to time to take into consideration the police system as now in force."[41] Though the proposal seems to have been rejected or ignored, the committee nevertheless proceeded to consider alterations of the police system, and in February 1855, it submitted an elaborate bill that specified even the stationery budget for the police chief's office. The bill's most significant provisions, however, were a consolidation of the day police and night watch under the chief's authority and a significant expansion of the police force to 300 "strong, able-bodied men of good moral character" who were not to attend the theatre or frequent "any public house or bar room where spirituous or malt liquor was served." After a few desultory amendments, a motion was introduced proposing "that the further consideration of the bill be permanently postponed." The motion passed by a vote of 10 to 8. The reason for the council's refusal to consider the ordinance may lie in another motion made by Democratic councilman J. S. Wright, one of those who voted to shelve the police bill. Wright moved that "in the present state of the finances of the city, and heavy burden of taxes imposed upon our citizens, we will not receive any business after the first day of April and adjourn 'sine die' at an early day thereafter."[42]

The council's second branch also considered the proposed expansion and reorganization of the police force. After several amendments, the bill passed. Councilman Krafft attempted to reintroduce the police ordinance in the first branch in March 1855. The branch's president declared his motion out of order, "a similar bill having been indefinitely postponed" earlier in the session. Krafft contended that because the bill had been amended in the second branch, it was not similar to the earlier measure. But the council upheld its president's ruling by a vote of 11 to 8.[43]

The bloody election riots of 1856 triggered a decisive shift in the city council. The Joint Committee on Police and Jail revived its plan to devise a "more efficient police system" and expanded on it. After declaring that the "present Watch and Police systems of the . . . City shall be abolished," the committee's report went on to order a sharp increase in the number of police officers. The new force would consist of "One Marshal, One Deputy Marshal, Eight Captains, Eight Lieutenants, 24 Sergeants, 347 Police officers, five detective Police officers, and eight Turnkeys." There would also be 42 lamplighters under the supervision of four superintendents of lamps. A city fire inspector would report on the origin of each fire and inspect new buildings to ensure that their construction complied with municipal ordinances. The marshal was to exercise sweeping authority over the police and law enforcement, but his power was closely tied to that of the mayor. One unusual provision of the ordinance required the marshal of police to meet with the mayor every day.[44]

Each of four police districts would be divided into "beats." After roll call, the sergeants would "lead forth their platoons" and assign each officer to his proper beat. For the first time, the officers would wear uniforms and numbered badges. Ordinarily, the police officers would be armed only with a wooden "battoon," 22 inches long and at least one and three-quarter inches thick. But in times of "great emergency" they would be issued revolvers or muskets. The mayor or the marshal could "at any time . . . call out the whole police." This time, the first branch of the council gave its unanimous approval to the police ordinance; the second branch passed it by a vote of seven to three, and Mayor Swann promptly signed it.[45]

POLICING IN PRACTICE

Opinion concerning the efficacy of Swann's new police department has been generally dismissive. A hagiographic history of the city's police force published in 1888 acknowledged that the reorganized and expanded department was "more efficient than the former ones," but "the new force was gradually filled with 'Know-Nothing recruits,' who, instead of maintaining the peace, became willing tools of violence and riot." More recent assessments have been no more favorable. The verdict is that "Baltimore's enlarged police force did little to restore election calm." The police stood by as "spectators" at election riots. When they did intervene, it was often as active partisans engaged in street-level hostilities against Democratic voters, especially naturalized citizens.[46]

The new police force would face its first practical test at the elections for magistrates and for the first branch of the city council in October 1857. Know-Nothing candidates for the council faced no opposition in 3 of the city's 20 wards—a sign, perhaps, of their party's success at intimidating challengers. A Democratic candidate in the Twelfth Ward withdrew the day before the election when he learned that the election judges had relocated his ward's polling place. It was now just two blocks away from the poll of the Know-Nothing Twentieth Ward. He was concerned that his supporters might have to brave bands of Plug Uglies to exercise the franchise.[47]

The October election of 1857 was markedly less deadly than the contest of the previous year, perhaps because many citizens decided that it was too dangerous to vote. The Know-Nothing vote declined by about 5,000, and Democratic turnout fell by 7,000, a reduction of about 50 percent from 1856. Still, a police sergeant was killed during a skirmish between Democrats from the Eighth Ward and Know-Nothings from the Fifth; another officer was wounded in the same engagement. Others were injured while trying to defend the Seventeenth Ward Democratic headquarters on Federal Hill against a Know-Nothing attack. At least some members of the enlarged and reorganized police department seem to have taken their responsibilities seriously. But they were unable to prevent the majority party in most wards from blocking the polls against the local minority.[48]

Elections for Congress, governor, the house of delegates, and other state offices were to be held in November. As in 1856, the disturbances that marred the October elections were seen as a portent of even greater trouble in November. Perhaps because of the carnage at the previous year's election, Governor Ligon asserted state authority more vigorously than in 1856. He again came to Baltimore, but this time he was prepared for a more extended stay. He took a room at Barnum's Hotel and dispatched a letter to Mayor Swann asking what measures had been taken to ensure the "personal security, and free exercise of the suffrage by legal voters" in the up-coming election. The violence of 1856 "conclusively established the inadequacy of the existing city police to secure the elective rights and personal safety of the voters." Ligon hinted at state intervention to ensure the integrity of the election.[49]

In a barely civil response, Swann rebuffed the governor's request to discuss his preparations for the November canvass, though he did not "object at any time to impart to you, or any other citizen, the fullest information in regard to matters con-nected with the government of the city." The mayor recognized his accountability to the people of Baltimore, not to state authorities. If he needed state assistance, he would ask for it. If the governor chose to place the city under "military supervision," the mayor could not resist, but he warned that "such a policy might seriously endan-ger the peace of the city."[50]

Ligon promptly ordered Major General John Spear Smith to enroll six regiments of 600 militiamen each to be ready for duty beginning on the Saturday preceding the election. The governor issued a proclamation asserting his constitutional duty to guarantee the right of Baltimoreans to cast their ballots in safety and promised "just retribution" for anyone who attempted to prevent citizens from voting, and also for citizens who voted excessively.[51]

The governor and the mayor exchanged a few more curt letters but chose not to confer face-to-face, even though they were within walking distance of one another. The most immediate effect of Ligon's proclamation was to arouse Know-Nothing anger. One American Party adherent claimed to have little interest in the election until he took offense at Ligon's pronouncement. The commander of the First Rifle Regiment, a Know-Nothing who had recently fallen out with his party, appeared at city hall to offer Mayor Swann the services of his regiment on election day. Governor Ligon's call to arms was generally ignored by the militia units that he summoned. Even if they had been willing, there were not enough weapons to arm all of them. Ligon sent a request to Virginia to borrow 2,000 muskets.[52]

The governor refused to withdraw his order to mobilize the militia, but he ex-pressed satisfaction with a face-saving alternative offered by Mayor Swann. To keep the peace on election day, the mayor agreed to appoint 200 temporary policemen drawn from both parties—10 officers for each ward. Swann then issued a stern proc-lamation threatening severe consequences for anyone creating a disturbance at a polling place or attempting to obstruct the polls. All firearms that might be "used to intimidate persons from voting" would be confiscated. Finally, all "drinking houses" would remain closed on election day.[53]

The proclamation and the special police may have reduced disorder at the polls. The only known fatalities occurred in the Seventeenth Ward, a frequent site of po-litical violence. A young man under voting age was "stabbed through the loins with a sword cane" and died a day later. His assailant was immediately struck by five shots and was not expected to survive. The *Sun* reporters circulating among the polling places told of "violent demonstrations" by gangs with partisan affiliations, and witnesses reported that voters were sometimes beaten. Naturalized citizens, in particular, were prevented from voting. The *Sun* reported that "as the day wore on

ORDER MAINTENANCE IN RETROSPECT

The conduct of Baltimore's congressional election in 1857 became the subject of an investigation in the US House of Representatives in the following year. Democratic congressional candidate William Pinkney Whyte charged that his American Party opponent, J. Morrison Harris, had secured a majority by blocking Democratic voters or discarding their ballots. Justices of the peace deposed witnesses in Baltimore. Thomas J. Rusk, a Democratic voter from the First Ward in southeast Baltimore, testified that he "attempted to vote; was pushed away from the window; told by the parties present that [he] could not vote that day; no fighting, no rioting, and perfectly quiet at the time."[55]

Vote suppression no longer required much overt violence. Most voters knew that the polls were overseen by partisans who "seemed pretty much to control the proceedings." It was pointless to challenge them. In the First Ward, voter intimidation had become nearly ceremonial. Thomas Rusk testified that the night before the election "between 9 and 10 o'clock p.m.; there were parties of some twenty or thirty persons armed with guns and muskets marching up towards the polls with a cannon . . . and the following day I saw the cannon close by the polls." It was fired, at nothing in particular, several times during the day, as if to announce that the American Party was still in command.[56]

David C. Piquett, a Democratic candidate for magistrate in the Second Ward in the October election, said that his experience in that contest convinced him not to vote in November because "I thought my life of more consequence than voting that day." A police officer had warned Piquett not to vote, but he tried to vote in spite of the implicit threat. He was, after all, a candidate. As he approached the polling place, he noticed 10 or 12 members of the Rough Skins standing in front of it. They were accompanied by the police officer who had previously threatened him. One of the gang members threw a piece of brick at him. He was able to avoid it. "I drew my revolver, and snapped it at the fellow who threw the brick . . . I snapped it at him twice before I was shot. Several shots were fired at me, and one of them struck me in the shoulder. I snapped my revolver twice after I was shot, but finding that it would not go off, I thought it better to get off myself, and left." Two men pursued Piquett—a member of the Rough Skins and the police officer. The officer overtook him and prepared to strike him with his "billet," but a storekeeper nearby persuaded the officer to desist.[57]

Not all polling places were controlled by gangs. A special police officer in the Democratic Eighth Ward testified that the voting "was perfectly orderly and quiet; and all persons had full, entire, and free access to the polls." Another special officer confirmed his account. In other wards, police officers actually tried to help voters by shouldering aside the Know-Nothings who blocked the polls, but were rarely successful. Far more frequently, the police made no attempt to arrest or drive off the ruffians, but they were not entirely passive. A special officer testified that when voters were beaten at the polls, "the general conduct of the regular police was to take the beaten parties in charge and persuade them to leave the polls." Some special police officers adopted the same approach.[58]

The advice of the policemen was probably the best that could be offered under the circumstances. The outnumbered officers, armed only with wooden "battoons," faced crowds of pistol-packing Know-Nothings. A concerted attempt to place the ruffians under arrest might provoke the violence that had made earlier elections so deadly. In counseling the battered and unsuccessful voters to go home, the officers were performing one of the vital and enduring jobs in police work: "order maintenance." Unlike law enforcement, order maintenance does not require apprehension of the guilty. Instead, it calls on officers to exercise their personal judgments to identify those persons—guilty or innocent—whose presence poses the most immediate threat to public order.[59] The safest way to preserve order around Baltimore's polling places was to remove the unfortunate citizens who provided targets for Know-Nothing assaults.

The expansion and reorganization of the police accomplished under Mayor Swann did not erase the city's reputation as Mobtown, but it was a distinct step forward in the struggle to sustain public order. With its badges, beats, battoons, uniforms, and administrative hierarchy, the new department provided a foundation for a modern police force.

Swann presided over a similar transformation of Baltimore's firefighting forces. Like mayors before him, he both complained about the disorder surrounding the city's volunteer companies and took care to blame the trouble not on the firefighters themselves but on the gangs that "ran" with the fire companies. His annual message in 1858 called on the city council to undertake a sweeping reorganization of the city's firefighters. The nine-member commission appointed to come up with a plan for a new fire department subsequently produced two of them. Both would have incorporated the latest technology in firefighting: the steam-powered pump engine and the fire-alarm telegraph. The steam engines were thought to require a level of technical expertise that part-time volunteers could not master, and the engines were too heavy to be pulled through the streets by anything less than 30 firefighters. The commission's majority therefore proposed that full-time, paid firefighters should staff seven companies with horse-drawn steam engines, while the rest of the department would continue to consist of unpaid volunteers on hook-and-ladder trucks or hand-powered pump engines. A minority report called for "total abolition of the present system, and the adoption in its stead of an entire paid department, in which steam and horse power shall be introduced to the greatest practicable extent." The minority consisted of Henry Spilman, a veteran volunteer firefighter from the Mechanical Company, the city's oldest fire company.[60] He would later become the chief engineer of Baltimore's full-time fire department.

Resistance to reorganization came from the Baltimore United Fire Department, which had represented the volunteer companies since 1833. It had been an experiment in self-regulation, pledged to discipline and control the most troublesome fire companies among its members. The organization was determined to preserve its member companies "inviolate from dismemberment by any proposed violent action by the mayor and city council." By way of self-defense, the group appointed its own committee to propose an alternative to the reorganization plans of the city commission, but the representatives of the volunteer companies voted against their committee's proposal, and some firemen submitted petitions endorsing Henry Spilman's demand for an "entire paid department,"[61] perhaps because they hoped to be its members.

The city council, however, passed an ordinance based on its commission's majority report, allowing a combination of paid and volunteer fire companies. Mayor Swann vetoed it. In his message, he announced his opposition to any settlement that would leave obsolete, hand-powered fire engines in place. Perhaps more important, he suggested that the division between paid and volunteer fire companies would only add another axis of conflict to disturb the peace of the city. He called instead for *"an out and out paid department—to consist exclusively of steam machinery—under the management and control of the municipal authorities."* The council bowed to Swann's emphatic rejection of its ordinance and quickly submitted another along the lines suggested by the mayor and Spilman. Swann signed it shortly after beginning his second term.[62]

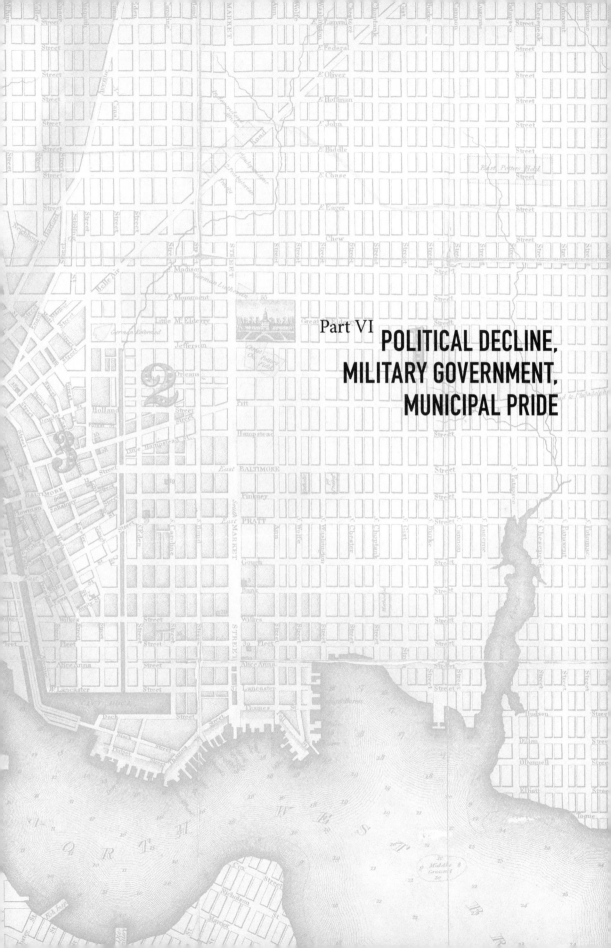

Part VI
POLITICAL DECLINE,
MILITARY GOVERNMENT,
MUNICIPAL PRIDE

Chapter 18 **AMERICAN PARTY RECKONING**

THOMAS SWANN CLAIMED that he did not intend to run for reelection as Baltimore's mayor in 1858 but was persuaded to do so by the American Party's convention. His name was the only one placed in nomination, and he was the unanimous choice of the delegates. Swann must have had some inkling of the outcome. According to the *Baltimore Sun*, when the nominee was ushered into the hall shortly after the vote, he "delivered a speech of considerable length, accepted [the nomination], and reviewed his whole political life."[1]

The Democrats nominated no candidate for mayor and only one for the city council—in Northeast Baltimore's Irish Democratic Eighth Ward. But the Know-Nothings faced a hastily organized opposition. A collection of independents, the nucleus of a new Reform Party, nominated a slate of candidates about three weeks before the general election. Their choice for mayor was Colonel Augustus P. Shutt, a son of German immigrants, former Whig, and respected officer in the local militia. He had served as high constable and then as warden of the city jail. An improbable swerve in his career took him to the B&O Railroad, where he was a conductor on passenger trains.

Shutt and his fellow independents ran against the violent reputation of the Know-Nothings and the culture that sustained it. He charged that people of "adjoining places" were reluctant to enter Baltimore for fear of being assaulted.[2] But his condemnation of Know-Nothing violence took an odd turn. He claimed that it was bad for business. It sapped "the foundation of commercial advantage by alarming merchants at a distance, and through the instrumentality of intestine feuds, terror, bloodshed, and death, diverts every description of business to other and more peaceful places." And the Know-Nothings "corruptly, for party reasons," increased the "burthens of municipal taxation" to support their lavish patronage system. For these evils, Shutt offered a familiar remedy: "It is a municipal government free from the bonds of faction."[3] Shutt ran against political parties, much as the Know-Nothings had done. Nonpartisan government, he argued, was the key to local peace and prosperity.

At about noon on election day, Shutt resigned his candidacy to avoid placing his supporters in danger of being assaulted by the Know-Nothings who controlled most of the city's polling places. As in 1857, however, there was comparatively little overt violence. A political dispute erupted in a group of workers on their way to a polling place. One of them was shot and killed. Another would-be voter in the Second Ward was "set upon" as he attempted to cast his ballot. Several shots were fired at him, and he took refuge in a nearby house. His assailants surrounded the place, but a "force of police" arrived and stationed themselves on the roof and at the doors and windows of the house to protect him.[4] The police may not have helped him to exercise his right to vote, but they did intervene to save his life.

Many shots were fired while the voting went on, some of which struck people, but most of the fighting ended soon after the polls opened. Once the Know-Nothings took control, their opponents knew better than to exercise their voting rights. Many of those who were prevented from voting in their own wards by American Party toughs went to the Eighth Ward, where they could cast their ballots under the protection of Democratic Party toughs. The Eighth was the only ward that Shutt carried."[5]

Swann and the American Party triumphed everywhere else, but the mayor drew little satisfaction from his success. Soon after his victory, he called the city council into special session to receive a morose message about the state of public order in the city. "Scenes of disorder and violence . . . which have transpired within a few weeks past" demonstrated that city authorities had to make further exertions "in maintaining the supremacy of the laws." Two police officers had been murdered. Their killing, Swann said, illustrated "the resolute and determined spirit with which these brave men . . . have stood up day and night in carrying out the requirements of their official oath." Swann urged the council to provide for the families of officers killed in the performance of their duties. While on the subject of police sacrifice and bravery, the mayor asked the council to authorize him to award one policeman, Officer Cook, with some appropriate recognition "as an appreciation of his gallant conduct."[6]

Three weeks before the municipal election, officers Benjamin Benton and Robert Rigdon struggled to take David Houck into custody. Houck appeared to be drunk, and he had attempted to crash a party against the wishes of its hostess. A friend of Houck's, either Henry Gambrill or Richard Harris, approached the police officers as they grappled with Houck and fatally shot Officer Benton in the neck. Gambrill, Harris, and Houck were all members of the Plug Uglies, a gang affiliated with the Mount Vernon Fire Company and the American Party.[7]

Gambrill's trial began two days before the election. It lent substance to the reformers' contention that Know-Nothing government floated atop an ocean of Know-Nothing violence. The trial became a public sensation. The *Sun* reported that the courtroom was "crowded to suffocation," and the case soon became even more heated. On November 5, Officer Rigdon, the principal witness at Gambrill's trial, was assassinated in his home on West Baltimore Street. The murder occurred on the day of Gambrill's conviction. Officer John Cook heard the shot that killed Rigdon and spotted the probable assassin as he left Rigdon's house. Cook exchanged fire with the killer, then pursued him for several blocks until he was finally able to knock him to the ground and, with the help of two other officers, take him into custody. Earlier on the same day, two of Gambrill's friends had created a disturbance in the courtroom. They were charged with causing a riot to give Gambrill the opportunity to escape. One of them was David Houck.[8]

The American Party's expanded and reorganized police department was at war with the party's own thugs. The Gambrill case was clearly on Mayor Swann's mind when he delivered his somber message to the council following his reelection triumph, now diminished by Plug Ugly police killers. The mayor plainly wanted to purify his party of any connection with the city's criminal class. The urban outlaws were "recognized and sustained by no party having any claim to respectability." They were the creatures of "low drinking establishments" that drew violent men together and dissolved their inhibitions. The danger they posed was magnified by the lack of any law against carrying concealed weapons. And, once they had been brought to justice for their crimes, punishment was neither swift nor certain.[9]

Swann held himself and his party blameless. They needed one another. The mayor gave the Know-Nothings respectability, not to mention his tireless and creative leadership. For his part, Swann needed solid Know-Nothing support to advance his plans for municipal improvement. The alacrity with which the city council bowed to his vetoes was a token of its loyalty. The Know-Nothings' support for his reorganization of the Fire Department, in particular, demonstrated their readiness to defer to his leadership even when it ran up against their partisan interests. Eliminating the volunteer fire companies, after all, removed one of the vital mechanisms of Know-Nothing organization and influence. But the Know-Nothing majority on the council marched behind its mayor. The party was not one of those exiguous organizations that came to life only during election campaigns and disappeared as soon as they were over. Swann could count on Know-Nothing support not only in getting elected but in winning approval for his policies. The party's durable political presence may have been grounded in secret lodges that continued to function between elections.

For Swann, however, the party was also a burden. Its electoral practices cast doubt on the validity of his victory. Near the end of his message to the council, he implicitly acknowledged Know-Nothing fraud and coercion at the polls, but added, "There are none who can doubt, with any prospect of being sustained, that I have been returned to this office by an overwhelming majority of the legal voters of the City." He hoped that those who observed his conduct in the election would "do me the justice to believe that I was sincere in my desire that the laws should be faithfully executed, and the humblest citizen protected in his right."[10]

TROLLEYS AND PARKS

Mayor Swann's campaign of municipal improvement lost no momentum to the unfortunate events of 1858. Having overhauled the public agencies that protected citizens against fire, crime, and riot, Swann turned to amenities. At the opening

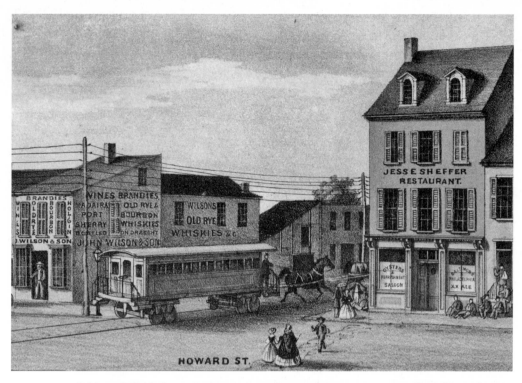

HOWARD ST.

Baltimore's first horsecar made its inaugural run in 1859. Just over 25 years later, the city became the first in the nation to introduce an electrified streetcar. Its route began outside the city limits and ended in Hampden, a distance of only two miles; it never reached the city center. The streetcar drew its power from a dangerous "hot" third rail. To avoid electrocuting pedestrians, the line used overhead wires at intersections and street crossings, but unlike streetcar lines in other cities, Baltimore's did not move to overhead wires citywide. Instead, the city abandoned the third rail for steam power. Trolleys were attached to underground cables driven by steam engines located in warehouses distributed across the city. A central powerhouse soon replaced the warehouses; its four smokestacks still punctuate the city's skyline. In 1896, after five years of expensive and unhappy experience with steam power, Baltimore finally abandoned it for overhead wires. The electric streetcars were retired in 1963. In 1992, a "light rail" line began operating, using an old railroad right-of-way and crossing the city on Howard Street, where this horsecar once traveled. *Courtesy Enoch Pratt Free Library, Cator Collection*

of its session in 1859, the city council considered a resolution instructing its Joint Committee on Highways to report on the feasibility of building a street railway for horse-drawn cars, extending from the western to the eastern boundaries of Baltimore. Two groups of investors petitioned the council for the street railway franchise. The council sent an ordinance to the mayor authorizing a group led by William H. Travers, a local attorney and Know-Nothing politician, to lay tracks on the city's streets for horsecars. Mayor Swann vetoed the measure.[11]

Swann was not opposed to street railways. In fact, he was convinced that they would add dramatically to the value of Baltimore real estate. Before the introduction of "omnibuses" in 1844, according to the mayor, "suburban property in and around . . . Baltimore was comparatively valueless." The horse-drawn coaches had made outlying areas accessible and "added millions to the basis of taxation." If the omnibus, struggling through muddy, cobbled streets, could prove so advantageous, "what might not have been anticipated from this more perfect mode of transportation?" But Swann hesitated. He claimed to be concerned about "the power of the city of Baltimore over her public highways." Echoing the debates provoked by the railroads 30 years before, Swann asserted that the city's authority over its streets was "the most important conferred by her charter."[12]

Such a crucial element of municipal power should not be compromised without adequate compensation, especially for horsecar railways because "the occupation of the streets . . . by a railway company," Swann argued, "is the exclusion of all other modes of transportation." Swann may have overstated his case. The tracks laid by trolley railways were usually embedded in grooves to minimize their interference with other uses of the streets. But it served Swann's purpose to cast the horse-car lines as monopolies in order to strengthen the case for municipal regulation. The mayor wanted, in particular, to control carfare. Swann observed that in most cities with street railways, passengers were charged a uniform fare of five cents. The companies bidding to build Baltimore's horsecar lines were offering fares of three to four cents. Given the other fees and exactions that the city council planned to impose on them, Swann wondered whether the trolley companies' revenues could keep them running. He recommended that Baltimore's horsecars, like those of other cities, charge five cents, and that the city should be "entitled to *one-fifth of the gross receipts for all passengers* . . . the same to be applied towards the establishment of a public Park in some convenient location to be fixed by the council . . . to cover an area of not less than 200 acres."[13]

Swann's vision of a park entailed something more than 200 acres. He resurrected a dream that had emerged from a committee of the city council six years earlier. His 200-acre park on the outskirts of the city was to be the centerpiece of a grand avenue—250 feet wide—that would encircle the entire city, beginning on the east "at the Patapsco River, on the Canton Company's grounds, and terminating at Fort McHenry," at the tip of Locust Point. This suburban Champs-Élysées would be 14.5 miles long and would tie together a necklace of parks and public squares on the city's outskirts. The entire scheme, according to Swann, would promote "the health of our whole population, and more especially for the industrial and working classes, whose pursuits confine them within the corporate limits."[14] The horsecars would allow the working classes to reach the promenade and parks along the city's boundaries. One penny of each fare collected would finance the parks.

On the same day that the city council's first branch received Swann's veto message, the members voted to table the ordinance they had earlier approved. Then a substitute was introduced incorporating the mayor's five-cent fare and devoting the revenue collected to the purchase of parkland. The council then voted to skip the first reading of the bill so that the branch could vote on it immediately. Not surprisingly, it passed, but without any provision for Swann's magnificent avenue. Like the original bill, the substitute assigned the horsecar franchise to a group of investors headed by William Travers.[15]

BALTIMORE BOODLE

Travers and his associates, however, were not the investors they pretended to be. A Philadelphia businessman, Jonathan Brock, seems to have given Travers and his four colleagues at least $500 each to pose as Baltimore-based trolley financiers, on the reasonable expectation that a local investment group would be more likely to win the franchise than capitalists from out of town—especially if the outsiders came from Philadelphia, Baltimore's longtime commercial competitor. While Brock and his backers provided the capital, Baltimoreans were to control the construction and operation of the trolley lines. Work began on a Broadway line in East Baltimore shortly after passage of the street railway ordinance. Two other lines were planned. One would carry passengers along Baltimore Street; the other would run north on Greene Street and then northwest on Pennsylvania Avenue.[16]

Rumors about the "sale" of the trolley charter circulated less than a month after the council passed the ordinance granting the Travers group the franchise. Hard-edged suspicions arose in June 1859, when the company was to offer its stock to investors. The more shares purchased in Baltimore, the fewer would be left for Brock's Philadelphia investors. Travers and his local "investors" therefore needed to minimize the sale of stock to Baltimoreans. When they opened the books to investors, they did not specify the number of shares available or the total amount of capital to be raised. Prospective investors had no way to calculate the price of the shares, the cost of building the street railway, or the size of their potential stakes in the company. On those terms, the stock attracted few customers.[17]

The street railway ordinance required that the subscription book remain open to the public for a minimum of five days. The number of subscribers increased as the deadline approached. But as soon as the fifth day ended, the subscription book was closed and spirited away to the state penitentiary. (The warden was an ally of Travers's fictive investment group.) When the book emerged from prison, it contained the names of two new subscribers for almost all of the remaining stock. One of them was a relative of the warden.[18]

In early June, after construction of the Broadway line was well under way, the mayor received a visit from Jonathan Brock, spokesman for the street railway's Philadelphia investors. He said he had come to answer any questions that Mayor Swann might have about Baltimore's passenger railway. Brock, presumably, was the person who had the authoritative answers. Swann had more complaints than questions. Most of them related to apparent failures of the Travers investment group and its Philadelphia sponsors to comply with the provisions of the street railway ordinance. If the Travers group had transferred control of the enterprise to Brock's investors, then the group had no authority to open the company's books for stock subscriptions. In effect, they were selling stock in nothing. The Philadelphia investors who actually owned the city's streetcar charter had the authority and obligation to open the subscription book, but they had never done so and therefore had violated the ordinance. The mayor observed that the real and supposed investors in the street railway might soon face a day of reckoning. The trolley company had yet to receive a corporate charter from the Maryland General Assembly.[19]

Before the request for a charter reached the legislature, Maryland politics suffered a sharp jolt. In October 1859, John Brown and his fellow conspirators launched their raid on Harper's Ferry. The attack itself horrified most Marylanders, but its more enduring political effect may have been shaped by the northern response to Brown. Northerners, according to the *Sun*, "seem desirous to invest him with something of the character of a martyr." In the reaction to Brown's crime, Marylanders could sense the depth of sectional discord. The man who seemed a monster to most southerners was embraced by many northerners. "Day after day," wrote the *Sun's* editorialist, ". . . we have cumulative evidence, furnished voluntarily by the press and the pulpit, that John Brown is in fact the representative man of a very large class of people of the North."[20]

Maryland elections for Congress and the state legislature came little more than two weeks after Brown's attack. In Baltimore, the Know-Nothings held fast, but almost everywhere else in the state, their party suffered severe reverses. The most dramatic of these occurred in the General Assembly. In the Maryland House of Delegates, where the American Party had enjoyed a substantial majority, the Democrats now held a majority just as comfortable. Control of the state senate shifted as well, but the Democrats held only a two-vote margin there.[21]

In the house of delegates, hearings on the Baltimore City Passenger Railway Company occupied the Committee on Corporations for 10 days. The committee confirmed what everyone already knew—that the "investors" who won the streetcar franchise had simply provided a Baltimore front for the Philadelphia financiers. The house committee members persistently inquired whether any member of the city council had received money for supporting the Travers franchise. All of the witnesses denied that there had been any bribery. But in the process, they also revealed the extent to which personal and political connections purchased success in the streetcar business. One of William Travers's four associates, for example, was the brother of a city council member and subsequently became superintendent of the city passenger railway. The brother of another council member won a contract to supply lumber needed for construction, and still another council member got a contract for laying the tracks.[22]

A Baltimore attorney, one of the committee's more candid witnesses, explained why he supported Philadelphia sponsorship of Baltimore's streetcar venture: "I was appealed to as a party man—an American—that it would be policy for Brock to get this charter from the Legislature." The critical consideration was political patronage. The Travers group and its fellow Know-Nothings "should have the entire control of the road—that all the contractors and appointees should be members of the American party . . . [the venture to] be an American measure altogether, as I understood it."[23]

That was the general understanding as well. Even Know-Nothing street fighters found employment on the streetcar lines. David Houck became assistant superintendent for construction of the Greene Street branch. John Wesley Gambrill, Henry's brother and a Plug Ugly captain, became a timekeeper on the Baltimore Street line, where Richard Harris served as assistant superintendent.

Harris, along with Henry Gambrill, had been a suspect in the murder of Officer Benton. Gambrill continued to declare his innocence even from the gallows, when he was hanged along with two men convicted in the murder of Officer Rigdon. Richard Harris fell gravely ill little more than a year after starting his job on the streetcar line. Shortly before his death, he confessed that he, not Henry Gambrill, had murdered Officer Benton.[24]

AMOUNTING TO NOTHING

The Baltimore street railway did not win its corporate charter from the state. It functioned without one until 1862. But the Know-Nothings had achieved a new level of political maturity. The party had become Baltimore's first political machine, controlling not only government offices but additional jobs running the city's street railway. The party's foot soldiers did not abandon street fighting. Muscle, after all, was an essential component of machine politics. But the party's access to government patronage made the Know-Nothings venal as well as violent. City jobs were rewards for service to the party, and those rewarded were expected to supply a significant portion of the funds that sustained the party's political operations. This expectation was so systematically enforced that the American Party's finance committee used a printed form to notify city employees of the sums they were obliged to contribute, indicating the location of the committee's offices and the hours during which municipal workers could drop off their "donations." Its message ended on a vaguely threatening note: "You will no doubt see the importance of an early and prompt attention to this request."[25]

The Know-Nothings' rapid rise from underground movement to political party and then to governing authority must have made them seem irresistible. Their Democratic opponents, after all, had simply abandoned active campaigning. But the very fact that the Know-Nothings could now offer jobs and offices to their adherents also fueled intraparty conflicts. Party members who lost out in the scramble for spoils became party malcontents. Partisan infighting was obvious as early as 1857, when the Know-Nothings held nominating conventions for court clerks and magistrates. Fights broke out at the meetings in the Sixth and Ninth Wards, and the police had to be summoned to keep things from getting out of hand. The citywide convention that followed did not need the police, but the delegates spent considerable time challenging one another's credentials, and when they finally got around to voting on nominees, they frequently needed multiple ballots to resolve deadlocks. The *Sun* floated the possibility that defeated Democrats and dissident Know-Nothings might combine to challenge the American Party's dominance.[26]

Something of the kind materialized less than a month after Augustus Shutt abandoned his campaign for mayor. A new City Reform Association delivered an "address" to Baltimore. It was signed by 166 men, including some of the city's most prominent residents, and declared that "a state of things exists in this community under which its members can no longer rest in safety or without disgrace." The association's members came together "for the purpose of vindicating their political, personal and civil rights" against a regime of "recognized violence and despotic ruffianism." Like Shutt, the Reform Association planned to overcome the corruption and violence by "the exclusion of partisan purposes" from municipal government.[27]

As the elections of 1859 approached, the American Party's internal fragmentation intensified. Know-Nothing nominating conventions degenerated into fist fights. In the Thirteenth Ward, a faction calling itself the "Regulators" seized the ballot box, and a Know-Nothing voter was badly beaten in the fracas. In the Nineteenth Ward, no nominee could be declared because the convention "broke up in a row" before the ballots could be counted. Know-Nothing violence and intimidation, once directed at opposition voters, now turned inward.[28] In the meantime, the Reform Association gained in solidarity and scale. It nominated only eight candidates for the first branch of the council, but it established Reform committees in all of the city's 20 wards and won 6 of the 30 seats in the city council.[29]

The Reformers made no gains in the November elections for the state legislature. The Know-Nothings took all 10 of Baltimore's seats in the house of delegates. But American Party losses in the rest of Maryland gave the Democrats a substantial majority in the house and exposed Baltimore's Know-Nothings to unaccustomed scrutiny in Annapolis. The 10 defeated Reformers contested the election of the 10 victorious Know-Nothings, and the hearings before the House Committee on Elections exposed the electoral practices of the American Party to relentless examination.

The evidence showed that the party's ruffians no longer confined their bullying to opposition voters. They used force to compel nonvoters to cast fraudulent Know-Nothing ballots. In the First Ward, a man sitting on a bench opposite the polling place was approached by several Know-Nothing foot soldiers. They handed him an American Party ballot and demanded that he submit it to the election judges. He refused. According to a witness, one of the gang members sat down beside him on the bench and "struck him with something (it could not have been his fist, it sounded too hard)." When he fell over, another of the Know-Nothings "kicked him in the face, and from the sound of it [the] witness thought that it wasn't a fair boot, there must have been something on the end of it." The toughs "continued kicking him in the side, and others beating him over the face." One of them pulled out a "horse pistol or blunderbuss" and placing its muzzle against the man's back "used the observation 'I'll put him through.'" At that point "a police officer rushed up and said, 'I'll be God damned if I can stand that.'" He wrested the pistol away from the assailant and discharged it into the air. But he made no attempt to arrest the would-be killer, who followed the officer as he walked away, asking if he could have his pistol back.[30]

William Mauer, "a cooper by trade," testified that he was at his business in the Second Ward when "five or six men came up to me and knocked me down, and put a ticket in my hand to vote it; I wouldn't; they drawed my clothes down and pulled me like a dead dog along; my neighbor Charles Beckert, came to help me, and one of them said, 'Shoot him! Shoot him!' and after they shooted, he falled and is dead and buried."[31]

The testimony of William Bartlett revealed a more systematic approach to the recruitment of involuntary voters, called "cooping." Bartlett was walking through Fell's Point on the evening of October 31. Three men came up behind him and demanded that he accompany them. He managed to shake off two of them, but the third "jerked out his blunderbuss," and Bartlett surrendered. He was taken to the cellar of a nearby house, where he was imprisoned together with about 60 other men; many more were kept in other rooms of the house. At about noon on election day, after more than 36 hours of captivity, Bartlett was escorted to the Second Ward polling place. Though it was directly across the street from the building in which he had been held, he was walked around the block so that he would not be seen approaching the polling place directly from the coop. Bartlett was given a Know-Nothing ballot and told to turn it in to the election judges. Though Bartlett was not a resident of the Second Ward, the Know-Nothing operative who had him in custody vouched for him, and the judge accepted his ballot.[32] Many of the men kept in coops would be forced to cast votes in several different wards.

MEASURES OF REFORM

The house of delegates did not immediately unseat the Know-Nothings from Baltimore. If it had expelled them before the end of the legislative session, a special election would be required to replace them, and the Democratic legislators were reluctant to authorize another election under the auspices of Baltimore's Know-Nothing government. Expulsion of the Baltimoreans was delayed until the last day of the session.[33] By that time, the General Assembly had enacted two pieces of legislation to break the Know-Nothings' hold on Baltimore. The bills were drafted by members of the City Reform Association. One of them virtually eliminated municipal control over the police department. It placed the force under a four-member board of police to be appointed jointly by the two houses of the General Assembly. The mayor would serve ex officio on the board, but his authority was limited. The absence of the mayor, for example, was not to be taken into account in determining whether the board had a quorum. No "officer or servant of the Mayor and City Council of Baltimore" was to interfere with the operation of the city's police department under state authority. (The prohibition presumably applied to the mayor.) The board was not to appoint or remove any police officer on account of his political opinions, but the statute made a conspicuous exception for abolitionist "Black Republicans," who were not to be hired for any position in the police department.[34]

The Baltimore Reformers sent a second bill to Annapolis that would transfer authority over city elections from the municipal government to the board of police. The board was to divide each ward into precincts and appoint three election judges for each. The increase in the number of polling places would shrink the number of Baltimoreans who congregated around each poll. Diminishing the size of the crowd reduced the likelihood of riots and the massing of enough rowdies to block access to the polls.[35] Passage of the two reform bills was followed by a purge of Baltimore's police that eliminated most Know-Nothing officers. Mayor Swann challenged the new legislation in court.[36] But it could not be blocked.

The measures that transformed the organization and control of the city's police had a parallel in New York. In 1857, Republican reformers in the New York State Assembly and a Republican governor created a state-controlled police force for New York City—the Metropolitan Police—whose commissioner was appointed by the governor, not by New York's Democratic mayor Fernando Wood. Though both cities confronted attempts at state control of the police, Baltimore and New York differed in their responses to the provocation. Instead of going to court, like Mayor Swann, Mayor Wood persuaded the city council to establish the "Municipal Police," consisting of all the officers then in New York City's force. It was under the direct control of the mayor. The Municipals and the Metropolitans fought in the streets for control of the city. The Metropolitans finally prevailed, but only with the support of an infantry regiment.[37] In both New York and Baltimore, the city-controlled forces were finally defeated. New York's Democrats, however, had put up a fight. Baltimore's Know-Nothings, who did not shrink from violence, put up a lawsuit, perhaps because they realized that reliance on street fighting had become a political liability, or because Baltimore did not have the political clout and autonomy of New York City.

In Baltimore's municipal election of 1860, the Democrats stood aside in all but one ward so that opposition to the Know-Nothings could unify behind the Reform Association. Though their party was on the ropes, the Know-Nothings might find consolation in the party's achievements. Little more than a month before the election, Mayor Swann informed the council that the city's park commissioners had succeeded in purchasing the land for his great park—Druid Hill. It would be three times as large as the 200-acre preserve he had originally envisioned and included a picturesque lake that doubled as a city reservoir. It would be named after the mayor—Swann Lake. At about the same time, commissioners had been appointed to look into the construction of a real city hall. Construction of a new city jail was nearing completion.[38]

The American Party struggled through one more municipal election in October 1860. The Reform candidate for mayor was George William Brown. The Know-Nothings had ballots printed with the name of William George Brown, an obscure resident of the Fourteenth Ward. The ruse fooled almost no one, and George William Brown was elected mayor by a vote of more than two to one. Reformers also took every seat in both branches of the city council.[39]

Chapter 19

BALTIMORE IN THE DIVIDED NATION

B Y 1860, BALTIMORE HAD PLAYED host to 12 presidential nominating conventions. Philadelphia, its nearest competitor, had attracted only three. Centrality and accessibility contributed to Baltimore's status as America's convention city. It was somewhat north of center on the Eastern Seaboard, close to the population concentrations of the Northeast, but further south and west than any of them. From the urban, industrial Northeast, Baltimore reached out to the rest of the country. The National Road connected Baltimore to the Ohio River, and steamboats on the Ohio and Mississippi connected the road with much of the West. Delegates from the Northeast and South could travel to Baltimore by water, and eventually by railroad. Baltimore's principal attraction, however, may have been its proximity to Washington, to which it was linked by the B&O. But the city's political placement may have seemed just as advantageous as its geographic location. Baltimore, as Eugene Rosenboom observed, was in "a border slave state but near enough to the Mason-Dixon line to be regarded as sectionally neutral. Hardly any local abolitionists were present to anger southern visitors. Nor would the harshest features of the slave system be in evidence to affront those from the free North."[1]

Toward the end of its run as the country's convention city, Baltimore became the city where parties went to break apart and die. A forlorn fragment of the Whigs gathered in Baltimore for a final meeting in 1856. Nine states sent no delegates at all. The Whigs had no presidential candidate of their own. They endorsed Know-Nothing Millard Fillmore for the presidency, but rejected his platform.[2]

In April 1860, the Democratic convention met in Charleston rather than Baltimore. Its platform committee produced three different platforms—one for the committee's majority and two endorsed by minorities. A majority of the convention adopted one of the minority reports. It failed to commit the party to protection of slavery in the territories and reflected candidate Stephen Douglas's demand for "popular sovereignty"—allowing each territory to decide whether it would be slave or free. Delegates from the Deep South walked out of the convention. The remaining Democrats tried to settle on a presidential candidate. The chairman ruled that victory required a two-thirds vote of the entire convention, not just of the delegates present. Stephen Douglas needed 202 votes of the 250 delegates remaining after the southerners departed. After 57 ballots, he remained unnominated. Maryland delegate William S. Gittings introduced a motion that the convention reconvene in Baltimore. He reassured his fellow Democrats that "Baltimore was no longer a Plug Ugly town and promised the delegates a hospitable welcome." The convention rejected Gittings's proposal three times before agreeing to reconvene in Baltimore for one more effort at harmony. After much persuasion, most of the southerners who seceded in Charleston agreed to rejoin the party in Baltimore.[3] The city was their accustomed gathering place. Perhaps a return to their old location might restore their old unity.

The home of Reverdy Johnson in Monument Square served as headquarters for Stephen Douglas. Democrats trying to prevent Douglas's nomination set up shop directly across the square at the Gilmor House, where fire-eating Alabaman William L. Yancey was staying. At night, after the convention had recessed, partisans of the two factions staged rival political rallies on opposite sides of the square, with band music and speeches. The convention itself met at the Front Street Theatre, where the Douglas and anti-Douglas forces, along with several other factions, quarreled for five days. The anti-Douglas Democrats then walked out once more and set up their own convention at the Maryland Institute. The Maryland Institute Democrats nominated states' rights candidate John C. Breckenridge of Kentucky, and the Front Street Theatre Democrats nominated Douglas.[4]

As the Democratic Party fell apart in Baltimore, another party was approaching its final days in the city, and still another was in Baltimore to gather itself together. By 1860, the American Party of Maryland retained its grip on political authority only in Baltimore and the governor's office in Annapolis. But Know-Nothing governor Thomas H. Hicks was already readjusting his party affiliation, and so were his fellow politicians in Baltimore. A new party, the Constitutional Unionists, offered them a replacement for the burnt-out remains of the Know-Nothing skyrocket. Their supreme concern now was preservation of the Union. That was also the objective of the new Constitutional Union Party, whose convention met in Baltimore.

The Constitutional Unionists recognized Senator John J. Crittenden of Kentucky as their founder, though he declined to accept their nomination for the presidency. At the end of 1859, Crittenden had called together 50 of his congressional colleagues who were affiliated with neither the Republican nor Democratic Party. Most were steadfast Whigs or disconnected Know-Nothings looking for a new political home. A committee of 10 was appointed to oversee construction of a new political party to accommodate them and others of like mind. Under the auspices of the committee, an appeal "to the people of the United States" was issued in February 1860, announcing the new party's platform—simply "Union and the Constitution." John Pendleton Kennedy was one of the authors of the appeal. It summoned Unionists to choose delegates from their states for a national convention in Baltimore. Delegates from 16 states eventually assembled in a building on Fayette Street, the former First Presbyterian Church. Two delegations showed up claiming to represent Baltimore. The convention sidestepped controversy by seating both and splitting the city's votes between them.[5]

Another difference of opinion, however, was more difficult to avoid. Some of the delegates urged that the first order of business should be nomination of a presidential candidate; others insisted that it should be the drafting of a platform. A Pennsylvania delegate declared that if the new party succeeded politically, he "wanted that success founded upon a principle and not upon a man" — in other words, a "definite platform." Baltimore mayor Thomas Swann disagreed: "When Mr. Crittenden stood upon the platform to call the convention together, that was platform enough for Maryland." Murat Halstead, a Cincinnati journalist who watched from the gallery, observed that "the worthies here in Convention assembled all fell to abusing platforms. There was probably as much discretion as virtue in this, for the delegates would find it impossible to agree on an expression of principles." The delegates did agree that a committee consisting of one member from each state should consider all resolutions proposed on the floor of the convention, including the question of the party's platform.[6]

The committee reported at the start of the next day's session. The platform proposed, in its entirety, was "the constitution of the country, the Union of the States, and the enforcement of the law." The delegates gave it nine cheers and passed it unanimously. This outpouring of unanimity was followed by a difference of opinion about the method of voting to be adopted in nominating a presidential candidate. It was resolved by an ingenious delegate from Virginia who suggested a scheme so complex that it satisfied almost everyone, except the Maryland delegation. Maryland had withdrawn from the first roll-call vote because, according to Halstead, its delegation was mystified by the voting scheme, which it could not get "through its head without a surgical operation."[7]

Fortunately, it took only two ballots for Tennessee's John Bell to achieve a two-thirds vote. His principal competitor was Sam Houston. By the time the roll call reached Virginia on the second ballot, Bell had secured a simple majority of the convention. To make his nomination unanimous, states that had already cast votes for other candidates went through the formality of changing them. Each declaration of unanimity for Bell was accompanied by speeches and ovations. Halstead complained that the convention was a bore: "too much unity here . . . to make it interesting." It was unity sustained by deliberate ambiguity. "They propose to accomplish that political salvation so devoutly to be wished by ignoring all the rugged issues of the day." In particular, Halstead noted, slavery was not once mentioned during the convention.[8]

Though delayed by a rainstorm, a "ratification" rally was held in Monument Square after the convention had concluded its business by nominating Edward Everett for the vice-presidency. The speakers' platform erected in the square was 60 feet long with a 30-foot tower at each end. One tower bore a portrait of George Washington; the other, Henry Clay. An arch between the towers provided sufficient space to display the entire platform of the Constitutional Union Party: "The Union, the Constitution, and the Enforcement of the Laws." US senator and former Know-Nothing Anthony Kennedy acted as master of ceremonies.[9]

VISIONS OF UNION

Senator Kennedy's literary older brother tried to preserve the Union in his own way. At the end of 1860, he finished a long essay, later printed as a pamphlet: *The Border States: Their Power and Duty in the Present Disordered Condition of the Country*. It offered a brief against secession and a plan to defeat it without coercion. Much of John Pendleton Kennedy's argument was aimed at South Carolina—the only state to have seceded when he was composing his essay. Kennedy asserted that behind all the Carolina bombast lay the same grievance that had roused South Carolinians during the nullification controversy of 1832. It was a matter of taxation. The state had seceded because its residents could no longer bear the tariffs imposed to protect northern manufacturers against foreign competition. The fevered defense of slavery, he insisted, was "a parade of idle and mischievous debate . . . a mere artifice of politicians."[10] The true disagreements reflected disparate material interests, not conscience, constitutional doctrine, or sacred tradition—in other words, were subject to resolution by practical compromise.[11]

The achievement of that compromise, Kennedy claimed, was the duty of the border states (in which he included Virginia and North Carolina). Their task was to make North and South abandon fanaticism and see slavery for what it was. The border states were prepared for this duty because they had been "the chief and only sufferers from the inroads of organized abolitionists who had stealthily abstracted their slaves" and each year sent almost a million dollars' worth of human chattel on the Underground Railroad bound for freedom. The border states, moreover, were most troubled by the difficulties of enforcing the Fugitive Slave Act. Yet they firmly believed that the best response to such incursions was "the due exercise of the power of the government," not "resort to a covert revolution that seeks to legalize its action by taking the name of secession."[12]

If the border states could respond so temperately to such direct aggression, without secession or violence, surely they could work out a peaceful resolution of the complaints voiced in the deeper South by people less immediately exposed to northern insults and attacks. If the border states' mediation proved unsuccessful, and the Union disintegrated, then the border states might form a confederacy of their own. This would "serve as a centre of reinforcement for the reconstruction of the Union." Northerners, wrote Kennedy, were far from unified on the issue of slavery. The more moderate among them—in Pennsylvania, New York, New Jersey—might find they had more in common with a confederation of border states than with stern New England abolitionists. A southern confederacy might be even more susceptible to the appeals of moderation. A polity founded on secession, after all, was inherently unstable. The states of the old Union—North and South—would gradually regroup around the country's center.[13]

Kennedy's plan for preserving the Union was an articulate and inventive expression of Baltimoreans' more general determination to talk their way around the issue of slavery. But his attempt, like theirs, was ultimately a failure. After declaring slavery a mere pretext for disunion, Kennedy devoted much of his essay to a discussion of the subject. He had only to consider the results of the election held just a month before he finished his essay. Slavery was the pivotal factor in Maryland's electoral realignment. Democratic gains were concentrated in rural counties with substantial slave populations. The Know-Nothings held on only in Baltimore.[14]

Kennedy's attempt to sideline the issue of slavery overlooked the extent to which race itself was a source of rancorous division in his own state. In 1859, Colonel Curtis M. Jacobs, an Eastern Shore slave owner and a member of the General Assembly, introduced a bill to curtail the rights of Maryland's free black people. The announced objective of his proposal was the abolition of "free-negroism." The bill would require every African American in the state—both slave and free—to carry a pass, a document that might be used to restrict movement. It would also outlaw the manumission of slaves and prohibit the functioning of independent black church congregations. Free black people who fell into debt might be sold back into slavery, and those who left the state would not be allowed to return except as slaves. In short, Jacobs wanted to ensure that every black resident of Maryland lived in bondage.[15]

Baltimore's black churches mobilized to fight the bill. The congregation gathered at Bethel AME Church at 3:00 o'clock one morning for an entire day of prayer and fasting to summon up the strength to defeat the legislation. Though black Baltimoreans could not vote, they could lobby. The city's barbers, most of whom were black, urged their customers to sign a petition opposing the Jacobs bill. The General Assembly received a petition from 200 of Baltimore's "best" white women protesting the proposed impositions on the liberty of free black people, and two of Baltimore's most prominent attorneys circulated another petition among the city's male elite in support of the same position. None of Baltimore's newspapers endorsed the legislation. All of the bill's proposals were defeated in the General Assembly. Weakened versions were later presented as referenda, and they were defeated as well.[16]

CITY ON THE EDGE

Less than a week after Abraham Lincoln was elected president, Baltimore's new mayor delivered his inaugural message. George William Brown took note of his Reform Association's sweeping victory over the Know-Nothings. He emphasized that the voters had supported the Reformers "on the ground . . . that national politics should be entirely disregarded in the administration of municipal affairs." It took only a few moments for Brown to contradict himself. A period of "great prosperity" seemed to lie ahead for Baltimore, he said, "but the prospect has been suddenly clouded by the effect produced on some of the Southern states by the recent Presidential election." The "welfare of this community is inseparably bound up with the preservation of the Union."[17]

Like John Pendleton Kennedy, Mayor Brown struggled to avoid the questions that agitated national politics, but some of his constituents refused to let them go. Local organizations committed to Stephen Douglas and John C. Breckenridge continued to operate in Baltimore even after their champions had been defeated.[18] The disputes that threatened to fracture the Union threatened public order in Baltimore.

One of Brown's first acts as mayor was to invite the supervisory staff of the police department to his office. The mayor assured the marshal, his deputy, the department's eight captains, and eight lieutenants that he "would do everything on his part to assist the police in the preservation of order and the protection of property."[19] Legislation drafted by Brown's Reform Association had sharply reduced the mayor's authority over the police. The mayor had just one vote on the state-controlled board of police. Perhaps Brown hoped to increase his personal influence with the police by dealing with them directly rather than through the board. Weeks after his meeting with the police commanders, he visited the central police station, accompanied by the department's marshal. The mayor looked over the vagrants rounded up the night before and "expressed his approbation" for the marshal's order to arrest "all such characters."[20]

Because the police operated under the authority of the state, the mayor's informal influence might be needed to keep them responsive to local sensibilities. The mayor also needed their discreet assistance to contain local eruptions of sectional conflict. Shortly after Brown took office, many Baltimoreans began to run up a modified version of South Carolina's Palmetto flag. It bore the familiar palm, but with a rattlesnake coiled around the trunk, encircled by 15 stars—one for each slave state. The *Sun* announced that it was "all the rage," though Mayor Brown claimed that such flags were immediately hauled down wherever they appeared. One of the flags raised over a firehouse in West Baltimore attracted particular attention. It flew above a meeting of the "Southern Volunteers," whose members and prospective members filled the firehouse and spilled onto the streets outside. The deputy marshal of police and 20 officers stood by to ensure that the proceedings did not get out of hand. The volunteers' spokesman announced that the organization's purpose was "the maintenance of Southern honor and the equal rights of the States in the Union." Then a succession of resolutions won approval by acclamation. The *Sun* reported that these "were properly conservative in tone," but "nevertheless breathed the true Southern spirit." The organization enrolled 100 new members.[21]

Signs of impending trouble were difficult to ignore. But public officials in Baltimore and Maryland tried to overcome the difficulty rather than face the trouble. Governor Thomas Hicks, once a Know-Nothing but now a Unionist, resisted urgent demands that he summon the General Assembly into special session to determine how Maryland should respond to the national crisis. Hicks held his silence until he received an entreaty signed by a former governor and some of the state's most prominent citizens, imploring him to call the legislature into session immediately. The governor responded that assembling the legislature to discuss the crisis would only inflame the excitement already far too prevalent in Maryland. He offered the sensible advice that Marylanders should wait for the new Lincoln administration to show its hand before acting on their anxieties about the policies it might pursue.[22]

Severn Teackle Wallis, one of Baltimore's most eminent attorneys, could not wait. He attacked Hicks not only for refusing to call the legislature into session but for urging Marylanders to "cling to the Union." In the diminished Union, Maryland's political role would be marginal at best. It had originally entered a Union in which Maryland was "a Central State, the tendrils of her prosperity fastening, upon every side, to the confederated communities around her. You break that confederacy in the midst, leaving her a border province with a foreign nation and perhaps an enemy beside her." More to the point, clinging to the Union meant "clinging to the Republican party"—a partnership that few Marylanders could stomach.[23]

In Baltimore, the Brown administration did its best to obscure the perils of a border city as the country fell to sectional warfare. In January 1861, for example, the *Sun* reported that a police captain "with a large body of men" had been "hovering about Fort McHenry, and a vigilant watch is being kept from the land and water side." The official explanation for the police presence was that burglars were operating in the area, but there were hardly any houses to be burglarized in the vicinity of the fort, which had been defended by a single US Army sergeant until the police showed up. Two artillery companies, however, were on their way from Fort Leavenworth.[24] The police were holding the fort until the reinforcements arrived.

In the meantime, the municipality busied itself with familiar local issues. On January 8, 1861, the day before Mississippi seceded, Mayor Brown issued his annual message. A significant portion was devoted to the well-known irregularities by which the City Passenger Railway had secured the right to operate on Baltimore's streets. Then he discussed the city's water supply, the construction of a new jail, and the location of a new almshouse. Only at the end of his message did he mention the national crisis that was destroying the Union: "it is not within the province of the Mayor to make suggestions in response to proposed measures bearing on questions of national importance."[25]

Baltimore's political authorities seemed determined to carry on business as usual even in the face of radically unusual circumstances. Like Mayor Brown, they acknowledged that the political survival of the nation was under threat, but they insisted that "national politics should be entirely disregarded in the administration of municipal offices." This parochial principle carried less weight among Baltimore's citizens than its public officials. The Southern Volunteers and the partisans of Bell and Breckenridge brought sectional loyalties and national issues into local politics. But some of Baltimore's citizens seemed just as resolutely focused on local concerns as the city's officials and just as resistant to the distractions posed by the crisis in national politics.

At the end of February 1861, after all the "cotton" states of the Deep South had seceded, some of the city's residents felt that the time was right to construct a city hall. Their appeal, signed "Many Baltimoreans," was published in the *Sun*. Baltimore had never had a proper city hall. It made do with buildings designed for other purposes. The city had leased a parcel of land on Holliday Street intended for such a structure, but had not yet secured the funds needed to build it. In the meantime, the officers of the municipality were housed in buildings already standing on the property, most of which had been private dwellings. According to "Many Baltimoreans," these accommodations were "a disgrace humiliating to city pride and offensive to architectural taste." Baltimore was the third largest city in the nation but did not have a city hall appropriate to its status. Its backwardness in this respect undermined its prospects in the competition for commerce and industry. "Many Baltimoreans" acknowledged the "national difficulties" of the time, but insisted that work on a city hall should proceed "whether the Union be permanently severed, peaceably or not."[26]

A few days before this plea, Abraham Lincoln passed through the city in the middle of the night on the way to his inauguration. His travel plans had originally included a stop in Baltimore, where he would deliver some reassuring remarks, as he had in the many towns along his route to Washington. On the advice of detective Allan Pinkerton, however, the presidential party traveled through Baltimore at night and in secret. Pinkerton had been retained by the Philadelphia, Wilmington, and Baltimore Railroad to investigate a rumored plot to assassinate Lincoln during his stop in Baltimore. The plot, writes David Stashower, "stands as a defining moment marking a crucial transition from civilized debate to open hostilities."[27] In less than two months, Baltimore would experience another crucial transition—from the threat of death to actual fatalities.

FIRST BLOOD

The war started at Fort Sumter, but the killing began in Baltimore. On April 18, 1861, state and local public officials finally acknowledged the possibility of a violent eruption. Governor Hicks issued a proclamation noting that Maryland's "peculiar position" at the junction of North and South shaped its residents' sharply divergent views about secession, union, and slavery. He urged them to "abstain from all heated controversy . . . to avoid all things that tend to crimination and recrimination." Mayor Brown's proclamation concurred and expressed his support for the governor's pledge that no troops would be sent from Maryland except to defend Washington. In other words, the state's soldiers would not participate in the "coercion" of the South, a touchy point even for local Unionists. In fact, it was the point that divided them. Constitutional Unionists opposed secession but insisted on conciliation of the wayward states. Unconditional Unionists insisted that secession was unconstitutional and should be met with force. The mayor, a Constitutional Unionist, stood for a moderate and conciliatory response, with the hope that "the storm of civil war which now threatens the country will at least pass over our beloved State and leave it unharmed."[28]

A day after the proclamations, a Baltimore mob attacked Massachusetts troops passing through the city on their way to defend Washington. The Massachusetts soldiers were among the first to respond to President Lincoln's call for 75,000 men to protect the capital. Soldiers traveling by rail from northern states to Washington had to change trains in Baltimore. The Philadelphia, Wilmington, and Baltimore line delivered them to the President Street Station just south of East Pratt Street. The troops continued their journey in horse-drawn passenger cars along tracks on Pratt Street, west to Howard Street and then south to the B&O's Camden Station, where they could board trains for Washington. The distance was something over a mile. The inconvenience was the product of a municipal prohibition against steam

President Street Station, the starting point for the Pratt Street Riot of April 19, 1861. The riot resulted in the first fatalities of the Civil War.

locomotives on city streets and the B&O's success in preventing other railroads from building direct lines from Baltimore to Washington.

Before the arrival of the Massachusetts regiment, several hundred volunteers from the North had marched through the city from various rail depots to Camden Station, with adequate police protection and little trouble. The Sixth Massachusetts together with some unarmed volunteers from Pennsylvania arrived at the President Street Station on the morning of April 19, and seven companies completed the journey from one station to the other. A growing crowd jeered and threw stones at them but could not block them. As the mob expanded, a load of sand was dumped on the tracks near the intersection of Pratt and Gay Streets, topped with anchors dragged from nearby docks and a mound of cobblestones. When the next passenger cars reached this obstacle, the team of horses was hastily shifted from the front to the rear of the cars in order to retreat to the President Street Station.[29]

On their return to the depot, four companies of the Massachusetts regiment—about 220 men—disembarked and formed up to march to Camden Station. Outside, a small force of city policemen struggled with the mob. From the moment they stepped onto President Street, the soldiers had difficulty maintaining their formation as the crowd pressed around them. A member of the mob marching ahead of the soldiers unfurled the South Carolina flag, possibly a copy of the ones that had recently flown over the city, and for a moment the Union troops were marching behind a symbol of secession.[30] Then "a whirlwind of stones" swept over the soldiers In the short distance from the station to Pratt Street, three members of the regiment were knocked to the ground by bottles or rocks, but all managed to keep up.[31]

As they crossed the bridge that carried Pratt Street over the Jones Falls, the soldiers may have been held up by construction debris left behind by workmen who were making repairs to the bridge. It was here that the troops began to fire their muskets into the crowd that pursued them; members of the mob had reportedly been firing pistols at the troops for some time. The officer in command of the detachment, Captain A. S. Follensbee, ordered his men to march at double quick time. As they reached the west end of the bridge, they encountered Mayor Brown, who had received word about their situation while he waited for them at Camden Station. Brown, armed only with an umbrella, took a position beside Follensbee at the head of the column, with the hope that his presence might temper the rage of his fellow Baltimoreans. He suggested that the captain rescind his order to march at quick time because the troops' hasty attempt to escape the mob might only encourage its pursuit. A member of the police board who had been waiting with Brown at Camden Station sent a message to Marshal George Kane instructing him to bring as many police officers as he could to protect the Union troops. Kane met them with about 40 policemen after the troops crossed Charles Street. His men formed a line, allowed the soldiers to pass through their ranks, and then pointed their revolvers at the pursuing mob. According to Mayor Brown, "The mob recoiled like water from a rock."[32]

The mob, however, had already killed four soldiers—two killed by gunshot, one beaten to death, and one who died of head injuries sustained in the "whirlwind" of missiles. Twelve civilians were dead. Thirty-six soldiers and an unknown number of civilians were injured.

The mob that met the soldiers was not the usual collection of Baltimore ruffians. More than half of those who can be identified held nonmanual occupations and owned more real and personal property than average Baltimoreans. Most were merchants or clerks or engaged in other commercial pursuits.[33] Customhouse clerks seem to have been active participants in the disorders. A witness who later testified in a court hearing said, "The people who were putting ankers [*sic*] on the track & abetting were as respectable in appearance as this Grand Jury."[34]

CHOOSING SIDES

Late in the afternoon, after the Sixth Massachusetts had boarded trains for Washington, a crowd gathered in Monument Square. Mayor Brown and other speakers condemned secession but also denounced the use of military coercion against the states of the Confederacy. Governor Hicks expressed his hope that the Union could be preserved, a hope that met a hostile response from the audience. Hicks then added that "I love my state and I love the Union, but I will suffer my right arm to be torn from my body before I will raise it to strike a sister state."[35]

The governor and the mayor had already sent a telegram to President Lincoln notifying him about the day's violence and requesting that no more troops be sent through Baltimore. A few hours later, they sent a more detailed letter to the White House repeating the request. A trio of prominent Baltimoreans (one of them a Republican) carried the letter to Washington on a late-night train. They were followed by US Senator Anthony Kennedy and Congressman J. Morrison Harris, who met with the president, the secretaries of state, treasury, and war, and Commanding General Winfield Scott. That evening, a small group of men gathered at the home of Mayor Brown, where Hicks was an overnight guest. There had been no reply to the telegram sent to the president, and the conferees had heard that more Union troops were set to pass through the city. They decided to send out a detachment of police officers and the Maryland Guard, a military force of doubtful loyalty to the Union, to burn the railroad bridges north and northeast of the city so that no more federal troops would be able to reach Baltimore.[36]

The next day, President Lincoln sent a telegram to Mayor Brown and Governor Hicks. Though he insisted that "troops *must* be brought" to Washington, he was not determined to bring them through Baltimore. General Scott had already suggested that federal troops could be marched around Baltimore rather than through it. "By this," wrote Lincoln, "a collision of the people of Baltimore with the troops will be avoided unless they go out of their way to seek it. I hope you will exert your influence to prevent this."[37]

But Hicks and Brown had already burned their bridges. In trying to keep Baltimore peaceful, they had temporarily cut Washington off from the North and prevented troops from reaching the capital, where they were badly needed. The destruction of the railroad bridges might be construed as a hostile act against the Union. It was not the only one. Very soon after the meeting in Monument Square, Governor Hicks had called out the militia to keep order. Some had already mobilized themselves. At best, the troops' loyalty to the Union was uncertain, and once mobilized, they might refuse to demobilize. Marshal Kane requested help from his friend Bradley Johnson in Frederick: "Streets red with Maryland blood; send expresses over the mountains of Maryland and Virginia for riflemen to come without delay. Fresh hordes will be down on us tomorrow. We will fight them and whip them, or die." Johnson arrived the next day with 70 men. He later became a Confederate general.[38]

Additional military manpower came from citizens spontaneously organizing into "associations for the defense of the city." On April 21, Charles Howard, president of the board of police commissioners, requested that Colonel Isaac Trimble "take charge of all organized Bodies who may choose to place themselves under your orders." Trimble would also become a Confederate general. Crowds ransacked hardware stores for firearms and ammunition. Trimble sought to obtain arms from several seceded states.[39]

Some US Army officers in Baltimore resigned their commissions. One of them, Colonel Benjamin Huger, later a Confederate general, was given command of the Maryland Guard and another militia regiment, the Independent Grays. The city council appropriated $500,000 for the "defense of the city."[40] There was no need to identify the aggressors.

Governor Hicks finally called a special session of the General Assembly. Baltimore's aroused secessionists demanded it. They threatened to take matters into their own hands if he refused again,[41] perhaps to summon up a convention of their own for a vote on secession.

Baltimore, it seemed, had shifted decisively toward the South. On April 24, a special election chose state legislators to replace the Know-Nothings expelled at the end of the last session, and it produced a solidly states' rights delegation. There were no other candidates. But there was something out of character about Baltimore's swing toward the South. The commercial and industrial city was an odd ally for the predominantly agricultural and slave-owning Confederacy, especially since the city's economy did not depend on slavery and its residents were not powerfully committed to the institution. The South's attachment to free trade was also out of joint with Baltimore's interest in the protection of domestic industry by tariff.[42]

Frank Towers suggests that the city's realignment was an artifact of local politics. The Reformers who took control of Baltimore's government in 1860 had defeated the Unionist Know-Nothings with the help of electoral reforms enacted by Democrats from the agricultural, slave-owning counties of Southern Maryland and the Eastern Shore. If the city's Reformers turned away from the South, they would undermine their alliance with their legislative allies and find themselves isolated in their confrontation with Baltimore's former Know-Nothings, now Unionists, who would gain strength from the federal patronage of the Lincoln administration.[43]

For President Lincoln, the loss of Maryland to the Confederacy meant that the nation's capital would be an isolated outpost in Confederate territory, cut off from troops and supplies from the North. After a White House meeting with Mayor Brown and another with Senator Anthony Kennedy, the president decided to avoid another confrontation with Baltimore's southern sympathizers. The War Department directed the Union commander in Philadelphia to put Washington-bound troops aboard steamboats near the mouth of the Susquehanna. The boats would circumvent Baltimore and land the soldiers at the Naval Academy in Annapolis, where they could board trains for the short ride to the capital. The president wanted to avoid provoking Baltimoreans, according to his aide John Hay, because "if quiet was kept in Baltimore a little longer, Maryland might be considered the first of the redeemed" for the Union.[44]

OCCUPIED CITY

Among the first units to arrive in Annapolis by the water route was the Eighth Massachusetts under the command of Brigadier General Benjamin Butler. Instead of proceeding to Washington, Butler's soldiers occupied Annapolis, over the protests of Governor Hicks. The presence of federal troops made the capital an inappropriate venue for the upcoming special session of the General Assembly; Hicks shifted the location to Frederick. In the days before the meeting of the legislature, the Union's military presence in Maryland grew rapidly. In Baltimore, however, secessionists were openly recruiting troops for the Confederacy. General Butler reported that the recruits were being marched south within a few miles of his position, and he asked whether he should try to stop them. He was ordered to intercept provisions headed for the South, but to let the men pass. An unknown number of secessionists of military age—the very men who might mount a violent resistance to the Union presence in Baltimore—were thus subtracted from the city's population.

Union troops on Federal Hill, their cannon trained on Baltimore. The city's residents were regarded as unreliable supporters of the Union. *Courtesy Maryland Historical Society, Item CC969*

By the time Hicks met with the General Assembly at Frederick on April 26, the legislators must have recognized that an ordinance of secession would be unenforceable. Maryland was occupied territory. The Union troops flowing through the state to Washington would not permit Maryland to leave the Union peacefully, and they had the strength to prevent it. The *Sun* reported that all of the railroad lines linking Baltimore to the rest of the country were controlled by federal troops.[45] It was now Baltimore's turn to face the possibility of isolation in enemy territory. The legislators who convened in Frederick had no choices to make. Hicks opened the session with a somber speech that set out no clear course for Maryland. The General Assembly as a whole was no more forthright. Both houses denied that they had authority to pass an act of secession.[46]

The General Assembly's inability to shape the course of events did not dampen the legislators' secessionist sympathies, but they found expression in largely symbolic resolutions complaining of the state's treatment by the federal government and its military forces. In Baltimore, a decided shift in the political climate was under way. In cutting the railroads that brought northern troops to Baltimore, the city had also damaged its own commerce, and there were second thoughts about the course that the city's leaders had chosen. The surge of southern spirit that followed the hostilities on Pratt Street only briefly obscured a base of support for the Union. Before the riot, a petition signed by 1,300 residents and business firms expressed support for Governor Hicks's refusal to convene the legislative session that Maryland's secessionists demanded, and another memorial signed by 5,000 citizens expressed the same view. Unionist sentiment resurfaced after the impact of the riot faded. Colonel Trimble dissolved the companies that had mobilized for defense of the city. The US flag flew once again over the customhouse. And, on the day the legislature adjourned, Hicks authorized the enlistment of volunteers to meet Maryland's quota of troops to defend Washington.[47]

The governor tried to salvage some vestige of neutrality by stipulating that Maryland's soldiers were not to serve outside Maryland and the District of Columbia. But Hicks must have found it difficult to sustain even this gesture of detachment from sectional discord as Union troops extended their occupation of his state. They made Maryland a part of the Union—willing or unwilling. On the same day that Hicks called up the state's volunteers for service in Washington, Baltimoreans woke to find Union guns atop Federal Hill and trained on the city.

General Butler, now commanding the Department of Annapolis, had taken control of the rail lines from the state capital toward Washington and those that led north to Baltimore. Not long before dusk on the night of May 13, Butler boarded a train with 1,000 infantry and half a dozen cannons, bound for Camden Station. The Sixth Massachusetts Regiment, with its Pratt Street veterans, was part of the detachment. At nightfall and under cover of a thunderstorm, they occupied Federal Hill. Butler gave orders that, if attacked, the artillery pieces on the hill and at Fort McHenry should target Monument Square, the traditional assembly point for Baltimore's mobs and mass meetings. He then issued a proclamation insisting that "rebellious acts must cease" and forbidding assemblies of armed men except for the city police and militia. But there was no trouble—except for Butler, who had occupied the city without explicit orders. General Scott removed him the day after his "hazardous occupation" of Baltimore and transferred him to the command of Fortress Monroe in Virginia.[48]

General Scott and his staff were not opposed to the occupation of Baltimore, but they were wary about leaving the operation to the discretion of a local commander. Instead of ordering federal troops to leave the city, Scott ordered Brevet Brigadier General George Cadwalader, in command of four Pennsylvania regiments, to replace Butler. Cadwalader's base was Fort McHenry, but his men occupied the rest of Locust Point, and their camps extended to Federal Hill, reaching the emplacement begun there by General Butler.[49]

Butler's departure marked a shift in the federal government's treatment of Baltimore's residents. President Lincoln had suspended the writ of habeas corpus in Maryland. Military commanders were empowered to place civilians under arrest without warrants and without specifying the charges against them, and to hold them in custody without regard to the demands of their attorneys or orders of courts. Butler had exercised this authority to arrest only one Baltimorean—wealthy indus-

Baltimore residents view General Butler's emplacement on Federal Hill.
Courtesy Enoch Pratt Free Library

trialist Ross Winans, who manufactured locomotives and other equipment for the B&O but had recently turned to the production of munitions. Winans was also a staunch states' rights secessionist who had been a member of Baltimore's delegation to the special session of the General Assembly in Frederick. He was arrested on the train while returning to Baltimore. Acting on instructions from Washington, Cadwalader freed Winans from confinement at Fort McHenry after the prisoner signed an oath of loyalty.[50]

MILITARY GOVERNMENT

General Cadwalader arrested John Merryman on the same authority that Butler had used to imprison Winans. Merryman was a militia officer who had participated in the destruction of railroad bridges after the Pratt Street riot. He was also suspected of communicating with the enemy and belonging to an underground secessionist cell possessing weapons belonging to the United States. Merryman was arrested without a warrant at his home near Cockeysville at 2 a.m. This time, however, Roger B. Taney, chief justice of the US Supreme Court (and a prominent Marylander), traveled to Baltimore to deliver, in person, a writ of habeas corpus to secure Merryman's release. Cadwalader refused to honor the writ and maintained that he was authorized to do so by President Lincoln. Taney then sent US Marshal Washington Bonifant to take Cadwalader into custody to face a charge of contempt. On arriving at Fort McHenry, the general's headquarters, Bonifant found that no one would let him in. The case made its way to the US Supreme Court, where Chief Justice Taney wrote the opinion in *Ex Parte Merryman*, denying that Lincoln's suspension of habeas corpus was lawful. Among other things, the Constitution provides that only Congress, not the president, can suspend habeas corpus. But Taney, like Marshal

Bonifant, who stood helpless outside the gates of Fort McHenry, had no means to enforce the law. He could only send a copy of his opinion to President Lincoln.[51]

Merryman was eventually brought to court, charged with treason, released on bond, and never tried. Long before that time, Cadwalader had left Baltimore. He was replaced by General Nathaniel Banks, commander of the new Department of Maryland. In June, General Scott ordered Banks to arrest Marshal Kane. Banks sent a force of 1,000 men to Kane's home on St. Paul Street. Every Baltimore police officer encountered on the way was taken into custody (and released after Kane's arrest). Kane answered the door himself, observed the size of the force that had come for him, and said that he would have complied just as promptly to a note from General Banks.[52]

By midsummer, Major General John Dix had replaced Banks. Dix knew Baltimore by reputation. "There is no city in the Union," he wrote, "in which domestic disturbances have been more frequent or carried to more fatal extremes, from 1812 to the present day."[53] He arrived just before the news that Confederate forces had decisively defeated Union troops at the battle of Manassas, or Bull Run. Dix and his staff were concerned that the victory might reignite secessionist spirit in the city. Though the general had 17 regiments and a battery of artillery to deal with such contingencies, he nevertheless ordered the arrest of elected officials suspected of holding southern sympathies. Mayor Brown was taken into custody along with 10 members of the state legislature and a congressman, all from Baltimore. (Ross Winans added a second arrest to his record.) At least 18 legislators from other parts of Maryland, including the Speaker of the house of delegates, were also arrested. Many were released after they signed a loyalty oath to the US government. Few legislators were paroled, however, until after the state election in November 1861.[54]

Mayor Brown, Marshal Kane, and the police commissioners were not so fortunate. Their confinement lasted a year longer. In the meantime, they appealed to Congress to protest their imprisonment. The House passed a resolution asking President Lincoln to explain why the police officials had been arrested. He responded that "it is judged to be incompatible with the public interest at this time to furnish the information called for in the resolution."[55]

Perhaps the "information" was just too complicated. Shortly after General Banks had Kane arrested, he dismissed the police commissioners. An army provost marshal would assume authority over the police. The commissioners ignored their dismissal and continued to meet and issue orders to their officers. The full board of commissioners, including the mayor, "put the officers and men off duty for the present, leaving them subject, however, to the rules and regulations of the service . . . and to the orders which the Board might see fit thereafter to issue, when the present illegal suspension of their functions should be removed."[56] General Banks charged that the commissioners had furloughed the police "intending to leave the city without any police protection whatsoever." The commissioners, as Banks saw it, still held "subject to their orders, a large body of armed men, for some purpose not known to the government."[57] For Banks that was sufficient to justify the commissioners' arrest.

The status of the idle officers was unresolved. It was a subject on which Mayor

Brown and General Dix exchanged sharp words. Brown, without consulting Dix, had ordered the city register to pay the off-duty police officers for two weeks' "arrearages" in salary. In fact, the "old police" apparently received their wages from the time they went on leave until at least January 1862, in spite of Dix's prohibition of further payments. Dix had written to Brown ordering a halt to these disbursements, adding that "the continued compensation of a body of men who have been suspended in their functions by the order of the Government, is calculated to bring its authority into disrespect." Brown claimed that he had been unaware of Dix's instructions because the general's letter had arrived at his city office when Brown was at his country house, but he expressed his determination to make the payments to the policemen: "I feel it to be my duty to enter my protest against this interference, by military authority, with the powers lawfully committed by the State of Maryland to the officers of the city corporation." He would inform the police officers that they could expect no further payments from the city, but he would grant them their back pay "unless prohibited by your further order."[58]

General Dix launched another letter: "I cannot, without acquiescing in a principle, assent to the payment of an arrearage to the old city police." This time, Brown responded that the letter had been forwarded to his country house while he was in the city, and he had not seen it until he had already approved, and the off-duty officers had received, their two weeks' pay. He added that he saw no "violation of principle" in making this payment. "I recognize in the action of the Government of the United States nothing but the assertion of superior force."[59] Brown was arrested three days later. The city continued to pay his salary during his "absence from the city" for at least five months. Brown was succeeded, after a brief interval, by the Constitutional Unionist president of the council's first branch, John Lee Chapman, who would later be elected mayor in his own right.[60]

Baltimore surely harbored southern sympathizers and even traitors. The city, after all, had welcomed Union troops with a riot. Many of the town's sons and husbands had enlisted with Confederate forces, and the families and friends they left behind cannot have been reliably devoted to the Union cause. But the conflicts that flared up between Union authorities and local officials probably reflected something more than the enmity between North and South. Mayor Brown's inaugural assertion that "national politics should be entirely disregarded in the administration of municipal affairs" was not entirely obliterated by military occupation, and it continued to generate friction between the military and civilian governments. Parochialism was Baltimore's strategy for sealing itself off from the nation's Armageddon, which had made Maryland the geographic center of a civil war and threatened to transform the state into a battleground.

Union authorities made at least one concession to the town's uneasiness about dealing with national authorities and issues. After Marshal Kane's arrest, a native Baltimorean was appointed provost marshal to take command of the police—Colonel John Kenly, a respected local attorney, a veteran of the Mexican War, and the popular commanding officer of the First Maryland Volunteers. When Kenly assumed control of the police department, he indicated that current members of the force could continue to serve, but they would take their orders from him, not from Kane or the board of police commissioners. The commissioners challenged his usurpation as an "arbitrary exercise of military power at variance with the laws of Maryland." When they placed the police force on "temporary leave," Kenly immediately recruited 400 new police officers—the "federal police"—who would serve under military authority. Congress appropriated $100,000 to cover their pay, an expense that would soon be transferred to the City of Baltimore.[61]

Kenly seems to have found his duties difficult and awkward. After three weeks, he asked to be relieved as provost marshal so that he could resume command of the First Maryland Volunteers. Mediating between the demands of the federal military authorities and the placebound sensibilities of his fellow Baltimoreans had evidently proven too much to bear.[62]

Chapter 20 **CITY AT WAR**

President Lincoln called a special session of Congress in 1861. His purpose was to win congressional approval for the funds he needed to wage war. On June 13, Maryland held a special election to choose its representatives for the session. To rule out apprehensions about military interference at the polls, General Banks assured Mayor Brown that Union soldiers would be confined to their posts on election day "except for those who are voters under the Constitution and laws of Maryland." This category was rather large. Three Maryland regiments were granted leave to exercise the franchise. In spite of their presence, secessionists and southern sympathizers seem to have campaigned freely and without military interference. A Southern Rights convention nominated a former ambassador to Mexico to run in Baltimore's Fourth Congressional District.[1] But Unionists carried every district in the state.

In Baltimore, the Unionist candidate in the Fourth Congressional District was Henry Winter Davis, the Know-Nothing orator and current incumbent. His popularity had suffered since his last election. When he first took his seat in the House, in 1856, he had conceived a grand strategy for averting the crisis about to consume the country. Davis envisioned a coalition of southern Whigs and Know-Nothings with northern Republicans, uniting to defeat secessionist Democrats. The southern Democrats had already shown their hand by threatening to walk out of the country if abolitionist Republican John Fremont should be elected president.[2]

In one of several attempts to forge his alliance between southerners and northerners, Davis became the only representative from a slave state to vote for New Jersey Republican William Pennington for Speaker of the House, in a closely fought contest. Without Davis's vote, Pennington would not have become Speaker. Northern newspapers hailed Davis as a hero. The Maryland House of Delegates censured him by a vote of 62 to 1.[3]

Davis's constituents turned against him as well. He lost the Fourth District to Henry May, who styled himself an "Independent Unionist."

May had previously been a Democratic member of Congress, who backed up his claim to party loyalty by declaring that he had never voted for a Whig in his life. He was ejected from his seat when Davis rode the Know-Nothing tide into the House of Representatives in 1855. May's first public appearance as a Union man occurred when he turned up at a Unionist meeting in Baltimore about 10 days before he won the party's nomination in the Fourth District.[4]

Congressman May's return to office began badly. Before he could take his seat, a Wisconsin congressman introduced a resolution instructing the House Judiciary Committee to investigate allegations that May had been "holding criminal intercourse and correspondence with persons in armed rebellion against the Government of the United States." The evidence against him came from articles in Richmond and Charleston newspapers suggesting that May visited Richmond to discuss the possible secession of Maryland and the readiness of 30,000 armed Marylanders to join the Confederate cause. The Judiciary Committee was unwilling to condemn May on the testimony of Confederate newspapers, and May himself was not present to defend himself because he was still in Richmond recovering from an illness.

When May finally occupied his seat in the House, he was invited, by unanimous consent, to offer a "personal explanation" of his recent activities. May complained that the charges made against him were "an unparalleled outrage on the privileges of a Representative." But he quickly veered from self-justification to a condemnation of the military authorities who had become the tyrants of Baltimore. His constituents, he said, were "bound in chains; absolutely without the rights of a free people in this land; every precious right belonging to them under the Constitution, trampled into the dust." A succession of congressmen rose to complain that May had strayed from personal explanation to political denunciation. But he was allowed to proceed. He presented a memorial from the imprisoned police commissioners of Baltimore. Then he instructed the clerk to read into the record Marshal Kane's report of his efforts to protect the Sixth Massachusetts on its march along Pratt Street. Asked directly what he was doing in Richmond, May explained that he was linked to Virginia by ties of family and friendship, and he had gone there "to inquire into the disposition of the people of the South; to mingle freely with them . . . and in the sacred office of pacificator, endeavor to avert, assuage, or terminate this awful civil strife."[5]

Congressman May voted against the $100,000 appropriation to pay federal police in Baltimore. He was not the only Marylander to do so. Senator Anthony Kennedy also opposed it, arguing that Baltimore's own police force should return to service. May, however, referred to the police appropriation as the "wages of oppression." He introduced one of several resolutions demanding that President Lincoln explain the arrest of Baltimore's police commissioners. Another of his resolutions called for an armistice between the Union and the Confederacy and negotiations "to preserve the Union, if possible, but if not, then a peaceful separation."[6]

In September 1861, Henry May was arrested by order of the secretary of war. May's brother wrote to President Lincoln pleading for the congressman's release. May had been confined to a casemate at Fort McHenry with 32 other prisoners, but later transferred to Fort Monroe and then Fort Lafayette. He was set free on the grounds of failing health, but returned to his seat in the House. An attempt to expel him from Congress was unsuccessful.[7] But the Fourth District's voters removed him from office at the end of his term and gave his seat back to Henry Winter Davis.

DISAPPEARING DEMOCRATS

Just as Henry May found it expedient to leave his Democratic past behind and re-invent himself as an Independent Unionist, Baltimoreans in general abandoned the Democratic Party. In October 1861, there were no Democratic candidates for the first branch of the city council. One Unionist candidate stood for election in each of the city's 20 wards. Only four of them faced any opposition, and the challengers, like Henry May, identified themselves as Independents, not Democrats. The Unionist candidates defeated all four of them.[8]

Baltimore's Union Party held itself apart from the small contingent of local Republicans because it regarded Republican free-soilers—"Black Republicans"—with as much distaste as it did secessionist fire-eaters. Abolitionists and secessionists were held responsible for the rift that resulted in warfare between North and South. The objective of Baltimore's Unionists was to sidestep the issues that would drag Baltimore into the deadly center of the storm consuming the nation. To that end, the party sought candidates with neutral political records or none at all. Baltimorean Augustus Bradford was one of these. He had been elected clerk of the city's circuit court as a Whig, but retired from politics during the 1850s and was conveniently free of any public record on the nasty divisions of that decade. He was elected governor overwhelmingly at the end of 1861, succeeding Thomas Hicks, the last Know-Nothing governor, who went on to become a Unionist US senator. The Unionists (including many former Know-Nothings) also swept the state legislature and judicial elections. There was little evidence that the result reflected military interference. Even states' rights sympathizers described the election as "quiet" and "free from molestation."[9]

In fact, Baltimoreans themselves seemed just as ready as the military to impose restrictions on the political freedom of local residents. In July 1862, Governor Augustus Bradford presided over an "immense Union meeting" in Monument Square, where one speaker after another warned the audience to be vigilant in detecting the treasonous crimes of their disloyal neighbors. Bradford himself warned of "the horde of traitors in our midst." Another speechmaker equated insufficient dedication to the Union cause with treason. This was, he said, "no time to hesitate and doubt . . . to hesitate was to die and to doubt was to be damned. To hold back was treachery, and treachery should meet the traitor's doom." The meeting closed with the approval of a resolution recommending, among other things, that the property and slaves of rebels should be confiscated. It also charged that some recipients of local government patronage and contracts were "men and firms notoriously disloyal, and not a few of them actually engaged in aiding the enemies of the government." The resolution's final section demanded that the commander of the local military district administer an oath to all men over 18 years old. They were to pledge "true allegiance to the United States, its Constitution and its laws," renounce any "faith or

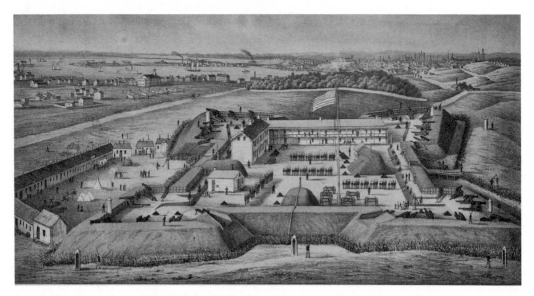

Fort Marshall, one of several federal strong points in occupied Baltimore. The fort was located in the city's southeast, in a neighborhood known to current residents as Highlandtown.
Courtesy Enoch Pratt Free Library, Cator Collection

fellowship with the so-called Confederate states," and pledge "property and life to the sacred performance of this oath of allegiance."[10]

A few days later, the first branch of the city council adopted a resolution of its own, requesting General John E. Wool, commander of the "Middle Department," to administer the oath "to all the citizens of the City of Baltimore at the earliest possible period." General Wool had been seated on the platform at the Monument Square rally. His remarks were notable for their brevity. He said that his business was not to speak but to conquer the enemies of his country. When presented with the city council's proposal for a "test oath," he declined to make use of the loyalty pledge. Its enforcement, he said, might "send twenty thousand men to swell the army of Jefferson Davis."[11]

Wool was not averse to intervention in local politics. Shortly before the mass meeting in Monument Square, he suggested that a majority of the city council's second branch should resign because they had failed to approve an appropriation of $300,000 to provide bounties for local volunteers who enlisted in the Union Army. All of those who had opposed the appropriation followed his suggestion.[12]

Union military authorities had begun their occupation of Baltimore by making arrests to crush subversion. Now they made suggestions. Suggestions succeeded for much the same reason that Know-Nothing thugs had been able to suppress opposition voters without resort to physical force. Like the Know-Nothings, the Union Army had demonstrated that it was in control of the city and that defiance of its authority was futile. In fact, the Union Army had transformed Baltimore into something just short of a military base. By war's end, there were nine military hospitals in the city. At least a dozen Union camps occupied the parks, squares, and fields in and around Baltimore. There were almost as many fortified positions, most of which were defended by artillery pieces. The most important of these were Fort McHenry (72 guns), Fort Federal Hill (47 guns), and Fort Marshall (60 guns), on high ground in southeast Baltimore in the area later known as Highlandtown. Taken together, these three fortresses could rain shells on the entire city and all of its rail lines.[13]

The artillery pieces remained silent. Baltimore's political authorities needed no prompting from Union generals to embrace the Union cause. Political circumstance had engendered a new consensus. Many Confederate sympathizers had left town, and those who remained seem to have recognized that staying put meant staying quiet.

WAR AND POLITICS

The Unionists' one-party rule in Baltimore was a bit less than it seemed. The Unionists never achieved unity. The only principle they held in common was opposition to secession.[14] Some opposed both secession and slavery. Others opposed secession but not slavery. Still others opposed secession but also opposed the use of coercion against the Confederacy as a means of defeating it. There were Regular Unionists, Independent Unionists, Conservative Unionists, Unconditional Unionists, and Conditional Unionists.[15]

Military conflict, however, constrained factional strife. Confederate incursions into Maryland kept the city and its military forces on alert. The deadly encounter at Antietam in 1862 did not directly threaten Baltimore. The battlefield was 75 miles away in Washington County, but some residents claimed they could hear the rumble of artillery, and Antietam's wounded flooded the city along with Confederate prisoners. Gettysburg hit closer to home. J. E. B. Stuart's cavalry was reported to have come within eight miles of Baltimore's city limits. Thousands of militiamen were put to work on the city's fortifications. Six thousand pro-Union members of the Loyal Leagues were armed, issued three days' rations, and posted to the outer defenses. Mayor John Lee Chapman urged residents to meet in their wards to organize companies for defense of the city. Major General John Schenck, who commanded the US Army's Middle Department from his base in Baltimore, imposed martial law and announced that "peaceful citizens are required to remain quietly in their homes."[16]

Another scare came in 1864, when Confederate General Jubal Early raided Maryland to relieve Union pressure on Richmond. A Marylander under Early's command, Major Harry Gilmor, led a detachment of Confederate cavalry on raids around Baltimore, approaching the city's limits on Charles Street, where his men burned Governor Bradford's country home—retaliation for Union troops' burning the home of Virginia's governor. On York Road they clashed with a Union cavalry detachment. Riding east to Magnolia Station in Harford County, Gilmor's men captured and destroyed two trains and burned several bridges. After the war, Gilmor would become a Baltimore police commissioner.

The proximity of the Confederate forces during the Gettysburg campaign may have contributed to a new severity in the military rule of Maryland. Preparing for the state election of 1863, General Schenck issued "General Order No. 53." It repre-

sented a departure from his predecessors' announced policy against military interference in elections. Schenck's order instructed his men to arrest anyone "found at,
or hanging about, or approaching any poll." If voters were suspected of disloyalty,
Schenck's men could demand that the election judges administer an oath of allegiance, as specified in Order No. 53. This included a pledge to adhere to the federal
government and its Constitution in preference to any law or resolution of the state
legislature and prohibited "communication with . . . any person . . . within . . . insurrectionary States" unless approved by "the lawful authority."[17]

Thomas Swann, chairman of the Union State Central Committee, wrote to President Lincoln expressing his apprehensions about military interference in the election, and Governor Bradford sent a letter on the same subject. Lincoln responded
that he had consulted General Schenck, who had assured him that violence would
almost certainly erupt on election day. The president modified Schenck's draconian
order such that only those actually engaged in violence or disruption at or near the
polls would be subject to arrest, but Lincoln let the other provisions stand. Bradford
issued a proclamation declaring Schenck's order "most obnoxious and entirely without justification." It was all the more offensive "in view of the known fact that at least
two of the five provost marshals of the State are themselves candidates for important
State offices." Bradford reminded the election judges that they could "summon to
their aid any of the executive officers of the county" in addition to the "whole power
of the county itself to preserve order at the polls"—implicitly putting the military
authorities on notice that they might be headed for confrontations with county officials. The military authorities responded by prohibiting the publication of Bradford's
proclamation in any newspaper. The governor issued his protest as a pamphlet.[18]

In the election campaign of 1863, the multiple factions of the Union Party divided
into two camps, ostensibly on the question of slavery. The Unconditional Unionists
favored immediate and uncompensated emancipation. The Conditional Unionists,
led by Thomas Swann and John P. Kennedy, also came out for immediate emancipation, but in a manner "easiest for master and slave." Masters, for example, might
be compensated for their slaves, and slaves who had not yet reached adulthood
might serve a period as their masters' "apprentices."[19] The Conditional Unionists
acknowledged the inevitability of emancipation, but they did not want to burden
the paramount goal of restoring the Union by linking it to the abolition of slavery.
They were also put off by the Lincoln administration's use of constitutionally questionable measures to suppress dissent and by the intrusive military presence in state
elections. The Unconditionals, on the other hand, professed full support for the
president and his war with the South.[20]

Unconditional Unionists dominated the legislature elected in 1863. They approved a bill providing for a special election in April 1864, at which Maryland voters would decide whether to call a state convention to draft a new constitution,
replacing the one approved in 1851. The 1851 constitution had protected slavery by
prohibiting the General Assembly from "abolishing the relationship of master or
slave." The determination to overturn this restriction had helped to promote the
movement for a constitutional convention.[21]

By 1864, however, Maryland's defenders of slavery had little left to defend. Almost half of Maryland's black population was already free when the war began. And slavery receded as the war proceeded, especially after 1862, when slavery was abolished in the District of Columbia, putting freedom close at hand for the large slave populations of Prince George's County and Southern Maryland.[22] Union forces contributed to the further erosion of slavery when they conscripted both slaves and free blacks as laborers. The enlistment of black soldiers exposed a complex web of interests among whites who owned slaves and those who did not. Slaves had originally been exempt from recruitment. Their exclusion raised resentments among whites who employed free black workers. Enlistment of free blacks in the army reduced their supply in the private labor market and drove their wages higher. But slave owners themselves were apprehensive about recruitment of free black men; they worried that the visible presence of black soldiers, in uniform and bearing arms, might make their slaves restless and insolent.[23] A further complication was a ruling by the secretary of war that black recruits would count as "credible" against the state's enlistment quota, thereby reducing the likelihood that white Marylanders would have to be conscripted to meet the state's allotment of Union recruits. Unconditional Unionist Henry Winter Davis shrewdly made the case for African American recruitment by referring to the black soldier as the poor man's substitute.[24]

The uncertainties that accumulated around the institution of slavery led to a collapse in the price for slaves. In 1863, an Eastern Shore newspaper estimated that slaves commanded only one-third the prices they had fetched five years earlier. In 1864, appraisers in Hagerstown assessed the value of 17 slaves at just five dollars apiece.[25]

RECONSTITUTION

A movement to draft a new state constitution in 1864 alarmed and reanimated the disorganized Maryland Democrats and prompted them to summon a convention of their own party, the first since the beginning of the war. They had little chance of salvaging slavery but hoped to influence how it was abandoned. Democrats were also concerned that a constitution drafted in wartime, with Unionists in power, might give permanence to restrictions and proscriptions that were chiefly disadvantageous to Democrats.[26] Emancipation, after all, could have been achieved by an amendment to the state constitution of 1851. By insisting on a constitutional convention, the Unconditional Unionists hinted that they had larger objectives.

The popular vote was heavily in favor of calling a convention, especially in Baltimore, where the vote for the convention was a suspiciously lopsided 9,102 to 87. But turnout was sharply reduced in the city—only a third as large as in the presidential election of 1860. Unconditional Unionists dominated the convention's deliberations, although Democrats managed to elect 35 of the convention's 96 members. All of the Democrats came from the state's southern counties with the largest slave populations, none from Baltimore.[27]

After addressing matters of organization and procedure, the delegates took up proposed changes in the Declaration of Rights, the statement that had preceded the body of the document since Maryland adopted its first constitution in 1776. The declaration included provisions concerning slavery and the tests of loyalty required of voters and officeholders. These issues were central to the convention's agenda, and debate about changes in the declaration would continue, with interruptions, for two months. The proceedings were suspended so that members could attend the Republican convention in Baltimore, interrupted again during the last week of June and the first week of July so that farmers could harvest their crops, and adjourned again when General Early invaded the state.[28]

The Democratic minority was on the defensive from the start of the convention. Early's raid further undermined their position, while giving the Unionists an occasion to suggest that Maryland's southern sympathizers were somehow complicit in the attack. They argued that their Democratic opponents should compensate the state's Union loyalists for damages suffered during the raid. The Unionists approved a resolution that all who refused to take an oath of loyalty to the United States should be held "to have taken part or openly expressed their sympathy with the recent invasion of the state" and that the federal government should send these disloyalists through the Confederate lines to the South or confine them to prison.[29] The federal government ignored these pronouncements.

The committee responsible for revising the Declaration of Rights made few changes, but touched on vital issues. A new article abolishing slavery in Maryland was debated for a week. Although it was clear that the institution had no future, Democratic delegates launched a spirited defense of bondage, supported by lengthy passages from the Old Testament, which their opponents matched with quotations from the writings of founding fathers and framers of the Constitution. Much of the discussion simply echoed the longstanding national dialogue about slavery, but the debate moved into new territory when the partisans of slavery suggested that owners be compensated for the emancipation of their slaves. One proposed that slavery be abolished in Maryland on January 1, 1865, provided that the federal government appropriated $20 million to cover the losses of Marylanders whose slaves were freed. The idea was quickly rejected. Hardly anyone was confident that the federal government would approve the reimbursement. Other Democrats raised the possibility that Maryland's government might pay for the freedom of slaves. Baltimore delegates were among the most determined opponents of this proposal because their city would have to provide much of the tax revenue needed to cover its cost, and since its residents owned few slaves, they would get little of the compensation.[30]

The debate on compensated emancipation ended with adoption of a near-meaningless resolution ensuring that if the federal government decided to compensate slave owners for their slaves, Maryland would see that the funds reached their intended recipients. But the state would not authorize an indefinite continuation of slavery on the uncertain likelihood that the federal government might eventually reimburse former slaveholders for their losses.[31]

The subject of loyalty oaths generated the most acrimonious debate of the convention, interrupting what one historian described as the "great cordiality" of deliberations notable for their "remarkable lack of personal abuse and recrimination."[32]

An early portent of the later disputes arose when the convention considered a proposed article of the Declaration of Rights holding that "every citizen of this state owes paramount allegiance to the Constitution and Government of the United States, and is not bound by any law or ordinance of this state in contravention or subversion thereof."[33] This apparent renunciation of states' rights roused the Democratic minority, who saw no necessary conflict between national authority and state sovereignty. The ensuing debate dragged on for the better part of two weeks but failed to move the majority.[34]

A far more serious controversy erupted after the delegates completed work on the Declaration of Rights and began to draft article I of the constitution itself, which governed the "electoral franchise." It permanently denied the right to hold public office to anyone who had "at any time been in armed hostility to the United States . . . [or] in any manner in the service of the so-called 'Confederate States of America.'" The ban extended beyond members of the Confederate government or military forces to anyone who had "given any aid, comfort, or support to those engaged in armed hostility . . . or in any manner adhered to the enemies of the United States." The article also excluded from office anyone who had ever communicated with the rebels or expressed approval of their cause.[35] The proscription was so broad that hardly anyone who stopped short of unconditional unionism could lay claim to loyal citizenship.

At first, the proscription applied only to the holding of public office. An amendment then extended its exclusions to voters. The article directed the General Assembly to approve statutes extending these restrictions to "the president, directors, trustees and agents of corporations created or authorized by the laws of this State, teachers or superintendents of the public schools, colleges or other institutions of learning; attorneys-at-law, jurors, and such other persons as the General Assembly shall from time to time prescribe." Critics argued that the measure might deny civil rights to loyal unionists who took exception to the Lincoln administration's deviations from the US Constitution. An amendment that would have ended the restrictions with the end of the war was defeated. Some adherents of the amendment warned that its rejection might prevent the postwar reconciliation essential to the reconstruction of national unity.[36]

The new constitution and the legislation carrying it into effect prescribed an oath of allegiance that election judges were required to administer to all prospective voters. Failure to do so could subject the judges to fines and imprisonment. In Baltimore, at least, the election judges needed no inducements to exclude allegedly disloyal residents from the voting rolls. Days before the presidential election of 1864, the election judges met in a local courtroom and decided that the oath was not sufficient to establish voters' adherence to the Union. Judges were "instructed to put such other questions to voters outside of those prescribed by the Constitution as shall satisfy them that the party offering to vote is not a Rebel or a Rebel sympathizer." A list of 25 such questions followed.[37]

Though the constitution's voting provisions would not become law until it had been approved by the voters, only those voters who met the restrictions in the proposed constitution and took the oath that it prescribed would be permitted to vote. Even this exercise in anticipatory disenfranchisement failed to win overwhelming support for the document. It passed by a vote of 30,174 to 29,799. And, without the votes of Maryland soldiers on active duty with the Union Army, the constitution would have been rejected.[38]

Baltimore City did profit politically under the new constitution. Under the formula finally adopted, the city got three state senators (up from one) and 18 seats in the 80-member house of delegates (up from six).[39]

RECONSTRUCTION

The Maryland State Constitution of 1864 backfired on its framers. Instead of solidifying the rule of the Unconditional Unionists, its "registry law" angered and eventually mobilized the state's dormant Democrats, while exposing breaks in the ranks of the Unionists themselves. Congressman Henry Winter Davis had emerged as the voice of the Unconditional Unionists. He squared off against Conservative Unionist Montgomery Blair, postmaster general in President Lincoln's cabinet and a leader in state politics. Both supported emancipation, but they disagreed on how to achieve it and what would follow. Blair wanted slave owners compensated for their slaves, opposed the recruitment of black soldiers for the Union army, and recommended that free blacks be required to emigrate to Haiti or elsewhere. Davis and the Unconditionals disagreed with Blair on all three issues and advocated racial equality. As postmaster general, however, Blair controlled 500 patronage jobs in Maryland, and Davis's political career ended with his death in 1865. Blair became principal leader of the Unionists and continued his effort to strengthen the new political organization by appealing to Democrats and former Democrats.[40]

By war's end, however, Blair's leverage with Democrats was evaporating. The new state constitution of 1864 freed the slaves and all but ruled out the compensation that Blair sought for their owners. The equal protection guarantees of the Fourteenth Amendment to the US Constitution pushed even more white voters away from the Unionists and into the ranks of the Democrats. When national Republican leaders expressed support for the enfranchisement of African Americans, they prompted still another wave of defections from Blair's Conservative Union Party to Maryland's more rigorously racist Democrats.[41]

The constitution of 1864 and its registry law sustained a politically artificial and ultimately untenable Unionist regime. The Civil War had helped to hold the Unionists together. Once the war was done, so were the Unionists.[42] Baltimore's election results showed the extent to which Unionist rule depended on manipulation of the electoral process. In 1860, Abraham Lincoln finished last of the four presidential candidates in Baltimore, with 3.6 percent of the city vote. Four years later, he carried Baltimore with nearly 84 percent of the city vote. The difference, as the *Sun* remarked, reflected not so much a mass conversion of Democrats into Republicans as a 40 percent drop in voter turnout between 1860 and 1864.[43]

A shadow electorate waited on the political sidelines, having been turned away from the polls, or unwilling to expose themselves to the oaths and interrogations of election judges and registrars. Other potential voters soon appeared. Approximately 20,000 Confederate Army survivors were returning home to Maryland. The first of them—paroled prisoners of war—happened to appear in Baltimore at the time of President Lincoln's assassination. Some Unionists feared that the ex-Confederates planned to redeem their military defeat with a campaign of political murder. Local military officials imposed martial law on the city, but only for a day. The Confederate veterans were instructed to report to the provost marshal and forbidden to wear their old uniforms. Their presence hardened the determination of the Unconditional Unionists, now called the Radicals, to defend the registry law. It would permanently bar southern soldiers and southern sympathizers from becoming voters.[44]

Unionist measures to exclude their opponents from the voting rolls became more severe. The names of all adult white males were entered in the registration books, so that even those who had not attempted to vote could be challenged if they presented themselves at the polls. The failure to vote was now reason for suspicion, a sign of a voter's reluctance to face the election judges and their questions. The electorate continued to shrink. Unionist candidates won the legislative elections of November 1865. But in Baltimore, only 10,842 registered voters remained on the rolls, and almost half of these did not vote. Little more than two months later, a petition protesting the registry law arrived in Annapolis from Baltimore. It carried 11,274 signatures.[45]

Baltimoreans had struggled to insulate their city from the country's deadly division over slavery. But the conflict took possession of the town. Baltimore was occupied by federal troops, its elected government was displaced, its officials were imprisoned, and a purged electorate imposed an alien political regime on the city.

Chapter 21 **DEMOCRATIC RESURRECTION**

B Y 1866, THE ATTENUATED ELECTORATE IN MARYLAND must have included few voters who were not Unionists, but they were divided between Conservative Unionists and Radical Unionists. The situation presented the Conservatives with an obvious opportunity to depose their Radical rivals. The Conservatives could reach out to the thousands of would-be Democratic voters who had been exiled from the electorate or had withdrawn from it. These potential voters were sharply at odds with the Radicals but had much in common with the Conservative Unionists.

Thomas Swann, formerly Baltimore's Know-Nothing mayor and now the state's ostensibly Unionist governor, recognizing that the Unionist coalition was split and sinking, denounced the Radicals and redirected state patronage to Democrats. He fired Unionist election judges and instructed their replacements (often Democrats) to interpret the registry law as liberally as possible, opening the rolls to voters previously excluded. In Baltimore, the Radicals who ran the municipality faced an election in October 1866. With the support of the city solicitor and the state attorney general, they held that the new voter lists created under Swann's direction were invalid and that the only legal registration rolls were those used in the election of 1865. Though challenged by Democratic attorneys, the election went forward under the Radicals' ground rules. They won every office in town. But fewer than 8,000 citizens turned out to vote. In 1860, more than 27,000 citizens had voted in the city's mayoral election.[1]

The state and congressional elections of 1866 followed closely on October's municipal contest. The Conservatives would have to act quickly to prevent another Radical sweep in Baltimore. Less than a week after the municipal election, a "Conservative City Convention" met in Baltimore, alleging misconduct by the board of police commissioners—especially its refusal to appoint any Democrats as election officials. The convention urged Governor Swann to put the commissioners on trial, as he was entitled to do under state law. The convention's resolutions reached

Swann along with a petition signed by 4,300 Baltimoreans demanding that the police commissioners be dismissed. Swann issued a summons demanding that the commissioners appear before him for trial. They sent their attorneys instead.[2]

Two days after the Conservative City Convention, the Radical (formerly Unconditional) Unionists assembled to protest Swann's interference in Baltimore's electoral arrangements and to proclaim the formation of a new organization—the "Boys in Blue"—consisting entirely of Union Army veterans. The men were summoned "to assemble in massed column to resist the attempt of the traitors in our midst to deprive the loyal men of our city of the control of our affairs and to hand them over to the tender mercies of our deadliest enemies."[3]

The new organization hinted at something more forceful in the way of electoral politics than oaths of allegiance, perhaps a reversion to the violence of the Know-Nothing era. The state had no militia to mobilize against such threats—a lingering consequence of federal occupation—and Radicals still controlled the local police force. Governor Swann turned to President Andrew Johnson, who had already been in touch with Maryland's aggrieved Democrats. The Marylanders wanted presidential support in their battle with their Republican antagonists; Johnson wanted Maryland's support for his reconstruction policy.[4]

Early in 1866, Maryland's Democrats and Conservative Unionists jointly sponsored a rally at the Maryland Institute in Baltimore to declare their support for the president's reconstruction policy. By summer, the alliance of Unionists and Democrats had become a single party under the Democratic Conservative label. Days after the pro-Johnson rally, the Radical Unionists sponsored a counter-rally at the Front Street Theatre to announce their opposition to presidential reconstruction. By some accounts, the meeting marked the birth of the state's Republican Party.[5]

The nascent parties, already at odds with one another on race, slavery, and the right to vote, now resolved to disagree about national reconstruction as well. Johnson responded to Governor Swann's request for support by instructing General Ulysses S. Grant to "look into the nature of threatened difficulties in Baltimore." Grant, the Army's commanding general, ordered General Edward Canby, commander of the military department that included Maryland, to visit Baltimore. Canby reported that there was no danger of riot in the city unless Governor Swann dismissed the Radical police commissioners and replaced them with his own appointees. Grant consulted with Swann, who seems to have agreed with this assessment. A week later, however, Swann completed the trial of the Baltimore police commissioners, found them guilty of malfeasance and misconduct in office, and dismissed them. On the following day, he appointed William Thomas Valiant and James Young to replace the Radical commissioners, deliberately creating the very conditions that Grant and Canby saw as the formula for civil disorder. With the assistance of the local sheriff, Young and Valiant attempted, unsuccessfully, to occupy the offices of the police commissioners. But there was no riot. Instead, on November 3, the Radical Unionist judge of Baltimore's criminal court, Hugh Lennox Bond, issued a warrant for the arrest of Young and Valiant.[6]

Young and Valiant refused to post bail and landed in the city jail. A team of attor-

Thomas Swann, president of the B&O, mayor, governor, and almost US senator; Whig, Know-Nothing, Unionist, and Democrat

neys, including John H. B. Latrobe, applied to the Maryland State Court of Appeals for a writ of habeas corpus to set them free. The writ was granted, but under state law the warden of the city jail could delay their release for four days so that the respondents would have the opportunity to contest the writ. The release of the new police commissioners was therefore postponed until after the election. Grant and Canby arrived in Baltimore for discussions with the Republicans, who remained in control of the city's electoral apparatus. Canby reported that the Republican officials had agreed to appoint one Democratic election judge and one clerk in each of the city's precincts. A list of proposed judges and clerks had already been prepared by the Democratic Conservatives, but when it was delivered to the office of the police commissioners, their attorney declined to receive it. Through a half-opened door he announced that the judges and clerks had been appointed, and no changes would be made.[7]

BREAKTHROUGH

Though the Republicans had not been dislodged from their oversight of Baltimore elections, the results of the state and congressional contests of 1866 ran powerfully in favor of the city's Democrats. They had acquired the courage to vote and had presented themselves at the polls in such numbers that the Republican election judges and registrars may have feared that turning away so many aspiring voters might provoke a riot. A. Leo Knott, secretary of the Democratic State Central Committee, maintained that the Democratic Conservatives were moved to brave the perils of the polls because they were outraged by the Republicans' "contemplated crime against the electoral franchise and the rights of citizens deliberately planned by the Republican party and aided by Judge Bond." But they may also have been emboldened by the challenge that Governor Swann posed to the Boys in Blue and their Republican backers. Two weeks before the election, the governor issued a proclamation warning them that their "illegal and revolutionary combinations against the peace and dignity of the State" would be "held to strict accountability in the event of riot and bloodshed."[8] In effect, Swann's proclamation converted the Radical Unionists into rebels, and his condemnation, together with his dismissal of the Radical police commissioners, provided a context of legitimacy for Democratic Conservative voters and the encouragement of official support. In the background, there was also the possibility that President Johnson might order federal troops to add steel to Swann's threats.[9]

On the morning of November 8, two days after the election, Swann was walking from his home on Franklin Street to his nongovernmental job as president of the First National Bank on Gay Street. By the time he reached Baltimore Street, he was surrounded by a sea of Baltimoreans who greeted him with "hearty cheers." Those who could get close enough reached out "to shake him cordially by the hand." The crowd grew so dense that the governor could make scarcely any progress toward his office. The mass of Baltimoreans propelled him toward the Merchants' Exchange, where he tried to escape by entering the building, with the hope that he might retreat either to the adjacent customhouse or the post office, at opposite ends of the building, and make his escape. But the crowd filled the exchange's rotunda and cut off his exits. Swann mounted a stairway to address them. Though it seemed unnecessary, given the celebratory spirit of his audience, Swann offered a detailed justification for his dismissal of the Radical police commissioners. But he emphasized, above all, the dignity, courage, and law-abidingness of Baltimore's Democratic voters in the face of Radical provocation.[10]

That night, a band marched to Swann's home to serenade him. He eventually emerged to deliver another version of the speech he had made earlier in the day.[11] The gratitude of Baltimore's Democrats was due in part to the most recent transformation in his political identity—having changed from Whig to Know-Nothing, then to Unionist, then, in May 1866, to Democrat. His electoral exertions had given the Democrats a two-thirds majority in the house of delegates, for which he expected something more than serenades and ovations. It had been understood that his newly adopted party's legislators would elect him to the US Senate, which they did.[12]

After more than a decade in purgatory, Baltimore's Democrats were back in control of their state, but not the US Senate. Thomas Swann's enemies were determined to deny him the seat bestowed by Maryland's Democratic legislature. A suspected plotter in the affair was Lieutenant Governor Dr. Christopher Columbus Cox, who was, like Swann a political nomad, but one who had finally come to rest with Maryland's Republicans. The office that he held had been created under the state constitution of 1864. Swann's elevation to the US Senate would make Cox governor. The

Exchange Place, ca. 1855. The Merchants' Exchange, in the background, was designed by Benjamin Latrobe and completed in 1820; it was demolished in the early twentieth century. At various times it housed a US customhouse, a stock exchange, a bank, and a post office. It frequently served as the site for public meetings to discuss municipal problems. *Courtesy Enoch Pratt Free Library, Cator Collection*

Senate's refusal to seat Swann would give Cox the opportunity to appoint his own candidate to that Senate seat. Cox, according to rumor, would then do what he could to block the movement for a new constitutional convention to undo the Unconditional Unionist constitution of 1864, and if he failed, there was the possibility that federal troops would be sent to the state to ensure that loyalists were in command of its government. As the scheme unfolded, Cox stoutly denied any responsibility for engineering it. And he may have been telling the truth. Maryland's Republicans generally detested Swann as a traitorous Unionist turned Democrat. Any of them might have conspired with the Republican majority of the US Senate to keep Swann from occupying his seat there.[13]

For the Republicans, spite had trumped political sensibility. Swann inevitably got wind of the scheme and announced that instead of trying to occupy his Senate seat, he would remain governor in Annapolis, where he could do far more damage to Maryland's Republicans than he could as a US senator. The two police commissioners whom he had appointed were out of jail and in charge of Baltimore's police officers. In his message to the General Assembly at the start of its 1867 session, Swann recommended that the legislators consider holding a new municipal election in Baltimore to correct the "flagrant injustice" of the one held the previous October. He also urged the formation of a new state militia, which would give the state's Democratic government the muscle needed to counter Republican threats. Finally, Swann asked the assembly to summon a new convention to replace the constitution imposed on the state just three years earlier.[14]

The General Assembly soon approved a bill restoring voting rights to those who had lost them under the Radicals' registry law. It also approved legislation requiring a new municipal election in Baltimore, to be held just 16 days after the bill passed. Baltimore's Democrats needed only four days to assemble a nominating convention to select its candidates for municipal office. Robert T. Banks, a glass and crockery merchant who had never held elective office, led the ticket as the Democratic Conservative candidate for mayor. He was a native Virginian with Democratic attachments and southern sympathies.[15]

A LITTLE CIVIL WAR

Baltimore's Republican city council unanimously approved a $20,000 appropriation to litigate its way out of the new municipal election. The money was to pay attorneys "to test the validity of the action of the General Assembly, in their recent legislation, for the removal of the existing city government." Mobilizing lawyers of their own, Baltimore's Democrats secured an injunction to prevent expenditure of the $20,000.[16]

Disputes concerning Baltimore's new municipal election erupted next within the Democratic Conservative coalition in Annapolis. The Conservative Unionists had restored the voting rights of Democrats in order to defeat their Radical Unionist rivals. When Democrat Robert Banks defeated a Conservative Unionist candidate to win the mayoral nomination in Baltimore, Conservatives discovered that even in a city where Conservative Unionists seemed strong, their new Democratic allies were stronger. Conservatives did not intend to become junior partners in the alliance. Conservative Unionists still exercised sufficient control in the General Assembly to derail the new municipal election in Baltimore, and Conservative Unionists in the state senate could also deny the two-thirds majority needed to call a constitutional convention. The convention bill had been introduced early in the session and called up twice, but its consideration was suspended on both occasions when the necessary majority failed to materialize. The assembly's Democrats chose, for the moment at least, to sacrifice the special election in Baltimore City in return for Conservative Unionist support on the constitutional convention (which could once again address the political status of Baltimore). The state senate repealed the municipal election bill, which had not yet been signed by Governor Swann, and two-thirds of the legislators voted for a referendum on a new constitutional convention.[17]

Maryland voters went to the polls in April 1867 to vote for the convention and to choose delegates. The Republicans, who rejected the exercise as unconstitutional, nominated no delegates. Since the start of the year, they had pursued a radical line of attack against the state's government. Their goal was to persuade the Republican majority in the US Congress to assume authority over Maryland, either because the state did not have a republican form of government, as required by the US Constitution, or because it was governed by disloyalists and, like the former Confederacy, was in need of federal reconstruction.[18]

The document that emerged from the constitutional convention contained few surprises. As expected, it did away with the test oath and the proscriptions that barred so many Democrats from becoming voters, but it retained one of the most significant innovations of 1864: creation of a statewide system of public education, overseen by a state board of education and financed, in part, by state taxation. Under the 1867 constitution, representation in the General Assembly was to be based on total population, not just white population as prescribed by the constitution of 1864. The change benefited the state's southern counties—home to a significant population of ex-slaves. Southern Maryland gained seven delegates when nonvoting African Americans were counted as part of the population to be represented. The new constitution also created a new county, Wicomico, on the Eastern Shore to accommodate the town of Salisbury, which until then had been divided between two counties. The addition of Wicomico gave the southern counties a majority in the state senate, even though they accounted for less than a third of the state's population.

In the matter of race, the constitution made one departure that might not have been expected of its Conservative authors: it opened the courts to black witnesses. But the delegates made it clear that this concession to racial equality was not a step toward general equality. African Americans might have civil rights, but they were not the political equals of white men.[19]

Article XI of the new constitution was devoted to the governance of Baltimore. It was brief. Baltimore would elect a new municipal government in October 1867. In this respect, the city's elected officials faced the same prospect as state officeholders in general, all of whom would step down after ratification of the constitution— except Governor Swann, who would serve out the remainder of his term. The only significant change in the powers of city government reduced its authority to incur debt to pay for internal improvements. It would be able to finance projects such as railroads and canals only with the approval of the General Assembly, followed by the approval of city voters. The restrictions could not have aroused much opposition among Baltimoreans. The city's investments in internal improvements had yielded disappointing returns, and its relationships with railroads in particular had passed from distant to acrimonious.[20] The B&O, Baltimore's great civic venture in the conquest of distance, had transformed itself into an aggressively private corporation.

CITY AT PEACE

For Baltimore's government, peace brought new stresses. Prices had risen sharply since the beginning of the war, and one class of city employees after another demanded pay increases consistent with the higher cost of living. Most got raises.[21] Similar demands unsettled the private sector. B&O machinists went on strike to demand higher pay for overtime work. The city council instructed its representatives on the railroad's board of directors to look into the sources of the work stoppage and possible ways of ending it. And the council went further. The first branch took the side of the machinists and supported their wage demands. The second branch tabled the resolution.[22] The intractable labor-management dispute was an early sign of more severe conflict to come between railroad workers and railroad capitalists. The intervention by the council's first branch anticipated the politicization of these struggles.

The city's longstanding engagement with railroads continued—and continued to be a source of trouble. In 1865, for example, the B&O raised its rates for the shipment of coal. Coal was Baltimore's staff of life. It powered the steam engines that animated the city's industries. The city council passed a resolution of protest holding that the increase was unjustifiable and asked the city's representatives on the B&O board to report. All of the council's representatives on the board had opposed the increase, but neither their protests nor those of their colleagues diverted the B&O from its new rate schedule.[23]

The municipality's relations with the Northern Central Railway had degenerated into lawsuits and injunctions. The city had objected to the proposed route of the railroad's extension to the waterfront in Canton and then complained about the company's failure to complete the line on schedule. In laying its tracks through other parts of the city, the Northern Central had illegally changed the grades of city streets, rousing the anger of local property owners and their council representatives. City officials also charged that the Northern Central had failed to meet its financial obligations to Baltimore. They were also unhappy that the railroad had moved its headquarters from Baltimore to Harrisburg. The city council ordered the Commission on Finance to sell the city's entire stake in the Northern Central for not less than $800,000. The city's interest in the company was reported to be worth $1 million.[24]

The city had no investment in the Philadelphia, Wilmington, and Baltimore Railroad, but the company managed to antagonize municipal leaders in the worst possible way—by contributing to Baltimore's urban inferiority complex. The PW&B had repeatedly sought permission to lay a double track along Boston Street to its President Street Station. The double track would leave scarcely any room for other street traffic. In 1865, the railroad renewed its request. This time it claimed that it was building a straight-as-the-crow-flies line from Washington to New York—the so-called Air Line Railroad. If Baltimore refused to allow a double track on Boston Street, the PW&B would have to bypass the city, leaving it disconnected from the most efficient route linking the biggest cities of the northeast corridor. The city needed the railroad, in other words, but the railroad and the big cities it served could do without Baltimore. Mayor John Lee Chapman found the railroad's position dishonest and insulting. He noted that the PW&B had not asked Philadelphia to allow double tracks through its streets but had taken a detour around the city. It appeared, moreover, that the Air Line Railroad was little more than air. "The Baltimore Representatives of this Company," wrote Mayor Chapman, "seem to be blind to all interest[s] but those of Stockholders, and have concluded that Baltimore is a Country

Town." Chapman's hostility was not limited to the PW&B. He took "a determined position . . . in opposition to the continued efforts of Railroad Corporations to take every advantage" of Baltimore and its citizens.[25] Railroads, once seen as Baltimore's salvation, were now regarded as predators.

Baltimoreans found new sources of disagreement among themselves. Their differences on questions of race and secession persisted, but they had dropped beneath the surface of local politics after Appomattox and left room on the local political agenda for debates about less weighty issues. One of the most controversial questions in the years just after the war was whether to renumber the city's houses. Mayor Chapman, in his annual message for 1867, explained that since the city had last assigned street addresses, a large population of new buildings had sprung up to complicate the numbering system. Strangers and residents alike were often unable to find their way around. Worse yet, the confusion complicated the work of city officers and tax collectors.[26]

Competing petitions for and against renumbering carried the names of hundreds of citizens and business firms.[27] The volume of popular expression seemed to paralyze the city council. The committee assigned to report on renumbering was unable to reach consensus. It submitted a majority report in favor of renumbering and a minority report against. The council's second branch "indefinitely postponed" consideration of the first and rejected the second.[28]

CITY HALL: URBAN STATUS SYMBOL

While the renumbering exercise stalled, Baltimore's long-delayed drive to get its own city hall finally moved forward. The municipality had never had a purpose-built city hall to house its public officials and solidify its fragile sense of civic pride. For several decades, the city council held its sessions in a former museum. Founded by Rembrandt Peale in 1814, the museum had once held an eccentric collection of portraits, fossils, and animal specimens. Peale was unable to make the museum a going concern, and the city purchased it in 1830. The first branch met in a former picture gallery; the chamber occupied by the second branch had previously held stuffed dead animals.[29]

Before the Civil War interrupted the project, the General Assembly had authorized the city to issue up to $400,000 in stock to build a city hall. A special committee of the city council selected a site on Holliday Street not far from the Peale Museum, but nothing happened until 1860, when Mayor Swann announced that the municipality had leased the property. Under an ordinance approved by the council, Swann appointed commissioners to select a plan for the building. They did so, and the council authorized the appointment of another commission to oversee construction. The second commission reported that the plan chosen by the first commission would cost much more than the city could spend. On the recommendation of Mayor Swann's successor, George William Brown, the council postponed further work on the building because the city could not afford it.[30]

During this postponement, city officials made do with the buildings that already stood on the intended site of their imagined building. The mayor's office was in the back parlor of "an old-fashioned private residence." His secretary occupied the front parlor, which also served as a waiting room for contractors, politicians, and job seekers who wanted to meet with the mayor. The city's tax appeal court held its sessions in a chamber measuring 12 by 15 feet, and some of the tax collector's clerks labored in sheds and outbuildings.[31]

Mayor Chapman restarted the city hall project with his annual message in 1864. The city council appointed a new commission to select a new architect for the building. It chose the design of George A. Frederick, an unknown in his early twenties embarking on his first independent project since completing his apprenticeship. The land once leased for the building was now purchased. Chapman and the council approved an ordinance appointing a new building committee to oversee completion of the work, and once again asked state approval to sell the bonds needed to pay for the project. This time the General Assembly authorized Baltimore to issue $600,000 in bonds. As required by the state constitution of 1867, Baltimore's voters approved the sale of the bonds by referendum, and construction began almost immediately— more than a dozen years after the city council first sought the assembly's approval for the building.[32]

The laying of the cornerstone occurred just after the municipal election of 1867. Only a small part of the building was finished in time for the ceremony—barely enough to support a cornerstone. Mayor Chapman attended, but he had just been voted out of office. The *Sun* suggested that his administration's unrepresentative, lame-duck status had been essential to the advancement of the long-delayed city hall project: "it required such temerity as only an expiring administration could summon to initiate the work just now, especially on so stupendous a scale as has been projected."[33]

John H. B. Latrobe served as orator for the cornerstone ceremony. His speech reviewed the city's history, perhaps to demonstrate why it deserved a city hall and why the improvised arrangements for housing Baltimore's government were "unbecoming to the character of our people." He closed by recounting the achievements of its recent mayors. Most were the accomplishments of Thomas Swann. Latrobe mentioned Chapman's expansion of the city's water supply but gave him no credit for restarting the construction of city hall.[34]

It proved to be a false start. Chapman's Democratic successor, Mayor Robert T. Banks, challenged the authority of the building committee, largely because he was not one of its members. According to Banks, the building committee operated in violation of the law, which required the mayor, register, and comptroller to open bids and determine the amount of the bond that contractors were supposed to post as security for fulfillment of their contracts. Worse yet, the cost of the "latitudinarian" contracts already signed by the building committee far exceeded the amount the General Assembly had authorized for the project. The members of the building committee rejected the mayor's demand that they resign, but they agreed to stop all work on city hall until the courts ruled on their legitimacy and their contracts.[35]

The city's superior court decided in favor of the building committee. Mayor Banks prevailed in the Maryland Court of Appeals, which found that the state leg-

Eighty years after it became a city, Baltimore finally built a city hall.

islation authorizing Baltimore to issue bonds for city hall was insufficiently explicit about the committee's authority to make contracts with suppliers and builders, all of which were declared invalid.[36]

The decision had no effect. Two months before the appeals court announced its decision, the General Assembly empowered the city to issue as much as $1 million in bonds to pay for its city hall. With the approval of the voters, the city council approved a new bond issue and appointed a new building committee—chaired by Mayor Banks.[37]

Less than a year later, the city council formed a special committee to investigate charges of fraud in the operations of the new building committee. After completing its inquiry, the committee submitted a resolution demanding the resignation of the building committee. All of the contracts it had made were to be annulled, and the city register was to make no further payments for the construction of city hall until instructed to do so.[38]

Baltimoreans who bothered to read the committee's report to the very end learned that it had found no evidence of fraud. No one on the building committee had "any interests in any contracts awarded by them." The special committee concluded instead that the building committee had made errors in judgment, perhaps a result of a "too great reliance on the representations and opinions of others, and want of proper knowledge or experience to discharge properly the duties of their respective positions." To avoid such errors in the future, the building committee would have to include three "practical mechanics." Mayor Banks and his associates on the committee offered a lengthy response and had it printed as a 38-page pamphlet for public consumption. They acknowledged that they had occasionally decided not to award contracts to the lowest bidders, because they did not regard the low bids as "responsible." In a contract for brick work, for example, the committee had passed over the lowest bidder to give the job to the mayor's brother-in-law. They also rejected the low bid in a contract for lumber, which went to a firm in which the mayor's brother was a partner. The lowest bidder for excavating the city hall cellar was L. D. Gill, but another contractor got the job. N. Rufus Gill chaired the investigating committee.[39]

Chairman Gill delivered his committee's response to Mayor Banks's statement, emphasizing that the issue was not one of corruption. The investigators saw nothing improper, for example, in awarding the lumber contract to the firm in which the mayor's brother was a partner. Their complaint was that the lumber had been of substandard quality and ordered so far in advance of its use that the building committee incurred additional expense for its storage.[40]

The council passed an ordinance that embodied the recommendations of its investigating committee, including the requirement that Banks's committee resign.[41] Banks rejected it. His remarkable veto message came out in another printed pamphlet, an indictment of the council's committee of investigation as the "offspring of those seasons of public excitement which have produced so many monstrous things in the history of our city." The inquiry, Banks insisted, belonged to the same family of "monstrous things" as the Bank Riot of 1835 and the deadly violence of the Know-Nothing movement—animated by rumors of conspiracy, much like the rumors of corruption in the city hall building committee. In short, the mayor and his committee were victims of Baltimore's mob politics.[42]

Banks portrayed himself as a public official whose conscientious decisions to veto previous ordinances had set the council against him: "Indignant that *he* should thus stand in the way of their sovereign will and pleasure . . . determined to strip him of his prerogatives, as well as to crush and humble him at the foot-stool of their power. Indeed the two Branches of the Council have treated the Mayor of Baltimore not otherwise than Andrew Johnson was treated by the two Branches of Congress. This determination on the part of the Council to crush him and humble him in the dust, has culminated at last and reached its climax, in the ordinance . . . now under consideration."[43]

The council declared that Banks's veto was invalid because it was printed and did not carry his signature, but it took the additional precaution of overriding it. Banks contested the council's action but could not prevent its approval of a new ordinance for the construction of city hall and its appointment of a new building committee. The committee elected as its president Joshua Vansant, a local hat maker who served as chairman of the Democratic Conservative State Central Committee. Vansant reported that Mayor Banks refused to administer the required oaths of office to the members of his committee.[44]

The mayor and his building committee finally surrendered. The new building
committee took office and restarted construction on city hall. In March 1870, however, Vansant reported that the $1 million authorized by the General Assembly would
be exhausted by the end of the year, and while he could not precisely calculate the
additional money needed, he supposed that it might amount to another $1 million.
In the end, the building's total cost would come to about $2.5 million, with another
$110,000 for furnishings. Though the city council began to hold sessions in its new
chambers in April 1875, the building would not be completed and dedicated until
the following October. The *Sun* ventured the hope that the council members would
live up to the grandeur of their new chambers.[45]

Part VII **PUNGENT POLITICS AND THE
FAINT SMELL OF MONEY**

Chapter 22
EX-SLAVES, EX-CONFEDERATES,
AND THE NEW REGIME

T HE CIVIL WAR AND ITS AFTERMATH reshaped Baltimore's population. During the 1850s, the city's foreign-born population increased by almost 50 percent, providing an easy target for the
Know-Nothings. But the city's African American population scarcely
grew at all, and the number of slaves declined.[1] The war, of course,
eliminated slavery. It also brought a sharp reduction in foreign immigration. Most new arrivals in Baltimore were migrants from agricultural areas of Maryland; smaller numbers came from Virginia
and North Carolina. These new arrivals were predominantly African
American. Between 1860 and 1900, the African American population
nearly tripled; the foreign-born population scarcely grew. A wave of
European immigration did continue to flow through Baltimore. More
than 600,000 arrived at the port during the last third of the nineteenth
century, but the vast majority landed at the B&O's immigrant dock on
Locust Point then boarded trains for destinations further west, where
local economies were growing more rapidly than Baltimore's. After
1880, Baltimore's African American population equaled or exceeded its
foreign-born population. Baltimore had a larger black population than
any big city save the District of Columbia and a smaller percentage of
foreign-born residents than any of the 10 largest cities in the country.[2]

Thousands of ex-slaves and black soldiers had arrived in Baltimore
at war's end. By 1866, the city's trustees of the poor acknowledged their
inability to care for "all worthy persons without regard to nation or col-
or." Local Quakers did what they could, but the Friends' Association for
the Aid of Freemen found employment for only a few hundred migrants.
The principal burden of caring for the newly freed arrivals was taken
up by Baltimore's black community. Institutions built by the city's free
African Americans since the beginning of the nineteenth century now
provided support for newly freed slaves and discharged black soldiers.
African American orphan asylums, a home for aged women, several
black churches, and the Lincoln Zouaves all provided money or care for
ex-slaves and ex-soldiers. Twenty-five years after his escape from slavery,

Frederick Douglass returned to deliver a lecture sponsored by the Colored State Fair Association; the revenue went to sick and wounded black veterans. Black Baltimore took care of its own.[3]

Though the population of transatlantic immigrants was no longer growing rapidly, black workers and white workers (many of them immigrants) continued to compete for jobs, and black workers usually lost out to whites. Oyster shucking, for example, had traditionally been a job for black men, but immigrant women took it over during the late 1870s. By the 1880s, according to the state's Bureau of Industrial Statistics, immigrant women were being hired as domestic servants, "driving the old colored domestic servant out of the field."[4]

In the Baltimore shipyards, racial conflicts were frequent a full generation before the Civil War. After Emancipation, interracial competition for waterfront jobs intensified. Between 1865 and 1867, white stevedores attacked black stevedores or forced them off the job on at least four occasions. A few months after the war's end, white workers at an East Baltimore shipyard went on strike to force the firing of 75 black caulkers. The yard's owner held out for more than a month, but finally agreed to phase out the black workers. Black caulkers at all of the East Baltimore shipyards walked off the job. Every local newspaper sided with them, but the weight of editorial opinion did not change the outcome.[5]

The black caulkers invented an outcome of their own. One of them, Isaac Myers, assembled 15 African American entrepreneurs who helped to accumulate $40,000 so that the black caulkers could open a shipyard of their own—the Chesapeake Marine and Drydock Company. About $10,000 more was raised in black churches. The company would eventually employ 300 workers, including some white caulkers and carpenters when they were needed. Within five years the company had repaid its entire debt. In 1869, Myers became the founder and first president of the Colored National Labor Union. Half a dozen years later he organized the Colored Men's Progressive and Cooperative Union of Baltimore. Its aim was to open white unions and apprenticeship programs to African Americans. The effort was largely unsuccessful, and the black-owned shipyard went out of business in 1884 after prolonged litigation.[6] While it lasted, it was one more sign of black Baltimore's capacity to generate autonomous institutions outside the range of white prejudice.

JIM CROW LITE

Emancipation did not bring radical change for Baltimore's African Americans. Most of them, after all, were already free. Postwar legal reforms did eliminate some racial inequalities. After the state's 1867 constitution made it legal for black witnesses to testify in cases involving whites, the US Supreme Court ruled that Maryland's exclusion of African Americans from service on juries violated the Fourteenth Amendment.[7]

Baltimore followed many southern communities in its imposition of Jim Crow restrictions, but with less consistency and vigor. The city's hotels and schools were rigidly segregated. Public transportation was supposed to be, too, but white riders were not sufficiently patient to wait for whites-only trolleys to maintain racial sep-

residents without any discernible protest from whites who frequented the same venues. Baltimore's black community was also largely spared the terror, mob violence, and lynching suffered by African Americans farther south. In Maryland, 43 lynchings occurred between the 1860s and 1930s—none in Baltimore, although two took place just outside the city limits.[8]

The regime of Jim Crow did not prevail unopposed. Though the US Freedmen's Bureau did most of its business in the "insurrectionary" states of the former Confederacy, it opened a Baltimore office on Calvert Street in a building owned by Senator Reverdy Johnson. One of the bureau's missions in Maryland was to take action against former slave owners who tried to retain control of their younger slaves through fictive "apprenticeships."[9] Most of these "apprentices" were indentured to farmers of Southern Maryland and the Eastern Shore, not Baltimoreans.

The emancipation of young African Americans, however, increased the number in need of education and made them part of the larger constituency for the Freedmen's Bureau's comprehensive campaign to provide schooling for freed slaves. Baltimore was not only a command post for this effort but one of its principal fields of endeavor. The state legislature approved the establishment of "colored schools" in 1867, but the level of state support to Baltimore remained below $5,000 annually as late as 1870. The General Assembly pegged its support for black schools at the amount that black residents had paid in school taxes.[10] More substantial assistance came from the Baltimore Association for the Moral and Educational Improvement of the Colored People, founded shortly after emancipation of Maryland's slaves in 1864. In 1865, the association turned to the municipality for financial support. The city council's education committee recommended an appropriation of $10,000. It was, the committee reported, "not only a wise . . . moral and Christian duty to provide an Educational system for the Colored race among us . . . but a sheer act of justice to a class of people who have so long been paying taxes to the School Fund of the City without receiving one cent of benefits from such taxation."[11]

Though it also received funds from out-of-state organizations such as the New England Freedmen's Aid Society, the Baltimore Association for the Moral and Educational Improvement of the Colored People lacked the money to keep up with the demand for black schools. An alliance with the Freedmen's Bureau helped to sustain its efforts. The bureau provided funds for the purchase of land and supplied lumber (from dismantled military hospitals and barracks) for the construction of schoolhouses. Other schools occupied space in black churches or on church grounds. Maryland's African Americans provided both money and labor for the construction of schools and support of teachers. In 1866, for example, they raised $10,000—twice the subsidy provided by the state. By the end of the year, the association reported that it was supporting 23 schools in Baltimore and another 51 in the counties. Almost all had just one teacher. The association was running a deficit of more than $10,000.[12]

In January 1867, the association turned once again to the city council, this time with a request for $20,000.[13] The council did not immediately respond, but in July it voted to assume responsibility for the education of Baltimore's black children, and the board of school commissioners took charge of the African American schools, with some misgivings.[14] A committee of the board reported that the "colored schools" were in poor condition. Their students ranged in age from 6 to 30. Boys and girls were mixed together. Some schools had only white teachers; others, only black teachers; and still others, teachers of both races. The report concluded that the colored schools would need a vigorous sorting out of teachers, students, and curriculum. After receiving the committee report, the school board voted that only white teachers should work in the city's black schools.[15]

AMBIGUITY AND EQUALITY

Though Maryland acknowledged African Americans' right to education, to serve on juries, and to practice law, it did not grant them full equality with whites. They could not vote or hold public office. The debate on adoption of the Fourteenth Amendment, beginning in 1866, made it more difficult to maintain this position.

The critical provision of the amendment declared that people born or naturalized in the United States were citizens and entitled to all the privileges and immunities of citizens. Some of the amendment's proponents, such as Senator Thaddeus Stevens of Pennsylvania, maintained that voting was one of the privileges to which all citizens—including black citizens—were entitled. The *Baltimore Sun* held otherwise. Women and children were citizens, after all, but not entitled to vote. Like them, African Americans could be excluded from the electorate.[16] Even the state's Radical Unionists initially insisted that their support for the Fourteenth Amendment did not commit them to support black suffrage. Conservative Unionists such as Governor Thomas Swann had no doubts about the political status of African Americans. He was "utterly opposed to universal negro suffrage." Montgomery Blair, Swann's rival for leadership of the Democratic Conservatives, complained that the governor's opposition was not universal enough. Rejection of *universal* black suffrage left open the possibility that *some* black Marylanders might be permitted to vote. Blair denounced any such possibility. Black voters, he argued, would diminish democracy because they would fall under the control of Radical Republicans, part of a "plot of Radicals to keep themselves in power and tyrannize over the rest of society."[17]

The Fourteenth Amendment held further complications for Baltimore and Maryland. Under Section Two, any state denying voting rights to a portion of its citizens would suffer a proportionate reduction in representation.[18] Democrats charged that the amendment compelled Maryland to choose between enfranchising black men and losing a congressman. Radicals argued that the loss of representation was deserved. It would be borne by sections of Maryland where ex-Confederates presided over numerous nonvoting plantation hands.[19]

RACIAL POLITICS

The Maryland General Assembly refused to ratify the Fourteenth Amendment. Maryland was one of six states outside the South to reject it. (Four southern states had to accept it in order to get back into the Union.) The assembly was even more

A parade of 10,000 Baltimoreans, marking ratification of the Fifteenth Amendment, marched to Monument Square, where distinguished speakers—including Frederick Douglass—celebrated the extension of voting rights to African American men. *Courtesy Maryland Historical Society*

emphatically opposed to the Fifteenth Amendment's mandate to grant voting rights to black men. Its opposition was unanimous. For their part, Maryland's Republicans no longer had any reason to back away from black suffrage. They hoped that African American voters might give them some prospect of success against a Democratic Party that enjoyed wide support among white Marylanders. Debates on the two constitutional amendments were exercises in party definition. Southern sympathizers were readmitted to Maryland politics, and blacks became voters. Former Unionists joined either the former slaves or the former Confederates. After choosing their allies, Marylanders confronted one another as Republicans and Democrats.

Baltimore's black community organized a huge parade in May 1870 to mark the ratification of the Fifteenth Amendment. About 10,000 African Americans marched in the procession to Monument Square. Near the front came carriages carrying notables, including Frederick Douglass, Judge Hugh Lennox Bond, and several members of Congress. Following them were several black military units, with a special dispensation from the commissioners of police allowing them to parade with their weapons. A crowd of at least 10,000 spectators, including thousands of whites, lined the streets. It took about an hour for the procession to pass. In Monument Square, Douglass and other speakers mounted a platform, but before the first of them could address the crowd, the platform collapsed. No one was injured, and Douglass mounted the pile of broken boards to propose three cheers for the Fifteenth Amendment. The speakers delivered their remarks from the balcony of a nearby hotel. The *Sun*—no advocate of the amendment—reported that the "entire affair was well and satisfactorily managed." According to the *Baltimore American*, "On the thousand banners that were borne along there was not one inscription that could wound the feelings of friend or foe." When the event was over, the "thousands of persons present, about one-third of whom were white, then dispersed, having listened to the speeches for more than two hours with scarcely a break in their ranks."[20]

No black voters participated in Baltimore's first municipal election following adoption of the Fifteenth Amendment. The Maryland General Assembly had given localities a November 1870 deadline to prepare new voter lists that incorporated African Americans; Baltimore's city council election came in October. The city's first test under the new amendment occurred in November's congressional elections. Though white politicians across a wide spectrum had stood in opposition to black suffrage, black voters encountered little resistance at the polls. Party leaders were intent on avoiding conflict. Several days before the election, the chairmen of the local Republican and Democratic parties wrote to the election judges suggesting a "fence or barrier at least six feet in length, extending from the poll window to the curb should separate the lines of black and white voters."[21] Election officials rejected the suggestion, but the voters arrived at informal arrangements for avoiding interracial contact at the polls. Most African Americans voted early in the day; white voters waited until they were gone before lining up. The *Sun* reported that the election was carried off with "remarkable quiet, considering the excitement of the campaign . . . heightened by the first appearance of the colored man with a ballot in his hand."[22]

White politicians had recently railed against voting rights for African Americans. Once the Fifteenth Amendment gave the vote to black men, however, Baltimoreans tried not to make a public fuss about it. They reacted to black enfranchisement in much the same way that Henry Winter Davis had approached the issue of slavery: the best way to deal with the problem was to remain silent about it.

The aftermath of the Civil War brought a large population of former slaves to a city where most black people had been born free. The two groups, understandably, held different perspectives on politics and race in Baltimore. Blacks born free, like Isaac Myers, tended to see progress as a matter of self-improvement and economic organization. "The colored man will not enjoy equal rights with whites," he said, "until they are mechanics and merchants of means. Then the men will put their prejudices in their pockets."[23]

Former slaves were more likely to see white racism as an obstacle to self-improvement. Life experience had radicalized them. A prominent example was Harvey Johnson. He emerged from slavery in Virginia near the end of the war, attended a seminary in Washington, and in 1872 became pastor of Union Baptist Church in Baltimore, where he remained until his death in 1923. Under Johnson's leadership, the Union Church soon became the state's largest black congregation. It also seceded from the Maryland Baptist Union Association, in which the state's white Baptists exercised control over the denomination. Johnson organized the Colored Baptist Convention of Maryland, and in 1885, he and several other Baptist clergymen launched a political organization: the Mutual United Brotherhood of Liberty. At first, it supported lawsuits to overcome the exclusion of black attorneys from Maryland's state and local courts, but that was only the opening step in a more general program of litigation and lobbying that attacked segregation in public transportation, Baltimore's refusal to hire black teachers, Maryland's discrimination against black women in payment of child support, and the absence of a high school for black students. The brotherhood's success in getting black attorneys admitted to the state bar also prompted the University of Maryland Law School to admit two black students, one of whom—Harry Sythe Cummings—would win a seat on the Baltimore City Council in 1891 to become the first black elected official in the state. Shortly after Cummings graduated, the law school again shut its doors to black applicants.[24]

Disagreements between recently freed slaves and free black Baltimoreans opened a new axis of dissension in African American politics. On the surface, the issue in dispute was black support for the Republican Party. The new militants denounced not only the party's failure to fulfill its commitments to racial equality but its refusal to reward the loyalty of black voters with a proportionate share of party leadership positions, elective offices, and patronage appointments. A black newspaper in New York, the *Age*, lamented the "jealousy and competition for leadership" that fractured Baltimore's black electorate, the largest in the nation. "With that large voting strength, were the Afro-Americans united, they would far outstrip their brethren in other States and materially benefit the race." "It is with them at all times a warfare of slander, abuse, political throat cutting, and desertion." After Cummings's triumph, "not a dagger is in its scabbard, but every one drawn and aimed at this young man."[25]

The postwar political settlement among whites seemed just as difficult to achieve as consensus among blacks. Weeks after Robert E. Lee's surrender at Appomattox, the first branch of the Baltimore City Council was still issuing charges of disloyalty against perceived traitors to the Union. The alleged seditionists were Methodist churchmen. Their offense was their refusal to join in prayers of thanksgiving for the return of peace and, by implication, the defeat of the Confederacy. The council's first branch complained that these men had "made themselves exceedingly obnoxious to our people" and noted that "a similar spirit of hostility to our Government has been manifested by these parties on former occasions." The branch requested that "the Military Authorities in command of this Department be requested to remove" the Methodist clergymen "from our midst and all such dangerous persons as are inimical to our Government."[26]

The return of Confederate veterans to Baltimore provoked a similar but more strident response. Both branches of the city council approved a resolution protesting "the Policy of allowing men, who left our City, for the purpose of cooperating with the so called Southern Confederacy against our lives, our property and our Nationality," to return to live "among us." The presence of the ex-Confederates, according to the resolution, would "in all probability result in collisions, terrible in their consequences." Voters from the city's fashionable Eleventh and Twelfth Wards assembled not long afterward to enter their own "solemn protest against the continuance of such wicked and unlawful men amongst us who have returned unrepentant and traitors in all their principles," and whose hands were "dyed with the Blood of our Brothers."[27]

In a city with Baltimore's rich history of riot, the presence of Confederate fighters may well have been a legitimate cause for concern. It was more than likely that some of them had taken part in the attack on the Sixth Massachusetts in Baltimore five years earlier. Now they returned, their military skills sharpened by four years of warfare. Exiling the southern veterans, of course, would also have been a political convenience to Republican municipal authorities who maintained their grip on government only by excluding large numbers of Democrats from the polls. If they remained in town, those soldiers might eventually become voters.

THE POLITICS OF ACCOMMODATION

Race and the rebellion continued to structure political divisions in postwar Baltimore, but during the 1870s, the role of the party organizations changed. Long before the days of the Know-Nothings, Baltimore's parties had been vehicles for political combat, often violent. Sometime after the Civil War, however, the dominant Democratic Party evolved into an institution for the management of conflict, while the Republican Party nearly disappeared.

The principal architect of the new regime was Isaac Freeman Rasin, a member of a prominent, prosperous Eastern Shore clan whose ancestors arrived in Maryland in the seventeenth century. In the early 1860s, when he was about 30 years old, Freeman—or "Free"—Rasin went into business, opening a "straw goods" shop near the intersection of Charles and Lexington Streets. At first, he sold bonnets, parasols, children's hats, and hoops for skirts, but his merchandise expanded to include cloth, velvet, and felt hats, French corsets, and kid gloves.[28]

Rasin also branched out into politics. In his postadolescent years, he had been secretary of the Ashland Square American Club, a Know-Nothing organization. Ashland Square is the site of a monument to Henry Wells and Daniel McComas, the two young volunteers killed in the battle of North Point in 1814, where they were supposed to have shot down British General Robert Ross and turned the tide against the British attack on Baltimore. The shrine was an appropriate focus for the patriotic Know-Nothings, but the Ashland Club's location in East Baltimore's Seventh Ward was a political handicap. East Baltimore leaned Democratic even when Baltimore leaned in the opposite direction. In 1854, for example, the year the Know-Nothings swept into control of the city council, Democrats managed to win four of the wards east of Jones Falls as well as the Ninth Ward, just across the Falls, but no wards west of Howard Street. The Democratic candidate for mayor won 49 percent of the vote in East Baltimore, but only 39 percent west of Howard.[29]

A Know-Nothing politician trying to build a political base would have found more opportunities to recruit adherents in West Baltimore than in the east, where the city's immigrant population was concentrated. Rasin stayed in East Baltimore but became a Democrat. Political opportunism is unlikely to have prompted his conversion. He drifted away from the Ashland Club as the Know-Nothings drifted into the Union camp. The Rasin family had strong southern affinities. Freeman's father suffered 28 months of imprisonment for refusing to take a loyalty oath to the United States.[30]

Freeman Rasin completed his political transformation in 1864, when his friends in the Seventh Ward elected him as their representative to the city's Democratic Executive Committee—by a one-vote margin. Three years later, under the new state

Isaac Freeman Rasin,
Baltimore's sometime Democratic
boss, at midcareer

constitution of 1867, the Democrats reconquered Baltimore, and Rasin reached the pinnacle of his career in electoral politics. He was elected clerk of the Maryland Court of Common Pleas, this time by a margin of almost 15,000 votes of approximately 25,000 cast. He held the job for 18 years. Its modest title suited him. Rasin managed to run Baltimore while remaining almost invisible. His obscurity was legendary. It was said that he delivered only one stand-up political speech in his life.[31] He made his career in politics largely by advancing the careers of others.

Even as he got himself elected clerk, Rasin was spreading his influence beyond his own office. At the same Democratic convention that nominated him for his clerkship, Rasin supported John W. Davis, a political adviser employed by the B&O, for nomination as sheriff. Rasin managed to have the sheriff's nomination moved to last place in the proceedings. The maneuver gave Rasin and his allies the opportunity to bargain with aspiring nominees for all other local offices, offering support to those candidates who agreed to back Davis at the end of the evening. Davis succeeded, and his defeated opponent is reported to have warned, "Boys, you have made a mistake. You have given Free Rasin a grip in politics, and mark my words, he will never let go."[32]

Rasin's courthouse job came with the authority to make several patronage appointments—two bailiffs, a crier, a cashier, a messenger, and a few clerks and copyists. Though most jobs went to his Seventh Ward friends and relatives, he also reached out to potential allies in West Baltimore's Eighteenth and Nineteenth Wards and to the heavily Irish and Democratic Eighth Ward, known as "Limerick." Several of Rasin's appointees had been delegates to the Democratic judicial convention that had nominated him. The jobs may have been rewards for their support. Rasin's subsequent appointments also gave him connections with the political leadership of the Second Ward—Fell's Point—and its community of German-Americans.[33]

Rasin's salary as clerk was $3,500 a year, paid out of the fees that his office collected for the issuance of various licenses, including marriage licenses. The fees amounted to more than $300,000 a year. The custom of Rasin's predecessors was to deposit these funds in a bank, at interest, until the time came to turn them over to the state; they kept the interest. Rasin continued the practice, augmenting his personal income and possibly adding it to the resources that extended his influence and attracted adherents.[34]

One of Rasin's youngest recruits was John J. "Sonny" Mahon. At 19 years of age, Mahon was the leader of a juvenile gang in the tough Ninth Ward on Baltimore's waterfront. "Politics in those days wasn't any kid-glove business," Mahon later recalled. "It was rough, and we were as rough as you make them. It was not very long before the leaders uptown began to take notice that they could not carry the Ninth ward in the primaries without us." Mahon was 20 when he was summoned to Rasin's office at the courthouse. Half a century later, he remembered their meeting: "That first conversation was a funny one. We talked about things in the Ninth ward and about the fall campaign. The old man cussed out a lot of people and I listened. The upshot of that conversation was that I became Rasin leader in the ward and got a job in the State tobacco warehouse at $2 a day."[35]

Muscle still mattered in Baltimore politics. Gang leaders like Sonny Mahon were vital members of the Democratic coalition and essential to its control of polling places. The era's partisan political parades were mass demonstrations of muscle. But money and jobs had come to occupy a more central role in city politics. Mahon himself would master the finer arts of politics and patronage, get elected to the city council, and emerge as principal boss of Baltimore when Rasin died in 1907.[36] Ethnicity also continued to be politically relevant, though not as prominent as it was under the Know-Nothings. Immigrants were not sufficiently numerous in Baltimore to carry elections, but in combination with southern-sympathizing Democrats, they could master the municipality. Material inducements helped to seal the alliance, but there were also attempts to manufacture a sentiment of kinship in the coalition. Residents of the Irish Eighth Ward were told that the nation's treatment of the South during Reconstruction was no different from England's abuse of Ireland.

Rasin consolidated his control over the city in 1871, when his candidate for mayor easily won nomination. The victor was Joshua Vansant, chairman of the city hall building committee and the state Democratic Conservative committee. Though there had been some support for the reelection of Mayor Banks, all the Democratic delegates elected in ward primaries were committed to Vansant, and the Democratic Conservative convention dispensed with the usual roll call to nominate him unanimously. At a preelection mass meeting of Democrats in Monument Square, Vansant pledged strict economy in municipal expenditures but made a special point of condemning the Republican administration in Washington for treating "the Southern States as a barbarous power would treat conquered provinces."[37]

In the general election that followed, Baltimore's Democratic Conservatives won every seat in the city council's second branch and all but one in the first. Vansant carried every ward. His biggest margins were in Rasin's Seventh and in the Irish Eighth, but his citywide majority was much narrower than Robert Banks's four years earlier. The Fifteenth Amendment took effect in Maryland a month after Banks was elected. Vansant was the first mayor to face an electorate that included black men, and they generally cast their ballots against the Democratic candidate. They could not vote Republican, however, because there were no Republican candidates on the ballot. Their stand-ins presented themselves to the electorate as candidates of the "National Reform Party."[38] Republicans had fallen into such disfavor that they dared not speak their name. During Vansant's administration, the residents of Republican Street would petition, successfully, to change its name to Carrollton Avenue.[39]

THE CITY AROMATIC

One municipal problem emerged as the focal concern of the Vansant administration: Baltimore smelled bad. It became the mayor's mission to track the odor to its sources and vanquish it. The city had been odiferous for some time. The aroma oozing up from the harbor in the summer months was so overpowering that some were willing to sacrifice the Inner Harbor itself to put an end to the odor. In 1858, a local physician, Thomas H. Buckler, had advocated neutralization of the noxious Basin by simply filling it in with soil, creating a new tract of real estate extending from the mouth of the Jones Falls west to Light Street and south to the foot of Federal Hill, which would no longer exist because Buckler proposed using the soil from the hill to fill up the Basin.[40]

Apart from its obvious cost to the city's shipping, the problem with Buckler's solution was its failure to deal with the Jones Falls, which delivered its own contribution to the harbor's stench. In 1863, Mayor Chapman had complained about the emanations of the Falls. It was the "receptacle of a large number of sinks on the line of its passage through the heart of the city," and in the dry summer months, "being filled with a black mud to nearly the surface of the water, it leaves exposed at the slightest depression of the tide a large mass of putrid pestilential matter." The mayor recommended dredging to remove the offensive layer of muck.[41]

Under Buckler's plan to fill in the Basin, the Jones Falls would have continued to add its murky burden to a diminished body of water, intensifying the pollution of the "outer" harbor off Fell's Point. Without the Basin to serve as a receptacle for the city's waste, Baltimore would need some other system of sewage disposal. In 1870, the city created the Commission for the Improvement of the Jones Falls to address both the stream's odor and, more catastrophic, the flood damage caused to properties along its banks. The commission's proposal to deepen the bed of the Falls would increase its capacity to accommodate storm water and remove the sediment responsible for its "fetid exhalations and disgusting exhibitions."[42]

By the end of Robert Banks's term as mayor, in 1871, the city stench had risen toward the top of the local agenda. The board of health convened a committee of prominent physicians to evaluate the well-being of the city. The committee delivered

The Centre Street bridge across the Jones Falls, when the stream served Baltimoreans as a sewer

its report at the office of the mayor in late August, the city's most odorous season. In general, the report was encouraging. Mayor Banks summarized it for the city council, declaring "cause for earnest congratulation that we can . . . maintain by comparison of vital statistics that our city ranks as one of the healthiest in the country." The claim was dubious. Baltimore's mortality rates for the early 1870s were lower than those of New York and Brooklyn but scarcely different from those in Boston, Philadelphia, and Cincinnati.[43]

According to the doctors, however, one "great problem" threatened the public health of the city: "How Most effectually to abate the grave nuisance made by our basin and docks during the heated term of every year, this year, more serious, it is believed, than ever before." The mayor offered no program to cope with the nuisance but urged the city council to "set about devising at once a proper remedy to be applied during the fall and winter months" in anticipation of the smelly spring and the even more noxious summer. Banks suggested to the council that it possessed "a means of very decided amelioration of the evil in your power to withdraw the privilege, now enjoyed by some of the City's hotels and private homes of discharging their water-closets through sewers communicating directly with the basin." The issuance of sewer permits fell within the council's authority; they were favors for friends and political patronage for constituents. Their cancellation would be an embarrassment and would reduce the political working capital that council members used to get elected and stay elected. Mayor Banks held out an alternative: "If however the plan of relief of the nuisance made by the basin . . . shall consist in causing the water therein to be active an[d] frequently changing, then it seems that these sewers might discharge into the basin with impunity."[44]

The physicians' report cited one further problem: the "manner of disposing of night soil," a practice "affecting injuriously the condition of the basin, as well as many parts of the city." For years, "night men" made the rounds of Baltimore with buckets, barrels, and horse-drawn carts, periodically removing the content of privy vaults and depositing it outside the city limits. Their excavations inevitably stirred up the deposits that they mined, releasing gases thought to be foul or even fatal. According to the physicians' committee, the collection and disposal of night soil might spread epidemic disease. In 1867, the city contracted with the Baltimore Fertilizing Manufacturing Company to collect all of the city's garbage and night soil. The night soil was moved to a site four miles downstream from Baltimore on the Patapsco River, where the waste was mixed with ashes, dried, deodorized, and converted into "poudrette," which the company sold as fertilizer.[45]

The arrangement with the fertilizer company solved some of the problems arising from the disposal of night soil. But the night men continued to drive their carts through the streets trailing clouds of essence excremental. In 1871, the municipality's attorneys arranged to terminate the contract under which Baltimore paid $18,000 a year to provide the Fertilizing Company with its raw material. The agreement would expire in 1872. Mayor Banks urged the council to use this interval to "mature some better way of managing these offensive matters . . . which shall be void of the disgusting and offensive features of the present plan."[46]

Baltimoreans were hardly the only urbanites assaulted by the odors of their city. London had been overcome by the smell of the Thames during the 1850s. The Houses of Parliament, on the bank of the river, were directly exposed to the nuisance and powerfully disposed to eliminate it. To overcome "the Great Stink," Parliament approved the construction of many miles of sewers to carry the wastes of the city far downstream.[47] Other American cities also reacted to the smells of sewage. In the 1850s, Chicago and Brooklyn abandoned the "privy-vault cesspool system of waste disposal" and constructed sewer networks that relied on water flow to carry off the offensive burden produced by their concentrated populations. Other cities followed their lead. Baltimore was not one of them. It would be the last of the country's major cities to build a sanitary sewer system.[48]

DOWN AND DIRTY

Challenged by Mayor Banks to save the city from its sewage, the Baltimore City Council made the subject one of its preoccupations after Mayor Vansant took office. In May 1872, the second branch of the council turned to the board of health for expert advice on eliminating "the stench emanating from the basin." The board's first priority, it seemed, was "calming the anxiety of our citizens many of whom suppose that the emanation is of a highly pestilential character." Though less alarmed about the "emanation" than its own committee of eminent physicians, the board acknowledged that the harbor's noxious emissions were "not conducive to a high state of health, and therefore ought to be removed or prevented as far as possible."

The solution, according to the board of health, was "plain and simple." Fifteen years earlier, the city's water supply had been "sufficient to allow all the water plugs to run once or twice a week in the afternoon during the summer months to flush out the gutters and after them the sewers and tunnels and lastly aiding in yielding to the docks and harbor a supply of fresh water, and then we had no stenches as is now experienced."[49]

The plain and simple problem was the "rigid economy of water" that Baltimore had to observe to accommodate a population that had grown by more than a quarter between 1860 and 1870. In the early 1870s, the city was also contending with successive summer droughts, when the only water that ran through the gutters was "dish and other filthy water, loaded with vegetable and animal matter some of which lodges in the interstices between the stones and there festers and rots in the hot sun thus contaminating the atmosphere." Without a substantial increase in the city's water supply, the board could only suggest the use of "chemical agents" to deodorize the harbor, and it could not guarantee their efficacy.[50]

Some local experts questioned the board of health's plain and simple understanding of the problem. Charles P. Kahler, a civil engineer and one-time city surveyor, argued that fresh water and harbor water might not mix. The two could differ in specific gravity because their temperatures differed or because the Basin's water was burdened with sediment. The fresh water might pass through the harbor and join the cooler, deeper, and cleaner Patapsco, doing no good at all for the Basin itself. Besides, Kahler concluded, Baltimoreans had better uses for pure water than to dump it into their malodorous harbor.[51]

Kahler submitted his observations at the end of the city's second consecutive summer drought. The city council, in response to the water shortage, was considering how to engineer a vast increase in Baltimore's water supply by drawing on the Gunpowder River—northeast of the city—pumping its water over a rise and into an existing city reservoir at Lake Roland in Baltimore County. The proposal had been in circulation for at least five years. Mayor Chapman and the council had spent $225,000 to purchase water rights along the Gunpowder, and in 1869, the *Sun* closed a lengthy review of the city's water resources with the prediction that it would "not be many years before the supply of water from the Gunpowder will become a necessity." In its annual report, issued early in 1871, the city water board repeated the prediction and added that "nothing remains but to determine, when the proper time arrives, and the best mode of conveying the water to the city."[52]

By 1872, mayor, council, and water board agreed that the time had come. The council's sense of urgency moved it to create a Joint Special Committee on the Introduction of the Water of the Gunpowder River and the Purification of the Harbor. The committee eventually solidified behind a resolution "to procure the opinion of an Eminent hydraulic Engineer as to the most certain permanent and prompt removal of the annoyance occasioned by the Stench of the Basin."[53]

By the end of the year, the committee submitted an ordinance authorizing the water board to begin drawing water from the Gunpowder River to feed the Lake Roland reservoir. The board had already dispatched a civil engineer to lay out the conduit connecting the two bodies of water, and Mayor Vansant had given his blessing to the enterprise in September, partly because the city was confronting another year of severe drought, but also because the "inner basin of the harbor . . . during the present exceedingly warm and dry season has exhaled a most offensive odor, and has alarmed the citizens of Baltimore because of an apprehension that it could engender disease of an infectious and malignant character."[54]

The council was distinctly impatient with the water board's progress in bringing the Gunpowder to bear on the city's noxious Basin. In September 1873, the council's second branch asked "how much progress has been made by the contractors for the introduction of the temporary supply of water . . . from the Gunpowder" and what action the water board was taking to deal with contractors who fell behind schedule. A resolution introduced not long afterward was charged with urgency: "Whereas the largest attainable supply of water by natural flow from the Gunpowder River is absolutely necessary at the earliest possible moment," the council wanted to assure Mayor Vansant and the water board that it was prepared to submit "the most liberal plan" to the Maryland General Assembly "for the power to issue Water Stock to secure the permanent supply of water from the Gunpowder River."[55]

By April 1874, the council's first branch wanted the water board to explain "what retards the speedy introduction of an additional supply of water into the City of Baltimore." Mayor Vansant responded on behalf of the board. The delay was not the fault of feckless contractors or unforeseen engineering problems. The difficulty was legal. The pumps, conduits, and pipes needed to carry the water of the Gunpowder to Lake Roland had been completed. But a property owner along the line of the conduit obtained an injunction prohibiting the city and its contractors from opening the system so that the water could flow into Lake Roland.[56]

The legal obstacles were manageable. Bernard Carter, attorney for the intransigent Baltimore County landowner and an ally of Freeman Rasin, wrote to Vansant to explain how an appropriate sum of money might solve the problem.[57] Other obstructions proved less moveable. The council's plan to freshen up the Basin called for the Gunpowder water to be pumped into Lake Roland and then to reach the city "by natural flow." Engineering an unnatural flow was likely to be expensive and time-consuming. As it happened, getting the water from Lake Roland to the harbor would require six miles of underground conduit lined with brick, along with several new reservoirs, not completed until the 1880s at a total cost of $8 million.[58] But the water cure collapsed in the face of a more fundamental problem.

The city council's Joint Standing Committee on the Harbor reviewed 15 proposals for flushing the stench out of the Basin—some of them appallingly implausible.[59] The committee unanimously rejected 13 of the plans. The plan proposed by Milo W.

Locke won the support of all but one committee member. Locke was a local contractor who proposed to draw sewage from the Basin through a tunnel extending under Locust Point and emptying into the main channel of the Patapsco. The fetid waters would be drawn into the tunnel by a pair of large propellers rotating at its far end; the current would be propelled by a jet of fresh water pumped into the bottom of the Basin to prevent the accumulation of sediment. The committee's lone dissenter offered a lengthy, point-by-point critique of the Locke plan as an "engineering conception," not a scheme tested in practice. He preferred the plan of F. H. Hambleton, who proposed a sanitary sewer system for the city as a whole. The council's first branch voted to reject this minority report. But the report's indictment of Locke's proposal was thorough and compelling. For that reason, perhaps, the second branch rejected a proposal to grant Locke funds to construct a model of his two-propeller plan. The water cure for the harbor had evaporated. The council faced the politically distasteful necessity to cut off all sewers draining into the Basin, including the one that served city hall, and revoking its constituents' permits to befoul the Inner Harbor.[60]

Only a fraction of the city's sewers discharged waste directly into the Basin. The Jones Falls may have received the effluent from the water closets of as many as 15,000 or 20,000 private homes and businesses. But the Jones Falls Improvement project included the construction of high walls along the length of the stream for flood control,[61] and the walls would make it difficult to connect household water closets with the Falls. Deprived of opportunities to drain their wastes directly or indirectly into the harbor, Baltimoreans were left with two options. They could support the construction of a comprehensive sanitary sewer system, or they could rely on privy vaults and the "night men" who cleaned them out.

Some Baltimoreans, like Hambleton, had the comprehensive vision needed to conceive a citywide sewer system, but Baltimore lacked the political integration necessary to build it. Instead, the municipality reacted disjointedly to one localized sewage crisis after another, fashioning partial solutions on a neighborhood scale.[62] Without a comprehensive sewer system, the night men remained indispensable. But the city's renewed reliance on them was accompanied by a determination to minimize the offensive by-products of their work. In his annual message of 1875, Mayor Vansant complained that the "intolerable nuisance" of the night carts "should be abated if it cannot be altogether averted." The city council created the Special Committee on Night Soil to recommend steps that might reduce the odors that resulted from the night men's operations and the supposed threat to health.[63]

An innovative technology offered hope that the night soil nuisance might be averted. A new business firm, the Odorless Excavating Apparatus Company, introduced itself to the mayor and city council. The company's patented equipment pumped privy contents through a hose into an airtight tank with a capacity of as much as 640 gallons. At the top of the tank was a small vent, opened when the equipment was in operation. A small charcoal furnace placed over the vent burned off the noxious gases that Baltimoreans found so objectionable.[64]

City agencies were among the earliest clients of Odorless Excavating. The school system signed on in 1874 and found that the company charged less than the night men. The health department issued permits exclusively to the company to pump out privy vaults during the summer, when strict regulations governed the removal of night soil. The health commissioner condemned "the old bucket and night cart system" as a danger to public health. He felt bound by his professional standards to use a method that reduced the "nuisance to the minimum." He asked the council to sustain him "and confer a blessing upon the people" of the city.[65]

The Odorless Excavating process was controversial because it could eliminate the jobs of night men, but the city council eventually granted the company a monopoly of the night soil business. The jobs lost were replaced by hundreds added in companies operating under Odorless Excavating franchises. The company's reign over the privies of Baltimore also had an unanticipated consequence. By mitigating the unhealthful stench associated with the excavation of privy vaults, the company reduced one of the irritations that might move Baltimoreans to demand a sanitary sewer system. And the company, its franchisees, and their workers naturally emerged as an interest group opposing such a system.

Demands for a sewer system continued. In 1876, the General Assembly had empowered and required the city to construct one or more "intercepting sewers" that would divert watery waste from the Basin "to some point so distant from the said Harbor as not to be liable to be returned thereto by the operation of tide water." Two years later, a bill was introduced in the first branch of the city council to provide for the construction of a sewer system along the lines of the one proposed by F. H. Hambleton. It was tabled.[66]

The work of Odorless Excavating had hardly solved the city's sewage disposal problems. The company needed a place to dump the waste that it pumped from Baltimore's privies. In 1872, the municipality had leased several sites in Baltimore County for this purpose and for disposal of garbage in general. The arrangement raised understandable objections in the county. The city's health commissioner urged the council to produce some "wise legislation" by which the city could be "relieved of this dilemma, and a permanent arrangement be decided upon by which all complaints will be removed."[67] The council's wisdom operated more slowly than the county's outrage. In 1873, county officials made their point by ordering the arrest of nine city health department employees for creating a nuisance by depositing night soil in the county. The city council eventually settled on an alternative plan for disposal without arousing Baltimore County officials. The night soil would be conveyed in "air-tight barges" to city-owned land in Anne Arundel County.[68]

Chapter 23
THE RING

WHILE BALTIMORE BATTLED ITS STENCH, Isaac Freeman Rasin extended his reach in local politics, but only faint hints of his influence broke the surface of the city's business. In 1873, for example, the city council took special pains to maintain and improve the Wells and McComas Monument in Ashland Square. It appointed a committee to "arrange for a celebration of the successful defence of the city in 1814—and the dedication of the Wells and McComas Monument."[1] No other city monument got so much attention at the time. The monument, of course, was located in Rasin's Seventh Ward. More important, both square and statuary had served as the symbolic and patriotic focus of the Ashland Square American Club, the organization that introduced Rasin to politics. In 1880, the city council's Joint Standing Committee on Highways proposed a new street in southeast Baltimore to be called Rasin Street. But the street never got beyond the proposal stage.[2]

While maintaining his roots in the Seventh Ward, Rasin extended his operations to the city at large, and then beyond. In 1870, at a conference of Democratic leaders in his office, Rasin met Arthur Pue Gorman, a member of the Maryland House of Delegates from Howard County. After the meeting, Gorman and Rasin had lunch together at Barnum's Hotel, along with B&O lobbyist John W. Davis, who had been elected sheriff, with Rasin's help, four years earlier. Gorman's political career had begun at the age of 11 when he was appointed a page in the US Senate. The experience ignited his determination to return to the Senate as an elected member. Rasin assisted his progress toward that goal in 1871, when his support helped to lift Gorman to the speakership of the house of delegates.[3] Until ratification of the Seventeenth Amendment in 1913, state legislatures elected US senators, and leadership in Maryland's General Assembly provided a platform for vaulting into the upper house of Congress.

The alliance between Gorman and Rasin—later known to their opponents as the Gorman-Rasin Ring—breached the boundary between Baltimore politics and state politics. Together, the two bosses arranged the election of William Pinkney Whyte as Maryland's governor in 1871. Whyte, an antebellum member of Congress, was already a commanding presence on the Baltimore City Democratic Committee when Rasin was elected a committeeman from the Seventh Ward. Rasin served part of his political apprenticeship as one of the older man's allies. Whyte had gotten a whiff of the US Senate when he served out the term of an incumbent who had been appointed ambassador to Great Britain, and he badly wanted to be elected a senator in his own right.[4] As governor, he could woo state legislators with patronage and favors.

Railroad politics probably figured more immediately than legislative politics in Whyte's election. The incumbent governor and Whyte's rival for the nomination was Odin Bowie. Before winning the governorship, Bowie had joined other citizens of Prince Georges County to secure a charter for the Baltimore and Pope's Creek Railroad. The charter permitted the company to build branch lines, and Bowie approached the Pennsylvania Railroad to propose that one of the branches might reach out to Washington, thus breaking the B&O's monopoly on rail traffic between Baltimore and the capital. The Pennsylvania Railroad backed Bowie's election and provided a $400,000 loan to help with construction of the Washington branch. The B&O wanted Bowie out of the governor's mansion before the line could be built. Whyte was a good friend of B&O president John Work Garrett and many of the railroad's directors. In 1871, the railroad put its considerable resources behind his campaign to prevent Bowie's reelection.[5]

According to Frank Kent, the *Baltimore Sun*'s foremost commentator on state and local politics, the election of 1871 marked a seismic shift in the character of Baltimore politics—the first election in which vote buying played a significant role. The practice followed the addition of African American men to the state's electorate under the Fifteenth Amendment. The city's Democratic organization countered black voters' understandable affinity for the party of Lincoln by paying them to stay away from the polls. Rasin may not have invented the arrangement, but he made it habitual. The boss's chief operative in the black community was Thomas A. Smith. The day after an election, Smith would appear at Rasin's courthouse office to count up the registered black voters who had cast their votes. Smith would be paid according to the number of black voters who had failed to show up at the polls. Smith's dilemma, in other words, was to maximize black voter registration but minimize black voting. He and his associates sometimes depressed African American turnout by arranging grand picnics or Chesapeake Bay excursions on election day. "From buying the negroes," wrote Kent, "the next step was buying the white men, and it did not take much of this sort of thing before the politics of Maryland became thoroughly steeped in corruption."[6]

Though undeniably corrupt, vote buying represented a far more civilized means of managing the electorate than the homicidal violence of the Know-Nothings, and it was certainly preferable to the vote blocking practiced further south by the Knights of the Ku Klux Klan.

If Baltimore's Democratic leaders would pay Thomas Smith to keep black men away from the polls, they might also be willing to pay black voters to support Democratic candidates. The possibility of such bargains and the estrangement of black voters from the Republican Party also suggested to white Democratic politicians a strategy of restraint on matters of race. While Democrats elsewhere in Maryland sought to bar black voters from the polls, most of Baltimore's Democratic politicians prudently avoided racial aggravations that might rouse the city's substantial African American electorate to renew its loyalties to the Republicans. Skillful bartering might turn them out for Democrats.

CHALLENGES OF MACHINE BUILDING

Arthur Gorman profited far more handsomely from the election of Governor Whyte than did Thomas Smith. Whyte fired the incumbent president of the Chesapeake and Ohio Canal and appointed Gorman in his place.[7] Gorman gained not only a substantial salary but control of the numerous jobs connected with maintenance and management of the canal. His leadership of the C&O, however, also had politically awkward implications for his (and Rasin's) corporate affinities. The C&O operated in competition with the B&O. Having just helped to elect a friend of the B&O as governor, the Gorman-Rasin Ring now embraced the C&O and its occasional political ally, the Pennsylvania Railroad. The Pennsylvania's counsel, Bernard Carter, entered Rasin's circle of political associates. When the B&O engaged his canal in a rate war, Delegate Gorman maneuvered in the General Assembly to achieve rough parity between canal and railroad rates.[8]

Rasin's connections with Governor Whyte and Arthur Gorman gave him leverage beyond the city limits and helped to compensate politically for the city's gross underrepresentation in the state legislature. With half the state's population, Baltimore held less than 20 percent of seats in the house of delegates and 12 percent of the state senate. Governor Whyte was generous in his distribution of state jobs to Rasin allies—among them, John J. "Sonny" Mahon's job in the state tobacco warehouse.[9]

Though Rasin had augmented his patronage resources, his Democratic organization faced an energized Republican opposition able to draw on the federal patronage of the Grant administration. In 1872, instead of running under the National Reform alias, Republican candidates for the first branch of the city council ran openly as Republicans, and they increased their representation from one council seat to three. In the congressional election, both of Baltimore's Democratic incumbents won, but by smaller margins than in 1870.[10]

While the Republicans struggled back from obscurity, Freeman Rasin, though still deliberately obscure, quietly continued to build his organization. Since his political base was in East Baltimore, he worked steadily to extend his strength west of the Jones Falls. One Democratic strong point in West Baltimore was the old engine house of the New Market Fire Company. Though there were no longer any volunteer fire companies to provide election-day organization and muscle, the alumni of the New Market Company still maintained an organizational existence. As firefighters, they had fought Know-Nothings on behalf of the Democratic Party. Rasin recruited the New Market veterans and their leader, Augustus Albert. With Rasin's support,

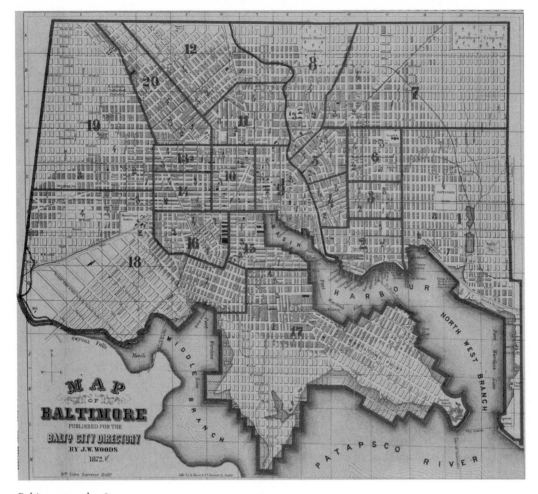

Baltimore wards, 1872

Albert won two terms as sheriff, and in the 1880s he became the city's fire commissioner.[11]

Rasin's respectable family background earned him a slot in Baltimore's social register and gave him access to heights of society out of reach for ward leaders like Sonny Mahon.[12] Rasin enjoyed access to the politics of the prosperous Eleventh and Twelfth Wards, embracing the mansions on Mount Vernon Place and the stately townhouses to its west, where he won friends at the top of the legal profession such as Bernard Carter. The attorneys were useful as wordsmiths, and they handled political litigation when Rasin's rivals alleged irregularities at the polls, as they frequently did.

Rasin's first six-year term as clerk of the Maryland Court of Common Pleas expired in 1873. He won reelection over his Republican opponent by a margin of two to one. In 1874, Rasin and Gorman used their influence in the state legislature to place Governor Whyte in the US Senate seat he had longed for. The legislature's vote for Whyte was unanimous.[13]

But, just a year later, the Democratic consensus that Rasin had achieved in Bal-timore was under attack and in danger of disintegration. A rally of independent reformers during the mayoral campaign of 1875 prompted the *Sun* to warn of "a popular movement, hardly yet defined and active, being worked into shape, and destined to protest against the shyster politicians and the incompetents who have had entirely too much control of public affairs." Rasin's Democratic candidate for mayor, Ferdinand Latrobe, declared that he was in favor of reform but had yet to learn whether any reforms were needed in the city or the state. He did, however, promise a parsimonious administration.[14]

The reformers achieved even greater strength than the *Sun* imagined. After the votes were counted, the first branch of the city council was evenly divided between organization Democrats and candidates running on the "merchants' and citizens' reform" ticket. The regular Democrats still held all but 2 of the 10 seats in the second branch. Latrobe managed to win the mayor's office by only 2,700 votes, with almost 54,000 cast.[15] His opponent, local merchant Henry M. Warfield, filed suit in Baltimore's superior court alleging fraudulent votes and intimidation at the polls. The evidence was rather thin. There had been some irregularities. Some "pudding ballots" were detected—contrivances by which organization men en-closed several fraudulent ballots inside a legitimate one, shaking the counterfeits loose as they dropped them in the ballot box. Warfield was unable to reverse his defeat, but the reformers would get another shot at the Ring in the state election only a month later.

"POTATO BUGS" AND PARTY POOPERS

Republicans, by themselves, posed no threat to the Ring. They were so weak, wrote Frank Kent, that "they would fuse with most any disgruntled element of the Dem-ocrats that chose to put up a set of candidates." But there was no shortage of dis-gruntled Democrats. Some of them gathered behind the gubernatorial candidacy of William T. Hamilton, the Western Maryland Democrat ousted from the US Senate to make room for Whyte. Hamilton made his move in the defining election of 1875, a contest that would shape the contours of politics in Maryland and Baltimore until the beginning of the twentieth century. Allied with the Republicans, the "reform" or "Independent" Democrats challenged the Gorman-Rasin ticket, from governor down to city council. The contest would be known as the "Potato Bug Campaign," after the insects that destroyed the crop of 1875. Democratic regulars likened Dem-ocratic adherents of the Reform Party to the yellow-striped pests—craven parasites who aimed to destroy the party that had nurtured them.[16]

Rasin, Gorman, and Senator Whyte supported the gubernatorial candidacy of John Lee Carroll. He owned a manor in Howard County, once the property of his great-grandfather, Charles Carroll of Carrollton. The younger Carroll also had a fashionable city address on Mount Vernon Place. His family name, his social prom-inence, and his reputation as a "fine southern gentleman" all contributed to his at-tractiveness as a candidate. He had another asset of special interest to Arthur Gor-man. Carroll represented Howard County in the state senate, and Gorman wanted the seat for himself so that he could advance his ambition to enter the US Senate.

299

The Ring

Gorman promised Maryland's other seat in the Senate to James Groome of Cecil County, a third Democratic aspirant to the governorship. Groome had become the gubernatorial stand-in after Governor Whyte moved to the Senate. In return for the promise that he would get a Senate seat of his own, Groome agreed to remain a candidate for governor until just before the Democratic state convention, when he would withdraw and throw his support to Carroll.[17]

William Hamilton had his own backers in Baltimore. Severn Teackle Wallis was a distinguished attorney and literary figure whose Confederate sympathies had earned him 14 months' imprisonment during the Civil War—and the admiration of the city's numerous ex-Confederates. His biting oratory stood in sharp contrast to the silence and invisibility of Boss Rasin. John K. Cowen provided more than oratory. He was chief counsel (and later president) of the B&O Railroad. His corporate interests set him at odds with the Gorman-Rasin Ring, which fed on the resources of the C&O Canal. A railroad tax imposed by the state legislature in 1872 was particularly galling to Cowen and the B&O. It was intended to quiet Democratic farmers, who charged that their lands were taxed too heavily while Maryland's wealthy corporations enjoyed low taxes or exemptions.[18]

The Ring swept both state and municipal elections in 1875, but not cleanly. The Democratic state convention had been reduced to riot. Die-hard adherents of William Hamilton delayed balloting and chipped away at Carroll's majority with a filibuster that extended over days and nights, persisting over catcalls and insults. Fistfights broke out, and the police were summoned. Through it all, Gorman remained imperturbable, until finally, the Hamiltonians were exhausted and John Lee Carroll won the gubernatorial nomination, his support augmented, as promised, by delegates originally committed to Groome.[19]

Carroll carried Baltimore by more than 15,000 votes of 60,000 cast. His margin of victory was suspiciously large, more than five times that of Ferdinand Latrobe in the mayoral contest just a month earlier. Accusations of electoral theft reverberated long after election day. Almost a month after the polls closed, the Reformers held an "Indignation Meeting" to protest the conduct of the election and point out evidence of fraud. Black voters, who had been expected to support the Reform candidates, had faced harassment and fistfights at the polls. But the most glaring indications of electoral irregularity lay in the voting results themselves. The total vote increased sharply in precincts where population had declined, with the bulk of these odd increases favoring Democrats. J. Morrison Harris, Carroll's Republican opponent, won a majority of the votes cast in the counties, but the margin of his defeat in Baltimore turned the election in favor of Carroll.[20]

The extent of the fraud came to light only seven years later when one of the Democratic election officers, in a voluntary statement before a local judge, confessed that on the night after the election, a court clerk had admitted him and other Democratic election officials to the basement of the courthouse where the ballots were secured. He and his colleagues sifted through them, removing reform ballots, burning them in a stove, and substituting votes for organization Democrats, taking care that the total vote count remained consistent with the figure reported when the polls closed. Several other election clerks corroborated his account.[21]

The state legislature did not wait for this evidence to come in. In 1876, the General Assembly enacted a new election law that, like its predecessor, applied only to Baltimore. It removed the supervision of elections from the purview of Baltimore's three police commissioners. The governor was to appoint, and the senate confirm, three supervisors of elections who would appoint three election judges in each precinct, one of whom had to come from the minority party.[22] Under the new law, Governor Carroll nominated the officials who were to prevent the frauds that allegedly got him elected in the first place.

TRAIN WRECK

Baltimore, which had given Carroll the governorship, would also present him with the most grievous trouble of his term in office. It began on July 16, 1877, at Camden Junction, just outside the city, where the B&O's Washington branch diverged from the main stem. A fireman abandoned his locomotive and walked off the job. July 16 was the day set by B&O president John W. Garrett to reduce the pay of railroad employees by 10 percent. Just before cutting his workers' wages, he had granted a 10 percent increase in dividends to stockholders. B&O workers were already in a bad way. Even before this latest pay cut, their wages were substantially lower than those paid by other railroads. It was the second pay cut in eight months. During the long recession following the Panic of 1873, B&O wages had dropped by almost 50 percent.[23] The July reduction converted workers' discontent into rage. More firemen joined the first striker at Camden Junction, and then 38 engineers walked off the job.

A surplus of unemployed workers meant that the B&O had no trouble recruiting replacements for the strikers, and the trains continued to roll. The strikers tried to dissuade their replacements from taking their jobs, but committed "no actual violence," according to the *Sun*. Mayor Latrobe, however, was readily persuaded to send his police officers beyond the city limits to Camden Junction, where they arrested three workers for threatening a riot—just before a Howard County judge ordered the city officers out of his jurisdiction. The B&O circumvented that problem by commissioning the city police as railroad constables.

B&O vice-president John King urged Governor Carroll to discourage any further disruption of rail traffic by mobilizing the state's National Guard, but Carroll did not think the situation serious enough to warrant military intervention. According to the *Sun*, after all, the strikers at Camden Junction "were all in good humor, and no bad feeling was exhibited."[24] But down the line, in Martinsburg, West Virginia, the mood was a good deal less mellow. The town's police force was smaller than Baltimore's, and railroad workers made up a larger share of its population. As crews jumped off incoming trains, hardly any railroad workers could be persuaded to replace them. B&O officials urged West Virginia's governor to call out the Berkeley Light Guards. Many of its members were railroaders themselves, however, and some of them were strikers. After a brief exchange of gunfire, the commander marched his Berkeley Guards back to town and dismissed them. Another guard unit, accom-

panied by West Virginia's governor, turned back at Grafton before it reached the defiant strikers at Martinsburg. Governor Mathews telegraphed President Rutherford
B. Hayes to request federal troops. B&O president Garrett did the same.[25]

Garrett also met with Governor Carroll to urge, once again, that the governor
mobilize the National Guard. This time Carroll agreed and called up two Baltimore
units—the Fifth and Sixth Regiments. They were needed in Cumberland, where a
motley crowd of railroad workers and others had stopped all train traffic. The two
regiments had to march through the streets of the city from their armories to Camden Station. To ensure a rapid response, the regiments' military commander insisted
that the 5–1–5 signal for militia mobilization be sounded on the bell at city hall and
on all the fire bells in town. They rang out just as factory and mill workers were
leaving their jobs for the day. The signal mobilized thousands of civilians as well as
soldiers. Crowds collected around the armories, and when the militia emerged, they
encountered a rain of brickbats and cheers for the strikers. Though 25 members of
the Fifth Regiment were injured, the unit managed to hold its formation and reach
the railroad station, only to find that a mob had torn up the tracks to stop any train
from moving.[26]

The Sixth Regiment faced a more difficult march to Camden Station. Its armory
was in East Baltimore, more distant from the station than the Fifth Regiment's. The
crowds here began to stone the armory even before the regiment emerged. The
soldiers' first attempt to break out failed, and when they finally began the march
to Camden Station, they encountered a sustained barrage of missiles. Against the
express orders of their commanding officer, they fired into the angry crowd, killing 10 people and wounding many more before a handful of soldiers reached their
destination. The rest—about two-thirds—had shed their uniforms and melted away
into Baltimore.[27]

The mayor, the governor, a number of police officers, and about 350 guardsmen
were now trapped inside the Camden depot surrounded by a crowd of approximately 15,000, some of whom seemed intent on setting the building afire. B&O
president John Garrett, perhaps the most hated man in Baltimore at that moment,
was nowhere to be seen. Among the notables held captive in Camden Station, the
only railroad executive was a B&O vice-president. Governor Carroll wired President
Hayes to request federal troops. Two thousand federal soldiers and 500 marines
were called in to reinforce the local regiments, and a US Revenue Cutter patrolled
the warehouses along the waterfront. But even before the regulars arrived, the forces
already gathered in Camden Station went on the offensive. National Guardsmen
advanced with fixed bayonets, and police officers waded into the mob to arrest the
most obvious troublemakers. Inside the station, the gentlemen's waiting room began
to fill up with arrested rioters. Outside, the crowd broke up and moved away. Only
the railroad strikers, who seem to have taken no part in the disorders, stood firm
at the depot with their grievances. Their strike collapsed. Management made no
concessions.[28]

The city added yet another riot to its record. It was succeeded by a 14-state contagion of railroad strikes and riots. Some observers saw the emerging outlines of an

American proletariat behind the disorders. In Baltimore, July's uprising produced a new contestant in October's municipal election—the Workingmen's Party. It offered a full slate of candidates, led by a charismatic blacksmith. The Workingmen's mayoral candidate, Joseph "Honest Joe" Thompson, addressed enthusiastic crowds in every ward and finished the election in second place, far ahead of the Independent Democrat, who received fewer than 1,000 votes. Thompson claimed that he had been denied victory by electoral fraud and his party lacked the money to challenge the outcome in court. He declared that he would never run for public office again, and was soon appointed deputy clerk of the court of common pleas, as Rasin's assistant. He was known thereafter as "Ex-Honest Joe" Thompson.[29]

POLITICAL PERFUMERY

The patronage and particularism of machine politics tended to dissolve working-class solidarity. But machine politics had no such effect on the town's reformers. Though the Rasin-Gorman-Whyte forces had defeated the "Potato Bugs" in 1875, they were chastened by the battle. Freeman Rasin adopted the practice of nominating reformers for visible municipal and state offices in order, he said, to "perfume" the ticket. That may have been Rasin's design when he supported—or permitted—the nomination of George P. Kane as Democratic candidate for mayor in 1877. Kane had been the city's police marshal during the Civil War until federal authorities arrested him. He was not one of Rasin's political creatures. In fact, he had run against Augustus Albert, Rasin's West Baltimore ally, in two primaries for sheriff and prevailed in one of them. Rasin himself was not in evidence at the city's Democratic convention in 1877—no surprise—but neither were any of his captains. In accepting the mayoral nomination, Kane asserted that he was "under no obligation to any man, or set of men. I have said repeatedly that I would make no promises nor enter any stipulations whatever regarding the trust for which you have put me in nomination."[30] It is more than likely that he was telling the truth.

Kane succeeded Mayor Ferdinand C. Latrobe, who was temporarily out of favor with the Rasin organization. He had run in 1875 as a candidate of the regular Democrats, but the *Sun* observed, hopefully, that he represented "the respectable members" of the organization. He was, after all, the son of B&O attorney John H. B. Latrobe and a B&O attorney himself. Latrobe may not have run as a reformer, but he behaved like one once in office. Perhaps the reformers' unexpectedly strong showing in the municipal election of 1875 and his own narrow victory moved him to reassess his position. He infuriated the Democratic regulars when he abolished the office of port warden and replaced it with an unpaid harbor board to oversee docks and dredging operations. At the same time, he closed the City Yard, the base of operations for the workers supervised by the port warden, and turned its work over to private contractors. Latrobe thus saved the city approximately $400,000, but also eliminated a fertile source of patronage for the city's ward bosses. In retribution, the organization denied him the Democratic nomination for reelection in 1877 and surrendered it, at Rasin's direction, to George Kane.[31]

Kane had sided with the Potato Bugs two years earlier and therefore provided

Rasin's municipal ticket with some of the reformist "perfumery" that the Democrats needed. But one of Kane's principal assets was his close friendship with Severn Teackle Wallis, who had run in 1875 as the reform candidate for state attorney general. Kane and Wallis had spent time in the same federal prisons during the Civil War. Rasin hoped that Kane's candidacy would mute Wallis's fierce attacks on the Ring. It did even more. Wallis deserted the Independents to support Kane and the rest of Rasin's ticket.[32]

Kane died after a year in office, but he had time enough to make it clear where he stood. Like Latrobe, he struggled to reduce municipal expenditures. He vetoed a city council ordinance that would have created an additional hook-and-ladder company in the Fire Department. He announced that he intended to reduce the size of the police force. Instead of building an expensive sewer system, he favored a good system of "surface drainage." He recommended an electrical system for igniting the city's gaslights to eliminate the need for lamplighters, and he insisted that the general economic malaise after the Panic of 1873 demanded a rigorous control or reduction of city expenditures to accommodate the decline in municipal tax revenues. Like his predecessors, he also noted that the city's considerable investment in internal improvements—chiefly railroads—was producing no return.[33]

On Kane's death, Ferdinand Latrobe returned to the good graces of the Rasin organization. He easily won a special mayoral election. In 1879, however, a reanimated Republican Party chose to run its own candidate for mayor rather than collaborate with the Independent Democrats. William A. Hooper fared better than any Republican mayoral candidate since 1867. Latrobe won, but his victory margin was less than half the one that carried him to his first term as mayor,[34] and he obligingly stood aside from the mayoral contest in 1881 so that William Pinkney Whyte could take his place. Arthur Gorman had incurred Whyte's enmity by taking his seat in the Senate. According to Frank Kent, Gorman believed that making Whyte mayor "would be the most effective way of permanently sidetracking him as a political factor and preventing him from coming again to the front as a State leader."[35]

Whyte, however, still exercised influence in some quarters. Most of the city's trial judges—known collectively as the Supreme Bench—stood ready to do the bidding of the mayor and the Rasin organization that stood behind him. One of the judges was Whyte's brother. In 1882, the terms of four judges expired. Some of the leading attorneys among the Independent Democrats and their Republican allies launched a "new judges" campaign to place the court beyond the "polluting touch of politics" by defeating the three judges most clearly identified with Whyte and Rasin. Although the Rasin organization united with Mayor Whyte in defense of the old judges, Gorman remained inactive and remote. Kent claimed that Gorman was secretly backing the reformers. One of Rasin's most distinguished allies, attorney Bernard Carter, also defected to support the new judges, though he subsequently rejoined the organization Democrats. In a campaign illuminated by the pyrotechnic oratory of the city's best lawyers, the reformers handed Rasin his first political defeat, while serving Gorman's purposes by destroying what was left of Mayor Whyte's influence. It was not just that Whyte lost his allies in the judiciary. By openly campaigning for them, he seemed to violate the principle of judicial independence and alienated many Democrats, as well as the *Baltimore Sun*. Whyte's brother won fewer votes than any of the judicial candidates.[36]

The "new judges" victory raised hope among the Independent Democrats that they might win a controlling share in local government. The struggle also convinced some prominent Democrats to desert the regulars and side with the Independents. The campaign was the first to enlist Charles J. Bonaparte among the machine's challengers. Bonaparte, grandson of Napoleon's youngest brother and Baltimore belle Betsy Patterson, would hit his stride as leader of Baltimore's progressive movement in the 1890s. His prominence among the reformers grew in the municipal election of 1883,[37] when even Whyte turned against Rasin's organization, repudiating the machine that had secured his election as mayor. Mayor Whyte supported his fire marshal, J. Monroe Heiskell, as his successor. Heiskell, who had served as Mayor Whyte's personal assistant, ran as a fusion candidate against Rasin's default mayor, Ferdinand Latrobe. Heiskell was another ex-Confederate—like George Kane and Severn Teackle Wallis—who somehow managed to find common ground with Baltimore's Republicans. Latrobe defeated Heiskell, but by less than 3,500 votes.[38] After his loss, Heiskell left town and moved to the far West. The Independents remained and looked forward to a showdown in the municipal election of 1885.

FADING TRIUMPHS

"By long odds," wrote Frank Kent, "it was the fiercest municipal election ever fought in Baltimore." The mayoral nominee of the reformers in 1885 was George William Brown, the city's Civil War mayor and one more local politician who had burnished his political credentials by serving time in a Union prison—where he kept company with Kane and Wallis. The Independents, who had been steadily narrowing the victory margins of the Ring's candidates, seemed to be closing in on electoral triumph. The most distinguished political orators in the city spoke on their behalf, and they were backed by Independent Democrat John K. Cowen—no mean orator himself—and his B&O Railroad. The reformers' prospects seemed so good that Rasin's last remaining rivals in the regular Democratic organization, Robert J. "Doc" Slater and J. Frank Morrison, deserted and went over to the Independents.[39]

Both men were Democratic ward leaders, but they had influence beyond their wards. Slater's base was in the First Ward on the eastern edge of the city, but he owned an upscale gambling casino downtown on Calvert Street. He was generous with cash, of which he seemed to have plenty. His hand-outs and contributions were made quietly, but widely recognized. Local opinion held that Slater "carried the whole of East Baltimore in his pocket."[40] Morrison had founded the Crescent Club in West Baltimore's Fourteenth Ward in 1874. By 1886, the organization had about 1,600 members and an impressive treasury. Morrison was a telegrapher, inventor, and successful businessman. A combination of expertise and political exertions earned him a position as superintendent of the police and fire departments' telegraph alarm systems. In 1878, he supervised the building of the world's first long-distance telephone line. At the request of Arthur Gorman, president of the C&O

Canal, Morrison extended the line along the route of the canal from Georgetown to Cumberland. Later, as Baltimore representative of the Brush Electrical Company, he won the contract to light Baltimore's streets with electric lamps.[41]

Before 1885, Morrison, Slater, and Rasin were generally regarded as a triumvirate that governed the city's Democratic organization, though Rasin was clearly paramount leader. The three bosses had not always been united. In 1871, Slater had supported Mayor Robert Banks against Joshua Vansant, Rasin's mayoral candidate. In 1884, soon after Rasin's defeat in the "new judges" election revealed his vulnerability, Slater and Morrison joined forces to challenge Rasin's control of the city Democratic convention.[42] In 1885, they declared their support for anti-organization candidate George William Brown. Rasin recruited James Hodges to run for mayor as the candidate of the Democratic organization. Hodges was a local businessman of high respectability who had never run for public office. Rasin also organized a political club of his own, the Calumet, to counter Morrison's Crescent Club and Slater's gambling palace, whose patrons could be mobilized for politics as well as other games of chance.

But even with the backing of Morrison and Slater, the Independents once more came up short. Their defeat was due in part to the meticulous management of Sonny Mahon, now Freeman Rasin's righthand man. Mahon assured Republican politicians who held federal patronage jobs that they would keep their positions under the incoming Grover Cleveland administration if they agreed to "lie down" on election day. Mahon was able to offer such assurances because his boss enjoyed close and cordial relations with President Cleveland. Rasin was an early beneficiary of the Cleveland administration's patronage. He abandoned his courthouse job in 1885 to take a comfortable customhouse appointment offered by the first elected Democratic president since James Buchanan. Mahon became a special agent of the US Treasury. A city hall purge replaced Slater and Morrison men with Rasin loyalists.[43]

The Independents and their Republican allies charged that the organization had once again fabricated its triumph through fraudulent electoral practices, and after the 1885 contest, some of the most prominent enemies of the Ring founded the Baltimore Reform League to sustain the campaign for clean elections. Charles Bonaparte was one of its early adherents. Electoral fraud was the leading issue in the city election of 1887, its importance underlined, just before the balloting, by the conviction of some city election judges and clerks for conspiracy to defraud. Though sentenced to two years' imprisonment, they were pardoned by the state's Democratic governor before serving half their terms. Other election officials were spared prosecution altogether when the General Assembly repealed the law under which they had been indicted and then reenacted it without making any provision for ongoing cases.[44]

The election judges who stood at the windows of the city's polling places seemed to play a more decisive role in determining the outcomes of municipal contests than the voters themselves. In one of his rare public statements, Rasin acknowledged as much: "Give me the windows, and I don't care who has the votes."[45]

The city's electorate was expanding. After several negative votes, residents of the "Belt," an area surrounding Baltimore on the north, west, and east, finally approved annexation to the city in 1888. A constitutional provision introduced in 1864 required that annexation be approved by the voters in the area to be annexed. Belt residents were initially wary about assuming the burden of city taxation, and business owners east of the city line were concerned about municipal regulations prohibiting coal oil refineries, distilleries, and slaughterhouses, many of which had been driven to the eastern suburbs by city ordinances. Becoming part of the city would also mean that the saloons and beer gardens of Highlandtown and Canton would have to close on Sundays. An annexation proposal was defeated in 1874, with voters in the eastern Belt voting nine to one against. Annexation succeeded in 1888 only because the three sections of the Belt—east, west, and north—voted separately, so strong opposition in the east could not cancel out support for annexation in the other sections. The suburbs were also promised substantial tax abatements if they joined the city. Like the absorption of the "precincts" 70 years earlier, the annexation of 1888 provided that property with less than five houses per acre would be deemed "undeveloped" and not subject to municipal property taxes. The northern and western suburbs voted in favor of annexation, but the eastern Belt rejected it. The tax exemptions for the two newly annexed wards imposed burdens on the 20 wards already in the city. Though the annexation added approximately 38,000 residents to the city's population, Baltimore won no additional representation in Maryland's General Assembly.[46]

The assembly, prodded by the city's Independent Democrats, enacted new electoral safeguards applying (again) only to Baltimore. The minority party was guaranteed a spot among the three election judges in each precinct, and to ensure the appointment of authentic Republican judges, minority representation was mandated for the citywide board of election supervisors that selected the judges. To prevent the majority Democrats from simply outvoting the minority Republican, each supervisor was to have a veto over proposed appointments. A final touch was the requirement that all of Baltimore's ballot boxes be made of clear glass.[47]

Chapter 24 **FIN DE SIÈCLE**

I N 1888, A RESOLUTION introduced in the second branch of the Baltimore City Council urged Maryland's General Assembly to take action against Chinese laundries. It charged that the "Mongolian aliens" who operated these establishments did "a serious injury to the industry of the citizens of this City and State" and contributed nothing "towards the support of the government that tolerates them and affords them protection." Moreover, the laundries were simply covers "for the introduction and encouragement of acts injurious to our civilization and detrimental to good morals and government." The resolution recommended a $25 annual licensing fee for each Chinese laundryman. The measure seems to have been stillborn. But the laundrymen had already aroused opposition elsewhere in the city. In 1885, at a meeting of the local Federation of Labor, the president of the Women's National Industrial Labor League distributed leaflets demanding that "Chinese laundries must go. They deprive the widows of the workingmen of their daily bread." At the same gathering, an African American member of the federation declared that he might have "a black skin, but [had] a white man's heart. If he had the power he said that he would drive the Chinaman out of this country in 24 hours."[1]

By 1889, animosity toward Chinese immigrants seems to have grown more general and vehement. A proposed council resolution lamented the "inroad upon our City" of the "Chinese Race," whose members were "practicing here the vile and abominable customs of their own land." They had "nothing in common with our refined civilization," and it was a "well known fact that their 'laundries' so-called" were "dingy opium smoking dens where infamous and un-American practices are resorted to . . . Where the vilest Mongolian practices have full sway." The courts could not deal adequately with the crimes of these aliens because it was so difficult "for a witness to distinguish one Chinaman from another." The resolution proposed that the council form a committee to ascertain "the best means, in accordance with United States laws, of relieving us of this evil . . . an incubus upon our fair fame as a model city." The council's second branch approved the measure, the first branch referred it to a committee, and there it died.[2]

The 1890 Census counted 178 Chinese residents—men, women, and children—in Baltimore's population of more than 434,000.[3] They were the minority that everyone could afford to hate, even those who were themselves borne down by prejudice of race or gender—an outlet, perhaps, for other animosities whose expression would be politically inconvenient or socially dangerous because they targeted larger, more powerful groups. As the century drew to a close, Chinese bashing may have created a moment of political unity in a town long accustomed to an underdeveloped and fragmentary public life, inhibited by the authorities in Annapolis and military occupation, and starved by misguided investments in "public improvements."

ETHNICITY AND CHARITY

German immigrants seemed less alien to Baltimoreans than did the Chinese, but they, too, were rather insular. They preserved their language, culture, and separateness long after their arrival in Baltimore, and passed them on to their children. Assimilation had held no appeal for the German revolutionary émigrés of 1848 because they regarded Baltimore as a temporary haven until political reformation would enable them to return home. They had little interest in learning English or adopting American ways. Their inclination to keep to themselves was soon reinforced by the assaults of the Know-Nothings. In response to persecution, the Germans "cut themselves off, founded their own societies, churches, schools, newspapers and built a wall around their German-American individualism that was to hinder acclimatization even to the next generation." Once the Know-Nothings faded, Baltimore's political authorities accommodated the separateness of the Germans. The General Assembly, for example, required that the text of every public law be published in at least two Baltimore newspapers, and one of them had to be a German-language paper.[4]

By 1900, Baltimore supported seven public schools that offered instruction in both English and German, and there were more than 30 German-language churches. The associational life of the German community extended to German Jews. They were among the founders of the German Society in 1817,[5] and their inclusion was one sign of the internal diversity that flourished behind the wall that separated German-speakers from other Baltimoreans. As in the city's African American community, the energetic construction of subcultural institutions in the German community led to subcultural disaggregation. There were competing choral societies and shooting clubs, separate organizations for immigrants from different regions of Germany, and religious divisions. A particular point of contention was observance of the Sabbath. Some German sects, such as the United Brethren, demanded strict observance of the day of rest and worship. The Turnverein favored Sunday concerts and lager fests. Denominational boundaries also figured in political affiliations. German Catholics leaned Democratic; the Protestants, Republican. Within each party, some Germans gravitated toward the reform wing, others to the regulars. But in their political diversity, they became no less German. In 1888, for example, the German-American

Democratic Central Association claimed the "right to petition the Authorities for the purpose of soliciting positions for such of its members who make application therefor and are duly qualified." Non-German office-seekers usually applied individually to the mayor. Some Germans applied collectively. In 1900, the various German labor unions, choral groups, Turnverein, and business associations united behind the Independent Citizens Union in an attempt to blend the multiple strains of German Americanism into a single voice.[6]

At the end of the nineteenth century, Germans accounted for almost two-thirds of Baltimore's foreign-born residents. They would not stand for the rough treatment dealt out to the city's minuscule population of Chinese laundrymen. The Germans may even have inspired imitation. They made up the core membership of early labor organizations. German associations of all sects and parties were notable for their charitable and social welfare programs. They founded orphanages, a home for the aged, and hospitals. German Jews supported the Hebrew Benevolent Society, which sponsored the Hebrew Hospital, where indigent Jews could adhere to the kosher diet they could not get at other charity hospitals. After the hospital came the Hebrew Orphan Asylum. Both hospital and orphanage were open to non-Jews "on an emergency basis."[7]

Other groups followed the German example, and city government added its own resources to the support of private and sectarian charities. Baltimore made contracts with a host of institutions, especially health care facilities, to provide services and sustenance to the indigent. In 1884, for example, the city granted subsidies to 17 private charitable institutions and reformatories, including seven medical dispensaries, three orphanages, the House of Reformation for Colored Boys, and St. Mary's Industrial School for Boys (where the young Babe Ruth would later serve time). By 1899, the number of city-supported charities had increased to 30, and city government had representatives on some of their boards.[8]

The city also maintained an asylum of its own—Bay View, a combined insane asylum, poorhouse, home for the aged, and hospital for the indigent, located just east of the city limits. By one account, it was a "magnificent edifice" named for "the expansive view it affords of the Chesapeake Bay and the surrounding country . . . its inner comforts, and the adoption of all modern improvements more suggestive of the ample means of some nabob . . . than of the home of the forlorn and helpless vagabonds which the seething cauldron of city life casts to the surface."[9] In 1898, the nabobs of the asylum were sustained on an average annual expenditure of $90 each—less than $2,500 in current dollars—and some observers thought the institution's design essentially flawed. An unsigned document in the city archives declares it "a mistake to have an asylum for the insane connected with one for the indigent and the sick. They should not only be separate buildings, but not in the same locality." The writer argued that the state, not the city, should "take charge of the indigent insane." If the state failed to assume its responsibility, then Baltimore must provide for the insane, even though the "Department of the Insane" at Bay View seems to have been chronically overcrowded.[10]

The handwriting in the document is Mayor Latrobe's, and the fragment seems to

The Bay View Asylum, a city-supported poorhouse, a hospital for the indigent and disabled, and an institution for the mentally ill

have been a discarded passage for his annual message of 1893. His views may have been influenced by a report on Bay View prepared, at the mayor's request, by Dr. Edward Brush, superintendent of the Sheppard Asylum, a private institution for the mentally ill. According to Brush, "the combination of institutions for paupers and the insane is wrong . . . experience has taught that such association results in the care of the insane sinking to the level of the care of the pauper." At Bay View he saw "children who were both mentally and physically crippled . . . in the corridors devoted to the insane contracting habits and tendencies of the most unfortunate and degrading character . . . presenting an appearance at once depressing and repulsive." The state did maintain an asylum at Spring Grove, four miles west of the city, which accepted some mentally ill patients. They were supported more generously than the inmates at Bay View—$150 rather than $90 a year for each person. The additional expense was probably due to the cost of therapy. Spring Grove was reserved for "hopeful cases," patients deemed curable if given appropriate treatment. The hopeless cases filled up the crowded corridors at Bay View, where they received only custodial care.[11]

UNBALANCED CITY

While the municipality struggled to provide care for Baltimoreans with mental and physical illnesses, its public officials also sought a new equilibrium for the city's troubled and unbalanced economy. It was heavily tilted toward commerce—moving things rather than making them. In 1877, the Baltimore City Council had appointed a commission to consider how to encourage the growth of local manufacturing. After a lengthy inquiry that extended to European as well as American cities, the commission recommended that all machinery, tools, and "implements of manufacture" be exempt from municipal taxation. Though it took more than five years, the recommendation eventually became an ordinance, and by 1887, the manufacturing exemption excluded almost $3.1 million in industrial equipment from local taxation, reducing the city's revenues by about $53,000.[12]

Baltimore industry needed encouragement. The city's economic life was sustained primarily by ships and railroads, not factories. The Civil War had seriously disrupted the city's commerce and temporarily stimulated manufacturing, but Baltimore's shipping sector resumed its rapid expansion after the South was restored to the Union. The value of the city's foreign trade grew from $33 million in 1870 to $130 million by 1900, enough to lift Baltimore from fifth to third place among American cities engaged in international commerce. In its seaborne trade with domestic ports, the city was outranked only by New York, and Baltimore's trade, in dollars and tonnage, outstripped all of its urban competitors in the South.[13]

The same railroads and steamship lines that carried goods through Baltimore could just as easily be carrying goods *made* in Baltimore, enabling the city to add the profits of manufacture to those of transport. To Ferdinand C. Latrobe, the city's perennial postbellum mayor, the opportunities seemed obvious. By 1887, he sensed that his fellow citizens had come to share his view and "generally conceded that the future wealth and prosperity of the city is dependent on manufacturing industries."[14]

The city's few manufacturing enterprises were frequently by-products of its commerce. When Baltimore ships unloaded their cargoes of flour in the Caribbean, they could refill their holds with sugar, providing the raw material for several Baltimore sugar refineries. Coffee grown in Latin America could be roasted in Baltimore. The coffee business would generate the capital for one of the country's first investment banks, Alex Brown and Sons. Baltimore ships sailed past guano-encrusted islands in the Caribbean and off the west coast of Latin America. Gangs of black laborers from Baltimore were sent to these desolate places, where, under hot sun and white overseers, they mined the bird manure for shipment to the city's fertilizer plants, to be processed and shipped out to enrich soil depleted by cotton and tobacco crops. Baltimore imported more guano than any other place in the world. The business would eventually expand from natural to chemical fertilizers. Just outside the city limits, in Canton, smelters refined Cuban copper ore. By the close of the nineteenth century, Cuban iron ore and Pennsylvania coal would converge on a massive mill in Sparrows Point to produce steel. In some cases, the Chesapeake itself provided the raw materials for industrial enterprise: Bay oysters were packaged at Baltimore canneries to be consumed far from salt water. The canning business later extended to local vegetables and fruits. The Pennsylvania oilfields filled B&O tank cars with petroleum, which sustained half a dozen locally owned refineries in Baltimore. Manufacturers of men's clothing, the city's largest employers, had turned out military uniforms during the war, and this helped them to develop standard sizes for men's suits, shirts, and trousers. The system paid off in peacetime.[15]

Warfare also boosted the production of sheet iron and shipbuilding. A foundry in Canton produced the armor plating for the USS *Monitor* and other ironclads. Textile plants just outside the city limits increased their output of sailcloth. By the 1880s, Baltimore and its environs accounted for about 80 percent of all the sailcloth produced in the United States.[16]

Growth prospects for the sailcloth industry were, of course, limited. In fact, most Baltimore industries—even the most expansive—lagged behind competitors in other cities. Some historians blame the stresses and upheavals of the Civil War as experienced in a border town. They argue that the war had traumatized the city's business community and "sapped the vitality of a generation." Baltimore had been the financial capital of the South, and the Confederacy's destruction made local bankers and investors more conservative, more easily satisfied with the meager returns generated by low-risk investments.[17]

There were also more tangible signs of the city's economic conservatism. In Baltimore, for example, manufacturing firms were less likely to be incorporated or to issue stock than in other East Coast cities. It was an "old-fashioned town" where factories were privately held and family-owned. Although the city's industrial output was growing, it was not growing as rapidly as in other cities. After 1880, in fact, its rank as a manufacturing center began to decline. On average, Baltimore manufacturers employed fewer workers than firms in other cities, and the amount of capital invested in local industries was below average when compared with the 10 largest cities in the United States. Perhaps most tellingly, Baltimore factories invested less money in machinery than factories elsewhere. This shortfall suggests not just technological backwardness but an impaired capacity to compete. Machinery usually meant lower prices.[18]

BRANCH-OFFICE TOWN

Baltimore industries were relatively undeveloped because the city came late to manufacturing. The town paid for its backwardness. Its manufacturing sector was immature and vulnerable at a time when monopolistic trusts were gobbling up weaker competitors around the country. In 1870, John D. Rockefeller was the first predator to strike the city's industrial base. He bought up or drove out of business all six of the independently owned oil refineries in Baltimore and eliminated them as competitors with Standard Oil. Rockefeller and Jay Gould joined forces to purchase the B&O Railroad's telegraph subsidiary and added it to Western Union. The town's two largest manufacturers of cigarettes and cigars were taken over by the American Tobacco Company. The capital stock of the Baltimore Sugar Refining Company was acquired by the American Sugar Refining Company, now known as Domino. The Baltimore Biscuit Company, the largest cracker factory south of New York, was bought out by the company later to become Nabisco. Eight local fertilizer factories were taken over by the American Agricultural Chemical Company, and the American Can Company acquired most of the locally owned canneries.[19]

Perhaps the most jarring shock to Baltimore's economy was the failure of the B&O Railroad, the city's signature enterprise. The company could not cover the bonds issued to pay for its construction costs. It stopped paying dividends in 1888. In his annual report for that year, the mayor listed the city's stock in the railroad as an "unproductive investment," but expressed hope that "this great corporation, which for so many years paid a large annual revenue into our treasury . . . may again take its place in the list of the City's income producing securities."[20] Instead, the railroad went into receivership. When it emerged from bankruptcy in 1899, its owners were the New York and Chicago investors who had been the railroad's creditors. Less than two years later, the Pennsylvania Railroad bought a controlling interest in what was left of the B&O; its president, John K. Cowen, was dismissed and replaced by a Pennsylvania Railroad executive.[21] Baltimore had become a branch-office town. It kept most of its factory and railroad jobs, but corporate control lay out of town, and profits flowed to the same destinations.

Local workers suffered a loss of status, along with their city. Industrial consolidation and mechanization undermined their bargaining power. For a time, trade unions had multiplied along with the factories. The Knights of Labor began to organize Baltimore workers in 1878; by 1886, the Knights numbered about 16,000 in Maryland at large. The year was the high watermark for organized labor. In 1886 alone, Baltimore workers formed 16 new unions, and the Maryland Bureau of Industrial Statistics and Information counted a total of 96 unions in the city, with a combined membership of about 25,000. Three overlapping labor federations consolidated the unions into citywide coalitions. On May Day 1886, 11,000 union members marched through Baltimore demanding an eight-hour day. Three days after the parade came the Haymarket bombing in Chicago. Public support for labor activism diminished. Baltimore labor organizations also operated under a distinctive handicap. As workers in a branch-office town, local unions were bargaining with multisite companies prepared to shift production to other locations if their Baltimore employees became too demanding. By 1890, the Knights of Labor had virtually disappeared from the city. Some craft unions fared better, but only 10 of the unions formed in the 1880s survived into the '90s. A brief resurgence in the labor movement in 1892 was cut short by the Panic of 1893, which thinned the ranks of almost all Baltimore unions, some of which simply disappeared.[22]

DERAILMENT

Baltimore was far from dead, but was developmentally inhibited. The city had bet heavily on railroads. The return on this investment had been disappointing, and the heavy commitment to railroads probably restricted investments in manufactures. The railroad men themselves did little to encourage factory production. When he ran for Congress as a Democrat in 1894, the B&O's John Cowen responded to the charges of his "Republican friends" that he was "inimical to American industries and labor" and was "a free trader, and this I do not deny." The alternative, he argued, was restricted trade, which would certainly handicap the local economy.[23] Free trade, of course, was just the thing for a city devoted to commerce, but not for a manufacturing town.

The city had already given up on railroads as "public improvements"—government-supported ventures devoted to municipal prosperity. In 1886, Mayor James Hodges vetoed a council ordinance to pledge the city's credit in support of a new railroad, the Baltimore and Eastern Shore. Railroads, he explained, had become decidedly private enterprises whose relentless pursuit of profit drew the investments of "the largest and most intelligent and enterprising capitalists."

"Hence, when a new railroad is needed by the expansion of trade, railroad men are generally ready to build it." They did not have to rely on public investment, and by implication, any venture needing public support was financially suspect — unable to attract the "most intelligent and enterprising capitalists." Hodges added that "the general sentiment of the community is now and has been for many years strongly opposed to the policy of lending the credit of the city to railroad enterprises. I believe it safe to say that the public mind, which has passed through a costly experience, is now thoroughly educated up to that point."[24]

However averse to new railroad investments, Baltimoreans could not simply brush off their old investments. Though the city had lost heavily on its railroad stock, it still held B&O shares worth almost $2.5 million. (The city pledged $3.5 million for them more than half a century earlier.) The city's stock holdings also made it the virtual proprietor of another railroad — the Western Maryland. Apart from the stocks, there were unpaid loans. The B&O still owed the city $5 million that it had borrowed in 1853. The loan was not completely unproductive; the railroad had been paying interest at the annual rate of 6 percent.[25]

In 1888, B&O president Samuel Spencer wrote to Mayor Latrobe requesting an extension of the loan — for 50 years, at only 4 percent. The railroad's lawyers had helpfully drafted an ordinance that would authorize the extension. One of the conditions of the original loan required that $500,000 of the amount borrowed be deposited with the city register as security — a sum that could be used to pay off part of the loan when it came due in 1890. A succession of city registers had managed to grow the half million dollars into $2.4 million. Since the requested extension meant that the loan would not be paid off in 1890, the "sinking fund" would not be used as originally intended, and B&O president Spencer therefore reasoned that the city should give his railroad the $2.4 million along with the extension and the interest rate reduction.[26]

Spencer explained how Baltimore would profit under his proposition. The city had issued $5 million in "city stock" to make the original loan. It could now exchange those certificates for a new issue of $5 million carrying 3.5 percent interest. Since the city would be receiving 4 percent interest from the railroad, it would come out 0.5 percent ahead — $25,000 a year. In case this inducement failed to persuade city officials, Spencer pointed out that the municipality was the B&O's largest stockholder, with about one-fourth of its common stock, and "as such . . . will derive nearly one-fourth of the benefit coming from such extension" of the loan. "Other reasons, of course," he added, "will readily occur to you why this fair arrangement should be made between the City and the Company."[27] In other words, it went without saying that if the city refused the loan extension and demanded repayment in 1890, it risked losing much of the value that remained in its B&O stock.

The railroad's request for a loan extension produced both controversy and confusion. Enoch Pratt, one of the city's finance commissioners, was decidedly opposed: "Good Heavens! Extend the loan for fifty years? Why should Baltimore be burdened with the debts of the Baltimore and Ohio for the next half century? . . . I do not see why the city should be run in the interest of the Baltimore and Ohio Railroad."

Mayor Latrobe seemed inclined to grant the company's request. If it were rejected, the railroad might have to borrow money elsewhere to pay off the loan, and the lender's demands might compromise the city's stake in the company.[28] (Latrobe was, of course, a B&O lawyer.)

In the city council, the Joint Standing Committee on Ways and Means was cautious, then confused. Its members worried that by extending the B&O loan, the city might lose its place in line among the railroad's creditors. After getting its $5 million loan from Baltimore in 1853, the B&O had piled up another $23 million in debt to other lenders. The committee asked for expert legal advice. City solicitor Bernard Carter (once a Pennsylvania Railroad lawyer) advised the ways and means committee that if the city surrendered the $2.4 million sinking fund to the railroad, it would lose its position among the B&O's creditors with respect to that portion of the debt. The committee reported that it was "unable to agree upon the subject" and sent the B&O's loan extension ordinance back to the full council without a recommendation.[29]

The city's leaders finally decided against the extension, and on December 31, 1889, municipal officials gathered in the mayor's office to receive repayment of the loan from B&O officials. Spencer sent an assistant.[30] Baltimore managed to recover its $5 million from the B&O before the company went into receivership in 1896. It also sold its stock in the railroad and reduced its own indebtedness in the process.[31]

The Western Maryland Railroad, though a much smaller enterprise than the B&O, consumed almost as much of the city's investment capital. As early as 1891, some Baltimoreans suggested that the city should rid itself of this burden by selling the railroad, and in 1892, the mayor and city council appointed a special commission to look into the condition of the Western Maryland. Mayor Latrobe, a member of the commission, was clearly concerned that the branch lines leased or built by the city-owned railroad would drain business from Baltimore. William Keyser, a B&O board member and owner of a local copper smelter, had also served as one of the Western Maryland's directors. He testified that the railroad had made a "disastrous financial showing" and that its management "was arrayed in hostile relations to its owner, the City." Keyser supported the sale of the Western Maryland.[32]

The commission did not embrace his recommendation, but its report seems to support his charges concerning the railroad's financial drag on the city. The commission concluded that the Western Maryland had cost Baltimore's taxpayers almost $8.5 million (more than $200 million in current dollars). Its report attributed almost $3.5 million of this sum to the railroad's failure to meet interest payments on city loans. The city's financial relationship with the Western Maryland had begun in 1868 with a bribery scandal that resulted in expulsion of three city council members—an early portent, perhaps, of a bad bargain.[33]

Chapter 25 **POLITICAL ECONOMY**

Isaac Freeman Rasin's democratic organization suffered decline along with Baltimore's factories, unions, and railroads. Its manipulation of the city's electoral system may have revealed its essential weakness: it might not have relied so much on stealing elections if it had been able to win them legitimately. The need for Freeman Rasin to "perfume" the machine's ticket by surrendering offices to reformers and other political innocents was another sign that Baltimore's boss was no Boss Tweed, and the uncertain loyalty of ward leaders such as J. Frank Morrison and Robert J. Slater was further evidence of his organization's weakness.

In other cities, immigrants and first-generation Americans provided reliable votes for machine politicians. But in 1890, Baltimore's foreign-born population, at 15.9 percent, was the smallest among the country's 10 most populous cities.[1] Rasin's organization also lacked the resources needed to win support of immigrants or anybody else. Toward the end of his political career, Rasin was still wondering how to win over the city's foreigners. He posed the problem to a visiting Tammany notable from New York City, Congressman Timothy "Silver Dollar" Sullivan, who stopped by for a visit on his way home from Washington. "You see," said Sullivan, "we have means of taking care of them in New York that perhaps you haven't got here. Of course, there's an awful lot of them, particularly Italians, but I guess we have more patronage in my Assembly district than you have in your whole city."[2]

The infirmities of the Baltimore Democratic organization arose not only from the city's limited electoral base of foreign-born voters but from its limited supply of tangible rewards to solidify their political support. The same commitment to "internal improvements" that burdened the city with debt also restricted its ability to generate patronage.

In other cities, alliances with the local business community may have been just as important to the emergence of political machines as the votes of ethnic groups. In a classic essay, Martin Shefter shows how the consolidation of the Tammany organization in New York depended on an alliance of Boss "Honest John" Kelly with a coalition of corporate lawyers and managers—the "swallowtail" faction of the Democratic Party, named for their fancy dress coats. They were the representatives of "mature" capitalism, not speculators or robber barons but solid corporate owners and managers who shared Kelly's interest in the order, predictability, and centralization of urban politics. Like Kelly, Rasin relied on businessmen to give his organization substance and respectability. Eventually, he would depend on committees of businessmen to sponsor the organization's candidates, while the boss himself stood on the sidelines pretending to be an uninvolved spectator.[3]

Baltimore's "branch-office" businessmen, of course, were hardly the hefty moguls that backed up machines in New York City, Chicago, and Pittsburgh. Strained relations between the Rasin-Gorman Ring and the B&O Railroad precluded a strong alliance between Baltimore's bosses and its most prominent business enterprise. Tension between the railroad and the Ring erupted into open hostility during the reformers' crusade for the "Australian ballot"—a standard ballot printed by the municipality, not by the parties, and cast in secret. The battle was condensed and personalized in the white-hot animosity between Arthur Gorman and John Cowen of the B&O. In the 1889 campaign for the Australian ballot, Gorman ignored all of his reform opponents except Cowen. In a vigorous stump speech, he accused Cowen of using the reform movement as a vehicle to advance the corporate interests of the B&O. Cowen responded with a four-column letter in the *Baltimore Sun*; Gorman's response provoked another letter. Finally, days before the election, Cowen produced a masterful piece of political theater. At the climax of a speech before a mass audience, he introduced two minions of the machine who had defected, and he carried the pair through a catalog of electoral crimes they had committed on behalf of Gorman and Rasin.[4]

Rasin's candidates carried the city as usual, but the struggle against the machine continued, and the fight over electoral reform became even more closely entwined in the personal feud between Gorman and Cowen. Gorman denounced the Australian ballot as a weapon to destroy the Democratic Party and empower its traitorous Independents, "selfish men, identified with corporate greed." The reform movement, he insisted, was "a corrupt scheme of Mr. Cowen's to get possession of the Legislature in the interest of the B&O R.R. Company, and to prevent its tax exemptions from being interfered with."[5]

Freeman Rasin's organization became the first casualty of the feud between Gorman and Cowen. Its collapse began with an attempt at reconciliation. In 1892, Gorman's second term in the US Senate would end, and he wanted to be elected to a third, but his ongoing feud with Cowen cast a shadow over his prospects. He turned to a colleague in the Senate who, like Cowen, was a railroad executive. Gorman asked him to approach Cowen with an offer of truce. Cowen agreed to end his attacks on Gorman so long as Gorman and his allies in Annapolis and Washington looked kindly on the interests of his railroad.[6]

Rasin was not covered by the treaty between Gorman and Cowen. He achieved a similar peace, however, by surrendering much of the Baltimore City Democratic ticket to the Independents. They predominated among his organization's nominees for the General Assembly, and while organization candidates were slated for most municipal offices, Independents were sponsored by Rasin for the city's judiciary—the Supreme Bench. His strategy virtually silenced charges of bossism in the city elections of 1893.[7]

The peace was brief. In 1894, the US Senate was considering a measure that would legalize railroad "pooling," an anticompetitive practice under which ostensibly competing lines divided their total earnings according to an agreement specifying the proportion each road should receive. The B&O belonged to a pool that covered railroads in the Northeast, and John Cowen, with the assistance of Rasin, was one of the lobbyists who succeeded in persuading the House of Representatives to pass this controversial bill. When the legislation was to come up for a vote in the Senate, Senator Gorman, chairman of the Democratic Caucus, argued that other pieces of legislation essential to the operation of the federal government should be considered before the railroad bill and, later, that there was insufficient time to consider the pooling bill before the close of the session. Cowen regarded Gorman's conduct as a violation of their truce and prepared for an all-out showdown with the Ring during the municipal election of 1895.[8]

Gorman had withstood such attacks in the past, but he undermined his support among regular Democrats in Maryland by breaking with President Cleveland on the issues of silver coinage and the tariff. As a Senate leader, Gorman practiced the art of compromise in an effort to build support for Democratic initiatives. President Cleveland, a Gold Democrat, was not inclined to compromise on a proposal to repeal the Sherman Silver Purchase Act. Gorman, as chair of the Democratic conference, sought to mollify the opponents of repeal by offering concessions, which Cleveland regarded as betrayals. An even more serious break with the president came when the Senate, in 1894, took up tariff reform. Gorman once again sought consensus through compromise and, in the process, mangled the president's declared intent to use the tariff merely as a source of revenue, not an instrument of protection from foreign competition.[9]

Relations between Cleveland and Gorman had cooled even before the tariff and silver disputes. Gorman had managed Cleveland's first campaign for the presidency in 1884. But in 1892, when Cleveland made his comeback, Gorman was rumored to be considering a run for president himself, and he kept his distance from the movement to put the ex-president back in the White House. By 1894, the break between the two men was complete, and Cleveland pointedly demonstrated his alienation from Gorman by pressuring Rasin to arrange the election of Gorman's archenemy, John K. Cowen, to the House of Representatives.[10]

Maryland's Democrats were solid supporters of President Cleveland. So was Freeman Rasin, but he now bore the burden of his long partnership with Arthur Gorman. Gorman would not face reelection to the Senate until 1898, but Rasin had to endure a municipal election in 1895, and many reform-minded Baltimoreans regarded the defeat of Rasin as a first step toward unseating Gorman. On the defensive, the Rasin organization reverted to election-day violence not seen since the

eral black voters were reportedly shot and killed, and Reform League poll watchers were assaulted by machine toughs. The *Sun* did not confirm the killings but declared that "rowdyism was rampant," especially in the Seventeenth Ward, and "gangs of repeaters were housed about town," but Reform League poll watchers could not get the police to take any action against them. This time, however, neither voter fraud nor the machine's muscle men could hold back the Republicans. They took control of both city and state governments, and grew even stronger after the election of William McKinley as president in 1896, when they gained the federal patronage that the Democrats lost.[11]

REFORM TRIUMPHANT

The new mayor, in 1895, was Alcaeus Hooper, proprietor of a textile mill in Wood-berry, just inside the city limits. In Baltimore, the putative Republican boss was William F. Stone, chairman of the city's Republican committee. The mayor and the chairman soon fell out. Stone had made his debut as a party activist in 1880, and only a year later he was elected executive of the Republican organization in the Seventh Ward, the district where Freeman Rasin began his career as a Democrat more than a decade earlier. Unlike Rasin, however, Stone labored for years with little hope of achieving state or local office. Democrats monopolized those rewards. Republicans had to make do with federal patronage, and perhaps because the spoils were so scanty, the competition was fierce. The party's internal factions were organized around federal jobs. "Post Office" Republicans squared off against "Customhouse" Republicans.[12]

Stone stood with the Post Office crowd, and when Republican McKinley succeeded Democrat Cleveland in 1897, Stone gathered endorsements to support his appointment as the city's postmaster. The incumbent, however, was an Independent Democrat who had campaigned vigorously for McKinley, and the president reappointed him. Stone became Baltimore's customs collector, a position he retained as long as Republicans controlled the White House.[13]

Access to city and state jobs did little to reduce Republicans' internal quarrels about patronage. Mayor Hooper was an energetic advocate of municipal efficiency. He was also stubborn and difficult. His efforts to improve and rationalize the delivery of public services ran headlong into the patronage demands of his fellow Republicans on the city council. The council wanted paying jobs for the Republican loyalists who had been steadfast party workers during the barren years of Democratic hegemony. The mayor wanted competence, and he was willing to hire Democrats or Independents in order to get it. The Republican council was shocked at first, then outraged, and according to the *Sun*, "the seeming indifference of the Mayor to the storm he . . . aroused by his appointments" only accentuated "the anger of his opponents in that body."[14] In 1896, the council passed an ordinance depriving the mayor of his appointive power. Hooper vetoed it. The council overrode his veto and proceeded to appoint a slate of department heads. Hooper refused to administer the oaths of office. The combatants carried their dispute into the courts, where the council's position initially prevailed, but the Maryland Court of Appeals sided with Mayor Hooper. It was an empty victory. He still had to get council approval for his appointments.[15]

Hooper found the work of the mayoralty as obnoxious as the council found him. After six months in office, he complained that a term as Baltimore's chief executive meant "two years of turmoil, trial, and trouble. There is scarcely a minute which is free of worry. The worst of it is that the worry is usually of a trivial nature about which the executive officer of a big city should not be bothered." In private corporations, he claimed, executives were never troubled with so much operational detail. The mayor had to oversee 25 municipal agencies. Eleven were governed by boards or commissions; the mayor was required to serve on eight of them and to be president or chairman of five. An obstreperous city council multiplied the miseries of the mayoralty. "A Mayor's lot," said Hooper, "is made almost a continuous nightmare if every movement of the executive branch . . . is combated by the legislative branch."[16]

A particular point of contention between the mayor and the council was the appointment of the city's school commissioners. Under the existing arrangement, the councilmen of each ward nominated one of its residents for the board of school commissioners, and then the council as a whole approved the nominees. The practice produced an unwieldy school board of 24 members, most having no particular expertise in matters of education. Early in 1897, before the council began its annual session, Mayor Hooper dismissed most of the school commissioners and appointed six commissioners to replace them. One of them was a woman; another was president of Johns Hopkins University, who served as president of the commission; three of the six commissioners came from a single ward—the Twelfth, the city's silk-stocking district. The commissioners dismissed by Hooper refused to step down, and for several months, Baltimore had two school boards. When the council reconvened, its members voted to challenge the mayor in court, and this time the court of appeals sided with the council.[17]

Baltimore's Reform League, under the leadership of the sharp-tongued aristocrat Charles J. Bonaparte, was fighting in the General Assembly for a more general reform of public employment in the city—a civil service law limited to Baltimore that would embody Mayor Hooper's commitments to competence and nonpartisanship. Patronage-starved Republicans and Democratic spoilsmen resisted, but instead of rejecting the measure outright, they shrewdly proposed a constitutional amendment that would extend the merit system to the entire state and require the approval of voters in a referendum. The amendment was rejected overwhelmingly. Less than one-fifth of Baltimore's voters supported it.[18]

Apparently emboldened by the public's rejection of civil service reform, the Post Office and Customhouse Republicans united behind William Stone to deny Mayor Hooper renomination in 1897. By some accounts, at least, Hooper was not much inclined to seek a second term anyway. Before he left city hall, however, several hundred of his friends gathered for a testimonial dinner at the Rennert Hotel. The speakers tried to give a positive spin to Hooper's irascibility. One of them proclaimed that "we want a Mayor who doesn't care . . . about 'harmony' . . . no sensible community elects and pays its chief officer to 'harmonize' with its plunderers or its vermin."[19]

REPUBLICAN INSURGENCY

William Stone's Republican organization, its plunderers and vermin, decided not to endorse anyone to succeed Hooper as mayor. Stone was initially inclined to support J. Frank Supplee, Republican loyalist, militia officer, prohibitionist, local dry goods merchant, a founder of the Merchants' and Manufacturers' Association, and locally famous as enthusiastic organizer of parades for almost any occasion. His chief opponent was William T. Malster, a man with little or no formal education who had worked his way from deckhand on a steamship to ownership of the Columbian Iron Works and Dry Dock Company, with a 13-acre shipyard on Locust Point where workers built naval vessels and some of the earliest oil tankers. While he campaigned for the mayor's office in 1897, his shipyard would launch one of the first practical submarines. He was founder and leader of a relatively new Republican organization, the Columbian Club, and had support among many of the party's ward organizations and workers, including many African Americans. Chairman Stone and the city's central Republican committee chose to let the Republican voters decide which of the two mayoral aspirants would be the party's nominee.[20]

They soon had reason to regret their neutrality. According to the *Sun*, the "intense bitterness of factional feeling . . . engendered in the red-hot contest between Col. J. Frank Supplee and William T. Malster" threatened to tear the party apart. A committee of Republican businessmen urged Stone and the city's Republican committee to endorse a unity candidate and press Malster and Supplee to withdraw in the interest of party consensus. The compromise nominee was millionaire businessman Theodore Marburg, who, like Mayor Hooper, stood with the party's reform wing, but seemed far more agreeable than the mayor. He was described as a "man of great gentleness," "the greatest tact and consideration," who wrote poetry, campaigned for world peace, and later headed the Municipal Art Society.[21]

Neither Malster nor Supplee would stand down. Malster filed suit to challenge the rules laid down for the primary by the Republican committee. The court denied his request for an injunction on the grounds that it had no jurisdiction. The dispute had to be resolved within the party. Malster decided to have a primary of his own. As its only candidate, he won easily. One of his more devoted followers was arrested when he tried to vote twice.[22]

Marburg and Supplee ran against one another in a separate Republican primary. In the interest of party harmony, the two candidates were allocated different wards in which to campaign so that they would not have to confront one another. Supplee won more votes, but Marburg got the nomination when delegates from two of Supplee's wards defected at the convention, on the evening after the primary. More significant than the outcome, however, was the difference in voter turnout between the two Republican primaries. Malster drew more than 18,000; Marburg and Supplee, roughly 4,000 less. Later that summer, the Republican state convention in Ocean City threw out the results of both primaries. Supplee abandoned his candidacy because Malster seemed to be the choice of most Republican voters, and it was "useless for any one to enter the lists against him." He declared that he was finished with politics and made a point of resigning from all the Republican clubs to which he belonged. (The next year he would secure appointment as city register.) Marburg also stepped aside. His disavowal of politics was permanent.[23]

The Reform League, though uncertain of Malster's progressive credentials, preferred him to the candidate of the Gorman-Rasin Ring, whose inclinations were well-known.[24] Malster won and promptly confirmed the reformers' worst suspicions. A legion of Republican office seekers marched behind him into city hall. Local reformers, usually advocates of municipal improvements, were leery of Malster's proposals for public works because they suspected that the projects were pretexts for patronage. But they welcomed another mayoral initiative. Malster appointed a bipartisan commission to draft a new city charter to overcome the administrative disjointedness and inefficiencies of ward-based government and increase his own power as mayor. The commission included Daniel Coit Gilman, president of Johns Hopkins University; former Democratic mayor Ferdinand Latrobe; and the venerable William Pinkney Whyte, ex-governor, ex-senator, and ex-mayor.

The committee's draft, approved by the General Assembly in 1898, was a significant step toward the centralization of Baltimore City government. It extended the mayor's term in office from two to four years. A three-quarters vote of the city council would be needed to override a mayoral veto. The new charter created a five-person board of estimates, chaired by the president of the second branch of the city council but generally dominated by the mayor. Two of the board's five members—the city solicitor and the city engineer—were mayoral appointees, and their votes, along with the mayor's, made for a prevailing mayoral majority. The board would prepare the city's budget for the approval of the council and vote on major city contracts. The council might reduce the budget prepared by the board of estimates, but it could not increase any item of expenditure. The charter also gave the mayor unambiguous authority to appoint the heads of all city departments and the key role in appointing school commissioners. There were also changes in municipal elections, which were to be held in May instead of October to separate them more fully from state and federal contests in November. In addition to the mayor, the president of the council's second branch ran for office citywide, as did candidates for the office of city comptroller. The charter also redrew the boundaries of the wards, disrupting the neighborhood power bases of the ward bosses, another step toward political centralization.[25]

By the time Baltimore's new charter took effect, the General Assembly's Republican majority had voted Arthur Pue Gorman out of the US Senate.[26] George L. Wellington, Republican state chairman and architect of Democratic defeat, had already captured Maryland's other Senate seat. The Ring seemed vanquished. "By the time it was all over," Sonny Mahon recalled, "you couldn't find a Democratic officeholder with a finetooth comb."[27] To make matters worse, the presidential contest of 1896 scrambled Democratic loyalties in Maryland, where most Democrats decried the silver coinage plank on which William Jennings Bryan grounded his campaign. Baltimore gave McKinley almost 61,000 votes to Bryan's 41,000.[28]

With Bryan's defeat, Baltimore's Democratic organization lost the federal patronage that had helped to sustain it under Grover Cleveland. Rasin's organization began to unravel. Sonny Mahon, Rasin's chief lieutenant, had drifted away from the boss in a quest to become a boss in his own right. Arthur Gorman seemed ready to part company with Rasin, too.[29]

But the Republicans faced serious internal schisms. Mayor Malster's 11 stalwarts in the General Assembly refused to enter the Republican caucus, thus preventing the Republican majority from electing a Speaker. The Malster Republicans allied with the Democratic minority to place a Malster man in the leadership position. (The new Speaker was later convicted as a jewel thief.) Malster's preemption of his party's attempt at legislative leadership was regarded as a gambit to advance his own unannounced ambitions for a seat in the US Senate.[30]

In the Republican mayoral primary of 1899, Malster defeated Alcaeus Hooper's attempt at a comeback, but Baltimore's voters were as fed up with Malster as they had been with the Democratic Ring. Freeman Rasin was shrewd enough to realize that his open sponsorship of any mayoral aspirant might handicap the candidate. He made a show of indifference about the contest: "I'm getting tired of it. I'm going to wash my hands of the whole business. Let the rest of these fellows get their candidate." A new "Democratic Association of Baltimore City" would settle on a candidate and orchestrate a "people's campaign." In fact, Rasin stayed in close but quiet touch with the group's leader. But his power had clearly diminished. From this time forward, he would support Democratic mayoral candidates chosen by the Independent Democrats and settle for a share of city patronage.[31]

The 2,500 members of the Democratic Association agreed that their party's mayoral candidate should be Thomas G. Hayes, a former US attorney for Maryland and one-time Democratic candidate for governor. Gorman and Rasin gave their assent, but said nothing in public.[32] Hayes campaigned as an Independent Democratic reformer. His past denunciations of Arthur Gorman gave him credibility in the role. In the ensuing election, the Democrats won not only the mayor's office but also the comptroller's, every seat in the second branch of the city council, and all but 6 of the 24 seats in the first branch. The *Baltimore American*, which had endorsed Malster, acknowledged that the election was "the most orderly and the most honest ever held in Baltimore." But racial animosity played an undeniable role in the Democratic comeback. Malster's Republican administration, wrote Frank Kent, "with its political pirates and negro office-holders, had pretty well disgusted the public." The *New York Times* agreed that the "race question largely entered into the election, the feeling against the Negro being very strong."[33]

Race also figured in Arthur Gorman's plans for a political comeback as a US Senator. His strategy was to shrink the Republican electoral base by disenfranchising some of the state's 53,000 African American voters, many of whom turned out reliably for the party of Lincoln. Early in 1901, the General Assembly approved a new election law ostensibly aimed at illiterate voters but intended to disenfranchise black voters, many of whom were illiterate. It eliminated all party emblems from ballots, which, according to H. L Mencken, "became Chinese puzzles to the plain people, who had been voting for Abraham Lincoln's beard or the Democratic rooster for years." Candidates' names were grouped by the offices they sought rather than their party affiliations. Voters were barred from receiving any assistance at the polls.[34] The first outing for the new law occurred in Baltimore's council elections in May 1901. The ballot law backfired. Republicans held coaching sessions for illiterate voters so that they could recognize the names of Republican candidates for the council. The Democrats offered classes too, but Democratic illiterates were apparently less willing to accept instruction. Republicans won 17 of the 24 seats in the council's first branch, and all 4 in the second branch that were up for election.[35]

Gorman's chances of regaining his US Senate seat depended on the state legislative elections occurring later in 1901. He attacked the Republican Party for its dependence on the black vote, and then chided African American voters for being misled by "designing men" who used them for political advantage. Republicans held their own in Baltimore, in spite of the literacy law. But Gorman won sufficient support outside the city to return to the Senate.[36]

REFORM BOSS

While Arthur Gorman tried to alter the racial composition of the state's electorate, Freeman Rasin was left to cope with Independent Democratic mayor Thomas G. Hayes. To his regret, Rasin discovered that Hayes was not only a progressive reformer but a potential rival for the role of Democratic boss and prince of patronage. He was the Democratic counterpart of Republican William Malster—a Reform boss. Progressive reformers perceived the same duality in Hayes. Charles J. Bonaparte warned that the mayor's attempt "to combine a 'business administration' with the abuses of a 'spoils' politics is a task as hopeless as to build a fire in a vessel of water."[37] But for a time, at least, Hayes made the combination work. Reformer Hayes appointed the president of the Reform League to head the school board and advocated the insulation of public schools from partisan politics; he named professionals as city engineer and health commissioner and introduced civil service examinations for applicants to the Fire Department. He was the first mayor to organize a municipal cabinet. It met once a month. But Boss Hayes used patronage appointments to win over some lesser Democratic bosses, including Sonny Mahon, in an effort to build his own machine for the next mayoral election.[38]

Hayes, however, was no good at maintaining alliances. Mencken, then a young city hall reporter for the *Baltimore Herald*, later described him as "an extremely eccentric and rambunctious fellow, so full of surprises that he had already acquired the nickname of Thomas the Sudden . . . There never lived on this earth a more quarrelsome man." "He was," Mencken added, "a really first-rate public official." He also had an unusual appetite for detail. His first annual message in 1900 went on for 72 typed pages and included observations about the chapel ceiling at the city jail and the supply of ice for the Quarantine Hospital.[39]

Hayes was the first mayor to take office after approval of the city's new charter in 1898. He made the most of the enhanced powers of his office, but failed to achieve success in several of his most significant projects. His health commissioner was powerfully convinced that the city needed a special hospital for patients suffering from infectious diseases — diphtheria, scarlet fever, and measles. (The Quarantine Hospital was for sick passengers and crew members from arriving ships.) Mayor Hayes supported the project, which also had the support of physicians at local medical schools.[40] No one seemed to oppose the project in principle. But no one wanted to live in the vicinity of a hospital for patients with infectious diseases. A majority of the city's delegation in the General Assembly supported a bill introduced by Republican delegate William Broening that prohibited construction of the hospital within half a mile of any public park. The measure prevented the city from using a parcel of land already purchased for the infectious diseases facility.[41]

The mayor faced more complicated hindrances in his pursuit of another high-priority project: construction of a municipal sewer system. Mencken reported that cesspool leaks, overflows, and illegal drains converted the Basin into an open sewer and gave Baltimore "a powerful aroma every spring and by August [it] smelled like a billion polecats."[42] Almost every big city already had a sewer system, but Baltimore continued to rely on belowground cesspools and a fragmented collection of half a dozen neighborhood sewers. Privy vaults were usually "dug to water." Many residents relied on neighborhood pumps that drew on the same aquifer. Aside from the associated smells and diseases, cesspools reduced the land area for building construction, diminishing the space available for development in a growing city and hindering the growth of municipal property tax revenues.[43]

The status quo had its friends. The Odorless Excavating Apparatus Company and its franchise holders profited from the council's longstanding failure to build a citywide sewer system. By 1900, the company virtually monopolized city contracts for the disposal of "night soil" and employed hundreds of workers. According to Mencken, two members of the city council held Odorless Excavating franchises, and the company spread its good fortune by selling its accumulated sludge to local fertilizer firms.[44] Freeman Rasin's brother owned one of them, but there is no hard evidence that he was an Odorless Excavating customer.

The city's chief expedient for both wastewater and storm-water management had been to "tunnel" some of the streams that passed through the city, waterways now invisible, unsmellable, and long forgotten. Tunneling was a less costly but less effective alternative to a sanitary sewer system, which might require the expenditure of $10 to $12 million.

In 1901, Mayor Hayes secured authority from the General Assembly to borrow up to $12 million for such a system. The bill that Hayes proposed also authorized him to appoint a sewerage commission that would oversee planning and construction. As mayor, he would lead the commission. Under questioning from members of Baltimore's legislative delegation, Hayes disclosed a curious feature of his tenure on the commission: he would continue to be its chairman even if he were no longer mayor — with a voice in decisions about spending millions of dollars and hiring

The Odorless Excavating Apparatus Company at work.

hundreds of workers. The vote was close in the General Assembly, but the measure passed.[45]

Hayes secured additional funds for his sewer scheme. He orchestrated the sale of the city's railroad—the Western Maryland—for more than $8.7 million. In 1902, the mayor sent an ordinance to the city council providing for a sanitary sewer. It included a provision that would authorize him to use "the unexpended balance of the purchase money of the Western Maryland Railroad, which is not needed by the Commissioners of Finance to meet . . . the outstanding indebtedness of the Mayor and City Council"—about $4.4 million.[46] One of the city's habitual misjudgments—a bad railroad investment—had unexpectedly yielded the resources to address one of its chronic embarrassments: the municipal stench.

Freeman Rasin fumed on the sidelines. While Hayes was mayor, according to Frank Kent, Rasin "was wont to sit in his office and curse him fervently by the hour. It was about the only fun he had at that time." And, since the 1898 charter extended the mayor's term to four years, Rasin would have to endure Hayes at least until 1903. But the members of the city council stood for election every two years, and Rasin went on the offensive in the council primaries of 1901. Rasin Democrats challenged Hayes Democrats. In the general election the two factions turned on one another, and Republicans won control of the council.[47]

The city council that received Mayor Hayes's sewerage ordinance in 1902 was therefore controlled by a new Republican majority, and while most Republicans supported the building of a sewer system, they wanted it to be done under their auspices, not Mayor Hayes's. They approved a bill to appoint a sewerage commission of their own in preference to the one headed by Hayes. But there was also a third option. In 1893, during one of his seven terms as mayor, Ferdinand Latrobe had appointed his own sewerage commission. It completed the first stage of its unhurried deliberations in 1897 with a 230-page report containing a plan for a sewer system that would cost over $10 million. Debate about the report dragged on for almost two years. The principal dispute concerned the disposal of sewage—whether it should be dumped into the Bay ("dilution") or undergo filtration through a 500-acre bed of sand and soil in Anne Arundel County. Latrobe's sewerage commission submitted a second report dealing with these questions during the Malster administration, not long before Hayes became mayor.[48]

The Hayes administration used the old commission's reports to preempt the sewerage commission contemplated by the Republicans. The board of public improvements, a body created under the city charter of 1898 and appointed by the mayor, sent the Republicans' ordinance back to the council "with our disapproval on the ground that it would cause a delay in sewer construction" that was "both inadvisable and unnecessary . . . Every phase of the sewerage question" had been "studied, investigated, and reported" by Mayor Latrobe's sewerage commission, which had "six years' time and the benefit of the study and advice of the best sanitary experts in this country and in England." Another commission would accomplish little more and waste both time and money.[49] But the unresolved disagreement between the Republican council and the Hayes administration about the sewerage commission meant that there would be no progress at all.

Part VIII **DEVASTATION: RACIAL DIVISION, MORAL AND MUNICIPAL BOUNDARIES**

Chapter 26 **FIRE, SMOKE, AND SEGREGATION**

THE CONSTRUCTION OF A SANITARY SEWER SYSTEM was a top priority for Baltimore's new mayor, Robert M. McLane, when he took office in 1903. He was one of the Democratic reformers that Freeman Rasin had recruited to "perfume" his ticket. McLane looked nothing like his predecessors in office—slim, with no moustache, chiseled jaw, impeccable attire. Local tailors pronounced him one of the city's best-dressed men and reported that many of their customers were trying to match the mayor's look.[1] He had other qualifications. He came from a distinguished family of ambassadors, US senators, members of Congress, and a B&O president. An uncle had been the state's governor, and McLane himself was formerly state's attorney for Baltimore. He won support from both organization and reform Democrats. After his unhappy experience with Mayor Hayes, Rasin was willing to support McLane, but only if the remaining positions on the Democratic ticket were assigned to loyal organization men. Rasin chose a longtime loyalist from the Twelfth Ward, W. Starr Gephart, to run for presidency of the upper house of the city council; Gephart had already been president of the lower chamber. The search for a city comptroller was more difficult. Several eligible organization men declined the position, and the search finally settled on an obscure candidate recommended by two ward leaders as "true blue" and a "Muldoon" (Baltimore's term for Democratic straight-ticket voters). He was Harry Hooper, an $18-a-week clerk at an ice company. When the young man received the news of his anointment from his ward boss, he was so surprised and delighted that he wept.[2]

The 1903 primary was the first conducted under state law rather than the auspices of the political parties. The Democratic forces were badly divided. Freeman Rasin and Sonny Mahon were going through one of their periods of political estrangement. McLane benefited from the support of both bosses, but Mahon's forces fought to defeat Rasin's candidates for comptroller and council president.[3]

McLane easily defeated Mayor Hayes, but he won the general election by only a narrow margin over Republican congressman Frank C.

Baltimore City Hall and the ruins left by the fire of 1904, between Calvert Street and Guilford Avenue. *Courtesy Maryland Historical Society, Item MC4709*

Wachter, who had seized his party's nomination in opposition to the choice of William Stone and his organization. Stone's Republican candidates for comptroller and council president defeated both of McLane's Democratic running mates. Gephart and Hooper, according to Frank Kent, were fatally tainted by their association with Rasin.[4]

McLane took office, therefore, with two city officials of the opposition party and a Republican opponent who challenged his 520-vote victory as a product of electoral fraud. Things would soon get even worse for the new mayor. On the morning of Sunday, February 7, 1904, a fire broke out in a dry goods store on the western side of Baltimore's business district. At first only billows of smoke were visible, but the first firefighters on the scene reported a sudden explosion, and then a strong southwest wind carried embers and flames eastward across the center of the city. Another explosion occurred when the fire reached a wooden box on the sidewalk in front of a hardware store. The box was filled with gunpowder and cartridges, and its detonation damaged several nearby buildings, exposing their inflammable interiors. More fire companies responded, but their hoses were ineffective. The flames were so hot that it was difficult to get sufficiently close to play water on them. The firefighters soon resorted to explosions themselves, after receiving authorization from Mayor McLane, to destroy buildings in the path of the conflagration with dynamite. Additional firefighters arrived from Pennsylvania, New York, Delaware, Washington, and Maryland counties. Because the fire had broken out on a Sunday when hardly anyone was at work downtown, no one was killed and few were seriously injured. But by the time the fire had finally burned its way to the Jones Falls and the harbor more than a day later, 140 acres of the city lay in blackened ruins—including the 60-acre plot laid out 175 years earlier as Baltimore Town.[5]

RECOVERY

Mayor McLane appointed a 63-member Citizens Emergency Committee to devise a rebuilding program for the "Burnt District." Its chairman was local industrialist William Keyser. The committee was an assembly of the city's elite, all but a dozen of its members listed in the social register. Keyser appointed subcommittees. Only days after its formation, the legislative subcommittee produced a draft bill for the General Assembly that would create a Burnt District Commission, its five members to include the mayor and two members of each political party. The bipartisan commission would carry out the reconstruction plans of the emergency committee. Its chair was Sherlock Swann, a former city council member and grandson of Governor Thomas Swann. Since the fire had destroyed most downtown office space, the commission operated out of the janitor's room in city hall. The city council appropriated $1 million of the funds generated by the sale of the Western Maryland Railroad to get the commission started on its rebuilding plans.[6]

The state legislature authorized Baltimore to borrow another $6 million to pay for reconstruction of the city's streets and waterfront. Less than a month later, the General Assembly empowered the city to issue yet another $10 million in city stock to finance construction of the long-delayed sewer system. Work on the street and sewer projects had to be pursued in tandem. It made little sense, after all, to repave the streets and then dig them up again to lay sewer mains. City officials hoped not just to rebuild Baltimore but to improve it. The council, for example, wanted to replace cobblestones with paving of a less bone-jarring sort, and it passed a bill appealing to the General Assembly to outlaw cobblestones. Mayor McLane vetoed the ordinance, not because he favored cobblestones, but because he insisted that the city should make its own decisions about paving materials.[7] McLane also made it his policy to return all contributions for the relief of the city that came to Baltimore from around the country. He thanked the donors for their kindness, but seemed to see recovery from the fire as an opportunity for the city and its residents to test their own resources, perhaps to overcome the disjointed politics that had handicapped the town since its founding.

In addition to the $16 million in borrowing approved by the state legislature and the funds remaining from the sale of the Western Maryland, the Burnt District Commission could impose an assessment on any property owner who benefited from improvements made in the course of reconstruction. As much as one-third of the cost of these improvements could be charged to the landowners who profited from them.[8]

Like the British invasion of 1814, the Great Fire animated Baltimoreans to marshal their city's constructive energies in the face of a crisis that lifted their city out of its chronic inertia and fragmentation. But, in some respects, the rebuilding of Baltimore proved to be more complicated and contentious than defending it against the British. Simply finding property lines and street levels beneath the rubble kept city surveyors busy for months. The task of removing debris occupied 10,000 workers. The Burnt District Commission was empowered to take property by eminent domain, but the exercise of this power was complicated by recalcitrant property owners, often backed by the Republican majority of the council's second branch. Wider streets were needed, not just to ease the flow of traffic, but to retard the spread of future fires. The street-widening proposals met with opposition among property owners who objected to the downsizing of their lots and anticipated increases in their taxes. The plans for Baltimore Street provoked particular contention and aroused property owners and their attorneys to fight condemnation of their real estate. The skirmish kept the Burnt District Commission from acquiring the property that it needed, and Baltimore Street today, unlike Lombard and Pratt, is no wider than it was before the fire.[9]

Baltimoreans living outside the Burnt District worried about the effect of the redevelopment plan on their tax bills. Residents in the area annexed to the city in 1888 complained that the diversion of resources to rebuilding the city center would delay the public improvements they had been promised.[10]

Some of the city officials who worked with Mayor McLane noted that "his entire appearance at times told too well of the heavy strain under which he was laboring." After a Friday meeting in May between the Burnt District Commission and the board of estimates, one of the participants asked, "I wonder what is wrong with the Mayor? He is certainly not himself to-day." But by the following Monday, Memorial Day, the mayor seemed to be in good spirits while he chatted with his wife of two weeks. At about three o'clock, he excused himself, went to a bedroom, retrieved a pistol from a wardrobe, and shot himself in the head.[11]

REPUBLICAN RECOVERY

Speculation about the mayor's state of mind filled the columns of local papers. A few prominent Baltimoreans, along with his family, insisted that his shooting was accidental. But there was no uncertainly about the custody of the mayor's office. It fell to a Republican. Under the city charter, the Democratic mayor was to be succeeded by the president of the second branch of the city council, Republican E. Clay Timanus, a loyal lieutenant of party boss William F. Stone. The city charter prevented Timanus from replacing McLane's Democratic department heads. As lesser offices fell vacant, however, Timanus and Stone filled them with their own partisans, and Timanus chose the members of the sewerage commission to oversee the long overdue construction of the city's $10 million sewer system.[12]

Rebuilding of the Burnt District proceeded more rapidly than expected. Mayor Timanus was intent on avoiding controversies. When the city council proposed to intervene in the contentious territorial disputes along Baltimore Street, he exercised his veto because the measure "would lead to no end of legal complications and great expense to the City, accomplishing no object whatever."[13] Timanus intervened in other disputes between the Burnt District Commission and recalcitrant property owners to break logjams in the commission's efforts to acquire strategic pieces of real estate.[14]

At the close of 1906, the commission managed to return more than half a million dollars to the city. By that time, 800 new buildings had arisen to replace 1,343 destroyed by fire. Many of the new structures, however, were considerably larger than the old ones, and they were assessed at $25 million, almost twice the value of the buildings they replaced. The reduction in the number of buildings also reflected the movement of some firms out of the city center; having been forced to leave the Burnt District during reconstruction, they decided to remain in outlying locations.[15]

Timanus recognized that the fire had created a new horizon of municipal opportunity. At the end of 1904, he invited 39 local organizations to send representatives to meet with a committee of the city council for a "General Conference on Public Improvement." Neighborhood associations were prominent among the participants. Though most of the city's residential areas had created such organizations as early as the 1880s, they had seldom concerned themselves with the future of the city as a whole. The conference's chief objectives were construction of the long-awaited sewage system and substitution of smoother paving materials for the city's cobblestones.[16]

The rebuilding effort engendered a more general civic momentum that pushed beyond mere restoration. Timanus appointed the Commission for the Encouragement of Manufacturing Plants in the City of Baltimore.[17] In clearing the way for construction of a sewer system, the fire also eliminated the septic tanks and privy vaults that had restricted the land area available for building. After the sewer mains came new streets, many of them wider than before, paved with modern materials that allowed smoother passage through the city at higher speeds than cobblestones permitted. Waterfront destruction gave the city an opportunity to take possession of and improve Baltimore's harbor facilities.[18]

The fire proved a fortunate disaster. It unleashed a new era of urban development while killing no one, except, perhaps, Mayor McLane.[19] In September 1906, the Greater Baltimore Jubilee and Exposition initiated a weeklong celebration of the city's recovery from its ordeal and launched a more permanent display of the facilities and advantages that the town could offer to industry. One of the honored guests on the first day of the jubilee was Charles J. Bonaparte, now secretary of the navy in the Roosevelt administration, who joined the governor on the reviewing stand at Baltimore Street and Hopkins Place (temporarily renamed McLane Place) to view the military procession. On the following day, the "Industrial Parade" marched. It was led by its chief marshal, the owner of a local distillery and commander of the militia's Fifth Regiment, in front of his "staff" of more than 50 business executives clad in black derbies, black coats, white trousers, and white gloves. Next came German social, musical, and athletic associations; then 5,000 B&O employees; and, finally, an extravagant "Artistic Division." This was led, on horseback, by local parade enthusiast and former mayoral candidate Colonel J. Frank Supplee. Punctuated by marching bands and exotically costumed fraternal organizations, it was a procession of the city's business firms, their workers, and executives. The companies displayed their products and services on floats. The William Knabe Piano Company had nine of them. The Joseph Wernig Transfer Company marched with 14 floats depicting "the general transfer business in its various forms" and illustrating "the handling of giant pieces of machinery and other articles difficult of management in removal from place to place."[20]

Mayor Timanus had gone far toward rebuilding his city. But it was still Baltimore, an underfunded, underrepresented, and underpowered municipality. In 1908, for example, a grand jury report compared the size of the local police force with those in five other cities. Baltimore's force was not only smaller than the others but smaller in relation to the population it had to protect and police. The city had one officer for every 742 residents. Boston had one policeman for every 333 citizens. New York, St. Louis, and Philadelphia also had higher police-to-civilian ratios than Baltimore. Chicago, with a ratio lower than that in the other four towns, still put one officer on the streets for every 529 residents — almost 30 percent more than Baltimore.[21] Baltimore did not even control its own police force. The board of police commissioners held their appointments from the state.

POLITICS AS USUAL

William Stone's Republican organization supported Timanus for a full term as mayor in the election of 1907. It could hardly do otherwise. As in 1903, the organization's candidate faced a primary challenge from George Wachter. This time, however, Wachter was defeated. But the battle between Wachter and Timanus made an issue of race. Each Republican tried to outdo the other as a champion of the city's black population and suggested that his opponent was a covert racist.[22] Two politicians declared themselves candidates for the Democratic nomination. Freeman Rasin dithered, uncharacteristically, and then approached former governor Frank Brown. Rasin pledged his organization's support to any candidate that Brown chose. After extensive discussions with members of Baltimore's political class, Brown settled on J. Barry Mahool, president of the city council's first branch. Rasin agreed to the selection. Shortly after Frank Kent interviewed the boss about the new mayoral candidate, Rasin collapsed. A few days later he was dead.[23]

Tribute came from an unexpected source. The *Afro-American* acknowledged that Rasin "was a Democrat of the most virulent type, [but] he always had a good side for the colored man." He had helped to give Baltimore's black students a high school of their own, and he overcame the school commissioners' resistance to the hiring of black teachers. "Whatever else he did, Mr. Rasin was never known to come out in abuse of colored people, and it is also known that he cared for more than one colored person who came under his notice. It is fair to assume also, that if Mr. Rasin had not set his face against it, the iniquitous Poe Amendment to disenfranchise the Negroes of this state would have become law." Rasin "had a warm spot in his heart for the despised race" even though most of its members voted against him.[24]

The Poe amendment was the Democratic Party's most ambitious attempt to reduce the Republican electoral base among black Marylanders. It was drafted by John Prentiss Poe in 1905 under the general direction of Senator Gorman, who aimed to shrink the state's Republican electorate. Poe was dean of the University of Maryland Law School. His amendment would have granted voting rights to men who were qualified to vote before ratification of the Fifteenth Amendment or were lineal descendants of such voters. All others would have to demonstrate that they could explain a portion of the state constitution to the satisfaction of the election judges.[25]

Maryland voters defeated the Poe amendment by slightly less than 35,000 votes of 104,000 cast. Almost two-thirds of the margin of defeat was rolled up in Baltimore, where the measure lost in 23 of the city's 24 wards. States further south had successfully used the "grandfather clause" to disenfranchise African Americans, but there were few white immigrants in the South. In Baltimore, however, foreign-born whites made up more than 15 percent of the population, and the grandfather clause would exclude them and their sons from the electorate along with their black fellow citizens. Most of the immigrant voters were Democrats, and an array of white ethnic organizations joined forces with the black Maryland Suffrage League to oppose the Poe amendment. The reform wing of the local Democratic Party launched an Anti-Poe Amendment Association, which claimed 500 members, and Freeman Rasin quietly shifted the weight of his organization against the measure. Four ward bosses openly disowned the Poe amendment. Rasin advised the city's Democratic candidates to keep quiet about it. When it was all over, the Gorman-Rasin alliance was finished. Rasin claimed that the city's Democratic organization "did all that could be done for it," but characterized the Poe amendment as a political burden that had lost votes for the party. An embittered Arthur Gorman died a year after the defeat of his amendment, for which he blamed Rasin, who expired a year later. The imperishable William Pinkney Whyte, ousted from the Senate to make room for Gorman, served out the rest of Gorman's term.[26]

PARTY PREJUDICE

Sonny Mahon now succeeded to the leadership of Baltimore's Democratic organization, along with two other sub-bosses: Frank Kelly and Robert Padgett. Kelly was leader of a ward organization in West Baltimore and a saloonkeeper frequently in trouble with the police for selling liquor on Sunday or maintaining a disorderly house; he usually managed to get out of trouble. Robert "Paving Bob" Padgett was a city contractor who acquired his nickname and his wealth from his work on the city's streets. The three Democratic leaders followed through on Rasin's commitment to Mahool as their mayoral candidate, though as a Presbyterian deacon and church treasurer, homebody, "politically and personally clean, straight, sincere, independent, earnest, and thoroughly devoted to the interests of the city," he was not a candidate of their sort.[27] He was, in short, rather colorless, which may explain why he had few enemies and why, in turn, he was chosen as the party's unity candidate for mayor.

Mahool faced two challengers for the Democratic nomination. George Stewart Brown was a council member. J. Charles Linthicum was a state legislator. They paid no attention to one another. Instead, both attacked Mahool as the candidate of bossism. Their assault was somewhat blunted by the two candidates' own reliance on the Democratic organization in past campaigns and by the near certainty that either one would seek organization support if he managed to reach the general election. The charge of bossism had also lost some of its efficacy because Freeman Rasin was no longer available as a target, though Linthicum tried to cast Frank Brown as the new boss. George Stewart Brown supported municipal ownership of utilities and streetcar lines and had the backing of the Socialist Workers Party. He tried a variant on Linthicum's theme. He made Frank Brown the agent of corporate capitalism and Barry Mahool his puppet.[28] Mahool's vote count in the Democratic primary exceeded the combined total for Brown and Linthicum by more than 13,000. He would not do so well against Mayor Timanus in the general election a month later. Mahool had little more to promise the voters than a continuation of the rebuilding and public improvement campaign already begun by his Republican opponent. But there was also the issue of race. It seemed to provide an angle of attack on Timanus, since both he and Wachter had appealed so vigorously for black votes in the Republican primary. Its debut as a campaign theme in the general election was staged to command attention.

Ex-mayor Thomas Hayes had kept to the private practice of law since his defeat for reelection four years earlier. He abruptly resumed the practice of politics days before the general election when he rose to address a crowd of 500 Democrats at a hall in the Eighteenth Ward. Frank Brown joined him on the platform. Hayes declared that he had nothing bad to say about Mayor Timanus. He concentrated instead on the character of Timanus's political party. The Democratic Party, said Hayes, belonged to "the bulk of the small house owners who pay the principal part of the taxes." Democratic officeholders were therefore "more likely to be on the lookout for the welfare of this large constituency as to the honest, wise, and economic expenditure of taxes." Hayes then compared the composition of the Democratic base with the makeup of the Republican constituency. "Who takes the place in the Republican party of the Democratic laboring masses in the Democratic party? Everyone knows it is the colored man, and the bulk of them, we all know, pay no taxes." Hayes claimed that he was no "enemy to the colored man," his equal before the law, but said that he was "positively opposed to giving the colored man the franchise until he is properly educated, both morally and mentally."[29]

Hayes said nothing new. His speech for the Mahool ticket echoed themes already implicit in Arthur Gorman's repeated efforts to shrink the black electorate. Gorman, of course, had packaged his prejudice as a concern about voter literacy. Hayes made no secret of his contempt for black voters. It was something he had in common with ex-governor Frank Brown, the Democratic Party's maestro of the moment who sat behind him on the platform. Brown had voiced similarly candid views about race when he campaigned for Robert McLane in 1903. "What will become of Baltimore," he had asked, "which has now one-fifth of its population, or 100,000 of the colored people, a larger number than any city in the United States . . . and the only Southern city and State in which the colored people have unrestricted right of suffrage?" The time had come, Brown said, to raise the race issue, because Maryland had "become the chief dumping ground of this worthless class of colored people from the South," who competed for jobs held by white workers and burdened "our courts, prisons, and asylums."[30]

Baltimoreans hesitated to make an issue of race when it threatened to disrupt established relationships and institutions. But when disagreements about race defined the differences between Republican and Democratic candidates, Democratic politicians were prepared to exploit the issue for partisan advantage. They were more guarded, however, when racial offensives were directed against the voting rights of black Baltimoreans, some of whom voted Democratic.

The General Assembly would make two further attempts to win voter approval for constitutional amendments designed to disenfranchise black voters. The Straus amendment, named for Maryland's attorney general and constructed by a committee of respected Democratic attorneys, was designed to avoid the Poe amendment's pitfall: excluding foreign-born voters from the polls along with African Americans. The Straus version granted voting rights to foreign-born citizens naturalized after ratification of the Fifteenth Amendment and their direct descendants. The remainder of the state's would-be voters—black voters—could qualify by owning and paying taxes on at least $500 in real or personal property or by filling out an application form. The form required them to write out not only personal information but the names of the president, at least one justice of the US Supreme Court, the state's governor, one member of the state court of appeals, and (in the case of Baltimore residents) the mayor. The measure was sold to the voters as a means to elevate the electorate by excluding the illiterate or politically ignorant. A majority of the voters of Southern Maryland and the Eastern Shore supported the proposal, but opposition in Baltimore and the northern counties was strong enough to defeat it. Baltimore City alone accounted for almost two-thirds of the amendment's margin of defeat.[31]

Democratic supporters of the Straus amendment nevertheless took encouragement from the outcome. The measure had come closer to victory than the Poe version. It had carried four of the city's wards instead of just one, and the strong Democratic majority elected to the General Assembly gave them hope that they would have another chance to drive most black men out of the state's electorate. Their opportunity came in 1911 with the Digges amendment, drafted by Charles County delegate Walter Digges. It gave the vote to all white men who were legal residents of the state and at least 21 years old. Other men had to prove that they had paid taxes on $500 or more in real or personal property for the previous two consecutive years. To enhance the amendment's prospects, the legislature passed a temporary registration law that excluded all black men from the polls. In other words, the state's African American voters would not be permitted to vote on the law that deprived them of the vote. But the registration law seemed so outrageous that the governor (who had originally endorsed it) felt compelled to veto it.[32]

In Baltimore, the Digges amendment lost by almost twice the margin that defeated the Straus amendment. The Republican gubernatorial candidate carried the city, which also elected Republicans as sheriff and state's attorney. The city's *Afro-American* offered its own explanation for the amendment's defeat.[33] Voters — even white Democratic voters — might want to ensure that their party had to compete for their support. A crippled Republican Party might reduce the Democratic Party's responsiveness to its own "laboring masses."

LIVING APART

In July 1910, a Yale-educated African American attorney, George W. F. McMechen, rented a house on McCulloh Street. His new home was only 10 blocks east of his old one, but his family's arrival roused nearby residents to form the Madison Avenue, McCulloh Street, and Eutaw Place Improvement Association. Their objective was to prevent black families like the McMechens from moving into their white neighborhood. Milton Dashiell, a white lawyer who lived on McCulloh Street, drafted an ordinance designed to achieve the organization's aim. He outlined its provisions for his fellow residents at a meeting of the new association. The ordinance would prohibit African Americans from moving to blocks where a majority of the residents were white, and whites from moving to blocks with African American majorities. It sounded even-handed, and Dashiell justified it by referring to Baltimore's racially segregated schools. If white children could not be required to spend part of each day with black children, why should white adults have to live day and night with black neighbors?[34]

The ordinance was an improvised response to an immediate grievance. The proposed measure did not cover the entire city, just a section of Northwest Baltimore.[35] But it made Baltimore the first city in the country to attempt residential segregation by law. Inquiries came from Roanoke, Richmond, Norfolk, Winston-Salem, Atlanta, and elsewhere asking for copies of the law. As the audience grew, so did the ordinance. It was extended to the entire city.

The segregation law was introduced by Councilman Samuel L. West of the Thirteenth Ward. Dashiell and his aroused neighbors were residents of the Seventeenth, but West's home was just a few blocks from McCulloh Street. Citizens who spoke at hearings on the proposed ordinance were overwhelmingly in favor of its passage. Some suggested that it would preserve the city's tax base by forestalling white flight to the suburbs. Two of West's colleagues, however, raised objections. One councilman suggested that restrictive covenants in property deeds would achieve residential segregation more effectively than a city ordinance that was sure to face legal challenges. The only black councilman, Harry Cummings, raised just such a challenge. He moved that consideration of the West ordinance be suspended until the city solicitor could rule on its constitutionality. His motion was defeated.[36]

Hearings were extended so that the bill's opponents might be heard. Emma Traxton, representing the Federation of the Colored Christian Women of Maryland, argued that "intelligent negroes" were "moving away from hovels to avoid disease from

Biddle Alley in 1911. Before they were confined to ghettoes, many of Baltimore's African Americans were confined to alley housing within walking distance of the white households and business firms that relied on their labor. Biddle Alley was notorious as Baltimore's "Lung Block," with the highest rate of tuberculosis in the city. *Courtesy Maryland Historical Society*

spreading among them and that they are anxious to uplift their race." A black clergyman, A. L. Gans, offered a similar explanation: black Baltimoreans "moved to the streets where white people lived simply to better their condition and environment."[37]

The council approved the West ordinance and sent it to Mayor Mahool, who referred it to city solicitor Edgar Allan Poe (the author's grandnephew) for an opinion on its constitutionality. Poe ruled that the ordinance represented a legitimate exercise of the city's police powers—a measure designed to preserve public order against the "disorder and strife" likely to erupt in racially mixed neighborhoods. The mayor then signed "An Ordinance for Preserving Peace, Preventing Conflict and Ill-Feelings Between the White and Colored Races, And promoting the General Welfare of the City of Baltimore By Providing As Far As Possible for the Use of Separate Blocks By White and Colored People For Residences, Churches, and Schools."[38] City officials were making an issue of race, in other words, to avoid the interracial friction that might compel them to address the issue of race.

The segregation ordinance endured as many reversals as had the various amendments designed to disenfranchise black voters. This time it was the courts, not the voters, who proved obstructive. The first version of the West ordinance failed to make it out of the city. Two judges on the Baltimore Supreme Bench ruled it improper because of its much-too-long title. Under the city charter, the title of an ordinance was supposed to specify a single subject to which it was addressed. The ordinance went back to the council for revision. Councilman West turned to a new legal adviser, William Marbury, to replace Dashiell. In addition to fixing the title, Marbury exempted racially mixed blocks from the law's provisions, but the legal verbiage he used was open to several interpretations. Dashiell, who was ill and unable to attend the hearings on the new version of his ordinance, wrote to Mayor Mahool urging that the ambiguous section be scrapped. Racially mixed neighborhoods, he argued, were precisely the ones "creating a condition for conflict, which the Ordinance is designed to obviate." Mahool signed it anyway, but it was repealed and reenacted by the council a month later because of a procedural error in its approval, and new provisions were added that applied to the location of churches and schools belonging to the two races. Mahool signed this on May 15, 1911. It was the last official act of his term as mayor.[39]

For two years, the West ordinance stood legally undisturbed. Then, in 1913, John E. Gurry, a "colored person," was charged with occupying a house in a white block. He was represented by W. Ashbie Hawkins, a law partner of George W. F. McMechen and the owner of the house on McCulloh Street that McMechen had rented. The case against Hawkins's client was dismissed in Baltimore's criminal court on the grounds that the ordinance's provisions made no sense. William Marbury's language concerning racially mixed blocks could be interpreted as making it illegal for anyone—white or black—to move in. The case went to the state court of appeals, which interpreted Marbury as he intended, but rejected the West ordinance all the same because it could prevent a white person who already owned a house on a majority-black block from occupying it. The same was true for a black owner of a house on a white block. The city council stood ready with a fourth version of the West ordinance, revised to preserve property rights already in force before enactment of the law.[40]

Baltimore's experiment with residential segregation by law was taken up in other cities, but not for long. In 1917, the US Supreme Court considered a case from Louisville, which had its own version of the West ordinance. The law was held unconstitutional, not because it was racially discriminatory, but because it infringed on the rights of property by dictating the race of the persons to whom landlords or homeowners could rent or sell their real estate.[41]

Baltimore's prolonged legal struggle to secure its residential segregation ordinance was notable not just because the law was the first of its kind but because the politicians who orchestrated the effort could hardly be portrayed as reactionary racists. Mayor Mahool endorsed female suffrage, the eight-hour day, utility regulation, a minimum wage, playgrounds for poor children—and residential segregation.[42]

Reformers in Baltimore adhered, like progressives elsewhere, to the encouraging hypothesis that the physical environment of the slum produced the deviant behavior of slum dwellers. A reduction in overcrowding and improvements in air circulation, toilet facilities, water supply, and exposure to sunlight would mitigate the poverty, immorality, and criminality of the people who lived in substandard housing. But the reformers' faith in environmentalism wavered when confronted with the black slum. The Baltimore Charity Organization Society and the Association for Improving the Condition of the Poor jointly sponsored a study of local housing conditions, completed in 1907. Its findings in two districts of "alley housing" inhabited by "light-hearted, shiftless, irresponsible" African Americans set the investigators "wondering to what extent their failings are the result of their surroundings, and to what extent the inhabitants, in turn, react for evil upon their environment."[43]

The housing study, however, did not recommend racial segregation, and Baltimore's foremost progressive reformer, Charles J. Bonaparte, was an outspoken opponent of the West ordinance.[44] Other members of the progressive elite remained silent and left the defense of white Baltimore to "middling whites who had vested interests in a neighborhood." In its assaults on the ordinance, the *Afro-American Ledger* made a point of emphasizing the inferior social standing of the whites who turned out for meetings in support of the segregation law. Gretchen Boger finds that the *Afro*'s assessment of the segregationists' status is confirmed by evidence from city directories and the social register.[45] The segregationists may have appropriated progressive rhetoric about public health or eugenics to advance their campaign, but their chief concern was to defend their neighborhoods from racial change and to protect the market value of their homes. The residents of elite Mount Vernon faced no such threat. Few blacks could afford to live in the neighborhood except as domestic servants. Roland Park, the sylvan, Olmsted-designed development on the city's fringe, relied not only on home prices but on restrictive covenants in property deeds that prevented residents from selling their homes to African Americans, Jews, or Catholics.[46]

Progressivism, according to Boger, was not the ideology that drove Baltimore's innovative campaign to achieve residential segregation by law.[47] Nor was segregation simply a measure to protect property values in white neighborhoods. Whites' concern about property values was inseparable from widespread Negrophobia. On that subject, one of the local experts was William Cabell Bruce, city solicitor, sometime mayoral candidate, and, eventually, US senator. In 1891, he had published a pamphlet titled *The Negro Problem*. It explained that emancipation had provoked the impulse toward segregation. The slave owner could allow "a considerable latitude of personal intercourse between himself and his slaves" because "no individual familiarity or indulgence could possibly efface the line of deep demarcation that the law had prescribed." Once that boundary disappeared, "it became impossible for the whites to allow themselves the same liberality without running the risk of having their race susceptibilities irritated in many different modes." When black men gained political citizenship, the gulf between the races grew even wider. "What the negro has gained in political privileges," wrote Bruce, "he has lost twice over in social. The freer his access to the polls, the more difficult has become his access to all the human relations that law cannot touch."[48] Rev. Harvey Johnson delivered a spirited refutation of Bruce on the question of African inferiority, but he did not address Bruce's observations about the etiology of white prejudice—its intensification in response to the removal of racial barriers.[49]

White Baltimoreans were long accustomed to living with free black people. Many whites regarded them as undesirables, but in a pedestrian city it was difficult to avoid contact with them, except by persuading them to leave for Liberia. Physical separation became feasible when streetcar lines enabled whites of the better sort to sift themselves out from less prominent Baltimoreans. Whites of middling or lower status may have felt abandoned and racially vulnerable as a result, but the demand for residential segregation rose only as the drive for black disenfranchisement collapsed. There may have been something in Bruce's contention that African Americans' access to the polls intensified white demands for racial separation.

City solicitor Poe hinted at a similar motive for segregation in the opinion he prepared for Mayor Mahool. He justified it as a measure for the preservation of public order among blacks and whites because "close association between them on a footing of absolute equality is utterly impossible . . . and invariably leads to irritation, friction, disorder, and strife."[50] Poe's rationale seems one more instance in the city's longstanding effort to prevent race from becoming a subject of political contention.

I N 1917, MAYOR JAMES H. PRESTON appointed a committee to investigate the living conditions of Baltimore's 90,000 black residents. Disease was a particular concern. Though they made up only 15 percent of the city's population, African Americans accounted for 40 percent of deaths from tuberculosis. The mayor suggested that the disease might have something to do with housing conditions. African Americans were crowded "into small houses in alleys and narrow streets . . . living under conditions extremely unsanitary and unhealthful."[1]

Racial segregation did not figure in the official diagnosis of the problem, even though it aggravated overcrowding in black neighborhoods by artificially restricting the supply of housing available to a growing African American population. The mayor considered building new housing for blacks in areas of the city set aside for members of their race, but neither he nor his committee considered abrogating the ordinance that prevented African Americans from moving into existing houses in white neighborhoods. The ordinance would soon become irrelevant, however, because of the US Supreme Court's ruling that it was unconstitutional. Residential segregation would then depend on restrictive covenants and the practices of realtors. The mayor sent a copy of a Chicago segregation plan to Baltimore's real estate board, apparently hoping that realtors could enforce segregation after it could no longer be sustained by city law.[2]

Unlike several of his predecessors, Preston did not lend "political perfumery" to the Democratic ticket. He had been a loyal soldier of Freeman Rasin's Democratic organization. He served two terms in the house of delegates and was briefly its Speaker, in 1894. And his political career might have taken a further turn upward had Republicans not swept the state in the Democratic disaster of 1895.[3] Preston served as a member of the board of police commissioners and made an unsuccessful run for Congress in 1910. After Sonny Mahon announced that he was backing Preston for mayor in 1911, against incumbent mayor Mahool, the *Baltimore Sun* let loose a condemnatory editorial dismissing

JOHN J. ("SONNY") MAHON

John J. "Sonny" Mahon succeeded to the uncertain leadership of Baltimore's Democratic organization after Freeman Rasin's death in 1907.

the candidate as a creature of the "Ring." When first elected to the house of delegates in 1889, Preston was "a young man, who should have had high ideals and honorable aspirations." Instead, he had "allied himself with 'the machine' which was then omnipotent at Annapolis and corrupt without limit." During his brief term as Speaker, according to the paper, he had prepared the way for the Democratic defeat of 1895 by advancing nefarious legislation that granted monopoly status to the local gas company and a firm that disposed of sewage and solid waste. On what grounds, the editorialist asked, "can Mr. Preston expect the support of Democratic voters who desire public officials to be public officials and not servile politicians wearing the collar and doing the bidding of corrupt bosses?"[4]

For Sonny Mahon, the choice of Preston was a high-stakes gamble. If the voters rejected him, the Democratic machine would suffer a decisive reduction in political influence, perhaps extinction. But continuing deference to reformers and Independents may have seemed only slightly preferable to utter defeat. Mahon was ready to roll the dice, but his lieutenants apparently lacked his nerve. Democrats who held offices under the Mahool administration worried that if Preston won the Democratic nomination, the city's electorate would turn to the Republicans, who would oust them from their city jobs. Other party loyalists were willing to abandon Mayor Mahool, but urged Mahon not to choose Preston, who was too obviously an organization man. The *Sun* contended that Mahon himself was "frightened by the outlook" and that "his followers, big and little, are scared to their wits' end."[5]

Mahon may have been less frightened than the *Sun* imagined. His selection of Preston confronted his organization's foot soldiers with stark alternatives: a victory pregnant with patronage or a defeat that might eliminate what remained of their access to municipal offices and contracts. It was a frightful choice that would elicit their maximum effort to avoid political extinction. As Rasin's chief deputy, Mahon had demonstrated his expertise in engineering elections, and he used his characteristic care in the campaign for Preston. A few days before the primary, for example, Mahon ordered his workers to test the candidate's strength by canvassing their precincts. The exercise served not only as an internal opinion poll but as a means to identify Democrats who supported Preston. These were the voters who would be targeted by the organization's "runners" on election day. To motivate its foot soldiers, the machine offered not just the prospect of city jobs but the more immediate inducement of election-day cash. In the Democratic strongholds of South and East Baltimore, the Preston campaign was expected to spend $25 to $40 per precinct for the runners.[6]

The organization lived up to the boss's expectations. Turnout in the Democratic primary reached 80 percent, an all-time high, and among the 50,000 Democrats who voted, Preston defeated Mahool by more than 9,000. The machine's triumph, however, was tarnished by the usual charges of electoral fraud. A grand jury ordered a recount of votes from precincts where irregularities were alleged, and a judge ordered that the sealed ballot boxes from those precincts be delivered to the court. But the board of election supervisors and board of police commissioners reported that the ballots from April's Democratic primary had been emptied into sacks because the ballot boxes were needed for the state primary in August. The police commander of the district where the boxes had been stored told a different story. He claimed that the boxes were emptied only days before they were to be delivered to the grand jury. If his account were true, then the dumping of the ballot boxes would have violated the judge's order. If the dumping occurred in August, it may have violated a state law requiring that ballots remain sealed in their boxes for six months after an election. While a convenient ambiguity enveloped the violation, the consequence was clear: the recount was impossible because, once the ballots had been dumped into sacks, there was no way to tell which precincts they came from.[7]

RULE OF THE RING

The resurrection of the Ring without Rasin may not have been achieved by fraud, but it was an unexpected triumph. The *Sun* had confidently predicted a defeat of the Democratic organization. What came next, however, was no surprise. City hall became a patronage clearinghouse for the political friends of the mayor and Sonny Mahon. Preston began by appointing his law partner, Steven S. Field, as city solicitor. "Little Danny" Loden, a Mahon loyalist, was named collector of water rents and taxes, but his main job was to oversee the administration's lesser patronage appointments. Rewards of a more substantial value would flow to political lieutenant Robert "Paving Bob" Padgett, who won lucrative contracts to cover the city's cobblestone streets with smooth asphalt. Mahon became a bonding agent for Padgett and other city contractors. He wrote to members of the city council announcing that he had entered the bonding business and would appreciate any clients they might refer to him.[8]

The new administration arrived at city hall along with a freshly authorized loan of $6 million to pave the city's streets. The F. E. Schneider Paving Company was one of the leading bidders for these funds. Schneider was the company's general manager, but he held just one share of its stock. The rest belonged to Robert Padgett and his wife. The company's legal business was handled by the law firm of the mayor and the city solicitor, Preston and Field.[9]

Padgett came relatively late to political prominence. He had been a novice in Rasin's Seventh Ward. While Rasin ruled, Padgett's highest public office was sergeant at arms in the house of delegates. His political status improved abruptly with the rise of Sonny Mahon. When Mahon succeeded Rasin in 1907, Padgett became the party's candidate for sheriff and, with Mahon's support, got elected. He also became a member of the city's Democratic committee. Paving Bob continued to conduct his private business while sheriff, and it was rumored that Mahon provided him with the capital to buy out a competing company and upgrade its asphalt plant. Padgett's term as sheriff ended as Preston became mayor, but the job left him with a hangover. To cover his salary as sheriff, he had been entitled to keep $3,000 annually of the fees and fines he collected. After he retired as sheriff, the state filed suit against him to recover about $11,000 that he had allegedly kept in excess of what was due to him. The commissioners for the opening of streets also filed complaints accusing the paving company of repeatedly violating the eight-hour labor law that covered city contractors.[10]

If any of this bothered Sonny Mahon or Mayor Preston, their apprehensions never became public. But Padgett's paving business soon became a political liability. His troubles began when the city's paving commission passed over William Elder, the low bidder on two major projects, and gave the jobs to Padgett instead. The commissioners had disqualified Elder's bids because his company had paved (at bargain rates) the concrete walkways at the home of the commission's assistant chief engineer, and the engineer had subsequently been accused of "padding" city contracts to increase payments to Elder. Padgett, it turned out, had given the same assistant engineer a $6,200 loan for the purchase of his home. One of the engineer's duties was to certify that paving jobs met specifications; Padgett's work had previously been cited for repeated failures to meet these specifications. Since Elder's firm had been disqualified as a bidder for paving contracts, Padgett seemed to merit similar treatment. Mayor Preston was reported to be furious with him, and the paving commission disqualified Padgett's firm as a bidder on its contracts. Padgett offered to resign from his corporation to preserve its eligibility for city contracts, but the commission and the mayor stood firm. So did Mahon. Though he had sponsored his friend's political career, he disowned Padgett in order to preserve his own alliance with Preston. Paving Bob withdrew from the paving business and leased his asphalt plant to a firm from New York.[11] The mayor expelled Padgett from his inner circle of lieutenants—temporarily.

VISIONARY BOSS

Mayor Preston had plans for Baltimore far grander than graft and much more original. The most ambitious of his ventures envisioned a radical extension of the city's boundaries.

Preston's plan was not simply an annexation proposal; in fact, he deliberately avoided the term. He proposed to add four self-governing and semi-independent "boroughs" to Baltimore, one in each quarter of the compass. They would increase the city's land area from less than 32 to more than 172 square miles. In each of the proposed boroughs, the registered voters would decide whether to join the city. Each borough approving the plan would get one representative on the city council, and the residents of each would elect three commissioners of their own to oversee taxation, expenditures, and services within the borough limits. The boroughs would be subject to the supervision of only the city's health department and school commissioners, and they would fall under the jurisdiction of the city courts. In return for this oversight, they would pay the city 5 percent of their revenue from taxes and fees. (Later versions called for 10 cents per $100 of assessed property valuation.) By negotiation with the city, the boroughs could also consolidate their police or fire departments with those of Baltimore or have their garbage collected along with the city's.[12]

Preston was proposing a gradualist annexation policy, thus avoiding the usual objections raised by suburbanites who would be absorbed by an extension of the city's limits and its taxes. He noted that "opposition always at first develops owing to the advance of taxation." But he believed that "if the Borough System which I have proposed is carefully thought out and all the money collected within the annexed limits is spent in the main in the territory in which the money is collected it will remove opposition on this score."[13]

The borough plan could play a significant role in Baltimore's continuing campaign to attract manufacturing firms. It would give the city access to prime industrial real estate on the waterfront in Baltimore and Anne Arundel counties. The city's factory site commission, headed by A. S. Goldsborough, worked with local realtors to identify property suitable for industrial uses. Water supply was a critical factor for manufacturing firms. The mayor sought to meet this problem by finding waterfront sites for factories so that they could draw water directly from the Patapsco instead of relying on a more expensive supply from the city's reservoirs.[14]

The borough bill made its debut in the General Assembly at the 1912 session, where it quickly dropped from sight. A *Sun* reporter later suggested that Mayor Preston had merely been sending out "a feeler" to expose the measure's enemies and reveal potential allies.[15]

Preston's gradualist approach to annexation seems to have made headway among the suburbanites affected by it. The Hamilton Improvement Association invited him to speak about his plan at its annual dinner. George A. Frick, a banker and state legislator who had drafted the borough plan for Preston, promoted the proposal before the Pikesville Improvement Association and reported a favorable reception, not only among the area's residents, but from Roland Park and Highlandtown community leaders who had attended to learn about the borough plan. The Roland Park Civic League appointed a committee to review the proposal. It issued a strong, unanimous endorsement. And a meeting of the Homestead Improvement Association unanimously declared its support for Preston's proposal.[16]

Support also came from a number of city leaders and organizations. The Merchants' and Manufacturers' Association supported the plan from the time it became public. The City-Wide Congress—a progressive organization founded in 1911 to promote government efficiency, planning, and social reform—also endorsed the proposal, but urged that it should include a provision creating a metropolitan planning commission.[17]

Mayor Preston hitched his borough plan to an appeal for more equitable representation of the city in the General Assembly and more autonomy in the management of its affairs. He advanced his case for the city in a pamphlet—"Fair Play for Baltimore City: An Appeal to the Counties by the Mayor of Baltimore"—and embarked on a statewide speaking tour to stir up support for the city and the borough plan in the very backwaters of Maryland that produced the legislators who voted down the city's pleas for equitable representation and taxation.[18] The tour was timed to coincide with the state election campaign and provided Preston with a succession of opportunities to earn the good will of fellow Democratic politicians by promoting their election to the General Assembly, along with the borough plan.

The *Sun* never endorsed Preston's plan. It harbored a longstanding suspicion about members of the Ring and their works. Preston regarded the newspaper with similar mistrust. The *Sun* made his attacks on the paper a centerpiece of its coverage.[19] The mayor faced more potent opponents among the politicians of Baltimore County. His borough plan would take away their richest sources of revenue. Some of them had spoken out against the plan even before the bill was introduced in the house of delegates. County congressman J. F. C. Talbott attacked the plan because, he said, the borough residents would not have an opportunity to vote on it.[20] Since the proposal included an explicit provision for voter approval, Talbott may not have read it—or was confident that no one else would.

As Preston prepared the borough plan for its second appearance in the legislature, Talbott struck again. Like the *Sun*, Talbott accused Preston of using his appearances on behalf of the borough plan "to further his own political ambitions." The plan's prospects deteriorated rapidly thereafter. Ten days after Talbott's denunciation, the Roland Park Civic League met to consider its committee's unanimous endorsement of the borough proposal. According to the *Sun*, the vote went two-to-one against the mayor. (In January 1914, the league reversed its decision on the grounds that many of those who voted in October were not league members.) In November, the Confederated Improvement and Protective Associations of Baltimore County voted against boroughs. By December, Preston faced opposition within the city itself. One of Baltimore's state senators, William J. Ogden, attacked the borough plan because it would allow the boroughs "to get their hands into the city treasury" and drain reve-

counties. Ogden supported some extension of the city's boundaries, but he wanted to achieve it by simple annexation and on a much smaller scale than the borough plan.[21]

Shortly after the opening of the General Assembly's 1914 session, the *Sun* renewed its editorial assault on the borough plan. It repeated Senator Ogden's apprehensions that the boroughs would gain disproportionately at the city's expense, then went on to predict that the Ring and its minions would somehow control the borough commissions to secure "luscious 'pickings' for the 'asphalt kings' and other such politician-contractors," and a host of jobs for the Ring's dependents. By the end of the legislature's session, the paper reported that "the famous borough plan of enlarging Baltimore's boundaries was merrily and enthusiastically stomped to death in the House and never saw the light of day in the Senate."[22]

Preston continued to promote his boroughs, but even Field, his law partner and city solicitor, advised him to drop it.[23] The politically inventive plan remained a road not taken in the development of metropolitan Baltimore. It succeeded, however, in arousing a coalition for municipal expansion on both sides of the city line, and it made extension of the city's boundaries an ongoing issue in both local and state politics.

PRELUDE TO PROHIBITION

In 1912, as Mayor Preston and George Frick were shaping the borough plan, the Anti-Saloon League came to town. The league had been a presence in Maryland for some time and had already failed in its first attempt to get the state legislature to pass a local option bill that would allow individual counties, municipalities, or districts to vote themselves "dry." The league's Maryland superintendent, William H. Anderson, blamed his organization's defeat on "the pressure of the Baltimore machine."[24] Now he ventured into enemy territory to confront the machine's mayor, characterized in league publications as a pawn of the liquor interests. Anderson and two of his colleagues met with Preston when the league's local option proposal was headed toward its second outing before the General Assembly. The mayor claimed, implausibly, to be uninformed about local option. Anderson followed up by sending him a brief "digest" of the local option bill, along with a letter that was not brief.

While he disavowed any hostility toward Mayor Preston, Anderson noted that he was "not especially fond" of some of the mayor's supporters—in particular, the city's representatives in the General Assembly. There was also Sonny Mahon, who was reputed to accept large contributions from the liquor interests, but he stood outside the immediate range of the league's vengeance because he held no public office. The Anti-Saloon forces, wrote Anderson, did not charge Preston with responsibility for his political colleagues' fealty to the liquor industry. The mayor's silence on local option, however, created the impression that he stood with his organization's operatives in opposing the league's proposal. If he remained quiet on the subject, the temperance forces would hold him accountable for everything that the city's legislators did to block local option. Preston, as the machine's principal officeholder, would be an obvious target for the wrath of the drys. The league, said Anderson, did not expect Preston to come out in favor of prohibition. He need only announce "that questions of this kind ought to be handed back to the people" so that they could vote their localities dry if they wished. Behind the league's push for local option, Anderson warned, was the influence of Protestant churches. For a politician of Preston's evident ambition, Anderson's message was simple: "There is no political future for the man who becomes identified in the public mind with opposition to this movement."[25]

Preston remained noncommittal on local option, and Anderson wrote again, charging that the mayor was orchestrating the defeat of local option in the house of delegates and warning that the league was prepared to make this charge publicly in testimony before the House Temperance Committee. The letter carries Preston's handwritten notation, "No answer." Anderson wrote again advising Preston, "[you] might just as well come out into the open and have a run for your money, for unless you undo the damage you have already done, we are going to make your responsibility . . . so clear that the most unsophisticated will understand." The mayor responded not to Anderson but to the public at large, announcing that he had not asked any member of the General Assembly to oppose local option and that he would "take no part either for or against the Local Option bill." Preston responded to letter writers who supported the bill with the disingenuous claim that Anderson had asked him to "keep 'hands off' the matter."[26] In the General Assembly, local option died again.

CULTURE WARS

Baltimore was morally agitated about a variety of subjects other than strong drink. The proliferation of "moving picture parlors" provoked consternation. A parish priest wrote to the president of the council's first branch in 1911 to protest the opening of a movie house near his church and its school, because he deemed "such an enterprise detrimental to the morals of the youth under my charge." A slightly different complaint came from a Walbrook resident. Movies, he wrote, "foster too much the spirit of daydreaming, the unreal . . . Too many, otherwise bright and useful lives, are spoiled by their blighting influence." Hundreds of other Baltimoreans protested against the movies, not always for moral reasons, but with consistent outrage. They complained about "the annoyance and inconvenience that follow such a business." Others mixed moral and material complaints. Movie houses reduced property values, and also had a corrupting influence: "In former years the young had their minds influenced by getting hold of the dime novel and reading its contents in some out of the way place, but now in these modern days the moving picture machine has taken the place of the old dime novel, and we extend to them an invitation to do the very thing that we tried so hard to prevent."[27]

In these modern days, the city council approved a bill allowing Baltimoreans to play baseball on Sundays, igniting a furor in 1914 even more passionate than the moral anxiety prompted by moving picture parlors. On behalf of the Maryland Sons of the American Revolution, J. Frank Supplee announced his organization's opposition. "The character of this American Republic," he argued, was "based upon the moral obligation of a religious instinct and anything that lowers this standard will be deplored." Sunday baseball was deplorable. For the Society of the War of 1812, the pursuit of America's pastime on Sundays introduced a European decadence to Baltimore—"a Continental Sabbath"—that threatened to "loosen the discipline of parents over children" and "to create neighborhood disorder." The Fuller Memorial Baptist Sunday School, "a body of men, women, and children 525 strong," protested that Sunday baseball would "seriously erode the Spiritual development of those participating in such practices on the Lord's Day." And, in Hampden and Woodberry, two mill towns added to the city in 1888, a mass meeting of Protestant church congregations with 4,500 members entered an emphatic protest against the bill and expressed apprehension that "Sunday Amateur Baseball . . . is but the entering wedge for a wide open Sunday."[28]

According to city solicitor Field, it was doubtful whether the city council had the authority to make law on the subject. The state legislature had already spoken on the matter of Sunday pastimes, and the council could not contravene state law.[29]

Mayor Preston confided that he had no personal objection to Sunday baseball, and one of his aides, A. S. Goldsborough, suggested that he approve the council's proposed ordinance but announce that he was doing so only to "test the validity of the ordinance" in the courts. Preston declined to shift the decision to the judiciary. He sent Goldsborough the "great mass of letters and resolutions received from churches, Sunday schools, improvement associations, patriotic associations and individuals protesting against the establishment of Sunday baseball." Professional baseball, played on occasional Sundays, in one isolated stadium with high fences, might prove no great irritant to the opponents, wrote the mayor, but amateur baseball in most of the city's parks and empty lots would pose an immediate and weekly annoyance to rigorous observers of the Sabbath. He also had misgivings about what lay behind the support for Sunday baseball, because "the whole question has grown up in the last few weeks, and I am led to believe that there is some sinister purpose behind it," perhaps a "wide open" Sunday. Preston did not feel that he could approve the ordinance.[30]

His veto message to the council cited the solicitor's opinion about the legality of the ordinance, but also expressed apprehension that Sunday baseball might "open the doors for wide changes in our Sunday laws. Baltimore now has an orderly and quiet Sunday. In my judgment we should not do anything to bring about a change in these conditions until there has been a distinct expression of the people on the subject, either by a referendum or an election of City officials in which the issue could be determined."[31]

Preston's veto earned him a torrent of congratulatory letters from constituents and may have contributed to the ease of his reelection in 1915. In spite of the Anti-Saloon League's attacks, the mayor faced no opposition in the Democratic primary and easily defeated his opponent, a member of the city council's Republican minority. His defense of the Sabbath's sanctity may have blunted attempts to portray him as an agent of the "liquor interests."

COMBATING THE "SOCIAL EVIL"

The mayor managed to remain on the sidelines in another campaign for moral improvement until after his reelection. This movement targeted Baltimore's houses of
prostitution. In 1911, a Johns Hopkins physician, Donald Hooker, charged that at
least 296 brothels were operating in the city. Dr. Hooker's estimate was one finding
of a study conducted by his Committee on the Social Evil. The City-Wide Congress
had appointed the committee, and Hooker was its chairman. He complained that his
committee lacked the resources needed for an adequate examination of the problem, and its report recommended that the mayor appoint a city commission to investigate prostitution in Baltimore. The response came not from Mayor Preston but
from Maryland's Republican governor, Phillips Lee Goldsborough. Prostitution, after all, fell within the purview of the police department, and Baltimore's department
operated under commissioners appointed by the governor. Goldsborough created
the Maryland Commission on Vice in 1912 to investigate Baltimore's prostitution
problem and recommend remedies.[32]

The police had treated prostitution as a necessary evil in need of regulation rather
than a moral abomination demanding abolition. By local custom, each house of
ill fame in Baltimore was subject to one fine annually. A receipt for that payment
served as a license to operate without undue police interference until the time for
the next year's fine, an annual event known in the city's courts and police stations
as "Ladies' Day."[33] For years, the practice had provoked little outrage even among
members of the city's Society for the Suppression of Vice, which concentrated on the
evils of gambling and saloons and confined action against houses of prostitution to
cases in which neighbors complained.[34]

Two of Baltimore's reform associations, however, had redefined the issue of prostitution so as to support the argument for abolition rather than regulation. Hooker was a founder of the Maryland Society for Social Hygiene in 1908. The society
emphasized prostitution's threat to public health. Mere regulation of prostitution,
according to Hooker, would not reduce the spread of venereal diseases. Syphilis
and gonorrhea were difficult to detect and could not be controlled by periodic tests
of women who had multiple customers in the course of an evening. Abolition was
the only cure for the problem.[35] The Baltimore Women's Civic League, founded in
1911, focused on prostitution as a business and came to the same conclusion. Urbanization brought thousands of women into the city's workplaces, liberated from the
protective insularity of family homes and exposed to what a later generation would
call sexual harassment. The Women's Civic League was concerned not only with the
vulnerability of working women but with the transformation of prostitution in the
big-city economy. Like the monopolistic trusts that held sway over other industries,
"consolidated capital" might organize the market in vice and draw the growing supply of candidates for prostitution into vast new commercial enterprises catering to
male lust.[36] Regulation would only sanction the industrialization of vice. Abolition
was the only remedy.

In 1916, Governor Goldsborough's vice commission would issue its report on prostitution—a five-volume investigation that covered almost every detail of the business from the rents paid by brothels to the sexual sensations of their occupants, their earnings, amusements, religious denominations, personal cleanliness, family backgrounds, and venereal diseases. But the commission recommended action before completion of its report. In March 1915, almost a year before it issued its five volumes, it wrote to the police department to urge "a continued enforcement of police regulations" to shut down Baltimore's bordellos and "assignation houses."[37]

The commission may have rushed its recommendation to avoid being overtaken by events. In 1912, the Society for the Suppression of Vice had criticized the city's judges—the Baltimore Supreme Bench—for their failure to enforce statutes prohibiting prostitution. In a speech before the society's annual meeting, board member Charles J. Bonaparte charged that any judge interfering with enforcement of these laws should be impeached. As a former US attorney general, his words carried weight. The judges responded that they could enforce the law only when the police initiated prosecutions against the merchants of flesh. The judges thus succeeded in shifting the society's attention to the board of police commissioners, which responded with a crackdown on houses of prostitution. According to the Society for the Suppression of Vice, the last of the city's brothels was closed on September 12, 1915.[38]

The state vice commission detected the change in the municipal climate while still collecting evidence for its report. In 1914, the commission had assigned a woman as an undercover investigator to pose as someone interested in opening a "boarding house" that rented rooms to couples for short stays. She was to explain her plans to police officers, "but she told them that she would be extremely circumspect and that in acknowledgment of their . . . discretion, she would expect to pay them a certain amount of money." None of the policemen took up her offer, and most warned her against opening her business in the neighborhoods that they patrolled. Several mentioned that their superiors and the board of police commissioners had recently become much less tolerant of such arrangements. According to one, there "was a time when things could be fixed up but there was nothing doing now."[39]

Mayor Preston exploited the vice commission report to attack the state's control of his city's police force. Relying on an informant, the mayor charged a police lieutenant with drinking on duty and other unspecified offenses "unbecoming an officer." At trial before the board of police commissioners, the case against the lieutenant collapsed when the informant disowned his testimony on the grounds that he had provided it while drunk. Preston, before a hostile audience of police officers, "was subjected to probably the most unpleasant experience any mayor of Baltimore has known for years," according to the *Sun*. Rather than give ground, he simply shifted his attack from the police lieutenant to the police commissioners, citing the vice commission's report as evidence that the commissioners did not know what went on in the city or their department. According to the mayor, Daniel Loden, a Mahon loyalist and former district magistrate, had brought the problem of prostitution to the board's attention long before creation of the vice commission: "Judge Loden came in here to this particular Board—I think I am right—Judge Loden was not appointed by the Governor, but was elected by the people of the city of Balti-more . . . He told you these things were widespread in this community. Did you look it up? Did you take one step to correct it?"[40]

Preston was explicit about his intentions. He was determined, he said, to end state control of his city's police department: "The government of the police force . . . is fundamentally wrong. It ought to be in the hands of the people of Baltimore, not the Governor of Maryland . . . and I am going to be on the job to see it is corrected, and that the police of Baltimore is run by the people of Baltimore."[41] In fact, the adjustment would not be made for almost 60 years after Preston left his job as mayor.

Chapter 28 **WORLD WAR AND MUNICIPAL CONQUEST**

B Y THE TIME MAYOR PRESTON staged his confrontation with the police commissioners, the country was waging war in Europe, and Baltimore's moral climate became the business of the federal government. The secretary of war, Newton Baker, wrote to the mayor requesting that no illicit diversions should tempt the recruits in military training camps around the city, especially amusements likely to spread sexually transmitted diseases. Baltimore's recent efforts to suppress vice and preserve the Sabbath undoubtedly figured in Preston's confident assurance "that there is not a house of prostitution in Baltimore." Local liquor laws, he added, included a prohibition against the sale of alcoholic liquors to sailors or soldiers in uniform.[1]

Half a century earlier, the Civil War had divided Baltimore. Its politicians had responded by trying, in vain, to isolate local politics from national politics. This war was clearly different. It would eventually sweep the city into a national mobilization that, according to Sherry Olson, "diminished Baltimorean identity."[2] But, initially, the city's politicians were reluctant to take sides in the European conflict. In mid-1915, Mayor Preston joined William Howard Taft's "League of Peace." In Preston's view, "the jingoe [sic] of today is the worst enemy of our country . . . Let us tend to our own business." He supported Henry Ford's ill-conceived mission to end the war by international mediation, and he declined an invitation to become a vice-president of the Maryland League for National Defense because he was "unwilling . . . to join in the hysteria of the present time toward military armament." Only one month before President Wilson urged Congress to declare war, Preston was still against universal military training and "opposed to war or militarism in the United States, Germany, France, England, or anywhere."[3]

Neutrality was not just a matter of international relations. Baltimore had a significant population of German immigrants and German Americans, and the city's ideological and ethnic schisms provided the raw material for civil disorder. A meeting of pacifists in April 1917 triggered a riot when attacked by a mob of young men ready to join the Allies in the trenches.[4]

Once the United States entered the war, Preston's most immediate concern was to keep peace at home. He urged Baltimoreans to do what they could "to prevent any disorder and to preserve the fair name of our beloved city." The president and Congress had declared war against Germany, and the time had passed "for any American citizen to discuss the subject." "The place to fight," he continued, "is in the Army of the United States . . . and not in our homes or streets or public gathering places." There was no room in the city "for anyone who wants to take sides with the German Imperial government." Baltimoreans of "German birth or descent, who are loyal to our country and the Stars and Stripes . . . may feel secure from any harm or injury . . . from citizens of other lineage."[5]

Between 1914 and 1917, the local German press energetically backed the Central Powers and predicted their victory. But a week after America's declaration of war, the German-language *Baltimore Correspondent* published a statement in English above its masthead affirming its status as an American newspaper. Its turn toward patriotic Americanism failed to save it. After 77 years of publication, the paper went out of business in 1918. Clubs, churches, and other German organizations dissolved. Two months before the armistice, the Baltimore City Council voted to change the name of a major downtown thoroughfare from German Street to Redwood Street, named after the first Maryland officer to be killed in France.[6]

BALTIMORE'S BATTLE PLANS

The municipal side effects of total war did not distract Preston from his continuing campaign to increase the city's autonomy and territory. A constitutional amendment granting a modest increase in home rule was introduced by Baltimore legislators in 1914 and approved by the voters in 1915. It allowed Baltimore and Maryland's 23 counties to amend their charters without seeking state approval, so long as they did not extend their powers beyond those granted by the legislature. Since the amendment added nothing to municipal authority, neither the mayor nor the city solicitor, Steven S. Field, regarded it as a significant opportunity to enhance city government.[7]

Preston was more immediately concerned about the state constitution than the city's charter. In 1915, he proposed a constitutional convention to address the state government's financial problems. Preston charged that a succession of state deficits might be brought to an end if Maryland adopted a centralized budget process that matched expenditures to expected revenues, instead of the "harum-scarum way we have been passing appropriation measures . . . no one knowing exactly where the money is to come from." He recommended the creation of a "board of control" to prepare state budgets, much as the city's board of estimates proposed annual budgets to the city council.[8]

The mayor's call for a convention roused opposition that had little to do with budgets, stemming instead from suburban anxieties about municipal expansion. A newspaper in Towson, just north of the city line, charged that the city hoped to gain through a constitutional convention what it could not get from the state legislature: "a larger representation in Annapolis, a larger proportion of State taxes, and freedom from control by the State Government, and incidentally the privilege of enlarging its boundaries from time to time without the consent of the persons in the annexed territory."[9]

Strong support for the mayor came from a Democratic gubernatorial candidate, US Senator Blair Lee. Lee endorsed not only the constitutional convention but Preston's proposal for state budgetary reform and extension of Baltimore's boundaries. Lee, however, was defeated in the Democratic primary, and the party convention was silent on a new state constitution. It did pass a resolution favoring Baltimore's annexation of suburban territory. The measure was the work of Frank Furst, a popular elder statesman in Democratic politics.[10]

Furst, a German immigrant, had risen from obscurity to wealth, prominence, and local renown. A longtime friend of both Arthur Gorman and Freeman Rasin, he had often been singled out as a favored prospect for public office—at least once for the governorship—but never campaigned for any office more elevated than delegate to national Democratic conventions. Furst was the superintendent of grain elevators for the Northern Central Railroad, and after retiring from the railroad started a dredging business that won contracts to maintain the depth of Baltimore's harbor and eventually grew into the Arundel Corporation, a company that worked on canals and ship channels around the world and expanded into the sand and gravel business. Furst also had extensive landholdings in Curtis Bay, a mixed residential and industrial tract on the waterfront southwest of Baltimore and just outside the city limits in Anne Arundel County. It was an area to which Baltimore had long banished "undesirable" land uses—gambling houses that sold liquor on Sundays, chemical and fertilizer plants, and a "pest house" for victims of an 1871 smallpox epidemic. After 1900, black migrants from the South who were unable to find housing in Baltimore landed in nearby Fairfield. Under Furst's annexation plan, all this would become part of the city.[11]

It was said that "no other man in the State" was "so well known personally as Mr. Furst," and no other man numbered "so many acquaintances and friends among all sorts and conditions of men." Though not an officeholder, he helped his friends win offices. In 1915, he chaired the gubernatorial campaign committee for Emerson Harrington, the Democratic state comptroller who defeated Preston's candidate Blair Lee in the party's primary. Harrington had run almost as much against Preston as against Lee. He warned Maryland's Democratic voters that a Lee victory might mean that the state would be "run from City Hall," and he came out against annexation for Baltimore, winning the support of voters in Anne Arundel and Baltimore counties, which he carried by substantial margins.[12] He also carried the city, though more narrowly, perhaps because his campaign manager was so popular there. He went on to win a narrow victory in the general election against Republican governor Goldsborough. According to the *Sun*, Furst had "antagonized some of his closest friends by refusing to go with the city machine in the primary" in support of Blair

Mayor James H. Preston, a product of the city's Democratic machine. He proved unexpectedly innovative in his approach to extending Baltimore's boundaries and made unexpected allies among the Protestant clergy.

Lee. But the antagonism faded because the "Democratic party understands very well that it owes its escape from defeat in the November election to [Furst's] straightforward and honest attitude and his uncompromising independence."[13]

Furst called Mayor Preston and the president of the council's second branch to a conference at his home on Thanksgiving Day, 1915, to work out the details of the annexation provision that Furst would propose for the Democratic Party platform. Their proposal would extend the city limits in all directions to a distance of five miles from the center of Baltimore. Furst urged Preston to "put aside the hostility which has prevailed between the state people and the city administration," and he assured the mayor that Governor Harrington was prepared to treat the city fairly. Preston gave Furst full authority to represent the interests of the city on annexation and agreed to support any plan that Furst approved. Unlike the mayor's earlier borough plan, Furst's proposal pointedly omitted a provision for a vote on annexation by the residents of areas to be absorbed. The mayor agreed that leaving the decision to the suburbanites would only "mean marching up the hill and marching back down again."[14]

The opposition's response was swift and hard. Less than three weeks after the conference at Furst's home, the newly formed Anti-Annexation Association of Baltimore County was soliciting funds for a campaign against the city's expansion. The group sought support not only from residents in the area to be annexed but from

of the City limits would cut about sixty million dollars . . . off the assessable basis of
Baltimore County, and necessarily greatly increase the present county tax rate over
the entire County." The group issued a special appeal to the mostly working-class
residents of Canton and Highlandtown, just east of the city, claiming (without evidence) that annexation would triple their tax bills.[15]

While Furst and Field drafted the city's annexation bill, the City-Wide Congress
was writing one of its own. The chairman of its annexation committee was state
senator William J. Ogden, who had earlier promoted his own annexation proposal
in opposition to Mayor Preston's borough plan. He persuaded his committee to proceed with its annexation proposal independently of the mayor. It differed from the
plan drafted by Furst and Field in leaving Anne Arundel County intact, an omission
that left crucial stretches of waterfront in Curtis Bay outside the city's jurisdiction.
The Ogden committee also required that annexation be approved by a majority of
voters in the territory to be annexed.[16]

ANNEXATION AT LAST

During the 1916 legislative session, the Furst and Ogden annexation bills were referred to the Senate Committee on Judicial Proceedings. Its chairman was Senator Ogden. The mayor and other supporters of the Furst annexation bill were now
engaged in a two-front war. They had to overcome resistance to annexation in the
counties—Baltimore and Anne Arundel—while trying to defeat the annexation
proposal of Ogden and the City-Wide Congress.[17]

State legislators from districts beyond Baltimore could hardly be expected to
support an annexation bill if the city's own representatives disagreed on what they
wanted. Furst rushed to Annapolis to take charge of the negotiations for the proposal that he and Field had designed. He was preceded by Mayor Preston and almost
150 of the city's businessmen, who boarded a special train for the state capital to
promote the Furst bill before the Committee on Judicial Proceedings. Baltimore
County congressman J. F. C. Talbott, critic of Mayor Preston's borough bill, also took
off for Annapolis to defeat annexation.[18]

Furst and Talbott met with Governor Harrington separately, trying to pull him in
opposite directions on the annexation issue. But the governor was evasive. According to the *Sun*, "when the Governor does not want to make up his mind he can sit
longer and misunderstand oftener and ask more irrelevant questions than any man
in the civilized world." The governor finally decided that his attachments to Congressman Talbott and Dr. George Wells, the Democratic leader of Anne Arundel
County, precluded his endorsement of the Furst annexation plan, even though Furst
"did more to nominate and elect the Governor than any other man." But he would
support an annexation bill that gave Baltimore the entire harbor and its waterfront,
including the sections currently lying in Baltimore and Anne Arundel counties.[19]

The governor's response made political sense. The annexation pledge in the
Democratic platform had declared the party's support for "legislation that will secure to the City of Baltimore complete control of the harbor and will best promote

the commercial and industrial welfare of the city." In his appeal to the legislature, Mayor Preston had emphasized the city's interest in the waterfront. He sought to bring its members to his side by inviting all of them on an inspection tour of the harbor onboard the city's "ice-boat," the *Ferdinand Latrobe*. The trip took place in a driving snowstorm, but the participants seem to have been drawn into some sort of unanimity. They ended the chilly cruise with a rendition of "Maryland, My Maryland," followed by "The Star-Spangled Banner."[20]

Control of the harbor was clearly central to the case for annexation, and a Baltimore delegate, William Purnell Hall, introduced yet another annexation bill that took in the entire harbor but added nothing beyond the city's North Avenue boundary. The governor embraced Hall's bill. Furst later brushed it aside as a "counterfeit" and an "insult to the city." He must have expected more from the governor whose election he had worked so hard to achieve, and he abandoned Annapolis without making any further public statement.[21]

Furst was soon back in the capital for one last thrust. He met again with Governor Harrington, who reportedly told him that, while he could not endorse Furst's bill, he would not intervene to defeat it. Furst "believed there was still a ray of hope and that he would not quit the fight as long as he could see that ray." The fight would be a fierce one. Senator Ogden stood firmly behind his own bill and, just after Furst's return to Annapolis, took the senate floor to deliver a long speech on its behalf. Just offstage, Congressman Talbott likened the annexation of Baltimore County to the German invasion of Belgium.[22]

In a desperate attempt to win acceptance for annexation, Solicitor Field announced that the city was prepared to amend its bill so that the extension of its boundaries would be submitted to statewide referendum. The change would allow legislators to avoid responsibility for the outcome, but Field justified it as recognition that the issue should be regarded "not as a mere local matter" to be decided by the voters in the territory to be annexed, "but as a statewide matter." At 4 a.m. on March 31, the advocates of annexation finally broke the opposition's filibuster and forced a senate vote on their bill, with its new provision for a statewide referendum. The result must have come as a shock. The annexation bill was recommitted to the Committee on Judicial Proceedings by a vote of 14 to 13. Two of Governor Harrington's adherents from the Eastern Shore had switched sides at the last moment.[23]

The outcome revived the old Baltimore animus against the government in Annapolis, a vein of rancor that stretched back to the regime of the Lords Baltimore. A bitter editorial in the *Sun* promised retribution and delivered a scorching attack on the legislature, the state Democratic Party, and Governor Harrington—especially Harrington. "Every consideration of right and fairness should have dictated his support of a proper annexation bill . . . all considerations of political expediency and personal interest urged him in the same direction . . . Yet he sits quietly by while the annexation bill is being done to death by grossly unfair tactics." The paper also observed that the legislative session had approved a $2.5 million bond issue for highways. Baltimore, with 50 percent of the state's population generating 70 percent of the state's tax revenue, would get only 20 percent of the proceeds. Once again, the Annapolis politicians had made Baltimore "the Goat."[24]

Frank Furst, though a declared Democratic loyalist, hinted that the party's violation of its platform pledge to Baltimore might lead the city's loyal Democrats to mistrust their party in the future—perhaps to renounce it.[25] Solicitor Field went a bit further, ridiculing the state Democratic candidates who made campaign promises to be "fair to Baltimore," only to increase the city's tax burdens and prevent its expansion. "The only way this city will ever get what it is entitled to is to form a non-partisan league that will put the interest of the city above party and demand justice for Baltimore."[26]

Field promptly made good on his suggestion. Days after defeat of the annexation bill, he won approval from the city's board of estimates to organize a "Greater Baltimore League" to carry on the struggle for city expansion. By the end of April 1916, the league—now called the Greater Baltimore Non-Partisan League—had signed up the East Baltimore Businessmen's Association, and Field had handed out membership cards at a luncheon of the City Club after giving a speech on annexation.[27] Field's declared intention to appeal for support without regard to party meant that the city solicitor could proselytize and enlist recruits even where Republicans congregated.

Other unlikely allies may have been drawn to the annexation struggle by Mayor Preston's early stand against Sunday baseball. W. W. Davis, general secretary of the Lord's Day Alliance, offered to bring in "one preacher from each county and put the organization of annexation up to them." Preston was wary of the ministers. Some were "tied up with the Anti-Saloon League"—reason enough to "doubt their sincerity"—but Preston wrote that he would be glad to meet with Davis's "friends any day to talk over the matter" of annexation.[28]

By the end of August 1917, the league—now called the Non-Partisan Greater Baltimore Extension League—had 10,000 members. Its membership chairman reported that most league members lived in Baltimore, but almost 1,000 had been recruited "in the counties."[29]

The City-Wide Congress, however, remained hostile. At its annual meeting in 1916, congress president A. R. L. Dohme charged that his organization's annexation bill had been dragged down to defeat by the city administration's bill—"a hodgepodge of the worst possible kind, and behind it, besides, was the game of politics, in which Frank A. Furst played a very prominent part."[30]

ROYAL FAMILY FEUDS

As the annexation controversy subsided, another kind of dispute threatened to fracture the core of the local Democratic machine. Baltimoreans referred to its central figures as the "Royal Family." Even Mayor Preston was excluded from this inner circle. Its patriarch was John J. "Sonny" Mahon, with a knowledgeable grasp of the entire city's politics at the ward level. His lieutenants included Daniel "Little Danny" Loden, the commissioner of water rents and taxes, city hall patronage broker, and first among equals in the Nineteenth Ward. Loden endeared himself to Freeman

Rasin by shifting his ward from the Republican to the Democratic column. Another member of the Family was Robert "Paving Bob" Padgett, restored to good standing as one of the city's favored contractors and apparent legatee of Boss Rasin's Seventh Ward. Finally, there was Frank Kelly. His base was in Southwest Baltimore's Eighteenth Ward and its United Democratic Club, but his influence often extended into the Sixteenth, and he would eventually contest control of wards across the city. Kelly held court in the backyard of his home at 1100 West Saratoga Street, but he was an obscure presence in the Royal Family. Virtually illiterate and publicity-shy, he stood in Mahon's shadow, not just because of his educational deficiencies, but because he ran a saloon on the shady side of the law.[31]

Kelly was clearly dissatisfied with his standing in the Royal Family and dreamed of ruling an independent kingdom of his own, perhaps in the unobtrusive style of Freeman Rasin. One of the first hints that he was turning against the Family came in 1915, when Kelly was rumored to be backing a candidate of his own for city council in the Seventh Ward, in opposition to the incumbent, who was Robert Padgett's man. Kelly's candidate won the primary, and his adherents defeated council candidates backed by Mayor Preston in two other wards as well.[32]

Kelly's next move came later that year in the gubernatorial primary, when the Mahon machine endorsed Senator Blair Lee. Kelly was at first noncommittal, then announced for Emerson Harrington just a few days before the September primary. Though the move had been a subject of speculation for months, the *Sun* hyperventilated: it was "the most sensational event of the entire campaign, and one of the most sensational in the political history of Baltimore in decades." The Mahon forces, however, "lassoed him, threw him, applied the brand again," and by late evening Kelly told the *Sun* that he was once again a Mahonite. He did not stay lassoed for long; later the same evening, he told the *Baltimore American* that stories of his recantation were empty rumors. For almost a year, Kelly had managed to keep politicians guessing about his intentions, and he continued to do so up to the last possible moment, when he issued orders to his ward leaders and precinct workers to turn out their voters for Harrington. Danny Loden pronounced him the "Judas Iscariot of the Democratic organization"—also the Benedict Arnold, the Brutus, and the Catiline. But by helping Harrington to carry Baltimore, Kelly put himself and his friends in line for gubernatorial patronage.[33]

The local machine's venture into nonpartisan politics in the cause of annexation had undermined party solidarity. Baltimore's machine drew closer to local Republican businessmen and "dry" clergymen while distancing itself from the state Democratic Party, which had reneged on its pledge to extend Baltimore's boundaries. Frank Kelly took advantage of the estrangement between city and state Democrats to form an independent alliance with Governor Harrington and to build his own organization outside the Royal Family circle. On one issue, however, Kelly stood with his former friends. He assembled his adherents in his backyard on an evening in late August 1917 and told them "to line up . . . for the Annexation bill of the Greater Baltimore Extension League." He may have supported annexation as a matter of policy, or he may have calculated that sentiment for annexation was so powerful in Baltimore that no candidate could survive without endorsing it.[34]

The day after Kelly's backyard assembly, 150 Democrats and Republicans gathered for a luncheon meeting at the headquarters of what was now called the Greater Baltimore Nonpartisan Extension League. They were members of the league's campaign committee, assembled to make plans for the state primary in September and the legislative session that followed, when the city administration would once again present a bill to expand Baltimore's territory. Mayor Preston reminded his bipartisan audience that annexation was a nonpartisan cause. "The business and well-thinking people of the city and the State are behind it." He immediately demonstrated the irrelevance of party by launching a fierce attack against fellow Democrat William Purnell Hall, a "traitor" to the city whose "counterfeit" annexation bill had helped to sidetrack the city administration's proposal during the last session of the General Assembly. His heated denunciation of the Democratic delegate put Preston at odds with his political patron Sonny Mahon, who supported Delegate Hall's renomination.[35]

Solicitor Field delivered an impassioned speech warning the league members that if they were defeated again, the next opportunity for annexation might not come along for another generation. It had been almost 30 years, after all, since the 1888 annexation. The meeting's presiding officer, Republican E. Clay Timanus, praised Democrat Field as "the best informed man in Maryland on the subject of annexation and the man best fitted to represent the league in the next Legislature." Field had become a candidate in the Democratic primary for the house of delegates so that he could carry the case for annexation to the floor of the General Assembly. He contested the seat occupied by William Purnell Hall.[36]

RESOLUTION AND DISSOLUTION

The city's annexation bill would face its first test at the state Democratic convention in September 1917. Mayor Preston thought the "question of city extension" would "probably be determined by the platform declarations of the two parties." The Republicans were likely to endorse the bill proposed by the city. If the Democrats did the same, then the issue would be "removed from the campaign" and the election would be "contested upon issues which divide the two parties, as it should be." If the Democratic platform fell short on annexation, it would open a schism between Baltimore Democrats and Democrats outside the city limits. Preston was pessimistic about his party's prospects.[37]

The Democrats met and delivered what the *Sun* termed "a mocking denial" of the city's annexation demand. Backed by Congressman Talbott of Baltimore County and Dr. Wells of Anne Arundel County, the proposal declared the party's support for annexation, but required that the city's expansion be approved by the voters in the territory to be annexed—and so virtually ensured the proposal's rejection. Preston called it a "covert attempt to kill any city extension legislation." The Republican state convention approved a platform that endorsed the city's plan.[38]

The mayor turned against his own party: "We arraign the Democratic State organization . . . as an enemy of the public welfare of the State of Maryland." Preston was in no mood for restraint. The state Democrats, he said, had won control of Maryland in 1915 "by the votes of Baltimore City, upon a promise to give the city a reasonable and fair extension of its limits, and violated that promise." They had allied themselves with the politicians of Anne Arundel and Baltimore counties "and with those who fatten upon the law breaking and vice that infests certain sections near the city's limits."[39]

Attached to the mayor's denunciation are several pages of handwritten notes signed by Preston. They quote a passage from the *American Cyclopedia* of 1863 citing the provincial assembly's legislation of 1745 that annexed Jones Town to Baltimore and, in particular, its inclusion of "an express provision that there was nothing in the act recognizing a right to 'elect delegates to the Assembly as representatives of the town.'" Preston underlined the next sentence: "*This was the earliest manifestation of the singular jealousy which has ever since been shown in the Legislature by the Maryland County members against the City of Baltimore.*"[40]

Baltimore was not the only city confronting a state legislature in which representation tilted toward rural communities and interests. A few states even controlled municipal police departments. Missouri, for example, took over the St. Louis police department in 1860 and did not return it to municipal control until 2013.[41] Since Baltimore was a free-standing unit of government, outside the jurisdiction of any county, it might be expected to enjoy a high degree of autonomy. But instead of being subject to a county's authority, Baltimore was vulnerable to interference from the more distant state authorities. In addition to the police department, the state controlled the board of police examiners, the board of election supervisors, and the liquor licensing board, and though the mayor and council appointed the members of the park board, the state determined its budget. The office of legislative reference, established by the city in 1906 to do research on pending legislation, was taken over by the state in 1916.[42] Preston's underlined sentence from the *Cyclopedia* highlighted what was singular about the General Assembly's "singular jealousy" toward Baltimore: it began long before the town became a city. It was a condition of the town's existence, part of its civic identity.[43]

In another setback for the mayor, Delegate Hall defeated Solicitor Field in the Democratic primary. Field attributed his loss to the "unexpected strength of Frank Kelly," who had backed Hall against the city administration's champion. Like Kelly, however, Hall had endorsed the administration's annexation proposal, abandoning the bill he had introduced in the previous session of the legislature and leaving Field's campaign without a clear line of attack. Proponents of annexation also prevailed in the general election, but it was a curious victory for the city's Democratic mayor. Two-thirds of Baltimore's representatives in the house of delegates were now Republicans. Republicans were also within one vote of controlling the state senate.[44]

Though its opponents tried to prevent a vote, annexation passed the house of delegates by almost two to one, thanks to the Republican members' unanimous adherence to their platform pledge on the issue. The senate vote was just as lopsided. Governor Harrington delayed signing the bill as long as possible, but after stating his reservations, finally approved it.[45] Mayor Preston and his city had won a momentous victory that added 75,000 to 100,000 to its population, doubled its land area, and extended its authority over the waters of the harbor.[46]

The Democratic Party was a wreck. Frank Furst had seen it coming. He had said little in public during the final round of the annexation fight. After the victory of the annexation bill in the house, but before the vote in the senate, a reporter asked Furst if he might say a few words in support of the cause. "No," said Furst, "I'll be damned if I will . . . I'm not going to humiliate myself any further by begging men to do what it is their duty to their party and their State to do . . . If they want to go ahead and wreck their party and ruin all chances of party success they can do it for all I care."[47]

Chapter 29

CIVIL SERVICE AND PROHIBITION

HAVING LOST THEIR BATTLE in the Maryland General Assembly, the opponents of annexation challenged expansion of Baltimore City in the courts, but the city's possession of its former suburbs stood undisturbed. Mayor Preston was not so fortunate. Though originally elected as a Democratic warhorse, he had so scrambled the bonds of party during his long campaign of municipal imperialism that he had unraveled the political network on which he depended and sacrificed control of the grander city that he now governed. Republicans had won annexation for him, and their next step was to refashion the character of his city. A new city charter was submitted to the voters in November 1918. Its principal feature was civil service reform.

Under the home-rule amendment adopted in 1915, the city could amend its own charter.[1] The mayor and city council could begin the process of revision by nominating a charter commission for voters' approval. But the amendment also allowed Baltimore's citizens to place a charter commission on the ballot by petition of 10,000 registered voters. A committee of the City-Wide Congress collected the requisite number of signatures. The commission nominated by the congress included William J. Ogden, former city solicitor Edgar Allan Poe, the president of the Merchants' and Manufacturers' Association, an assortment of respected judges and attorneys, medical and academic luminaries from Johns Hopkins University and Hospital, and portrait photographer David Bachrach—but no party politicians.[2] The city's voters put the commission to work on a new charter in November 1917. The home-rule amendment did not permit the commission to endow the municipal government with any powers beyond those granted by the state legislature, but within those limits it could amend the city charter without submitting the changes to the General Assembly.[3]

The central provision of the proposed charter created the City Service Commission to oversee the hiring and promotion of all city employees not appointed by the mayor and city council. Both political parties would be represented on the commission, and its members would clas-

Preston Gardens, an early venture in slum clearance. Mayor Preston proposed it as a means to replace a concentration of African American housing in close proximity to the central business district and city hall. *Courtesy Enoch Pratt Free Library*

sify all city jobs. For those in the "competitive class," the commission would design a system of examinations.[4]

Baltimore's Democratic and Republican organizations both opposed the new charter; its merit system might destroy the patronage system on which they fed. In fact, as Joseph Arnold observed, the merit system posed no great threat to the spoils system. The level of competence required for municipal employment was not beyond the reach of most party activists. Civil service regulations might, however, impede a new administration's efforts to rid itself of an old administration's appointees. Sonny Mahon later complained about the difficulty of sustaining his political organization with "a law that keeps a lot of Republicans in office after you win an election . . . The people don't want that. That isn't what they vote for, and it's against all principles of our government."[5]

Frank Furst found little that was objectionable about the new charter. He abandoned his Democratic friends and supported it. The voters did the same, approving the new charter by more than three to one. It carried all but one of the city's wards.[6]

DEMOCRATIC DOWNFALL

In April 1919, Mayor Preston wrote to architect Thomas Hastings in New York, urging him to complete his comprehensive plan for the city. Among other projects, Hastings designed a widening of St. Paul Street that included a park and a sunken garden, just blocks from city hall and the courthouse. The new development replaced a neighborhood of black Baltimoreans that threatened to envelop the city center and surround the seat of municipal government. Preston described the area as "stagnant and out of touch with its vicinity." He ordered the homes to be leveled—an early exercise in slum clearance. The civic amenities that replaced them would eventually be known as Preston Gardens. Preston wanted his plan for the city as a whole to take effect as soon as possible. His letter to Hastings explained why. "We had bad luck last week, and we will have a new Mayor down here about the first of May."[7]

Preston had not even been able to get past the Democratic primary. He had lost by 4,000 votes, and once again it was his struggle to achieve annexation that helped to defeat him. The residents of the newly annexed territory voted solidly against him and, according to the *Baltimore Sun*, his opponent in the primary enjoyed the backing of the state Democratic organization, which had fought Preston on the issue of annexation. Yet the hostile *Sun* had been moved to enhance its estimate of the mayor in spite of his ties to the Mahon machine. Preston sent his last annual message to the city council in the autumn of 1918. Without abandoning its animosities toward the Ring, the *Sun* paused to pay him a kind of tribute. It expressed "a certain measure of respect for the turbulent genius" whose "record of achievement . . . evidences very clearly that the present boss of City Hall is really the boss."[8]

Preston's Democratic challenger was George Weems Williams, who enjoyed not just the backing of the state party organization but the support of Frank Kelly and his local Democratic insurgency. Williams was a Baltimore aristocrat and one of the city's leading attorneys. His family owned a steamboat company, and he was educated in private schools and at Princeton. His campaign for mayor was his first and only descent into electoral politics. Though he prevailed in the Democratic primary, he came up short in the general election against Republican William F. Broening.

Broening was no aristocrat. He grew up in South Baltimore's Fifteenth Ward, one of 10 children of German immigrant parents. His father was a tailor, and Broening left public school after the primary grades to add to the family's income. His first job was in the office of a company that made and sold stoves. He later became an apprentice in its manufacturing operation and for four years learned to be a sheet-iron worker and coppersmith. In the evenings after work he would read law books; he eventually left the stove factory for the University of Maryland Law School, graduating in 1897 at the age of 27. In the same year, the Fifteenth Ward elected Broening to the first branch of the city council, as a Republican. One of his early accomplishments as a councilman was an ordinance establishing a municipal "subway" system. It carried no passengers but provided a network of conduits beneath the streets that carried electrical, telegraph, and telephone lines, reducing the need for aboveground wires and utility poles. The rental fees for space in the conduits became a significant source of municipal revenue.[9]

Broening left the city council after one term to serve in the house of delegates for one term, then became secretary to Republican congressman George Wachter, and in 1911 he won the first of two terms as state's attorney of Baltimore. In the Republican mayoral primary of 1919, he faced no opposition. He portrayed his Democratic opponent as the agent of the state party organization and warned that election of the Democrat might strengthen the state's hand in the management of Baltimore's affairs. Williams, according to Broening, was also the creature of corporate power. As an attorney, he had represented railroads that laid claim to city streets and petitioned the municipality to provide space for sidings and terminals.[10]

A *Sun* columnist suggested that Broening lacked an independent program and that he conducted his campaign by matching the moves of his opponent: "If Mr. Williams offers the people an issue today, does Mr. Broening bite his fingernails and walk the floor, and finally decide to tell the people there is nothing in that? Not at all! Not at all! He calmly steps to the front the next day or the day after that, and tells the people the same thing Mr. Williams had told them before . . . What is more William F. Broening has his fingers in the armholes of his waistcoat and his face plainly shows that he is saying to himself: 'Come on, you George Weems Williams! Come on and try to say something I cannot repeat! Dare you, dare you, dare you.' "[11]

Broening began his campaign with an appreciation of Mayor Preston's record. Preston's "sole thought," he said, was "in developing Baltimore, and through his aggressive efforts he has pushed to a successful conclusion many improvements begun under his predecessors, and initiated others." His "great outstanding achievement," of course, was expansion of Baltimore by annexation, which he accomplished only with Republican support.[12]

It was politically convenient for Republicans to praise Preston and his record. In the Democratic primary, Williams had run against the mayor's record. Exalting Preston diminished Williams. And Preston's record was substantial. In addition to annexation, Preston could claim much of the credit for founding the Baltimore Symphony Orchestra and almost all the credit for construction of the municipal auditorium and War Memorial Plaza, which stretched out in front of the auditorium, styled by some civic boosters as Baltimore's own Place Vendôme. He also played an early role in creation of the Baltimore Museum of Art. He buried the troublesome Jones Falls under a new thoroughfare, the Fallsway, and wrapped another major artery, Key Highway, around the base of Federal Hill and across Locust Point. Former Republican mayor Timanus went so far as to deplore the defeat of Preston in the Democratic primary. It is unlikely, however, that the Republicans would have preferred to face Preston in the general election. Their embrace of the defeated mayor seemed calculated to win over the Democrats who backed Preston in the primary.[13]

Democratic city councilman William Purnell Hall, like the *Sun*, noted Broening's tendency to echo the positions of his opponent and characterized his campaign as "silly." Hall observed that during his two terms as state's attorney, Broening had never tried a case on his own. The *Sun* seemed to agree with Hall's assessment when it noted that Broening was "never thought of as an able man."[14] He seemed a step down in political stature from Mayor Preston.

Broening's victory was a surprise. Even his fellow Republicans had not expected it. The day before the election, the betting odds had run two to one against him. But his success was decisive. He led Williams by almost 10,000 votes of a total of 111,000, one of the heaviest turnouts in the town's history. The *Sun* pronounced it "the most remarkable of any election held in Baltimore in a generation," but could not account for its outcome. The paper could only surmise that voters favored Broening because he "worked his way to the front from humble origins." At the time of Broening's death, in 1953, the *Sun* would recall that he was "certainly not the liveliest mayor." His two terms in office were "placid, even sluggish," but he was "the best-loved of Baltimore mayors" in the twentieth century. "Everyone liked him."[15]

Heavy turnout among black voters certainly contributed to Broening's triumph, though it may not fully explain the election's outcome. Black Republican candidates won two seats in the first branch of the city council, more than at any previous election. Broening won both of these council districts by margins greater than expected.[16] Yet he seems to have done little to attract black voters. The Democrats, however, did much to alienate them.

Albert Ritchie, Maryland's Democratic attorney general, delivered a speech in Baltimore warning white voters that "if Mr. Broening is elected Mayor, not only will negroes be appointed as laborers and in other branches of the city service, but because of the merit system, which goes into effect on January 1, 1920, it may be perfectly possible for them to stay there indefinitely."[17] Mayor Preston did even more to turn away black voters. Long before the *Afro-American* criticized Preston for leveling black housing to make way for Preston Gardens, it called attention to his conduct at the commencement exercises of the city's black high school, where he handed out diplomas but avoided shaking hands with the graduates. Finally, one young woman managed to slip her hand into Preston's; the black audience erupted in applause. During his campaign for reelection in 1919, while addressing an audience of ship caulkers, Preston had asked those who supported his reelection to raise their hands. When he noticed that some black workers had raised theirs, he added that he was speaking only to the white men. A full year before the election campaign began, the *Afro* announced that "eight years of Preston's 'lily white' government is enough," and before there were any other candidates to support, the paper decided that it wanted "NO MORE PRESTON."[18]

Mayor Broening may have regarded his black support as more burden than bonus. In 1922, he would erase the impression that he was the favorite of Baltimore's black voters. Against the protests of black clergymen, he authorized a Ku Klux Klan parade through the city.[19]

THE CIVIC AGENDA

Mayor Preston managed to unveil his comprehensive plan for the city and its newly annexed territory just before the inauguration of his successor. It was a close thing. A box carrying the final map of the future city, though nine feet long, had somehow gone astray in the mail between the New York architects and Preston's city plan commission. He was able to publish the commission report with maps and drawings just before he left office.[20] Mayor Broening's inaugural address held little beyond Preston's plans. Broening acknowledged as much. He embraced the "program in physical and industrial upbuilding which has given Baltimore a new place among the cities of our country, and . . . cheerfully [accorded] credit in competent leadership for the success already achieved."[21]

Broening's principal task was to raise the money to pay for all the projects he had inherited. He mobilized the municipal elite and the local press in a vigorous campaign to win voter approval for four bond issues. One would generate funds to build new schools and renovate old ones—an agenda item borrowed from George Weems Williams. Another was to finance an expansion of the city's water supply and extend water service to the newly annexed parts of the city. A third was for the harbor improvements that had been a focus of Preston's annexation initiative and a major subject in his comprehensive plan for the city. The fourth was to pay for extension of essential public services in the new annex. A sharp increase in the property tax rate was predicted if the loans were not approved. Democrats Frank Furst and James Preston endorsed the city loans. A parade of 10,000 adults and schoolchildren marched in support of the bonds. Local movie theaters showed a film in silent support. A general executive committee of almost 200 prominent Baltimoreans stood behind the loan proposal. The strenuous promotional campaign seems to have worked—or perhaps it had been unnecessary. Voters approved the four loans overwhelmingly. The harbor loan, for example, passed with more than 95 percent of the vote.[22]

On another matter, however, the city failed to win a vote of confidence. A ballot question asked whether Baltimore's police department should continue under the control of the governor or whether authority over the department should be transferred to the mayor. A majority of 54 percent indicated a preference for the governor, affirming an arrangement made familiar by almost 60 years of experience.[23]

Broening's administration brought a change of party in the mayor's office but few other changes. Facing heavy Democratic majorities in both branches of the city council, Broening would probably have won little support for initiatives of his own. The mayor did appoint a committee to consider combining the council's two branches into a unicameral body of 18 members, 3 members to be elected from each of six districts. The city charter was amended accordingly, and the council's Democratic majority became even more lopsided.[24]

The mayor's municipal construction campaign encountered at least one serious snag. The Allied Building Trades Council objected to the employment of nonunion labor on some of the city's projects, and its members at work on those sites walked off the job in June 1921. A year later, a city council member from Southeast Baltimore (a "Kelly Democrat") reignited the city's labor troubles when he introduced an ordinance defining the wage rates to be paid on city construction projects. Existing legislation called for workers to receive the "current rate of per diem wages." The proposed ordinance would have defined the "current rate" as "the wages paid by any recognized organization of workingmen"—in other words, the union rate. The proposal generated controversy both inside the council and out. The council rejected the proposal decisively. Edward Bieretz, business agent of the Allied Building Trades Council, announced that "labor must get into politics."[25]

BREWING STORM

The national Prohibition amendment (Eighteenth Amendment) became effective on January 17, 1920. By early March, Mayor Broening was in Annapolis leading a Baltimore-based assault on the law, demanding that the General Assembly rescind its ratification of the amendment and that Maryland challenge Prohibition before the US Supreme Court. Noting that the amendment allowed the states "concurrent power" with the federal government in enforcement of Prohibition, Broening also argued (implausibly) that Maryland should exercise this power by declaring the Volstead Act void within its boundaries.[26]

The country had already been legally dry for six months before Prohibition, under the provisions of the Wartime Prohibition Act, perversely approved by Congress a week after Armistice Day and then passed over President Wilson's veto. It was justified as a measure to conserve foodstuffs for the war effort, especially grains used in the brewing of beer and distillation of liquor. Baltimore, however, remained moister than most towns. One Prohibition agent later described the city as "dripping wet." The characterization came in his letter of resignation, which also complained about the difficulties that Baltimore posed for making arrests and securing convictions under the Volstead Act.[27]

William H. Anderson, the Anti-Saloon League's superintendent for Maryland, had detected the city's distinct hostility to his organization's cause.[28] In 1916, after Anderson had left Maryland, the league and its allies seemed close to victory. A bill requiring the state's remaining "wet" counties and Baltimore to vote on Prohibition had been introduced in the house of delegates. Lopsided overrepresentation of dry, rural counties in the General Assembly made it likely that the measure would pass. Four delegates from Baltimore—three Democrats and a Republican—submitted a plea that Baltimore be exempt from the law. Prohibition, they argued, never worked in big cities. Its enforcement would cost Baltimore tax revenues and liquor license fees and would destroy the jobs of residents who worked in the city's breweries, distilleries, and bars. But the bill passed as written.[29]

The Baltimore delegates need not have worried. Not a single one of the city's 24 wards voted dry. In the ethnic neighborhoods of Southeast Baltimore, the margins of defeat were staggering. On the city's southeast fringe, the First Ward voted 97.7 percent wet. In the city at large, nearly three-fourths of the voters cast their ballots against Prohibition.[30]

When the General Assembly considered ratification of the Eighteenth Amendment in 1918, the House Temperance Committee recommended that the legislature delay its vote until the next session so that a state referendum could determine where Maryland's voters stood on Prohibition. But the drys had learned their lesson two years earlier. Baltimore, with half the state's population, would dominate any popular vote on drying up Maryland, and the city's electorate had left no doubt about its position on Prohibition. The General Assembly chose not to consult the voters and ratified the Eighteenth Amendment. Only two of Baltimore's 23 representatives in the house of delegates voted in favor of it.[31]

Dry legislators soon had second thoughts. Republican state senators from dry counties on the Eastern Short introduced a bill that urged Congress to legalize 3.5 percent beer. They had not anticipated that Congress would define "intoxicating beverages" as those with alcohol levels of more than 0.5 percent. For Baltimore's beer-drinking German population, the restriction came as a shock. Many had expected that the Volstead Act would outlaw only distilled spirits. Even for Maryland drys, Prohibition seemed more drastic than anticipated. Sharp turnover in the membership of the General Assembly in 1918 may also have contributed to a change in the legislature's stand on alcohol.[32]

The shift in mood may explain why Maryland was the only state that never enacted legislation to support enforcement of the Volstead Act. For this distinction Maryland earned its title as the "Free State," bestowed in 1922 by *Sun* editor Hamilton Owens. Governor Albert Ritchie embodied Maryland's resistance to Prohibition. Ritchie objected to the cost of its enforcement and to its imposition on Maryland without a popular vote, but above all he regarded it as an "encroachment of Federal power upon the functions of the States." It was one of many such encroachments. "Just now," he added, "it holds the stage and holds it so prominently as to obscure the fact it is simply one phase of the only question of principle upon which the American people can with consistency divide politically today."[33] Ritchie opposed Prohibition because he was a principled advocate of states' rights.

Many Baltimoreans needed no principle. They simply ignored federal encroachment. Restaurants carried signs bearing red crabs to signal customers that they sold beer. The Belvedere Hotel's Owl Bar used its iconic bird to notify patrons about the availability of alcohol. If both of the owl's eyes were illuminated, only fruit juices and soft drinks were on sale, but when the owl winked, there was booze. Organized crime of the kind that bloodied Chicago and Detroit never took hold in Baltimore. It was unnecessary. Baltimoreans could get drunk without much in the way of organized criminal conspiracy.[34]

Illegal alcohol production was a major local industry. In March 1922, federal agents raided a moonshine plant on East Pratt Street that was alleged to produce 300 gallons of liquor a day. At the time, it was thought to be the largest bootlegging operation in the United States. But then, just two months later, agents raided a building on East Street and found 22 stills and 3,500 gallons of mash. Even some ostensibly legitimate businesses found it difficult to resist the profitable possibilities of Prohibition. The US Industrial Alcohol Corporation produced alcohol for industrial and medicinal uses at its waterfront plant in Curtis Bay. Both kinds of spirits were legal under the Volstead Act, but the company modified its industrial alcohol to make it nonlethal and drinkable. A gallon of its 185 proof product sold for about three dollars. After diluting it with a gallon of water and adding glycerine for flavor, a bottle of the concoction could be rolled on the floor with one's foot to mix the contents, aged for half an hour, and then consumed as "gin." The company's waterfront location made it easy to export immense quantities of its bootleg output by ship, though it also used Baltimore's railroad facilities. Prohibition agents found a car carrying 8,000 gallons of Industrial Alcohol product at the President Street Station. It was labeled "olive oil."[35]

In addition to their defiance of Prohibition, some Baltimoreans fought to bring about its repeal. There was, of course, the "ombibulous" H. L. Mencken, who drank beer for breakfast. One of Mencken's less voluble friends was William H. Stayton, president of the Baltimore Steamship Company and, in 1918, founder of the Association Against the Prohibition Amendment. Stayton came to the city from his native Delaware by way of the Naval Academy, achieving the rank of captain. He retained the title for the rest of his life. Captain Stayton's objections to Prohibition had much in common with Governor Ritchie's. He thought that the regulation of alcohol was the business of state and local governments and no concern of federal authorities. His organization quickly attracted a national membership of 30,000, including about 1,000 Baltimoreans, one of whom was Frank Furst. Beyond Baltimore, Stayton's organization enlisted Kermit Roosevelt, Vincent Astor, and John Philip Sousa.[36]

By 1926, the association claimed 726,000 members nationwide. But Stayton had begun to concentrate less on mass recruitment and more on enlisting "quality" members, wealthy men who could finance the association's political campaigns against dry candidates. They included Marshall Field, Pierre DuPont, Stuyvesant Fish, and John J. Raskob of General Motors. The plutocrats shouldered Stayton aside. DuPont and Raskob, in particular, wanted to steer the campaign for repeal toward their objective of reducing the income tax. Federal taxes on alcohol, they hoped, would generate sufficient revenue to make the progressive income tax unnecessary or innocuous to people of their class.[37]

But Stayton was not overlooked when repeal was won and its grateful advocates named their heroes. Stayton's friend Mencken was one such advocate. "The hero of the day is Capt. William H. Stayton," he wrote, "organizer of the Association Against the Prohibition Amendment. He was bearing the heat and the burden at a time when nine-tenths of all the politicians were skulking. He has done the American people a vast service, and I only wish that I could hope that they will not forget it."[38] Unlike Mencken, Stayton was a teetotaler, and his next public project after repeal was to devise systems of alcohol regulation for the nation's states.[39]

Other Baltimoreans joined the crusade along with Stayton. In 1924, US Senator William Cabell Bruce, former Baltimore city solicitor, advocated repeal of the Volstead Act, though not revocation of the Prohibition amendment itself. He was, at this point, only a "modificationist" who wanted to allow each state to impose its own regulations for the sale and consumption of alcohol, subject only to the provisions of the Eighteenth Amendment itself. Two years later, Bruce's position had evolved, and while he did not explicitly advocate repeal, a major change in the Prohibition amendment seemed to follow from his argument. He advocated adoption of the "Quebec System," under which the provincial government operated a government liquor monopoly. Wine and beer would be sold by licensed restaurants, hotels, and grocery stores, but only state governments could sell distilled spirits.[40]

Senator Bruce laid out his position in a lengthy treatise delivered before a subcommittee of the Senate Judiciary Committee—35 years after his treatise *The Negro Problem*.[41] He had since taken to attacking the Ku Klux Klan of Alabama for its lawlessness. Senator Hugo Black of Alabama reciprocated by condemning Maryland's lawlessness with regard to the Volstead Act.[42] Lawlessness was one of Bruce's principal concerns about Prohibition. It made outlaws of thousands of imbibing Americans, created a class of gangster bootleggers, and opened opportunities for bribery and corruption among Prohibition agents, who were not covered by civil service regulations. Bruce's objections to Prohibition were largely practical, not principled like Albert Ritchie's, though they led him to support Ritchie's preference for state regulation.

Congressman John Philip Hill of Baltimore was a more flamboyant warrior for the wets. He delighted in publicity. *Time Magazine* claimed that "if newspapers were abolished, he would curl up and die." One of his first pitches for the headlines was a bill proposing that the House finance a veterans' bonus by taxing beer and light wines, which would obviously require an overhaul of the Volstead Act. Baltimore's city council passed a resolution supporting his bill, which was defeated, but got Hill into the *New York Times*.[43]

Hill next attacked the disparity in Prohibition's treatment of farmers and city folk. Farmers could legally produce hard cider, an indulgence denied to urbanites. Hill renamed his house on West Franklin Street "Franklin Farms," had a picture of a cow painted on his fence, and planted apple saplings and grape vines. He pressed fruit (probably purchased elsewhere) and entombed their juices in his basement. Their fermentation, he claimed, was not his responsibility. The apples and grapes, not Hill, violated the Volstead Act. He regularly invited Prohibition agents to measure the alcohol content of the wine and cider maturing in his cellar. He wanted to compel the federal government to specify just what levels of alcohol were permissible for homebrew under the Volstead Act, even if he got arrested in the process. He did. But a jury decided that his concoctions were not intoxicating, even though they exceeded 12 percent alcohol by volume. And federal district judge Morris Soper decided that Hill's homebrew was not covered by the Volstead Act's 0.5 percent limit for beverages commercially manufactured and sold.[44]

Hill, Stayton, Ritchie, and Bruce agreed that the regulation of alcohol was a state or local matter. While all four did not elevate the issue to the principled altitude attained by Ritchie, they reflected a general sentiment that it was not the federal government's business to tell people what they could drink. They shared their partiality for states' rights with many southern Democrats. But most southern Democrats did not share Maryland's openness to alcohol. Southern fundamentalists disapproved of strong drink. But the conjunction of southern sentiments on states' rights and northern drinking habits made Baltimore one of the wettest cities in the country.

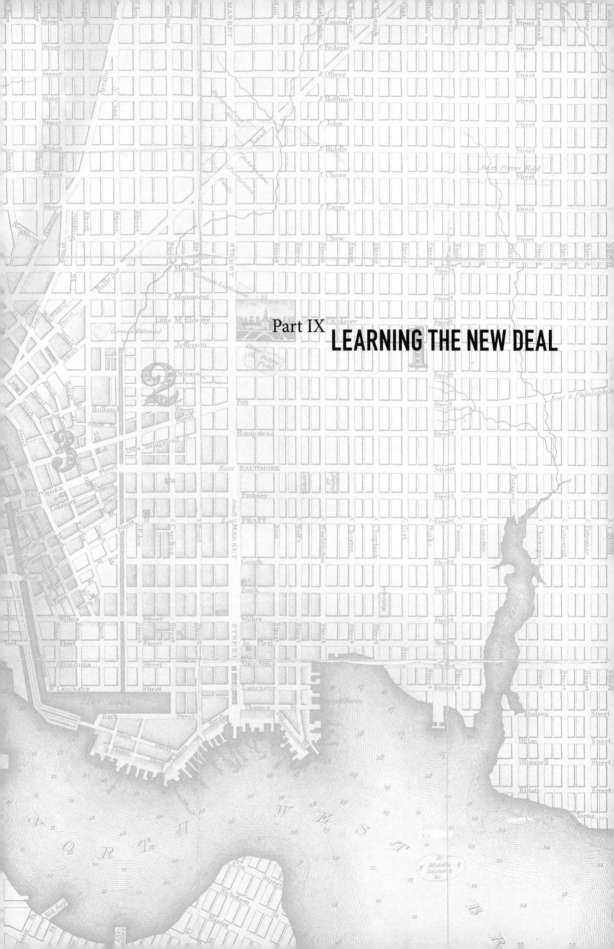

Part IX **LEARNING THE NEW DEAL**

Chapter 30 **BOOM TO BUST**

T HOUGH THEY MIGHT STAND TOGETHER against Prohibition and for states' rights, Baltimore's Democratic politicians were at odds with one another. Sonny Mahon and Frank Kelly, now aging, were still rivals. The two bosses had not spoken to each other in four years when Albert Ritchie made his first run for the governorship in 1919. The campaign and Ritchie's victory afforded an occasion for a fragile and expedient truce between Democratic factions. By 1920, Mahon and Kelly were sparring again, competing for seats on the Democratic State Central Committee. But Governor Ritchie attempted, through an evenhanded treatment of the bosses and an equitable division of state patronage, to mend the intraparty schism in Baltimore. In 1921, he negotiated an electoral compromise between the two factions. They would support the reelection of Mahonite Howard Jackson as register of wills and Kelly adherent Edward Gross as clerk of the criminal court. By 1923, Ritchie was able to bring the bosses together in support of Howard Jackson, the party's mayoral candidate.[1]

Jackson was a bookkeeper. He started an insurance business and was elected to the city council in 1907 from Freeman Rasin's Seventh Ward, where his sponsor was Robert Padgett.[2] He served on the council until 1909, when he was elected register of wills; he remained in that position until Ritchie, Mahon, and Kelly called him to the mayor's office in 1923. He also had the support of Frank Furst, and the Association Against the Prohibition Amendment rated him "100 percent wet." Mayor Jackson came to the post peculiarly suited to carry on the city's crusade against Prohibition. He was a steady adherent of states' rights and an alcoholic.[3]

Jackson's drinking habits do not seem to have interfered with his efficiency as register of wills. He surpassed all previous occupants of the office in his collection of fees. His revenues had to be surrendered to state government, but in 1911 it was estimated that if the city had kept the proceeds of his office, it would have reduced the city property tax by 10 cents.[4]

One of Jackson's first projects as mayor was creation of the Commission on Economy and Efficiency, devoted to elimination of waste in municipal operations and reduction of the city's tax rate.[5] Drunk or sober, Jackson's inner bookkeeper never rested. He instructed the commission to rationalize and centralize the municipality's accounting and payroll operations. The commission also recommended a less costly telephone system for the city (employing female switchboard operators) and a comprehensive proposal to reorganize all of city government, requiring a referendum to amend the city charter. The plan consolidated about 40 departments into 14. The Charter Revision Commission approved a reorganization ordinance drafted by the city solicitor, Philip Perlman. The centerpiece of the plan—and its most controversial element—was a new Baltimore Department of Public Works that absorbed the functions of the paving commission, the water board, the electrical commission, the harbor board, and the topographical survey commission. It would also be responsible for public buildings, street cleaning, the sewer system, and building inspection. Boards and commissions were to be replaced by administrative executives who were professional engineers.[6]

Members of the city council were understandably leery of the proposal. The plan for the Department of Public Works would abolish many city jobs; the new department would control hundreds of remaining appointments and millions of dollars in city contracts—the currency of city politics. Deliberations about the reorganization plan dragged on for more than a year while the council introduced amendments to protect the jobs of various political appointees. The influential corporate executives on the Commission on Economy and Efficiency finally weighed in to warn the council that its amendments might undo all their labors. Mayor Jackson was not available to reinforce the commission's admonition. He had been absent from his office for several days. According to the *Sun*, "His frequent absences in the last two or three weeks, often for days in succession have caused comment in municipal and political circles."[7]

Jackson reappeared to urge passage of the reorganization ordinance, reminding the council that he and council members had won election on a promise to enhance municipal efficiency and reduce taxes. The council capitulated and withdrew or defeated virtually all the amendments that had drawn the criticism of the mayor and his commission.[8]

CAPITAL AND LABOR

While Jackson struggled to make city government more businesslike, Baltimore's business community was attempting to do the same within its own sphere. In 1924, the Merchants' and Manufacturers' Association, the Board of Trade, and the Export and Import Board completed negotiations to consolidate themselves into a single Baltimore Association of Commerce. Its by-laws made the city's mayor a member of the organization's board of directors, recognizing the close relationship between the fortunes of the city's businesses and the success of its public authorities.[9]

Mayor Jackson was active in the business executives' ongoing campaign to bring new companies to Baltimore. The most prominent result of the effort was acquisition of Montgomery Ward's Eastern Plant. Its construction would cost $2 million (almost $25 million in current dollars). Once completed, it would employ between 1,200 and 1,500 Baltimoreans, with an annual payroll of $1.5 million. The company estimated that it would purchase $3 to $5 million in goods annually from Baltimore merchants and place additional orders with local industries for the manufacture of its "quantity purchases."[10]

In 1923 alone, Baltimore added 44 new industrial plants, representing an investment of almost $4.5 million and employing over 2,700 workers. More than $11.5 million was spent during the year on the expansion of existing plants, which added 2,235 jobs.[11]

Baltimore had come out of the Great War riding a wave of economic expansion. It became a center for the new aircraft industry and recovered some of the ground it had lost to other industrial centers before the war. Bethlehem Steel's Charles Schwab declared that there was "no place in the United States so susceptible for successful industrial development." Still, the city of trade and commerce never disappeared beneath the city of industry. Baltimore's ranking in export-import trade rose along with its status as an industrial powerhouse.[12]

The transport of coal was essential for the city's industrial prosperity. Coal yards ringed the harbor. The world's largest copper refinery, in Canton, was a ravenous consumer of electricity. The Consolidated Gas and Electricity Company depended on coal delivered by rail from Western Maryland to meet the plant's appetite. Other industries were gas-powered, and that too was a coal by-product. The coke ovens at Sparrows Point consumed mountains of coal, and the methane generated was piped to the local gasworks. Baltimore's industry, as Sherry Olson points out, was a creature of its "coal-hauling system." But the system did not belong to Baltimore. Both the B&O and the Pennsylvania Railroads were owned by the Kuhn-Loeb banking group based in New York. The Consolidation Coal Company was controlled by the Rockefellers, who also held the Western Maryland and the Wheeling and Lake Erie Railroads. The Baltimore Copper Smelting and Rolling Company had been bought out by the American Smelting and Refining Company in 1907, which, like Baltimore's oil refineries, was controlled by Rockefeller interests.[13] Baltimore might prosper, but it would still be a branch-office town.

While Mayor Jackson cemented his connection with local business, he faced an extended struggle with local labor. Members of unions belonging to the Building Trades Council went on strike against city construction projects in July 1925. The dispute centered on a city charter provision requiring employees who worked for the city (or city contractors) to be paid at "prevailing rates of wages." The mayor had convened a committee of engineers from the new Department of Public Works to set wages for workers on city projects. Edward Bieretz, business agent of the Building Trades Council, charged that the committee had established "a negative wage rate" lower than the union schedule. The strike idled about 3,000 union members and halted construction on new police and fire department headquarters, repairs at the city's Bay View Hospital, electrical work at city hall, and the building of six new public schools.[14]

Work on the projects resumed when the city and the Building Trades Council agreed to submit their dispute to an arbitration committee consisting of representatives of the municipality, the unions, city contractors, and the Public Improvement Commission—a body created to generate support for city loan referenda and to oversee expenditure of the borrowed funds. These four members of the committee were to select an economist to serve with them. They chose William C. Weyforth of the Political Economy Department at Johns Hopkins.[15]

A *Sun* editorialist warned Mayor Jackson that it was "a difficult job to outtalk the business agent of a labor organization," and Edward Bieretz came close to proving it impossible. As business agent for the Building Trades Council, he was the only union man on the Wage Arbitration Commission. For a year and a half he argued tirelessly for the union wage at the commission's tiresome weekly meetings. Its minutes record a steady stream of Bieretz's objections, rebuttals, challenges, and points of order.[16]

Resolution came finally in January 1927, at a meeting where Bieretz was uncharacteristically absent and the mayor unusually unguarded. The city, said Jackson, was fortunate that the Building Trades Council had suspended its strike while the arbitration commission deliberated. The union members continued to work on new buildings for the city's male high school, Baltimore City College, and one of its two high schools for girls. Construction also continued on the new police headquarters and a municipal office building, and work was soon to begin on the Baltimore Museum of Art. All of these projects were in jeopardy. Mayor Jackson proposed a solution: "There is only one thing to do to prevent a strike in my mind . . . this committee has either got to support me in approving the standard or union rate of wages on City work or I have got to say yes or no to the Building Trades Council and it will either result in my saying yes or in my saying no and that would result in a strike tying up of City work."[17]

Stated in a less roundabout way, either the commission would support the mayor in making the union wage the prevailing wage, or the mayor would do the same unilaterally. The commission issued a resolution in support of the union wage. One city bureaucrat, chief of the Bureau of Buildings in the Department of Public Works, refused to abide by the agreement. Jackson could not be located to respond to this insubordination. He was reported to be in Philadelphia on "personal business."[18]

Mayor Jackson's term ended after the municipal election in May. He was criticized for his drinking and for awarding about a third of the city's fire insurance coverage to his own firm. He had not indicated that he would seek another term, but Governor Ritchie and Frank Kelly took the decision out of his hands and denied him renomination in 1927. They chose instead one of Kelly's more promising adherents—William Curran, the son of Irish immigrants, a successful attorney, and a former state senator and city council member. Curran faced no opposition in the primary, but he lost the general election to the resurrected Republican William F. Broening. The restlessness and ambitions of the Kelly and Mahon loyalists may have contributed to Curran's defeat. The two leaders were aging, and their lieutenants were jockeying uncertainly in preparation for politics without the bosses. They may have seen Curran's elevation as a threat to their own prospects for leadership when the current leaders were gone.[19]

There was something else. Curran's disappointment in 1927 foreshadowed Al Smith's in the presidential election of 1928. Curran's Catholicism had divided the electorate. The *Sun*, in fact, regarded the mayoral race as a local test of Al Smith's electability. At a Broening rally just days before the mayoral election, a handbill was distributed listing the religious affiliations of all candidates. Only Curran's faith was printed in upper case: CATHOLIC. In reliably Democratic Northeast Baltimore, all three Democratic candidates for the city council were Roman Catholic. All were defeated. The *Sun* reported that "religion played a very important role in the election. Mr. Broening polled extremely well in the sections in which anti-Catholicism is regarded as finding its most vigorous expression in politics." The paper's editorialist hoped for other explanations of the outcome, but conceded that it might "be due to religious prejudice exerted through a whispering campaign" because Curran was Catholic.[20]

THE NEW DISORDER

In the year of Smith's defeat, rival bosses Frank Kelly and John J. Mahon died, and Baltimore entered a new era of political factionalism. The city was a political crazy quilt. The First, Second, and Third Wards in the city's southeast were Italian, Polish, and Democratic. The Fifth Ward, just to their northwest, was African American, Eastern European Jewish, and usually Republican. Working-class, native-born whites in the Sixth and Seventh Wards were usually Democratic. The Tenth (known as the "Old Irish") was generally Democratic, but 17 percent of its residents were African American and Republican. The Eighth Ward in East Baltimore and the Fifteenth in West Baltimore held concentrations of the city's ethnic Germans; they were politically independent. The city's north central wards—the Ninth, Eleventh, Twelfth, Thirteenth, and Twenty-Seventh—were home to Baltimore's most substantial citizens, Gentile and Jewish; many of them were attached to the GOP, but others were ideological Democrats committed to states' rights, low tariffs, and racial segregation. The Fourteenth and Seventeenth Wards, at the city's heart, were African American and Republican.[21]

Baltimore was the politically volatile center of state politics. Its disparate political fragments could realign themselves to produce variable coalitions and political outcomes, and its large population of voters meant that its electoral instability had statewide consequences. Between 1872 and 1948, the city's presidential vote showed less consistency from one election to the next than any other subdivision in Maryland.[22]

The presidential election of 1928 marked a striking discontinuity across the state. Al Smith's Catholicism drove longtime Democrats of the Eastern Shore and Southern Maryland into the arms of Herbert Hoover. Baltimoreans moved in the opposite direction, though Hoover managed to win a bare majority in the city. The contest brought a surge in turnout and a reshuffling of party attachments that would solidify under the New Deal.[23]

After losing to Broening, William Curran abandoned the pursuit of elective office to pursue politics as a factional leader within the local Democratic organization. "I play politics," he said, "because I like the game. Politics is my golf, my country club." His political base lay in Southeast Baltimore's "ethnic" neighborhoods, but Curran no longer lived there. As a successful attorney, he could afford to move his home base to genteel Roland Park.[24]

After 1930, Curran's chief political rival was his fellow Democrat, former mayor and reformed alcoholic Howard W. Jackson. Curran represented ethnic and mostly Catholic Democrats; Jackson's constituents were primarily old-stock Protestants.[25] In 1929, however, the two rivals joined forces in a doomed campaign to oppose Albert Ritchie's bid for an unprecedented fourth term as Maryland's governor. But Governor Ritchie, widely regarded as a contender for the presidency, was too popular to stop. Curran and Jackson capitulated. In the Democratic state primary, the original backers of Ritchie squared off against late arrivals to the governor's cause, and both opposed putative "anti-Ritchie" operatives. Ritchie himself refused to endorse anyone running for state office, to avoid complicating his presidential ambitions with factional entanglements. "Democrats fight among themselves," noted the *Baltimore Observer*, "without having any real factions. There are groups but they are loosely knit. It is next to impossible to tell where one group ends and the next one begins . . . The Democratic situation in Baltimore is now more of a mess than it is anything else."[26]

For Republican William Broening, the Democratic "mess" created a Republican opportunity. His second tour as mayor began under more auspicious circumstances than his first. In 1919, he had faced lopsided Democratic majorities in both branches of the city council. In 1927, the unicameral council was evenly divided between Democrats and Republicans, and one dissident Democrat occasionally voted with the Republicans.[27] This time Broening built an agenda of his own instead of carrying out the plans of his Democratic predecessor.

His aims were modest. One of his early priorities was a new city dog pound. Movie star and dog lover George Arliss, while in Baltimore for a theater engagement in 1919, had pronounced the pound "the worst I have ever seen in this country or in England." The existing dog shelter was run for the city under contract by the Baltimore Society for the Prevention of Cruelty to Animals at a facility near Franklin Street and Calverton Avenue in West Baltimore, but for several years the society had sought to build a new pound at a different location.[28]

In 1928, the SPCA announced that it planned to build a new shelter on land adjacent to Roosevelt Park. The society had acquired the site several years earlier, but the plan had been rejected by Mayor Jackson because the project aroused such vehement protest among nearby residents of Hampden and Woodberry. The society apparently hoped that the new city administration would view its project more favorably. But Broening signed an ordinance authorizing condemnation and purchase of the SPCA's land as a city park, preempting the society's plans for a dog shelter. The city budget, however, held no funds to cover the acquisition. And there was an additional complication. Only the park board could make decisions about the purchase of parkland, and the board's chairman announced that it had no interest in acquiring the property.[29]

The SPCA's agreement with the city was scheduled to expire in 1929, and Broening announced that the city would invite competitive bids for the animal shelter contract. He allowed, perhaps unwisely, that he would not object to "the 'proper use' of dogs in medical colleges for scientific investigation if a humane method of killing them was employed."[30] A torrent of mail rained down on city hall, fearful that stray dogs and cats might suffer painful experimentation before humane death. Broening drafted a form letter explaining his position.[31]

The mayor then floated another plan for the dog pound. It would dispense with contractors. The municipal government would operate its own dog shelter at a site near Back River outside the city limits. The city had already imposed its sewage-treatment plant on the area's residents, and they now rose up in fury against this new indignity. Led by the pastor of the neighborhood's Lutheran church, the Back River community threatened litigation. The clergyman denounced the decisions that had made Back River "a rubbish pile for Baltimore city," and threatened that his community would protest "violently" against the dog pound. The city decided to drop the Back River option.[32]

Its next proposal called for a temporary shelter not far from the original site of the SPCA dog pound in West Baltimore. The contract to operate the shelter was awarded to E. T. Forman, who operated a garbage-hauling company. But the new shelter would be adjacent to the House of the Good Shepherd, which housed a community of cloistered nuns and about 100 African American children. In a letter to Mayor Broening, the institution's attorney complained that it would be "difficult, if not impossible, for the Sisters or inmates to secure their proper rest during the night and they would be constantly harassed by the howling of the dogs during their religious services and periods of study." The mayor admitted that he was weary and did not know what would be done about the shelter.[33]

Forman surrendered his contract, which once again became the responsibility of the SPCA, and the city built a permanent shelter not far from the society's former facility, years after the mayor retired from city hall.[34] Broening, in short, got nowhere.

In his second term, Broening seems to have acquired the pugnacity to start fights, but he—or the city itself—lacked the capacity to resolve them. Baltimore was boss-less. Broening's next battle would prove even more intractable than the dog-pound fight. It centered on the selection of a route for the so-called East-West Viaduct. The project was designed to ease the flow of automobile traffic across the city and disentangle the routes of cars from those of trolleys and trains. The viaduct would carry traffic east from the city's center, over the tracks of the Pennsylvania Railroad and across the Jones Falls valley to the vicinity of the Johns Hopkins Hospital in East Baltimore. At the end of 1928, city engineer Charles Goob considered three trajectories for the elevated thoroughfare. One would extend Franklin Street to the northeast; a second would extend Franklin due east; and a third would run eastward from St. Paul Street along Bath Street (now Orleans Street). Engineer Goob chose the Bath Street option because, he said, it offered the cheapest and most direct route to East Baltimore.[35]

A surprisingly large number of persons and organizations had decided opinions about Goob's recommendation. Representatives of the Baltimore Association of Commerce and some neighborhood-based business organizations wanted the viaduct to run northeast from Franklin Street, where it could link up with an existing streetcar line. Engineer Goob opposed running streetcars on the viaduct. Trolleys slowed automobile traffic. The business groups were confident that they and the city could resolve their differences.[36]

Nearly four months later, however, the mayor appointed a special committee in an attempt to resolve the deadlock. At the end of 1929, the city council declared itself unable to decide which of two alternatives it preferred. Some of its members proposed that the question be decided by public referendum, but the city solicitor advised them that the law ruled out this evasive alternative. The Municipal Art Society retained Frederick Law Olmsted, Jr., to provide an outsider's detached assessment of the choices. Olmsted and his brother had designed the exclusive neighborhoods of Roland Park and Guilford and submitted a plan for parks and parkways in the area annexed in 1918. Olmsted expressed surprise at the "amount of heat and partisanship . . . on both sides of this [viaduct] question." But it was obvious, he said, that the intensity of the dispute had led both sides to exaggerate the advantages and disadvantages of the two remaining viaduct alternatives. Olmsted concluded that Charles Goob's Bath Street option was preferable to the Franklin Street alternatives, but added that the "merits of the general alternative propositions appear to me much more closely balanced . . . than the proponents of either have been willing to concede or even been able to recognize."[37]

The Federation of Republican Women of the Twelfth Ward opted for the Bath Street plan. The Young Men's Bohemian Democratic Club urged the mayor to adopt the Franklin Street alternative. The representative of the Old Town Merchants' and Manufacturers' Association came out for Bath Street but later changed his mind and endorsed Franklin Street.[38]

A compromise at the end of 1929 moved the city council to approve the Bath Street plan, but further disputes about the viaduct's location and prolonged condemnation proceedings delayed construction. The opening ceremonies for the Orleans Street Viaduct would finally occur at the end of 1935, more than four years after Broening left city hall.[39]

Broening's proposal to build a waterfront airport on landfill just east of Canton was held up even longer. The mayor initiated discussions on construction of a city airport in 1927. Controversies about its location, cost overruns, and construction problems prevented its completion until 1941.[40]

The economic consequences of construction delays grew more serious as the national economy faltered. After the stock market crash of 1929, Baltimoreans saw the city's stalled building projects as an untapped source of urgently needed jobs. The president of the Baltimore Federation of Labor sent the mayor a resolution adopted by the Building Trades Council. It complained of the "unreasonable" delay in building the East-West Viaduct and requested that Broening immediately begin construction. The mayor responded that "we are anxious to expedite the work," but nothing happened. More than a year later, a state senator urged the mayor to start construction of the viaduct, which had been "in the public mind for too long a time without a spade having yet actually turned. Put to work those who are needy . . . By all means, put an end to this present chaotic state."[41]

Chapter 31

RELIEF, REPEAL, NEW DEAL

O N THE BRINK OF THE GREAT DEPRESSION, the Baltimore Association of Commerce saw only a golden glow in the city's future. It predicted that the local population would pass one million by 1930 and boasted of the city's attractiveness as a site for manufacturing. The experience of the 1920s no doubt sustained the association's confidence. Western Electric, Proctor and Gamble, Lever Brothers, American Sugar, Glenn L. Martin, and McCormick Spice had all opened new plants in the city. Bethlehem Steel embarked on a $100 million expansion of its mill in Sparrows Point. Between 1920 and 1926, Baltimore rose from seventh to third most active port in the nation. Its construction industry produced about 6,000 homes a year.[1]

Mayor Broening shared the business community's confidence. Months after the stock market crash, he breathed boosterism at a conference he had called for 100 executives representing "the cream of Baltimore industry." If there were a depression, he told them, it would be brief, and Baltimore had little to fear. The Association of Commerce sought to spread this sentiment. It distributed 250,000 copies of a pamphlet titled "197 Reasons Why You Should Enthuse over Baltimore."[2]

Just as Baltimore discovered reasons to "enthuse," the Great Depression banished enthusiasm. By March 1930, the state commissioner of labor and statistics reported that between 13,000 and 15,500 usually employed Baltimoreans were out of work. The city's situation was not so dire as that in other parts of the country. Job losses in manufacturing and among unskilled workers were offset by gains in the construction trades, but a decline in new construction contracts suggested that harder times lay ahead. In May, Broening appointed the Commission on Employment Stabilization to consider ways of dealing with the problem.[3]

Private charities—the Family Welfare Association, the Salvation Army, Catholic Charities, and Associated Jewish Charities—met the leading edge of the crisis while the city's business leaders continued to minimize its magnitude. The Baltimore Police Department had also transformed itself into a relief agency, providing food, clothing, and shelter to households unable to provide for themselves. By the end of 1930, the Baltimore Association of Commerce recognized the urgency of the situation and followed its enthusiastic pamphlet with a circular on emergency employment. The association also prodded Baltimore's government to preserve and generate jobs, and in 1931, when local unemployment was estimated at 19 percent, the association took the lead in organizing the Citizens Emergency Relief Committee. Mayor Broening was one of its members.[4]

The committee's objective was to raise $300,000 to replenish the funds of private charities and the police department. Mayor Broening pledged $50,000 on behalf of the municipality, but private contributions lagged. W. Frank Roberts, chairman of the relief committee and president of the Association of Commerce, attributed the disappointing response "to the feeling . . . on the part of a great many people that the City should take care of most of this emergency relief through the tax rate." Mayor Broening agreed that the "tendency today seems to be toward paternalism. Business with its ailments and individuals with their problems are turning to Government for a solution."[5]

Frank Roberts turned to Governor Albert Ritchie for a state contribution to Baltimore's relief fund. Ritchie declared himself willing to help in any way he could, but proved no help at all. He pointed out that if Baltimore received state aid, Maryland's 23 counties would expect to receive assistance as well, and Ritchie was clearly unwilling to invite such requests.[6]

Mayor Broening had run out of time and money. Acknowledging that the city had not done enough to reduce unemployment, he announced that he would not run for reelection. One of Baltimore's few clear accomplishments under his administration was the congressional designation of Francis Scott Key's "Star Spangled Banner" as the national anthem in 1931.[7]

RETURN OF THE DEMOCRATS

Howard Jackson made a startling comeback. A coalition of district leaders backed him for a second shot at the mayor's office. He had held the job before, after all, and now he was sober. His political rival, William Curran, joined other Democrats in a "frenzied hunt" for some other candidate. But no plausible alternative emerged, and the anti-Jackson politicians fell to fighting among themselves. One by one, they announced their support for Jackson. He faced no opposition in the Democratic primary and only token competition in the general election.[8]

Curran's political prospects seemed dim. His candidate for council president was defeated, and most of those he backed for city council were beaten too. His friends would get no patronage appointments in the Jackson administration. His only remaining allies were in the city's delegation in Annapolis and on Baltimore's Democratic committee.[9]

Mayor Jackson shrewdly maneuvered to solidify his influence. Instead of dictating patronage appointments in the city's judicial system, for example, he deferred to the city council in choosing clerks, bailiffs, and criers. For two months the hopelessly factionalized council debated inconclusively, and then it willingly surrendered the patronage decisions to Jackson. By deferring to the mayor, the council seemed to recognize him as the boss of Baltimore, the leader to whom Democrats turned for resolution of their many squabbles.[10]

But the boss seemed reluctant to put his political influence to work. Jackson insisted that support of the city's unemployed was not a municipal responsibility. It was a job for private charities. His initial response to the economic crisis was to reduce the salaries of city employees and the size of the municipal budget. Jackson and his Commission on Governmental Economy and Efficiency embraced retrenchment to secure Baltimore's favorable bond rating. Early in 1932, however, the private Family Welfare Association announced that it had reached the limit of its resources. Mayor Jackson expressed doubt at first that the agency had exhausted its funds, but he was convinced when the association closed its offices and stopped accepting cases. In response, Jackson arranged an appropriation of $50,000 to support the unemployed, acknowledging that the sum would last no more than a few weeks. By the time the money was exhausted, Jackson had requested and received emergency powers from the city council. He borrowed $3 million to sustain the unemployed through the end of 1932 and announced that the city's 1933 budget would require an increase in the property tax rate for unemployment relief. At public meetings, the Taxpayers' War Council shouted down his proposal. Jackson next hinted that a city sales tax might enable Baltimore to meet its relief expenditures, but gained little support for the proposal. The economy and efficiency commission announced that the city would have to cut its current expenditures for the remaining months of 1932 by 11 percent or face a deficit. Governor Ritchie seemed to offer Jackson a way out of his dilemma. The governor promised to urge the 1933 session of the state legislature to authorize a bond issue that would cover Baltimore's current and future relief expenditures.[11]

Ritchie's presidential prospects overshadowed the Democratic primaries in the spring of 1932. The hope that a Marylander might reach the White House muted intraparty strife. But Ritchie's presidential boom fizzled, and then he reneged on his pledge to see that Baltimore was reimbursed for its relief expenditures, suggesting instead that the city achieve greater economy in its own expenditures. Mayor Jackson followed up on the governor's suggestion by eliminating almost all relief expenditures from the city's 1933 budget, deliberately steering the city toward crisis. Ritchie backtracked, and the General Assembly grudgingly approved his request for a $12 million bond issue to offset relief expenditures in Baltimore.[12]

Jackson had called the governor's bluff, and next went after his job. The mayor began by using patronage to consolidate Baltimore's fluidly factionalized Democratic organization—even if it meant giving jobs to William Curran's allies. The new union of Baltimore Democrats was sufficiently influential to dictate the choice of the Speaker at the 1933 session of the house of delegates. Back in Baltimore, after the session ended, the coalition achieved consensus on patronage appointments in the people's court and the office of the register of wills. The first hint of discord was Governor Ritchie's appointment of Curran's Fourth District leader, James H. "Jack" Pollack, to the State Athletic Commission. Pollack's earlier career as a prizefighter presumably qualified him for the job, but his extensive police record made the appointment both questionable and controversial. Ritchie conceded that Pollack "used to be quite a bad boy once"—a "bad boy" phase that included a charge of murder. But the governor claimed that Pollack's marriage and family responsibilities had transformed him into a solid citizen. Ritchie's appointment of a Curranite triggered speculation that he was trying to entice the Curran faction to desert Mayor Jackson. Curran's delighted response only strengthened that impression.[13]

MAYOR VS. NEW DEAL

While Mayor Jackson prepared to make his bid for state leadership, he was also trying to accommodate national policy. Creation of the Federal Emergency Relief Administration in mid-1933 made federal authority a fiscal presence in local politics. The FERA was to spread half a billion dollars in federal funds among state and local relief agencies. Jackson's emergency relief committee would not qualify for grants because it was not a fully public agency. Jackson had discussed the need for a welfare department during his 1931 campaign, but as late as 1933, he opposed the city's entry into the relief field because he feared that once a relief agency became a part of municipal government, it would "cling there as a budgetary barnacle most difficult to scrape off when normal business conditions are restored." Instead, he appointed leaders of private charities and business executives from the Baltimore Association of Commerce's emergency relief committee to a Baltimore Emergency Relief Commission, and then shifted most of the private charities' caseworkers to the public payroll. Federal field observers were not deceived by his repackaging of the organization, and they filed unfavorable reports about the city's unsystematic and inequitable relief practices, noting in particular discrimination against African Americans. Jackson finally relented and announced plans for a new welfare department in January 1934. It was the only way to qualify for federal funds.[14]

The director of the new agency was Judge Thomas Waxter, a member of Baltimore's social elite with an extensive record of service in charitable causes, including free legal representation of the poor. He remained welfare director for 20 years, and his prominence gave the agency an autonomy and freedom from political interference that it might not have enjoyed with a less prestigious leader.[15]

Jackson supported some federal initiatives more readily than the social welfare policies. On March 22, 1933, President Roosevelt signed the Cullen-Harrison Act allowing the sale of beer with an alcohol content of 3.2 percent. On the same day, Jackson sent a bill to Annapolis legalizing 3.2 percent beer in Baltimore. His constituents were eager to abandon Prohibition. In October, 94.3 percent of them voted for repeal. Not a single one of the city's 471 precincts produced a majority in favor of the Eighteenth Amendment.[16] It was one of the few issues on which Baltimore fell into line with the Roosevelt administration.

Clashes with federal authorities were far more common. The city's relations with the Civil Works Administration were even more troubled than those with the FERA. The work program's implementation was marred by graft. The president of the Maryland Democratic Club was sentenced to two years in prison for accepting bribes in return for CWA jobs.[17] The CWA offered unusual attractions for urban patronage brokers, though it had been designed to address the views of social workers—most notably, FERA director Harry Hopkins. The social workers argued that work relief was preferable to welfare checks, but the jobs should not be demeaning. CWA jobs paid locally prevailing wages, and applicants did not have to prove poverty to qualify for them. But the CWA was an emergency measure to carry Americans through the hard winter of 1933–34. It was replaced by more traditional work relief programs such as the Works Progress Administration, which required proof of poverty, and although WPA workers were paid prevailing wages, the program capped their weekly work well below 40 hours.[18]

Mayor Jackson exhibited a "studied ambivalence, if not outright hostility, toward every jobs program created by the New Deal." In 1935, the mayor pronounced the new Social Security Act "the most asinine thing I have ever read in my life." Jackson's reaction to the federal public housing program in 1937 was almost as negative, and he resisted creation of a city housing authority until pressured do so by a prestigious citizens' committee.[19]

Governor Ritchie, like Mayor Jackson, was hostile to federal intervention and reluctant to acknowledge that government should bear significant responsibility for unemployment relief. As the dimensions of the Depression unfolded, Ritchie called on the business community "to recognize that the problem belongs to it and not the state."[20]

Jackson's decision to challenge Ritchie's bid for a fifth term as governor in 1934 had little if anything to do with disagreements about public policy. Nor was William Curran moved by considerations of policy when he endorsed Ritchie over Jackson. Both were hostile to the New Deal, as were most Democratic politicians in Maryland. Ritchie defeated Jackson in the Democratic primary, then lost the general election. The victory of Harry W. Nice finally gave Maryland a New Deal governor—a Republican. Nice campaigned on "A New Deal and a Square Deal for All," and a band played "Happy Days Are Here Again" as he accepted his party's nomination.[21]

DEMOCRATS IN DISARRAY

Howard Jackson and William Curran were left to fight it out with one another for control of the city. The balance of power shifted between them as the city's district leaders deserted Curran for Jackson and then redefected. One of the Curranites who switched to Jackson in the 1935 mayoral election explained his move as a step toward political order: "We have had too many political leaders. I think Howard Jackson will be able to bring everybody together now and unite the party."[22] It was a vain hope.

During the presidential campaign of 1936, Baltimore boasted two Roosevelt campaign headquarters: one was Curran's; the other, Jackson's. Curran had moved first by organizing the Maryland for Roosevelt League, calling attention to the strained relationships between Mayor Jackson and the New Deal. Jackson then launched his own campaign for FDR, to validate his questionable New Deal credentials.[23]

Jackson soon regained the initiative and launched his second drive to become governor. His prospects looked good. The city's Democratic committee deserted

Curran and collaborated with Jackson in a "purge" of ward executives. But Mayor Jackson had exhausted his political resources. He had already distributed what there was of city patronage, and there were more claimants than he could satisfy, perhaps because the Depression had created a widespread hunger for jobs. There were also the purged ward executives to contend with. They drifted toward Curran, who still controlled the city's legislative delegation in Annapolis. Jackson's second bid for the governorship, if successful, would yield enough jobs to solve his problems. But Herbert R. O'Conor, a proven vote-getter as Baltimore state's attorney and Maryland attorney general, emerged as a Democratic alternative to Jackson. Curran announced that O'Conor could defeat Jackson in all six legislative districts of Baltimore. The state's Democratic politicians converged behind his candidate.[24] Since Curran had no gubernatorial ambitions of his own, he could choose to back the most promising candidate for the office. Jackson, who wanted very much to be governor, was stuck with himself.

The consequences of the 1938 gubernatorial election revealed, once again, the fractured character of politics in Baltimore. O'Conor, with Curran's backing, won both primary and general elections. At the same time, however, Curran lost control of the city's delegation in Annapolis to Jackson allies. But Jackson gained little. His supposed partisans in the General Assembly wanted to cooperate with the popular new governor, not only because he was popular, but because he controlled state patronage. They found it expedient, therefore, to accommodate "Willie" Curran, O'Conor's principal political sponsor in Baltimore. Though they had been elected with Mayor Jackson's endorsement, the city's representatives chose a Curran ally to chair the city delegation. Another became Speaker of the house. Baltimore's Democratic committee, whose members had defected to Mayor Jackson, now redefected to nominate a slate of Curran men to serve on the city's board of election supervisors.[25]

In a party organization where factional loyalties changed so readily, no alignment was likely to last. Howard Jackson was back in charge in time for the mayoral election of 1939. Jack Pollack, powerful and independent boss of West Baltimore's Fourth District, shifted his organization from Curran to Jackson; other district leaders followed his lead. Jackson outpolled Curran's mayoral candidate in 26 of the city's 28 wards, and Jackson's candidates for city council won all but 3 of its 18 seats. In the general election, Jackson ran against a popular Republican, Theodore McKeldin, who had served as secretary to Mayor Broening. Though Jackson defeated McKeldin, the outcome suggested that his popular support was declining. His total vote was about 5,000 less than in 1935.[26]

The resistance of Baltimore politicians to New Deal policies was not unusual. State and local politicians across the country reacted much as Ritchie, Jackson, and Curran had. What distinguished Baltimore was the disjointed factionalism of its Democratic Party. In other cities, the coming of the New Deal provided the resources that political bosses used to build or strengthen powerful organizations. In Chicago, after the death of Mayor Anton Cermak, the Kelly-Nash machine imposed order and centralization in city politics. In Kansas City, Thomas Pendergast flourished even though Franklin Roosevelt tried unsuccessfully to unseat him; he fell only when he was convicted in 1939 for failing to pay income tax on a bribe. In Memphis, boss Edward Crump and his Democratic organization thrived under the New Deal. At the same time, Joseph Guffey was building a Democratic machine in Pittsburgh, converting the town from a Republican to a Democratic stronghold, while in New York, Fiorello La Guardia, with the support of FDR, built a reform coalition that transformed his city.[27]

By comparison, Baltimore seemed politically disabled—unable to gather itself together. What distinguished the city's politics, according to Edwin Rothman, was "the lack of binding ties of loyalty between city leaders and district leaders." Baltimore had always been short on political patronage, and the supply diminished after introduction of the civil service system. No political leader controlled sufficient political capital to build a unified political machine.[28] State patronage may also have contributed to the city's political fragmentation. As long as Howard Jackson hungered for the governorship, incumbent governors were likely to direct state patronage to his local political rival, William Curran.

RACIAL REALIGNMENT

Before the New Deal, the Democratic Party, lacking a Lincoln and burdened by its Confederate heritage, had limited leverage among Baltimore's African American voters. Patronage and favors attracted a minority of black Baltimoreans to the Democrats. The party focused its resources on keeping black Republicans away from the polls on election day. By the 1930s, however, Baltimore's African American voters were abandoning the party of Lincoln for the party of FDR. The newly converted black Democrats enlarged the party's constituency but also threatened its unity. A party that hoped to accommodate both African Americans and white voters with racist inclinations could be fractured if race became a political issue.

Race may have been much on the minds of Baltimoreans, but they were generally wary of discussing it in public. In the era of slavery, the town's social and political elites were divided on the subject and generally avoided the issue. Prominent Baltimoreans supported the African colonization movement because it offered something to both sides of the slavery controversy and exported the race issue back to Africa. The Know-Nothings struggled to sidestep the issue of slavery in an effort to maintain the Union. Even Baltimore's residential segregation ordinance of 1910 was justified as a way to avoid the frictions that might make race a matter of public contention. But as African American voters transferred their loyalties to the Democratic Party in the 1930s, the avoidance of racial politics became not just a matter of preserving domestic tranquility but an essential condition for preserving the city's majority party. Even Franklin Roosevelt had to tread carefully around the issue of race to avoid antagonizing southern Democrats.[29] In Baltimore, where black and white populations were more nearly equal than in the nation at large, the perils to the party were even greater.

The organizational and institutional depth of the black community helped the Democrats sidestep the race issue. If Baltimore's African Americans had arrived in a giant wave of migrants from the South, uprooted from home communities and disconnected from one another, they would have had only their race in common, and appeals to race would have been the principal means to mobilize them as voters. But Baltimore was home to the largest population of free black people half a century before the Emancipation Proclamation. They had the freedom and the numbers to sustain a dense network of community institutions decades before the Civil War. The many-stranded connections that tied black Baltimoreans together through churches, schools, fraternal groups, labor organizations, and social clubs enabled leaders to draw them to the polls through direct or indirect acquaintance-ship rather than appeals to racial solidarity. "Unlike African American communities in other cities, especially to the North," observes Andor Skotnes, "Baltimore's Black community was never largely a transplant from distant rural areas, and even the Great Migration failed to demographically disrupt its processes of community- and culture-building."[30]

Black political aspirants in West Baltimore formed the Citizens Democratic Club, whose principal role was to round up black votes for white candidates. In East Baltimore, Clarence "Du" Burns was doing the same for the all-white Bohemian Democratic Club. His efforts won him a job as a locker room attendant at a black high school gym. A trio of like-minded black politicians approached Howard Jackson with an offer to mobilize black voters behind his gubernatorial campaign if he would grant them city jobs. Race was not an issue for these pragmatic African Americans. According to Verda Welcome, a member of the Citizens Democratic Club and the first black woman elected to the state legislature, race was not mentioned explicitly in electoral politics until the 1970s.[31]

The ability to mobilize African American voters without making appeals to race enabled black politicians to form alliances with white politicians and deliver black votes to white candidates. The most notable beneficiary of such an alliance was Jack Pollack, the white political boss of West Baltimore's Fourth District, who controlled judges, state legislators, and city council members. Baltimore's "bad boy" continued get white candidates elected long after his district's electoral majority had become African American. His chief lieutenant was Loyall Randolph, a black hotel and tavern owner who escorted white candidates through West Baltimore's African American neighborhoods, distributed the patronage that came his way, and helped local merchants cope with zoning or liquor license problems.[32]

Thurgood Marshall and Clarence Mitchell, Jr., both grew up in Pollack's district. They graduated together from Frederick Douglass High School (known then as the Colored High School), and by the time they returned to Baltimore from Lincoln University in Philadelphia, Pollack was in full command. Unlike other politically ambitious members of West Baltimore's black community, they did not join Pollack's Citizens Democratic Club. Mitchell and Marshall both became members of the City-Wide Young People's Forum, an organization affiliated with the local branch of the NAACP. It could attract as many as 2,000 young African Americans to its Friday evening meetings. Juanita Jackson, a 19-year-old University of Pennsylvania graduate, started the forum in 1931. The group met at the Sharp Street Methodist

Church, but moved to Bethel AME when the pastor at Sharp Street thought the organization had become too radical. Mitchell joined in 1932, soon became vice-president, the forum's premier orator and debater, and, later, Juanita Jackson's husband.[33]

Marshall and Mitchell would become leading actors in the forum's most ambitious offensive against racial discrimination. In 1933, Prophet Kiowa Costonie, a visiting religious exotic and black activist from New York, encouraged Juanita Jackson to organize a campaign against retailers in black neighborhoods who refused to hire African American workers. The Buy Where You Can Work campaign was initially aimed at the A&P and another supermarket chain, the American Sanitary Company (ASCO), both of which refused to employ black workers. The Young People's Forum coordinated a boycott with the support of at least 40 black churches. Five hundred adherents of the forum took turns picketing the markets, and many of their elders participated as well. A&P agreed to hire three black clerks and promised more. But a few weeks later, the chain fired several black employees as "inefficient." The community reaction was seismic, and by December 1933, A&P had hired 32 black clerks and promised jobs for two black managers.[34]

The Buy Where You Can Work movement next targeted three locally owned stores on one block of Pennsylvania Avenue, the principal shopping and entertainment thoroughfare for West Baltimore's black community. Not long after the picketing began at this new location, the demonstrators encountered trouble. Counterdemonstrators appeared in support of the store owners. Another contingent of picketers, allegedly Communists, showed up with signs demanding that the stores hire only black employees. The store owners got a temporary injunction to end all picketing.[35]

Trouble also emerged within the Buy Where You Can Work campaign. Black churches were divided on the extension of the boycott, and Prophet Costonie became a polarizing figure who contributed to contention within the coalition supporting the protest. Costonie announced that he had "a list of names of persons who were traitors" to the boycott, adding that "the Ark is about to leave, and I am going to give all backsliders a last chance to get on." The pose alienated Clarence Mitchell, now a reporter for the *Afro-American*. No conspiracy of African American traitors, he argued, was responsible for the situation of black Baltimore. The real enemy was a racist social and political system. Thurgood Marshall presided over a meeting between Costonie's supporters and black ministers who were trying to reach consensus on the boycott. The attempt at conciliation dissolved into a free-for-all. Some of the clergy were indignant about Costonie's conflation of faith healing and fundraising. The prophet's advocates allegedly set off stink bombs to disrupt the assembly. The divisions then spread jaggedly beyond the meeting itself as charges of treason spread among the churches and clergy for and against the boycott.[36]

The movement soon suffered another setback. In May 1934, the Pennsylvania Avenue merchants returned to court to get a permanent injunction against the boycott movement. The judge held that since the pickets were not employees of the stores where they demonstrated, their protest was not covered by the Norris–La Guardia Act. The advocates of the boycott fought the injunction to Maryland's highest court, where they lost again.[37]

The boycott, however, was not a failure. It had won jobs for some African Americans. More important, perhaps, it stirred a new energy in black Baltimore's fight against discrimination. Earlier struggles had been defensive reactions to residential segregation and disenfranchisement. This time, black Baltimore took the offensive against racial discrimination. The Buy Where You Can Work campaign, as Larry Gibson points out, "became a milestone and a turning point in political activism for Baltimore's black community. For the first time, the community undertook a proactive protest."[38] Boycotts and demonstrations, however, would not serve as the principal vehicles for protest.

LITIGATION AND LOBBYING

For Thurgood Marshall, little more than a year out of Howard University School of Law, the obvious alternative to demonstrations was litigation. Filing suit against discrimination circumvented the organizational difficulties of mass protests — difficulties that Marshall had confronted personally in the Buy Where You Can Work campaign. Litigation did not depend on maintaining a consensus among Baltimore's African Americans. It did not require mass mobilization. It required only a lawyer and someone to pay court costs and attorney's fees.

Marshall's first venture in civil rights litigation sought to reopen the University of Maryland School of Law to African Americans. His client was Donald Murray, a member of the Young People's Forum and a graduate of Amherst. He had applied to the law school and, like every black applicant since 1889, had been rejected. In anticipation of the lawsuit, the Maryland General Assembly approved a bill that would pay tuition for black students to attend graduate and professional schools outside the state.[39]

Marshall argued that requiring black students to earn their degrees outside Maryland was inherently discriminatory, and he prevailed at trial and on appeal. But his case was not simply his own. It was part of a strategy designed by Charles Hamilton Houston, one of Marshall's teachers in law school and an attorney for the NAACP. Houston sought to demonstrate that the "separate but equal" formula was a fiction — that segregated facilities for blacks were inherently inferior. Houston was Marshall's associate counsel in the Murray case. Marshall also relied on Carl Murphy, publisher and president of the *Baltimore Afro-American*. Murphy was a member of the NAACP's national board of directors and a leader in the organization's Baltimore branch. He was also an early advocate of Houston's litigation strategy.[40]

Thurgood Marshall moved from his first successful suit against Jim Crow to a series of others aimed at equalizing salaries for black and white teachers in one Maryland county after another, cases that also served as rallying points in the organization of NAACP branches across the state. His next case, *Williams v. Zimmerman*, carried far-reaching implications for the NAACP strategy of contesting racial discrimination in schools, foreshadowing *Brown v. Board of Education*. It was the first of the civil rights cases in Maryland that Marshall lost.

The defendant was the principal of an all-white Baltimore County high school. The county had no high schools for black students, and that was why the NAACP filed suit on behalf of student Margaret Williams. The county had required her to take a test after she completed the seventh grade. If she passed, the county would pay her tuition at a black high school in Baltimore City. Margaret had not passed the test, though she had successfully completed the seventh grade. Marshall argued that the test was a transparent attempt by Baltimore County to deny Margaret equal access to a high school education, and he sued for her admission to a white high school. But, on the advice of NAACP counsel Charles Houston, he claimed that his real purpose was to get Baltimore County to open a black high school. The NAACP lawyers were concerned that a flat demand for school integration would carry them too far ahead of the courts. In the end, they got neither integration nor a black high school. The Maryland Court of Appeals argued that the remedy Marshall should have requested was abolition of the test or creation of a fair test for tuition. Reflecting on the result, Marshall noted that "for the first time, a court has admitted that some inequalities are inevitable in a separate school system. It is significant and valuable to have a court recognize and state the mere existence of a separate system, in itself, imparts inequalities."[41]

Carl Murphy's newspaper rallied its readers behind Marshall's efforts, and the publisher provided more tangible support. Marshall's embryonic practice left him time to litigate on behalf of the local NAACP, but he earned little from private clients. Murphy hired him to handle the *Afro*'s legal work. The editor also backed the Young People's Forum, while reviving the Baltimore branch of the NAACP, which had dwindled to no more than 100 members. The branch president was Lillie Carroll Jackson, Juanita Jackson's mother. Thurgood Marshall's victory in the Murray case increased the NAACP branch's visibility and membership. A lynching on the Eastern Shore triggered outrage and yielded more members. Clarence Mitchell, Jr., like Marshall, relied on the *Afro-American*. He was one of its columnists, and he served simultaneously as publicity director of the NAACP branch. His task was not just to give visibility to the reinvigorated organization but to hold together the coalition of groups that backed the branch. Baltimore's NAACP was not a free-standing organization. As David Terry points out, "Though an examination of the rank-and-file of the city's 'active' black citizens would reveal various organizational and institutional backgrounds, that which can be characterized as a core leadership displayed a penchant for multiple affiliations, with the common denominator being the NAACP." All of the branch's ventures were "multi-organizational undertakings."[42] Constant negotiations held the coalitions together, and that was part of Mitchell's job.

While Marshall was preparing the Murray case, Mitchell ran for the state legislature, his first and only venture in elective politics. Neither of the major parties appealed to him. To Mitchell, it seemed, "the Democrats are a lot of high pressure artists, who will tolerate gambling dens, drinking dives, and houses of prostitution, but refuse to support anything that means uplift and justice." But the Republicans were not much better—"a bunch of shilly-shallying reprobates who need to undergo a complete metamorphosis." Mitchell ran as a socialist and got 1,700 votes—far less than he needed to win, but a respectable showing for a socialist.[43]

Having tested the limits of mass protest and electoral politics, Mitchell the nego-

Juanita Jackson Mitchell and
Lillie Carroll Jackson. Mother
and daughter served as presidents
of the Baltimore branch of the
NAACP. They stand in front
of Freedom House, once the
headquarters of the local NAACP.

tiator and Marshall the litigator would carry their work beyond Baltimore. Marshall
served as lead attorney for the NAACP. Mitchell became the NAACP's chief lobbyist
in Washington. Baltimore contributed two vital leaders to the national struggle for
racial equality. They were not architects of protest or masters of oratory like Martin
Luther King or Malcolm X. The operating styles that made Mitchell and Marshall
figures of national importance seem to have originated as responses to the distinctive racial politics of Baltimore. Backed by a wave of protest, Marshall's litigation
would lead to *Brown v. Board of Education*; Mitchell's negotiation and lobbying
would aid the passage of the landmark Civil Rights Act of 1964.

Chapter 32

DEMOCRATIC HARMONY, REPUBLICAN VICTORY

N OT LONG AFTER HOWARD JACKSON began his fourth term as Baltimore's mayor, Franklin Roosevelt was nominated for a third term as president. Mayor Jackson was not one of his adherents. At the state Democratic convention, Jackson had urged Maryland's delegation to the national convention to support, instead, US Senator Millard Tydings of Maryland, one of the anti–New Deal Democrats targeted in FDR's ill-fated "purge" of 1937. In a concession to political reality, the state convention decided that if Roosevelt appeared to be succeeding in winning his third nomination, the Maryland delegates should vote as they pleased.[1]

Roosevelt's nomination was clearly a setback for Jackson, and he seemed unwilling to accept it in silence. Little more than a month after the national convention, he gave a speech condemning the fiscal policies of "this Government," expressing concern about "the erosion of citizenship, the erosion of local governments, State, city, and county, by virtue of their dependence upon the national Government, the erosion of the moral fiber of the American people by their dependence upon government rather than their own independence." Jackson proceeded to raise questions about foreign policy: "I am not afraid of Hitler. I haven't got the jitters as a lot of people have. What I am concerned about is our local and domestic affairs. What I am worried about is that this government is spending $2 and taking in $1."[2]

Speculation and criticism followed the mayor's speech. Speculation centered on the possibility that he might desert Roosevelt for Republican Wendell Willkie. The mayor's mail was mixed. Three letters complimented him on his remarks; all came from out of town. The backlash was local, and much of it came from Jackson's supporters. A local book publisher wrote that as one of Jackson's "most ardent supporters [I am] all the more grieved at your untimely speech. I might almost say tirade . . . Even if you are opposed to the New Deal administration, you should be politician enough to know that this is no time to show it."[3]

At a labor rally a week before the election, the *Baltimore Sun* reported that Jackson was "heckled persistently as he attempted to recount the achievements of his administration in the labor and welfare fields." Finally, someone shouted from the back of the hall, "Are you for Roosevelt?" When the mayor hesitated, the roar of the audience grew louder, until Jackson finally responded that he had voted for Roosevelt as a delegate to the Democratic National Convention and pledged his support for the Democratic ticket.[4] Coming as it did, so soon before the general election, the endorsement seemed belated and half-hearted.

At Democratic campaign headquarters on the night of the election, many of the celebrants were Mayor Jackson's longtime political associates and allies. But Jackson was conspicuously absent. The *Sun* reported that there was considerable criticism of Jackson, "forced to declare for Roosevelt at the labor meeting."[5]

During the following year, Jackson sent several telegrams to FDR in support of his foreign policy.[6] Jackson saw to it that his telegrams received wide publicity, along with a letter of thanks that he received from the president. The mayor was attempting to mend his fences with local advocates of the New Deal.[7]

He was mending fences even with his political archrival. Jackson and William Curran cited the war as reason for their truce. A month after Pearl Harbor, the two men agreed on a candidate to fill the vacant chairmanship of Baltimore's Democratic Central Committee and engineered his unanimous election. Not long afterward, a local reporter noticed that Curran and Jackson greeted one another with a hug at a public banquet. Jackson explained: "Willie and I have always been good friends, personally." They were becoming good political friends too. Curran endorsed Jackson's reelection as mayor, and the two leaders agreed on a common slate of candidates for the state legislature. "People are not interested in ordinary politics at this time," said Curran. "Those who have boys in the armed forces scattered over the world don't want to talk politics." Even Governor O'Conor reached out to Jackson. The Herbert O'Conor Democratic Club cancelled its Jefferson-Jackson Day Dinner so that the governor and his friends could attend the banquet held at the mayor's Concord Democratic Club. All of the speakers emphasized the need for political unity. A "harmony conference" met in July 1942, at which Curran, Jackson, and O'Conor were able to agree on a partial slate of candidates for the General Assembly from Baltimore City. The participants expressed a hope that further conferences would extend the list of "harmony" candidates.[8]

World War II increased municipal responsibilities. Even before Pearl Harbor, the city had to expand its public services to accommodate thousands of new workers in local defense plants and shipyards. The public schools had to provide for their children. Mayor Jackson became director of civil defense for the Baltimore metropolitan area, but wanted some assurance that his new office did not make him subordinate to the state's director of civil defense, Governor O'Conor. It took a ruling from Fiorello La Guardia, the national director of civil defense, to put the mayor in his place.[9]

Harmony had its limits. While Curran and Jackson made peace with one another, they revealed how little control they exercised among their supposed followers. The Democratic primary of 1942 brought out not only "harmony" candidates for the legislature but also recalcitrant Jackson candidates and Curran candidates, along with some who supported both Jackson and Curran but not O'Conor, and still others who ran under the banners of district leaders such as Jack Pollack. In one Baltimore legislative district, 17 candidates ran for three seats in the house of delegates. The election produced a motley collection of Democratic legislators and only a narrow victory for Governor O'Conor over Republican Theodore R. McKeldin. Pollack crowed that the results disclosed the "dead leadership" of William Curran.[10]

Curran and Jackson, however, continued to cooperate. Curran reiterated his support for Jackson's reelection as mayor in 1943, and Jackson endorsed Curran allies for the offices of comptroller and city council president. Harmony, however, did not extend beyond these three citywide offices. Neither Curran nor Jackson endorsed any candidates for the city council, perhaps because they recognized just how little influence they exercised in district-level politics. Jackson won the Democratic primary with a 6,000 vote margin over all four of his opponents combined. Curran's candidates for comptroller and city council president were also successful. But in the general election, Jackson lost his bid for a fifth term as mayor to Theodore McKeldin by more than 20,000 votes, while every other Democratic candidate was victorious.[11]

The mayor's defeat was generally attributed to "long continuance in office," though McKeldin's final campaign attacks on Jackson suggested a variety of other reasons for retiring him—his use of the mayor's office to enhance his insurance business, for example. But the new alliance between Jackson and Curran may have given McKeldin his most effective ammunition. He pointed out that Jackson had waged his last campaign "to keep Mr. William Curran out of the City Hall. This time he takes the same William Curran to his heart and into City Hall despite the past smears he has put upon him."[12] When the city's two most powerful Democratic bosses joined forces, Baltimoreans may have had reason for apprehension. Rapprochement between the two also deprived Democratic district bosses of the opportunity to win patronage and perquisites by shifting from Curran to Jackson and back again.

MINORITY OF ONE AND THE RACIAL MINORITY

Mayor McKeldin commanded no machine. A lone Republican in an otherwise Democratic government, his influence depended almost entirely on his personal political skills. The unanimously Democratic city council went its own way. Curran and Jackson had agreed that the council's patronage should be divided evenly between their two camps. Instead, the supposed partisans of Howard Jackson deserted their fallen leader and joined three council members controlled by Fourth District boss Jack Pollack to deny the Curran faction any share of the spoils.[13]

At first, McKeldin dispensed mayoral patronage among council members and their retainers without much regard to faction, a strategy designed to maintain good will with the council as a whole, but one that infuriated the mayor's fellow Republicans—who gained almost nothing tangible from his victory. When McKeldin made appointments outside the council's Democratic factions and their backers, the jobs usually went to Jews, African Americans, women, or independent liberals, thus creating an intensely loyal personal constituency for the mayor among people usually denied access to leadership positions in city government.[14] To his fellow Republicans, the mayor offered only a plea to rise above partisanship. In a speech to the Alexander Hamilton Club of Maryland, he urged his party to "forget its special party interest and support first and foremost the interests of the nation, the State, and the city." Some Republicans, at least, believed that the mayor had betrayed his party "by selling out to the Jackson wing of the Democratic party."[15]

An alliance with the council's Jackson faction made sense for the mayor. Pollack, in one of his politically exquisite acts of betrayal, had shifted his district's three stalwarts from the Jackson to the Curran side of the council, thus creating a new council majority and securing the tangible gratitude of the Curranites. For Mayor McKeldin, an alliance with the pro-Jackson minority was an exercise in balance-of-power politics designed to offset the influence of the Curran-Pollack majority.[16]

War may have inspired Baltimore's rival Democratic bosses to strive for unity and to compose "harmony" tickets, but it seems to have heightened tension between the city's black and white residents. Mayor McKeldin was apprehensive that Baltimore might have a race riot like the one that exploded in Detroit in 1943.[17] The first stirrings of interracial violence emerged in Baltimore barely two months after the attack on Pearl Harbor, when a police officer killed a black soldier, Private Thomas Broadus. Patrolman Edward Bender shot him in self-defense, according to the Baltimore Police Department, when attacked by Broadus and two other black men, one of whom seized the officer's nightstick and used it to beat Bender over the head. Initial reports said that Bender had suffered a broken arm and a possible skull fracture, but neither the police department nor hospital officials offered further confirmation of his injuries. He was released from the hospital after just over a week, and a grand jury declined to indict him on a charge of homicide. Not long afterward, a judge acquitted Private Broadus's alleged accomplices of assaulting Bender or interfering with a police officer. Neither of the defendants testified; the judge dismissed the charges on the basis of the patrolman's testimony that Broadus was the person who had beaten him with his nightstick.[18]

The Baltimore branch of the NAACP initiated its own investigation of Broadus's death; so did the state's attorney, the medical examiner, and military authorities. Eyewitnesses reported that Broadus had been running away from his fight with the police officer when he was felled. The soldier was killed by two shots in the back.[19]

Broadus was the second black man killed by Officer Bender in his five years on the force. His death and the exoneration of the police officer responsible for it triggered a mass protest in the city's black community. Led by the *Afro*'s Carl Murphy, 2,000 African Americans joined a caravan of cars and buses to confront Governor O'Conor. (The Baltimore Police Department still operated under the governor's authority.) The protesters demanded not just an end of police brutality but the hiring of more black officers (there were only three) and appointment of black police magistrates. O'Conor listened, and a month later appointed the Commission on Problems Affecting the Negro Population.[20]

The commission's subcommittee on the police submitted a preliminary report demanding that Officer Bender's case be resubmitted to the grand jury on the grounds that Bender had killed Broadus while he was fleeing and the patrolman was no longer in danger. The report criticized the handling of the case by the state's attorney. He had allowed the grand jury to dismiss charges against Bender before it had heard from all witnesses to the shooting. The report was even more critical of the police commissioner, Robert F. Stanton, who had not taken any disciplinary action against Officer Bender. Since his appointment as commissioner, Stanton had hired no black police officers. During the preceding 12 years, police officers had killed 14 black men—9 of them since Stanton had become commissioner less than three years earlier. None of the nine officers had been brought to trial or disciplined.[21]

The 18-member commission continued to work on its final report for almost a year. It recommended the hiring of black police officers and appointment of blacks to government bodies such as school boards. It did not, however, challenge the regime of segregation. It urged greater financial support for teacher training at black colleges. The commission paid particular attention to housing for African Americans, perhaps because it was the black problem most likely to disturb whites. Black neighborhoods were already overcrowded, and wartime migration to Baltimore aggravated the housing shortage for blacks, much of which was substandard. Overcrowding in black neighborhoods threatened to push blacks into white neighborhoods. As the commission pointed out, housing was "at the root of many of the stresses that arise between the white and colored races." It called for additional black housing, with the proviso that it be "contiguous to existing Negro neighborhoods."[22]

The commission had little to say on the issue of black employment. Its members had split on the question of initiating a fair employment practices investigation of Baltimore industry. The mere proposal drove some members to resign in protest.[23] An investigation would have shown that barriers to black employment persisted even in the face of wartime manpower shortages. The *Afro* celebrated the employment of 13,600 blacks in Baltimore-area defense plants "as job barriers fall." But by the end of 1942, African Americans accounted for less than 7 percent of the city's war workers, though they made up more than 20 percent of Baltimore's labor force. In many cases, even employment did not lead to desegregation. The Glenn L. Martin plant and the Koppers Company confined black workers to separate facilities. Attempts to create integrated workplaces at Western Electric and Maryland Drydock triggered strikes by white workers.[24]

The migrations set in motion by World War II changed Baltimore's ethnic composition. The percentage of the population born abroad was shrinking. Ethnic political and social organizations were in decline. Baltimore's new immigrants were from Appalachia and the South. About 89 percent of the new arrivals—150,000 to 200,000—were white; their arrival reduced the demand for black workers. Employers refused to hire African Americans or assigned them to the least desirable jobs. When pressed, writes Kenneth Durr, they explained that they were deferring to the wishes of their white workers. They were mostly right. The massive influx of southern whites, says Durr, reinforced racist sentiments among native Baltimoreans.[25]

RACE AND PLACE

Mayor McKeldin escaped responsibility for police misconduct, but he stood directly in the line of fire when it came to the deficiencies in black housing cited in the final report of the governor's Commission on Problems Affecting the Negro Population. The Committee on Post-War Planning, originally appointed by Mayor Jackson, released its report on the same day that the commission announced its findings and called attention to the same conditions. Both reports took care to propose that any new housing for black Baltimoreans should be adjacent to existing black neighborhoods.[26]

The federal government's wartime need for defense workers intensified the problem of housing black Baltimoreans. Months before McKeldin's election, the federal War Manpower Commission had directed the Federal Public Housing Administration (PHA) to build as many as 2,000 temporary housing units in Baltimore for African American workers in defense plants and shipyards. The Baltimore City Plan Commission immediately objected to the construction of temporary housing. Baltimore already faced a shortage of decent, affordable housing. A survey of low-rent units conducted in 1941 found that even in housing rated as "standard," over 30 percent of the renters had no inside toilets or baths, and the percentage of households unable to afford decent housing was growing, especially among African Americans. City officials wanted wartime housing that would continue to serve after the war was over.[27]

More controversial than the durability of black housing was its location. The federal housing agency selected a site for the project in industrial East Baltimore, convenient to many of the city's mills and factories. The announcement provoked immediate protests from white residents nearby and from the Baltimore Association of Commerce, which complained that the area was a prime location for railyards and manufacturing and too valuable for residential development.[28] The Baltimore Housing Authority then suggested a different site on the same side of the city, just east of Herring Run Park. The authority's chairman emphasized that his agency was not recommending the site, only calling attention to it, because "the selection of the site or sites, the determination of all questions of policy and the planning and actual construction" were matters to be decided by the federal housing agency. Another eruption of protest meetings followed the mention of the Herring Run site. The chairman of the city's housing authority stood before one gathering of angry protesters and denied that his agency had any authority to decide where to put the federal government's housing project for black defense workers. For his part, Mayor Jackson claimed that "it has not yet been demonstrated, in my opinion, that there is a need . . . that would warrant the building of temporary Negro war workers' housing."[29]

Candidate McKeldin had criticized Mayor Jackson for failing to "take any part in the discussion of the Negro housing project." Mayor McKeldin appointed the Inter-racial Commission on Negro Housing to consider the matter and to resolve the impasse between local and federal officials. The mayor took care to emphasize, however, that he had "no authority to determine where these houses shall be built."[30]

The mayor's Inter-racial Commission met with officials of the PHA to consider Mt. Winans, a predominantly black neighborhood in a remote corner of Southwest Baltimore, as a location for black housing. Mayor McKeldin declared it "an ideal place for the project." A week later, the chairman of the Inter-racial Commission mentioned, hopefully, that he had heard no protests about the site. Two days later, however, residents of adjoining neighborhoods announced that they would oppose the use of Mt. Winans for black housing. Two hundred of them gathered the next evening and voted to send a delegation to Washington to protest use of the site. But there was no need for protest. In a meeting with city officials, the regional director of the PHA had already eliminated the Mt. Winans site because of its isolation.[31]

Attention reverted to the Herring Run location. The City Plan Commission favored the site. The city's housing authority, which had earlier suggested but not recommended it, now announced its disapproval of the location.[32] Mayor McKeldin, whose sideline was paid, professional oratory, delivered a masterful performance before 750 white opponents of the Herring Run site at the War Memorial auditorium. When he rose to speak, he was greeted with boos. He quieted the crowd and pointed out that housing black defense workers had been a problem before he assumed office, and again emphasized that the federal government had the responsibility for selecting a site for housing those workers. On the proposed location near Herring Run Park, he declared, "If I had selected this site I would have had the courage to stand up here and say so." He won loud applause when he said that he "had been unalterably opposed to bringing Negroes here from the South and building housing for them to the exclusion of long-time residents." At the close of the meeting, members of the once hostile audience surrounded the mayor to get his autograph.[33]

A week later, Mayor McKeldin distanced himself even further from the racial uproar by announcing that the city solicitor, a mayoral appointee, had ruled that city agencies had no authority to select public housing sites. That initiative, he said, belonged to the city council. The mayor called a special session of the all-Democratic council and gave them 15 days to designate locations for African American housing. If they failed to do so, he said, he would present the federal authorities with the disparate site recommendations of the Baltimore Housing Authority, the City Plan Commission, and his Inter-racial Commission. The council made no decision. Instead, it enacted a legally absurd but politically expedient ordinance prohibiting the federal government from "constructing any war housing in Baltimore without the approval of the Mayor, City Council, and Board of Estimates."[34]

The mayor thus failed to saddle the city council with an onerous decision that was almost sure to anger white voters, or black voters, or both. But he may have succeeded in moving one or more members of the council to mobilize Maryland's entirely Democratic congressional delegation to intercede with the PHA. Maryland's two senators and two of its congressmen met with federal housing officials to express their opposition to the Herring Run location. Congressman Thomas D'Alesandro, Jr., from Baltimore's Third District in Southeast Baltimore, suggested that federal officials' "seizure" of the site against the protests of city officials might prompt a congressional investigation. Congressman Streett Baldwin of Baltimore County added that "if Congress knew the money . . . would be used for this kind of project, you would not have gotten it, and you would not get any more."[35]

Herbert Emmerich, commissioner of the PHA, next attempted to burden Mayor McKeldin with the responsibility for deciding where to put housing for black defense workers. He may have reasoned that the mayor would be vulnerable to pressure because, as a solitary Republican, McKeldin could not count on Baltimore's Democratic politicians or its congressional delegation to rise to his defense.

Emmerich's stern letter to the mayor noted that the Inter-racial Commission and City Plan Commission had both recommended use of the Herring Run site for permanent African American housing. The mayor had forwarded these recommendations to the PHA. Though McKeldin told the PHA's regional director that the city council had to decide on the location of housing for black workers, Emmerich was determined to compel the mayor to assume responsibility for it: "I find it necessary to request that you advise us definitively and promptly whether the recommendations which you transmitted to us actually represent the recommendation of the City." He gave McKeldin a deadline of August 25, 1943.[36] If McKeldin rejected the Herring Run site, or failed to take a position, Emmerich added, "only one course remains open to us: that of building temporary housing to meet the war need on sites selected by us. As a matter of law, war housing projects may be constructed without regard to municipal laws, rules, ordinances or regulations." The mayor was not cowed. He bridled at the "curt bureaucratic attitude" evident in Emmerich's "lengthy letter of ungrounded assumptions, patent omissions and mandatory requirements." It was, wrote McKeldin, a "panicky letter seeking to escape responsibility . . . on Negro housing . . . by shifting the same to me." Federal officials had repeatedly claimed authority to decide where to build housing for black defense workers. As for the mayor, he "had not indicated a preference for a site. I have never expressed and do not now express a preference, as that is my prerogative."[37] The mayor then informed Emmerich that the Herring Run site was unacceptable, not because he was personally opposed to it, but because the city council would never approve it. Choosing a location, he repeated, was not his job. Instead, it became the business of the federal district court: the federal housing agency initiated condemnation proceedings to acquire the Herring Run land by eminent domain.[38]

McKeldin went on vacation when the case went to court. The acting mayor criticized the federal officials for acting in a "most autocratic and dictatorial manner" and instructed the city solicitor to contest the condemnation suit.[39] For Baltimore's political class, however, settling the issue in the courts may have been preferable to selecting a site themselves. But the politically astute Thomas D'Alesandro, Jr., took advantage of a lull in the court proceedings to arrange a conference between Baltimore officials and the head of the PHA. The city's representatives resurrected one of their early proposals—a plan that distributed housing for black workers among four small sites located close to defense plants. Two of them were outside the city limits.[40]

The newly proposed sites did not escape criticism. The Baltimore Urban League, supported by the local branch of the NAACP, objected to three of the four locations, primarily because they were in isolated industrial areas remote from community facilities such as schools and stores.[41] But the remoteness that made some of these sites objectionable to African Americans was precisely what made them acceptable to white residents and politicians. Other cities decided to locate housing for African Americans at isolated or undesirable sites or confined them to preexisting black ghettoes.[42] Baltimore politicians tried to sidestep the decision altogether.

FEATS OF FOOTWORK

Local Republican leaders had feared that the mayor would be "jockeyed into an unfavorable position on the matter" of black housing and were uneasy about "subtle attempts . . . to create the impression that the city administration is responsible for the efforts to locate the development in the city." But Mayor McKeldin had proven capable of the political footwork needed to dance his way around a politically treacherous issue. Democrats, however, persisted in their attempts to maneuver him into hazardous positions or prevent him from building a record of accomplishments. Democratic state legislators torpedoed his proposal for a crosstown expressway.[43] With the help of the city's Democratic delegation in Annapolis, Baltimore's police commissioner, bypassing the mayor, proposed police pay increases directly to the state legislature. But the mayor would have to fund these increases from the city budget, along with increases for other city employees whose compensation was pegged to police pay scales.[44] The Democratic city council refused to back the mayor in a tax dispute with the private company that held the franchise for public transportation in the city because the council wanted to deny the McKeldin administration an opportunity to pose as "the champions of the people against the great vested interests."[45]

In the face of Democratic obstructionism, McKeldin nevertheless managed to ready the city for postwar renewal. He gave Baltimore an up-to-date airport that could handle a new generation of large passenger aircraft too big for the municipal airfield begun under Mayor Broening.[46] McKeldin launched a school construction program and initiated planning for a civic center to accommodate conventions and sporting events. He started a new reservoir to secure the city's water supply, and a tunnel to carry water to the city. He appointed a commission to revise the city charter, which produced the first major overhaul of the document since 1898. The mayor got authorization from the state legislature to create the Baltimore Redevelopment Commission.[47] Its assignment was to shrink the city's slums. McKeldin also introduced another innovation in city government. He appointed the first African American to the city's board of school commissioners: George W. F. McMechen, a local attorney. Thirty-four years earlier, his rental of a house on McCulloh Street had provoked the wave of white protest that led Baltimore to enact its residential segregation ordinance. His appointment to the school board incited no public protest, and Mayor McKeldin was named to the 1944 honor roll of the *Afro-American*.[48]

McKeldin might have expected difficulties with Democrats, but factional divisions in his own party deprived him of solid support in meeting the Democratic challenges. By 1944, the battle lines were clear. On one side were Mayor McKeldin and his executive assistant, Galen L. Tait, who was also chairman of the Republican State Central Committee. In opposition were the followers of Paul Robertson, chairman of the Baltimore City Republican Committee and candidate for his party's nomination to the US Senate. One of Robertson's backers demanded that Tait be dismissed as the mayor's deputy because he was using city time to manage the campaign of Robertson's chief opponent in the Republican senatorial primary. McKeldin's camp responded by demanding the resignation of a pro-Robertson member of the city's election board who allegedly pressured Republican election judges to support his candidate.[49]

The intraparty feud grew more intense when McKeldin became a candidate for the Republican gubernatorial nomination in 1946. Fellow Republicans charged that he had failed to report many of the campaign contributions received when he was running for mayor in 1943. They attacked him for failing to appoint Republicans to city offices and for his "political mismanagement" thereafter. Even after three years as mayor, McKeldin was still just "an amiable youngster," according to one Republican critic, "totally lacking in business or executive experience, as is exemplified by the various muddles of his administration." Another questioned McKeldin's eligibility for the Republican primary "on the grounds that he is not even a Republican."[50]

McKeldin lost the governorship by a wide margin. Other Republican losers blamed him for dragging them down to defeat. The fact that his most energetic Republican critics were concentrated in Baltimore may have affected McKeldin's decision not to run for reelection as mayor in 1947. Even more important, perhaps, was that he failed to carry the city as a gubernatorial candidate.[51]

Chapter 33

D'ALESANDRO AND HIS DEMOCRATS

I N POSTWAR BALTIMORE, the Democrats may not have been as sharply divided as the Republicans, but they were hardly at peace with one another. William Curran found himself competing with nonparty organizations for the loyalty of voters. The local CIO political action committee transformed itself into a campaign organization to mobilize voters in favor of a fourth term for FDR. Representatives of the labor organization showed up at the state Democratic convention, demanding that the party go on record in support of Roosevelt. Curran charged that they had no place in party business unless they could prove consistent party loyalty from the top of the ticket to the bottom: "Are you for Fallon? Are you for Tydings? You people will have to get right with the party before you come down here."[1] Curran regarded his party organization as a bulwark against the kind of political radicalism that he saw in the CIO.

But the Democratic organization split when the alliance between Curran and district leader Jack Pollack fell apart in a petty patronage dispute over the appointment of election judges. Pollack, in an unlikely pairing, joined with the CIO-PAC in opposition to Curran. In 1946, the two bosses aligned themselves with different Democratic gubernatorial candidates. The city's district leaders joined their colleague Pollack in his support of William Preston Lane, who won the Democratic primary, defeating Curran's Eastern Shore candidate, J. Millard Tawes. Curran was able to carry only one of the city's six districts for Tawes, and his candidate for state comptroller lost all six. A majority of his candidates for the General Assembly survived the Democratic primary, but once the legislature convened they could be expected to succumb to the patronage at Governor Lane's disposal.[2]

Curran's defeats in the state elections of 1946 may help to explain his shaky leadership as he approached the municipal elections of 1947. In February he called a meeting of the ward executives, party committee members, and elected officials who made up the Curran organization. The 83 politicians who gathered in the Emerson Hotel voted overwhelmingly that the organization should unify behind a single aspirant to the mayor's office, but they could not agree on a candidate. The leading prospect was Howard Crook, the unfortunately named city comptroller who was acknowledged to be Curran's personal choice as mayoral candidate. Congressman Thomas D'Alesandro, from Southeast Baltimore's Little Italy, was 10 votes back in second place. Curran expressed disappointment that "the vote wasn't more one-sided in favor of somebody" and confessed that he had no idea what could be done to avoid a wide-open primary that would fragment his own forces and Democrats in general. Less than two weeks later, a meeting of Democratic leaders not associated with Curran was also unable to unify behind a single mayoral candidate, though D'Alesandro, the only candidate to make a personal appearance, seems to have made some converts among those in attendance.[3]

Finally, Pollack declared his preference, beginning with a condemnation of his former ally William Curran and his mayoral candidate Howard Crook. The election of Crook, said Pollack, would make Curran the de facto mayor. "Crook is Curran," he shouted, "and Curran is Crook." The statement lent itself to more than one interpretation. Pollack followed up with an endorsement of Congressman D'Alesandro.[4] In the Democratic primary, D'Alesandro won 48 percent of the vote, a near majority over his nine opponents, and then won the spirited general election by more than 24,000 votes, defeating Republican Deeley K. Nice, nephew of former Republican governor Harry Nice. Democrats won every seat in the city council.[5]

Thomas D'Alesandro, Jr., was a different kind of Democratic mayor. Unlike his Democrat predecessors, he was a committed advocate of the New Deal. He named one of his sons Franklin D. Roosevelt D'Alesandro. Unlike William Curran, he did not distance himself from labor organizations such as the CIO-PAC. Instead he made the group part of his constituency. D'Alesandro was a mayor for Baltimore's working class, but mostly its white working class. In 1947, the city's white working-class wards gave "Tommy" two-thirds of their votes; in the black wards, he received only 44 percent.[6]

The mayor's election had been achieved by a "coalition of bosslets," and they were not ready to surrender their independence to the mayor or to any other boss.[7] Within the council, there were sharp debates about the deference to be shown to Mayor D'Alesandro's nominations to city offices. The members were especially aroused when one among the bosslets appeared to gain ground on the others. Jack Pollack, whose support had been critical to D'Alesandro's election, emerged as the principal beneficiary of mayoral patronage—and the chief object of attack in the council.

The appointment of the city solicitor generated especially sharp controversy. D'Alesandro first nominated a former state senator, Milton Altfeld, who had been identified in the *Baltimore Sun* as a Pollack crew member. Altfeld issued a statement denying that he was one of Pollack's followers. Pollack was furious that his lieutenant had disowned him and informed the mayor that he no longer supported Altfeld's appointment. D'Alesandro's next choice was Edwin Harlan, a young and promising attorney. Rumors circulated that Harlan, too, was a Pollack stalwart. Altfeld seems to have been a principal source of the rumors, which were probably correct, and Harlan became unacceptable to the council. D'Alesandro next turned to assistant state's attorney Thomas Biddison, who had no known associations with Pollack. Pollack insisted, and D'Alesandro agreed, that Harlan be appointed immediately as Biddison's deputy.[8]

The council continued to complain about Pollack's influence over mayoral appointments, but council members also squabbled among themselves about the allocation of city jobs among council districts. Almost everyone claimed to be short-changed. The vacancy created by the death of a councilman created a new source of dispute. Rejecting the candidate favored by the mayor (and allegedly by Pollack), the council named a replacement not identified with Pollack or D'Alesandro—then mobilized the new voting alignment to oust the council's clerk, a Pollack adherent, and replace him with a loyal Curranite. It was, said the *Sun*, "the first direct victory—and the only one in the present Council to date—for William Curran." Almost a year later, in the spring of 1949, the remnants of the Curran organization would come together as the council's majority coalition, united against Pollack and the mayor.[9]

PRIORITIES VS. PROBLEMS

A Democratic mayor with a solidly Democratic council might have expected gentler treatment than D'Alesandro received. A hint of the troubles that awaited him was evident in the Democratic primary of 1947, when he confronted nine opponents from his own party. Once in office, he found that the repeated formation and collapse of council coalitions limited progress on his policy initiatives. He had sketched out his priorities a few months after taking office, identifying three projects: construction of a crosstown expressway, construction of a new stadium (and, by implication, acquisition of a major league baseball team), and consolidation of the agencies concerned with the city's harbor into a single port authority.[10]

The mayor's vision of a crosstown expressway was a revival and revision of Mayor McKeldin's highway proposal. D'Alesandro's road suffered many cuts at the hands of the city council, but not death. As originally proposed by the mayor, the freeway would have crossed the city diagonally from northeast to southwest. One by one, council representatives from districts in the path of the road eliminated the segments that would have cut through their home territories. In the end, only a little more than a mile of highway would remain—enough to link up with a road being built by the federal government from Washington to a military base just southwest of Baltimore. The new link would give Baltimoreans easy access to the new Friendship Airport begun under Mayor McKeldin.[11]

At first, D'Alesandro's stadium project seemed more promising than his highway proposal. The voters had approved a $2.5 million stadium bond issue in the same election that made D'Alesandro mayor. The money was to finance the replacement of an existing city stadium built in the early 1920s and used primarily by college and high school football teams and, later, by the Baltimore Colts. The minor league Baltimore Orioles played at a nearby ballpark owned by the team, but the park burned down in 1944, and the city stadium on 33rd Street became their home field. D'Alesandro envisioned a new stadium on the same site that would increase seating capacity from about 40,000 to at least 60,000, and he wanted it to have a roof. Engineers and architects, however, estimated that a roofed ballpark would cost twice the $2.5 million approved by voters. The stadium's neighbors objected to the crowds, the noise, the parking, and the lighting needed for night games. The city hired a team of engineers to evaluate 22 possible sites for the new arena. The 33rd Street location was their first choice, and the state courts disposed of the neighbors' objections. Persuading voters to authorize an additional $2.5 million bond issue proved more difficult. Having approved a stadium loan in 1947, voters were unwilling to approve another in 1948, especially since the size and design of the new arena were still uncertain.[12] By 1950, after city leaders began to talk about getting a major league baseball team, the electorate was ready to approve the money for a bigger stadium. In the meantime, D'Alesandro had already been building as much stadium as he could afford with the money in hand. He would not get the roofed stadium that he wanted, but Baltimore would have the big-league park that would enable it to compete for big-league teams.

As a port city, Baltimore was already in the big leagues, but it was threatened by competition with East Coast and Gulf Coast cities and soon to face the St. Lawrence Seaway. After World War I, Baltimore had created the Port Development Commission. It issued bonds to finance loans to some of the railroads that radiated from the harbor; they used the money for construction of new piers, warehouse expansion, and development of rail access to shipping. The commission, however, shared its authority over the port with five other agencies and had undertaken only two major projects from the time of its formation in 1920 to the end of World War II.[13]

According to a special committee of the Baltimore Association of Commerce, "Large sums for new port development are being expended by our competition on the Atlantic and Gulf seaboards." The competition relied heavily on public funds provided by state or municipal port authorities that exercised general control over harbor facilities. Unlike its rivals, Baltimore had no port authority with the power to issue bonds, levy taxes for harbor improvements, or acquire property by eminent domain.[14]

Railroads generally controlled the maintenance and improvement of Baltimore's port facilities. The municipality had taken over several piers in the aftermath of the 1904 fire, but the city exercised only limited authority over the harbor. Mayor D'Alesandro appointed a committee to come up with a coherent program of port improvements, partly because "the division among the shipping people in Baltimore" made it "difficult to determine what is necessary here." The committee, noting that the railroad companies were "definitely opposed to the construction . . . of truck terminals or other facilities which may in any way compete with existing rail owned and operated facilities," proposed an independent study, financed by the city and the state, to estimate how much truck traffic the port handled and how much more it might attract with a program of improvements.[15]

Baltimore had been a railroad pioneer, but now the city's commitment to railroads had become a drag on its economic growth. The port specialized in the bulk cargoes that railroads carried—coal, grain, potash, or gypsum; it was short on facilities for handling the kinds of shipments that trucks carried—everything from

The B&O freight yard on Locust Point in the early 1950s, when railroads monopolized access to the waterfront. *Courtesy Maryland Historical Society*

bales of textiles to machinery and shoes. At the railroad-owned piers, wharfage fees discriminated against cargoes carried by truck and, it was argued, diverted business to New York, where fees and facilities were more favorable to the trucking industry.[16]

The Port Development Commission hired a New York engineering firm to conduct a comprehensive study of port operations and facilities. It recommended creation of a centralized port authority with the power to take property by eminent domain and to issue bonds to pay for harbor improvements. Nine port-related organizations and agencies picked the report apart before the mayor's port committee could issue its conclusions. The president of the Western Maryland Railroad was ready to state his views even before receiving the report: "Baltimore has become a great port primarily because the railroads have kept a steady, lower freight rate for goods handled through Baltimore. Let the trucks with their hodge-podge rates, which can never be relied upon, take control and see what a great port that will be."[17]

The harbor advisory board, one of the agencies to be phased out under the study's recommendations, delivered another negative verdict on the study. Not long afterward, the mayor expressed reservations about the condemnation powers assigned to the proposed commission, and the influential Baltimore Association of Commerce rejected almost all of the study's conclusions, arguing in favor of a slightly modified version of the existing Port Development Commission—one that was likely to increase private ownership of the port. Projects financed by commission loans would revert to private ownership once the borrowers paid off the debts.[18]

Some participants in the discussion that followed tried to preserve a measure of consensus by accepting the consultants' advice to create a Port District Commission and leaving it to the commission to hammer out the hard decisions on the other recommendations. But members of the new Port of Baltimore Commission soon complained that they lacked the powers to upgrade the port and were too dependent on the city government for approval of their spending and development plans.[19] By 1953, the commission members were discussing the authorization of yet another study, "the feasibility of a single body operating all harbor activities." Nothing happened. Two years later, a new city business organization, the Greater Baltimore Committee (GBC), persuaded the state legislature to create an independent Maryland Port Authority with its own earmarked stream of funds from state corporate tax revenues.[20] The port had long been one of Maryland's vital assets. Now it would be run by Maryland, not Baltimore. The city did not protest.

THE BALTIMORE PLAN

Baltimore's public improvements rose up against a background of private squalor. Much of the city's housing stock was old, deteriorating, and overcrowded. The redevelopment commission could only whittle away at the slums, and public housing could accommodate only a small fraction of their residents. A new civic organization, the Citizens Planning and Housing Association (CPHA), formed in 1941 to promote a new approach to the problem. It persuaded the city council to specify minimum standards for housing—basic plumbing, ratio of windows to floor space, square footage per occupant, and more. Fire, health, police, and public works officials were to carry out a strict enforcement program demanding that landlords bring their properties up to code. The campaign drew national attention. It was the "Baltimore Plan." In 1947, a city housing court, the first in the country, began to hear cases generated by the plan. Two and a half years later, it had cleared 90,000 complaints. In 1949, Mayor D'Alesandro created a special office of housing and law enforcement in the city's health department with sole responsibility for the Baltimore Plan.[21]

The plan's new bureaucratic location was not ideal. The priorities of the health department and those of its housing office were out of joint with one another, and now that the office fell within the jurisdiction of a single city department, it had difficulty drawing together the fire and building inspectors whose expertise was essential to its work. The director of the housing office, G. Yates Cook, lobbied for creation of an independent agency to carry on the work of the Baltimore Plan. He had the support of James Rouse, real estate developer and chairman of the office's citizen advisory board. The CPHA also backed him. But the mayor rejected the proposal for a new agency. Yates resigned early in 1953. Rouse followed, as did several other members of the advisory committee.[22]

Independent status may not have made the program successful. In 1951, the housing office had targeted a 27-block section of East Baltimore for strict enforcement.

Landlords complained of harassment. Instead of making needed repairs, they expelled hundreds of tenants and sold their buildings. Rents soared. A subsequent study of the Baltimore Plan estimated that the human costs of the code-enforcement campaign exceeded the benefits.[23]

The Baltimore Plan was classic Baltimore—an effort to conserve the old rather than build anew—and one of its unintended consequences may have served the city's traditional aversion to contentious public discussions of race and discrimination. Bringing slum housing up to code allowed the city's disproportionately black population to remain in segregated neighborhoods. A more ambitious program of slum clearance would have scattered black residents and risked the nasty reactions that broke out when African Americans landed in white residential areas. Such conflicts were not inevitable. Blockbusting real estate entrepreneurs could trigger white flight from racially changing neighborhoods, leaving few white residents to stand and fight the newcomers. Edward Orser's account of racial turnover in Baltimore's Edmondson Village neighborhood shows how 20,000 black residents replaced 20,000 whites in a decade. One of the new African American homeowners commented on the white departure: "They were friendly, but they were prejudiced. They didn't want to live where colored people did . . . They didn't tell you [why they moved]; they just moved." These white Baltimoreans, like many others, kept their prejudices to themselves. Race was a private problem, not a public issue.[24]

To cope with such issues if they arose, the mayor proposed creation of a 20-member commission on human relations. Among the commission's responsibilities would be the conduct of educational programs to eliminate discrimination based on race, religion, and national origin. On the day of the mayor's announcement, Baltimore park police broke up a baseball game in Easterwood Park between an African American team and a team of sailors from a naval ship undergoing repairs at a city dry dock. Two weeks earlier, the police had intervened to end an interracial tennis match between a team from Howard University and another from a nearby military base.[25]

Racially integrated athletic competition violated a longstanding policy of the board of recreation and parks. The board's chairman was Robert Garrett, grandson of B&O president John Work Garrett and a respected Baltimore banker. In 1948, Garrett and his board disqualified a boys' basketball team from competing in the city's recreation league because two of its members were African American. The board's action prompted a stream of protests addressed to Mayor D'Alesandro, including two letters from the formidable president of Baltimore's NAACP branch, Lillie Mae Jackson. She complained that the "Park Board, which you have appointed, is a disgrace to the democratic way of life."[26] In a letter of his own, Garrett outlined his reasons for sustaining the ban on interracial athletics: "I voted in favor of the old policy believing it wise to go slow in this difficult problem . . . In this case there is no adequate means of determining what the majority may desire. There are many thousands of persons involved in the work of the Department of Recreation and Parks and for us to put over a ruling covering a new practice would in my judgment involve an element of dictatorship."[27] Garrett added that race had been only one consideration in his decision. The basketball team in question had been sponsored by a local chapter of the Progressive Citizens of America, and "that organization by general reputation is subversive as to the government of the United States and the American way of life as is shown clearly in the pamphlet covering certain Hearings of the House Un-American Activities Committee."[28]

The mayor took issue with Garrett's position. "As public officials," he wrote, "our duty is to consider and decide questions that properly come before us, on the basis of merit regardless of sponsorship." While acknowledging Garrett's devotion to democracy, D'Alesandro dismissed his refusal to depart from established policy without a clear expression of majority opinion. Decisions "are made daily by public officials who are chosen for this very purpose, without opportunity for a referendum."[29] But the mayor did not attempt to reverse the board's ruling.

Three years later, the city council unanimously approved D'Alesandro's proposed human relations commission. On the same day, the park board announced the integration of the city's four golf courses. Interracial play would also be permitted at specifically designated tennis courts and baseball diamonds. But teams would have to secure a special permit from the parks department before engaging in interracial contests. Robert Garrett had resigned from the park board a year earlier.[30]

BROKEN MACHINES

Mayor D'Alesandro's reelection campaign began while the Port of Baltimore Commission was still being prodded into existence and shortly after creation of the mayor's human relations commission. The city council was in a state of paralysis. The resignation of one member created a numerical tie between the council's two factions, and they were unable to agree on a replacement. The mayor stood aloof from the council's squabbles; he did not even bother to take a position on the four-way contest for the Democratic nomination for council president. His ticket consisted only of himself and the incumbent city comptroller, J. Neil McCardell. Ward leaders from the mayor's own district unanimously announced their support of C. Lloyd Claypoole for the council presidency. Claypoole's sponsor was Fourth District boss and mayoral ally Jack Pollack. If successful, Claypoole's election would elevate Pollack even further above the city's other bosslets and aggravate the factional tensions that had divided the city council since Thomas D'Alesandro, Pollack's candidate, had become mayor. Two Sixth District bosslets from Southwest Baltimore—senate president George Della and municipal judge Joseph Wyatt—put forward Arthur B. Price, a former councilman, as candidate for the council presidency, and they declared war on Pollack.[31]

Virtually all of the Democratic combatants in the contest for the council presidency supported Mayor D'Alesandro for reelection, and the remnants of William Curran's organization advanced no candidate to challenge him. D'Alesandro steadfastly refused to take part in the many brawls that churned beneath him in the Democratic Party. Neutrality enabled the mayor to deflect the enmity of the politicians struggling to check Pollack's ambitions while being the quiet beneficiary of the Pollack machine's vote-mobilizing power. A frustrated reform candidate for mayor argued that the apparent independence of D'Alesandro from Pollack was an election tactic designed "to lull the Democratic party into a state of security."[32]

For Democratic politicians, there was little security. Old allies became antagonists, and longstanding enemies formed partnerships. The mayor coasted to easy victory in the Democratic primary, as did his candidate for city comptroller, but two incumbent council members were defeated. The Della-Wyatt organization was the second most significant winner in the primary. It picked up a seat on the city council, and its candidate for city council president, Arthur Price, unexpectedly defeated Pollack's candidate by just over 1,000 votes.[33]

Price's victory in the Democratic primary was followed by a more notable surprise. C. Markland Kelly, the incumbent city council president, filed with the board of elections as an independent candidate for mayor, submitting a petition signed by 2,800 registered voters (only 1,500 were required). The board rejected the petition on a technicality, but was overruled by a city court. As council president, Kelly had often been at odds with Mayor D'Alesandro. Now he launched a full-scale attack. Corruption, he said, was pervasive in the D'Alesandro administration, and his position as chairman of the city's board of estimates, he said, gave him a ringside seat on the unsavory processes by which municipal contracts were awarded. "There is no planning," Kelly complained, "most things are helter-skelter depending on the wishes of cheap, offensive politicians and paving contractors." According to Kelly, D'Alesandro simply failed to understand the problems of the city because he was "lacking in education and business experience."[34]

The voters apparently disagreed. D'Alesandro defeated his Republican opponent by a margin of two to one, and Kelly finished a distant third. The mayor was only the most prominent victor in a Democratic sweep of the municipal election. The party's success seemed to heal its most persistent internal divisions. Days after the election, the Curranites, who made up the council's Third District delegation from Northeast Baltimore, declared their readiness to cooperate with the mayor. The mayor reciprocated. He supported the delegation's senior member for a seat on the city's planning commission. A Sixth District Curran partisan who had lost his council seat in the Democratic primary gained a place on the mayor's staff, along with another from the First District.[35]

The D'Alesandro administration took care to monitor hiring in city government at large. During the first year of the administration, the number of African Americans working for the city had increased by about 7 percent. The gain would have been greater had there not been an inexplicable drop in total employment for the Department of Public Works.[36] But even African Americans who had won city jobs were dissatisfied. Late in 1951, they were considering a strike. A walkout would be unprecedented. The city had faced strikes by workers employed by city contractors, but workers employed directly by the municipality had never walked off the job. Black employees accounted for 1,300 of the 3,300 city workers who belonged to the Municipal Chauffeurs, Helpers, and Garage Employees, Local 825—affiliated with the Teamsters Joint Council of Baltimore and the national Teamsters Union. They wanted a raise from $1.10 to $1.60 an hour. The city offered $1.18. Noting that the mayor and the director of public works had recently won annual pay increases of $5,000 apiece, the members voted overwhelmingly to go on strike. But the union called off its strike at the last minute and grudgingly accepted a city offer to increase hourly pay by 12 cents.[37]

A year later the union resolved not to be bought off so cheaply, and Local 825 became the first public employee union in the history of the municipality to go on strike. The union's heterogeneous membership performed services essential to the life of Baltimore. They included collectors of garbage, janitors and furnace men in the public schools, street sweepers, and workers who repaired water mains. Others operated the water filtration and sewage treatment plants. The city dog pound had no one to drive the trucks that picked up stray animals. For a time, 104 of Baltimore's 174 schools had to send their pupils home because it was January and their buildings lacked heat. Uncollected garbage accumulated at the rate of 1,000 tons a day.[38] While the strike threatened essential city services, it also challenged Mayor D'Alesandro's status as a firm friend of labor. He sought to secure his political reputation by characterizing Local 825's job action not as a strike against an employer but as a strike against the public. "Even the most ardent friends of labor," he said, "recognize that the strike is not an appropriate weapon to be used by labor against the public." It was an attempt to "club the public into submission." If Baltimoreans would "stand firm and endure whatever temporary inconveniences may be involved, then these tactics will not succeed and the public interest will prevail."[39]

The union may have exposed the weakness of its position by the progressive reduction of its demands. It retreated from its insistence on an hourly raise of 50 cents to propose a 10 percent increase, then 9 percent. The mayor and board of estimates rejected all these demands because, they said, there was no money in the 1953 budget to pay for them. The union proposed that the administration take advantage of a city charter provision authorizing "emergency" borrowing when "the health, safety and sanitary condition of the city" were threatened. The mayor responded that borrowing money would increase the cost of raising laborers' incomes by adding interest payments to the wage increase. The city solicitor pointed out that the strike did not meet the judicial definition of an emergency because it "was not sudden, unexpected and unforeseen." The mayor offered the possibility of a cost of living increase in 1954 and "fringe benefits," such as an increase in the pay differential for night work from 5 to 10 cents an hour.

The union rejected the proposal. On January 14, the board of estimates unanimously voted to withdraw the city's recognition of the union. The mayor announced that men who returned to work would receive the package of fringe benefits previously offered. Those who failed to show up would be fired. Two days later, almost all of the workers were back on the job.[40]

D'Alesandro, a self-described friend of unions, had won a local reputation for his effectiveness in dealing with labor. About a year before he faced down Local 825, the mayor had gotten most of the credit for preventing a walkout by transit workers. Not long afterward, an "appreciation dinner" honored D'Alesandro for his prowess as a "skilled labor negotiator." It drew 800 guests. If any union officials attended, their presence escaped the notice of the local press. When transit workers later threatened another strike, the mayor was not on hand to dissuade them. For over three weeks he had been hospitalized with a respiratory infection and high blood pressure. His physician attributed his condition to "overwork" and agreed to discharge him only if he would immediately embark on a Caribbean cruise that would take him out of the city for another two weeks.[41] The mayor would also remain on the sidelines in what may have been Baltimore's most challenging case of conflict resolution.

RACE AND RETICENCE

I heard about the US Supreme Court's decision in *Brown v. Board of Education* while listening to the car radio from the backseat of my father's '49 Studebaker. I had just turned 11 years old and was about to finish sixth grade at a legally segregated, all-white elementary school. At the time, I thought that the Court's decision would take effect almost immediately. It was, after all, Supreme. In fact, the justices would hold the *Brown* case over for a year so that they could hear argument about implementation of their decision. The Baltimore Board of School Commissioners, however, acted more quickly than the Court. On June 3, 1954—just 17 days after the Court announced its decision—the school board voted unanimously to desegregate the city's schools when they reopened in September. The meeting was the first at which local department store executive Walter Sondheim served as board president. (His predecessor, Roszel Thomsen, was being sworn in as a federal judge on the same day.) The school commissioners' decision took up just a minute and a half of their meeting, and there was no public discussion.[42] My expectations about the speed of the integration process turned out to be roughly accurate. In September, I would be attending a racially desegregated junior high school named after Robert E. Lee.

Under the freedom-of-choice plan approved by the school board, the number of black students attending formerly white schools was small. In 1954, only about 1 percent of the city's black secondary school students attended junior or senior high schools previously reserved for whites. But they were concentrated in a relatively small number of schools. Several black children started with me at Robert E. Lee. We never talked about race. Neither did the teachers. In fact, no one discussed racial desegregation with the students.

The city at large was almost as quiet on this subject. It was so silent that one segregationist expressed his puzzlement at the absence of debate in a letter to the *Sun*. "Somewhere in this town of ours," he wrote, "there must be others with the urge to voice the opinion."[43] For four and a half months, however, Baltimore did nothing but congratulate itself, quietly. Such resistance as there was broke into the open at the beginning of the new school year. Then, in working-class Pigtown, about 30 white women picketed the neighborhood elementary school to protest its integration. A much larger crowd—mostly students—gathered at Southern High School, not far from the waterfront. Fistfights broke out, and there were several arrests. But the protests lasted for only three days and affected only about 3 percent of the school population. In a statement that would later be echoed by public officials in the deeper South to dismiss integrationists, Southern's principal blamed the segregationist disturbances on "agitators" who had spread false rumors about conditions at his school. Nineteen civic and religious organizations announced their support for the school board's decision to desegregate voluntarily. A superior court judge threw out a suit challenging desegregation.[44] The city's police commissioner delivered a televised statement in which he warned that the picketing of schools might constitute a misdemeanor under a state law prohibiting disruption of classes and that inciting children to boycott their classes was a crime.[45]

Baltimore, as Robert Crain pointed out, stood apart from other cities facing school integration. It had "no demonstrations of importance and hardly any public statements that suggested conflict."[46] The Maryland Petition Committee voiced opposition to school integration, but most of its supporters were outside the city. Its most prominent adherent in Baltimore was attorney George Washington Williams. According to a local Urban League official, Williams's racist rants actually "did a great deal to help our cause."[47]

The protests evaporated, and for the time being the debate about school integration in Baltimore was over. Prolonged discussion would have suggested uncertainty and encouraged resistance. Saying as little as possible was the conscious policy of the superintendent of schools. According to a subsequent review of school integration, sponsored by city and state human relations commissions, the superintendent "and his administrative staff, backed by the Board of School Commissioners, believed firmly that the less said in advance about integration the better, since talking about it would focus attention on presumed problems and create the impression that difficulties were anticipated." In a memorandum from headquarters, school staff members were instructed to carry out desegregation "by 'doing what comes naturally,' so that children would look upon it as a natural and normal development and hence nothing over which to become excited or disturbed."[48]

The silence that I encountered at Robert E. Lee was not just one school's response to integration. It was school system policy. Its aim was not just desegregation but conflict avoidance. The school board's early and abrupt compliance with the *Brown* decision was a preemptive strike designed to minimize political contention about race, and its short-term effect was to foreclose most public discussion of desegregation.[49]

The decision, however, may have been less precipitous than it seemed. Baltimore had been moving quietly toward integration for years. In 1952, Ford's Theater dropped its whites-only admission policy; most downtown department stores, which had discouraged if not excluded black customers, agreed to serve them—except in women's wear. In 1953, the Baltimore Fire Department hired its first black firefighters. Not long before the opening of schools in 1954, Baltimore's public housing agency dropped its segregation policy. Almost six months before the Supreme Court handed down its decision in *Brown*, a *Sun* reporter had asked Mayor D'Alesandro how the city might respond to court-ordered desegregation. D'Alesandro did not hedge. If the verdict was for desegregation, "it will be my duty and the responsibility of the Board of School Commissioners to carry out the mandate of the Supreme Court."[50]

The school system had been unobtrusively preparing for integration since the 1940s. In 1947, for example, school staff meetings were integrated. Integration of the citywide PTA council followed. Two years before the *Brown* decision, 16 black boys were admitted to a demanding college preparatory curriculum—the "A course"—at the all-male Baltimore Polytechnic Institute, one of the city's elite high schools. The local Urban League had insisted that nothing equivalent to the program could be created at any of Baltimore's black high schools. Thurgood Marshall argued before the school board that the desegregation of Poly's A course was required by law. There was talk of litigation, but none was needed. During the summer following the *Brown* decision, adult education classes were desegregated. The Baltimore Division of Colored Schools was abolished, and the administrator who headed it became assistant superintendent of the entire system. With the exception of the decision to admit black students to Poly, none of these preparatory steps had caused comment. While the Supreme Court was still deliberating about the *Brown* cases, Baltimore's school superintendent visited the headquarters of the city's NAACP branch to discuss desegregation plans with the organization's leaders.[51] Baltimore's quiet approach to integration had begun years before the *Brown* decision. It was settled policy.

Keeping quiet was not the same as doing nothing. The city's leaders had to make significant adjustments to minimize public debate about race in Baltimore. Integration of the schools may have been insignificant at first, but by 1957, 26 percent of the city's African American pupils were attending school with whites.[52]

Baltimore had to work hard to restrict the politicization of race. The acquiescence of Baltimoreans in general could not be taken for granted. Thousands of white southerners had migrated to the city during World War II to work in defense plants,[53] and many native Baltimoreans shared southern attitudes about race and segregation. The city, after all, had named one of its public schools after Robert E. Lee. For the most part, however, Baltimoreans made little or no trouble for their leaders. The muffling of racial conflict was not just a matter of elite convenience; it was a widespread political convention.

TAKING CARE OF BUSINESS

School board president Walter Sondheim told Mayor D'Alesandro about the desegregation decision only after the board had voted. Keeping the decision out of the hands of local politicians was an essential element of the board's low-profile approach to integration. It was also consistent with the board's conviction that its responsibility for the schools was "a cherished, sacred, and separate-from-politics duty."[54] The point, in short, was to prevent politicians from making an issue of school desegregation. One of them tried. A city councilman from Northwest Baltimore's Fifth District introduced a resolution asking that the school board retain racially separate schools as required by municipal ordinance. He had trouble getting anyone to second the measure, and when he asked for unanimous consent to bring his resolution to the floor immediately, no one joined him. His bill was eventually defeated.[55]

Important local policies were being made outside the reach of party politicians. The Baltimore Plan, like school desegregation, had emerged outside the realm of the bosslets. It began as an initiative of the CPHA, whose leaders "designed a precise plan for implementing and coordinating the different enforcement procedures and services needed" to prevent or reverse urban decay; the CPHA promoted the plan and sold it to Mayor D'Alesandro, who directed city agencies to cooperate in enforcement program. It was overseen by a citizens' advisory board that included several leaders of the CPHA.[56]

The CPHA was regarded with some suspicion by the Democratic regulars at city hall, and the organization soon clashed with the mayor over his appointments to the zoning appeals board. By one account, the mayor actively promoted this dispute to demonstrate to party loyalists that he had not gone over to the civic do-gooders.[57] The CPHA and the party politicians operated in different arenas. While the housing association launched programs to rescue neighborhoods from decay, the city's Democratic politicians fought a measure that would have consolidated Baltimore's courts and diminished the supply of clerkships available for distribution as patronage.[58]

The games played by party politicians seemed increasingly marginal to the city's existence. While the CPHA worked on the city's residential neighborhoods, the congregation of business firms that formed the Greater Baltimore Committee saw to the city's commerce and its downtown. After persuading the General Assembly to create the Maryland Port Authority in 1953, the GBC returned to Annapolis in 1955 to win legislative approval for a civic center authority with the power to issue bonds to finance a facility that would accommodate indoor sports, concerts, theatrical productions, and conventions. Originally, the authority was to operate independently, without relying on the city's credit. But financial advisers doubted that the authority could raise sufficient funds on its own. The civic center authority requested city financing; the board of estimates agreed to provide a home for the authority within the municipal bureaucracy. Its $6 million bond issue won the required voter approval. The authority considered several different sites for the civic center, including one in Druid Hill Park, where the building could rise on land donated by the city. But critics attacked the loss of valuable park land. The influential Baltimore Commission on Governmental Efficiency and Economy noted that the civic center "could offer a dramatic implementation of the City's developing plans to revitalize downtown Baltimore." Downtown land was expensive, but the commission uncharacteristically endorsed the additional cost with the expectation that it would yield more revenue than any of the other sites proposed.[59]

The GBC also formed a subcommittee, headed by developer James Rouse, to address the larger problem of urban deterioration. Its report, issued in 1955, noted that the city's loss of population and purchasing power meant a "loss of markets to the business enterprises in the central city." The future of city government looked no brighter. Decaying neighborhoods inhabited by needy residents would increase the cost of city services while property assessments and tax revenues diminished. Responsibility for reversing the city's physical decline, wrote the subcommittee, was divided among several city agencies. It recommended a thorough study "to determine what must be done to develop a program in scale with the problems the city faces."[60]

About two months later, the city's board of estimates approved $35,000 for the proposed study. A committee of six outside experts, headed by the director of the Institute of Urban Studies at the University of Pennsylvania, submitted its report in

November 1956. It called for a $900 million urban renewal program. Mayor D'Alesandro announced that he would immediately take steps to carry out one of the committee's recommendations. He got city council approval for an urban renewal superagency that would combine the functions of the redevelopment commission, the code enforcement office responsible for the Baltimore Plan, and the housing authority. He also designated Baltimore's first urban renewal area—Harlem Park—where the new Baltimore Urban Renewal and Housing Agency (BURHA) would begin work on its $900 million *magnum opus*.[61] Walter Sondheim would serve as chairman of the new agency's citizen advisory commission.

Baltimore's urban renewal effort moved into new territory. Originally, the federal renewal program was tailored to upgrade or replace housing in slum neighborhoods, but the Housing Act of 1954 made commercial areas eligible for federal subsidies. Mayor D'Alesandro designated the central business district as a renewal zone. Baltimore was the first city in the country to take such action. But the GBC, not city government, would oversee planning for downtown renewal. A new GBC Planning Council would hire its own planner and, together with an organization of downtown retailers, cover the costs of designing a downtown renaissance. Privatization, according to the *Sun*, would enable the business community to avoid making "its plans in a goldfish bowl, subject to the vagaries of public opinion." If renewal schemes had to be "watered down to meet all objections, there would be little to inspire the private developer to take a plunge."[62]

The GBC took the plunge when it announced plans for the Charles Center Project. This would include eight office buildings, an apartment complex, a hotel, a theater, a parking garage, and shops. It would link the department store and retail district on the downtown's west side to the financial district on the east. The new civic center would occupy a site just to the south. Charles Center would not rely on federal funds, at least at first, and the city would have to cover only about $20 to 25 million of its estimated $180 million cost. The rest would come from private developers.[63]

The city provided something even more essential than its financial investment: the power of eminent domain. Land for Charles Center had to be acquired from more than 200 property owners, some of whom were understandably determined to hold on to their parcels of real estate at the very heart of the city.[64]

In a 1956 speech before the GBC, Mayor D'Alesandro declared, not for the first time, his support for the renewal program outlined in the committee's report. He warmly endorsed its observation that the mayor's office must serve as "the essential center of leadership in this undertaking." But he had been something less than central in the early stages of Baltimore's urban renewal effort, which was dominated by local business leaders. Although he could expect to exercise more influence in the clearance and rehabilitation of deteriorating residential neighborhoods like Harlem Park, downtown renewal would proceed largely under the auspices of downtown business. The business district's chief planner, David A. Wallace, acknowledged the leadership of Mayor D'Alesandro and the facilitating role of Baltimore's consolidated urban renewal machinery. But the planning council that he led was "a wholly owned subsidiary of the Greater Baltimore Committee" and operated under a con-

Charles Center
Courtesy Maryland
Historical Society,
Item B95

tract with the Committee for Downtown, another organization of local business leaders. The contract was signed in the presence of the mayor, but he was not a party to it. City government had no representation on the planning council and covered none of its costs.[65]

D'Alesandro followed up his uncertain assertion of leadership with a character-istic Baltimore lament: "Why do we always seem so content with things as they are? Why do we never go quite far enough to round out an idea with the drive and the promotion essential to compete with other large urban centers?" "During the last several months," he added, "I have been prompted to make some pretty bad com-parisons between Baltimore and some other cities."[66]

The city's downtown redevelopment effort did compare favorably with those of other cities. Theodore McKeldin, who would succeed D'Alesandro, expanded on the Charles Center initiative while the project was still under construction. He urged extension of the downtown renewal effort to the Inner Harbor, with its rot-ting piers, empty warehouses, and derelict Chesapeake Bay steamers. Rehabilitation of the city's waterfront added 240 acres to Baltimore's downtown revival program. A private, nonprofit corporation—Charles Center–Inner Harbor Management Corporation—would oversee the planning and execution of the more ambitious enterprise under the general direction of the city's urban renewal and housing ad-ministration.[67]

Part X **BUILDING A BETTER BUREAUCRACY**

Chapter 34

I'M ALL RIGHT, JACK

WHILE BALTIMORE'S CIVIC ORGANIZATIONS and business leaders
became more prominent as urban policymakers in the 1950s, the
old party organizations faltered. Their mostly white constituents
decamped for the suburbs, one jump ahead of a growing African American population. In West Baltimore's Fourth District, where Jack Pollack
had exercised nearly absolute control for a generation, a black Republican candidate for city council, Harry Cole, came close to unseating
one of Pollack's stalwarts in 1953. Cole later defeated a Pollack man for
a seat in the state senate, and another black Republican, Emory H. Cole
(no relation), defeated a Pollack candidate for the house of delegates.
Pollack was already giving ground. In the 1954 general election, he threw
his support behind Truly Hatchett, a black candidate for delegate who
had survived the Democratic primary without Pollack's endorsement.
Hatchett got Pollack's support in the general election and joined the
Coles in the General Assembly.[1]

Pollack wasted no time in trying to rebuild his barony. Since his
Fourth District base was crumbling, he tried to colonize other districts.
In the 1954 Democratic primary, Pollack slated candidates for the state
senate, not just in the Fourth, but also in the Second, Third, Fifth, and
Sixth Districts. His objective was to elect four of the six state senators
from the city. Had his strategy succeeded, he would have been able to
control the flow of state patronage from Annapolis to Baltimore. Longstanding tradition gave senators veto power over gubernatorial appointments in their districts, and a majority of Baltimore's six senators would
have the final say on state appointments to citywide offices such as the
board of elections. Two of Pollack's colonizing candidates succeeded. If
he had been able to elect a state senator in his own Fourth District, he
would have commanded at least half of Baltimore's delegation in the
state senate. But Harry Cole's victory on Pollack's home ground left the
boss short of his objective.[2]

In 1957, Pollack mounted another offensive. As the black population
of the Fourth District grew, many of his former constituents moved to

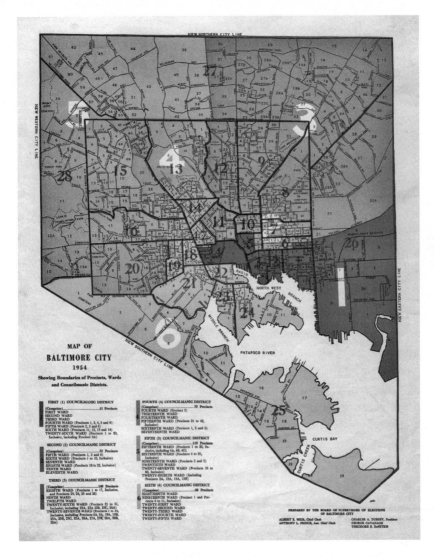

MAP OF
BALTIMORE CITY
1954

Showing Boundaries of Precincts, Wards
and Councilmanic Districts.

FIRST (1) COUNCILMANIC DISTRICT
(Comprises)_____61 Precincts
FIRST WARD
SECOND WARD
THIRD WARD
FOURTH WARD (Precincts 1, 2, 4, 3 and 6)
FIFTH WARD (Precincts 2, 3 and 4)
SIXTH WARD (Precincts 11, 12, 13 and 14)
TWENTY-SIXTH WARD (Precincts 1 to 20,
Inclusive, including Precinct 5A)

SECOND (2) COUNCILMANIC DISTRICT
(Comprises)_____33 Precincts
FIFTH WARD (Precincts 1, 5 and 6)
SIXTH WARD (Precincts 1 to 10, Inclusive)
SEVENTH WARD
EIGHTH WARD (Precincts 18 to 22, Inclusive)
TENTH WARD
ELEVENTH WARD

THIRD (3) COUNCILMANIC DISTRICT
(Comprises)_____140 Precincts
EIGHTH WARD (Precincts 1 to 17, Inclusive,
and Precincts 23, 24, 25 and 26)
NINTH WARD
TWELFTH WARD
TWENTY-SIXTH WARD (Precincts 21 to 51,
Inclusive, including 22A, 23A 23B, 23C, 26A)
TWENTY-SEVENTH WARD (Precincts 1 to 54,
Inclusive, including Precincts 6A, 5A, 19A, 19B,
25A, 25B, 25C, 25A, 26A, 27A, 27E, 28A, 28B,
32A)

FOURTH (4) COUNCILMANIC DISTRICT
(Comprises)_____70 Precincts
FOURTH WARD (Precinct 3)
THIRTEENTH WARD
FOURTEENTH WARD
FIFTEENTH WARD (Precincts 21 to 42,
Inclusive)
SIXTEENTH WARD (Precincts 1, 2 and 3)
SEVENTEENTH WARD

FIFTH (5) COUNCILMANIC DISTRICT
(Comprises)_____119 Precincts
FIFTEENTH WARD (Precincts 1 to 20, In-
clusive, including 4A, 4B, 4C)
SIXTEENTH WARD (Precincts 4 to 25,
Inclusive)
NINETEENTH WARD (Precincts 2 and 3)
TWENTIETH WARD
TWENTY-SEVENTH WARD (Precincts 35 to
42, Inclusive)
TWENTY-EIGHTH WARD (Including
Precincts 2A, 12A, 13A, 15B)

SIXTH (6) COUNCILMANIC DISTRICT
(Comprises)_____68 Precincts
EIGHTEENTH WARD
NINETEENTH WARD (Precinct 1 and Pre-
cincts 4 to 11, Inclusive)
TWENTY-FIRST WARD
TWENTY-SECOND WARD
TWENTY-THIRD WARD
TWENTY-FOURTH WARD
TWENTY-FIFTH WARD

PREPARED BY THE BOARD OF SUPERVISORS OF ELECTIONS
OF BALTIMORE CITY

ALBERT E. WEIR, Chief Clerk   CHARLES A. DORSEY, President
ANTHONY L. PRINCE, Asst. Chief Clerk   GEORGE CAVANAGH
                                       THEODORE E. DePETRIS

Baltimore's
councilmanic
districts in 1954.
*Courtesy of
Baltimore City
Department
of Legislative
Reference*

Northwest Baltimore's predominantly Jewish Fifth District. Two loyalists from Pollack's Trenton Democratic Club followed them, and they founded the Fifth District's Town and Country Democratic Club a year in advance of the 1958 election. The move was risky. The Fifth District already had a Democratic club—the Fifth District Organization for Better Government. Its leader was Irvin Kovens, owner of a furniture store and several bars. Kovens had been propelled into politics by his irritation at a state sales tax instituted under Governor William Preston Lane in the 1940s. His furniture store's 35 collection agents gave him a readymade political organization. They fanned out across the city's most densely populated neighborhoods to collect weekly installments on sofas and dining room sets. They began collecting political adherents, too.[3]

When Pollack mounted his assault on the Fifth District, Kovens was a member of the Baltimore Liquor Board, appointed by Republican governor Theodore McKeldin.

He had two influential lieutenants: state senator Philip Goodman, who was chair of the city's legislative delegation until pushed out of the position by Pollack allies, and John Luber, Speaker of the house of delegates. But only two months after Pollack's agents opened for business in the Fifth District, Kovens abruptly resigned from the liquor board and announced that his family and business obligations, together with his doctor's advice, had led him to withdraw from politics.[4]

In fact, Kovens's "retirement" from politics merely provided him with cover for a temporary withdrawal from the Democratic Party. Thomas D'Alesandro, Jr., who had become mayor with the support of Jack Pollack, was now running, with Pollack's backing, for the US Senate against the Republican incumbent, J. Glenn Beall. Free of his Democratic ties, Kovens backed Beall, not just to defeat D'Alesandro, but to curb the imperialistic designs of the mayor's political sponsor—Jack Pollack. During the election campaign, Kovens's lieutenant, Philip Goodman, oversaw the operations of his leader's political organization in the Fifth District. The "retired" boss was conspicuously present at his club's rally a week before the general election. Also conspicuous were campaign signs bearing the names of all Democratic candidates save D'Alesandro. Senator Goodman spoke in support of the party's nominees, except for the mayor. Goodman later denied charges that he and his organization planned to "cut" Mayor D'Alesandro from sample ballots, locally known as "palm cards."[5]

According to a Democratic election official, "a well-organized campaign of ticket-cutting" had operated in four of the city's six districts. Sample ballots in D'Alesandro's First District and Pollack's Fourth District were unaffected, but the mayor's name disappeared everywhere else. In some precincts, it was impossible to vote for D'Alesandro because the lever next to his name was jammed. In others, party labels had been removed from voting machines. Democratic leaders blamed Kovens. D'Alesandro managed to carry the city in spite of the irregularities, but not by enough votes to compensate for his unpopularity in the rural and suburban counties. After 23 consecutive election victories, D'Alesandro was a loser.[6]

Irvin Kovens emerged from his "retirement" in time for the municipal primary of 1959, when D'Alesandro ran for an unprecedented fourth term as mayor. D'Alesandro's opponents within the Democratic Party coalesced around J. Harold Grady, the state's attorney and a former FBI agent. Grady announced his candidacy in the Democratic primary by declaring that he had "not the slightest inclination or desire to become a political boss or to build a political machine in order to dominate the city." His ticket included Kovens lieutenant Goodman for president of the city council, and physician R. Walter Graham for comptroller—the "Three G Ticket." Grady urged Baltimoreans to turn out the "entrenched political machine" that had been running the city "pretty much as it pleased" during D'Alesandro's 12 years as mayor. Toward the end of the campaign, he became more explicit. The election would decide "whether Jack Pollack is going to take over Baltimore." Maryland's governor, J. Millard Tawes from the Eastern Shore, endorsed D'Alesandro but may have inadvertently supplied the ammunition that gave force to Grady's accusations. Days before the primary, Tawes announced a list of nominees for state offices. Pollack's son-in-law was to be chief magistrate of Baltimore's traffic court; the mayor's son was appointed president of the board of supervisors of elections. The mayor lost the primary by an astonishing 33,000 votes. Kovens, according to the *Sun*, was one of "the small headquarters group which helped Mr. Grady mastermind his campaign."[7]

Grady's Republican opponent in the general election was Theodore McKeldin. Each candidate claimed that the other was tainted by bossism. McKeldin wasted no time in linking Grady to Irvin Kovens, while naming Kovens as a "protégé" of Jack Pollack. "Mr. Kovens," he said, "is running the campaign because it is his intention to take over control of his party . . . and he intends to do it through the distribution of patronage that would be made available to him" with the election of the Grady ticket.[8] McKeldin's attack on bossism lost some of its force because of his so often being either a beneficiary or a benefactor of Democratic bosses himself. It was widely known that Boss Pollack had helped him win the governorship in 1950, and as governor, he had appointed Boss Kovens to the Baltimore Liquor Board.[9] Kovens reminded the voters of McKeldin's political history. Grady, having run as an anti-machine candidate in the Democratic primary, cranked up the same rhetoric to attack McKeldin.[10]

The conduct of Jack Pollack was extraordinary, perhaps desperate. He showed up at a $100-a-plate dinner for Harold Grady without being invited. Grady refused to speak to him. Pollack nevertheless endorsed him, but when the rebuffs continued, he changed course. At an end-of-campaign rally of his followers, Pollack failed to mention Grady. He announced that he was "releasing" his workers and urged them to vote for "the man with experience." Remarkably, the next step of the seldom visible boss was to book four 15-minute segments on a local television station for a series entitled "Meet Jack Pollack." On the first show, he introduced Mrs. Pollack along with his three grown children and their spouses. The program's purpose, he said, was "to remove the veil of secrecy from practical politics." He compared his Trenton Democratic Club's decisions about candidates to the deliberations of the *Sun* editorial staff in their "smoke-filled board room" to decide on the paper's endorsement of candidates.[11]

Grady capitalized on Pollack's new visibility by charging that the boss and his organization were covertly supporting McKeldin. Pollack added credibility to the claim by issuing a series of increasingly strident attacks on Grady. McKeldin never issued a categorical repudiation of Pollack, but some Republicans, possibly recalling McKeldin's dismissive treatment of his own party when he was mayor and governor, announced that they were repudiating him. The Republican candidate lost the city by a record 81,000 votes.[12]

THREE G'S MINUS TWO

As mayor, Grady never lived up to his landslide. He initiated a mayoral television program on Sunday evenings. One week, he took calls from constituents complaining about neighborhood nuisances; another, he and Baltimore legislators discussed the city's "tax crisis." But no remedies emerged. The program ended after four weeks.[13]

At the suggestion of Walter Sondheim, Grady applied for $15 million in federal funds to pay part of the city's $23 million investment in the Charles Center project. The Baltimore Urban Renewal and Housing Agency (BURHA) advisory commission, headed by Sondheim, took the initiative in applying for federal support. Grady provided only his acquiescence.[14]

In Harlem Park, where Mayor D'Alesandro's urban renewal program was supposed to make its debut, the Greater Baltimore Committee (GBC) found "major problems of coordination" in the enforcement of housing codes between the city's urban renewal agency and the bureau of building inspection. Fire and health inspectors added to the confusion. The GBC recommended that code enforcement for the urban renewal area be consolidated under the authority of the BURHA. An independent study conducted by the League of Women Voters arrived at the same conclusion, as did the Citizens Planning and Housing Association. Mayor Grady ignored all three, and the protests of the Harlem Park Neighborhood Council, by consolidating code enforcement in the bureau of building inspection.[15]

The mayor seemed insufficiently interested in his job. Two years into his term, he was considering the possibility of a federal judgeship.[16] Not long afterward, the city council lost patience. Grady had nominated his executive assistant to be chairman of the zoning board. Six council members linked to Jack Pollock opposed the appointment, but even Grady's allies turned against him. Council president Goodman and vice-president William Donald Schaefer—both Kovens loyalists—rejected the nomination, as did the city comptroller R. Walter Graham. The opponents acknowledged that the nominee was a "decent, honorable man" who was qualified to serve on the zoning board. The attack was aimed instead at the mayor for "his ineptitude, his lack of leadership, and his unwillingness to learn how to operate in the political field." His consideration of an appointment as a federal judge was a sign of his "disloyalty to the city."[17]

Grady did not receive a call to the federal bench, but in 1962 he was named to the Baltimore Superior Court and resigned as mayor.[18] Under the city charter, council president Philip Goodman succeeded him in office. During his brief tenure as mayor, Goodman built his reputation as a champion of civil rights, but without involving the city council, whose devotion to the cause was uncertain. Instead of urging his former colleagues to enact a public accommodations ordinance, for example, he negotiated directly with Baltimore's restaurant association to open the city's eateries to African American diners. Goodman also supported a venture sponsored by several private social welfare organizations working on "a comprehensive master plan for 'The Inner City and Human Renewal.'" The Community Chest, Associated Jewish Charities, and Catholic Archdiocese each contributed $5,000 to the planning effort, and the city matched their support with $15,000. Goodman appointed a new administrative assistant for human renewal, Stanley Mazer, who was to orchestrate the services of private and public agencies to address such problems as "high crime and delinquency; broken families; high unemployment; low level of education and early school dropouts; poor nutritional and health standards; low motivation for responsible citizenship; limited access to facilities for self-help."[19] While urban renewal attacked the physical decay of the inner city, "human renewal" would address its social deterioration. The program was an anticipation of the War on Poverty, aimed at the noneconomic handicaps that accompanied economic deprivation.

When Goodman moved up from council president to mayor, the council's vice-president was William Donald Schaefer. The city charter did not specify who should succeed to the presidency of the council when the position fell vacant. Schaefer may have hoped for elevation to the office. His vice-presidential status was not the only factor that made him a prospect for the promotion. As a loyal soldier in the Kovens camp, Schaefer had been asked to take on the risky assignment of challenging Pollack son-in-law Paul Dorf, an incumbent state senator, in the Democratic primary of 1962—though Kovens and Schaefer soon abandoned this inflammatory attack on Pollack's family, perhaps because Governor Tawes intervened to make peace.[20] But now Kovens passed over Schaefer and recruited ex-mayor D'Alesandro's son, Thomas D'Alesandro III, as his candidate for council president. Putting "Young Tommy" on the ticket would head off "Old Tommy's" opposition.[21] Schaefer played the part assigned to him.

The cooptation of Young Tommy enabled Philip Goodman to campaign for mayor in 1963 with the support of the D'Alesandro forces as well as those of the Kovens organization. He won an easy victory over Comptroller Graham in the Democratic primary. Theodore McKeldin's success in the Republican primary was just as decisive.[22]

McKeldin had followed his own distinctive path toward the Republican nomination. It included a stop at traditionally black Morgan State College for a symposium marking the centennial of the Emancipation Proclamation, and soon afterward he became the only mayoral candidate endorsed by the local chapter of the left-liberal Americans for Democratic Action. Samuel Culotta, McKeldin's opponent in the Republican primary, sent a telegram to the ADA accusing it of "deliberately attempting to sink the Baltimore Republican Party by [its] kiss-of-death indorsement of Theodore R. McKeldin." The ADA's support revived old questions about his Republican credentials. McKeldin, however, was running as a Republican in a city where Democrats enjoyed a four-to-one registration ratio. A telling sign of his cross-party appeal occurred on primary day, when election judges received repeated complaints that the lever next to McKeldin's name was jammed. In every case, the malfunction resulted from the attempt of a registered Democrat to vote for McKeldin in the Republican primary.[23]

One week after the primary, all of the Democratic candidates—winners and losers—came together for a demonstration of party unity. The harmony was temporary. Two weeks later, R. Walter Graham, who had lost the mayoral primary to Goodman, refused to endorse the victor. A week after that, another would-be Democratic mayor, the city treasurer, denied Goodman his support. In the meantime, Theodore McKeldin announced that his invitations to a $100-a-plate dinner had elicited "an amazingly open, unsolicited and enthusiastic response from the ranks of the city's registered Democrats." One Democrat who showed up was Hyman Pressman, a self-appointed political gadfly and civic watchdog. He had lost the Democratic primary for comptroller. After a lawsuit and appeal, he would turn up on McKeldin's Republican ticket for the same office.[24]

McKeldin lost no time in capitalizing on other Democratic desertions. Goodman, he said, had been repudiated by those who were in a position to know whether he was qualified to be mayor because they had been part of "his official family," like Graham. Goodman ducked a debate with McKeldin before the Junior Chamber of Commerce. He was in Florida "for a much needed rest." McKeldin, an accomplished orator, ridiculed Goodman for his "dread of departing from prepared scripts to comment on issues that he doesn't understand" and derided his "determination to keep the campaign as quiet as possible so that voter apathy will leave election-day in the hands of his paid muldoons."[25]

McKeldin beat the muldoons. Though Thomas D'Alesandro III outran both the Republican and Democratic tickets, McKeldin and Pressman both got by with margins of about 5,000 votes over their Democratic rivals, in a total turnout of over 200,000. Pressman would remain comptroller (as a Democrat) for the next 28 years. He also served as the municipality's unofficial poet laureate, reciting his truly awful verses whenever a ceremony or public occasion provided an opportunity to do so. Baltimoreans overlooked the literary shortcomings of his poetry and dubbed him "Rhymin' Hyman." The indefatigable Jack Pollack tried to parlay his five-man delegation on the city council into majority control by making an alliance with the new city council president. But there was too much bad blood between them. Pollack had tried to prevent the younger D'Alesandro from succeeding Goodman as council president, and they had clashed when D'Alesandro, as president of the board of elections, had purged many Pollack voters from the rolls.[26] The boss had no more cards to play.

ROAD WARRIORS

Mayor McKeldin came to office facing unfinished business. The Jones Falls Expressway was the continuation of an interstate highway that began at Harrisburg and was supposed to extend through the city to the waterfront. Mayor D'Alesandro, Jr., had proposed construction of the city segment of the highway in 1949. In the face of neighborhood protests about the route of the expressway, the city council killed at least three versions of the highway bill, until it finally approved one in 1955. Construction delays and additional controversies slowed completion. By the time McKeldin began his second term as mayor in 1963, the expressway was stalled more than a mile short of its planned destination on the waterfront, where it was to join a projected east-west expressway on an overpass above the Inner Harbor. No progress had been made on the Jones Falls since 1962, and the "East-West Expressway" was a longstanding figment of municipal imagination.[27]

The necessity for urban expressways followed from the business district renewal begun under Mayor D'Alesandro, Jr., and continued by McKeldin, who proposed to extend downtown renewal efforts to 470 acres just north of Charles Center.[28] Charles Center, the Baltimore Civic Center, and McKeldin's plans for downtown north and the Inner Harbor would all falter unless the city's transportation infrastructure offered Baltimoreans the means to get to, from, and around the new concentration of business and entertainment. Central business district renewal commanded general support. The highways needed to sustain it did not.

Threading six lanes of concrete through the heart of the city was difficult, not only because of building density, but for aesthetic reasons. Baltimore's decision makers did not want to introduce an architectural eyesore into their newly enhanced central business district or disturb the integrity of the historic buildings nearby. The plans of the highway engineers had to pass muster with the Expressway Design Advisory Committee headed by the ubiquitous Walter Sondheim. Mayor McKeldin insisted "on expressway designs which do not offend the sensibilities of either our citizens or our visitors."[29]

McKeldin's changeable sensibilities compounded uncertainties about the Jones Falls project and delayed its completion. In 1963, the mayor endorsed a plan for an elevated expressway that skirted the eastern edge of the central business district. It was the plan favored by the GBC and endorsed by the public works and the transit and traffic departments, which had completed most of the surveys and land-acquisition studies for this alternative. The project could therefore move forward quickly to get state approval and start land acquisition and construction. Promptness was important, said McKeldin, because "I don't want the State to have any idea that we are confused . . . that we don't know what we want."[30]

About six weeks later, McKeldin flatly rejected the plan for an elevated highway. Architectural drawings commissioned by the planning department persuaded the mayor that an elevated highway would be unsightly. The city planners opposed the Department of Public Works' proposal and supported an expressway route that ran west of the business district at ground level. A few weeks later, the director of public works produced drawings showing how a section of the eastside highway would look if supported by fill dirt rather than concrete piers. McKeldin was favorably impressed but wanted to see drawings of more sections.[31]

A month later, at a meeting with engineers and the head of the Maryland State Roads Commission, McKeldin once again seemed a man in a hurry to build the highway along the eastside route proposed by public works. But before the end of 1963, he discussed the possibility of a westward diversion of the road to make room for a new municipal office building, and in January 1964, he gave in to pressure from the city planning commission and the Citizens Planning and Housing Association to order a study of a westside route at ground level—but expressed a preference for an eastside route if it were "aesthetically suitable" and did not interfere with his plans for an eastside park and new municipal building. He also warned his department heads to "quit their public bickering" about where the expressway should go.[32]

The bureaucratic infighting continued. Toward the end of 1964, council president D'Alesandro asked the mayor to call a meeting between public works and city planning to stop the "constant bickering." He was concerned that Baltimore would forfeit federal highway funds if there were further delays in construction.[33] The summit meeting occurred two months later and included many more participants than D'Alesandro had suggested. McKeldin began by acknowledging that planning for the city's expressways had been "plagued with conflicts, differences of opinion, and personality clashes." "If we are to move ahead," he added, "these conflicts must be eliminated and common agreement achieved." The mayor offered a plan to achieve consensus. He would create the Expressway Policy Committee. Its membership would include the city solicitor, the commissioners of public works, transit and traffic, and urban renewal, and the chairman of the city planning commission. McKeldin himself would head the policy committee, which would "have formal responsibility for all phases of the implementation of our expressway program." Each member of the policy committee would appoint a representative to a subcommittee that would "handle day-to-day problems and situations as they arise." A team of consultants would be retained to provide advice on the expressway's path and design.[34]

Additional pressure to resolve the highway fights came from George Fallon, US congressman from Baltimore's Fourth Congressional District and chairman of the House Public Works Committee, which oversaw federal highway grants. He wrote to mayor McKeldin to express his concern "over the lack of progress shown by the City of Baltimore in construction of the Interstate System." He urged the mayor "to utilize the full prestige of [his] office to bring together those whose divergent opinions are responsible for the lack of decisions needed to move this work forward."[35]

The prestige of his office was one of McKeldin's few political resources. As the lone Republican among Baltimore's elected officials, he had few allies who could be counted on to support his attempts to bring feuding bureaucrats into line. If he fired errant department heads, the replacements he nominated would have to win approval of the all-Democratic city council. McKeldin faced a further problem. The bureaucratic contestants in the expressway wars had the backing of political actors who were largely independent of the mayor. The planning department was usually supported by the city planning commission, composed largely of eminent citizens who served without pay. Under the Baltimore City Charter, they could kill a projected highway if they deemed it inconsistent with the city's master plan. For his part, the director of public works routinely invoked the authority of state and federal highway officials to support his positions on expressway design. They controlled the money. Finally, Thomas Ward, a voluble council member, raised objections to the elevated expressway that were endorsed by many of his constituents who lived along the proposed route.[36]

By 1967, the GBC, one of the original advocates of the eastside highway, had shifted its attention from roads to mass transit. It apparently did so with McKeldin's encouragement.[37] Perhaps he and the committee were searching for an off-ramp from the conflict and confusion of expressway planning.

Once again, some of the confusion originated with McKeldin. In May 1965, a team of engineering and architectural consultants showed him a new design for an elevated expressway. The mayor noted that the distance between the piers supporting the road "would be greater than the usual distance." This, together with "the arching pattern in the expressway itself . . . would create an almost bridge-like span," which the mayor thought attractive. But McKeldin was especially drawn to inclusion of a park extending under the expressway and on either side. It even had a lake. "This open-space approach," he wrote, "would tend to unify areas on either side of the expressway, rather than separate them." There is no sign that he consulted the members of his Expressway Policy Committee before issuing a press release describing the new plan as "intriguing."[38]

The committee members were less charmed. One of them, Eugene Feinblatt, a respected attorney and chairman of the BURHA commission, complained that the architects had misunderstood their assignment. They were supposed "to design the expressway so that it would complement and blend in with its surroundings." Instead, they tried "to change the surroundings." He pointed out that their park would infringe on the site chosen for the city's new post office and require the demolition of a brand new building owned by an electrical supply company. Altogether, the park and lake would require the condemnation of 25 additional acres of urban real estate. Other participants in the expressway debate offered similar criticisms.[39]

Not long before the mayor proposed his "intriguing" design for the highway, the city planning commission introduced the formula that would eventually resolve the Jones Falls Expressway debate. The commission's proposal would follow the eastside route backed by the Department of Public Works, but bring the elevated portion of the highway down to the ground as a street-level boulevard well short of the waterfront; it ruled out an aerial cloverleaf linking the Jones Falls with the proposed East-West Expressway above the Inner Harbor. Further disagreements and construction delays would postpone completion of the Jones Falls Expressway until 1983.[40]

Chapter 35

SLOW-MOTION RACE RIOT

MAYOR THEODORE MCKELDIN was party to several other conflicts that rolled on beside the expressway fight. Shortly after his inauguration, the all-Democratic city council rejected two of his nominees for the Baltimore Equal Employment Opportunity Commission—created by Mayor Thomas D'Alesandro, Jr., and the city council in 1956 in the afterglow of the city's school desegregation effort. The council complained that McKeldin's nominees were "too liberal." The council relented and approved McKeldin's nominees just two weeks later. Apparently, the Democrats had wanted to flex their political muscles for the edification of the Republican mayor.[1]

Equal opportunity was to become one of McKeldin's chief preoccupations. While the council grumbled about his nominees for the Equal Employment Opportunity Commission, the mayor was negotiating with African American ministers to ward off "mass demonstrations" at city-financed building projects to demand more jobs for African American construction workers. Rev. Marion Bascom, spokesman for the Interdenominational Ministerial Alliance, announced that the protests would have "more 'grass-roots support' from the city's Negro community than any previous racial demonstration." McKeldin agreed to meet with the ministers to reach a "peaceful solution," which seemed within reach after his first session with the ministers, representatives of the construction unions, and the association of general contractors. Bascom praised the mayor for his part in reaching the agreement, including apprenticeship opportunities for young African Americans and immediate jobs for black workers.[2]

The black ministers kept up the pressure all summer. Representatives of the local chapter of the Congress of Racial Equality met with the mayor to demand the integration of public swimming pools. In August, McKeldin announced that he would submit a comprehensive civil rights ordinance to the council when it reconvened in the fall.[3]

Not long after the council returned to city hall, the NAACP's Juanita Jackson Mitchell arrived there at the head of a demonstration demanding nondiscrimination in public facilities. The mayor invited the leaders of the protest into his office—and then exploded. According to Mitchell, the mayor "became very excited." "He was damning and helling all over the place." McKeldin called the demonstration "ill-timed" because he was only a week away from submitting his civil rights bill to the council, including a provision that would prohibit discrimination in restaurants, bars, hotels, hospitals, bowling alleys, swimming pools, and vocational training. He had also announced his support for a fair housing ordinance proposed by Councilman Walter Dixon, one of the council's two black members.[4]

The legislation proposed by the mayor and introduced by council president Thomas D'Alesandro III was a comprehensive measure outlawing discrimination not only in public accommodations but in employment, housing, public and private (but not parochial) schools, and health and welfare services. Most of the bill's provisions do not seem to have elicited much controversy. At the hearing on educational institutions, for example, only one person spoke in opposition. Opposition to the fair housing guarantee, however, endangered the entire ordinance. The bill's proponents sacrificed the prohibitions against housing discrimination and agreed to an exemption from the public accommodations provision for establishments deriving more than 50 percent of their revenues from the sale of alcoholic beverages. Council members were said to fear that if black drinkers and white drinkers imbibed in one another's company, trouble was sure to follow.[5]

Mayor McKeldin had declared the civil rights ordinance his "top-most priority," and he continued to urge passage of an open-occupancy bill until the end of his administration. The failure to enact a fair housing ordinance, he said, left an "odious mark" on the city.[6]

Less than two weeks after the city council approved the modified version of McKeldin's civil rights ordinance, the mayor announced another top priority: the War on Poverty. On March 7, 1964, McKeldin and council president D'Alesandro issued a joint press release stating that "the number one priority for this City" should be "a massive attack on poverty." The mayor had already written to R. Sargent Shriver, soon to be director of the US Office of Economic Opportunity (OEO), to assure him that Baltimore stood "ready to move beyond the traditional approaches to poverty to immediately attack poverty in its broadest form." He noted that the city would not be able to deal effectively with the problems of its poor unless it received federal assistance, and he asked to meet with Shriver to discuss "the implications of President Johnson's attack on poverty, for the City of Baltimore." McKeldin earned points with Shriver by writing to his fellow Republicans in the US Senate to urge their support for the War on Poverty.[7]

The human renewal program initiated by Mayor Goodman had given Baltimore a head start on its poverty program. Three days before President Johnson sent the antipoverty bill to Congress, McKeldin presided over a meeting to outline the city's antipoverty strategy. In addition to city officials, the participants included the chairman of the Human Renewal Steering Committee and Walter Sondheim, the mayor's representative on the committee. Two members of the Health and Welfare Council of the Baltimore Area were also present. In 1962, the council had issued a plan similar to Goodman's in a "Letter to Ourselves," calling for an antipoverty effort that extended beyond welfare payments to attack the social sources of poverty.[8] Drawing on these preexisting plans, McKeldin was ready to submit his antipoverty ordinance to the city council by the end of 1964. The program would have a budget of $4.3 million; all but $300,000 was to come from the federal government. Baltimore's Community Action Program was one of the first in the country to qualify for federal funds.[9]

A WAR WITHIN THE WAR

The city's antipoverty agency was soon a focus of controversy. Juanita Jackson Mitchell, secretary of the Legal Redress Committee of the Baltimore NAACP, sent a telegram to OEO director Shriver demanding that the local program be suspended because African Americans had not participated in its planning. Stanley Mazer, now the mayor's staff assistant for the War on Poverty, responded that the president of the Baltimore NAACP, Ms. Mitchell's mother, Lillie Mae Jackson, had in fact served on the committee that drew up the program. The Interdenominational Ministerial Alliance also contradicted Ms. Mitchell's charge. The alliance, which included most of the city's African American clergy, had drafted a 207-page "Plan for Action" to provide guidelines for the city's antipoverty effort.[10]

Something more than misunderstanding and disarray may have been at work here. As portrayed by Peter Bachrach and Morton Baratz, the city's War on Poverty was a warmed-over social services program, not a venture in community organization and empowerment. Unlike its counterparts elsewhere, Baltimore's poverty agency was not an autonomous organization but a part of city government. Though it received its funds directly from the federal government and not through the municipality, it operated on a short leash.[11]

The arrangement may have been intended to minimize conflict between the Community Action Agency and city authorities, but it seemed to have just the opposite effect. The CAA had to operate inside city government, with the cooperation of city officials—an arrangement that multiplied occasions for friction between the poverty fighters and other municipal authorities.

The agency's first director, Dr. Melvin J. Humphrey, a former professor of economics at Morgan State College, was recruited from his position at the OEO in Washington. He resigned after three months, citing unspecified "differences of opinion" with the Community Action Commission that oversaw the local poverty program. All of the commission's African American members abstained from voting on the motion to accept his resignation.[12] Humphrey was succeeded by Parren J. Mitchell, a member of the clan that provided much of the leadership for the local branch of the NAACP. In his former position as executive director of the Maryland Commission on Interracial Problems and Relations, his annual salary was $9,500. As director of Baltimore's poverty program, he would receive $22,500; the mayor earned only $2,500 more. Mitchell's compensation became a point of contention, not only in Baltimore, but in the federal government, which announced that it would not provide support for the new director's salary above $17,000.[13]

Mitchell's salary triggered one of the controversies that punctuated his tenure as director of the CAA and spread to Washington and beyond. Mayor McKeldin sent a letter to each member of Maryland's congressional delegation in an effort to justify Mitchell's pay grade. He also had to respond to former vice-president Richard Nixon, who cited Mitchell's salary in a New York speech as a sign that the Community Action Program was a device for "making a profit out of the poor" and claimed that 70 percent of the Baltimore program's budget was devoted to administrative expenses. McKeldin responded that the agency's initial budget allocated only 2.2 percent of its funds to bureaucracy.[14]

The next attack on the leadership of the CAA was aimed at Morton Macht, chairman of the Community Action Commission. Macht was a local homebuilder and the owner of several apartment houses. Early in 1965, James Griffin, president of the local Congress of Racial Equality (CORE), complained that Macht's residential developments had "not offered equal access . . . to qualified Negro buyers." Griffin argued that antipoverty officials "connected with discriminatory housing developments" could not "identify with the people of the ghetto" because they bore the responsibility for keeping "the people of the ghetto walled in." He expressed hope, however, that "our impression of Mr. Macht is incorrect." "If he does practice equal opportunity in housing . . . you have our very best wishes."[15]

CORE renewed its criticism of Macht in August, when the leaders of its Housing Committee charged that his failure to open his apartment houses to black renters was inconsistent with his leadership of the Community Action Commission. Macht replied that he was "an advocate of open-occupancy in housing" but "felt that a voluntary system will not work unless every element in the housing industry is party to the agreement." Since this was unlikely, he had "advocated and continue[d] to advocate fair housing legislation for the City of Baltimore."[16] Macht implicitly shifted responsibility for residential segregation to the city council, which had repeatedly refused to pass open-housing legislation.

The programmatic expenses of Baltimore's War on Poverty drew fire along with its leadership. The city's director of finance recommended a reduction of almost 50 percent in the Community Action Commission's budget request. The commission appealed to the board of estimates, arguing that the city would lose millions of dollars in federal matching funds and that its program was only a modest start on what the city's poor people needed. The commission envisioned a Community Action Program in each of 119 neighborhoods where poor households were concentrated, but it was starting with just 20 of the poorest neighborhoods in East Baltimore. It was prepared to reduce its Neighborhood Youth Corps to cut its projected expenditures. But the council decided to reduce the municipal contribution to the poverty program by 30 percent and ruled that the entire sum should be taken from the CAA's program of legal aid for the poor.[17]

The legal services program was a flash point in relations between the CAA and the council. Before an audience of "about 100 lobbying attorneys," the council had voted unanimously to eliminate the legal services program from the CAA's "Plan of Action." The council itself included a number of lawyers, and their hostility to the antipoverty agency erupted when they discovered that the Community Action Commission had endorsed the "concept" of a legal services program. Though Parren Mitchell tried to calm them by emphasizing that only the "idea" of such a program had been approved, they denounced his program as "mismanaged," "arrogant," a "grab bag, and "a political organization to build up the McKeldin machine." Mitchell finally mollified them by pledging that no legal services program would be launched without the council's explicit consent.[18]

This was not the first time that Mitchell had become a target for the council's wrath. Only a week before explosion of the legal services controversy, he was summoned to the city council to explain the Community Action Commission's intention to expand its program's "action area" from East Baltimore to West Baltimore. Mitchell explained that if the CAA delayed its move into West Baltimore, other groups would get antipoverty grants and take over that side of town. Mitchell's principal interrogator was Councilman William Donald Schaefer, the council's representative on the Community Action Commission. Schaefer pointed out that the mayor and council had confined the program to an area of East Baltimore so that the antipoverty effort could prove itself in one target area before expanding to other parts of the city. Premature expansion, said Schaefer, was "the greatest danger the Baltimore program runs."[19]

At its next meeting, the Community Action Commission voted to defy the council and expand into West Baltimore. It was the same session at which it approved the "concept" of a legal services program for the poor. Schaefer attended the commission's executive session but left before any votes were taken, thinking that both issues had been settled as the city council wished. Schaefer was the first councilman to let loose his anger when Parren Mitchell appeared before the council to discuss the legal services program. Schaefer declared that the action of the commission had left him "completely embarrassed" and cast doubt on his integrity. He invited his council colleagues to remove him from the antipoverty commission if they no longer had confidence in him.[20]

Only Councilman Henry Parks came to the defense of Mitchell and the poverty program. He was one of the council's two black members. But Mitchell had other allies. Clarence Mitchell, Jr., Parren's uncle, wrote a column in the *Afro-American* that decried "the Council's churlish action of flatly rejecting a legal aid program for the poor and then trying to cover up by pretending that someone was using the anti-poverty program for political purposes." Richard Steiner, director of Baltimore's urban renewal agency, declared that the War on Poverty was "essential to the future health of Baltimore." From the hospital where he would soon die, Morton Macht expressed his strong support for the legal aid program. He also submitted his resignation from the Community Action Commission.[21]

After the council's two-hour tantrum, Schaefer sought to make peace with the commission. He suggested that council president D'Alesandro arrange a meeting between the commission and the council. The participants agreed that the commission could proceed, without council approval, to carry out any program included in the antipoverty agency's original "Plan of Action," but would submit to the council any program of legal services for the poor. Other initiatives would be referred to the council for its "advice." Schaefer pointed out that the legal services controversy had obscured the fundamental agreement between the commission and the council concerning the objectives of the antipoverty program. A few months later, the council approved the poverty program's expansion into West Baltimore.[22]

At the start of 1966, Mayor McKeldin made another attempt to get council approval for an open-housing ordinance—his third. He assembled a cross-section of the city's clergy to address a crowd of 2,000 in the War Memorial building in support of the open-occupancy bill. Lawrence Cardinal Sheehan, prelate of the oldest Catholic diocese in the United States and a native Baltimorean, was subjected to booing and catcalls. McKeldin condemned the crowd reaction as a "blot upon the name of Baltimore!" The scolding seems to have had no impact on the city council, which voted 13 to 8 to defeat open-housing legislation once again. The local CORE chapter sponsored a silent vigil outside city hall to protest the result.[23]

TARGET CITY

In April 1966, Floyd McKissick, national director of CORE, announced that his organization had selected Baltimore as its "target city" for the upcoming summer. Asked whether the city had the country's worst record on civil rights, he said, "If it's not the worst, it is very close to it. They're probably the only city where the Council has voted down a housing law three times."[24] The council, of course, had been able to vote down an open-housing bill three times only because Baltimore had a mayor who proposed it three times.

A local television station assembled a panel of 13 local African American leaders, both inside and outside city government, to comment on CORE's selection of Baltimore as its target. For more than two hours, they responded to questions on live TV. At first, local news reporters dominated the questioning, but they were soon sidelined by the representatives of black militant organizations. Parren Mitchell went through yet another hostile interrogation. He was asked to defend his antipoverty agency against a CORE official's charge that it was a "swill-hole." Next, he responded to a complaint that "too much federal money is going to 'traditional agencies' that have no understanding of Negro problems." The *Sun* reported that "the panelists uncovered more differences among themselves than with C.O.R.E. officials."[25] Once again, it seemed, no one could claim to speak for black Baltimore.

CORE's decision to target Baltimore had as much to do with its own organizational needs as with conditions in the city. McKissick had only recently assumed leadership of the group after the resignation of James Farmer, and his organization was more than $250,000 in debt. It needed to make a splash. The organization's national leadership had considered joining a civil rights crusade in Chicago, where Martin Luther King, Jr.'s Southern Christian Leadership Conference planned to mount a campaign against residential segregation, but CORE's leaders worried that King would steal the spotlight in Chicago and leave their organization in the shadows. CORE explained that it chose Baltimore as its target because the city embodied "all the evil attributes of the south and all of the more subtle and discriminatory patterns of the north." CORE was an organization in transition, trying to redefine its objectives. The new leadership wanted to shift its operations northward, but it had not yet worked out its new identity.[26] Baltimore, a border city, might be the place to accomplish this transition.

CORE's summer in Baltimore followed two summer race riots in other cities— Harlem in 1964 and Watts in 1965. Baltimoreans were apprehensive that CORE's protests in the summer of 1966 would trigger a riot. Some local residents and organizations wrote to the mayor to express their anxieties about a CORE-inspired riot or to offer their assistance in keeping the peace.[27]

McKeldin acknowledged that the city faced "almost insurmountable problems in meeting the legitimate demands of those segments of our population which have, for so long, been denied full access to the benefits of our culture." But "in spite of any demonstrations which occur, the lives and property of all citizens will be protected . . . those participating in civil rights activities are responsible persons who will not perpetrate any actions which are likely to end in violence."[28]

Interim police commissioner George Gelston, in his former role as adjutant general of the Maryland National Guard, had helped to restore order in the Eastern Shore town of Cambridge after race riots in 1963 and 1964. General Gelston met with local and national leaders of CORE to review their plans for "intense civil rights activity in Baltimore." CORE, he said, was a "responsible organization," and he was confident that it would work closely with the police to avoid the outbreak of violence. In a speech before the local chapter of the Sons of the American Revolution, Gelston told his audience that the spiritual descendants of the nation's revolutionary heroes were to be found in the streets among the civil rights demonstrators.[29] Gelston would later win praise from the secretary of the Maryland Interracial Problems Commission for telling his officers that their job was not to prevent civil rights demonstrations but to "protect the right to hold them while maintaining law and order for the entire community."[30]

Gelston embodied Baltimore's response to CORE's summer campaign. One of the participants in the CORE protest noted that it was difficult to sustain the emotional edge of the insurgency when subjected to a "constant barrage of accommodationism."[31] The Baltimore establishment embraced the revolution and absorbed it into the status quo. Mayor McKeldin was the architect of a velvet counterrevolution. In early June, he called a meeting of 100 civic leaders to announce an official attack on racial bias. Six committees were to be established, each with two co-chairs, one black and one white. They would address racial discrimination in housing, education, police-community relations, employment, public accommodations, and health and welfare.[32] The mayor thus coopted much of the city's black leadership, including the chairman of the Urban League and the president of the NAACP branch.[33] "Before CORE's organizers stepped off the train in Baltimore," write Bachrach and Baratz, "their planned campaign was aborted." The city's liberals, both black and white, had been preemptively recruited by Mayor McKeldin. CORE would find it difficult to use Baltimore's black leadership as a local political base.[34]

CORE's problems were aggravated by tensions between its national staff and the local chapter in Baltimore. The initiative for the Baltimore project had come from national leaders, who claimed that the impetus had come from local residents. National CORE and local CORE had different agendas. Strategists at the national headquarters wanted the chapter to set aside its "middle-class concerns" and mobilize the poor and working-class residents of the city's black ghetto. The local members wanted to protest the city's failure to pass an open-occupancy law that would open high-rise apartment buildings to black renters. One of the most experienced members of CORE's national staff encouraged them to expand their campaign from the high-rises to "slumlords and rats and roaches" in poor neighborhoods. CORE's national staff members soon shifted their emphasis from housing and slums to employment. The plan was to create an independent black labor union—the Maryland Freedom Union—concentrating on jobs in the retail and service sectors. Employers who hired retail and service workers in black neighborhoods might be vulnerable to consumer boycotts like the NAACP's Buy Where You Can Work campaign of 30 years earlier.[35]

A staff member sent to Baltimore to do research and data collection in preparation for CORE's campaign of unionization was distracted by reports of low wages and squalid conditions at nursing homes for elderly African Americans. He skipped the research stage and moved directly to the unionization campaign, which resulted in unsuccessful strikes at two nursing homes. (The strikers were fired.) Nursing homes were not vulnerable to consumer boycotts. CORE's Baltimore project, according to one of its participants, succumbed to "situational opportunism." The thrill of struggle triumphed over the more tedious work of research and strategizing. CORE also discovered that its venture in unionism trespassed on the turf of some labor unions and turned potential allies into enemies. In addition to encouraging the walkout at the nursing homes, CORE's Baltimore project staff persuaded the president of Local 195 of the International Union of Laundry Workers to take his organization out of the AFL-CIO and affiliate with the Maryland Freedom Union. Officials at the international office of the Laundry Workers got wind of the move and dispatched an official to Baltimore, who seized the local's bank account, closed its office, changed the locks, and "captured everything." After that, according to one Baltimore project staff member, the international union office "called the National Office of CORE and really raised hell."[36]

A NEW HORIZON

A dramatic development in the local CORE chapter's campaign to desegregate high-rise apartments turned the national staff away from its experiment in labor organization. Members of the Baltimore chapter had been picketing Horizon House, a downtown apartment building that excluded black tenants, when a white-robed contingent from the Ku Klux Klan showed up to conduct a counterdemonstration. They were accompanied by a team of booted, helmeted Klan "sentries," each with a police dog. Some Klansmen carried sticks or long, heavy flashlights.[37]

The appearance of the Klan provided CORE's Baltimore project staff with an opportunity to stage the kind of dramatic confrontation they had been unable to elicit from the accommodating Mayor McKeldin and nonconfrontational Commissioner Gelston. The opportunity grew even more attractive when a local judge issued an injunction applying equally to the CORE and Klan demonstrators. It limited the number of pickets to 10 for each group, required that they remain at least 10 feet apart, banned the use of police dogs, and banned loud singing (a standby at CORE protests). The presence of the Klan gave CORE and its nonviolent demonstrators a chance to occupy the moral high ground against notoriously violent racists. But the court's treatment of CORE and Klan protests as equivalents offered an even more promising protest objective. Dramatic defiance of the injunction could lead to mass arrests of CORE demonstrators, filling city jail cells. The organization would show local authorities just how much trouble it could create. Leaders of the local CORE Housing Committee sent a telegram to Mayor McKeldin threatening more serious disruption. By depriving them of their only means of protest—nonviolent demonstrations—the city judge had opened the way for violence. The restrictions on CORE's pickets at Horizon House had to be lifted immediately "if this nonviolent indignation is to be maintained." "The Negro community is at fever pitch from suffering under this yoke of segregation." A subsequent telegram from the local CORE chapter threatened actions to disrupt "Civic Center events and conventions." It charged that the court's injunction "added to an already explosive situation . . . by equating and treating alike non-violent protests and Ku Klux Klan intimidation. They have joined forces with the Klan's efforts to put CORE out of business. They have told CORE that non-violence does not pay. By removing our only means of protest and self expression . . . the courts are also removing our only means of releasing pent up emotion and hate created by a bigoted inhuman society . . . putting more strain on human endurance than can be tolerated without explosion."[38]

McKeldin reminded CORE of his repeated attempts to get the city council to pass an open-housing ordinance. As for the court injunction, he pronounced it "completely outside my jurisdiction as mayor," but he would forward the text of the telegram to the judge who had issued the order, the city solicitor, and the state attorney general.[39]

The mayor, however, was preparing to seize the initiative from the demonstrators while circumventing the city council's rejection of open-housing legislation. He opened direct negotiations with the owners and managers of the city's largest high-rises and asked CORE to suspend its protest at Horizon House while he attempted to secure desegregation there and at eight other large apartment buildings. The organization asserted that the mayor could not "call the shots on when we will use direct action," but agreed to withdraw its pickets while McKeldin conducted his negotiations. None of the apartment-house owners wanted to be alone in accepting integration. Each owner's agreement to open occupancy was contingent upon the acceptance of the other owners. By early June, McKeldin had succeeded in getting all nine owners to open their buildings to African Americans. At the same time, he negotiated an agreement with 22 bar owners on the notorious Baltimore Street "Block," under which their establishments would serve African Americans.[40]

CORE's summer campaign lost several prominent targets for protest. According to Louis Goldberg, it was left "floating in a planless vacuum with an uncertain future." Its ability to mount a coherent campaign was further handicapped by a shortage of funds. But one of its problems seemed to have been resolved. Having achieved success in desegregation of the city's biggest high-rise apartment houses, the local chapter of CORE voted to disband all of its committees for the duration of the summer so that members could work directly for the national organization's Target City Project.[41]

Deprived of its target at Horizon House, however, CORE's street rallies and demonstrations subsided. The pullback may also have followed from a demonstration at the end of May that had turned violent. CORE was picketing a white-owned bar in a black neighborhood of East Baltimore. The owner would not seat black customers. They could buy beer and liquor, but only to carry out. In the last week of May, the proprietor shot and wounded a young black man who had apparently created a disturbance at the tavern. A crowd estimated at 2,500 to 3,000 assembled around the bar. Then a contingent of the Klan showed up. Bricks, rocks, pieces of concrete, and other missiles were hurled at the counterdemonstrators. It took a force of 50 policemen to escort the Klan members from danger. Two police officers were injured.[42]

CORE's Target City staffers were also diverted from demonstrations when they abruptly acquired other responsibilities. CORE had planned to hold its national convention in St. Louis, but at the last minute decided to move it to Baltimore. The Target City headquarters on Gay Street was filled with workers preparing a convention site and arranging food, lodging, and entertainment for several hundred delegates. A more troubling problem was to ensure that out-of-town activists did not get out of hand and aggravate CORE's already troubled relations with black and white Baltimoreans. The group adopted the recommendation of one imaginative staff member who suggested that the visiting delegates be recruited to conduct a door-to-door voter registration drive in East Baltimore.[43]

The city administration tried to be helpful. Commissioner Gelston offered the auspices of his department to arrange a picnic for the delegates in the Maryland countryside or a cruise on the Patapsco, complete with refreshments. The CORE leadership declined the invitations, perhaps to avoid giving out-of-town activists the impression that the Target City Project had gotten too cozy with local law enforcement. CORE leaders did invite McKeldin to address their convention. On the first day of the gathering, Stokely Carmichael of the Student Non-Violent Coordinating Committee addressed the delegates to urge them to embrace "black power." It did not matter, he said, how white liberals or powerholders understood the term. "We understand what it means," he shouted, and his audience responded with loud applause. Earlier that day, a closed session of the convention had adopted a resolution holding that "black power," not integration, was "the only meaningful way to total equality." The measure endorsed the position already expressed by the group's new director, Floyd McKissick, in an interview before the convention. The delegates also reconsidered their organization's commitment to nonviolence, narrowly defeating a resolution that would permit CORE demonstrators to respond with violence when attacked. They approved a substitute that permitted CORE to act in cooperation with other civil rights organizations that approved the use of force in self-defense.[44]

Mayor McKeldin arrived at the convention to deliver his speech while Carmichael was reaching the end of his remarks. The mayor was told that he had arrived too late to address the delegates and was turned away, unable to present CORE with the key to the city. He returned two evenings later. His address began by acknowledging that those in Baltimore who labored in the cause of equal rights knew "there was much unfinished business to complete in this field." He recounted the progress that Baltimore had made toward racial equality—much of it the work of his own administration—but conceded that the city would not have been able to move ahead without "the boat-rockers and the agitators," and he won applause when he said that he was glad CORE had come to town, "because we need you, and you need us."[45]

At summer's end, McKeldin wrote to McKissick to express his "appreciation for the contributions which CORE made to the cause of equal rights, and the sense of responsibility which your organization displayed in carrying out its program in Baltimore." Though he remained peeved at McKissick's springtime characterization of the city as the "worst . . . in the country in terms of race relations," he also conceded that the work of his 200-member task force of civic leaders had been helped by the protest. Without CORE's presence, it would have been "difficult to achieve such a dramatic response and such dedicated activity." The mayor asked McKissick to extend his "thanks and appreciation to the Target City Staff for the splendid and effective role that they played in helping to avert a violent reaction." McKissick wrote back to "express our sincere appreciation" for McKeldin's "statements of support and congratulations." He added that CORE would have a continuing presence in Baltimore and hoped for the mayor's further cooperation.[46]

Baltimore's other civil rights organizations expressed far less favorable views of CORE. CORE's decision to take advantage of the opportunities for confrontation at Horizon House exposed the organization to the same kinds of criticism once voiced by its national staff about the local CORE chapter. As the campaign drew to a close, the leader of a grassroots organization in West Baltimore complained, "We wanted them to get off the high-rise apartment bit and picket a slumlord." Walter Lively, a leader of East Baltimore's Union for Jobs or Incomes Now, had cooperated with CORE in some of its protests, but he argued that the Target City Project had "weakened the effectiveness of the civil rights movement by promising so much and doing so little. I think they have made the power structure more cynical about the power of the Negro community." CORE, said Lively, had "dulled the direction of the movement by carrying on integration of high-rise apartments instead of [confronting] the problems of unemployment, slum housing and welfare." Juanita Jackson Mitchell, president of the state chapter of the NAACP, conceded that CORE had accomplished some good things, "but on the debit side there has been a definite hardening of segregationist and anti-Negro sentiment which was precipitated by cries of 'black power.'" Parren Mitchell was dismissive of CORE's summer offensive: "The nature of inner-city problems is such that they can't be solved on a crash basis."[47]

POVERTY CRASH

Parren Mitchell, his Community Action Agency, and its grassroots ghetto supporters rose to challenge the city authorities just as the CORE insurgency was waning.
The new pressures originated with the OEO, which urged the city to broaden the
membership of the Community Action Commission and grant it more independence from the mayor and city council. To comply with federal guidelines, Mayor
McKeldin had appointed two representatives of "the poor" to the 15-member commission. The OEO regional director advised that new members should be appointed
in a selection process in which the commission itself, rather than the mayor, took the
lead. In a move likely to raise hackles in the city council, the OEO regional director
also recommended that the Community Action Commission have independent authority to adopt new programs.[48]

At the close of 1966, a convention of delegates from Baltimore's low-income, inner-city neighborhoods sounded the new, assertive voice of the poverty program's
local constituency, and the activists received open encouragement from the CAA's
administrative staff. Members of the city council countered the new independence
of the poverty program by reining in a proposed "self-help" housing program that
would employ about 90 residents to make household repairs in poor neighborhoods
and clean trash from the streets. The council insisted that all administrative and
clerical employees be hired through the city's civil service system and that the program's 80 laborers be hired from a list provided by the Department of Public Works.
Council members frequently placed their friends and supporters on this list. The
council also cut the salaries of the program's three administrators. Councilman John
Pica was reported to have asked CAA director Parren Mitchell to allow him to name
the occupants of these three positions. After the votes, Pica told him, "You wouldn't
give 3, so now you lost 90." Another council member commented, "We'll be perfectly frank . . . we think that Parren Mitchell is building a political organization."
McKeldin had been quietly promoting the idea that Mitchell might join him on the
Republican ticket in 1967 as candidate for city council president.[49] Mitchell did not
accept the invitation, but he resigned from the CAA to run successfully for Congress
in 1970. Perhaps he had been building a political organization.

In response to the council's effort to seize control of CAA jobs, about 200 supporters of the local poverty program demonstrated in front of city hall. It was the
first occasion on which a protest was openly orchestrated by the administrative staff
of the CAA. The crowd was addressed by Juanita Jackson Mitchell, president of the
state NAACP and Parren Mitchell's sister-in-law. The council backed down at its
meeting later that evening when its members learned that the OEO would withdraw
all funds for the self-help program if the city insisted on the hiring restrictions that
the council had imposed.[50]

The council seemed reconciled to a wider role for the poor in the city's poverty
program. William Donald Schaefer, still the council's representative on the Community Action Commission, introduced a bill to enlarge the commission to 21 members
and give residents of poor neighborhoods 10 of the 21 seats. A predicted battle over

the proposal never occurred. Even those council members normally hostile to the antipoverty program fell silent.[51]

In cooperation with local civil rights and advocacy groups, CAA organizers were mobilizing inner-city residents to confront Baltimore's welfare, health, and education departments and to pressure the city council. The antipoverty agency's organizing efforts had a tangible influence on the mayoral election of 1967, when "the large black population was for the first time openly courted by the top of the Democratic ticket."[52]

McKeldin, citing "deep divisions" among Baltimoreans on such issues as taxes and civil rights, announced that he would not run for reelection. "While I consider my administration to have been productive and progressive," he said, "these issues I have just cited and others do not appear to have made my administration popular."[53]

Chapter 36

RACIAL BREAKDOWN

MAYOR MCKELDIN'S ENDORSEMENT of a one-time Republican congressional candidate failed to avert intraparty factionalism in the mayoral contest of 1967. A former Republican state legislator challenged McKeldin's choice. Both men appealed for black votes. But Democratic city council president Thomas D'Alesandro III was generally recognized as the heir apparent.

A former city council member, Peter Angelos, was D'Alesandro's principal challenger in the Democratic primary. The Angelos ticket included an African American for city council president—state senator Clarence Mitchell III. His counterpart on the D'Alesandro ticket was council member William Donald Schaefer. Mitchell's West Baltimore political rival, state senator Verda Welcome, endorsed the D'Alesandro ticket.[1]

As in previous municipal elections, bossism emerged as the principal focus of the campaign. Peter Angelos announced his candidacy with an attack clearly aimed at D'Alesandro: "We can no longer endure elected officials born in bondage to political factions and whose sole concern is their selfish interest rather than the needs and hopes of a million people." Hyman Pressman, candidate for city comptroller on the D'Alesandro ticket, responded in kind. Jack Pollack, he charged, "was the architect of the Angelos ticket." Francis Valle, who ran with Angelos as candidate for comptroller, had long been associated with the Fourth District boss. Angelos not only denied any connection with Pollack but said that his ticket would reject any support that the infamous boss might offer. Pollack issued a press release: "I have followed closely the childish efforts of Peter Angelos and Hyman Pressman to stir interest in their lagging campaigns by using me as a whipping boy." The release ended by announcing that "I have no interest in the campaign." In his own handwriting Pollack added, "at this time."[2]

Beneath the talk about bossism lay the more seismic issue of race. D'Alesandro walked into a meeting of the all-white Young Men's Bohemian Democratic Club just as a speaker declared, "We've got the guts to stand up for you—the white people." When D'Alesandro stood up to speak, he said, "What we want and need is a guarantee all men can live in peace and dignity—I hope you can agree." Later in the campaign, he rejected the endorsement of the National States Rights Party "with distaste and disgust" for "its philosophy of bigotry."[3] Mayor McKeldin defended D'Alesandro against Republican attacks questioning his commitment to racial equality. As city council president, D'Alesandro had been the chief sponsor of McKeldin's failed open-housing ordinance. But Baltimore's black electorate leaned toward the Angelos ticket, possibly because it included a black candidate for council president. Schaefer won the primary, but lost every black precinct to his African American opponent, Clarence Mitchell III. Though his victory over Angelos was overwhelming, D'Alesandro nevertheless trailed him in most black neighborhoods.[4]

D'Alesandro and his ticket outpolled their Republican opponents by approximately 110,000 votes, and the city council that took office with D'Alesandro was entirely Democratic. Four of its 18 members were African Americans, up from two in the outgoing council. In his inaugural address, the new mayor promised to "root out every cause or vestige of discrimination." One of his first official acts was the appointment of a new city solicitor. He chose George Russell, who had been the first African American judge of the Superior Court. The mayor announced that he would propose new ordinances to outlaw discrimination in housing and public accommodations and would establish neighborhood "mayor's stations" where citizens could file complaints and make inquiries about city programs. There would also be neighborhood development corporations and neighborhood centers where public and private agencies would offer a range of services.[5]

The *Afro-American* saw D'Alesandro stepping up to the mayor's office in a "mean Baltimore"—"a time when civil unrest is extremely high in this city."[6] After the eruptions in Harlem and Watts, race riots had wracked Newark, Detroit, Chicago, and Cleveland. Baltimoreans seemed torn between self-congratulation for having avoided collective violence and apprehension that it might break out at any time. D'Alesandro did what he could to avert the explosion. Just two months after his inauguration, he opened the first of the mayor's stations. He compromised with black militants who demanded control of the local Model Cities program. He asked leaders of public and private agencies to plan for "a coordinated fully programmed summer" for the city's young people. He submitted bills to the General Assembly that would eliminate all exceptions from the open-housing and public accommodations statutes. He met with the members of the Greater Baltimore Committee to urge that they create jobs for the city's unemployed.[7]

He also recommended measures aimed more directly at the prevention of civil disorder. A new loitering ordinance was introduced in the city council. It was designed to disperse street-corner congregations of young people after dark, an echo of similar concerns voiced a century earlier. But six prominent black leaders issued a statement suggesting that this measure and other crime-fighting initiatives were aimed at African Americans, noting that they emerged in the aftermath of "ghetto rebellions." "The coincidence of these phenomena," they charged, "suggest[s] that the real concern is for the property and persons of whites rather than the blacks who ostensibly are to benefit most by the proposed measures." The *Sun* raised the possibility that enforcement of the proposed anti-loitering ordinance might become the "potential spark" igniting the riot that the measure was supposed to prevent. A month later, the mayor directed city council president Schaefer to cancel hearings on the loitering bill, and a "high city official" predicted that the proposal would die in committee, adding that "it was a potential source of trouble, that bill." The mayor said that it was "just not the right time."[8]

DIVIDING HIGHWAY

Like Theodore McKeldin, Thomas D'Alesandro III arrived in the mayor's office to face an unfinished and controversial expressway. D'Alesandro's road project, however, was much less finished and more controversial. It was the East-West Expressway first proposed by a team of engineers in 1942, though such crosstown transportation ventures had antecedents dating to the eighteenth century.[9] By the time D'Alesandro took office in 1967, the original plan for the freeway had been followed by nine more. In 1944, the city had brought the imperious Robert Moses from New York as a consultant, with the hope that he might envision a highway that would command sufficient reverence to reach the construction stage. He proposed an east-west route that would displace 19,000 residents, most of them black and living in slums. The elimination of their neighborhoods was one of his plan's selling points. According to Moses, "the more of [these neighborhoods] that are wiped out, the healthier Baltimore will be in the long run." The Baltimore Association of Commerce saw similar benefits in expressway construction. Freeways were the means by which the central business district might be "rescued and redeemed" because they "would pass through blighted areas" or "sections approaching blighted conditions."[10]

Moses estimated that his east-west highway would cost the city about $40 million. Attorney Herbert M. Brune charged that the real cost would be much higher. Brune served on a mayoral committee created to study the problem of traffic congestion in Baltimore. Moses's cost estimate, he noted, omitted the expenditures needed to replace the five schools and 12 churches that would be demolished if his highway were built. There was also the cost of housing the 19,000 people that the expressway would displace. Brune concluded "that the carrying out of this project will be disastrous for the city of Baltimore, socially, financially, and from the standpoint of well-rounded traffic improvement." H. L. Mencken was more concise. He predicted that Moses's expressway would be approved because "it has everything in its favor, including the fact that it is a completely idiotic undertaking."[11]

The city council rejected the Moses plan, not because it was idiotic, but because even at $40 million it was too expensive for the municipal budget. But the Federal Highway Act of 1956 changed the way freeway builders counted their costs. Expressways that complied with federal specifications and connected with the interstate highway system could qualify for federal funds covering up to 90 percent of the outlay for condemnation, clearance, and construction. By 1957, the Baltimore City Planning Commission had come up with a complex expressway proposal to take advantage of federal funding. Its chief components were an east-west freeway that intersected a north-south freeway—the Jones Falls Expressway (I-83), which would extend southward on a bridge across the Inner Harbor, over or around Federal Hill, and then continue as the so-called Southwest Expressway. The plan also included an inner beltway that circled the central business district, which would sprout a Southeast Expressway passing through Fell's Point and Canton, tying the central business district to much of the city's heavy industry. Yet another highway (I-95) would approach the city from the south and cross the harbor from Locust Point to Southeast Baltimore by means of a tunnel, then continue northward to connect with both the East-West Expressway and the Southeast Expressway. Both I-95 and I-83 were to make connections with the Baltimore County Beltway, then under construction.[12]

Completed in 1962, the Beltway circled the city and linked its various suburbs to one another, enhancing their collective autonomy from the city. That, at least, was the threat that Baltimore's highway planners perceived in it. Philip Darling, director of the planning department, likened the potential economic impact of the Beltway to that of the Erie Canal in the 1820s. It imperiled the city economy. Much as Baltimoreans of the 1820s found salvation in railroads, those of the 1950s would save their city from decline by building freeways that sent taproots out to the Beltway and beyond the city limits. The Jones Falls Expressway made one of these connections to the north; I-95 made another to the south. The proposed East-West Expressway would not only speed the flow of traffic through Baltimore but connect the city center with the Beltway's suburban traffic on both the east and west. Like Darling, the Committee for Downtown claimed that the East-West Expressway would "lend a powerful force toward restraining decentralization." It was part of a more general strategy "to revitalize the city now endangered by shopping malls and suburban growth along the outer beltway."[13]

The planning commission's 1957 plan competed with two other versions of the East-West Expressway. One emerged from a regional planning agency and another from an engineering firm hired by the Maryland State Roads Commission. The city hired three more engineering firms—known as the "Expressway Consultants"—to combine the plans into a single, revised standard edition. They had scarcely begun their work when the planning commission proposal ran into trouble in both Washington and Baltimore. Federal highway authorities objected to the steepness of the grade required to make the connection between a depressed section of the planned highway along Biddle Street and the elevated Jones Falls Expressway. The planning department adjusted the plan so that the depressed section on Biddle Street became elevated—and almost immediately ran into the determined opposition of the nearby Mount Vernon Neighborhood Association, whose upper-crust constituency included some of the most influential residents of the city. The organization's president referred to the elevated section of highway as a "monstrosity." Darling and his staff shifted their highway's route south to Pratt Street, along the waterfront and beyond the range of these attacks. The southern route had an additional advantage: it would require the demolition of only a third as many houses as the Biddle Street alternative. The planners would achieve this reduction by building a portion of their expressway over the wharves along the margin of the Inner Harbor.[14]

In the meantime, the Expressway Consultants conceived an east-west route, labeled 10D, that ran even further south than the planning department's proposal. It stayed south of the Inner Harbor until it reached Federal Hill, where it crossed the harbor on a 14-lane bridge, then traveled east through Fell's Point and Canton. This was the first of the two expressway plans to receive a public hearing. In late January 1962, about 1,300 people gathered in a high school auditorium to shout down and heckle city officials and business executives who spoke in favor of the 10D route. Four members of the city council attended—all of them opposed. One managed to seize the microphone from the president of the Junior Chamber of Commerce, who, he charged, was a suburbanite. "About 15,000 are going to be put out on the street because of this expressway," he shouted. "They are the people who ought to be heard, not those who live in the County." The director of public works managed to wrestle the microphone away from the councilman, but the crowd yelled, "Let him talk!" One local businessman spoke against the expressway. He was Henry G. Parks, founder of the Parks Sausage Company, at the time the largest black-owned business in the United States. Parks, however, was present as the representative of the Baltimore Urban League. The Expressway Consultants, he said, had "put too much emphasis on engineering and not enough on human beings."[15] Little more than a year later, Parks would challenge one of Jack Pollack's protégés to win a seat on the city council from West Baltimore's Fourth District.

Mayor Thomas D'Alesandro III inherited the east-west mess a decade after the planning commission submitted its first plan. Though the city had acquired much of the property needed for the expressway, it had yet to pour its first batch of concrete. But the battle lines had hardened. A ground force of citizen organizations had mobilized to stop the road, notable for their acronyms as well as their militance: the Movement Against Destruction (MAD), the Relocation Action Movement (RAM), the Southeast Council Against the Road (SCAR), and Volunteers Opposed to the Leakin Park Expressway (VOLPE). John Volpe was the US secretary of transportation. The Society for the Preservation of Fell's Point, Montgomery Street, and Federal Hill disdained acronyms but not protest.

Baltimore's deadlock was not unusual. By the late 1960s, city residents across the country stood in angry opposition to the extension of urban freeways. But Baltimore's road war seemed to stand out from the wider fracas. "Baltimore's interstate history," observes Raymond Mohl, "provides a fascinating case study of how not to build expressways." Though the federal government stood ready to bestow hundreds of millions of dollars on cities that united behind expressway projects, Baltimore's business and political elites seemed unable to come together on a single plan. Highway engineers differed with one another about expressway routing. The departments of planning and public works scarcely ever agreed. "Political infighting in Baltimore," writes Mohl, "and between city and state muddied the waters for years." Baltimore was distinctively "factious."[16]

As city council president, the younger D'Alesandro had overseen the contentious process by which the council passed the condemnation ordinances to clear a route for the highway. It did so in modest steps, one segment at a time. D'Alesandro later recalled that "every condemnation ordinance was a real blood bath." The public hearings verged on civil disorder. William Donald Schaefer, chairman of the council's judiciary committee, presided over them. One session in 1965 got so far out of control that Schaefer simply walked out, declaring, "The hell with it all."[17]

Municipal agencies expressed criticism of the expressway more decorously, but with just as much determination. By 1967, the chairman of the Baltimore City Planning Commission argued that the entire expressway plan needed revision, especially the southward extension of I-83 to Pratt Street. The Baltimore Park Board held up further extension across the Inner Harbor to Federal Hill. It alone had the authority to condemn parkland, and Federal Hill was a city park.[18]

DESIGN INTERVENTION

The federal Bureau of Public Roads attributed Baltimore's stalled highway project to "city hall politics." In an effort to sidestep further city hall complications, the federal highway bureau created a new agency, the Baltimore Interstate Division. Officially, it was a state agency, but most of its money came from the federal government, and its decisions were subject to the city government's veto. It was to coordinate the design and construction of Baltimore's expressways and mediate disputes between state and municipality under the general guidance of a policy advisory board chaired by the mayor. Both the federal highway agency and the Maryland State Roads Commission were concerned that the city might not be able to come up with an acceptable plan in time for the 1972 cutoff date for the funding of interstate highway projects.[19] The chief obstacle was not the squabbling between city and state but public opposition.

Archibald Rogers, president of the city's chapter of the American Institute of Architects, suggested a more comprehensive approach to expressway design that might address the concerns of neighborhood residents who stood in its path and ease the highway's progress through the city.[20] Rogers proposed that a team of architects, sociologists, engineers, and planners reexamine the expressway plan to see whether it might be refashioned to "reform and revitalize the city" so as to blend the highway into a better Baltimore. Rogers's suggestion held the hope that the resistance of residents along the path of the road might be softened by ancillary projects and "joint development" ventures designed to enhance their neighborhoods and diminish the expressway's intrusiveness. State highway officials were skeptical but willing to try almost anything to break the deadlocks. Federal highway officials were similarly inclined to support and finance an experiment in public pacification that might prove useful in overcoming the increasingly widespread opposition to urban freeways.[21]

The federal Bureau of Public Roads provided $4.8 million to sustain an Urban Design Concept Team (UDCT) for two years. The team's job was to reconcile the city with the road. One of the team's principal subgroups was spearheaded by missionaries from the San Francisco office of the Skidmore, Owings, and Merrill architectural firm (SOM). The team included not only architects but political scientists, sociologists, behavioral scientists, and urban planners. At the insistence of the State

Roads Commission, a local engineering firm, the J. E. Greiner Company, joined the team in its reevaluation of the expressway plan. Greiner had received more than $20 million from the roads commission for helping to create that plan, and state highway officials evidently hoped that its participation in the review would prevent the UDCT from veering too far from the consensus the engineers had achieved. A further restriction on the team was the requirement that it could not depart from the route already plotted for the East-West Expressway and its offshoots. In addition, team participants were not to release any information to the public.[22]

These and other restrictions may have reflected changing currents in state politics. Republican Spiro T. Agnew was elected governor in 1966. He had close ties with Maryland's engineering firms. Some of them had paid him kickbacks during his stint in Baltimore County government, and he appointed one of his confidants from those days, Jerome Wolff, to head the State Roads Commission. Wolff would later head a Greiner subsidiary, and later still would accept a plea bargain to testify at Agnew's trial for extortion, conspiracy, and tax evasion. Bernard Werner, director of the Baltimore Department of Public Works, found in Wolff an ally to help him rein in SOM's founding partner, Nathaniel Owings, who took charge of his firm's outpost in Baltimore. Owings finally signed a memorandum of understanding, accepting the limits imposed on his firm's work for the UDCT. He had no choice. The city council had approved the route laid out by the engineers with only one dissenting vote—Thomas Ward's.[23]

Changes in national policy, however, may have strengthened Owings's hand. The Federal Highway Act of 1962 called for state and local governments to develop "a cooperative, continuing urban transportation planning process." Creation of the US Department of Transportation in 1966 placed a new level of supervision over the federal Bureau of Roads (now the Federal Highway Administration), and for the first time, the highway administrator, now Lowell Bridwell, was not an engineer.[24]

Conflict between the highway engineers and the UDCT caused such disruption and delay that the US Department of Transportation threatened to cut off the funds it had promised for the work of Owings's team. Federal officials announced that the subsidy depended on resolution of the struggle between the engineers and the design team, and they saddled the state and the city with responsibility for achieving peace. The director of the Baltimore office of the US Bureau of Public Roads noted that the concept team's role "as initially proposed by the State and the city [has] been changed in scope, responsibility, and output." Owings later met with the secretary of transportation in an effort to clarify his team's sphere of operation.[25]

Owings's Washington visit infuriated Jerome Wolff and Bernard Werner. He had gone over their heads. Owings, said Werner, must "accept our dicta . . . or we don't think he can properly be part of [expressway planning]." "We are his clients. If he can't accept that fact, he won't be our architect . . . Mr. Owings is not the one to go to the national level. We are. I don't care if he knows Lady Bird or the President himself. It makes no difference to me."[26]

In Baltimore, tension between Greiner and SOM led them to work separately. SOM would address the "urban design" issues; Greiner would then incorporate these modifications, when possible, into the highway plans. The arrangement freed SOM to work on its own with Baltimoreans fighting the expressway and to evade some of the restrictions under which it had agreed to operate. Its efforts did little to reconcile residents to the road. While meeting with citizen groups to find out what they wanted, team members from SOM "educated interested residents about highway engineering and planning" and provided them with "the technical knowledge they needed to effectively organize against the highway."[27]

The Relocation Action Movement came together in 1966 at about the same time that state and federal officials were making arrangements for creation of the UDCT. RAM's members and supporters lived in and around the Franklin-Mulberry corridor—a strip of real estate that extended west of the central business district. The corridor had figured in every proposal for an East-West Expressway going back to 1942. It would run through Rosemont, a stable, African American neighborhood where 72 percent of the residents owned their homes, and clip the southern edge of Harlem Park, the testing ground for Baltimore's urban renewal, code enforcement, and rehabilitation programs. Relocation confronted the black residents of the two areas with the acute problem of finding new homes in a residentially segregated city where a rapidly growing population of African Americans was confined to already congested neighborhoods. Homeowners whose property had been condemned for the expressway could not expect compensation sufficient to purchase comparable housing. Under state regulations, they were entitled to their homes' "market value," but real estate that had lain under the shadow of condemnation for more than 20 years commanded little value in the market. Rosemont houses that had sold for $6,500 in 1948 brought only $4,000 in 1967.[28]

While forced to bear the disruption and displacement of expressway construction, black residents of Rosemont and Harlem Park were largely excluded from its benefits. RAM's president, Joseph Wiles, complained that "this system . . . is being built for the convenience and exclusive use of white suburbanites to gain easy access to downtown districts." The organization's "Position Statement" was even more pointed: "For too long the history of Urban Renewal and Highway Clearance has been marked by repeated removal of black citizens. We have been asked to make sacrifice after sacrifice in the name of progress, and when progress has been achieved we find it marked 'White Only . . . Unless black people's demands are satisfied the Expressway WILL NOT be built."[29]

But the expressway was already being built. The city had acquired most of the property needed to push the highway through the Franklin-Mulberry corridor, and demolition was under way. The cleared land lay vacant years before road construction would begin and created another set of inconveniences for remaining residents. The condition of the corridor's housing deteriorated as property owners gave up on maintenance in anticipation of condemnation. In a 1967 petition to Mayor McKeldin, RAM demanded that the city "correct the negligent method of condemnation which often left one or two families on a block of vacated, boarded-up, garbage infested, city-owned housing causing increased problems of vandalism, rats, and an unreasonably large amount of additional upkeep on their own homes." The Harlem

Park Neighborhood Council warned that the vacant houses posed fire hazards. It proposed that the vacant land be used for playgrounds or other community amenities until it was covered with concrete.[30]

The Harlem Park Council had only positive things to say about the "team of sociologists, planners, architects, economists, acoustical experts, urban designers, landscape architects, and others" who gave "technical assistance to residents of the city." The SOM wing of the UDCT had been meeting with neighbors of the Franklin-Mulberry corridor to identify interim uses of land cleared for the expressway. The team also got permission for a tentative departure from the policy that required them to work within the existing highway alignment. After being permitted to study alternatives to the Rosemont segment of the road, they identified three routes that circumvented the neighborhood, one of which the team members recommended unanimously. This alternative would cost less to build than the original alignment and would spare more houses, but it would have to slice through a cemetery, and under Maryland law cemeteries were not subject to condemnation. The restriction, however, did not apply to the federal government, the highway's principal funding source. But the policy advisory board that oversaw the road project ruled that the cemetery was sacrosanct. Residents of Rosemont contended that dead white people were accorded more deference than live black ones.[31]

COMBAT IN THE STREETS

One can only guess whether Baltimore might have avoided a race riot had Martin Luther King, Jr., not been assassinated in Memphis on April 4, 1968. After two days of shock and mourning came four days of looting and arson. On April 4 and 5, the only portents of disorder were a few isolated firebombings. The first major outbreak of collective disorder occurred in East Baltimore on Saturday, April 6, just after 5:00 p.m. A mob had assembled on Gay Street. Someone threw a firebomb into a vacant house. The crowd grew as it moved up the street. Two furniture stores on North Gay Street were set afire. The uprising spread west to Harford Road, where there was extensive looting. The next day, according to Emily Lieb, "along a spine formed in part by the old expressway corridors, the disturbances made their way to West Baltimore via the Franklin-Mulberry corridor." By 4:00 a.m. on April 7, less than 24 hours after the mob formed on Gay Street, official reports counted 300 fires, 404 arrests, and five deaths.[32]

The Harlem, Watts, Detroit, and Newark riots had alerted state and local authorities to prepare for a possible uprising in Baltimore. They did not assume that a Baltimore race riot was inevitable. Little more than a month before the first firebombing, Mayor D'Alesandro had reassured his constituents that the city was "not programmed for war in the streets." Instead, Baltimore was "programmed for services," and though the services might bear fruit for African American residents only in the long run, D'Alesandro hoped "that the show of good faith and the tangible results so far will head off any trouble here." "We have good dialogue with all segments of the community," he added, "and Negro leaders have indicated that they are ready to move along without violence."[33]

In 1966, when Donald Pomerleau became Baltimore's police commissioner, succeeding interim commissioner George Gelston, he expanded the force's community relations department and established a string of police service centers where officers were on duty from noon to 8:00 p.m., seven days a week, to respond to residents' problems and complaints.[34] Together with the mayor's stations established by D'Alesandro and the various neighborhood centers of the antipoverty and Model Cities programs, these outreach efforts might intercept private complaints and grievances before they could coalesce into contentious issues and collective protests. A month before the city's civil disorders, a *Reader's Digest* article had cited Pomerleau's police service centers in an article titled "How Baltimore Fends off Riots."[35]

City and state authorities would not rely on such measures to keep the peace. Two months before the riot, Mayor D'Alesandro issued an executive order reviving the Baltimore Office of Civil Defense, once responsible for shielding Baltimoreans against atomic bombs, but downsized and sidelined when public authorities concluded that local government could not do much to protect against nuclear holocaust. The mayor had a new mission for the office. It was to lead other city agencies "in drawing up a workable plan for handling any type of crisis situation which might occur to, and within, the City of Baltimore." The first test exercise, based on a hypothetical explosion of a hydrocyanic tank car in a railyard, took place in late March of 1968. The test was designed to prepare the city for "practically every kind of problem, such as fire, rioting, looting, critical food supplies, and medical supplies, etc."[36]

When the riot erupted, the civil defense plan specified how the city was to marshal its resources to meet the disorder. School buses, for example, were first employed to transport Maryland National Guardsmen from outlying armories to the centrally located Fifth Regiment Armory. The buses were then used to bring residents displaced by the riot to an improvised shelter in a public high school, where they received food stockpiled and prepared in school cafeterias. The buses went into service again to carry arrested looters and curfew violators to detention centers, and later to courts. The arrestees and the forces of law and order were fed from school cafeterias restocked, in part, by private donations.[37]

Major General George M. Gelston had continued to serve as adjutant general of the Maryland National Guard while he was Baltimore's temporary police commissioner. In November 1967, he announced that the Guard had been working with the US Army to develop "quite detailed contingency plans" in case civil disorders broke out in Baltimore. The plans included the use of teargas rather than bullets. The Guard added three new military police units and an emergency headquarters group to serve as a command center in the event of a riot.[38]

Weeks before the outbreak of violence in Baltimore, the state legislature approved a measure giving the governor sweeping powers to mobilize the forces of the state in the face of riots and other emergencies. Under the new law, Governor Agnew could declare a state of emergency and designate the area to which the declaration applied. He could then impose curfews, close streets to automobiles and pedestrians, ban the sale of gasoline or alcohol, prohibit public assemblies, and call up the National Guard and state police for riot duty.[39] Agnew signed the law on April 5, just in time to make use of it at 8:00 p.m. on April 6, when he declared a state of emergency in Baltimore.

Two hours later, at Mayor D'Alesandro's request, the governor imposed a curfew in the city, banned the sale of alcohol, and dispatched the National Guard to patrol the streets. Once the Guard was activated, General Gelston assumed command of Baltimore's police officers and the Maryland state troopers already on duty in the city. The forces of order did not operate in perfect harmony with one another. Commissioner Pomerleau suggested that the National Guard troops "be more aggressive in initiating repressive control." Guardsmen reportedly stood by while looters ransacked stores.[40] But the agents of public order shared a general commitment to restraint. The National Guardsmen carried ammunition, but their weapons were not loaded. Police officers received a message from Pomerleau reminding them of "the established Firearm Policy." They would shoot only "in defense of themselves, fellow officers, military personnel, and citizens." Looters were not to be shot "except in self defense."[41]

In spite of the mobilization of the National Guard on Saturday evening, the disorder continued to grow. A Guard unit had to request assistance in dealing with a large crowd on Gay Street. At Preston and Greenmount, another mob stoned Guardsmen and police officers. Firefighters on Guilford Avenue asked for protection from rioters. The restoration of order was complicated by unfounded reports of snipers, looting at a hospital, and bomb scares. Governor Agnew requested the assistance of federal troops at about 6:00 p.m. on Sunday. The first contingent arrived three hours later, and overall supervision of the forces fighting the riot passed from General Gelston to Lieutenant General Robert York, Fort Bragg's commanding officer.[42]

Mix-ups and miscommunication seemed to increase after the arrival of federal troops. Both D'Alesandro and Gelston had issued passes to black activists allowing them to engage in peace-restoring efforts during curfew hours. Federal troops ignored the permits and arrested their carriers. As the disorders subsided, an afternoon peace rally authorized by the city police was broken up by troops wearing gasmasks.[43]

On April 10, the *Sun* announced that the "backbone" of the riot had been broken. Six people had been killed: one in an auto collision with a police car, two in fires, one shot by a bar manager, one found with a fatal gunshot wound in a burned building, and one killed by a police officer. About 600 people were injured, but according to the *Sun*, only 19 were so seriously hurt that they were admitted to hospitals. Thirty-five alcoholics cut off from their usual beverages were hospitalized with delirium tremens. Over 5,700 people were arrested, a majority of them curfew violators, many of them held for trial at the civic center. Estimates of property damage ranged from $8 million to more than $13 million.[44]

William Donald Schaefer tried to distinguish Baltimore's riot from the ones that broke out simultaneously in approximately 100 other cities. "We had looting," said Schaefer, "but not with the vengeance they had elsewhere. Tommy had done things for civil rights."[45] In the aftermath of the riot, the things that "Tommy" had done seemed insufficient or irrelevant. The mayor was jeered by local businessmen at a

Mayor Thomas D'Alesandro III, in foreground, views wreckage left by the 1968 riot following the assassination of Dr. Martin Luther King, Jr. *Courtesy Lt. James V. Kelly and Baltimore City Police Department*

meeting where he had hoped to offer assistance in repairing riot damage. A new organization, Responsible Citizens for Law and Order, attracted a crowd of 1,200 to a meeting where speakers criticized D'Alesandro for his restrained response to the riot. The group spokesman suggested that small businesses refuse to pay their property taxes because of the city's inability to protect them from civil disorder. "Taxpayers' Night" at the city council turned nasty. Councilman Dominic "Mimi" DiPietro described the audience as "a hatred crowd. They hated the way the riot was handled. They want to force the Police Department to carry a big stick."[46]

Complaints about police restraint were commonplace. Councilman Thomas Ward wrote to the mayor while the rioters were still in the streets: "You don't handle an insurrection as if it were a civil rights demonstration. By 4 o'clock yesterday this city was . . . particularly bad due to the fact that word got around in the streets that you could get away with it . . . I suggest in the future that you handle looters (who were certainly not children) the only way looters understand—with force." Ward complained that his neighborhood was completely without protection during the riot. The residents, he reported, provided for their own defense.[47] One of his neighbors recalled that the councilman spent much of his time during the disorders on the roof of his building, armed with a shotgun.

Governor Agnew's response to the riot received more attention than most. He called more than 125 African American leaders to a meeting at his Baltimore office.

No militant leaders or advocates of Black Power were invited. Many of those attending had spent much of the previous five days on the streets, trying to get rioters to go home. Instead of thanking them for their efforts, the governor accused them of capitulating to the black militants who, he maintained, had engineered the city's riot. Most of his audience walked out before he completed his remarks, and many of those who remained were waiting only for the opportunity to denounce him and his explanation of the riots.[48]

Mayor D'Alesandro wasted no time in taking exception to the governor's remarks, which he described as "somewhat inflammatory." "This is a bad time to say what he said"; it was a time when "we should be emphasizing reconciliation and harmony, not divisiveness." Some Baltimoreans appreciated D'Alesandro's position. One resident of an all-white neighborhood expressed "heartfelt support for your policy of restraint in controlling riots, and your courageous refusal to bow to demands for the kind of 'control' that would only make the situation worse." State senator Verda Welcome was grateful for his "positive communication and action . . . you spoke out for peace and reconciliation. To me, your actions were phenomenal, because how can one be sure that he is right under such trying circumstances? To most Baltimoreans you have been right and we love you for it."[49]

Within 24 hours of his scolding of Baltimore's black leaders, Agnew received 1,117 telegrams supporting his "honest" and "courageous" stand. Many urged him to run for president. Only 69 took issue with his remarks.[50] For white Baltimoreans, as Kenneth Durr observes, the riot "discredited a Democratic political leader and made a Republican a hero." In ethnic, blue-collar Southeast Baltimore, some white residents had armed themselves to defend their neighborhoods during the riot. Civil authorities who granted leeway to looters, they reasoned, could no longer be trusted to protect law-abiding citizens. The governor had brought a new clarity to their social situation and legitimacy to their politics. His denunciation of Black Power activists as the architects of civil disorder targeted a new, black racism for white working-class Baltimoreans who had often been cast as racists themselves.[51]

ON THE ROAD AGAIN

The *Sun* had once referred to D'Alesandro the younger as the "Super-Charged Mayor," "undaunted by the magnitude of the city's problems and convinced that Baltimore is of a size to be manageable." But manageable cities do not have riots, and there was more chaos to come. In the aftermath of the uprising, the city's antipoverty agency unraveled when its three top administrators resigned. The agency's remaining staff members complained that city government had "betrayed" them. They resented, in particular, that the council viewed them "as a watchdog agency to prevent riots." The council rejected the mayor's nomination of a former CORE activist to lead the agency—an act that D'Alesandro regarded as "a personal affront." Almost half of the Community Action Commission resigned. A long-running dispute between the director and board of the local Model Cities agency delayed the launching of programs and services. And D'Alesandro had to address garbage, transit, and symphony orchestra strikes.[52] After the riot, Mayor D'Alesandro was frequently absent from the city. Council president Schaefer served as acting mayor.

The East-West Expressway was still suspended somewhere between conception and construction. The controversy about it expanded and intensified as though echoing the anger of the riot. In August 1968, more than 30 organizations met to form a citywide coalition to fight the freeway. Representatives of both RAM and Rosemont attended. Social workers employed by the Catholic archdiocese had organized the gathering, which convened at the Catholic Center next to Baltimore's Basilica. A representative from a coalition of neighborhood improvement associations announced that they were "unalterably opposed to the expressway and are not willing to accept a compromise." They were prepared, he said, "to lie down in front of the bulldozers" if necessary. According to Parren Mitchell, now a candidate for Congress, "Everybody in the path of this monstrosity ought to be angry because that's the only way you're going to get something done." The group chose a steering committee and elected its temporary chair. He was Stuart Wechsler, CORE's Maryland field secretary, former associate director of CORE's Target City Project in Baltimore two years earlier, and one of those arrested for curfew violation during the riot.[53] The coalition that he headed became MAD — the Movement Against Destruction.

Plans for the East-West Expressway had continued to shift in the ongoing debate between the UDCT and the highway engineers. The engineers had operated on the assumption that most of the east-west flow would be local traffic headed for the city center. The design team's surveys indicated that 47 percent of the volume would be through-traffic, with no need for access to downtown. The Interstate Policy Advisory Committee, chaired by Mayor D'Alesandro, gave the team $48,000 and about five weeks to come up with detailed plans for alternatives to the expressway route proposed by the engineering consultants. The team produced two options. One plan (3C) provided for two East-West Expressways. One route was designed to provide drivers with access to the central business district. It ran through the Franklin-Mulberry corridor, turned south before reaching downtown, turned east to Federal Hill, bridged the Inner Harbor, and then proceeded east through Fell's Point and Canton to join I-95 east of the city. It resembled the original design by the Expressway Consultants, except that the bridge over the Inner Harbor would shrink from 14 lanes to 6. The reduction in size would be made possible by a second leg intended for through-traffic: this entered the city from the southwest and crossed the harbor well south of downtown at Locust Point, not far from Fort McHenry, then passed through Canton and also met I-95 east of the city. By rerouting through-traffic south of the city, the planners could reduce the number of lanes required in the Franklin-Mulberry corridor, saving about 500 homes in Rosemont and another 900 along the rest of its route.[54] This was the plan favored by Jerome Wolff, Bernard Werner, and the highway engineers.

The alternative option (3A) gave drivers access to the western side of the central business district by means of a boulevard rather than a limited-access expressway.

On the east was the Jones Falls Expressway, already under construction. Like 3C, this plan included an outer-harbor crossing at Locust Point to handle through-traffic, and it also provided for a Southeast Expressway that started at the southern end of I-83 and extended east through Fell's Point and Canton, but there would be no bridge above the Inner Harbor. This was the option supported by the UDCT and the chairman of the Baltimore City Planning Commission.[55]

Two days before the scheduled release of the design team's recommendations, Nathaniel Owings presented them prematurely to an audience of 500 at a banquet of the Citizens Planning and Housing Association. Mayor D'Alesandro and several council members were in the audience. Owings likened Baltimore's decades-long entanglement in expressway planning to the nation's long, muddled venture in Vietnam. "Everyone sensed that it was wrong," he said, "but no one knew what to do about it." His design team had devised an alternative that minimized disruption in the city's neighborhoods and its central core. The Expressway Consultants' plan, he argued, would "be wholly disruptive upon the inner city . . . The forcing of twelve or more traffic lanes with massive interchange structures through this area . . . would be physically destructive and operationally disastrous." He recommended the 3A option—"*one that does not cross the Inner Harbor.*"[56]

Owings paid for his attempt to upstage the highway engineers. Less than two weeks after his speech to the CPHA, the director of Baltimore's Interstate Division, Joseph Axelrod, eliminated the UDCT's community relations staff. "The professionals," he said, "have gotten emotionally involved with the people." He noted that some of the people had questioned the design team about the need for any expressway at all. "We're not looking for feedback where [residents] don't want an expressway," he said," because they're going to get an expressway." He presented Owings with an ultimatum: support the 3C option endorsed by the highway engineers or be fired. Owings capitulated. The Interstate Division's payments to his architectural firm were already $700,000 in arrears. They were frozen several months earlier when Owings hired some consultants not approved by Axelrod. In closed-door meetings, the policy advisory board settled on the 3C plan endorsed by Wolff, Werner, and Axelrod.[57]

Owings's open insurgency, though brief, had lasting influence. In public, at least, Owings and his team disowned their favored expressway alignment, but the 3A option won the support of city council president Schaefer and planning commission chair David Barton. Robert Embry, commissioner of the Baltimore Department of Housing and Community Development, endorsed the plan because it minimized destruction of the city's housing stock, and a sizeable number of citizens voiced their backing of the plan in preference to the one embraced by the highway engineers.[58]

By the time the policy advisory board announced its recommendation in favor of the 3C route, an array of public officials and citizen organizations had already mobilized against the decision. Mayor D'Alesandro came down on the side of the critics. "If all of you are in favor of 3C," he told the members of the policy advisory board, "it's got to be wrong. I am adopting 3A, and I don't want to hear any more about difficulties. I want to hear how it will be done." The mayor's decision included the UDCT's boulevard access to the west side of downtown. The boulevard would be named after Martin Luther King.[59]

The changes came too late for Rosemont. The neighborhood had already been devastated. RAM had undermined its own opposition to the road. On the one hand, it tried to stop the expressway; on the other, it lobbied to increase compensation for residents whose homes stood in its path. State legislation approved in July 1968 granted homeowners replacement value for their houses rather than market value and provided up to $5,000 to cover residents' relocation expenses. The Federal Highway Act of 1968 supplied much of the money to cover the new costs. Residents of Rosemont and Harlem Park who had once stood firm against the highway took advantage of the legislation to clear out.[60]

Robert Embry's Department of Housing and Community Development bought condemned houses from the Interstate Division, spent an average of $16,000 to rehabilitate them, and resold 366 of them to Baltimoreans for the cost of renovation; 59 others were rented as public housing.[61] Rosemont has a monument to memorialize its encounter with the road gang—a disconnected stretch of highway that never made its intended rendezvous with I-170 on the far side of Leakin Park. Baltimoreans call it the "Road to Nowhere" or "Interstate Zero."

Mayor D'Alesandro earned some praise for his "courage" in overriding the roadbuilders to spare Rosemont and kill the Inner Harbor bridge, but the mayor soon confronted intense public anger on the east side of town, and the UDCT—once the covert ally of citizen organizations—became a target of popular attack. MAD charged that the new 3A alignment was simply "a palliative to placate those who opposed this present expressway." The opponents included not just residents who would be uprooted by the road but preservationists determined to defend the neighborhood where William Fell had opened his shipyard almost 250 years earlier. A tourist from Long Grove, Illinois, wrote to the mayor that "Fells Point with its background of clipper ships, its waterfront residential area, its stable community would be a unique source of tourist income . . . you just don't know what a wonderful city you have."[62]

Sun reporter James Dilts, who chronicled the twists and turns of the roadbuilders, helped to ensure that the protestors would be heard far beyond the public hearings in their neighborhoods. One of the most prominent voices belonged to Barbara Mikulski. She grew up in Southeast Baltimore, where her parents owned a bakery, and became a social worker for the Catholic archdiocese. Apart from speaking up at expressway hearings, she and Alex Ticknor, pastor of a Methodist church in Canton, along with other local activists, began to plan the organization of a coalition that extended across the neighborhoods of Southeast Baltimore, a group whose agenda would extend from the expressway to other issues that faced the aging communities. In the process of creating the Southeast Community Organization (SECO), they and their allies transformed the politics of the area. Since the days of Freeman Rasin and Sonny Mahon, Southeast Baltimore had been the reliable anchor of the city's Democratic organization. It provided an electoral base for Mayor D'Alesandro. But the highway controversy had turned the residents against their bosslets.[63]

At one expressway meeting in 1969, a red-faced city councilman thundered, "Let's get something straight. Not you or the Pope or nobody else is going to stop the road from going through these neighborhoods. It's passed. It's done." The audience's booing and shouting could be heard two blocks away.[64] And it was hardly done. The expressway controversy generated a new kind of neighborhood activism. One resident recalled that the "first anti-road meeting I attended . . . took place in Canton . . . and it really turned into a raucous upheaval, and I had never been to a meeting like that in East Baltimore—anti-politician, anti-establishment, anti-everything—over the road. But it was not just the road. Everything was blasted out at those [city councilmen] . . . And you really resented those politicians." East Baltimoreans were ready for new politicians. In 1971, Barbara Mikulski ran for city council. She stood outside her family's bakery after Sunday mass, handing out campaign literature. One voter told her that if she was half as good as Mikulski's doughnuts, she ought to be okay. She was. Mikulski defeated the organization and seven other Polish-American candidates to win the Democratic primary for the city council and then the general election.[65]

Little more than a year after taking office, Mayor D'Alesandro was said to be telling friends and financial backers that he did not want to run for another term. In public, he dismissed such talk as "premature" and claimed that he had not given much thought to reelection.[66] But he did hint that he might seek higher office. This suggestion damaged his relationship with Governor Marvin Mandel. The mayor complained of being "ostracized" from deliberations of the Democratic Party and charged that the governor had not consulted him concerning the appointment of a new state party chairman. A poll commissioned by the mayor showed him trailing Mandel. D'Alesandro took himself out of contention and endorsed the governor's reelection.[67]

In April 1971, the mayor finally announced the decision that political observers had expected for more than two years: he would not run for reelection. He refused to give reasons for his decision. "Because these reasons are personal and concern only my family and me, I do not intend to elaborate on them now or in the future."[68] In addition to the expressway wars, D'Alesandro had confronted racial protest and conflict from the time he took office. Even more than Mayor McKeldin, he had tried to meet what he plainly regarded as legitimate black complaints against racial discrimination. In the face of an overwhelmingly white city council, D'Alesandro was a consistent advocate of the antipoverty and Model Cities programs. And he won some credit for what one black journalist called "an honest effort to bring Baltimore into the 20th Century." In his first three months on the job, the mayor had appointed the first African Americans to serve on the zoning and fire boards, as well as the first black city solicitor, and he increased African American representation on the park board and the civic center commission. On the heels of these gains came the race riot of 1968. D'Alesandro, wrote *Sun* reporter C. Fraser Smith, "took the upheaval personally . . . He fell into despair."[69]

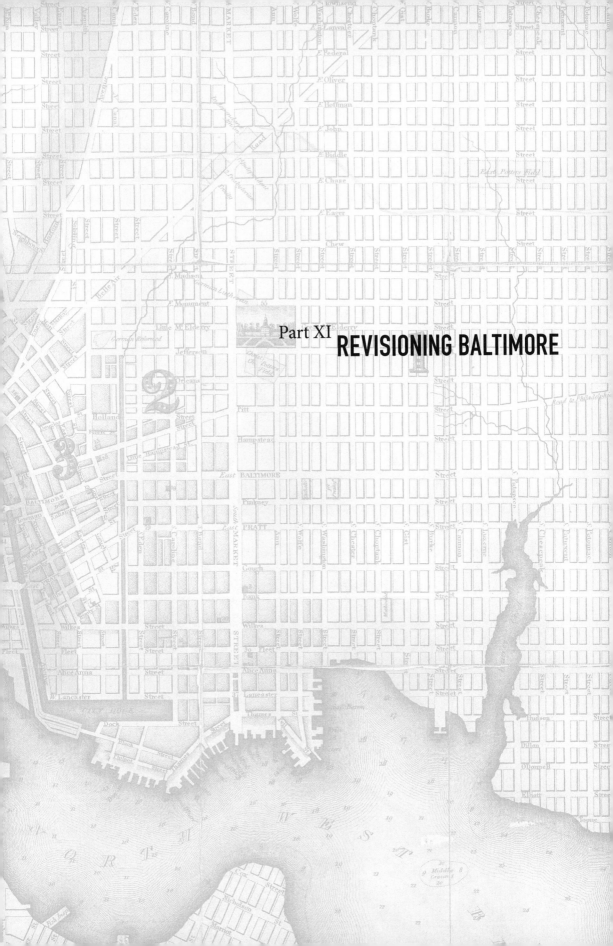

Part XI **REVISIONING BALTIMORE**

Chapter 37 **BALTIMORE'S BEST**

THOMAS D'ALESANDRO III's renunciation of politics in 1971 brought out a collection of aspirants to succeed him as mayor. Council president William Donald Schaefer announced his candidacy two days after D'Alesandro bowed out. But Schaefer had to overcome considerable uncertainty before entering a confident bid for the mayor's office. Self-doubt had been an enduring feature of his political career. His original political sponsor, Fifth District boss Irvin Kovens, had nicknamed him "Shaky" because of the worry and personal insecurity with which he contested elections.[1]

Schaefer confided his doubts about running for mayor to William Boucher, executive director of the Greater Baltimore Committee. His expressed diffidence may in fact have been a shrewd bid for a pledge of financial support from the city's business community. Kovens had retired to Florida, and Schaefer was shopping for a new source of organized support. Boucher asked an acquaintance to call Kovens to get him back in Baltimore to orchestrate Schaefer's mayoral campaign, which was managed by a young operative, Theodore Venetoulis, who would later win election as Baltimore County executive. But Schaefer's campaign for mayor needed high-level political expertise and contacts as well as money and energetic management. Schaefer would enter the race as a political hybrid, combining the backing of a party organization with the support of newer civic organizations. In addition to the Greater Baltimore Committee, he had backing in the Citizens Planning and Housing Association, of which he was a member of long standing and recipient of its first Annual City Statesmanship Award.[2]

Schaefer faced half a dozen announced candidates in the Democratic primary. City comptroller Hyman Pressman was one of them, until he decided to abandon his quest for the mayor's office and seek reelection as comptroller on Schaefer's ticket. Kovens appears to have engineered the shift. One by one, other white candidates for mayor dropped out, leaving Schaefer with only one white competitor, a representative of Jack Pollack's former empire who was given no chance of success.[3]

Two prominent black candidates ran against Schaefer—and one another. George L. Russell, city solicitor and former judge, was first to announce his interest in the mayor's office. State senator Clarence Mitchell III declared a few weeks later. Many black political leaders decried the anticipated division of the African American vote between the two black candidates. Milton B. Allen had been elected in a citywide contest a year earlier as Baltimore's first African American state's attorney when other black candidates for the office stepped aside. "What is about to happen in this election," Allen warned, "will totally destroy that sense of unity and deny us further entry into the decision making inner sanctum for many years to come." Its aftermath would be a prolonged "political vendetta."[4]

Judge Joseph C. Howard had won a seat on the Baltimore Supreme Bench in 1968, with solid black support, the first African American to win a citywide election. Not long before the filing deadline for the 1971 election, black political leaders hoped to make him the "consensus" candidate for black Baltimore, an outcome that hinged on withdrawal of both Russell and Mitchell. Howard could not be persuaded to run while the two other black candidates remained in the contest, and neither Mitchell nor Russell could be persuaded to step aside.[5]

Their persistence may have been anchored in the diffuse expectation that the time had come for a black mayor in Baltimore. Other cities with large black populations—Newark, Cleveland, and Gary, Indiana—had recently elected black mayors. According to the 1970 Census, African Americans made up 47 percent of Baltimore's population, and the proportion was growing as a result of natural increase among blacks and migration of whites to the suburbs. Prognosticators nodded at Baltimore as the next city to elect an African American mayor.[6]

George Russell drew considerable support outside black Baltimore. About half of the donors attending his $50-a-person fundraiser were white. They felt comfortable with him. He was a Roman Catholic in a city with a large population of Polish, Italian, Lithuanian, and German Catholics. And he shared their socially conservative outlook. Russell did not seem to represent a threat to white Baltimore. One of his supporters—a retired white businessman—said as much. Acknowledging that the election of a black mayor would come soon, he favored Russell because we "would rather do it now with someone we know than later with someone we do not know, after some eruption." Clarence Mitchell III had little white support and did not seek it. He ran on his record as a civil rights activist. His campaign biography noted that he was one of the founders of the Student Nonviolent Coordinating Committee and had been arrested at several demonstrations.[7]

Mitchell may have been running not to win but to prevent Russell from becoming mayor. His defeat would mean that Mitchell could run for mayor in 1975 without having to face a black incumbent, and by 1975, African American voters would almost certainly represent a bigger slice of the electorate. Mitchell himself added to the credibility of such speculation in his concession speech, when he announced, "I am a candidate for the mayoralty in Baltimore City in 1975."[8]

The election results in 1971 may explain why Mitchell's second bid for the office never materialized. The combined votes of the two black candidates fell almost

30,000 short of Schaefer's total. Mitchell came in last with slightly over 6,500 votes of more than 166,000 cast. One imponderable is the extent to which the mutual recrimination between the two black candidates may have depressed black turnout and contributed to the defeat of both. Mitchell denied that the "bitterness" of his fight with Russell had anything to do with individual animosity. But it was hard to square this denial with his contention that the ill feeling was due "to the racist exploiters who achieved division in the black community by running one of their showcase puppets." The candidate's uncle, Clarence Mitchell, Jr., denounced Baltimore's white-owned newspapers for endorsing Schaefer, a "mediocre" candidate, but charged that the *Afro-American* was "the worst of them all" for supporting Russell while closing its columns to his nephew. The black-owned paper, he said, was "a dictatorship."[9]

Schaefer carried almost all of the city's white precincts by wide margins, but he also picked up about 20 percent of the African American vote. When the white residents of his West Baltimore neighborhood had fled to the suburbs, Schaefer and his mother remained beside their new black neighbors in the row house where the mayor had lived since birth. As a city councilman, he earned the gratitude of his black constituents. One of his young African American supporters remembered "all those times when my grandmother asked him to get something done in our block, and it was always done."[10]

"SHAKY" TAKES CONTROL

For Schaefer, the general election was a speed-bump on the way to the mayor's office. He defeated his Republican opponent with 87 percent of the vote. Because Mayor D'Alesandro was absent from the city, Schaefer was already acting mayor and had begun to issue mayoral pronouncements even before the campaign was over. He announced that he would create four new posts in the mayor's office—a development coordinator and liaison officers for education, drug problems, and national relations. He also urged voters to support a $3 million industrial development bond referendum that shared the ballot with him. And, before an audience of commercial realtors, he revealed his plans for the money. He identified 13 underused sites for industrial development. The $3 million would be used to purchase them in succession. After clearance and improvements, each site would be sold for industrial development, and the proceeds would finance the purchase of the next site on the list.[11]

By the end of 1972, the bond issue provided the financial wherewithal to create the Baltimore Industrial Development Corporation, a new quasi-public, nonprofit venture that operated largely outside the scope of Baltimore's city charter, civil service commission, and city council. It was, however, overseen by the five-person board of estimates, where the mayor controlled three of the five votes. The executive vice-president of the BIDC worked at the headquarters of the local chamber of commerce, which contributed $75,000 toward the corporation's operating expenses. The city put up another $150,000. A mixture of Baltimore business executives, attorneys, and city bureaucrats sat on the corporation's board. The BIDC opened a new sector of Schaefer's municipal *imperium*, a "corporate branch" of government.[12]

Shortly after inauguration, Schaefer announced another initiative: the Outer City Conservation Program. It would provide loan and grant funds for the mostly white neighborhoods left out of the antipoverty and Model Cities programs. To take part in the program, neighborhoods would have to organize.[13] Schaefer's goal was to prevent sound, stable neighborhoods from deteriorating, but his program also mobilized a political constituency that could enhance his control of the city and its government. Though he drew support from black Baltimoreans, white residents of the outer city were his core constituency. Unlike programs for poor neighborhoods, the Outer City initiative came with relatively little federal oversight, though it would eventually exploit federal funds.

The same insecurity that led Kovens to call him "Shaky" may have driven Schaefer to insist on close control of the city's operations and detailed information about them. Control began with the members of his own staff. Early in his administration, he asked them to supply him with material for a speech by preparing outlines of what they had been working on. A few weeks later, he issued a request for updated outlines of their activities every month.[14] His governing strategy combined a systematic drive to centralize power in his own office with a decentralization of municipal responsiveness to neighborhood mayor's stations, service centers, and programs such as his Outer City initiative. The contrary combination of consolidation and devolution seemed designed to prevent development of any bureaucratic power blocs between the mayor and his constituents. The four mayoral staff officers whose appointment he had announced before he was elected were part of his program of "institutionalizing executive authority and accountability." There was also an inner circle of administrative assistants who rose to prominence partly because they managed the mayor's schedule and therefore controlled access to him. He later appointed one of them, Bailey Fine, as president of the school board. Another, Joan Bereska, became deputy mayor and de facto chief of staff.[15]

The mayoral cabinet, however, became the principal mechanism of executive oversight. Schaefer was not the first mayor to meet regularly with a cabinet of bureau chiefs. Mayor Preston had initiated the practice in 1911.[16] But Schaefer launched a plurality of cabinets. The principal cabinet had two wings: one concentrated on physical development; the other, on "human resources." The cabinet as a whole met once a month, but each of its two components met more frequently "to discuss policy matters in great detail." The cabinet also had interdepartmental and ad hoc committees. Schaefer complained that "many agencies were not really working together." His cabinet was supposed to foster interagency cooperation, but Schaefer also used it to enhance mayoral control over city agencies.[17]

The cabinet's regular meetings occurred monthly on a Thursday, but in 1976, Schaefer created the "Special Tuesday Cabinet." It included some high-level agency chiefs such as Robert Embry, commissioner of housing and community development, and Francis Kuchta, director of public works. Embry and Kuchta were accompanied by some of their staff members. The mayor brought most of his own staff to meetings, along with the city solicitor and Charles Benton, the influential director of finance. Initially, the Special Tuesday Cabinet seems to have concentrated on city finances. One of its first meetings focused on guidelines for laying off municipal employees. The cuts were a response to a shortfall in city revenues.[18]

Soon the Tuesday Cabinet moved beyond financial issues to address a wider range of municipal business. The mayor's other cabinets expanded their agendas in much the same way. In 1972, for example, the mayor introduced a cabinet for the chairs and presidents of city boards and commissions—the "Mini Cabinet." Its first item of business was a council bill governing the conduct of boards and commissions, but the discussion quickly moved to parking garages, the policing of downtown, and bringing conventions to Baltimore. In 1973, Schaefer called the first meeting of "second-level personnel" in city agencies, known (for reasons not recorded) as the "Maxi-Mini Cabinet." The mayor wanted to advise midlevel managers "of some of the policies of the present administration," in particular "changing the image of the city from a negative to a positive one." At subsequent meetings, Schaefer discussed the importance of rapid and courteous responses to citizen requests. He saw the Maxi-Mini Cabinet as a vehicle for interagency coordination, and he introduced a program that assigned second-level personnel to work for short periods in agencies other than their own to learn something about the departments with which they were supposed to cooperate.[19]

The Maxi-Mini Cabinet and the Cabinet of Commissions and Boards were short-lived. They disappeared after a year or two. A new "Executive Cabinet," convened in 1975, apparently survived for only one meeting.[20] But Schaefer seemed to have long-term plans for the Special Tuesday Cabinet. He ordered one of his staff members to come up with a format for the group that would maximize the effectiveness of the meetings. He approved the memo on the new format, but indicated that he did not want it distributed to members of the Tuesday Cabinet.[21]

Schaefer's management strategy, with its multiple cabinets and secret memos, seemed calculated to keep his bureaucrats off-balance and on their toes—just as insecure as Mayor "Shaky" himself. Administrators faced repeated demands for progress reports and briefings about current programs and future plans, and exposure to questions and criticisms from the mayor and his staff. During his early years as mayor, Schaefer added to their insecurity by keeping several key members of his cabinet on "acting" status. In other words, the mayor did not submit their names to the city council for confirmation. They were "temporary" employees, and Schaefer could fire them without explanation. If council members wanted to get rid of an acting appointee, they could have voted the official out of office. They never did.[22] But a commission appointed by the mayor to review the city's charter criticized Schaefer for departing from the conventional process for approving nominees. Some council members also complained about the practice, and two years into his term, Schaefer finally submitted several appointments to the council for approval as regular city officials.[23]

Schaefer continued to tinker with his cabinets up to the end of his administration. In 1984, he complained that the "Cabinet has not been as productive or satisfactory as it should be." His solution was to "rearrange" it into four separate units: Discussion Cabinet, General Interest Cabinet, Physical Development Cabinet, and

Human Services Cabinet. The four panels met on successive Tuesdays each month. The mayor clearly hoped that the new arrangement would induce the municipal bureaucracy to respond more promptly to his authority. He complained that "things are not getting done on time" and that a "memo from the Mayor means nothing." At the first meeting of the General Discussion Cabinet, he told his administrators that the appearance of the city was bad and suggested that they were hiding "behind excuses" rather than taking responsibility for its unsightliness.[24]

The mayor enlisted his top administrators in his campaign to improve grassroots service delivery. He required each of them to spend at least two hours a week out on the streets, "noting and reporting items such as abandoned cars, potholes, downed traffic signs, dead trees, etc." Municipal employees with city-owned automobiles were expected to conduct similar inspection rounds and to meet a quota of at least one problem per week.[25] The mayor did not exempt himself from such duties. On weekends he drove around the city looking for urban eyesores and infractions. He would then report these problems to the appropriate agencies, but not their locations. His complaints would send municipal workers roaming across Baltimore to find and eliminate the particular urban abomination that had offended their sadistic mayor.

Mayor's stations and multiservice centers offered more systematic mechanisms for grassroots surveillance and service delivery. Both had precedents in the administration of Mayor D'Alesandro, but Schaefer increased their number, redefined their functions, and imposed central direction. The stations and centers were to see that "the full range of needed services are provided and coordinated in the local neighborhood." But they were also to function as data-collection points that would provide city hall with profiles of neighborhood needs. Schaefer created an office to oversee these municipal outposts by combining the remnants of the antipoverty and Model Cities programs into a new department: the Urban Services Agency. The service centers were located in the city's poorer neighborhoods, while mayor's stations served "slightly more well-off" areas.[26] Eventually, the two types of neighborhood offices would be renamed "multipurpose centers" under the supervision of the Urban Services Agency.

Schaefer was a mayor suspended between the old politics of the urban machine and the new politics of municipal bureaucracy. The party organization and its patronage appointees no longer gave him reliable control of city administration. The influence of urban bureaucracies, as Theodore Lowi pointed out, arises from their "cohesiveness as a small minority in the midst of the vast dispersion of the multitude."[27] Mayor Schaefer countered bureaucratic power and independence partly by using multiservice centers and his Outer City Conservation Program to organize and mobilize Baltimoreans in their neighborhoods, reducing the "vast dispersion of the multitude" and building himself a grassroots constituency.

By his second term, he was working with 92 neighborhood advisory committees. The community groups soon discovered that when he responded to their demands, he usually had demands of his own. If they wanted a playground, they would have to raise money for swings and a sliding board. Protest demonstrations and posturing met stone-cold indifference. By the time he left the mayor's office in 1986, Schaefer had expanded his base to about 350 community groups. He appointed some of their leaders to city jobs and converted their neighborhood associations into a citywide political organization that embraced both white and African American communities. Schaefer had converted himself into "Citizen One, a man who represented the people before the bureaucracy."[28] The so-called shadow government, exemplified by the BIDC, gave Schaefer an alternative bureaucracy controlled by the board of estimates, which was controlled in turn by the mayor. Finally, Schaefer's multiple cabinets gave him multiple vantage points on the business of city departments and opened them up to his supervision and micromanagement.

THE POLITICS OF PERCEPTION

Mayor Schaefer used about as much political muscle to change the "image" of the city as he did to change the city itself. One of his early initiatives, for example, was the "Approachways Project." Travelers along the northeast corridor saw the worst of Baltimore. The view as they passed by, according to the mayor, was "punctuated with piles of junked cars and buses, tangles of overhead utility wires, clusters of signs that do little to guide you, roadways which have not been well maintained and roadsides totally lacking in landscaping. I am sure—just like me—you cringe." The city could not eliminate all of the eyesores, but many of them could be hidden behind almost a mile of "screening," which, along with improved signs and strategic landscaping, would enable Baltimore to make a better impression on motorists and passengers riding by on their way to someplace else.[29]

For Baltimoreans themselves, Schaefer launched a strenuous program of celebrations and festivals, not just to lift their spirits, but to engender pride of place. Schaefer did not invent the Baltimore City Fair. It was initiated by an official in Robert Embry's Department of Housing and Community Development, a year before Schaefer became mayor, as "a little world's fair of neighborhoods." Schaefer doubled its size and made it a city institution—a celebration of the town's diverse and numerous residential areas, but also a reminder of Baltimore's "oneness." The site of the first fair was Charles Center, but it soon outgrew this location. An expanded version began with a parade of neighborhood floats and high school bands that marched through downtown to the Inner Harbor, where dozens of neighborhood associations had erected booths on city piers to introduce their communities to the city at large. At the 1974 fair, the Ednor Gardens–Lakeside organization turned its booth into a representation of one of its neighborhood's typical row houses. Union Square's residents reproduced an "old-fashioned corner store selling homemade pickles, jellies, and jams." Its volunteers dressed in "Victorian-period costumes." The civic league of upscale Roland Park decked out a booth to look like a "Victorian summer house with wicker porch furniture." More than 60 neighborhoods were represented at the fair, along with more than 90 city agencies and nonprofit organizations.[30]

The neighborhood exhibits might look back to a Victorian past, but the spirit of the fair convinced Baltimoreans that their city was alive and flourishing in the present. A local television station's editorial cited the fair as the answer to critics who claimed that "the City is dead . . . it simply doesn't work anymore as a place where large numbers of people can live comfortably and peacefully." A mother wrote to the mayor to thank him for all of his "efforts in trying to make our city a lovely place to live. Our family went to 'The Fair' on that rainy grey Saturday afternoon. But just being with everyone black and white and seeing how people enjoyed themselves made it a sunny day for Baltimore." A survey of 1974 fairgoers found that 79 percent thought Baltimore was "a better place today than it was in 1972."[31]

Baltimoreans who turned out for the fair might have been more upbeat about their city's progress than the stay-at-homes. But the testimony of the fairgoers undoubtedly reflected Schaefer's success in changing the way Baltimoreans perceived their city at least as much as his achievement of tangible changes in the city itself. The mayor himself said as much. At the midpoint of his first term, he issued a statement to his department heads outlining "what we have accomplished in the past two years." According to the mayor, if "there is one overall achievement of my Administration, it has been to awaken a feeling among our citizens that they are important, they have much to contribute, and they are heard and involved." In his meetings throughout the city, "this theme is repeated: Baltimore is on the move."[32]

The city fair was only the beginning of Schaefer's assault on Baltimore's inferiority complex. Five years after becoming mayor, he introduced his signature celebration of Baltimore and its residents. Thousands of bumper stickers announced "Baltimore's Best / Baltimore Is Best." The program distributed awards every three months to Baltimoreans who had gone "out of their way to express their enthusiasm for the 'Big B.'" At the end of each year, one of the winners was honored as the "Best of Baltimore's Best." Those cited included an unofficial cheerleader at Orioles games, a bank that provided financing for rehabilitation of inner-city housing, and a cab driver who promoted the attractions of Baltimore while driving travelers between the airport and the city. The *Sun* called the Baltimore's Best program "mass therapy for Baltimore's famed inferiority complex."[33]

Schaefer was convinced that the elevation of Baltimore's self-image required careful and constant attention to the everyday contacts between citizens and city government. Little more than a year into his first term, he had asked his development coordinator, Mark Joseph, to remind the members of his cabinet to devote special attention to these interactions. "You will recall," wrote Joseph, "that the Mayor expressed a concern that the Administration over the past several months has not been dramatizing its concern for everyday matters—people kinds of concerns." Schaefer asked his agency heads to suggest how he might demonstrate his own attentiveness to those everyday concerns. It was all very well to manage the municipal budget in the face of declining federal aid, make peace with increasingly aggressive unions, and announce ambitious plans for a new expressway or downtown development project—he had done all of these things during his first year. Schaefer wanted the next year "to be more clearly dedicated to the people, to little things; the year of the neighborhood."[34]

It was not just the theme of one year. Schaefer was resolutely focused on "the 'little things' that are important to taxpayers." In the middle of his second term, the

Mayor William Donald Schaefer promised that if the National Aquarium were not completed on schedule, he would take a dip in the seal pool. It wasn't, and he did—one in a long list of stunts designed to call attention to the city and its attractions. *Reprinted with permission from* The Baltimore Sun.

human resources unit in the mayor's office was engaged in a "Little Things Mean a Lot" initiative, with its own monthly newsletter in which staff members reported the special efforts made to investigate and resolve the complicated problems of individual Baltimoreans.[35] The mayor's fixation on little things produced results. In 1977, the National Municipal League named Baltimore an "All-America City," notable in particular for a high level of citizen participation. A year earlier, a study of 22 cities found Baltimore to be the most responsive to neighborhood organizations.[36]

The mayor's propensity to think small, though thoroughly Baltimorish, seemed out of joint with the big projects and programs that made his administration memorable. According to his biographer, C. Fraser Smith, some of Schaefer's top administrators doubted whether the mayor really understood the big programs. "They also began to see that it didn't matter. *He* was the program, the common element in everything that happened." His staff members tolerated his petulance and endured his abusive treatment because they had begun to see him as the "human counterforce" against urban decline.[37] From time to time, he also allowed Baltimoreans to see him as a clown—and they liked him for it. He stood ready to wear silly hats or mug for the cameras or take part in ridiculous stunts to call attention to worthy municipal enterprises. His comic turns were all the more effective because his usual demeanor was so humorless, and they reassured Baltimoreans that he, like them, did not take himself too seriously. This was almost certainly a false impression.

Chapter 38 DRIVING THE CITY

MAYOR SCHAEFER WAS COMPLETELY SERIOUS about building the East-West Expressway, but incompletely successful. Like the two mayors before him, he came to office facing the challenge of constructing a controversial, unfinished highway. The task may have carried more urgency for Schaefer than for either Theodore McKeldin or Thomas D'Alesandro, Jr. The city and federal governments had already sunk millions of dollars into planning, condemnation, clearance, and construction. Unless he could sell the highway scheme to his constituents and fellow politicians, the bits and pieces of the road already finished or under construction would become what city finance director Charles Benton called "tombstones"—useless monuments to wasted expenditures.

Less than two weeks after his election in November 1971, Schaefer received a letter from Thomas Perkins III, president of the Citizens Planning and Housing Association. Perkins noted that "the resolution of the current highway dilemma" was perhaps "the most pressing and complex assignment facing your new administration." But, he added, the CPHA, and especially its transportation committee, were "concerned that there appears to be . . . a significant lack of consensus among government planning officials and consultants with regard to major elements of the proposed highway system." He suggested that Schaefer stage a public forum at which city officials could present a clear and comprehensive plan for the East-West Expressway that would resolve the confusion and convey to the public "a clear understanding of the design and objectives of the system as a whole."[1]

Two months later, a quartet of the mayor's department heads appeared before the city council and an audience of about 100 citizens to explain the expressway. Planning director Larry Reich traced the long history of the east-west highway, with maps to illustrate the changing outlines of the project. Public works director F. Pierce Lineaweaver and housing commissioner Robert Embry presented the case for the highway as a vital ingredient in the city's downtown development projects and its economic base.[2] But their presentations hinted at a shift in the case for the new expressway.

Finance director Benton delivered the most explicit acknowledgment of this new perspective on the road. The highway's role in speeding traffic to and around the central business district was still part of the argument, but Benton now emphasized the road's vital part in keeping Southeast Baltimore's industries in Baltimore. He was not the first public official to arrive at this view. Mayor D'Alesandro III had become an expressway believer after he heard industry representatives at a board of estimates session complain that transportation problems might compel them to abandon Baltimore for locations with better highway access. Benton's presentation now made this problem an explicit and official focus of the Schaefer administration's transportation policy. "Certain large industries," he warned, "now located in the City have made it perfectly clear that their commitment to remain in the City is contingent on the provision *now* of adequate transportation facilities of which the Interstate System is the cornerstone." Baltimore's mills and factories had once relied on railroads to move their raw materials and finished goods, but trucks and highways had become essential to industry. The city, he promised, would not neglect the transportation needs of commuters and transit riders. Its highways would accommodate the region's motorists as well as interstate 18-wheelers, and a new rapid transit system would increase mobility for Baltimoreans at large.[3]

As finance director, of course, Benton's principal concern was whether the city could afford the proposed expressway, with a total cost of $1.1 billion. He estimated that the federal government would pay for all but $213 million, which would mostly be covered by the state's issuance of transportation bonds; Baltimore would have to pay back the principal with interest. But Benton assured Baltimoreans "that the *entire* burden of the Interstate System, as well as all other highways in Baltimore City, is being financed not from the tax on real estate, or any other tax imposed by Baltimore City." The money would come from Baltimore's share of the state's automobile revenues—auto registration and titling fees, together with the proceeds of the state gasoline tax. Benton claimed that by 1978, when the expressway was to be completed, annual debt service on the transportation bonds would be $22.5 million, but the city's share of the automobile revenues would exceed $50 million.[4] Money was not a problem.

Although the CPHA did not oppose the mayor's new highway system, it challenged Charles Benton's assurances about the city's ability to pay for it. Not long after the finance director's presentation at the public hearing, the CPHA treasurer subjected Benton's estimates to a searching analysis. Some of Benton's assumptions were undermined by the rising cost of the highway and increases in interest rates on state transportation bonds. But the organization's sharpest criticism questioned Benton's plan to cover the cost of the expressway with the city's share of automobile revenues. According to the CPHA, this would push other transportation expenses—for building, maintaining, lighting, and cleaning the city's streets—into the general funds budget and draw on property tax revenues, which Benton had declared sacrosanct.[5]

Benton had articulated a new, industrial-strength justification for building the East-West Expressway but had also introduced a new problem. The highway project was judged financially feasible after passage of the Federal Highway Act of 1956 because the federal government would underwrite most of its cost. Now the city's ability to cover even its own relatively small share of the cost was open to question. Soon, members of the Schaefer administration were forced to acknowledge that the city might not have the money to complete the mayor's expressway plan. By early 1974, for example, they were considering abandonment of the segment through Little Italy, Fell's Point, and Canton. The route through Fell's Point had run up against steely opposition, not just in the neighborhood itself, but among historic-preservationists across Baltimore and beyond. To mollify them, the mayor and his highway planners proposed burying the highway in a tunnel that would run beneath the Inner Harbor just offshore from Fell's Point, at a cost of $145 million. Mollification was expensive, and housing commissioner Robert Embry, among others, proposed abandoning the entire eastern leg. It was too costly.[6]

Elimination of this leg would be an awkward step. The eastward extension was designed to handle much of the truck traffic generated by the industrial plants in Southeast Baltimore. Canceling it would undermine the Schaefer administration's argument that the 3A system was needed to keep manufacturing firms from leaving Baltimore. But there was still some mileage left in the administration's case. The 3A plan included a harbor crossing that would link the tip of Locust Point, close by Fort McHenry, to the Canton waterfront. It would reach Southeast Baltimore industries while diverting through-traffic away from downtown.[7]

ROADBLOCKS

The East-West Expressway and its Fort McHenry crossing were a prominent issue in William Donald Schaefer's first campaign for mayor in 1971. At a debate before the Locust Point Civic Association, mayoral candidate and city solicitor George Russell called Schaefer "the cement king of Baltimore . . . steeped in programs favoring highways and interstate systems." The expressway was a touchy issue in Locust Point because the area's residents were united and vehement in their opposition to the Fort McHenry crossing. All of the candidates at the debate—even Schaefer—declared themselves opposed to the crossing. Schaefer claimed that the highway would subside into an entirely imaginary and previously unmentioned tunnel somewhere west of the Inner Harbor, pass beneath the Basin, and resurface somewhere east of Fell's Point.[8]

After winning the election, Schaefer resumed his advocacy of the less fanciful Fort McHenry crossing and confronted the united opposition of the three councilmen from the Sixth District, who represented Locust Point. They were supported in their defiance by local bosslet and state senator Harry "Soft Shoes" McGuirk, known for his political stealth—it was said that no one ever saw him, but he was always there. McGuirk introduced a bill to prohibit construction of the highway through Federal Hill or near Fort McHenry. Locust Point residents picketed the Monday night meetings of the city council, some dressed in military garb of the War of 1812, linking the protection of their neighborhood to Fort McHenry's historic defense of Baltimore. Others dressed as clowns.[9]

The councilmen of the Sixth District rarely made trouble for the mayor. Because of their compliant and cooperative approach to politics, they were known collectively as the "Silent Sixth." But Schaefer's harshly punitive response to their defiance on the expressway issue took no account of their previous agreeability. He rejected all requests for city support of projects in their district—right down to a $7,500 appropriation to equip a playground. Having made his point, the mayor agreed to a modest realignment of the tunnel to an underwater path just offshore from Fort McHenry. Some Pointers continued to object, but the plan reduced the tunnel's intrusiveness and contributed to Schaefer's reconciliation with the Silent Sixth.[10]

Other highway-related battles awaited the mayor. The Movement Against Destruction promoted an alternative to Schaefer's expressway—no expressway. At first, MAD's constituency had embraced black residents of Rosemont and Harlem Park together with white liberals and leftists attached to CORE. But the highway builders' designs on East Baltimore extended the organization's membership base to white working-class residents of Little Italy, Fell's Point, Canton, Highlandtown, and Washington Hill. The expressway gave MAD's divided constituency a common enemy and helped to override past disagreements on matters of race that had intensified in the wake of the 1968 riot, along with more recent tensions roused by federal pressure to achieve racial balance in the public schools.[11]

Though highway construction had not yet touched Southeast Baltimore, the expressway had already wounded Canton. The city had acquired hundreds of the neighborhood's row houses by condemnation to clear a corridor for the road, uprooting their residents and stiffening the opposition of those who remained. More than a decade after the condemnation ordinance, one Canton resident still felt that "the road and the torn-down houses are a very touchy subject in our neighborhood. The elderly people are very bitter, because a lot of people died. They were born and raised down there."[12] The neighborhood's trauma drew its inhabitants together in the Southeast Council Against the Road (SCAR), a constituent in the MAD federation.

MAD itself had been temporarily stymied by the road-building tactics of Mayor Schaefer, who attempted to initiate work on as many segments of the expressway as possible. By multiplying the targets for highway resisters, the tactic tended to fragment the opposition and left MAD to play whack-a-mole with no focus for protest. So MAD adopted a new tactic of its own. Along with other anti-expressway groups (and former city councilman Thomas Ward), it sued. To sue, plaintiffs had to show that they had standing. In other words, they had to demonstrate that they would suffer some tangible harm as a result of the highway's construction. Owning property that would be taken or damaged by the road would be the most obvious way to establish standing. But taking the city to court had become an option for a host of other expressway opponents after Congress passed the National Environmental Policy Act of 1969. It required every project financed or sponsored by the federal government to file an Environmental Impact Statement. Organizations like MAD could sue city hall simply by claiming an interest in the environmental damage likely to result from the highway — air pollution, for example.[13]

No one won the suit that finally stopped the expressway. MAD, the Sierra Club, and Volunteers Opposed to the Leakin Park Expressway (VOLPE) all sued officials of the city and its Interstate Division in federal district court, arguing that the hearings held on an essential section of the expressway to be built through Leakin and Gwynns Falls Parks had not given adequate attention to the social, economic, and environmental impact of the project. The Leakin Park segment would connect the expressway with I-170, which approached the city from the west. In June 1972, Judge James Miller issued a temporary injunction halting all work on this stretch of highway until new hearings were held. In his written opinion, however, the judge expressed confidence that the defendants in the suit would be able to meet all the objections of the expressway opponents. At the hearings in December, more than 150 people signed up to speak, many from nearby Dickeyville, a prosperous, white neighborhood on the city's western, semi-suburban fringe. Only three speakers supported the highway. One lived in the area; the others were the president of the Baltimore Chamber of Commerce and William Boucher of the Greater Baltimore Committee.[14]

In January 1973, the Environmental Protection Agency criticized a draft of the new environmental impact statement submitted by the Interstate Division as "inaccurate and misleading." By early summer of 1975, the revised environmental impact report filled three loose-leaf binders, and highway officials predicted that they would return to court and ask Judge Miller to lift his injunction by the end of the year. The report had cost $198,000. The cost of the expressway had risen by $26 million. By early fall, the city's Interstate Division reported that the stretch of highway leading from downtown toward Leakin Park — the Franklin-Mulberry segment — had doubled in cost over the previous three years, to $50 million, and new storm drains would add another $20 million. By mid-autumn, the expressway's total price had risen to $1.4 billion. In 1977, an official of the Interstate Division announced that his agency had been preoccupied with the stretch of road that was supposed to carry I-83 east across Little Italy, around Fell's Point, and through Canton, but would soon turn its attention to the Leakin Park section. Because of the "time lapse" since the last hearings, he said, "we will definitely hold the hearings over again. I would say next fall." He added that one of the options to be considered was a "no expressway" alternative.[15]

City council president Walter Orlinsky had already introduced a bill scrapping the Leakin Park section of the highway, and at the inauguration ceremony following Schaefer's reelection in 1979, he urged the mayor to abandon both the route through the park and the eastward extension of I-83. The next day, Schaefer uncharacteristically admitted doubts of his own about building the road through the park, and though frequently at odds with Orlinsky, the mayor complimented him on "a good speech." In 1980, finance director Benton announced that because of runaway inflation and falling automobile revenues, "We have no money to do any more than we have currently committed." The city had not spent its full allotment of federal highway funds, but it intended to request that the remaining money be transferred to local rapid transit projects.[16] The East-West Expressway was finished.

Mayor Schaefer was far from finished, but he had ridden the East-West Expressway straight into a political dilemma. A supportive coalition of mobilized neighborhoods had lent political substance to the formal power of his office, but the expressway had antagonized people in many of those neighborhoods—Canton, Highlandtown, Fell's Point. Little Italy, Dickeyville, Harlem Park, Rosemont, Locust Point, and Washington Hill. Baltimore's all-too-numerous neighborhoods seem to have splintered the city's comprehensive expressway plan in much the same way that Baltimore's political incoherence had held back completion of its sanitary sewer system generations earlier.

The incomplete highway was only one of Schaefer's frustrations. During his first year in office, he had presented his mayoral agenda in a speech and slide show at a Baltimore Advertising Club luncheon. Like the admen, he said, he had a product to sell—Baltimore. He was determined to create a "positive attitude" about the place, but he had plans for the city's physical as well as psychological redevelopment. In addition to the 3A expressway, the mayor mentioned his Approachways project and Outer City initiative. He announced that the city would build a pyrolysis plant to dispose of Baltimore's garbage and reduce its reliance on the shrinking capacity of landfills. The plant would incinerate solid waste at low oxygen levels to limit air pollution emissions and sharply reduce the volume of the remaining waste, which could be mined to recycle metals. Pyrolysis failed for technological reasons, however, and the city wrote off its investment in the process. Schaefer had also begun his mayoral tenure with an attempt to augment the city's middle-class population by building a residential "new town in town" at Coldspring, near an arboretum in Northwest Baltimore. It had fallen well short of its 3,700 planned housing units because of financial problems. Housing commissioner Embry launched a more successful effort to attract middle-class households by selling abandoned homes in selected neighborhoods for a dollar apiece, provided that purchasers would renovate the buildings to bring them up to the housing code. The city offered low-interest financing to cover the costs of rehabilitation.[17]

STRUGGLE OVER SCHOOLS

Not surprisingly, some of the most difficult issues for Schaefer were the ones that did not appear on his own agenda. After a period of adjustment following the *Brown* decision of 1954, for example, the city had rested on its open-enrollment version of school desegregation. Given that the city's residential areas were segregated, its neighborhood schools would remain largely segregated too. In 1968, city solicitor George Russell issued an opinion stating that the city's school integration policy did not comply with recent opinions of the US Supreme Court. City council president Schaefer argued against a review of the policy because it would lead to discussion of the race issue.[18]

Black parents and the local branch of the NAACP, however, insisted on talking about it. They complained that the school system's practices stalled progress toward integration. The parents registered their complaints with the US Civil Rights Commission, but stopped short of filing suit. Perhaps, as Howell Baum suggests, Baltimore's African Americans were constrained by the same liberal ideology that sanctified freedom of choice or saw the limited changes in public schools as first steps toward more sweeping racial integration.[19]

The issue was taken out of local hands in 1970, when the NAACP Legal Defense Fund sued the US Department of Health, Education, and Welfare. It alleged that HEW was violating Title VI of the Civil Rights Act of 1964, which prohibited discrimination based on "race, color, or national origin" in any "program or activity" financed by the federal government. Under the Elementary and Secondary Education Act of 1965, local school systems received billions of dollars in federal funds to reduce the educational handicaps of children from low-income or minority-group households. For Baltimore, the act meant that federal aid rose almost immediately from 1 percent of the school budget to 10 percent. The NAACP charged that HEW had an affirmative responsibility to ensure that school systems receiving federal support did not practice racial segregation. A federal district court decided in favor of the NAACP, and the result was sustained on appeal. Baltimore's school system was one of those covered by the decision in *Adams v. Richardson.*[20]

Roland Patterson had become Baltimore's superintendent of schools in 1971, not long before Schaefer was elected mayor. In April 1973, Patterson received a letter from Peter Holmes, director of HEW's Office of Civil Rights, calling on the school system to meet the integration standard set out in the *Adams* case. Patterson would have to explain why any of his schools deviated by more than 20 percent from the overall percentage of black children in the system. Baltimore's public school population was 70 percent black, so to qualify as integrated, a school's African American enrollment could range from 50 to 90 percent. Of more than 200 schools in Baltimore, almost half operated outside this range. Teachers were also segregated. One school's staff was all-white; nine had only black teachers. The results of Baltimore's open-enrollment plan were unsatisfactory to HEW and the federal judiciary.[21] The school system had to adopt a desegregation plan acceptable to the department's Office of Civil Rights or lose millions of dollars in federal aid.

Superintendent Patterson labored under several burdens. First, he was not a Baltimorean. He had come to the city from Seattle and had only a short time to adjust to the city's peculiarities—especially its longstanding reluctance to make race an issue of public discussion. He had caused a stir at his job interview when he charged that large numbers of political prisoners were being held in America's prisons. Some school board members were "visibly upset" by the remark, but it provoked applause among African American members of the community panel invited to participate in the interview process.[22] Second, the demands from Holmes and HEW arrived just as Patterson's teachers went on strike. Third, Patterson's operating style may have alienated important figures in city government. He told finance director Benton, for example, that he would need $7.5 million in additional funds to cover the cost of desegregating the schools. According to the budget analyst assigned to review the request, it could be "separated into three categories: related to the desegregation plan; related to previously denied FY 75 budget request; and not related to anything at all." The analyst concluded that no more than $297,000 could be attributed to the desegregation process.[23] In other words, the superintendent seemed to be exploiting the desegregation issue to beef up his budget. And finally, Patterson's problems may have been magnified by the fact that he was Baltimore's first black school superintendent. Other black educators had served as interim superintendents, but Patterson was the first to receive a "permanent" appointment as superintendent. He would not be permanent much longer.

Patterson insisted—and HEW agreed—that a legally sufficient response to HEW's demand for integration need not include busing. Baltimore's new integration plan proposed school "pairings" as a remedy for racial imbalance. Elementary schools with large white student enrollments would be matched with geographically proximate schools where black students predominated. Pupil transfers between the paired schools would aim to increase racial balance. The elementary schools would be designated as "feeders" to junior high schools so as to increase desegregation there, and some senior highs would become magnet schools with educational specialties that would draw students from the city at large.[24] But in the white working-class neighborhoods of Southeast Baltimore, anger and anxiety boiled up in protest against "forced busing"—even though no public official had proposed it. It may have been an anticipatory protest. Southeast Baltimore was so solidly white that some of its leaders and many of its residents assumed that busing to distant neighborhoods would be necessary to satisfy the requirements of HEW. A city councilman told an audience of 1,200 protesters that "school pairings" proposed under the city's new desegregation plan was "just another code word for busing."[25]

Many of Baltimore's black residents regarded the antibusing protests in white neighborhoods as encoded racism. Against the background of heightened racial tension, city council president Walter Orlinsky demanded an audit to determine whether Patterson had shifted funds for supplies and materials to pay school system salaries. Patterson responded that the audit was a racist ploy intended to undermine any desegregation plan that he might propose to HEW. Mayor Schaefer made things worse. George Russell, his opponent in the Democratic primary, submitted a frosty letter informing Schaefer that he would resign as city solicitor on June 30, 1974. Without informing Russell, the mayor appointed a successor to take over on June 4. Russell regarded this as "tantamount to a firing" and complained that he "didn't even get the courtesy of a letter."[26]

The discourtesies added to the racial antagonisms of the moment and offended the sensibilities of the city's black leaders, some of whom met at the offices of the *Afro-American*. They issued a statement asserting that "black citizens take these rude dismissals as an insult to each and every black citizen." They went on to complain about the underrepresentation of African Americans on the city's boards and commissions, and finished with a dozen demands concerning the conduct and composition of the school board, the treatment of Roland Patterson, and increased financial support for schools.[27] An article in the *Sun* hinted that the city might be headed for another race riot. With racial tensions at the boiling point, Schaefer faced an outburst of militant unionism among city employees. The sanitation workers walked out in July, leaving piles of garbage to ferment in the summer heat. Soon they were joined by groundskeepers at the city schools, many guards at the city jail, and the sewer workers. The police began a "job action," issuing nuisance tickets. The mayor's limousine got one. When Schaefer failed to respond to their pay demands, many officers stopped showing up for work, especially in West Baltimore. While 50 policemen picketed the Western District police station, looters were carrying off the merchandise of liquor stores just two blocks away. Schaefer chose this moment in 1974 to announce a new promotional campaign to present Baltimore as "Charm City," a tourist destination.[28]

In 1975, William Donald Schaefer faced reelection. Parren Mitchell, formerly director of the local antipoverty program and now a congressman, declared himself a candidate for Schaefer's job. But he hinted that he might be willing to withdraw if Schaefer invited a black candidate to displace one of his white ticket-mates for city council president or comptroller, and some observers suggested that Mitchell's candidacy might also be related to the renewal of Roland Patterson's contract. Mitchell's venture assumed that the city's African American leaders and voters would unify behind him, but his base was in West Baltimore, and one of the deepest fissures in black Baltimore ran between the east and west sides of the city. State delegate John Douglass and city council member Clarence "Du" Burns, both East Baltimore leaders, hoped that Mitchell's challenge might push the mayor in their direction. Schaefer took the hint. The mayor's office steered hundreds of Neighborhood Youth Corps summer jobs to Burns and groups associated with his Eastside Democratic Organization.[29] Schaefer's political alliance with black politicians from proletarian East Baltimore helped to reinforce the division that separated them from the college-educated political dynasts of West Baltimore.

State senator Julian Lapides filed a complaint with the US Labor Department concerning Schaefer's allocation of Youth Corps jobs. Lapides headed the Mount Royal Democratic Club, whose candidates for city council regularly competed with those of Burns's organization; both groups operated in the city's Second District. Lapides charged that the mayor's lopsided allocation of summer jobs made a fair election in the district impossible. He had earlier indicated that he might challenge Mayor Schaefer's bid for reelection. Schaefer and Burns had more than one reason to join forces.[30]

Patterson's contract as school superintendent came up for renewal in the same year that Mayor Schaefer faced reelection. During his first term as mayor, Schaefer had appointed several new members to the school board, which now had an African American majority. Supporters of Superintendent Patterson held prayer vigils outside school headquarters while the board discussed his future inside. But Schaefer's appointments had undercut black support for Patterson. Now that there was a black majority on the school board, Patterson's retention seemed less essential to African Americans, and the new balance on the board also increased the likelihood that any successor to Patterson would be black.

The board fired Patterson in June 1975. Three of the board's black members supported his dismissal. Parren Mitchell withdrew as mayoral candidate not long afterward, and Mayor Schaefer and his ticket prevailed in what was generally regarded as a dull campaign. Its most prominent issues turned on proposals to construct a subway line and a downtown baseball stadium. If approved, the two projects would be completed so far in the future that they generated little immediate excitement. Voter turnout, according to one election official, was at its lowest in 15 years. "It's not that people don't care," said Mayor Schaefer. "The people of Baltimore are satisfied. There are no problems, no issues. Everything is okay." A *Sun* editorial responded by enumerating respects in which Baltimore was not okay, but one of the municipality's most immediate vexations was about to dissolve.[31]

In May 1975, the HEW's Office of Civil Rights had initiated administrative proceedings to cut off $23 million in federal aid to Baltimore's school system on the ground that the school board had failed to produce an acceptable desegregation plan.[32] In January 1976, the city filed suit in federal court to obtain an injunction that would halt HEW's action against its school system. The city's attorneys argued that the Office of Civil Rights had never specified exactly what was wrong with the city's desegregation plans or what should be done to make them acceptable. The Baltimore School Board prevailed in the federal district court, but HEW appealed. The appeals court heard the case *en banc* and initially voted four to three to reverse the lower-court decision. But one of the judges in the majority died of a heart attack before having an opportunity to read the minority opinion, and Baltimore's attorneys summoned up the precedents to ensure that his vote could not be counted. The tie vote meant that the district court's decision stood undisturbed. Justice Department lawyers refused to appeal to the US Supreme Court to avoid the risk that a decision applying only to Maryland might be extended to the entire country.[33]

BUILDING THE RECREATIONAL CITY

Schaefer's defense of the school system against HEW seemed to exhaust his interest in public education, though he continued to rely on the school system as a source of patronage jobs for his African American adherents.[34] While city and federal officials were squabbling over desegregation plans, the proportion of African American students in the public schools had risen from 70 to 77 percent, further reducing the prospects for real racial integration. To Schaefer, perhaps, the work of rebuilding an urban school system to educate the children of the poor seemed just too complicated to succeed.[35]

But the passion that Mayor Schaefer invested in public sanitation and pothole repair rose to grander projects designed to uplift both the city's spirit and its economy. Harborplace was the symbolic integration of these goals, an expression of civic pride and commercialism. The idea of harbor-side development had been in the air at least since Mayor McKeldin mentioned it in his 1963 inaugural address. By the time Schaefer's second term approached its end, the old warehouses and rotting piers had been cleared away, leaving a desolate emptiness on the city's doorstep. The mayor demanded that something be done. The Charles Center / Inner Harbor Management Corporation landscaped the area. Its beautification efforts created a waterfront park so attractive that it became a popular gathering place for Baltimoreans, especially those who worked in downtown office buildings. Schaefer, however, had other plans for the location.

The mayor had already received approval and full or partial financing for a convention center several blocks west of the Inner Harbor, a science center to the south, and an aquarium on the east, and the city had become a shareholder in a new Hyatt Regency to be built near the convention center. The lynchpin that transformed these isolated projects into an integrated development was the strip of parkland where Baltimore met the water along the north and west margins of the Inner Harbor.

Schaefer backed a scheme conceived by developer James Rouse. It would create a $22 million "festival mall" on 3.2 acres of the 29-acre waterside park—two pavilions at right angles to one another, north and west of the harbor. They would house shops and restaurants. Along with the aquarium, the convention center, the science center, and the Hyatt Regency, the Rouse plan would convert the Inner Harbor into a tourist destination. The idea had taken hold among Baltimore's planners and developers two years earlier during celebration of the nation's bicentennial. In Baltimore, the festivities included the arrival of eight tall ships in the Inner Harbor. Their visit drew more than 100,000 spectators, who lined the waterfront from Fell's Point around the Basin to the top of Federal Hill.[36]

The success of the event set Baltimore's business and political leaders thinking of the Inner Harbor as a tourist attraction, and that led to the plan for Harborplace. But the proposal ran up against general opposition among Baltimoreans, including some of the city's more prominent residents. Eugene Feinblatt, chairman of the Urban Renewal and Housing Commission, thought the parklike "Baltimore Common" on the waterfront had achieved the objective envisioned in Rouse's plan for commercial development. It had drawn Baltimoreans to the Inner Harbor. "At the time the Plan was adopted," he wrote, "we did not, in our wildest dreams, envision the present appeal, popularity and utilization of the Inner Harbor as a gathering place." Feinblatt argued that the waterfront park was an "almost unique environment and its scope, sweep and its openness should be preserved without undue physical impediment or visual distraction." Attorney and investor Zanvyl Krieger was concerned about the impact a Hyatt Regency would have on his stake in the Lord Baltimore Hotel, to which he had provided financial support "in the interest of the city."[37] A variety of less prominent Baltimoreans stood against any commercial encroachment on the public space to which they had staked their claim by collective use. Citizens for the Preservation of the Inner Harbor embarked on a petition drive for a ballot question to prevent any commercial development on the Basin's perimeter. Mayor Schaefer countered with a ballot question of his own that would preserve 26 acres of open space while permitting construction of Rouse's pavilions. The Citizens for Preservation needed 10,000 signatures to put its proposition on the 1978 election ballot. Schaefer needed only the support of 10 city council members to get his measure before the voters.

In Baltimore, at least, the battle of the ballot questions drew far more attention and emotion than the contests for governor or state legislature. But it also confused voters. To express their preferences effectively, they had to vote in favor of one of the two propositions and against the other. The Citizens for Preservation charged that the mayor had deliberately attempted to mystify the electorate, and it stepped up its efforts to defeat Schaefer's proposition, especially in the neighborhoods of South Baltimore. According to the *Sun*, the group portrayed its crusade as a David-and-Goliath struggle—"Big City Hall, Big Mayor Schaefer, Big Rouse Company versus little man and little woman." But the preservationists' claim to speak for the city's grassroots was vigorously contested. The mayor's long cultivation of community and civic organizations paid off. The CPHA sided with Schaefer and Rouse, as did a diverse array of neighborhood associations that belonged to the mayor's political base. About 100,000 citizens cast their votes on the Harborplace ballot questions. The mayor's question won by about 17,000 votes; the Citizens for Preservation's question fell short by less than 10,000.[38]

After the victory of Harborplace, the mayor's reelection in 1979 seemed anticlimactic. His opponents in the Democratic primary were political nonentities. But the criticisms were more prominent than the candidates. The mayor's "Charm City" offensive seemed to overlook those citizens whose lives were short on charm. While the city courted middle-class households for its dollar-a-house homesteading program and Coldspring Newtown development, 24,000 Baltimoreans were on the waiting list for public housing, and Schaefer had no plans to build additional public housing. In its effort to attract tourists and taxpayers, the city had spent one-third of its federal urban renewal and community development aid on Harborplace and a new housing development for middle-income residents.[39] Federal authorities would later rule that some of these expenditures were illegal. Under Schaefer, the public schools' share of the budget remained constant, but only because of increased state aid for the city's educational system. The local contribution to the education budget actually declined during his administration. An article in the *New Republic* criticized the mayor for neglecting the city's low-income and African American residents, but conceded that his "positive thinking" had engendered "a genuine atmosphere of achievement and hope."[40]

The hopeful atmosphere had begun to take hold in Baltimore even before Harborplace provided a focus for the city's aspirations. In 1976, Baltimore's *Daily Record* announced that the city was providing a "model for 'new' U.S. Cities." Baltimore had accumulated budget surpluses for three consecutive years; it was retiring more municipal bonds than it was issuing. As the journal of the city's business and legal communities, the *Record* naturally made much of budgets and bonds, but it also claimed that Baltimore, more than most cities, had "managed to heal the racial, social, and physical wounds of the turbulent 1960's" by being "responsive to its own internal needs." Its inward-looking parochialism helped its residents come to terms with one another. The city's mayor "had no charisma at all . . . [he was] just low key, down to earth and very effective." His approach "fit in well with Baltimore's traditional style, and made communication easier between neighborhood residents, business, labor, state and local governments."[41]

Baltimoreans, of course, might be prone to see their city as a model for others, but out-of-town observers were also finding that Baltimore, once regarded as "hopelessly dull," had undergone a "dramatic renaissance," beginning downtown and spreading to the margins of the harbor and beyond to the city's many neighborhoods. Baltimore, according to the *New York Times*, had "lain in the shadow of bigger and better known neighbors"—Philadelphia and Washington. But the city was "holding its head higher these days," not only because of downtown renewal but because of neighborhood preservation: "Above all, extensive renovation in Colonial-era neighborhoods like Federal Hill and Fells Point has given the city a new national image." The *Wall Street Journal* looked behind the national image to the city's inner life. Baltimore had its cultural attractions but opted out of competition "for national attention with major cultural centers." Instead, it was "free to concentrate its efforts inward to improve the aesthetic lives of its own inhabitants." The city's vitality, according to the *Journal*, was a by-product of its internal diversity, its multiplicity of ethnic and neighborhood cultures.[42]

Seen by travelers on the way from Washington, DC, to New York, Baltimore was "Factory Town, a chuckhole in the eastern megalopolis." But when a writer for *National Geographic* stopped to explore Baltimore, he found it "mellow, antique, friendly. Riding the gentle slopes of the land, waves of row houses—neighborly, Victorian, of enduring brick—line the streets in subtly changing patterns." It was the "city with a thousand footnotes." F. Scott Fitzgerald (Francis Scott Key Fitzgerald) had lived here while Zelda was treated at the Phipps Psychiatric Clinic at Johns Hopkins Hospital. "Baltimore," he wrote, "is so rich with memories . . . it is nice to look up the street and see the statue of my great uncle and to know that Poe is buried here and that many ancestors of mine have walked in the old town by the bay. I belong here, where everything is civilized and gay and rotted and polite."[43]

Chapter 39

TURNING POINT

A S BALTIMORE GAINED NATIONAL VISIBILITY, it lost jobs and population. In 1977, Mayor Schaefer appointed Johns Hopkins professor Abel Wolman to head the newly created Task Force on Population Migration. Its report found that residents were leaving the city at an accelerating pace. In the 1960s, Baltimore lost population at an average rate of about 3,000 a year. In the 1970s, the annual exodus averaged 11,000 to 12,000. On paper, at least, the city had lost no jobs. From the mid-1960s to mid-'70s, the number had remained steady at over 400,000. But by the mid-'70s, Baltimore City residents held only about half of those jobs. The rest were filled by commuters from the suburbs, largely because they had training or skills that city residents lacked.[1]

The jobs for which many Baltimoreans could qualify were disappearing. General Motors and Bethlehem Steel, two of the metropolitan area's biggest industrial employers, eliminated 12,000 jobs between 1978 and 1982.[2] Mayor Schaefer's urban renaissance coincided with Baltimore's decline.

Like other American cities, Baltimore was undergoing deindustrialization. But even as the Schaefer administration moved the city toward a new, tourist-based economy, it also struggled to save industrial jobs. Its highway plans, after all, had taken account of the needs of manufacturing firms. Schaefer's people also took more direct steps to prevent the decline in industrial employment. The city's economic trajectory could be traced in the fortunes of Bethlehem Steel's Key Highway Shipyard. Until the 1980s, the ship repair facility reliably employed 1,000 workers, but then the workforce declined to 400, and at the end of 1982, Bethlehem Steel closed the yard and put it up for sale. The Schaefer administration was committed to the site's continued use as a shipyard. Bernard Berkowitz led the city's efforts in that direction. He was president of the quasi-public Baltimore Economic Development Corporation (BEDCO) and formerly the mayor's development coordinator. BEDCO offered to arrange financing to potential buyers who would reopen the yard as a ship repair facility. The city's endeavor had the support of the Council of

Peninsula Organizations, a coalition of Locust Point community associations originally formed to oppose the city's plans for Harborplace. Timothy Murphy, one of the area's city council representatives, also endorsed the plan to get a new owner for the shipyard on Key Highway.[3]

In 1984, the yard was purchased by a Baltimore real estate developer, Richard Swirnow, in conjunction with a local bank, Fairfax Savings Association. BEDCO encouraged the new owners to use the site for a "marine industrial park." The city's development corporation identified potential clients for the ship repair facility and referred them to Swirnow and Fairfax, but the new owners apparently did not follow up on these leads. Berkowitz offered to meet with some of the prospects himself. Only two months after the purchase of the yard, Berkowitz "was informed that the owners had concluded that marine industrial use was not feasible." Mayor Schaefer had become deeply suspicious of Swirnow. "I think he saw it as an opportunity to buy waterfront land," said the mayor, "and I don't think he was ever very serious about trying to reopen it as a shipyard."[4]

Swirnow and his partner continued to assure the mayor that they were serious about reviving the shipyard. "To the best of my knowledge," wrote Swirnow, "I have done everything within my power to comply with all your wishes." But his efforts, he claimed, had run up against economic conditions that doomed the yard. Swirnow and the president of Fairfax wrote repeatedly to Schaefer to reaffirm their commitment to his vision. The mayor did not respond. The partners had already started to sell off the yard's equipment. Three years later, Swirnow unveiled plans for a marina, a yacht club, and a cluster of high-rise condominiums with spectacular views of the harbor and the city skyline. The Council of Peninsula Organizations announced its opposition. But the city had already given preliminary approval to the plan.[5]

Baltimore seemed destined to become a city of tourism, recreation, and entertainment, struggling to attract residents of middle-class status or above. Even when its political establishment was bent on preserving the working-class city of factories, mills, and shipyards, the town drifted in the direction set by Harborplace and its environs. What Swirnow was trying to accomplish on the south side of the Inner Harbor roughly matched what Schaefer was attempting on the north. It was all part of the Baltimore renaissance.

"SHAKY" CHALLENGE

In 1983, a credible black candidate challenged Mayor Schaefer's bid for a fourth term. William H. ("Billy") Murphy, Jr., was a circuit court judge. His great-grandfather founded the *Baltimore Afro-American* in 1892, and the paper was still in the family, one of the most prominent black dynasties of West Baltimore. Murphy attacked the mayor for giving too much attention to building projects for tourists and too little to the people of his city, especially its low-income black people. He emphasized the importance of the city's public schools in improving African American lives. Julian Bond, Jesse Jackson, and Atlanta's first black mayor, Maynard Jackson, visited Baltimore to promote Murphy's candidacy. As in previous elections, Schaefer was "Shaky" and anxious about defeat.[6]

He may have had reason for the jitters. In November 1980, Baltimore's African American leaders had convened at a westside banquet hall to create a new coalition, the Committee on Political Equality (COPE) '83. Its goal was to win control of the city at the next municipal election. Mayor Richard Hatcher of Gary, Indiana, was the keynote speaker. Congressman Parren Mitchell and some of the city's most prominent black pastors rounded out the program. A fact sheet distributed to the guests noted that African Americans made up about 60 percent of Baltimore's population but held less than a third of the seats in the city council and less than a fourth of the judgeships on the Supreme Bench. They were similarly scarce on city boards and commissions and in executive-level jobs in the city bureaucracy. In 1970, Baltimore had elected Milton B. Allen as state's attorney, the first elected black prosecutor in the country. But a white candidate sponsored by Jack Pollack defeated him for reelection in 1974 because only 24 percent of Baltimore's African American voters showed up at the polls. There were signs of recovery, however. In the judicial election just a few weeks before the banquet, a black candidate, Judge Robert Bell, finished first in a field of six candidates, and Billy Murphy came in third. About 55 percent of the city's registered voters were African American, but they had to show up on election day if COPE '83 was to realize its ambitions.[7]

In the months before the banquet, a committee of black political leaders had drawn a detailed program and timetable for the election of 1983. It set a fundraising goal of $500,000 to support voter registration and mobilization efforts as well as candidates' campaigns. An executive committee would oversee the program and identify candidates worthy of support.[8]

The organization showed its strength in 1982, when its support helped a young lawyer, Kurt Schmoke, win election as state's attorney, defeating the white incumbent who had beaten Milton Allen eight years earlier. But COPE's campaign fell behind its timetable. More than a year after its inaugural banquet, the group's leader, Samuel T. Daniels, conceded that the organization had raised only $72,000 of its planned half-million-dollar war chest. Daniels was a longtime civil rights crusader and political leader. Beginning in 1958, he had worked to wrest control of the Fourth District from Pollack. He had been chairman of the Community Relations Commission and a member of the school board, and for 20 years was executive director of the Black Council for Equal Business Opportunity. In May 1983, five months before the primary election, Daniels announced that he was supporting Mayor Schaefer's reelection.[9] A majority of Baltimore's black electorate went along. In the Democratic primary, the voters gave the mayor his fourth term by his biggest majority so far. In the general election, he won 90 percent of the votes. A local community organizer suggested that Billy Murphy may have made a mistake by bringing in civil rights celebrities such as Jesse Jackson and Julian Bond to campaign for him. "Baltimore is a parochial town," he said. "If anything, outsiders might have hurt him more than help him."[10]

But an *Afro-American* columnist condemned COPE: "The old leadership faked out the masses in the black community by toying with [the] idea of COPE '83 which was supposed to organize the black community for taking citywide elective office.

When confronted with their fear of the white political establishment this old line leadership backed the mayor with a servility that was both embarrassing and revealing."[11]

RENAISSANCE MEN

Baltimore voters had given the mayor's urban renaissance a vote of confidence, but some had misgivings. Schaefer's campaign to restore the economy of his drab metropolis seemed out of joint with the *Daily Record*'s claim that Schaefer "fit in well with Baltimore's traditional style." Schaefer's style could be dictatorial, impatient, and secretive, and he had engineered an unprecedented and decidedly un-Baltimorish concentration of bureaucratic authority.[12]

Financing Baltimore's renaissance had been a problem for Schaefer. He might prod the slow-moving council to get a bond issue onto the ballot and then persuade the voters to go along. But the process was time-consuming, and there was no guarantee that the outcome would be positive. The city's first attempt at winning voter approval for Inner Harbor development had failed in 1964.[13] Federal grants for city projects were similarly encumbered by lengthy application processes and regulations.

At the end of 1976, the mayor created a bureaucratic mechanism designed to circumvent these hindrances to urban rejuvenation by creating a "corporate" government. At its center stood the "trustees"—finance director Charles Benton and treasury manager Lawrence Daley. Since they were already city employees, they did not need council approval to assume their new duties. The board of estimates granted them authority to oversee city loans to builders, developers, or quasi-public corporations created by the city itself. By 1980, the trustees controlled a "bank," or loan fund, of $100 million largely outside the purview of the city council and beyond the reach of the city charter. The money had originally come from federal grants, proceeds of bond issues approved by voters, and funds from the capital budget. The trustees initially drew on these funds to make loans to developers and contractors, most of which were earmarked for specific projects approved by the council, the board of estimates, or the federal government. Once the loans were repaid, however, the funds fed an accumulation of "clean" money that the trustees and mayor could use with few restrictions, needing only the approval of the board of estimates.[14]

The board did not keep the trustees on a short leash, and at times the dynamic duo ran wild. For example, the trustees withdrew $2.75 million from a federal community development block grant they were supposed to use as a loan to cover construction of a shopping center in Walbrook, a predominantly African American neighborhood. The trustees invested the money instead. Their financial acumen yielded a $209,000 return. But they had violated a federal regulation that prohibited withdrawal of community development funds more than three days before they were needed for their intended purposes. The trustees were obliged to surrender their investment earnings to the federal government, along with $786,000—the unspent balance of the funds for the shopping center.[15]

Fred Durr, a Johns Hopkins undergraduate writing his senior thesis, conducted the first comprehensive investigation of what he called the "corporate branch" of city government. He presented his findings to a city council committee in the summer of 1979 and later rewrote his thesis as a report to the council's Policy and Planning Committee, while serving as an intern to Councilman Thomas J. Waxter. One of the pivotal agencies of the "corporate branch" was BEDCO, created by Arthur Held, a former executive of the Rouse Company and a member of the Greater Baltimore Committee. On Held's recommendation, the city dissolved its Economic Development Commission and the Baltimore Industrial Development Corporation. In their place, the city incorporated BEDCO to manage Baltimore's economic development efforts as a city contractor. Contracts were approved not by the city council but by the board of estimates, where the mayor was in control.[16]

Durr's report raised worries about the accountability of city government's corporate extensions: "As the corporate branch gains strength, the City Council grows weaker . . . As more and more money is transferred to corporations outside the Council's control, there is less and less public accountability. Through the corporate structure, city government is short-circuiting various checks and balances established by the City Charter."[17]

Baltimore Sun reporter C. Fraser Smith used Durr's thesis as the starting point for an eight-part series in which Durr's "corporate branch" became Mayor Schaefer's "shadow government." "In the name of Baltimore's renaissance," wrote Smith, "a parallel—or 'shadow'—government has been formed, a kind of corporate Baltimore." An armada of 25 quasi-public corporations conducted municipal business outside the framework of the municipality and beyond the bounds of its charter. The National Aquarium, for example, operated as the Baltimore Aquarium, Inc., with an all-volunteer board. Its independent status placed it outside civil service regulations, which, it was claimed, would have impaired its ability to assemble the expertise necessary to run the facility.

Some problems required such prompt action that they could not wait for the council to pass an ordinance. The city urgently needed to find a place to dump its garbage. A landfill site favored by the Schaefer administration, near the Bayview hospital complex, was ruled out of bounds when the General Assembly, prompted by some East Baltimore delegates, made it illegal to locate a landfill within half a mile of a hospital. The city then used a $2.3 million bond issue for industrial development to purchase a 143-acre tract for a landfill. BEDCO was the vehicle for the transaction. The city's "trustees" lent the money to the corporation, which then bought the land. But 98 acres of the tract were in Anne Arundel County, which prohibited their use as a landfill. Normally, the purchase would have been part of the city's capital budget, drawn up by the City Planning Commission and approved by the council. Either or both of these bodies might have raised objections to acquiring unusable property in Anne Arundel County. The "shadow government" created a path around those potential impediments.[18]

The developer of Coldspring Newtown demanded that the city compensate him for $1.4 million in "construction losses," which he blamed on minority contractors. Though the project was aimed at bringing middle-class homeowners into the city, the trustees drew on federal funds for low-income housing to cover the alleged loss on the middle-income project. Once again, they proposed to channel the money through BEDCO. Arthur Held, the corporation's founder and CEO, resigned.[19]

The ambiguous public/private character of the "shadow" corporations carried marked advantages. As private corporations, they did not have to observe city requirements that contracts be assigned by competitive bidding. As agencies of government, they could qualify for the "nontaxable" interest rate on loans, several percentage points below the interest charged to private borrowers.[20]

In the absence of competitive bidding, the trustees could do favors for contractors and developers who were close to Mayor Schaefer. One of them was Mendel Friedman, mayoral friend and campaign contributor, who received $27 million in low-interest construction loans between 1977 and 1980, more than any other developer. His biggest venture was a $10 million project to build a new headquarters for the Municipal Employees Credit Union. (The city would rent 9 of its 10 floors.) Friedman formed a partnership to oversee the project and sold shares to wealthy investors, who would own the building when it was completed and then lease it back to the credit union and the city, while writing off the building's depreciation for tax purposes. The trustees would later bail Friedman out on two condominium projects that went bad.[21]

According to Smith, "The Schaefer administration has established, in effect, a corporate machine in which the trustees have become distributors of patronage in the form of low-interest loans to Schaefer supporters and politically important community corporations."[22]

Instead of provoking outrage, the public exposure of the shadow government initially prompted talk about revising the city charter to accommodate the trustees' operations. City council president Walter Orlinsky, one of Mayor Schaefer's most consistent political antagonists, attempted to get the state legislature to dismantle the "corporate" branch of city government through an amendment to the city charter, but hardly anyone seemed ready to follow him. The mayor did appoint an "unofficial" six-member committee of the council, including some of his more reliable allies, to meet with the trustees to discuss their operations and shine some light on the shadow government. Two years later, the committee's chairman, council member Carroll Fitzgerald, resigned in "total disgust" because, he said, the trustees had failed to inform the committee about two loans for condominium projects that had gone sour—the loans made to Friedman.[23]

Councilman Fitzgerald subsequently proposed an amendment to the city charter that would require the trustees to get council approval for any loan exceeding $1 million. It passed easily and seemed headed for consideration by the voters at the next election. Mayor Schaefer could have vetoed the bill. He simply chose not to sign it. His inaction would not keep the amendment off the ballot in the 1983 municipal election—unless the council recalled the measure. Councilman Clarence "Du" Burns, the mayor's floor leader, made a motion for reconsideration at a special meeting in the heat of August. Orlinsky ruled Burns's motion out of order. Burns challenged his ruling, thus requiring Orlinsky to abandon the chair while the council voted on his procedural decision. His place at the podium was taken by the council's vice-president—Clarence Burns. Since the council was meeting long after its regular session had ended, it was unclear just what procedures should be followed. Councilman Norman Reeves attempted a filibuster, reading aloud from the council's rule book—which he abandoned when several other members all tried to speak at the same time. Reeves repeatedly shouted, "Point of order!" until one of Burns's allies unplugged his microphone. After an hour of parliamentary anarchy, one councilman bellowed a motion to adjourn. Burns gaveled the meeting to a close.[24]

The charter amendment to rein in the trustees did not appear on the ballot in 1983. William Donald Schaefer and Clarence Burns did. Burns ran to replace council president Orlinsky.[25]

DOUBTERS

A year after Schaefer's reelection, *Esquire* published a long article naming him the best mayor in the country. The writer was Richard Ben Cramer, a Pulitzer Prize–winning reporter for the *Philadelphia Inquirer* after years of not winning a Pulitzer at the *Baltimore Sun*. Schaefer was displeased with the piece. He and his inner staff—described by Cramer as the "All-Girl Gestapo"—had expected to see another of the "glittering urban renaissance-up-from-the-ashes stories" that had celebrated the mayor's success in other newspapers and magazines around the country. Instead, Cramer profiled a mayor who cursed at his cabinet members, threw temper tantrums in his office, slammed down the telephone, stomped out of meetings. Readers got a glimpse of Schaefer at one of his first cabinet sessions after his reelection in 1983: "You think we've been in this job twelve years and we've done this and we've done that. Well you're wrong. This is a new administration . . . What has this government done for the city? Nothing. Not a thing. Where's the new ideas? WHERE? What's NEW? NEW! There isn't a damn thing new."[26]

Some observers echoed the mayor's complaint that there was nothing new in Baltimore—in particular, no urban renaissance. Urban historian Marc Levine argued that the chief beneficiaries of Baltimore's downtown–Inner Harbor development had been developers, financiers, real estate speculators, suburbanites, a few affluent condo dwellers, and tourists. Resident Baltimoreans—especially poor, black Baltimoreans—sank deeper into poverty and occupied increasingly dilapidated housing. Levine conceded that the success of Charles Center and Harborplace had stimulated $700 million in private investment and generated another $52 million in annual convention business. But little of that money had moved outside the central business district to uplift the economies of the city's blighted neighborhoods. When the municipality set its sights on the Inner Harbor, it seemed to turn its back on Baltimore's neediest residential communities. Adjusted for inflation, Levine charged, the city had cut its general funds budget by 20 percent between 1974 and 1984, but expenditures for economic development rose by 400 percent. Baltimore had set business development above social spending.[27]

BEDCO's Bernard Berkowitz, in response to Levine's critical appraisal, pointed out that Baltimore had not been obsessively focused on downtown development. It had also made a serious effort to retain and attract industrial firms; the Key Highway Shipyard was a case in point. The city promoted commercial development in its neighborhoods. His figures showed that between 1972 and 1987, the city had expended almost $62 million from its general funds budget and general obligation bonds on economic development, but only $4.3 million of that had gone for downtown redevelopment. Downtown development, of course, had been financed in large part by private corporations, generally reflecting corporate priorities. And Berkowitz's table of city expenditures did not include a line for the city trustees. By 1986, their "bank" held $200 million. But he maintained that the city had tried to create a linkage between downtown development and jobs for Baltimoreans. Projects receiving city support were required to do their hiring through the mayor's Manpower Program. Harborplace alone had generated 1,300 jobs; the Hyatt Regency, 320 more. Berkowitz acknowledged that poverty, unemployment, and blight remained, due in part to a national recession in the early 1980s, but the city had made "a tremendous effort and expenditure of resources to improve low- and moderate-income neighborhoods and to generate nondowntown economic development."[28] He did not report the results of this effort. His implicit point, perhaps, was that the Schaefer administration's exertions may not have improved the city's circumstances, but they may have prevented them from being much worse.

The evidence drew others to the same conclusion. Donald Norris commended the city's pursuit of tourism because no other option seemed to promise as much economic growth. No declining smokestack city had succeeded at reindustrialization or recovered from residential abandonment. Retail sales had migrated to the suburbs and were unlikely to return. Though the city's municipal, business, and academic elites had considered other avenues of economic renewal such as biotechnology and life sciences, none held as much promise for Baltimore's needy residents as did out-of-town visitors with money.[29]

While Levine and Berkowitz sparred about the city's recent economic performance, Peter Szanton speculated about what was to come. A local foundation had commissioned him to consult with a panel of local leaders, outline the objectives that Baltimore should pursue, and then chart a path that promised to reach them. Szanton's assessment was grim. He declared the school system a disaster. "There are more guns than books in some of those schools." Fewer than 30 percent of the students who made it through high school went on to college, and only a bare majority of the city's students made it through high school. Szanton's sole consolation was that the population and the economy of the city would continue to decline, but at a more gradual rate. The future of Baltimore politics seemed more uncertain. One of his informants told him that the "black community lacks glue." "It is divided," wrote Szanton, "by geography, and by church affiliation, and again by political loyalty." But one phrase from Szanton's report captured Baltimore's collective memory more than any other: "the rot beneath the glitter."[30]

Behind Harborplace and Charles Center, the city was dying or already dead. Desertion by the Baltimore Colts in 1984 seemed a symbolic commentary on the town's future status. How could the perennial Super Bowl contenders continue to play ball

ported that he was the most popular public officeholder in Maryland. It seemed only natural that he should become the state's next governor. His chief competitor in the Democratic primary would be Stephen Sachs, Maryland's attorney general. Schaefer defeated him easily and went on to carry the general election with 82 percent of the vote, a Maryland record.[31]

RACIAL UN-POLITICS

Schaefer's victory in the gubernatorial election elevated Clarence Burns from the city council presidency to the mayor's office. The governor-elect seems to have done little to help Burns prepare for his new responsibilities. Schaefer held on to the may-or's office until the day he was inaugurated as governor. Perhaps Burns needed lit-tle preparation. He made it plain that he intended no significant departures from the policies of the Schaefer administration. But as the city's first African American mayor, Burns represented a break with the past. Even more remarkable was that he became Baltimore's first black mayor without making an issue of race. Elsewhere, black mayors had come to office as outsiders, challenging white political regimes. Unlike the first black mayors of Newark, Birmingham, Atlanta, Philadelphia, and Chicago, Baltimore's first black mayor was already a political insider.[32]

Burns's next challenge was to become the city's first *elected* black mayor. The Democratic primary came only eight months after his inauguration. He expected to face two significant Democratic opponents: Kurt Schmoke, the state's attorney, and Robert Embry, former housing commissioner, who resigned as school board president to consider entering the race. If Schmoke and Burns split the black vote, Embry might be able to win on the strength of the white vote. But Embry eventually took himself out of consideration. "I felt it was not healthy for the city," he said, "and not likely that I could win."[33]

Baltimore, which had never elected a black mayor, was headed for a Democratic primary in which the two leading candidates were black. Yet they could hardly have been more different. Burns attended a high school in East Baltimore and spent 22 years handing out towels in the locker room of a high school in West Baltimore. His father, a one-time Republican who became a Democratic precinct worker in East Baltimore, had introduced young Du to politics. Long before he was old enough to vote, he was distributing campaign literature. He became a precinct worker himself and, in 1947, formed his own political club to round up votes for Thomas D'Alesan-dro, Jr. The job as locker room attendant was his reward. It took him 24 years to move up from precinct and locker room to district leadership; in 1971 he was elected to the city council.[34] Schmoke was a graduate of Yale and Harvard Law School and had been a Rhodes Scholar at Oxford. His talents were already evident when he attended high school at Baltimore City College. He was president of the student government and star quarterback on the football team, which won the state championship.

Early polls put Schmoke almost 30 percentage points ahead of Burns. Mayor Burns's campaign had money problems and organizational problems. His campaign coordinator resigned when it came out that he had defaulted on a business loan from the city and was charged with fraud and malfeasance for diverting some loan funds to his personal use. The coordinator had been recruited because many of Burns's backers in the Baltimore business community thought his campaign manager was not up to the job. Raymond Haysbert, CEO of Parks Sausage, was brought in to give the organization steady direction, but the campaign manager, a longtime Burns loyalist, refused to recognize his authority.[35]

Burns could not give full attention to the campaign for mayor because he was too busy being mayor. By most accounts, he put in a solid performance. The *Sun* commended the budget that he submitted to the board of estimates and city council. It showed that he was not just an extension of William Donald Schaefer. He shifted the emphasis from bricks, mortar, and economic development to "human needs and the provision of city services to its citizens." He gave special emphasis to public education and police protection, and settled the question of "whether Mayor Burns is carrying on the Schaefer administration after it is gone. He is not. The priorities are his own."[36]

Governor Schaefer occasionally created difficulties for Burns. In an uncharacteristic display of concern about Baltimore's educational system, the governor summoned the mayor and city school officials to a meeting in Annapolis, with four hours notice, at which he offered to pay a team of outside experts $1.6 million to work on school problems for four years. His proposal, introduced on a Wednesday, took the school administrators by surprise, but he wanted the city's response by Friday. The Baltimore officials balked. It seemed to them that the governor was telling the city how to run its schools. As mayor, Schaefer's own handling of the school system had not earned any standing ovations. Burns and school superintendent Alice Pinderhughes proposed an alternative program under which state and local experts would conduct a study of the city's school system. "They said they want autonomy," huffed the snappish governor. "So I'm not going to spend any more of my efforts there." Some of Burns's Baltimore allies were even less helpful than the governor. First District councilman Dominic "Mimi" DiPietro asserted that Clarence Burns had "lived amongst the white people all his life and he knows what the poor people want." "Kurt Schmoke," he said, "lived amongst . . . the wealthy Jews up there in Jew Town . . . , in Mount Washington, up where all the rich Jews live . . . He don't live with the people who work every day. He lives with the people who have factories, the fat cats." Burns tried to distance himself from DiPietro's remarks, but he could hardly repudiate the loyal Mimi.[37]

Schmoke apparently resolved to sit on his substantial lead in the polls and avoid saying anything that might alienate his supporters. Burns, by acting like a mayor, steadily gained support. By the closing weeks of the campaign, he had cut Schmoke's lead to 10 percentage points and was still gaining. On election day, Schmoke won by only 3 percentage points, and Burns carried the city's white voters by two to one.[38]

Baltimore had elevated its first black mayor and elected its second black mayor without making an issue of race. The issue was unlikely to arise, of course, when both mayoral candidates were black. Burns and Schmoke were not alone in the primary, but the four other would-be mayors, taken together, drew barely 2 percent of the vote. Had Robert Embry chosen to run, race might have become an issue. Embry said his "major reason" for not running was that he was "just not comfortable with the divisive aspects of it racially." But he also mentioned that poll results had figured in his decision. In a survey completed not long before he announced his non-candidacy, less than 6 percent of voters interviewed supported Embry. In other words, Baltimore's voters—including most of its white voters—were not searching for a white candidate. And no one anticipated that an Embry campaign would make an issue of race. Marie Henderson, Burns's campaign manager, said, "I've had the pleasure of knowing Bob Embry for so many years, and would never have foreseen his candidacy as being divisive." Schmoke's campaign manager, Larry Gibson, agreed. He did not think that race would dominate the campaign "unless some candidate campaigned on the basis of race—and certainly Bob would not have."[39]

Perhaps the candidates *should* have been talking about race. It was an issue that Baltimoreans had consistently sidestepped at least since the days of the African colonization movement, or perhaps as early as dissolution of the Maryland Abolition Society in 1800. By the late twentieth century, the issue acquired renewed urgency. The percentage of Baltimoreans who were black had increased, and as it grew, living circumstances in the city deteriorated compared with those experienced by Marylanders living outside the city limits—some of them former Baltimoreans, black and white, who could afford life in the suburbs. Baltimore's decline, in other words, resulted in part from the departure of its more fortunate residents, not just from the immiseration of its remaining population. Discussion of race in city politics could not make much headway partly because some of the essential participants in the dialogue—whites and middle-class blacks—no longer lived in the city. Annexation might have brought them into the conversation. But the city had not annexed any suburban territories since 1918, and a state constitutional amendment approved in 1948 made annexation practically impossible by requiring that voters in the territory to be annexed must approve it. Like avoidance of the race issue, political subordination of the city to state policy had been a defining condition of Baltimore's existence.

AFTERWORD: NOT YET HISTORY

ON APRIL 30, 2015, the Baltimore Orioles defeated the Chicago White Sox with a tenth inning homerun at the Camden Yards ballpark, built at the initiative of William Donald Schaefer. The homerun ball landed in empty stands. A riot a few days earlier had followed the arrest of 25-year-old Freddie Gray, who had suffered a serious spinal cord injury while in police custody and later died. The gathering of thousands of fans at the stadium seemed to pose a risk of further violence, either by or against the baseball crowd. Local authorities ruled that the game could proceed only if there were no spectators.

The Baltimore riot attracted a nation of spectators. It succeeded another disorder in Ferguson, Missouri, where the fatal police shooting of Michael Brown had ignited collective violence and looting. In Ferguson, as in Cleveland, Staten Island, and North Charleston, South Carolina, white officers acting under largely white political authorities had killed black men—in Cleveland, a 12-year-old boy. Baltimore seemed different. Its mayor, police commissioner, and state's attorney were African American, as were three of the six police officers charged in the death of Freddie Gray.

Institutional practices, of course, can persist long after the personnel change. But Baltimore's particularities got swallowed up in a national narrative of white racist law enforcement and black victimization. A *New York Times* editorial, "How Racism Doomed Baltimore," explained that the town was really a southern city where "the segregationist impulse . . . was particularly virulent and well-documented." Racial isolation and concentrated poverty created the conditions of unrest in many cities. "But the acute nature of segregation in Baltimore—and the tools that were developed to enforce it over such a long period of time—have left an indelible mark and given that city a singular place in the country's racial history."[1]

The *Times* editorialist seemed misinformed about the "acute nature of segregation in Baltimore"—and in New York. An analysis of residential racial segregation in America's metropolitan areas based on 2010 Census data found that Baltimore ranked forty-fourth, just outside the top 10 percent. Metropolitan New York was fourth in residential segregation.[2] The "tools" developed to enforce segregation over such a long time presumably referred to Baltimore's residential segregation ordinance enacted in 1910, thrown out three times by city and state courts, and finally invalidated by the US Supreme Court just seven years after its passage.

A post-riot report issued by the Brookings Institution described the Baltimore metropolitan region as rather affluent. It ranked seventh in per capita income among the 35 largest urban regions in the country and was home to a sizeable black middle class. Median household income for African Americans in the Baltimore area ranked second of the 35 urban regions, just behind the District of Columbia. But the disparity between the central city and surrounding suburbs was stark, and the capacity to reduce those inequalities was limited by the city's institutional independence. The separation of Baltimore City from Baltimore County by the constitutional convention of 1850 relieved the county of any direct responsibility for living conditions in the city and deprived the city of direct access to county resources. The city line also functioned as a racial divider—a barrier between the unequal schools, services, and perils of a majority black city and its majority white suburbs. A report issued by a local foundation in 1995 suggested that the downward spiral of the city might be irreversible and that the surrounding suburbs could be pulled into the whirlpool of the city's decline.[3] So far, "edge cities," industrial parks, and shopping malls have kept the suburbs afloat.

Within the city itself there were gaping inequalities between black and white residents in education, employment, and poverty. Still, income inequality in Baltimore was about average for big cities, the poverty rate among its black residents was lower than for most cities with large African American populations, and the employment rate for black adults was near the median for these cities. Nor did the spatial concentration of poverty set Baltimore apart. There was one respect, however, in which Baltimore was distinctive. A team of Harvard economists ranked the 100 most populous counties in America according to the social mobility of their residents—the likelihood that a child born into poverty would escape it as an adult. Baltimore placed last.[4]

The city's sorry showing was undoubtedly due, in part, to its status as a stand-alone unit of government, not included in Baltimore County. Baltimore County's population contained many of the upwardly mobile households that had left Baltimore City for life in the suburbs. The move did not carry them very far. Baltimore County, exclusive of the city, ranked sixty-first among the 100 counties included in the study.[5] The social mobility of Baltimore City and County residents combined would have placed well below that of the average county, probably a by-product of economic stagnation.

The city that Mayor Kurt Schmoke inherited from William Donald Schaefer in 1987 was in decline, notwithstanding Charles Center and Harborplace. Schmoke did not abandon Schaefer's focus on economic development, but he had other priorities. In particular, he shifted city hall's attention from Harborplace to the public schools, and he dropped Schaefer's "Baltimore Is Best" slogan in favor of "The City That Reads."[6] Education had been a pivotal issue in Schmoke's election. Governor Schaefer's proposal to bring in outside experts to study the school system had helped to focus attention on the subject. But, according to Marion Orr, the unsuccessful mayoral campaign of William H. Murphy four years before Schmoke's victory had elevated the issue of education on the city's agenda and made it the center of Schmoke's campaign. Murphy charged that Mayor Schaefer's preoccupation with downtown development had drawn attention and funds away from Baltimore's failing school system. Murphy's campaign theme helped to initiate a discussion on the state of schools between the city's corporate elite in the Greater Baltimore Committee and black leaders, mostly members of the clergy, who came together in Baltimoreans United in Leadership Development (BUILD). Schmoke embraced BUILD's educational agenda during his campaign and formed a working relationship with the group after he was elected.[7]

Mayor Schmoke's school improvement efforts were politically risky, a fact widely recognized from the start of his administration. No one had developed a formula for enhancing the educational performance of poor black children in a big city with thousands of single-parent households. Downtown development was relatively straightforward by comparison, and Schaefer had his reasons for concentrating on bricks-and-mortar projects while steering clear of the schools.[8]

Schmoke's educational initiative stumbled on his personnel choices. His first choice as president of the board of school commissioners, for example, seemed eminently qualified. Meldon Hollis, like Schmoke, was a graduate of Harvard Law School, and he had an inspirational biography. Hollis had worked his way up from childhood poverty in Columbus, Georgia, to a distinguished law firm in Baltimore. But the experience was, apparently, anything but humbling. Hollis created an important new administrative position—executive director of the school board—without taking a formal vote of his colleagues on the board. He then hired a person to fill the job before the board had approved a candidate. He admitted that he deliberately gave false information to board members and school officials so that he could find out who was leaking confidential matter to the press. Schmoke demoted him from board president to board member.[9]

Schmoke played an unusually active role in the appointment of a new school superintendent. The school board had the formal authority to make the choice, but the mayor persuaded its members to bypass their top candidate to hire the applicant that he preferred. He soon had reason to regret his choice. After months of vacillation, the new superintendent, Richard Hunter, finally rejected the school-based management plan worked out laboriously by the teachers' union, the Greater Baltimore Committee, and school administrators. His plan for reorganizing the system's headquarters bureaucracy would eliminate 119 jobs and require many demotions. Under union contracts, layoffs and demotions were to be made on the basis of seniority rather than performance. Some of the more able administrators looked for jobs elsewhere, and staff morale plummeted. Hunter vetoed one school's adoption of a rigorous private-school curriculum supported by a local foundation's grant.

He would allow adoption of only peripheral elements of the curriculum, and he demanded that the foundation give the school system an additional $4 million to reduce class sizes systemwide. Finally, he dithered for so long about Baltimore's participation in a national project to improve teaching in the sciences that the program finally went to Philadelphia. Hunter's contract was not renewed when it expired in 1991. In departing, he claimed that Schmoke had set him up "as the scapegoat to take the blame for this administration's failure to live up to the mayor's campaign promise to the voters of Baltimore."[10]

Schmoke's educational initiative eventually landed him in court. He sued the state of Maryland for the funds that Baltimore needed to provide its students with the "thorough and efficient" education required by the state constitution. The state countered by arguing that the city schools suffered not from insufficient state aid but from local mismanagement. Given the school system's recent history, it was difficult to refute the argument. Schmoke and the state finally concocted a bargain under which Baltimore got more money from the state, but the city had to surrender some of its authority over its school system. The governor and the mayor would jointly appoint the city's school board and the system's CEO. The school administration had to adopt a series of management reforms demanded by the state.[11] Baltimore's control of its own affairs once again gave way to state intervention.

By this time, Baltimoreans had recast Schmoke's "City That Reads" slogan as "The City That Bleeds." The homicide rate had surged in the years after his election. Baltimore was one of the deadliest cities in the country. Its murder rate might have been even higher had it not been for its cutting-edge emergency medical system and shock trauma center.[12] Although he had served for four years as the city's prosecutor, Schmoke did not place crime near the top of his mayoral agenda. *Sun* reporter David Simon wrote a four-part series about the deterioration of the police department under Schmoke's leadership. Though violent crime was on the rise, the mayor had ordered a reduction in the number of police officers as part of a budget-cutting effort made necessary by a reduction in state aid. Experienced officers and commanders retired or went to work for other police agencies with better salary scales. Morale sank, and patrol officers busied themselves with arrests for minor drug offenses instead of tackling tough cases of homicide, robbery, or aggravated assault. The arrests earned them time in court, for which they might be paid overtime. To many in the police department, Schmoke seemed "peculiarly passionless when it came to fighting crime." "In the past," said one commander, "when we got near 200 felonies a day in the city, you'd have Schaefer demanding that something be done. Now we're routinely over 300 a day, and no one bats an eye."[13]

Another subject on which Mayor Schmoke remained largely silent was race. As he prepared to leave the mayor's office in 1999, Schmoke complained that Baltimore was a "city where issues of race continue to be important, but they are issues that no one wants to talk about. It's almost as though people would like to ignore the fact that race continues to be a significant factor determining the quality of life in the city and metropolitan area."[14] Given that he had been mayor of the city for 12 years, one might ask what kept him from using his own office to promote discussion of

Baltimore's racial divisions. Perhaps it was the same culture of avoidance that had long kept the race issue from rising to the top of the city's political agenda. In an interview with an out-of-town newspaper reporter, Schmoke conceded that he tried to avoid making race a subject of city politics.[15]

The mayor had come closest to making race an issue in his 1995 reelection campaign, when his principal opponent was the white city council president, Mary Pat Clarke. The color scheme on Schmoke's campaign bumper stickers was black, red, and green—the colors of black nationalism. Though he said almost nothing about race in his campaign, whites accused him of playing the race card. The *Afro-American*, on the other hand, took offense at Schmoke's belated discovery of the race issue. The mayor's campaign manager denied that the bumper stickers had anything to do with black nationalism.[16] Baltimoreans have delicate sensibilities when it comes to the politics of color.

The election of Schmoke's successor could easily have ended Baltimore's long-standing avoidance of racial politics. Instead, it seemed to demonstrate more decisively than ever the independence of the city's political alignments from its racial divisions. At first, two black politicians presented themselves as leading candidates for the Democratic mayoral nomination: Lawrence Bell, city council president, and Carl Stokes, school board member and former councilman. Influential black leaders were not satisfied with either candidate and set out to recruit others. Howard "Pete" Rawlings was one of the chief recruiters. As chairman of the House Appropriations Committee in Annapolis, he was regarded by some as the most powerful black politician in Maryland. Rawlings at first tried to induce NAACP president Kweisi Mfume to declare himself a candidate for mayor, even though Mfume lived outside the city limits. Mfume's backers engineered modifications in mayoral residency requirements to accommodate his candidacy; they also increased the mayoral salary so that Mfume would find it easier to abandon the income he received as leader of the NAACP. But Mfume decided to stay where he was.[17]

With only two weeks remaining before the filing deadline, Martin O'Malley, a white city councilman from Northeast Baltimore, declared himself a candidate for mayor. The immediate response was racially heated. Black leaders attacked O'Malley as a political opportunist trying to capitalize on the expected division of the black vote among several African American candidates. A prominent black minister predicted that the election of O'Malley would be "devastating." In fact, O'Malley was one of the political notables who had tried to persuade Mfume to enter the primary, and race-related attacks faded when Rawlings and several other black leaders endorsed O'Malley. On the other hand, a substantial number of whites supported Carl Stokes. Polls showed that voters were less likely to cast their votes along racial lines than in the mayoral election of 1995.[18]

O'Malley concentrated on the crime problem. As councilman, he had been sharply critical of the city's police commissioner for alleged underreporting of violent crime and for refusing to appear before the council to respond to the Community Relations Commission's critical report on the police department. O'Malley announced his candidacy for mayor at a street corner notorious as a site for drug dealing. He stressed the connection between illegal drugs and Baltimore's high homicide rate and insisted that the city would be able to deal effectively with other problems, including education and jobs, only if it could bring crime under control. O'Malley won the Democratic primary decisively, with 53 percent of the vote, over 16 other candidates. But some black leaders were concerned about his emphasis on crime. They worried, in particular, about his advocacy of the "no-tolerance" policing strategy practiced in New York, which targeted minor offenses such as drinking in public, loitering, panhandling, and unlicensed street vending on the theory that they created an atmosphere of disorder that encouraged more serious offenses. After O'Malley won the general election in November, Delegate Rawlings arranged a city hall meeting between the new mayor and 20 black elected officials who were concerned that no-tolerance policing could lead to racial profiling or abusive police conduct. The new mayor promised to be "as vigilant in policing the police as in policing the streets."[19]

The no-tolerance strategy was based on the "broken window theory"—the observation that a building with one broken window left unrepaired would soon have all its windows shattered. The police, in effect, should repair the first broken window by making arrests for minor offenses that were thought to create the climate of disorder that led to more serious lawbreaking.

O'Malley's embrace of this policing policy reemerged as an issue in the aftermath of Baltimore's 2015 riot, when the former mayor was preparing to run for the presidency. The broken window theory had undergone searching criticism since O'Malley made it the model for policing Baltimore.[20] Among other things, critics suggested that such an assertive approach might aggravate animosities between the police and the communities in which they were supposed to maintain order. These tensions might help to trigger riots in response to police overkill—as in the case of Freddie Gray.

Reflecting on the Baltimore riot, sociologist Orlando Patterson suggests that it exploded out of the intersection of aggressive policing and a ghetto subculture that draws together disconnected young men, aged 16 to 24, who are not in school and are chronically out of work. It echoes the Wild West outlaw ethos of Jesse James and Billy the Kid, a ghetto version of "core American mainstream values: hypermasculinity, the aggressive assertion and defense of respect, extreme individualism, materialism, and a reverence for the gun, all inflected with a threatening vision of blackness openly embraced as the thug life."[21] Stuck at the bottom of Baltimore, with scarcely any hope of reaching the ranks of the respectable, the ghetto minority who choose "thug life" have fashioned a kind of knighthood with its own perverse code of honor. Under the regime of no-tolerance policing, the knights of the ghetto are likely to receive disproportionate attention from the police, and the seeds of civil disorder might easily germinate in the confrontation between overaggressive law enforcement and the minority of ghetto residents who take up "thug life."

Ta-Nehisi Coates, who grew up in Baltimore, sees something more behind "thug life": fear and vulnerability. In a soliloquy addressed to his young son, he counsels caution in the presence of police, who can "destroy your body" with impunity while

Demonstration at Baltimore City Hall after Freddie Gray's death. Used by permission of the Associated Press.

"enforcing the whims of our country." But he also warns that there is cause to be wary of other black boys. Venturing into a neighborhood controlled by a rival gang can be just as dangerous as a hostile encounter with law enforcement. The response to fear, Coates suggests, is to become fearsome oneself—to project "fearsome rage" as a deterrent to potential assailants.[22] That "fearsome rage" was plain to see in the young men who stomped on abandoned police patrol cars on the day of Freddie Gray's funeral. They gave Baltimore one of its rare moments of media attention.

But fearsome rage cannot account fully for all that happened in the late-April uprising that followed Gray's death. The looting of 27 pharmacies and two methadone clinics, most of them far from the television cameras and the scenes of violence, seemed to express a rage of acquisitive capitalism.[23] Media coverage understandably concentrated on images of angry young men pelting the police with rocks. CNN could hardly have been expected to report on the riot's significant non-events: no one was killed; not a single shot was fired (except for one accidental discharge when a careless rioter dropped his handgun). In fact, while the disorders lasted, there were no homicides in a city with one of the highest murder rates in the nation. (Killings spiked after order was restored.)

Though acts of violence naturally stood at the center of the nation's attention, nonviolent actions occupied the margins of media coverage. Many enraged Baltimoreans engaged only in peaceful protest. Thousands from all over the city converged on the sites of civil disorder to clean up the mess or restore order. Though the police reported that black gangs had targeted officers for attack, members of the Crips, Bloods, and Black Guerilla Family met with about 75 clergymen to discuss what could be done to end the violence, and some gang members joined the ministers in demonstrations and prayers for a restoration of order. Other gang members stood with the president of the city council to plead for peace. The members of a local antiviolence organization, the 300 Man March, broke up fights and stood between angry young men and lines of police officers. And there were more than a few instances when angry, rock-throwing young men were outnumbered by people dancing and singing in the streets. In the *Sun*, one letter to the editor suggested that the "disorders that followed Mr. Gray's demise were less protest than party."[24] Perhaps it is possible to be Mobtown and Charm City at the same time.

THIS BOOK HAS BEEN in the back of my mind for so long that I cannot possibly name all those who helped to shape it. One of that multitude is Richardson Dilworth, whose invitations to write essays about Baltimore in his edited collections helped to move this project from the back of my mind to the front. Edward C. Papenfuse did more than anyone to complete the project and make it a book. As Maryland State Archivist, Dr. Papenfuse took on the responsibility for managing the Baltimore City Archives. He and his staff enhanced the order and accessibility of this enormous collection, which has been my principal reliance in reconstructing Baltimore's political history. Dr. Papenfuse also provided detailed comments on an earlier and even longer version of this study, as did my colleague Tristan Davies. Howell Baum offered a candid and honest assessment, took apart my early attempt at an introduction, and induced me to start over. He was right, and I did. His advice helped to reshape my conception of the book.

Saul Gibusiwa ensured my daily access to the City Archives for more than three years. Rob Schoeberlein, Tony Roberts, and Anthony Freeman provided guidance and steered me toward materials that I might otherwise have missed.

I am especially grateful to Mary Jane Arnold. She gave me access to the papers of her late husband, Joseph Arnold, who never finished his history of Baltimore. His trove of documents and articles is now in the Special Collections of the Albert O. Kuhn Library of the University of Maryland Baltimore County. I thank Tom Beck and Lindsay Loeper of the Kuhn Library for their help in finding materials for this book.

Also helpful were Patricia Anderson at the Maryland Historical Society, Paul Espinosa at the George Peabody Library, the staff of the Maryland Room at the Enoch Pratt Free Library, and Tracy Melton, who shared materials he had unearthed in his own research about Baltimore.

The staff of the Sheridan Libraries at Johns Hopkins University were unfailingly helpful, and I want in particular to thank Rosemary Spellman, Chella Vaidyanathan, and Rosanne Liebermann for their assistance in collecting illustrations.

At Johns Hopkins University Press, Robert Brugger took an interest in this book long before it became a book, and his own scholarship concerning the history of Maryland added more than editorial expertise to his guidance. Linda Strange was an ever-attentive copy editor who caught every irregularity in my footnotes and every opportunity to sharpen my prose. And I am grateful to Kim Johnson of Hopkins Press for nursing my book to the point of publication and to Meagan Szekely for wrestling with the illustrations.

I would also like to express long overdue thanks to the late Vincent "Murph" Lanasa, who introduced me to street-level politics in Baltimore when I was an undergraduate collecting material for term papers.

Appendix A

POPULATION, RACE, AND NATIVITY, BALTIMORE, 1790–2000

YEAR	TOTAL POPULATION	NON-WHITE			FOREIGN-BORN	
		No.	% of total population	% Free	No.	% of total population
1790	13,503	1,578	11.7	—	—	—
1800	26,514	5,614	21.2	49.4	—	—
1810	46,055	10,343	22.4	54.8	—	—
1820	62,738	14,683	23.4	70.3	—	—
1830	80,620	18,910	23.4	78.2	—	—
1840	102,313	21,166	20.7	84.9	—	—
1850	169,054	28,388	16.8	89.6	35,452	20.4
1860	212,418	27,898	13.1	92.0	52,497	24.7
1870	267,354	39,560	14.8	—	66,484	24.9
1880	332,313	53,729	16.2	—	56,138	16.9
1890	434,439	67,296	15.4	—	69,142	15.9
1900	508,957	79,739	15.7	—	68,600	13.4
1910	558,485	85,098	15.2	—	77,662	13.9
1920	733,826	108,696	14.8	—	84,809	11.6
1930	804,874	142,760	17.7	—	75,448	9.4
1940	859,100	166,395	19.4	—	61,698	7.2
1950	949,708	226,053	23.8	—	52,645	5.5
1960	939,024	328,512	35.0	—	39,687	4.2
1970	905,787	425,950	47.0	—	28,710	3.2
1980	786,741	441,692	56.1	—	24,667	3.1
1990	736,014	435,768	59.2	—	23,467	3.2
2000	651,154	418,951	64.3	—	29,638	4.6

Appendix B

BALTIMORE MAYORS, 1797–2017

James Calhoun	1797–1804	James Hodges	1885–1887
Thorowgood Smith	1804–1808	Ferdinand C. Latrobe	1887–1889
Edward Johnson	1808–1816	Robert C. Davidson	1889–1891
George Stiles	1816–1819	Ferdinand C. Latrobe	1891–1895
Edward Johnson	1819–1820	Alcaeus Hooper	1895–1897
John Montgomery	1820–1822	William T. Malster	1897–1899
Edward Johnson	1822–1824	Thomas G. Hayes	1899–1903
John Montgomery	1824–1826	Robert McLane	1903–1904
Jacob Small	1826–1831	E. Clay Timanus	1904–1907
William Steuart	1831–1832	J. Barry Mahool	1907–1911
Jesse Hunt	1832–1835	James H. Preston	1911–1919
Samuel Smith	1835–1838	William F. Broening	1919–1923
Sheppard Leakin	1838–1840	Howard W. Jackson	1923–1927
Samuel Brady	1840–1842	William F. Broening	1927–1931
Solomon Hillen	1842–1843	Howard W. Jackson	1931–1943
James O. Law	1843–1844	Theodore R. McKeldin	1943–1947
Jacob G. Davies	1844–1848	Thomas D'Alesandro, Jr.	1947–1959
Elijah Stansbury, Jr.	1848–1850	J. Harold Grady	1959–1962
John H. T. Jerome	1850–1852	Philip H. Goodman	1962–1963
John S. Hollins	1852–1854	Theodore R. McKeldin	1963–1967
Samuel Hinks	1854–1856	Thomas D'Alesandro III	1967–1971
Thomas Swann	1856–1860	William Donald Schaefer	1971–1987
George William Brown	1860–1861	Clarence H. Burns	1987
John C. Blackburn	1861–1862	Kurt L. Schmoke	1987–1999
John Lee Chapman	1862–1867	Martin J. O'Malley	1999–2007
Robert T. Banks	1867–1871	Sheila Dixon	2007–2010
Joshua Vansant	1871–1875	Stephanie Rawlings-Blake	2010–2017
Ferdinand C. Latrobe	1875–1877		
George P. Kane	1877–1878		
Ferdinand C. Latrobe	1878–1881		
William Pinkney Whyte	1881–1883		
Ferdinand C. Latrobe	1883–1885		

ABBREVIATIONS

In citing works in the notes, short titles are generally used after giving the full source on its first citation in each chapter. Works frequently cited are identified by the following abbreviations or short forms.

AA   *American Archives* (online, Northern Illinois University Library).

AM   *Archives of Maryland* (online, Maryland State Archives).

Balto Financ.   Jacob H. Hollander. *The Financial History of Baltimore.* New York: AMS Press, 1982 [1899].

Balto Hist.   Clayton Colman Hall (ed.). *Baltimore: Its History and Its People.* New York: Lewis Historical Publishing Company, 1912.

Balto Nation   Gary Lawrence Browne. *Baltimore in the Nation, 1789–1861.* Chapel Hill: University of North Carolina Press, 1980.

BCA   Baltimore City Archives, Baltimore.
A Works Progress Administration (WPA) project in the 1930s put librarians and archivists to work cataloguing the Baltimore City Archives. Documents issued by different city agencies were assigned to different Record Groups (RG). Within Record Groups, documents produced in a particular year were assigned numbers. At the beginning of each year, the numbers started again at 1.

Bldg Balto   Sherry Olson. *Baltimore: The Building of an American City.* 2nd ed. Baltimore: Johns Hopkins University Press, 1997.

Chronicles   J. Thomas Scharf. *The Chronicles of Baltimore, Being a Complete History of Baltimore Town and Baltimore City from the Earliest Period to the Present Time.* Baltimore: Turnbull Brothers, 1874.

Continuity   Jean H. Baker. *The Politics of Continuity: Maryland Political Parties from 1858 to 1870.* Baltimore: Johns Hopkins University Press, 1973.

First Records   Wilbur F. Coyle (comp.). *First Records of Baltimore Town and Jones Town.* Baltimore: Mayor and City Council, 1905.

Maryland	Robert J. Brugger. *Maryland: A Middle Temperament, 1634–1980.* Baltimore: Johns Hopkins University Press, 1988.
Md. Hist.	Richard Walsh and William Lloyd Fox (eds.). *Maryland: A History, 1632–1974.* Baltimore: Maryland Historical Society, 1974.
Md. Negro	Margaret Law Callcott. *The Negro in Maryland Politics, 1870–1912.* Baltimore: Johns Hopkins University Press, 1969.
Md. Polit.	Frank R. Kent. *The Story of Maryland Politics.* Baltimore: Thomas and Evans Printing Co., 1911.
MHM	*Maryland Historical Magazine.*
Official Records	*The War of the Rebellion: Official Records of the Union and Confederate Armies.* 128 vols. Washington, D.C.: Government Printing Office, 1880–1901.
Schaefer	C. Fraser Smith. *William Donald Schaefer: A Political Biography.* Baltimore: Johns Hopkins University Press, 1999.

PROLOGUE

1. Robert David Sack, *Place, Modernity, and the Consumer's World: A Relational Framework for Geographic Analysis* (Baltimore: Johns Hopkins University Press, 1992), 29–53.

2. Dolores Hayden, *The Power of Place: Urban Landscapes as Public History* (Cambridge, Mass.: MIT Press, 1995), 15.

3 Edward Hungerford, *The Personality of American Cities* (New York: McBride, Nast, 1913).

4. Richard Florida, *Who's Your City? How the Creative Economy Is Making Where to Live the Most Important Decision of Your Life* (New York: Basic Books, 2009).

5. Harvey Molotch, William Freudenheim, and Krista E. Paulson, "History Repeats Itself, But How? City Character, Urban Tradition, and the Accomplishment of Place," *American Sociological Review* 66 (December 2000): 791–823.

6. Yi-fu Tuan, *Space and Place* (Minneapolis: University of Minnesota Press, 1977), 6.

7. Edward S. Casey, "How to Get from Space to Place in a Fairly Short Stretch of Time: Phenomenological Prolegomena," in Steven Feld and Keith Basso (eds.), *Senses of Place* (Santa Fe, N.M.: School of American Research, 1996), 15–51.

8. See Stephen Thernstrom and Richard Sennett (eds.), *Nineteenth-Century Cities: Essays in the New Urban History* (New Haven, Conn.: Yale University Press, 1968); Sharon Zukin, "A Decade of the New Urban Sociology," *Theory and Society* 9 (July 1980): 581; M. Gottdiener and Joe R. Feagin, "The Paradigm Shift in Urban Sociology," *Urban Affairs Review* 24 (December 1988): 172; James DeFillipo, "Alternatives to the 'New Urban Politics': Finding Locality and Autonomy in Urban Political Development," *Political Geography* 18 (November 1999): 973–990.

9. For a useful summary of the literature on these constraints, see Katherine Levine Einstein and Vladimir Kogan, "Pushing the City Limits: Policy Responsiveness in Municipal Government," *Urban Affairs Review* 52 (January 2016): 6–9.

10. Daniel Kemmis, *Community and the Politics of Place* (Norman: University of Oklahoma Press, 1990), 78–80.

11. Dominic A Pacyga, *Chicago: A Biography* (Chicago: University of Chicago Press, 2009), 4–5.

12. The other cities (besides Baltimore, New York, and Atlanta) were Boston, Chicago, Cleveland, Dallas, Denver, Detroit, Indianapolis, Los Angeles, Miami, Milwaukee, Minneapolis, New Orleans, Philadelphia, Phoenix, Pittsburgh, San Francisco, St. Louis, and Washington, DC.

13. One of New York's boroughs—Brooklyn—scores almost twice as many quirks as the city to which it belongs, a sign that quirk counts cannot serve as precise measures of civic eccentricity.

14. Quoted in *Baltimore Business Journal*, 6 June 2004.

15. Russell Baker, "The Biggest Baltimore Loser of All Time," *New York Times Magazine*, 21 October 1973, 34–35.

16. Stephen Hunter, *Washington Post*, 25 January 2001; William Manchester, *City of Anger* (Boston: Little, Brown, 1981 [1953]).

17. Quoted in *Washington Post*, 8 July 2005; *Baltimore Sun*, 13 November 2009.

18. *Sun*, 20 January 2000; Jeremy Kahn, "The Story of a Snitch," *Atlantic Monthly*, April 2007, 89.

19. Hungerford, *Personality of American Cities*, 106.

20. H. L. Mencken, *Baltimore Evening Sun*, 11 June 1934.

21. Quoted in *Washington Post*, 8 July 2005.

CHAPTER 1. SETTLING

1. Some European-born immigrants did arrive in Baltimore during its early years, but many of them came to the town after settling elsewhere in the Americas.

2. Ronald Hoffman, *A Spirit of Dissension: Economics, Politics, and the Revolution in Maryland* (Baltimore: Johns Hopkins University Press, 1973), 4; Clarence P. Gould, "The Economic Causes of the Rise of Baltimore," in *Essays in Colonial History Presented to Charles McLean Andrews by His Students* (New Haven, Conn.: Yale University Press, 1931), 226–227. The Chesapeake Bay has 48 major tributaries, and ships of the time could navigate some of them for up to 100 miles inland. These tributaries have 102 tributaries of their own, and some of these were navigable for up to 50 miles.

3. Jack Usher Mowll, "The Economic Development of Eighteenth Century Baltimore" (PhD diss., Johns Hopkins University, 1954), 73–74; Pearle Blood, "Factors in the Economic Development of Baltimore, Maryland," *Economic Geography* 13 (April 1937): 187.

4. Carville Earle, *Geographic Inquiry and American Historical Problems* (Stanford, Calif.: Stanford University Press, 1992), 91, 94; *Maryland*, 65.

5. Charles G. Steffen, *From Gentlemen to Townsmen: The Gentry of Baltimore County, 1660–1776* (Lexington: University Press of Kentucky, 1993), 29, 100; Paul Kent Walker, "The Baltimore Community and the American Revolution: A Study in Urban Development, 1763–1783" (PhD diss., University of North Carolina, 1973), 8–9; Dennis Rankin Clark, "Baltimore, 1729–1829: The Genesis of a Community" (PhD diss., Catholic University of America, 1976), 11.

6. Clark, "Baltimore, 1729–1829," 11; *Chronicles*, 18, 60–61.

7. Tim Thornton, "The Palatinate of Durham and the Maryland Charter," *American Journal of Legal History* 45 (July 2001): 235–255.

8. Ibid.

9. Newton D. Mereness, *Maryland as a Proprietary Province* (New York: Macmillan Co., 1901), 6–7, 49; David Curtis Skaggs, *Roots of Maryland Democracy, 1753–1776* (Westport, Conn.: Greenwood Press, 1973), 14; Coleman Clayton Hall, "Baltimore Town, 1730–1797," in *Balto Hist.*, 1:9.

10. Charles A. Barker, *The Background of the Revolution in Maryland* (New Haven, Conn.: Yale University Press, 1940), 1.

11. Bernard Bailyn, *The Origins of American Politics* (New York: Alfred A. Knopf, 1968), 121.

12. *Chronicles*, 20; J. Thomas Scharf, *History of Baltimore City and County from the Earliest Period to the Present Day, including Biographical Sketches of Their Representative Men* (Philadelphia: Louis H. Everts, 1881), 50, 223, 819, 924. Six of the first seven commissioners were justices of the peace in Baltimore County. All were landowners, but only one was a native of the county. Two were physicians. One commissioner, Richard Gist, was the provincial surveyor

for the Western Shore of Maryland, and another, Thomas Tolley, represented Baltimore County in the provincial assembly.

13. *First Records*, ix–xii, xx; *Bldg Balto*, 13–15; Clark, "Baltimore, 1729–1829," 25.

14. Thomas Waters Griffith, *Annals of Baltimore* (Baltimore: W. Wooddy, 1833), 13–14.

15. *First Records*, 1–3, 19, 24, 26; Steffen, *Gentlemen to Townsmen*, 139; *Balto Financ.*, 7.

16. Griffith, *Annals of Baltimore*, 13–14; *Maryland*, 66.

17. Hall, "Baltimore Town, 1730–1797," 1:12, 18.

18. *Chronicles*, 18, 32; Norman G. Rukert, *The Fells Point Story* (Baltimore: Bodine Associates, 1976), 12.

19. Aubrey C. Land, *The Dulanys of Maryland: A Biographical Study of Daniel Dulany, the Elder (1685–1753) and Daniel Dulany, the Younger (1722–1797)* (Baltimore: Johns Hopkins University Press, 1968 [1955]), 174–175; *Maryland*, 69, 89.

20. Gould, "Economic Causes," 231.

21. William Eddis, *Letters from America*, ed. Aubrey C. Land (Cambridge, Mass.: Belknap Press of Harvard University Press, 1969), 50.

22. *First Records*, xvii.

23. *Chronicles*, 36.

24. *First Records*, xix.

25. Ibid., xxii.

26. Ibid., 18–19, 23.

27. Mowll, "Economic Development," 128.

28. Gould, "Rise of Baltimore"; Griffith, *Annals of Baltimore*, 32–33.

29. Gould, "Rise of Baltimore," 232; Clark, "Baltimore, 1729–1829," 13; Walker, "Baltimore Community," 65, 74.

30. Earle, *Geographic Inquiry*, 104–106.

31. Ibid., 88–128. See also Tina Hirsch Sheller, "Artisans and the Evolution of Baltimore Town, 1765–1790" (PhD diss., University of Maryland, 1990), 20.

32. Barker, *Background of Revolution*, 23. One of the owners who stood to gain more than most was Charles Carroll of Annapolis. His family had originally sold the town commissioners the land on which to build Baltimore. In 1729, he was the first purchaser to select a lot there, a right granted him under the town charter. In 1736, perhaps seeing a future that was invisible to the Lords Proprietary or their functionaries, Carroll bought back 26 town lots. Until he began to sell off his holdings almost 10 years later, he held approximately 40 percent of Baltimore Town. Steffen, *Gentlemen to Townsmen*, 139–140.

33. *First Records*, 21; Griffith, *Annals of Baltimore*, 12–13.

34. *AM*, 44:664–665.

35. Clark, "Baltimore, 1729–1829," 60.

36. *First Records*, 35.

37. Griffith, *Annals of Baltimore*, 13; Thaddeus P. Thomas, *The City Government of Baltimore*, Johns Hopkins University Studies in Historical and Political Science, ser. 14, no. 2 (Baltimore: Johns Hopkins University Press, 1896), 13.

38. The commissioners might have chosen to deal with their town's muddy streets by paving them. As in many other new towns of America, however, this solution seems to have been regarded as too ambitious and expensive. See Eric H. Monkkonen, *America Becomes Urban: The Development of U.S. Cities and Towns, 1780–1980* (Berkeley: University of California Press, 1988), 94.

39. Griffith, *Annals of Baltimore*, 36.

40. Hall, "Baltimore Town, 1730–1797," 1:19–20.

41. Griffith, *Annals of Baltimore*, 36.

42. Steffen, *Gentlemen to Townsmen*, 147.

43. Hoffman, *Spirit of Dissension*, 10; Charles C. Steffen, *The Mechanics of Baltimore: Workers*

and Politics in the Age of Revolution, 1763–1812 (Urbana: University of Illinois Press, 1984), 4; Scharf, *History of Baltimore City and County*, 1:185.

44. *AM*, 61:521–522.

45. Ibid., 566–567.

46. Ibid., 64:198–200; Scharf, *History of Baltimore City and County*, 778; Thomas, *City Government of Baltimore*, 11.

47. Griffith, *Annals of Baltimore*, 45.

48. *First Records*, 37.

49. Douglas G. Carroll, Jr., and Blanche D. Coll, "The Baltimore Almshouse: An Early History," *MHM* 66 (Summer 1971): 138–139, 141; *Chronicles*, 73.

50. Clark, "Baltimore, 1729–1829," 23, 25–26.

51. Ibid., 30.

52. Francis F. Beirne, *St. Paul's Parish Baltimore: A Chronicle of the Mother Church* (Baltimore: St. Paul's Parish, 1967), 8, 13; Scharf, *History of Baltimore City and County*, 518.

53. Beirne, *St. Paul's Parish*, 15.

54. Ibid; *First Records*, 18–19.

55. Beirne, *St. Paul's Parish*, 19.

56. Ibid., 20.

57. Walker, "Baltimore Community," 98–99. On the population of Annapolis, see Edward C. Papenfuse, *In Pursuit of Profit: The Annapolis Merchants in the Era of the American Revolution, 1763–1805* (Baltimore: Johns Hopkins University Press, 1975), 155. On the basis of tax records, Papenfuse estimates that as late as 1783, Annapolis still had only about 1,280 residents, both slave and free.

CHAPTER 2. GOVERNMENT IN THE STREETS

1. Gary B. Nash, *The Urban Crucible: The Northern Seaports and the Origins of the American Revolution* (Cambridge, Mass.: Harvard University Press, 1986), 15.

2. George W. McCreary, *The Ancient and Honorable Mechanical Company of Baltimore* (Baltimore: Kohn & Pollock, 1901), 14.

3. Ibid., 15–16.

4. de Francis Folsom, *Our Police: A History of the Baltimore Force from the First Watchman to the Latest Appointee* (Baltimore: J. M. Beers, 1888), 18. The town commissioners retained this responsibility only briefly. The General Assembly transferred it, in 1793, from the commissioners to the Baltimore County Court.

5. Dennis Rankin Clark, "Baltimore, 1729–1829: The Genesis of a Community" (PhD diss., Catholic University of America, 1976), 81; McCreary, *Ancient and Honorable Mechanical Company*, 18.

6. Pamela Satek, "William Lux of Baltimore: 18th Century Merchant" (MA thesis, University of Maryland, 1974), 165, 172; Ronald Hoffman, *A Spirit of Dissension: Economics, Politics, and the Revolution in Maryland* (Baltimore: Johns Hopkins University Press, 1973), 38–39.

7. Hoffman, *Spirit of Dissension*, 41–43.

8. Ibid., 50–51; Charles C. Steffen, *The Mechanics of Baltimore: Workers and Politics in the Age of Revolution, 1763–1812* (Urbana: University of Illinois Press, 1984), 56–57; Paul Kent Walker, "The Baltimore Community and the American Revolution: A Study in Urban Development, 1763–1783" (PhD diss., University of North Carolina, 1973), 137; Charles A. Barker, *The Background of the Revolution in Maryland* (New Haven, Conn.: Yale University Press, 1940), 310–311; McCreary, *Ancient and Honorable Mechanical Company*, 25.

9. Hoffman, *Spirit of Dissension*, 82–83; Walker, "Baltimore Community," 143.

10. Charles G. Steffen, *From Gentlemen to Townsmen: The Gentry of Baltimore County, 1660–1776* (Lexington: University Press of Kentucky, 1993), 29, 157.

11. Walker, "Baltimore Community," 143–145; Hoffman, *Spirit of Dissension*, 85–87; Barker, *Background of Revolution*.

12. Satek, "William Lux," 175.

13. Walker, "Baltimore Community," 152–153; Robert Purviance, *A Narrative of Events Which Occurred in Baltimore Town during the Revolutionary War* (Baltimore: Joseph Robinson, 1849), 10.

14. Richard Walsh, "The Era of the Revolution," *Md. Hist.*, 74.

15. *Maryland*, 110–111; Daniel Dulany, *Maryland and the Empire, 1773: The Antilon-First Citizen Letters*, ed. Peter S. Onuf (Baltimore: Johns Hopkins University Press, 1974), 15–16.

16. Dulany, *Maryland and Empire*, 56.

17. Quoted in Barker, *Background of Revolution*, 351.

18. Walker, "Baltimore Community," 157–158. Correspondence between Charles Ridgely, a Baltimore County delegate, and Samuel Chase of Annapolis strongly suggests that the demonstration was planned in advance, probably without the cooperation of Baltimore's mercantile community. See Steffen, *Gentlemen to Townsmen*, 161–162.

19. Walker, "Baltimore Community," 158.

20. On the overthrow of the Calverts, see Lois Green Carr and David William Jordan, *Maryland's Revolution of Government, 1689-1692* (Ithaca, N.Y.: Cornell University Press, 1974); Michael G. Kammen, "The Causes of the Maryland Revolution of 1689," *MHM* 55 (December 1960): 293–333.

21. Aubrey C. Land, *Colonial Maryland—A History* (Millwood, N.Y.: KTO Press, 1981), chap. 5.

22. The Baltimoreans may also have hesitated to join the protest against the governor's proclamation because the principal protestors were the plantation aristocrats in the provincial assembly who had denied Baltimore any legislative representation and denounced the town's merchants for their abandonment of the non-importation agreement in response to the Townshend Acts.

23. Walker, "Baltimore Community," 154.

24. Though no official records survive for the Baltimore commissioners from 1754 and 1768, Scharf reports two meetings, one in 1763 and another in 1766. *Chronicles*, 56, 58.

25. Ibid., 46; Walker, "Baltimore Community," 103–104.

26. Quoted in *Chronicles*, 47.

27. *AM*, 59:306; italics added.

28. Ibid., 306–307.

29. Ibid., 64:236–238. On unhealthy conditions in the jail, see *Maryland Journal and Baltimore Advertiser*, 13–20 November 1773, 4 August 1778.

30. *AM*, 63:261–271; *First Records*, 40.

31. Jon Teaford, *The Municipal Revolution in America: The Origins of Modern Urban Government, 1650-1825* (Chicago: University of Chicago Press, 1975), chap. 2.

32. G. B. Warden, "Town Meeting Politics in Colonial and Revolutionary Boston," in Ronald P. Formisano and Constance K. Burns (eds.), *Boston 1700-1980: The Evolution of Urban Politics* (Westport, Conn.: Greenwood Press, 1984), 15–20.

33. Barker, *Background of Revolution*, 228–232.

34. Tina Hirsch Sheller, "Artisans and the Evolution of Baltimore Town, 1765–1790" (PhD diss., University of Maryland, 1990), 32.

35. Steffen, *Mechanics of Baltimore*, 6.

36. James Webb, *Born Fighting: How the Scots Irish Shaped America* (New York: Broadway Books, 2004), 153.

37. James G. Leyburn, *The Scotch-Irish: A Social History* (Chapel Hill: University of North Carolina Press, 1962), 305.

38. Ward L. Miner, *William Goddard, Newspaperman* (Durham, N.C.: Duke University Press, 1962), 49–53, 113–114.

525

Notes to Pages 29–33

39. *Maryland Journal*, 16–23, 23–30 October 1773.

CHAPTER 3. REVOLUTION

1. Samuel Adams to the Committee of Correspondence for the City of Philadelphia, 13 May 1774, Purviance Papers, Maryland Historical Society, Baltimore; Philadelphia Committee of Correspondence to Dr. Stevenson, Mssrs. Samuel Purviance, Alexander Lawson and Others, Principal Gentlemen in Baltimore, 21 May 1774, ibid.; Samuel Smith to William Lux, 13 May 1774, in Robert Purviance, *A Narrative of Events Which Occurred during the Revolutionary War* (Baltimore: J. Robinson, 1849), 110–111.

2. Andrew Buchanan, William Buchanan, John Moale, William Smith, William Lux, John Smith, Robert Alexander, Robert Christie, Sr., Isaac Vanbibber, John Boyd, and Samuel Purviance, Jr., "To the Freeholders and Gentlemen of Baltimore County," Purviance Papers; David Curtis Skaggs, "Maryland's Impulse toward Social Revolution, 1750–1776," *Journal of American History* 54 (March 1968): 780. Propertyless residents who could not qualify as freeholders were presumably excluded from such meetings.

3. "At a Generall Meeting of the Freeholders, Gentlemen, Merchants, Tradesmen and Other Inhabitants of Baltimore County Held at the Court House of the Said County on Tuesday May 31, 1774," Purviance Papers; *Chronicles*, 126.

4. Paul Kent Walker, "The Baltimore Community and the American Revolution: A Study in Urban Development, 1763–1783" (PhD diss., University of North Carolina, 1973), 173–175.

5. *Chronicles*, 126; Purviance, *Narrative*, 13. New York's Sons of Liberty and its Committee of Correspondence issued a similar call for a continental congress just two weeks before Baltimore's town meeting did so. See Barnet Schechter, *The Battle for New York: The City at the Heart of the American Revolution* (New York: Walker & Co., 2002), 40.

6. J. Thomas Scharf, *History of Baltimore City and County from the Earliest Period to the Present Day* (Philadelphia: Louis H. Everts, 1881), 70; Walker, "Baltimore Community," 183–185.

7. George W. McCreary, *The Ancient and Honorable Mechanical Company of Baltimore* (Baltimore: Kohn & Pollock, 1901), 22–25; Chronicles, 166.

8. Scharf, *History of Baltimore City and County*, 73.

9. Annapolis Committee of Correspondence to Baltimore Committee of Correspondence, 26 May 1774, in Purviance, *Narrative*, 117; Robert Alexander to Baltimore Committee of Correspondence(?), n.d., ibid., 125.

10. Ronald Hoffman, *A Spirit of Dissension: Economics, Politics, and the Revolution in Maryland* (Baltimore: Johns Hopkins University Press, 1973), 136.

11. Quoted in James F. Vivian and Jean H. Vivian, " 'A Jurisdiction Competent to the Occasion': A Benjamin Rumsey Letter, June, 1776," *MHM* 67 (June 1978): 144.

12. Philip A. Crowl, *Maryland During and After the Revolution: A Political and Economic Study*, Johns Hopkins University Studies in Historical and Political Science, ser. 41, no. 1 (Baltimore: Johns Hopkins University Press, 1943), 18–19. On the Revolution as a social upheaval, see Gordon S. Wood, *The Radicalism of the American Revolution: How a Revolution Transformed a Monarchical Society into a Democratic One Unlike Any That Had Ever Existed* (New York: Alfred A. Knopf, 1992).

13. Maryland Provincial Convention, 18 January 1776, *AA*, 4:762.

14. Robert Alexander to the Maryland Council of Safety, 30 January 1776, *AM*, 11:133.

15. Herbert E. Klingelhofer, "The Cautious Revolution: Maryland and the Movement toward Independence," *MHM* 60 (September 1965): 268–269; *First Records*, 41.

16. Walker, "Baltimore Community," 207.

17. Extract of a Letter from Robert Moreton Preventive Officer at Baltimore in Maryland to the Commissioners of Customs at Boston, 28 May 1773, *AM*, 63:427–428.

18. Aubrey C. Land, *Colonial Maryland—A History* (Millwood, N.Y.: KTO Press, 1981), 312–313; Hoffman, *Spirit of Dissension*, 158–159; Walker, "Baltimore Community," 210.

19. Frank A. Cassell, *Merchant Congressman in the Young Republic: Samuel Smith of Maryland, 1752–1839* (Madison: University of Wisconsin Press, 1971), 14–15.

20. Hoffman, *Spirit of Dissension*, 157.

21. Ibid., 164; Walker, "Baltimore Community," 210–213.

22. *Maryland Journal and Baltimore Advertiser*, 23 January 1775.

23. Purviance, *Narrative*, 46–47.

24. *AA*, 1:1146; *Maryland Journal*, 23 January 1775.

25. Proceedings of the Committee for the County of Baltimore, 2 May 1775, *AA*, 4:1710.

26. Tina Sheller, "Artisans and the Evolution of Baltimore Town, 1765–1790" (PhD diss., University of Maryland, 1990), 97.

27. Xing Lu, *Rhetoric of the Chinese Cultural Revolution: The Impact on Chinese Thought* (Columbia: University of South Carolina Press, 2004), 43–44.

28. Proceedings of the Committee for the County of Baltimore, 13 November 1775, *AA*, 4:1780.

29. *Maryland Journal*, 29 March 1775.

30. *AA*, 4:1719–1720 (3 July 1775).

31. Ibid., 6:1462 (17 June 1776).

32. Purviance, *Narrative*, 37.

33. *AA*, 4:1702 (17 January 1775); ibid., 4:1710 (2 May 1776); *Maryland Journal*, 10 May 1776.

34. Quoted in *Chronicles*, 155–156

35. Charles C. Steffen, *The Mechanics of Baltimore: Workers and Politics in the Age of Revolution, 1763–1812* (Urbana: University of Illinois Press, 1984), 66–67.

36. *AA*, 1:522 (23 July 1776).

37. Ibid., 1:668 (30 July 1776); *Maryland Journal*, 31 July 1776.

38. *AA*, 2:1652 (13 July 1775).

39. *Maryland Journal*, 19 July 1775.

40. *AA*, 2:1653 (13 July 1775).

41. Ibid. (14 July 1775).

42. Ibid., 2:1653–1654.

43. Ibid. (9 August 1775); *Chronicles*, 136.

44. Purviance, *Narrative*, 62–63; Hoffman, *Spirit of Dissension*, 190.

45. Robert Christie to Daniel of St. Thomas Jennifer, 10 December 1776, *AA*, 3:1147.

46. Steffen, *Mechanics of Baltimore*, 69–70; Dennis Rankin Clark, "Baltimore, 1729–1829: The Genesis of a Community" (PhD diss., Catholic University of America, 1976), 90.

47. Baltimore Committee of Observation, "Complaint of Cumberland Dugan against Dr. Henry Stevenson," 25 June 1775, AA, 6; J. R. Quinan, "The Introduction of Innoculation and Vaccination into Maryland, Historically Considered," *Maryland Medical Journal*, 30 June 1883, 116, 132.

CHAPTER 4. BALTIMORE AT WAR

1. "Charges against Vincent Trapnell and Others," 18 November 1776, *AM*, 16:87.

2. "James Bosley's Statement," 18 November 1776, ibid., 88.

3. Samuel Baxter to Council, 3 January 1777, ibid., 11–12.

4. Dennis Rankin Clark, "Baltimore, 1729–1829: The Genesis of a Community" (PhD diss., Catholic University of America, 1976), 90.

5. Council to Baltimore Committee, 9 January 1777, *AM*, 16:31.

6. Council to Baxter, 9 January 1777, ibid.

7. Council to Baltimore Committee, 18 January 1777, ibid., 59; Charles C. Steffen, *The Mechan-*

ics of Baltimore: Workers and Politics in the Age of Revolution, 1763–1812 (Urbana: University of Illinois Press, 1984), 70.

8. Steffen, *Mechanics of Baltimore*, 70; Paul Kent Walker, "The Baltimore Community and the American Revolution: A Study in Urban Development, 1763–1783" (PhD diss., University of North Carolina, 1973), 248–249.

9. Ward L. Miner, *William Goddard, Newspaperman* (Durham, N.C.: Duke University Press, 1962), 147, 152–154.

10. Steffen, *Mechanics of Baltimore*, 72; Walker, "Baltimore Community," 255–261; Miner, *William Goddard*, 152–154.

11. *Maryland*, 125.

12. Hamilton Owens, *Baltimore on the Chesapeake* (Garden City, N.Y.: Doubleday, Doran, 1941), 112.

13. Oliver Wolcott to Laura Wolcott, 2 January 1777, in Paul H. Smith (ed.), *Letters of Delegates to Congress, 1774–1789* (Washington, D.C.: Library of Congress, 1976–2000), 6:15. See also Matthew Thornton to Meshech Weare, 23 January 1777, in Smith, *Letters*, 6:15, 189.

14. John Adams' Diary, 8 February 1777, in Smith, *Letters*, 6:238.

15. *Maryland*, 125.

16. *Balto Hist.*, 1:39; Thaddeus P. Thomas, *The City Government of Baltimore*, Johns Hopkins University Studies in Historical and Political Science, ser. 14, no. 2 (Baltimore: Johns Hopkins University Press, 1896), 17.

17. Benjamin Rush to Julia Rush, 31 January 1777, in Smith, *Letters*, 6:184.

18. James Kendall Hosmer, *Samuel Adams* (New York: Houghton Mifflin, 1898), 148; John K. Alexander, *Samuel Adams: America's Revolutionary Politician* (New York: Rowman and Littlefield, 2002), 123–126; Samuel Adams to Elizabeth Adams, 26 December 1776, in Smith, *Letters*, 5:670.

19. "A Number of Prisoners Arrived at Baltimore from Philadelphia to Be Secured," 21 December 1776. *AA*, 3:1607.

20. Elias Boudinot, *The Life, Public Services, Addresses, and Letters of Elias Boudinot* (Boston: Houghton Mifflin, 1896), 1:182; George M. Curtis III, "The Goodrich Family and the Revolution in Virginia," *Virginia Magazine of History and Biography* 84 (January 1976): 49–74.

21. *AA*, 3:1609, 1616 (23, 30 December 1776).

22. Todd Cooper, "The Impact of the War on Baltimore's Merchants," in Ernest McNeill Eller (ed.), *Chesapeake Bay in the American Revolution* (Centreville, Md.: Tidewater Publishers, 1981), 292.

23. Robert A. East, *Business Enterprise in the Revolutionary Era* (New York: Columbia University Press, 1938), 151; Jerome R. Garitee, *The Republic's Private Navy: The American Privateering Business as Practiced in Baltimore during the War of 1812* (Middletown, Conn.: Wesleyan University Press, 1977), 15.

24. Stuart Weems Bruchey, *Robert Oliver, Merchant of Baltimore, 1783–1819*, Johns Hopkins University Studies in Historical and Political Science, ser. 74, no. 1 (Baltimore: Johns Hopkins University Press, 1956), 33.

25. Cooper, "Impact of War," 290.

26. William Elliot Griffis, "Where Our Flag Was First Saluted," *New England Magazine* 8 (July 1893): 581; Jack P. Greene and J. R. Pole (eds.), *A Companion to the American Revolution* (Malden, Mass.: Blackwell, 2000), 518.

27. Friedrich Eller, *The Dutch Republic and the American Revolution*, Johns Hopkins University Studies in Historical and Political Science, ser. 29, no. 2 (Baltimore: Johns Hopkins University Press, 1908), 51.

28. Garitee, *Republic's Private Navy*, 15.

29. Norman G. Rukert, *The Fells Point Story* (Baltimore: Bodine and Associates, 1976), 17.

30. Ibid., 8; Arthur Pierce Middleton, "Ships and Shipbuilding in the Chesapeake Bay and Tributaries," in Eller, *Chesapeake Bay*, 124.

31. Garitee, *Republic's Private Navy*, 17–18.

32. Howard Irving Chapelle, *The Baltimore Clipper: Its Origin and Development* (New York: Edward W. Sweetman, 1968), 103–104.

33. *Maryland*, 126.

34. East, *Business Enterprise*, 167.

35. David Lee Russel, *The American Revolution in the Southern Colonies* (Jefferson, N.C.: McFarland, 2000), 126.

36. Ibid., 164–165.

37. *Federal Gazette and Baltimore Daily Advertiser*, 5 December 1796.

38. Curtis P. Nettels, *The Emergence of a National Economy, 1775–1815* (New York: Harper & Row, 1969), 7–8.

39. Johann David Schoepf, *Travels in the Confederation* (New York: Burt Franklin, 1968 [1788]), 1:326, 329.

40. Myron J. Smith, Jr., and John G. Earle, "The Maryland State Navy," in Eller, *Chesapeake Bay*, 217–219; Captain Matthew Squire to Gov. Robert Eden, 8 March 1776, Purviance Papers, Maryland Historical Society, Baltimore.

41. "Committee Informed by Mr. Brown . . . ," 15 March 1776, *AA*, 5:1512.

42. "Memorial of Clarke and Others," 10 October 1776, *AM*, 12:333.

43. Robert Purviance, *A Narrative of Events Which Occurred in Baltimore Town during the Revolutionary War* (Baltimore: Joseph Robinson, 1849), 48; Smith and Earle, "Maryland Navy," 220; Baltimore Committee to Council, 16 March 1776, *AM*, 10:255–256.

44. Smith and Earle, "Maryland Navy," 221.

45. J. A. Robinson, "British Invade the Chesapeake, 1777," in Eller, *Chesapeake Bay*, 351–352, 362.

46. Russell, *American Revolution*, 201.

47. Ernest M. Eller, "Washington's Maritime Strategy and the Campaign that Assured Independence," in Eller, *Chesapeake Bay*, 475; Marshall Booker, "Privateering from the Bay, Including Admiralty Courts and Tory as Well as Patriot Operations," in Eller, *Chesapeake Bay*, 278; Robinson, "British Invade the Chesapeake," 357.

CHAPTER 5. FROM TOWN TO CITY

1. Gordon S. Wood, "Forward: State Constitution-Making in the American Revolution," *Rutgers Law Journal* 24 (Summer 1993): 911–921.

2. *AM*, 78:311.

3. Willi Paul Adams, *The First American Constitutions: Republican Ideology and the Making of the State Constitutions in the Revolutionary Era*, trans. Rita Kimber and Robert Kimber (Chapel Hill: University of North Carolina Press, 1980), 206.

4. Quoted in Gary B. Nash, *The Unruly Birth of Democracy and the Struggle to Create America* (New York: Viking Books, 2005), 286.

5. Beverly W. Bond, Jr., *State Government in Maryland, 1777–1781*, Johns Hopkins University Studies in Historical and Political Science, ser. 23, no. 3 (Baltimore: Johns Hopkins University Press, 1905), 11.

6. *Maryland*, 121–122; Philip A. Crowl, *Maryland During and After the Revolution: A Political and Economic Study*, Johns Hopkins University Studies in Historical and Political Science, ser. 63, no. 1 (Baltimore: Johns Hopkins University Press, 1943), 32–33; Ronald Hoffman, "Popularizing the Revolution: Internal Conflict and Economic Sacrifice in Maryland, 1774–1780," *MHM* 68 (Summer 1973): 130.

7. Robert Purviance, *A Narrative of Events Which Occurred in Baltimore Town during the Revolutionary War* (Baltimore: Joseph Robinson, 1849), 43.

8. Paul Kent Walker, "The Baltimore Community and the American Revolution: A Study in Urban Development, 1763–1783" (PhD diss., University of North Carolina, 1973), 237.

9. Ibid., 240.

10. Dennis Rankin Clark, "Baltimore, 1729–1829: The Genesis of a Community" (PhD diss., Catholic University of America, 1976), 95–96.

11. Tina Sheller, "Artisans, Manufacturing, and the Rise of a Manufacturing Interest in Revolutionary Baltimore Town," *MHM* 83 (Spring 1988): 3–17.

12. Ibid.; Charles C. Steffen, *The Mechanics of Baltimore: Workers and Politics in the Age of Revolution, 1763–1812* (Urbana: University of Illinois Press, 1984), chap. 4.

13. Walker, "Baltimore Community," 343–344; *Chronicles*, 201–202; Wilbur Coyle, *Records of Baltimore (Special Commissioners), 1782–1797* (Baltimore: Press of Meyer & Thalheimer, 1909), 99.

14. Thaddeus Thomas, *The City Government of Baltimore*, Johns Hopkins University Studies in Historical and Political Science, ser. 14, no. 2 (Baltimore: Johns Hopkins University Press, 1896), 12–13; T. W. Griffith, *Annals of Baltimore* (Baltimore: W. Wooddy, 1833), 42.

15. *AM*, 203:419–421.

16. Ibid., 422.

17. Walker, "Baltimore Community," 345–346; *Maryland Journal* quoted in *Chronicles*, 196.

18. Walker, "Baltimore Community," 332.

19. Gary L. Browne, "Federalism in Baltimore," *MHM* 83 (Spring 1988): 51–52.

20. Philip A. Crowl, "Anti-Federalism in Maryland, 1787–1788," *William and Mary Quarterly*, 3rd ser., 4 (October 1947): 462; Clark, "Baltimore, 1729–1829," 109.

21. L. Marx Renzulli, Jr., *Maryland: The Federalist Years* (Rutherford, N.J.: Fairleigh Dickinson University Press, 1972), 93–94; Steffen, *Mechanics of Baltimore*, 92–93; Crowl, *Maryland During and After the Revolution*, 159–160.

22. *Balto Nation*, 13. Boston, though larger than Baltimore, remained a town until the 1820s, but Boston's township government performed a much wider range of functions under much more extensive electoral and democratic control than Baltimore Town. See Leonard P. Curry, *The Corporate City: The American City as a Political Entity, 1800–1850* (Westport, Conn.: Greenwood Press, 1997), 2.

23. *New Jersey Journal*, 4 March 1789.

24. Quoted in Scharf, *History of Baltimore City and County*, 1:82.

25. Joseph B. Varnum, Jr., *The Seat of Government of the United States* (Washington, D.C.: R. Farnham, 1854), 11–12; Lee W. Formwalt, "A Conversation between Two Rivers: A Debate on the Location of the U.S. Capital in Maryland," *MHM* 71 (Fall 1976): 311.

26. William Bruce Wheeler, "The Baltimore Jeffersonians, 1788–1800: A Profile of Intra-Factional Conflict," *MHM* 66 (Summer 1971): 154.

27. Scharf, *History of Baltimore City and County*, 1:118; Renzulli, *Maryland Federalist Years*, 152–153.

28. Frank A. Cassell, "The Structure of Baltimore Politics in the Age of Jefferson, 1795–1812," in Aubrey Land, Lois Green Carr, and Edward C. Papenfuse (eds.), *Law, Society, and Politics in Early Maryland* (Baltimore: Johns Hopkins University Press, 1977), 278–279.

29. Clark, "Baltimore, 1729–1829," 118.

30. Wheeler, "Baltimore Jeffersonians," 159.

31. Clark, "Baltimore, 1729–1829," 36, 110; *Chronicles*, 280, 286; *Bldg Balto*, 13–15.

32. Wheeler, "Baltimore Jeffersonians," 166; *Chronicles*, 280.

33. Wheeler, "Baltimore Jeffersonians," 163; George W. McCreary, *The Ancient and Honorable Mechanical Company of Baltimore* (Baltimore: Kohn & Pollock, 1901), xi.

34. Thomas, "City Government of Baltimore," 19; *Balto Nation*, 38–39.

35. *Balto Nation*, 43–44.

36. Wheeler, "Baltimore Jeffersonians," 165–166; Frank A. Cassell, *Merchant Congressman in*

the Young Republic: Samuel Smith of Maryland, 1752–1839 (Madison: University of Wisconsin Press, 1971), 70–72. See also Steffen, *Mechanics of Baltimore*, 160.

37. Clark, "Baltimore, 1729–1829," 110; *Chronicles*, 248, 266–267; James Haw, Francis F. Beirne, Rosamund R. Beirne, and R. Samuel Jett, *Stormy Patriot: The Life of Samuel Chase* (Baltimore: Maryland Historical Society, 1980), 169–170.

38. Renzulli, *Maryland Federalist Years*, 195, 198, 200; Cassell, *Merchant Congressman*, 80–81.

39. Steffen, *Mechanics of Baltimore*, 73–75, 164; Renzulli, *Maryland Federalist Years*, 204; Cassell, *Merchant Congressman*, 83–88; Whitman H. Ridgway, *Community Leadership in Maryland, 1790–1840: A Comparative Analysis of Power in Society* (Chapel Hill: University of North Carolina Press, 1979), 77–78.

40. Steffen, *Mechanics of Baltimore*, 64; *Federal Gazette* quoted in Scharf, *History of Baltimore City and County*, 1:118.

41. *Chronicles*, 286.

42. Renzulli, *Maryland Federalist Years*, 218.

43. Ibid., 228–229; *Chronicles*, 294, 297–298.

CHAPTER 6. "CALAMITIES PECULIARLY INCIDENT TO LARGE CITIES"

1. *Ordinances of the Corporation of the City of Baltimore, Passed at Their First and Second Sessions, Held in February, 1797 and February, 1798, with the Act of Incorporation Prefixed* (Baltimore: John Cox, 1875), 7.

2. *Bldg Balto*, 49.

3. Mayor's Communication Respecting the Mud Machine, 7 July 1800, BCA, RG 16, no. 345b; Z. Burke to Mayor Calhoun, n.d., 1800, BCA, RG 9, no. 346; Report of the Committee Respecting the Mud Machine, n.d., 1801, BCA, RG 16, no. 262; Report of the Committee to Whom Was Referred the Resolution to Treat with Capt. Colver for the Purchase of His Mud Machine, n.d., 1806, ibid., no. 221; Report of the Joint Committee on the Petition of Jno. Evelett, 3 March 1806, ibid., no. 222; Mayor's Annual Message, 1807, ibid., no. 239.

4. Petition Relating to Fire Wood, 19 June 1797, BCA, RG 16, no. 98; [no title], 1798, ibid., no. 215.

5. Memorial of the Brickmakers, n.d., 1798, ibid., no. 150; Repeal of Brick Ordinance, 21 February 1798, ibid., no. 169.

6. Cumberland Dugan's Report on Inspection Law's Progress from Annapolis, 18 December 1803, BCA, RG 9, no. 200a.

7. Mayor's Annual Message, 11 February 1805, BCA, RG 16, no. 320.

8. *Ordinances of Baltimore*, 162–163.

9. *Chronicles*, 267; William Travis Howard, *Public Health Administration and the Natural History of Disease in Baltimore, Maryland, 1797–1920* (Washington, D.C.: Carnegie Institute, 1924), 47; John R. Quinan, *Medical Annals of Baltimore* (Baltimore: Isaac Friedenwald, 1881), 18.

10. Howard, *Public Health*, 50.

11. Quinan, *Medical Annals*, 20

12. *Federal Gazette and Baltimore Daily Advertiser*, 29 August 1797.

13. An Ordinance for the Establishment of an Hospital for the Relief of Indigent Sick Persons and the Reception and Care of Lunaticks, 20 February 1798, BCA, RG 16, no. 188.

14. Board of Health Report, 5 February 1799, ibid., no. 217.

15. *Federal Gazette*, 12 March 1799.

16. Ibid., 5, 12 August 1800.

17. Ibid., 22 August 1800.

18. Douglas F. Stickle, "Death and Class in Baltimore: The Yellow Fever Epidemic of 1800," *MHM* 74 (September 1979): 283, 287–288.

19. Ibid., 288–289.

20. *Federal Gazette*, 10 December 1800.

21. Ibid., 20 January 1802; Stickle, "Death and Class," 291.

22. *Federal Gazette*, 31 January 1801.

23. *Ordinances of Baltimore*, 265–266.

24. Ibid.; Howard, *Public Health*, 50–51.

25. Mayor Calhoun to City Commissioners, 23 August 1802, BCA, RG 9, no. 338.

26. Resolve, 9 March 1801, BCA, RG 16, no. 327; An Ordinance to Carry into Effect an Act of the General Assembly, 20 February 1802, ibid., no. 244.

27. Mayor's Communication, 9 February 1807, ibid., no. 239.

28. A. Fonerden, Secretary to the Board of Health, to Mayor, 11 February 1808, BCA, RG 9, no. 299.

29. Colin MacKenzie and James Smyth to Mayor Thorowgood Smith, 14 April 1808, ibid., no. 300.

30. An Ordinance for Leasing the City Hospital and the Grounds Belonging Thereto, 24 June 1808, City Council Ordinances and Resolutions, 1797–1838 and 1847, BCA, RG 16, ser. 5, p. 3.

31. Ibid., 240, 297. The agreement to cede the hospital to the state was formalized in successive resolutions from 2 April 1827 to 4 February 1828.

32. Louise Malloy, "Fire Protection," in *Balto Hist.*, 1:429.

33. Ibid., 430; Clarence H. Frost, *Official History of the Fire Department of the City of Baltimore: Together with Biographies and Portraits of Eminent Citizens of Baltimore* (Baltimore, 1898), 13–15.

34. Frost, *Fire Department*, 18–19; *Chronicles*, 279.

35. Frost, *Fire Department*, 19–20.

36. *First Records*, 23.

37. Ibid., 23, 35; Ordinance for Regulating the Sweeping of Chimneys, 3 December 1798, BCA, RG 16, no. 172.

38. Ordinance for Sweeping of Chimneys.

39. Ordinance for Preventing Fires in the City of Baltimore, 6 December 1798, BCA, RG 16, no. 178.

40. An Additional Supplement to the Ordinance to Diminish the Number of Dogs, 20 March 1810, ibid., no. 456.

41. Report on Watering the City, 13 June 1799, ibid., no. 213; James Sullivan to ?, 22 June 1799, ibid., no. 215.

42. Report on Watering the City; Communication from the Mayor, 10 February 1800, BCA, RG 16, no. 336.

43. Communication from the Mayor, 14 February 1803, ibid., no. 345.

44. An Ordinance Providing for Introducing a Copious & Permanent Supply of Water into the City of Balto., 24 March 1803, ibid., no. 260.

45. The Report of the Commissioners Appointed by an Ordinance for Introducing a Copious and Permanent Supply of Water into the City of Baltimore, 21 February 1804, ibid., no. 132.

46. Mayor's Communication to the City Council, 13 February 1804, ibid., no. 231; Alfred Quick, "Baltimore Water Works," in *Balto Hist.*, 1:413.

47. Petition of Water Company, 21 November 1805, BCA, RG 16, no. 242.

48. Report of the Committee on the Mayor's Communication, 13 November 1805, ibid., no. 290; Report of the Committee Appointed to Ascertain Terms upon Which the Directors of the Water Co. Are Disposed to Sell Their Stock & to Make Additional Contracts, 4 December 1805, ibid., no. 291.

49. Quick, "Baltimore Water Works," 414; Nelson Manfred Blake, *Water for the Cities: A History of the Urban Water Supply Problem in the United States* (Syracuse, N.Y.: Syracuse University Press, 1956), 220.

50. *Bldg Balto*, 49.

51. Quick, "Baltimore Water Works," 414.

52. Memorial of George Waddell to the Mayor and City Council, n.d., March 1806, BCA, RG 16, ser. 1, no. 166.

53. *Bldg Balto*, 49; Report of the Committee on the Mayor's Communication, 13 November 1805, BCA, RG 16, no. 290; Report of Committee Appointed to Ascertain Terms upon Which Directors of Water Co. Disposed to Sell; An Ordinance Relative to the Baltimore Water Company, 30 January 1806, BCA, RG 16, ser. 5, p. 31; John McKim to Mayor Thorowgood Smith, 10 May 1808, BCA, RG 16, no. 342; Blake, *Water for the Cities*, 76.

54. Resolution for Purchasing Permanent Springs of Water, 10 March 1807, BCA, RG 16, no. 436; Blake, *Water for the Cities*, 221.

55. Sam Bass Warner, Jr., *The Private City: Philadelphia in Three Periods of Its Growth*, 2nd ed. (Philadelphia: University of Pennsylvania Press, 1987), 3–4, 45, 202.

56. E. Digby Baltzell, *Puritan Boston & Quaker Philadelphia* (New Brunswick, N.J.: Transaction Publishers, 1999 [1979]), 372–373.

57. Robert J. Gamble, "Civic Economies: Commerce, Regulation, and Public Space in the Antebellum City" (PhD diss., Johns Hopkins University, 2014).

58. William J. Novak, *The People's Welfare: Law and Regulation in Nineteenth-Century America* (Chapel Hill: University of North Carolina Press, 1996). See also Novak's "The Myth of the 'Weak' American State," *American Historical Review* 113 (June 2008): 252–272.

59. An Ordinance for the Safekeeping of Gun Powder within the City of Baltimore and Precincts Thereof, 27 February 1801, BCA, RG 16, no. 293.

60. Mayor's Communication on the Subject of a House for the Superintendent of the Powder Magazine, 18 February 1804, ibid., no. 205.

61. Petition, 22 February 1802, BCA, RG 16, [no number]; Resolution, 26 February 1802, ibid., no. 230; An Ordinance to Suspend an Ordinance Entitled an Ordinance for Building a City Hall for the City of Baltimore, 11 March 1802, ibid., nos. 229–230.

CHAPTER 7. TRIAL BY COMBAT

1. Richard A. Fox, "Trouble on the Chain Gang: City Surveying, Maps, and the Absence of Urban Planning in Baltimore, 1730–1823; with a Checklist of Maps of the Period," *MHM* 81 (Spring 1986): 9.

2. Ibid.; Resolution Authorizing the Mayor &c to Contract for a Survey of the City, 9 March 1812, BCA, RG 16, no. 629. The price would later rise to $3,000. See T. Poppleton Contract, n.d., 1812, ibid., ser. 1, no. 208.

3. Copy of Letter to Comr(?) Howard, 23 May 1812, BCA, RG 3, ser. 1, no. 281; Howard's Letter, 25 May 1812, ibid., no. 277; Opinions of Former City Commissioners, n.d., 1812, ibid., no. 282. Stauffer prepared a lengthy statement outlining his reasons for supporting Bouldin and opposing Poppleton. See Henry Stauffer's Objections against the Appointment of Mr. Poppleton as Surveyor of the City, 20 April 1812, ibid., no. 283.

4. Fox, "Trouble on the Chain Gang," 15.

5. Concerning T. H. Poppleton's Survey of the City, Observations and Proposals Made by Him, n.d., 1812, BCA, RG 3, ser. 1, no. 208.

6. Mr. Poppleton's Proseadings of Surveying on 25th 27th & 28th of April 1812, ibid., no. 287; Mr. Poppleton's Resignation as Private Surveyer, 29 April 1812, ibid.

7. T. Poppleton's letter to Edwd. Johnson Mayor of the City of Baltimore, 4 May 1812, BCA, RG 16, ser. 1, no. 640.

8. Mayor Com'n, 26 May 1812, ibid., no. 558.

9. Mayor's Communication, 24 February 1812(?), ibid., no. 557. The uncertainty of the evidence has to do with the date of Mayor Johnson's letter, which is clearly inconsistent with its content. On February 24, there was no ordinance authorizing the survey and no contract with Poppleton. The letter was grouped with other documents of a later date.

10. Report of the Joint Committee on the Mayor's Communication, 8 June 1812, BCA, RG

16, ser. 1, no. 483; A Supplement to the Ordinance for Making a Correct Survey of the City of Baltimore, 9 June 1812, ibid., no. 593.

11. Stipulation of Contract, n.d., 1812, BCA, RG 3, ser. 1, no. 256.

12. Communication T. Poppleton, 25 July 1812, ibid., no. 421; The Board of Assessors for Opening Pratt Street, 30 September 1812, ibid., no. 427.

13. Walter R. Borneman, *1812: The War That Forged a Nation* (New York: Harper Collins, 2004), 22–23.

14. Hamilton Owens, *Baltimore on the Chesapeake* (Garden City, N.Y.: Doubleday and Doran, 1941), 156–159.

15. Frank A. Cassell, *Merchant Congressman in the Young Republic: Samuel Smith of Maryland, 1752–1839* (Madison: University of Wisconsin Press, 1971), 117–118. Ultimately, Smith voted for restrictions on trade with Haiti. By this time, however, he saw war with Britain as imminent and wanted to draw close to its French enemy.

16. Cassell, *Merchant Congressman*, 138–139.

17. Rhoda Dorsey, "Baltimore Foreign Trade," in David T. Gilchrist (ed.), *The Growth of Seaport Cities, 1790–1825* (Charlottesville: University of Virginia Press, 1967), 63.

18. Louis Martin Sears, *Jefferson and the Embargo* (Durham, N.C.: Duke University Press, 1927), 221.

19. *Chronicles*, 302; *Balto Nation*, 51–52; Dorsey, "Baltimore Foreign Trade," 65.

20. *Chronicles*, 303–304.

21. Cassell, *Merchant Congressman*, 178.

22. *Chronicles*, 306–309; William M. Marine, *The British Invasion of Maryland, 1812–1815* (Baltimore: Society of the War of 1812 in Maryland, 1913), 6.

23. Jerome R. Garitee, *The Republic's Private Navy: The American Privateering Business as Practiced in Baltimore during the War of 1812* (Middletown, Conn.: Wesleyan University Press, 1977), 31, 43–44; *Chronicles*, 374; William D. Hoyt, Jr., "Logs and Papers of Baltimore Privateers, 1812–1815," *MHM* 34 (June 1939): 165–174.

24. Quoted in Marine, *British Invasion*, 18–19.

25. E. P. Thompson, "The Moral Economy of the English Crowd in the Eighteenth Century," *Past and Present* 50 (February 1971): 76–136; Pauline Maier, *From Resistance to Revolution: Colonial Radicals and the Development of American Opposition to Britain, 1765–1776* (New York: Alfred A. Knopf, 1972), 20, chap. 3; Lloyd I. Rudolph, "The Eighteenth Century Mob in America and Europe," *American Quarterly* 11 (Winter 1959): 469; Gordon S. Wood, "A Note on Mobs in the American Revolution," *William and Mary Quarterly*, 3rd ser., 23 (October 1966): 635–642.

26. Quoted in Marine, *British Invasion*, 7. The first sentence is from Shakespeare's *Coriolanus*.

27. Donald R. Hickey, *The War of 1812: A Forgotten Conflict* (Urbana: University of Illinois Press, 1989), 59.

28. Steffen, *Mechanics of Baltimore*, 244; *Chronicles*, 310–311.

29. Paul A. Gilje, "The Baltimore Riots of 1812 and the Breakdown of the Anglo-American Mob Tradition," *Journal of Social History* 13 (Summer 1980): 551–552.

30. Steffen, *Mechanics of Baltimore*, 244; Hickey, *War of 1812*, 61. Hanson's newspaper charged the mayor and other local officials with complicity in the original attack on its office. See *Federal Republican*, 27 July 1812.

31. Steffen, *Mechanics of Baltimore*, 246; *Chronicles*, 312–329; Gilje, "Baltimore Riots of 1812," 554–556; Frank A. Cassell, "The Great Baltimore Riot of 1812," *MHM* 70 (Fall 1975): 241–259; Henry Lee III, *A Correct Account of the Conduct of the Baltimore Mob* (Winchester, Va.: John Heiskell, 1814).

32. *Chronicles*, 339; Joint Committee to Whom the Mayor's Communication Was Referred, n.d., 1812, BCA, RG 16, ser. 1, no. 485.

33. Joseph A. Whitehorne, *The Battle for Baltimore* (Baltimore: Nautical and Aviation Publishing Company of America, 1997), 160.

34. Walter Lord, *The Dawn's Early Light* (New York: W. W. Norton, 1972), 227–330; Cassell, *Merchant Congressman*, chap. 13; Ruthella Mary Bibbins, "The City of Baltimore, 1797–1850: The Era of the Clipper Ship, the Turnpike and Railroad," in *Balto Hist.*, 1:107.

35. Marine, *British Invasion,* 21; Frank A. Cassell, "Baltimore in 1813: A Study of Urban Defense in the War of 1812," *Military Affairs* 33 (December 1969): 356.

36. Cassell, "Baltimore in 1813," 351, 353.

37. Jehu Bouldin to Smith, 5 September 1814, Smith Family Papers, Library of Congress, Washington, D.C.; Lord, *Dawn's Early Light*, 234.

38. Smith to Armstrong, Third Division Order Book, 13 March 1813, Smith Papers; Cassell, *Merchant Congressman*, 182.

39. Cassell, *Merchant Congressman*, 165–171; Whitehorne, *Battle for Baltimore*, 9. Smith's relations with the Madison administration were not entirely friendly. An old feud with Madison's secretary of the treasury, Albert Gallatin, had reignited when Samuel's younger brother Robert entered the cabinet as secretary of the navy; it turned white hot when President Madison chose Robert Smith, instead of Gallatin, as his secretary of state in 1809. Madison dismissed Robert in 1811, partly because he suspected that his secretary of state had been reporting the internal deliberations of the cabinet to his brother in the Senate, and partly because Robert shared his brother's conviction that the administration's attempt to reach a diplomatic settlement with Britain had gone on too long.

40. Cassell, *Merchant Congressman*, 166. Hanson quoted in Marine, *British Invasion.*

41. Hickey, *War of 1812*, 64. Much of the evidence that partisanship blunted the city government's defense of Federalists in the riot of 1812 comes from a legislative committee report on the riot and depositions taken from witnesses. The committee members belonged to a legislature with a decisive Federalist majority—and only two representatives from Baltimore. See *Report of the Committee of Grievances and Courts of Justice of the House of Delegates of Maryland on the Subject of the Recent Mobs and Riots in the City of Baltimore* (Annapolis, Md.: Jonas Green, 1813).

CHAPTER 8. BALTIMORE TRIUMPHANT

1. Frank A. Cassell, "Baltimore in 1813: A Study of Urban Defense in the War of 1812," *Military Affairs* 33 (December 1969): 352.

2. Ibid., 353; Frank A. Cassell, *Merchant Congressman in the Young Republic: Samuel Smith of Maryland, 1752–1839* (Madison: University of Wisconsin Press, 1971), 186; Gen. Johnson to Maj. Beall, 21 March 1813, BCA, RG 22, no. 551; Johnson to Smith, 1 April 1813, Smith Family Papers, Library of Congress, Washington, D.C.

3. William D. Hoyt, Jr., "Civilian Defense in Baltimore, 1814–1815: Minutes of the Committee of Vigilance and Safety," *MHM* 39 (September 1944): 200.

4. William M. Marine, *The British Invasion of Maryland, 1812–1815* (Baltimore: Society of the War of 1812 in Maryland, 1913), 23.

5. Cassell, "Baltimore in 1813," 353–354; Cassell, *Merchant Congressman*, 187; Communication from the Mayor Recommending the Appropriation of $20,000 for the Defence of the City of Baltimore, 13 April 1813, BCA, RG 16, ser. 1, no. 460.

6. Council Chamber, 8 May 1813, BCA, RG 16, ser. 1, no. 461.

7. Mayor's Communication to Both Branches of the City Council, 10 May 1813, ibid., no. 462.

8. Cassell, "Baltimore in 1813," 356–357.

9. Ibid., 351, 355.

10. Ibid., 356.

11. Cassell, *Merchant Congressman*, 194–195.

12. Marine, *British Invasion*, 32–33.

13. Joseph A. Whitehorne, *The Battle for Baltimore* (Baltimore: Nautical and Aviation Publishing Company of America, 1997), 114–115.

14. Marine, *British Invasion*, 53–55; Cassell, *Merchant Congressman*, 195–196.

15. Frank A. Cassell, "Response to Crisis: Baltimore in 1814," *MHM* 66 (Fall 1971): 271–272. For some, the committee's military character was too pronounced. Days after it convened, one of its members resigned. Elias Ellicott, a flour merchant and member of a prominent Quaker family, found that "its duties were so much connected with Military Operations as to make it inconsistent with my Religious Principles." See A Letter from E. Ellicott, 27 August 1814, BCA, RG 22, no. 467.

16. Whitehorne, *Battle for Baltimore*, 116.

17. Walter Lord, *The Dawn's Early Light* (New York: W. W. Norton, 1972), 23.

18. Cassell, "Response to Crisis," 273; Ralph Robinson, "Controversy over the Command at Baltimore in the War of 1812," *MHM* 39 (September 1944): 180–181.

19. Robinson, "Controversy over Command," 184–186.

20. Cassell, "Response to Crisis," 275; Robinson, "Controversy over Command," 181–182; Lord, *Dawn's Early Light*, 231.

21. Whitehorne, *Battle for Baltimore*, 161.

22. Woman quoted in Lord, *Dawn's Early Light*, 235; Marine, *British Invasion*, 145–146.

23. Marine, *British Invasion*, 159–160.

24. James McCulloh to General Smith, 14 September 1814, Smith Papers.

25. Lord, *Dawn's Early Light*, 287–291.

26. Report of Col. Howard &c. Who Were Deputed to Wait upon the President, 23 September 1814, BCA, RG 22, no. 500.

27. A. J. Dallas to Edward Johnson, 24 October 1814, BCA, RG 16, ser. 1, no. 540.

28. Colin MacKenzie to Committee of Vigilance and Safety, 18 November 1814, ibid., no. 557; S. Sterrett to Edward Johnson, 25 November 1814, ibid., no. 567; William Thornton to Edward Johnson, 22 December 1814, ibid., no. 580.

29. R.W. Gill to George Stiles, 3 March 1818, BCA, RG 9, ser. 2, no. 72; Gill to Henry Payson, 2 February 1818, ibid., no. 731. Smith lays out the justification for charging his wartime expenditures to the federal government in a letter to John Montgomery some time during 1820. See BCA, RG 16, ser. 1, no. 594.

30. Armstrong to Smith, 3 April 1813, Smith Papers.

31. In retaliation for the War Department's demands, Mayor George Stiles presented the department with a bill for storing federal munitions in the city's powder magazine. Stiles thought the department should pay the same storage fees as private citizens. Since the War Department refused to reimburse Baltimore on the "frivolous Excuse that our accounts had not been regularly kept . . . I therefor think it becomes us to be just, before we are liberal, and let the Storage $889.28 be received." The War Department advised the mayor and city council to reconsider the storage charge because the munitions placed in the city's powder magazine were for the use of Baltimore in its own defense. The city withdrew the claim. George Stiles to City Council, 6 March 1818, BCA, RG 9, ser. 2, no. 730; Lt. N. Bader, 30 March 1818, BCA, RG 16, ser. 1, no. 735; Resolution of Mayor and City Council, 1 April 1818, BCA, RG 9, ser. 2, no. 734.

32. George Stiles to Samuel Smith, 27 January 1818, BCA, RG 9, ser. 2, no. 733; Henry Payson to Richard W. Gill, n.d., 1818, ibid., no. 732.

33. Peter Hagner to John Montgomery, 8 November 1820, BCA, RG 16, ser. 1, [no number]; Peter Hagner to David Harris, 31 March 1821, ibid., no. 1094; David Harris to John Montgomery, n.d., March 1821, ibid., no. 1095; Committee of Vigilance and Safety to James Monroe, n.d., 1814, ibid., nos. 602, 602a.

34. *Balto Nation*, 70–72; John Lauritz Larson, *The Market Revolution in America: Liberty, Ambition, and the Eclipse of the Common Good* (New York: Cambridge University Press, 2010), 40–41.

35. David Head, "A Different Kind of Maritime Predation: South American Privateering from Baltimore, 1816–1820," *International Journal of Naval History* 7 (August 2008): 1–33.

36. Gary L. Browne, "Baltimore and the Panic of 1819," in Aubrey Land, Lois Green Carr, and Edward C. Papenfuse (eds.), *Law, Society, and Politics in Early Maryland* (Baltimore: Johns Hopkins University Press, 1977), 212–227; Adams quoted in *Balto Nation*, 76.

37. Andrew L. Cayton, "The Fragmentation of 'A Great Family': The Panic of 1819 and the Rise of the Middling Interest in Boston, 1818–1822," *Journal of the Early Republic* 2 (Summer 1982): 143–167.

38. *Baltimore Patriot and Evening Advertiser*, 19 August 1813.

39. Wilbur Coyle (ed.), *Records of the City of Baltimore: Eastern Precinct Commissioners, 1812–1817; Western Precinct Commissioners, 1810–1817* (Baltimore: Press of the King Brothers, 1909), vii, 111.

40. *Balto Financ.*, 28, 76.

41. Joseph L. Arnold, "Suburban Growth and Municipal Annexation in Baltimore, 1745–1918," *MHM* 73 (June 1978): 110.

42. Quoted in *Bldg Balto*, 54.

43. Arnold, "Suburban Growth," 111; *Laws of Maryland*, December Session, 1816, chap. 209.

44. *Niles' Weekly Register*, 1 March 1817.

45. Arnold, "Suburban Growth," 111.

46. Anon., *An Inquiry into the Late Act of the Legislature for Incorporating the Precincts with the City of Baltimore* (Baltimore, 1817), 33. The claim that annexation had always required assent of the annexed voters is questionable; ibid., 21–22.

47. *Proceedings of the First Branch of the City Council*, 12, 21 March 1817.

48. Resolution Relative to the Appointment of a Joint Committee, 18 October 1817, BCA, RG 16, ser. 1, no. 583; Memorial of Mayor and City Council of Baltimore to the General Assembly of Maryland, 2 December 1817, ibid., no. 648.

49. *Proceedings of the First Branch of the City Council*, 15 December 1817; Resolutions of the Mayor & City Council Relative to the Removal of the Seat of Government, 15 December 1817, BCA, RG 16, ser. 1, no. 632.

50. Resolution Appointing a Joint Committee to Prepare a Memorial to the General Assembly of Maryland and for Other Purposes, 4 December 1817, BCA, RG 16, ser. 1, no. 584.

51. Memorial, 1 December 1817, ibid., no. 648.

52. Report of the Committee Sent by the C. Council to Annapolis, 25 February 1818, ibid., no. 502.

53. *Journal of the House of Delegates*, 5 February 1817.

54. Report of the Committee; Maryland General Assembly, Session Laws, 1817, *AM*, 636:60, 121–123, 158–160, 195; *Balto Nation*, 105–106.

CHAPTER 9. PUBLIC DEBT AND INTERNAL IMPROVEMENTS

1. Report of the Committee sent by the C. Council to Annapolis, 25 February 1818, BCA, RG 16, ser. 1, no. 502.

2. *Niles' Weekly Register*, 12 October 1822, put the margin at 18 votes, but according to Gary Lawrence Browne, the figure is incorrect. See *Balto Nation*, 107, 269.

3. *Balto Nation*, 107, 111.

4. Ibid., 83.

5. *Bldg Balto*, 72.

6. *Balto Nation*, 110.

7. Daniel Raymond, *Elements of Political Economy*, 2 vols. (Baltimore: F. Lucas jun. and J. Cole, 1823); Charles Patrick Neill, *Daniel Raymond, an Early Chapter in the History of Economic Theory in the United States*, Johns Hopkins University Studies in Historical and Political Science, ser. 15, no. 6 (Baltimore: Johns Hopkins University Press, 1897).

8. Raymond, *Elements of Political Economy*, 1:28–31.

9. Ibid., 47, 50.

10. Ibid., 125.

11. Ibid., 46.

12. Communication from the Mayor, 4 March 1819, BCA, RG 16, ser. 1, no. 444.

13. Mayor's Annual Communication on the Opening of the Session, 7 January 1822, ibid., no. 314; Communication from the Mayor on the Subject of a Loan, 11 February 1822, ibid., no. 312.

14. The Committee of Ways and Means Beg Leave to Report to the First Branch of the City Council of Baltimore, 24 March 1818, ibid., no. 568.

15. Resolution Authorizing the Payment of Certain Money to the Commissioners of the Sinking Fund, 4 June 1818, ibid., no. 692.

16. Report of the Committee on Ways and Means upon the Sinking Fund, 24 March 1818, ibid., no. 560; *Balto Financ.*, 196.

17. Mayor's Communication, 11 January 1819, BCA, RG 16, ser. 1, no. 437.

18. An Ordinance Relating to the Sinking Fund, 3 March 1819, ibid., no. 469; Resolution Sinking Appropriation for Extinguishment of City Debts, 2 February 1821, ibid., [no number]; *Balto Financ.*, 196–197.

19. John P. Kennedy to Mayor Johnson, 11 December 1822, BCA, RG 16, ser. 1, no. 492; *Baltimore Patriot*, 17 February 1817, 18 January 1820.

20. Committee Appointed on the Letter of John Barney Esquire, 4 January 1821, BCA, RG 16, ser. 1, no. 510; Resolution Regarding the Mayor to Select a Committee to Repair to Annapolis for the Purpose Therein Mentioned, 11 January 1821, ibid., no. 866. It is not clear that the delegation ever went to Annapolis. Delegate John Barney wrote to Mayor Montgomery a few days before the council resolution, advising him that it would not be wise to send a delegation from the city council to make its case to the General Assembly. He suggested that the council should "confidentially confer" and send their instructions to delegates Barney and Kennedy. See Letter from Mr. Barney Esquire a City Delegate, 8 January 1821, ibid., no. 957.

21. Quoted in *Patriot*, 11 January 1821.

22. Ibid.

23. Mayor's Annual Communication on the Opening of the Session, 7 January 1822, BCA, RG 16, ser. 1, no. 314; Resolution Authorizing Mayor to Borrow Money in Anticipation of City Revenue, 12/18 February 1822, ibid., no. 400; Resolution Authorizing Mayor to Borrow Money in Anticipation of City Revenue, 27 February 1822, ibid., no. 399.

24. *Patriot*, 19, 31 August, 7, 18 September 1822.

25. Mayor's Annual Message, n.d., 1823, BCA, RG 16, ser. 1, no. 469. Johnson's calculation of city debt departed from previous financial reports. After adding up all of the city's outstanding notes in anticipation of revenue, issues of stock, and other miscellaneous indebtedness, he subtracted all the money due to the municipality, including "war debt" from the federal government. Since there was no guarantee that these payments would ever be made or would be applied to the reduction of debt, the results may not provide an accurate statement of debt. They are clearly inconsistent with other statements of city indebtedness made in previous and subsequent administrations.

26. Mayor's Annual Message 1823; Resolution Authorizing the Mayor with the Concurrence of the Presidents of the First and Second Branches of the City Council to Issue Certificates of Stock &c., 28/31 January 1823, BCA, RG 16, ser. 1, no. 387; *Balto Financ.*, 177.

27. Mayor to Second Branch of the City Council, 20 January 1823, BCA, RG 16, ser. 1, no. 480; Mayor's Annual Message 1823; Ronald E. Shaw, *Canals for a Nation: The Canal Era in the United States, 1790–1860* (Lexington: University Press of Kentucky, 1990), 6; James Weston Livingood, *The Philadelphia-Baltimore Trade Rivalry, 1780–1860* (Harrisburg: Pennsylvania Historical and Museum Collection, 1947), 55; Alan M. Wilner, *The Maryland Board of Public Works: A History* (Annapolis, Md.: Hall of Records Commission, Department of General Services, 1984), 5.

28. Mayor to City Council, 10 February 1823, BCA, RG 16, ser. 1, no. 472.

29. *Patriot*, 27 February 1823.

30. Ibid., 3, 22 April, 25 November 1822.

31. *Chronicles*, 407.

32. *Report of the Maryland Commissioners on a Proposed Canal from Baltimore to Conewago* (Baltimore: Fielding Lucas, 1823), 5–7, 34–36, 83–84.

33. Ibid., 25, 40–42.

34. Ibid., 64.

35. The Potomac Company's first president was George Washington. Its purpose was to improve navigation on the Potomac River by deepening its channel and removing obstructions, not digging a canal. It did use short canals and locks to circumvent falls and rapids on the river. The company's efforts faltered after confronting the Great Falls of the Potomac. See James W. Dilts, *The Great Road: The Building of the Baltimore and Ohio, the Nation's First Railroad, 1828–1853* (Stanford, Calif.: Stanford University Press, 1993), 16–17.

36. Milton Zeitenstein, *The Economic History of the Baltimore and Ohio Railroad, 1827–1853*, Johns Hopkins University Studies in Historical and Political Science, ser. 15, nos. 7–8 (Baltimore: Johns Hopkins University Press, 1897), 10.

37. Livingood, *Philadelphia-Baltimore Trade*, 59–60; *Chronicles*, 408.

38. Livingood, *Philadelphia-Baltimore Trade*, 71–74, 77; Shaw, *Canals for a Nation*, 112.

39. *Balto Financ.*, 178.

40. An Ordinance Relative to the Public Debt of the City of Baltimore, 25 March 1826, BCA, RG 16, ser. 1, no. 923; *Balto Financ.*, 197; *Balto Nation*, 110.

41. Thomas Phenix, *Proceedings of the Convention of Internal Improvements Held in Baltimore, December, 1825* (Baltimore: William Ogden Niles, 1825), 5–6; Resolution Requiring the Mayor to Subscribe Two Hundred Copies of a Work Therein Mentioned, 11/12 January 1826, BCA, RG 16, ser. 1, no. 943.

42. Phenix, *Proceedings of Convention*, 9–10, 19–20, 26.

43. Ibid., 20–21. A year earlier, Secretary of War Calhoun had discussed a similarly grand project of canal construction in a letter to Robert Goodloe Harper. See Calhoun to Harper, 10 June 1824, BCA, RG 16, ser. 1, no. 838.

44. Phenix, *Proceedings of Convention*, 20, 28–29.

45. Wilner, *Maryland Board of Public Works*, 1.

46. Walter S. Sanderlin, *The Great National Project: A History of the Chesapeake and Ohio Canal* (Baltimore: Johns Hopkins University Press, 1946), 158–159.

47. It seems that the chief obstacle to be overcome by the Susquehanna Canal lay in the segment from Havre de Grace to Baltimore, where the waterway would have to cross three high and dry ridges. See Dilts, *Great Road*, 23; *Chronicles*, 445.

CHAPTER 10. WORKING ON THE RAILROAD

1. "Explosions of Steam Boilers," *Journal of the Franklin Institute* 9 (January 1832): 16; *Baltimore Patriot*, 30 March 1818.

2. *Chronicles*, 340–341; Suzanne Ellery Greene, *An Illustrated History of Baltimore* (Woodland Hills, Calif.: Windsor Publications, 1980), 74; Communication from the Mayor, 18 May 1826, BCA, RG 16, ser. 1, no. 623.

3. Thomas Phenix, *Proceedings of the Convention of Internal Improvements Held in Baltimore, December, 1825* (Baltimore: William Ogden Niles, 1825), 42–43; Alan M. Wilner, *The Maryland Board of Public Works: A History* (Annapolis, Md.: Hall of Records Commission, Department of General Services, 1984), 11; *AM*, 402:141.

4. *Proceedings of Sundry Citizens of Baltimore Convened for the Purpose of Devising the Most Efficient Means of Improving Intercourse between That City and the Western States* (Baltimore: William Wooddy, 1827), 3.

5. Ibid., 31.

6. John F. Stover, *History of the Baltimore and Ohio Railroad* (West Lafayette, Ind.: Purdue University Press, 1987), 14, 20.

7. Ibid., 17; *AM*, 437:97.

8. James D. Dilts, *The Great Road: The Building of the Baltimore and Ohio, the Nation's First Railroad, 1828–1853* (Stanford, Calif.: Stanford University Press, 1993), 47; Baltimore City Council, *Ordinances and Resolutions*, 20, 29 March 1827.

9. Edward Hungerford, *The Story of the Baltimore and Ohio Railroad, 1827–1927* (New York: G. P. Putnam, 1928), 1:30; Dilts, *Great Road*, 46; Gary John Previts and William D. Sampson, "Exploring the Contents of the Baltimore and Ohio Annual Reports, 1827–1853," *Accounting Historians Journal* 27 (June 2000): 6; An Ordinance Relating to the Baltimore and Susquehanna Railroad Stock, 22 June 1830, BCA, RG 16, ser. 1, no. 939.

10. Quoted in Dilts, *Great Road*, 47.

11. Stover, *History of the B&O*, 27; Hungerford, *Story of the B&O*, 1:70, 116.

12. Hungerford, *Story of the B&O*, 1:135–136; John E. Semmes, *John H. B. Latrobe and His Times, 1803–1891* (Baltimore: Norman, Remington Co., 1917), 337–343.

13. Stover, *History of the B&O*, 39; Dilts, *Great Road*, 218–220.

14. Mayor's Message (Annual), 7 January 1828, BCA, RG 16, ser. 1, no. 612.

15. Resolution Relative to Rail Road Stock, 12 February 1828, ibid., no. 1126.

16. Letter from S. Etting to Phil. Thomas as President of the Rail Road dated May 2, 1828, BCA, RG 9, ser. 2, no. 1234. Solomon Etting and his city council colleague Jacob Cohen were the first Jews elected to public office in Maryland under the "Jew Bill" of 1826. Until then, only Christians could qualify for elective office.

17. Letters from Solomon Etting Esqr to Mayor Jacob Small dated May 29, ibid., no. 1233.

18. Stover, *History of the B&O*, 23.

19. Mayor's Communication, 10 March 1828, BCA, RG 9, ser. 2, no. 513.

20. Resolution Authorizing the Mayor to Convey to the Baltimore and Ohio Rail Road Company Certain Property without Any Pecuniary Consideration, 3 April 1828, ibid., no. 1122.

21. Previts and Sampson, "Exploring B&O Annual Reports," 22.

22. Stover, *History of the B&O*, 31–32, 49–50; Hungerford, *Story of the B&O*, 1:73, 78–80.

23. *Baltimore American*, 2 January 1830.

24. Edwin G. Burrows and Mike Wallace, *Gotham: A History of New York City to 1898* (New York: Oxford University Press, 1999), 564; Norman G. Rukert, *Historic Canton: Baltimore's Industrial Heartland and Its People* (Baltimore: Bodine and Associates, 1978), 20. Cooper's iron rails could not compete with cheaper and better rails manufactured in Britain. See Dilts, *Great Road*, 92.

25. Stover, *History of the B&O*, 35–36; Hungerford, *Story of the B&O*, 1:174–175.

26. "A History of My Connection with the Baltimore and Ohio Railroad Corporation," 10–11, in "Sundries of Many Sorts," John H. B. Latrobe Family Papers, S 523, box 4, Maryland Historical Society, Baltimore; Thomas K. McCraw (ed.), *The Essential Alfred Chandler: Essays toward a Historical Theory of Big Business* (Boston: Harvard Business School Press, 1988), 185–189.

27. Hungerford, *Story of the B&O*, 1:112.

28. Milton Reizenstein, *The Economic History of the Baltimore and Ohio Railroad, 1827–1853*, Johns Hopkins University Studies in Historical and Political Science, ser. 15, nos. 7–8 (Baltimore: Johns Hopkins University Press, 1897), 310–311; Stover, *History of the B&O*, 39.

29. Reizenstein, *Economic History*, 315–316; Stover, *History of the B&O*, 51–52.

30. George Winchester to Mayor and City Council, 27 August 1829, BCA, RG 16, ser. 1, no. 636.

31. Report & Resolution Authorizing the Mayor and City Council of Baltimore to Subscribe for Two Thousand Shares of Stock in the B&S RR Company, 28 August 1829, ibid., no. 837.

32. Baltimore City Council, *Ordinances and Resolutions*, 3 May 1830, no. 37, p. 218.

33. Report of John Diffenderffer Director of the Baltimore and Susquehanna Rail Road,

3 January 1830, BCA, RG 16, ser. 1, no. 504; Letter to the Pres. & Directors of the Balto. & S.R.R. Co., 27 April 1830, ibid., no. 505.

34. Communication from Geo Winchester Esqr Pres Balto & Susquehanna Rail Road Company, 21 June 1830, ibid., no. 506.

35. Ibid.; Alex Nisbet, Presdt. Balto. & Susquehanna RR Co. to the Stockholders of the B&S RR Co., 19 October 1835, ibid., no. 728; George H. Burgess and Miles C. Kennedy, *Centennial History of the Pennsylvania Railroad Company, 1846–1946* (Philadelphia: Pennsylvania Railroad Co., 1949), 129.

36. Report from the Balto. & Susq Rail Road Company, 26 January 1835, BCA, RG 16, ser. 1, no. 727.

37. An Ordinance Relative to the Balto & Susq Rail Road Co., 10 April 1835, ibid., no. 1120; Copy of a Bond to the State of Md from the Balto & Susq Rail Road & City of Baltimore, 27 May 1835, ibid., no. 294.

38. *Balto Financ.*, 185–186.

39. Joint Committee of Ways and Means, 15 April 1836, BCA, RG 16, ser. 1, no. 793.

CHAPTER 11. CORPORATE CHALLENGE TO EQUALITY AND AN EDUCATIONAL RESPONSE

1. Alfred D. Chandler, *The Visible Hand: The Managerial Revolution in American Business* (Cambridge, Mass.: Belknap Press of Harvard University Press, 1977), 79, 87.

2. Matthew E. Mason, "'The Hands Here Are Disposed to Be Turbulent': Unrest among the Irish Trackmen of the Baltimore and Ohio Railroad, 1829–1851," *Labor History* 39 (August 1998): 254.

3. *Baltimore Patriot*, 1, 9 July 1831, 15 July 1834; *Baltimore Gazette and Daily Advertiser*, 2 July 1831.

4. Seth Rockman, *Scraping By: Wage Labor, Slavery, and Survival in Early Baltimore* (Baltimore: Johns Hopkins University Press, 2009), 8–10.

5. Mason, "Hands Disposed to Be Turbulent," 258–259.

6. *Balto Nation*, 96–97.

7. Dennis Rankin Clark, "Baltimore, 1729–1829: The Genesis of a Community" (PhD diss., Catholic University of America, 1976), 258; John Thomas Mason, *Life of John Van Lear McMahon* (Baltimore: John B. Piet, 1880), 41; John Scott to Mayor Montgomery, 21 January 1826, BCA, RG 16, ser. 1, no. 377.

8. *AM*, 402:100.

9. *Patriot*, 1 January 1826; Tina H. Sheller, "The Origins of Public Education in Baltimore, 1825–1829," *History of Education Quarterly* 22 (Spring 1982): 33–34.

10. Baltimore City Council, First Branch, *Proceedings*, 3 February 1826, 338.

11. *Patriot*, 29 September 1826. William Krebs would soon become one of the most active figures in the organization of Baltimore's Jacksonian Democrats. See Whitman H. Ridgway, *Community Leadership in Maryland, 1790–1840: A Comparative Analysis of Power in Society* (Chapel Hill: University of North Carolina Press, 1979), 100.

12. A lengthy legal argument for reintroduction of property requirements for voters appeared in the *Patriot*, 11 October 1826, signed "Stiles." The writer cannot have been former Mayor Stiles, who had died almost seven years earlier, but may have been one of his loyal supporters.

13. Baltimore City Council, First Branch, *Proceedings*, 16 March 1824, p. 75.

14. Ibid., 25 March 1824, p. 98

15. Sheller, "Origins of Public Education," 28. Other children could qualify for public education if their parents were at least 21 years old and residents of Baltimore for at least 12 months. Another standard required simply that the parents of schoolchildren had to be employed.

16. *Baltimore Gazette*, 31 October 1826.

17. Ibid., 25 October 1826.

18. See *Patriot*, 9 March, 19 September 1826.

19. *Baltimore Gazette*, 23 September 1826.

20. Mark Haller, "The Rise of the Jacksonian Party in Maryland," *Journal of Southern History* 28 (August 1962): 308–309.

21. *Baltimore Gazette*, 25 September 1826; Thomas Waters Griffith, *Annals of Baltimore* (Baltimore: W. Wooddy, 1833), 248; Ridgway, *Community Leadership*, 95–97.

22. See Eric Robert Papenfuse, *The Evils of Necessity: Robert Goodloe Harper and the Moral Dilemma of Slavery* (Philadelphia: American Philosophical Society, 1997), chaps. 1 and 2.

23. [Robert Goodloe Harper], *Plain Reasons of a Plain Man for Preferring Gen. Jackson to Mr. Adams as President of the United States* (Baltimore: Benjamin Edes, 1825), 3, 5, 12–13.

24. Haller, "Rise of the Jacksonian Party," 312.

25. Kate Mason Rowland, *The Life of Charles Carroll of Carrollton, 1737–1832: With His Correspondence and Public Papers* (New York: George Putnam, 1898), 2:334.

26. Charles H. Bohner, *John Pendleton Kennedy: Gentleman from Baltimore* (Baltimore: Johns Hopkins University Press, 1961), 56.

27. *Balto Nation*, 103–104; Whitman H. Ridgway, "McCulloch vs. the Jacksonians: Patronage and Politics in Maryland," *MHM* 70 (Winter 1975): 354.

28. *Baltimore Gazette*, 28 April 1827, 26 September 1832.

29. *AM*, 402:130–139.

30. Sheller, "Origins of Public Education," 37–38; A Bill Entitled an Ordinance Relating to the Public Schools, 25 February / 5 March 1828, BCA, RG 16, ser. 1, no. 1097; A Bill Entitled an Ordinance Relative to the School Fund, 26 June 1828, ibid., no. 1098. "Monitorial Plan" is explained in the text below.

31. *Ordinances of the Corporation of the City of Baltimore*, 1829, Ordinance no. 21, 13 March 1829, pp. 113–116.

32. *Baltimore Gazette*, 7 April 1829; *Patriot*, 8 April 1829.

33. *Patriot*, 11 April 1829.

34. Mayor's Communication, 4 January 1830, BCA, RG 16, ser. 1, no. 584; *Ordinances and Resolutions of the Corporation of the City of Baltimore*, 1830, Resolution no. 70, 30 April 1830, p. 257.

35. William B. Johnson, "Chanting Choristers: Simultaneous Recitation in Baltimore's Nineteenth Century Primary Schools," *History of Education Quarterly* 34 (Spring 1994): 1–23.

36. Communication, Commissioners, Public Schools, 31 March 1831, BCA, RG 16, ser. 1, no. 781; Commissioners of Public Schools, "Third Annual Report," in *Ordinances of the Mayor and City Council of Baltimore Passed at the Special Session of 1831*, pp. 88–94.

37. Communication, Commissioners, Public Schools, 31 March 1831

CHAPTER 12. ROAD HOGS

1. *Ordinances of the Corporation of the City of Baltimore*, 1812, no. 20, p. 231; ibid., 1816, no. 21, p. 82.

2. Ibid., 1821, no. 23, p. 317.

3. Mayor's Communication, 22 January 1828, BCA, RG 16, ser. 1, no. 1101.

4. Seth Rockman, *Scraping By: Wage Labor, Slavery, and Survival in Early Baltimore* (Baltimore: Johns Hopkins University Press, 2009), 178.

5. *Ordinances of City of Baltimore*, 1828, no. 23, pp. 24–25; ibid., 1831, no. 10, p. 275; ibid., 1838, no. 25, pp. 73–74.

6. *Baltimore American and Daily Commercial Advertiser*, 16 January 1842.

7. Ibid., 8 January 1834. For other mayoral complaints about the "roughness" of the streets, see Mayor's Communication, 7 January 1828, BCA, RG 16, ser. 1, no. 611; Mayor's Communication, 5 January 1829, ibid., no. 712.

8. Rockman, *Scraping By*, 96–97.

9. *Ordinances of City of Baltimore*, 1837, appendix, pp. 4–5.

10. Copy of Notice to Water Company, 6 August 1835, BCA, RG 16, ser. 2, no. 116.

11. *Baltimore American*, 6 January 1835; Columbus O'Donnell, President of B. W. Co. to Joshua Dryden, Chairman of the Water Committee, 3 February 1835, BCA, RG 16, ser. 1, no. 731.

12. Michael Feldberg, *The Turbulent Era: Riot & Disorder in Jacksonian America* (New York: Oxford University Press, 1980), 65–69.

13. *Baltimore American*, 3 January 1826; *Niles' Weekly Register*, 5 November 1831.

14. *Ordinances of the Mayor and City Council of Baltimore*, Passed at the Extra Sessions in 1830 and at the January Session 1831, no. 18, pp. 28–29; ibid., no. 33, pp. 42–43.

15. Letter from P. E. Thomas, Pres. B&O RR, 14 February 1831, BCA, RG 16, ser. 1, no. 782.

16. *Ordinances of City of Baltimore*, 1831, no. 18, p. 283; Philip E. Thomas to J. H. Dorsey (Clerk, City Commissioners), 12 May 1832, BCA, RG 3, ser. 1, no. 117.

17. Memorial from Alexander Grier and Others, 18 February 1831, BCA, RG 16, ser. 1, no. 577.

18. *Baltimore Patriot*, 13 October 1830.

19. *Ordinances of City of Baltimore*, 1832, no. 35, pp. 35–37.

20. Comm. of P. E. Thomas, Presdt. of the Baltimore & Ohio Rail Road Comp., 16 January 1835, BCA, RG 16, ser. 1, no. 725; Memorial of the Baltimore & Ohio Rail Road Company, 28 March 1837, ibid., no. 802; Report of John Diffenderffer Director of the Baltimore and Susquehanna Rail Road, 3 January 1830, ibid., no. 504.

21. Comm. from Saml. Moore, Esq. City Director &c. Enclosing the Agreemt. between the Balto. & Ohio and Port Deposit Rail Roads, n.d., 1837, ibid., no. 354 (includes extract from Port Deposit board minutes, 11 October 1831).

22. Resolt. to Furnish the City Directors in the Ohio Rail Road with a Copy of the Resolt. Relative to the Junctn. of the Depots, 7/8 March 1837, ibid., no. 1299; Report of the City Members on the Balt. & Ohio Board, 14 March 1837, ibid., no. 942A.

23. Report of City Members on Balt. & Ohio Board, 14 March 1837.

24. *Baltimore Gazette*, 6 July 1837; An Ordinance Relating to the Baltimore & Port Deposit Rail Road, 31 July 1837, BCA, RG 16, ser. 1, no. 1413.

25. *Baltimore Gazette*, 15 February 1832; Report of the Joint Committee on Rail Roads on the Sewer on Pratt St & the Rail Road in the Same Street, 6 March 1835, BCA, RG 16, ser. 1, no. 800.

26. *Baltimore Gazette*, 14, 16, 17 March 1835.

27. Report entitled "A Supplement to an Ordinance Relating to the Baltimore and Ohio Rail Road Company," 16 March / 7 April 1835, BCA, RG 16, ser. 1, no. 887; *Bldg Balto*, 74.

28. Report of the Minority of the Select Committee Relative to the Rail Way in the City, 19 March 1835, BCA, RG 16, ser. 1, no. 799.

29. Report & Resolution on the Petition of Sundry Hackneymen, Draymen and Carters for the Removal of the Rail Road out of the City, 19 March 1835, ibid., no. 805.

30. Ibid.

31. Bill no. 30, Report of resolution entitled "A Supplement to an Ordinance Relating to the Baltimore and Ohio Rail Road Company," 6/7 April 1835, ibid., no. 887.

32. Petition of A. K. Kennedy and Others, n.d., 1837, BCA, RG 16, ser. 1, no. 803. In fact, all three railroads that entered Baltimore during the 1830s eventually built waterfront depots in Canton but continued to use their facilities inside the city limits.

33. Select Committee on the Memorial by Peter Uhler and Others, n.d., March 1835, ibid., no. 804.

34. Edwin A. Gere, Jr., "Dillon's Rule and the Cooley Doctrine: Reflections of the Political Culture," *Journal of Urban History* 8 (May 1982): 274–276.

CHAPTER 13. POLICING THE DISORDERLY CITY

1. *Niles' Weekly Register*, 15 August 1835; *Baltimore Patriot*, 23 January 1834.

2. *Patriot*, 22 February 1834.

3. Mayor's Communication, 21 January 1828, BCA, RG 16, ser. 1, no. 617. Though Baltimore

was the first city to introduce gas streetlamps, it took some time to install them throughout the city. When Mayor Small outlined the responsibilities of the night watch, most of the streets that the watchmen patrolled were still illuminated by oil lamps. See *Baltimore American*, 4 January 1831.

4. This formulaic list of duties would eventually lead to trouble, in 1838, when watchmen were sued for false arrest for detaining a citizen who was merely suspected of disturbing the peace. Petition of James Mullen and James Dukes, 11 April 1838, BCA, RG 16, ser. 1, no. 573.

5. *AM*, 203:420; de Francis Folsom, *Our Police: A History of the Baltimore Force from the First Watchman to the Latest Appointee* (Baltimore: J. M. Beers, 1888), 16–17; Petition of Mullen & Dukes.

6. Folsom, *Our Police*, 23; *Patriot*, 26 February 1826.

7. *Baltimore Gazette*, 26 December 1826.

8. *Patriot*, 15 January 1829, 30 August 1830.

9. *Baltimore Gazette*, 2, 25 April 1831, 25 September 1832, 25 March 1833.

10. *Ordinances of the Mayor and City Council of Baltimore*, 1834, appendix, pp. 8, 12; ibid., 1835, pp. 9–10.

11. Ibid., 1835, no. 10, pp. 14–15.

12. David Grimsted, "Robbing the Poor to Aid the Rich: Roger B. Taney and the Bank of Maryland Swindle," *Supreme Court Historical Society Yearbook*, 1987, pp. 54–55.

13. Ibid., 59; Robert E. Shalhope, *The Baltimore Bank Riot: Political Upheaval in Antebellum America* (Urbana: University of Illinois Press, 2009), 32–33.

14. Shalhope, *Baltimore Bank Riot*, 33–34.

15. Ibid., 14; Grimsted, "Robbing the Poor," 64.

16. Grimsted, "Robbing the Poor," 68–73; *Balto Nation*, 122–123.

17. Shalhope, *Baltimore Bank Riot*, 34; Grimsted, "Robbing the Poor," 76; *Baltimore Gazette*, 25 March 1834.

18. Grimsted, "Robbing the Poor," 77.

19. Ibid., 79–80; Shalhope, *Baltimore Bank Riot*, 38–39.

20. Grimsted, "Robbing the Poor," 78, 80; *Niles' Weekly*, 12 April 1834.

21. *Balto Nation*, 23; Shalhope, *Baltimore Bank Riot*, 89.

22. Shalhope, *Baltimore Bank Riot*, 13, 23–29.

23. Grimsted, "Robbing the Poor," 86–92.

24. Reverdy Johnson and John Glenn, *Final Reply to the Libels of Evan Poultney, Late President of the Bank of Maryland and a Further Examination of the Causes of the Failure of That Institution* (Baltimore: Lucas and Deaver, 1835); Evan Poultney, *Appeal to the Creditors of the Bank of Maryland and to the Public Generally* (Baltimore: John D. Toy, 1835).

25. Shalhope, *Baltimore Bank Riot*, 46; David Grimsted, "Democratic Rioting: A Case Study of the Baltimore Bank Mob of 1835," in William L. O'Neill (ed.), *Insights and Parallels: Problems and Issues in American Social History* (Minneapolis: Burgess Publishing Company, 1973), 132; *Patriot*, 8 June 1826.

26. Shalhope, *Baltimore Bank Riot*, 49.

27. Ibid., 49–52; *Niles' Weekly*, 15 August 1835; *Baltimore Gazette*, 8 August 1835.

28. Shalhope, *Baltimore Bank Riot*, 54; Grimsted, "Democratic Rioting," 134.

29. Shalhope, *Baltimore Bank Riot*, 54–55.

30. Ibid., 56; Grimsted, "Robbing the Poor," 94; Grimsted, "Democratic Rioting," 135.

31. Shalhope, *Baltimore Bank Riot*, 57–58.

32. Ibid., 66; Grimsted, "Robbing the Poor," 94; Grimsted, "Democratic Rioting," 136.

33. "William E. Bartlett to Edward Stabler, 12 August 1835," *MHM* 9 (June 1914): 158, 160.

34. *Baltimore Gazette*, 10 August 1835; *Niles' Weekly*, 15 August 1835; *Chronicles*, 478.

35. *Baltimore Gazette*, 11 August 1835; Shalhope, *Baltimore Bank Riot*, 68; Bartlett to Stabler, 160.

36. Shalhope, *Baltimore Bank Riot*, 68.

37. Capt. Deems Co., 3rd Ward, 11 August 1835, BCA, RG 9, ser. 2, no. 396; Capt. McConnick's Co., 4th Ward, 14 August 1835, ibid., no. 397; Letter from J. K. Stapleton on the Subject of the Fire Companies Being Ready for Service as Military, n.d., 1835, ibid., no. 395; Copy of letter to Genl. Smith, 17 August 1835, ibid., no. 397.

38. *Baltimore Gazette*, 14 August 1835.

39. Ibid., 4, 8 September 1835; David Grimsted, "Rioting in Its Jacksonian Setting," *American Historical Review* 77 (April 1972): 388–389.

40. Report from the Jail, n.d., August 1835, BCA, RG 16, ser. 1, no. 401; Shalhope, *Baltimore Bank Riot*, 77–78.

41. *Baltimore Gazette*, 6 November, 8–29 December 1835, 2–29 January 1836.

42. David Grimsted, *American Mobbing, 1828–1861: Toward Civil War* (New York: Oxford University Press, 1998), 4; *Niles' Weekly*, 5 September 1835.

43. Michael Feldberg, *The Turbulent Era: Riot & Disorder in Jacksonian America* (New York: Oxford University Press, 1980), 100.

44. Grimsted, "Democratic Rioting," 136–137.

45. *Niles' Weekly*, 22 April 1837.

46. Feldberg, *Turbulent Era*, 101. Studies of more recent riots confirm the impression that civil disorder depends on preexisting social networks. In the Watts riot of 1965, for example, newcomers to Los Angeles were less likely to have participated in the disorders than those born in the city, probably because long-term residents were more likely to belong to local social networks. Neighborhood networks also figured significantly in a study of violence between Christians and Muslims in Nigeria. See David O. Sears and John B. McConahay, "Participation in the Los Angeles Riot," *Social Problems* 17 (Summer 1969): 3–20; Alexandra Scacco, "Who Riots? Participation in Ethnic Violence," http://politics.as.nyu.edu/docs/IO/9568/jobpaper.pdf.

47. Grimsted, "Democratic Rioting," 144.

48. Edward Pessen, "The Egalitarian Myth and the American Social Reality: Wealth, Mobility, and Equality in the 'Era of the Common Man,'" *American Historical Review* 76 (October 1971): 1012–1014.

49. *Niles' Weekly*, 22 April 1837.

50. *Ordinances of Mayor and City Council of Baltimore*, 1836, Resolution no. 30, pp. 91–93

51. *AM*, 214:192–194; Preamble and Resolution Relative to the Indemnity Bill, 24 March 1836, BCA, RG 16, ser. 1, no. 988; Joseph Nelson and Walter Constable to Samuel Barnes, 22 April 1836, ibid., no. 628; Walter Johnson to Samuel Barnes, 18 June 1836, ibid., no. 626.

52. James Warner Harry, *The Maryland Constitution of 1851*, Johns Hopkins University Studies in Historical and Political Science, ser. 20, nos. 7–8 (Baltimore: Johns Hopkins University Press, 1902), 14–15.

53. *AM*, 214:107. On the politics behind these changes, see A. Clarke Hagensick, "Revolution or Reform in 1836: Maryland's Preface to Dorr's Rebellion," *MHM* 57 (December 1962): 346–366.

CHAPTER 14. RACIAL BORDERS

1 James Silk Buckingham, *America: Historical, Statistic, and Descriptive*, 2 vols. (New York: Harper & Brothers, 1841). Buckingham also published *Autobiography of James Silk Buckingham, Including His Voyages, Travels, Adventures, Speculations, Successes, and Failures* (London: Longman, Brown, Green and Longmans, 1855). He apparently intended to write a multivolume account of his life, but died after publication of the first volume.

2. Buckingham, *America*, 1:255, 289.

3. Harriet Beecher Stowe, *Men of Our Times or Leading Patriots of the Day* (Hartford, Conn.: Hartford Publishing Company, 1868), 161–162.

4. David K. Sullivan, "William Lloyd Garrison in Baltimore, 1829–1830," *MHM* 68 (Spring

1973): 67; Buckingham, *America*, 1:268; H. E. Shepherd (ed.), *History of Baltimore, Maryland from Its Founding to the Current Year, 1729–1898* (Baltimore: S. B. Nelson, 1898), 89; Paul Finkelman, *Slave Rebels, Abolitionists, and Southern Courts* (Clark, N.J.: Law Book Exchange, 2007), 303, 307; Steven Deyle, *Carry Me Back: The Domestic Slave Trade in American Life* (New York: Oxford University Press, 2005), 179–180.

5. See Barbara Jeanne Fields, *Slavery and Freedom on the Middle Ground: Maryland during the Nineteenth Century* (New Haven, Conn.: Yale University Press, 1985), 42.

6. See Ralph Clayton, *Cash for Blood: The Baltimore to New Orleans Domestic Slave Trade* (Bowie, Md.: Heritage Books, 2002), 74.

7. On Baltimore's influential Quakers, see Leroy Graham, *Baltimore: The Nineteenth Century Black Capital* (Lanham, Md.: University Press of America, 1982), 16–18.

8. T. Stephen Whitman, *Challenging Slavery in the Chesapeake: Black and White Resistance to Human Bondage, 1775–1865* (Baltimore: Maryland Historical Society, 2007), 69–70. In 1850, it was estimated that escapes cost the border counties of Maryland about $10,000 in slave property every week. Group escapes were common. On some occasions, as many as 30 or 40 slaves would abscond at once. Not all of them headed for Pennsylvania. Baltimore was a popular destination for escapees because they could blend in with the city's large population of free African Americans. See Ralph Clayton, *Slavery, Slaveholding, and the Free Black Population of Antebellum Baltimore* (Bowie, Md.: Heritage Books, 1993), chap. 7.

9. Frederick Douglass, *My Bondage and My Freedom*, ed. William L. Andrews (Urbana: University of Illinois Press, 1987 [1855]), 199–202.

10. James M. Wright, *The Free Negro in Maryland, 1634–1860* (New York: Columbia University Press, 1921), 78–79.

11. Christopher Phillips, *Freedom's Port: The African American Community of Baltimore, 1790–1860* (Urbana: University of Illinois Press, 1997), 40–56.

12. Douglass, *Bondage and Freedom*, 93.

13. Phillips, *Freedom's Port*, 58–61, 104.

14. Eric Robert Papenfuse, *The Evils of Necessity: Robert Goodloe Harper and the Moral Dilemma of Slavery* (Philadelphia: American Philosophical Society, 1997), 55n11; *A Letter from Gen. Harper, of Maryland, to Elias B. Caldwell, Secretary of the American Society for Colonizing the Free People of Colour in the United States with Their Own Consent* (Baltimore: R. J. Matchett, 1818), 8.

15. Quoted in T. Stephen Whitman, *The Price of Freedom: Slavery and Manumission in Baltimore and Early National Maryland* (Lexington: University Press of Kentucky, 1997), 141.

16. *Harper to Caldwell*, 8–9.

17. Whitman, *Price of Freedom*, 140; Phillips, *Freedom's Port*, 58.

18. P. J. Staudenraus, *The African Colonization Movement, 1816–1865* (New York: Columbia University Press, 1961), 19–20; Richard L. Hall, *On Afric's Shore: A History of Maryland in Liberia, 1834–1857* (Baltimore: Maryland Historical Society, 2003), 11.

19. *Harper to Caldwell*, 18.

20. Ibid., 11.

21. Ibid., 14.

22. Ibid., 18–19.

23. John E. Semmes, *John H. B. Latrobe and His Times, 1803–1891* (Baltimore: Norman, Remington Co., 1917), 139–142; Penelope Campbell, *Maryland in Africa: The Maryland State Colonization Society, 1831–1857* (Urbana: University of Illinois Press, 1971), 7–8.

24. In some states with large slave populations, the issue was not simply black political equality but the apprehension that free black voters might outnumber whites. See Eugene S. Van Sickle, "A Transnational Vision: John H. B. Latrobe and Maryland's Colonization Movement" (PhD diss., West Virginia University, 2005), 25–26.

25. *Harper to Caldwell*, 19.

26. Staudenraus, *African Colonization Movement*, 20–21, 28, 33, 193–206; Eric Burin, *Slavery and the Peculiar Solution: A History of the American Colonization Society* (Gainesville: University Press of Florida, 2005), 26; Joseph Garonzik, "Urbanization and the Black Population of Baltimore, 1850–1870" (PhD diss., State University of New York at Stony Brook, 1974), 231.

27. "Colonization," John H. B. Latrobe Family Papers, MS 523, box 4, Maryland Historical Society, Baltimore.

28. Ibid.

29. Ibid. Several of the dissenters later met with Latrobe and Harper, who agreed to strike every passage in the "address" to which its African American critics took exception. Semmes, *Latrobe*, 143.

30. Staudenraus, *African Colonization Movement*, 110–112; Campbell, *Maryland in Africa*, 11.

31. Aaron Stopak, "The Maryland State Colonization Society: Independent State Action in the Colonization Movement," *MHM* 63 (September 1968): 276; Van Sickle, "Transnational Vision," 44.

32. Papers of the Maryland State Colonization Society (MSCS), reel 1, minutes, 26 March 1831, 12 April 1831, Maryland Historical Society, Baltimore.

33. Ibid., 4 May 1831, 14 November 1831; Campbell, *Maryland in Africa*, 23–25.

34. MSCS Papers, reel 1, minutes, 4 May 1831.

35. Van Sickle, "Transnational Vision," 57.

36. *AM*, 213:342–346. On the impact of the Nat Turner uprising in Maryland, see also Wright, *Free Negro in Maryland*, 267–273.

37. Wright, *Free Negro in Maryland*, 346–347.

38. MSCS Papers, reel 1, minutes, 30 April 1832, pp. 21–22.

39. MSCS Papers, reel 3, Corresponding Secretary's Books, Latrobe to Cortlandt Van Rensalaer, 10 July 1833; Hall, *On Afric's Shore*, 27.

40. MSCS Papers, reel 1, minutes, 4 February 1833.

41. Ibid., 30 April 1833; Campbell, *Maryland in Africa*, 51–53.

42. MSCS Papers, reel 1, minutes, 28 June 1833.

43. Ibid., 19 July 1833; *Baltimore Gazette*, 17 September 1831.

44. Burin, *Slavery and the Peculiar Solution*, 66; Campbell, *Maryland in Africa*, 60–61; Hall, *On Afric's Shore*, 27.

45. Phillips, *Freedom's Port*, 145–146; Bettye J. Gardner, "The Institutional and Organizational Life of the Baltimore Black Community," University of Baltimore Archives (online).

46. Phillips, *Freedom's Port*, 133–134. Phillips suggests that Coker's secession may have been motivated in part by his frustration about his own status as a deacon rather than an ordained minister at the Sharp Street church.

47. Jeffrey R. Brackett, *The Negro in Maryland: A Study of the Institution of Slavery* (New York: Negro Universities Press, 1969 [1889]), 177–178; Wright, *Free Negro in Maryland*, 114.

48. Wright, *Free Negro in Maryland*, 204–205.

49. Petition of Mr[s] Ross to Have a Supper 24th Dec. 1838, BCA, RG 9, ser. 2, no. 1221; Petition of John Miller for a Ball &c. 22nd Nov 1838, ibid., no. 1222; Petition of George Presstman for John Ford, Coloured, for a Pass, 14 November 1838, ibid., no. 1285; Petition of Thomas Walsh & Others for a Pass for Perry Boardley, 16 November 1838, ibid., no. 1285.

50. Gordon J. Melton, *A Will to Choose: The Origins of African American Methodism* (Lanham, Md.: Rowman and Littlefield, 2007), chap. 3.

51. Phillips, *Freedom's Port*, 213.

52. Ibid., 38; Graham, *Baltimore*, 75–77; Floyd J. Miller, *The Search for a Black Nationality: Black Emigration and Colonization, 1787–1863* (Urbana: University of Illinois Press, 1975), 55, 58–59.

53. Bettye J. Gardner, "William Watkins: Antebellum Black Teacher and Anti-Slavery Writer," *Negro History Bulletin* 39 (September/October 1976): 623.

54. *Baltimore Gazette*, 14 December 1826.

55. A Coloured Baltimorean, letter, *Genius of Universal Emancipation*, 3 March 1827. Black resistance to emigration persisted, despite state financial support for the colonization society. During the 1850s, fewer than 1,200 Maryland blacks emigrated to the Maryland colony in Liberia, and those who did were denounced by other African Americans as traitors. See Garonzik, "Urbanization and Black Population," 232.

56. A Coloured Baltimorean, "Colonization Society," *Freedom's Journal*, 6 July 1827.

57. William Lloyd Garrison (ed.), *Thoughts on African Colonization* (Boston: Garrison and Knapp, 1832), pt. 2, pp. 52, 55–56.

58. Ibid., 22.

59. Graham, *Baltimore*, 119–120.

60. *Colored American*, 17 June 1837.

CHAPTER 15. BETWEEN MOBS AND CORPORATIONS

1. *Baltimore Sun*, 26 April 1839; *Chronicles*, 497–498.

2. *Balto Nation*, 147.

3. General Report of the Joint Committee on Internal Improvements, 6 March 1839, BCA, RG 16, ser. 1, no. 1155, pp. 1–2.

4. Ibid., 2–3.

5. Ibid., 4.

6. Milton Reizenstein, *The Economic History of the Baltimore and Ohio Railroad, 1827–1853*, Johns Hopkins University Studies in Historical and Political Science, ser. 15, nos. 7–8 (Baltimore: Johns Hopkins University Press, 1897), 46; Communication from the Registrar Relative to the Three Million Subscription to the Baltimore & Ohio Rail Road, 11 March 1845, BCA, RG 16, ser. 1, no. 384.

7. James S. Dilts, *The Great Road. The Building of the Baltimore and Ohio, the Nation's First Railroad, 1828–1853* (Stanford, Calif.: Stanford University Press, 1993), 271.

8. Reizenstein, *Economic History*, 46–47.

9. Copy of a letter to L. Marshall, 30 December 1841, BCA, RG 16, ser. 1, no. 403.

10. Report of a Resolution of the Joint Committee on Police Relative to Small Stock Transfers of the Baltimore & Ohio Railroad Company, 19 January / 22 February 1841, ibid., no. 592.

11. Mayor's Annual Communication, 17 January 1841, ibid., no. 458.

12. Carter Goodrich and Henry Segal, "Baltimore's Aid to Railroads: A Study in the Municipal Planning of Internal Improvements," *Journal of Economic History* 13 (Winter 1953): 8–9; *Sun*, 8, 10 January 1842.

13. *Sun*, 10 March 1842.

14. Reizenstein, *Economic History*, 47–48; Dilts, *Great Road*, 274.

15. *Balto Nation*, 134.

16. Dilts, *Great Road*, 274, 283, 299.

17. Letter from the Register, 22 July 1840, BCA, RG 9, ser. 2, no. 138. Contrary to Hunt's claim, Mayor Leakin had taken action to meet the city's deficit. Only five days after the register reported the city's desperate state, Leakin called the city council into special session to approve "a temporary loan to meet with the promptness that has been customary and is desirable, the quarterly demands on the City Treasury." Hunt may have thought it politic to suggest that Leakin had been unresponsive. Leakin was a Whig. Brady was a Democrat, as was Hunt. See To the Members of the First & Second Branches of the City Council, 27 July 1840, ibid., no. 408.

18. *Chronicles*, 502; *Sun*, 4, 5 November 1840.

19. Mayor's Communication, 6 January 1840, BCA, RG 16, ser. 1, [no number]; *Sun*, 20 March 1839.

20. *Sun*, 19 August 1839; Jack Tager, *Boston Riots: Three Centuries of Social Violence* (Bos-

ton: Northeastern University Press, 2001), 111; Jean H. Baker, *Ambivalent Americans: The Know-Nothing Party in Maryland* (Baltimore: Johns Hopkins University Press, 1977), 4–5.

21. Goodrich and Segal, "Baltimore's Aid to Railroads," 12.

22. On this difficulty in Philadelphia, see Michael Feldberg, *The Philadelphia Riots of 1844: A Study of Ethnic Conflict* (Westport, Conn.: Greenwood Press, 1975), 8.

23. Report & Resolution on So Much of the Mayor's Communication as Relates to an Increase of Police Officers, 20/21 January 1840, BCA, RG 16, ser. 1, no. 510.

24. Louis McLane to Henry A. Sandaman, 31 January 1842, ibid., [no number].

25. Communication from L. McLane, President of the Balto. & Ohio railroad Co., 12 February 1842, ibid., no. 405; Letter from Louis McLane, Esq. Rec'd on April 7th Answered Same Day. An Interview Had on Friday 8th as Requested, BCA, RG 9, ser. 2, no. 844.

26. A Resolution Relative to the Directors of the Balto. & Ohio Rail Road, 30 March 1843, BCA, RG 16, ser. 1, no. 663.

27. Report of the Committee of Ways & Means on the Petition of Stephen R. King & Others, 22 March / 9 April 1838, ibid., no. 849.

28. Mayor's Communication, 4 January 1841, ibid., no. 452.

29. de Francis Folsom, *Our Police: A History of the Baltimore Force from the First Watchman to the Latest Appointee* (Baltimore: J. M. Beers, 1888), 23; Samuel A. Eliot to Samuel Smith, 6 February 1838, BCA, RG 9, ser. 2, no. 1288.

30. *Sun*, 8 March, 28 August 1843, 6 March 1844; Mayor's Communication, 15 January 1844, BCA, RG 16, ser. 1, no. 593; A Report Requested from the Joint Committee on Police Relating to the Calling of the Hour, 27 March 1843, ibid., no. 530; Folsom, *Our Police*, 23.

31. *Sun*, 27 September 1841, 19 January, 22 November 1842.

32. Ibid., 19 April 1841, 31 October 1842.

33. Mayor's Communication, 15 January 1844, BCA, RG 16, ser. 1, no. 593.

34. *Sun*, 9 December 1837; R. J. Breckenside Complaining of Nuisance, 19 August 1844, BCA, RG 9, ser. 2, no. 288; Matthew O'Reilly, Balto., 18 November 1844, ibid., no. 291.

35. *Sun*, 4 December 1843; *AM*, 212:61–64; Report of the Select Committee Relative to Altering or Enlarging the Jail, 22/23 April 1845, BCA, RG 16, ser. 1, no. 689. See also Report of the Joint Committee to Whom Was Referred So Much of the Annual Communication of the Mayor as Relates to the Jail, 28 February / 5 March 1845, ibid., no. 500.

36. *Sun*, 4 March 1841, 16 February 1842.

37. Amy S. Greenberg, *Cause for Alarm: The Volunteer Fire Company in the Nineteenth-Century City* (Princeton, N.J.: Princeton University Press, 1998), 22, 84–88; *Sun*, 2 September 1844.

38. *Ordinances and Resolutions of the Mayor and City Council of Baltimore*, 1841, pp. 63–64; Communication to the Presidents of the Fire Companies with a Resolution of the City Council, 1 June 1841, BCA, RG 9, ser. 2, no. 875 (incorrectly listed in WPA inventory with records of 1842).

39. Mayor's Communication, 15 January 1844, BCA, RG 16, ser. 1, no. 593.

40. *Ordinances and Resolutions of Mayor and City Council*, 1844, pp. 39–40, 63.

41. Report & Resolution from the Joint Committee on Police and the Resolution Directing Them to Inquires into the Subject of the Numerous Burglaries Committed during the Last Year, 11/12 March 1844, BCA, RG 16, ser. 1, no. 861; Report & Resolution from the Joint Committee on Police on the Petitions of William Harrison & Others, 28/29 March 1844, ibid., no. 699.

42. Communication from the Mayor, 4 April 1844, ibid., no. 594.

43. Thaddeus P. Thomas, *The City Government of Baltimore*, Johns Hopkins University Studies in Historical and Political Science, ser. 14, no. 2 (Baltimore: Johns Hopkins University Press, 1896), 26n2.

44. *Ordinances and Resolutions of Mayor and City Council*, 1844, pp. 10–11, 35; ibid., 1847, p. 6.

45. Report of the Joint Committee on Fire Cos upon the Application for Special Appropria-

tion, 7 March 1843, BCA, RG 16, ser. 1, no. 501; Report from the Joint Committee on Retrenchment, 23 July 1843, ibid., no. 587.

46. *Ordinances and Resolutions of Mayor and City Council*, 1846, p. 8; Petition of John McCormick, Jos. Christopher, & Others for an Increase of Compensation for Watchmen, 26 January 1846, BCA, RG 16, ser. 1, no. 453.

47. "Sixteenth Annual Report of the Commissioners of the Public Schools," in *Ordinances and Resolutions of Mayor and City Council*, 1845, appendix, pp. 63–68; Communication from the Commissioners of Public Schools, 27 March 1845, BCA, RG 16, ser. 1, no. 460.

48. Communication from the Commissioners; To the President of the Board of School Commissioners, n.d., April 1845, BCA, RG 16, ser. 1, no. 461.

49. *Ordinances and Resolutions of Mayor and City Council*, 1845, pp. 26–28; Report and Resolution from the Joint Committee for Education, 19/24 February 1845, BCA, RG 16, ser. 1, no. 966.

50. Mayor's Communication, 15 January 1844, BCA, RG 16, ser. 1, no. 593.

51. Mayor's Communication, 17 January 1848, ibid., no. 642.

52. Report of the Committee on the Jail, 11/16 February 1848, ibid., no. 716.

53. Mayor's Message, First Branch, 20 November 1850, ibid., no. 654.

54. *Sun*, 5 October 1850.

55. Ibid., 31 August 1849, 17 January, 5 October, 28 November 1850.

56. Ibid., 17 August 1850; Tracy Matthew Melton, *Hanging Henry Gambrill: The Violent Career of Baltimore's Plug Uglies, 1854–1860* (Baltimore: Maryland Historical Society, 2005), 33–34.

57. *Sun*, 10 October 1850.

58. Ibid., 11, 14 October, 1 November 1850, 1 February 1851.

59. Ibid., 7, 11, 14 November 1850.

60. Mayor's Message, 20 November 1850.

61. Mayor's Message, in *Ordinances and Resolutions of Mayor and City Council*, 1848, appendix, p. 10; ibid., 1849, p. 7.

62. Mayor's Message, 20 November 1850.

63. *Ordinances and Resolutions of Mayor and City Council*, 1850, pp. 7, 11.

64. Mayor's Communication, 20 January 1851, in *Ordinances and Resolutions of Mayor and City Council*, 1851, appendix, p. 4; *Sun*, 17 September 1852.

65. *Balto Nation*, 200–201.

66. Mayor's Communication, 19 January 1852, in *Ordinances and Resolutions of Mayor and City Council*, 1852, appendix, pp. 3–7.

CHAPTER 16. PIGS AND POLITICIANS

1. See "Reckoning" in chapter 13.

2. James Warner Harry, *The Maryland Constitution of 1851*, Johns Hopkins University Studies in Historical and Political Science, ser. 20, nos. 7–8 (Baltimore: Johns Hopkins University Press, 1902), 8.

3. Michael F. Holt, *The Rise and Fall of the American Whig Party: Jacksonian Politics and the Onset of the Civil War* (New York: Oxford University Press, 1999), 459–461.

4. Harry, *Maryland Constitution*, 21, 42.

5. Ibid., 9, 29; *Baltimore Sun*, 2 January 1850.

6. Harry, *Maryland Constitution*, 46–47; *Md. Hist.*, 3:242–243.

7. J. Thomas Scharf, *History of Baltimore City and County from the Earliest Period to the Present Day: Including Biographical Sketches of Their Representative Men* (Philadelphia: Louis H. Everts, 1881), 62–63, 201; *Bldg Balto*, 135; Report of the Joint Standing Committee on Police and Jail Enclosing Resolutions Relating to the Reorganization of the Night Watch and Police Systems, 25 February 1851, BCA, RG 16, ser. 1, no. 771; Report of the Joint Standing Committee on Police & Jail to Which Was Referred That Portion of the Mayor's Communication Relating

to the City & County Jail, and Reorganization of the Police & Night Watch, also the Report of the Board of Visitors of That Institution, 16 April / 19 May 1851, ibid., no. 1071.

8. See Roland J. Liebert, *Disintegration and Political Action: The Changing Functions of City Government in America* (New York: Academic Press, 1976).

9. An Ordinance Relating to Swine, n.d., March 1852, BCA, RG 16, ser. 1, no. 1126.

10. *Sun*, 25 March 1852.

11. Report of the Joint Committee on Health on the Petition for Restraining Hogs from Running at Large, 18 March / 23 May 1851, BCA, RG 16, no. 676; *Ordinances and Resolutions of the Mayor and City Council of Baltimore*, 1852, p. 17.

12. To the Honorable Mayor and Council of Baltimore, n.d., 1853, BCA, RG 16, no. 599.

13. The council received at least eight copies of this petition signed by hundreds of residents. See Petition for the Repeal of the Ordinance Relating to Swine, 17 January 1853, ibid., no. 569.

14. Report of the Committee on Health, 9 February 1853, ibid., no. 1480; An Ordinance Respecting Swine, 15 February 1853, ibid., no. 1481; An Ordinance Respecting Swine, 3 February 1853, ibid., no. 1479.

15. An Ordinance Respecting Swine, 11 February 1853, ibid., no. 1480; An Ordinance Respecting Swine, 3 February 1853, ibid., no. 1481; Substitute for an Ordinance to Permit Swine to Go at Large within the Limits of the City, 24 February / 7 March 1853, ibid., no. 1481.

16. *Sun*, 19 January 1853.

17. Baltimore City Council, *Proceedings of the First Branch*, 17 April 1852 to 10 March 1856, pp. 89, 99, 102, 507, 537, 541, 544, 548, 551, 553, 576, 648, 669, 788, 798–799; *Proceedings of the Second Branch*, 20 March 1854 to 18 January 1858, pp. 17, 30, 44, 91, 121, 129–132, 255, 257, 275, 277; *Sun*, 23 June 1854.

18. Oscar Handlin, *This Was America: True Accounts of People and Places, Manners and Customs, as Recorded by European Travelers to the Western Shore in the Eighteenth, Nineteenth, and Twentieth Centuries* (Cambridge, Mass.: Harvard University Press, 1949), 217; Ted Steinberg, *Down to Earth: Nature's Role in American History* (New York: Oxford University Press, 2002), 160; Catherine McNeur, "The 'Swinish Multitude': Controversies over Hogs in Antebellum New York City," *Journal of Urban History* 37 (September 2011): 639–660; Edwin G. Burrows and Mike Wallace, *Gotham: A History of New York City to 1898* (New York: Oxford University Press, 1999), 477, 786.

19. Burrows and Wallace, *Gotham*, 353–354.

20. See Jerome Mushkat, *Fernando Wood: A Political Biography* (Kent, Ohio: Kent State University Press, 1990), 38–40.

21. Burrows and Wallace, *Gotham*, 637; Reports and Returns, 1845, BCA, RG 33, ser. 8, nos. 1341–1528; *Balto Nation*, 149. See also William J. Evitts, *A Matter of Allegiances: Maryland from 1850 to 1861* (Baltimore: Johns Hopkins University Press, 1974), 58.

22. Communications from Register, 7 June 1853, 22 November 1853, BCA, RG 16, ser. 1., nos. 746A, 746B.

23. Minority Report of the Committee of Ways & Means upon the Disposition of a Portion of the Dividend Stock of the Balto & O RRoad, 4 April 1851, ibid., no. 567.

24. John Joseph Wallis, Richard E. Sylla, and Arthur Grinath III, "Sovereign Debt and Repudiation: The Emerging-Market Debt Crisis in the U.S. States, 1839–1843" (National Bureau of Economic Research, Working Paper 10753, Cambridge, Mass., September 2004), 32.

25. Leonard P. Curry, *The Corporate City: The American City as a Political Entity, 1800–1850* (Westport, Conn.: Greenwood Press, 1997), 43.

26. Quoted in Carter Goodrich, "The Revulsion against Internal Improvements," *Journal of Economic History* 10 (November 1950): 153.

27. *Bldg Balto*, 105.

28. Resolution Relative to the Annual Report of B&O. R.R., 8 December 1854, BCA, RG 16,

ser. 1, no. 944; Substitute Proposed for Resolution Relative to 28th Annual Report of the Balto. & O. RRoad, 19 December 1854, ibid. no. 947.

29. Substitute Proposed in the First Branch June 13th, ibid., no. 950; *Ordinances and Resolutions of Mayor and City Council*, 1854, p. 62.

30. John F. Stover, *History of the Baltimore and Ohio Railroad* (West Lafayette, Ind.: Purdue University Press, 1987), 93.

31. *Ordinances and Resolutions of Mayor and City Council*, 1854, pp. 83–88.

32. Message of the Mayor, 11 July 1853, BCA, RG 16, ser. 1, no. 798.

33. Report of the Joint Committee of Police & Jail on the Resolution of Inquiry as to Furnishing the Police with Revolvers, 23 April 1852, ibid., no. 859.

CHAPTER 17. KNOW-NOTHINGS

1. William J. Evitts, *A Matter of Allegiances: Maryland from 1850 to 1861* (Baltimore: Johns Hopkins University Press, 1974), 66, 100; Jean H. Baker, *Ambivalent Americans: The Know-Nothing Party in Maryland* (Baltimore: Johns Hopkins University Press, 1977), 1–2; *Continuity*, 5.

2. Laurence Frederick Schmeckebier, *History of the Know Nothing Party in Maryland* (Baltimore: Johns Hopkins University Press, 1899), 13–14.

3. *Baltimore Sun*, 26 April 1852.

4. Baker, *Ambivalent Americans*, 18; Evitts, *Matter of Allegiances*, 72–73; Frank Towers, *The Urban South and the Coming of the Civil War* (Charlottesville: University of Virginia Press, 2004), 86.

5. See Towers, *Urban South*.

6. *Balto Nation*, 191; Towers, *Urban South*, 95.

7. Schmeckebier, *Know Nothing Party*, 47–52.

8. Kennedy to S. N. Spencer, 24 November 1855, John Pendleton Kennedy Papers, Peabody Institute, Johns Hopkins University, Baltimore.

9. Kennedy to Robert C. Winthrop, 21 February 1856, Kennedy Papers.

10. Baker, *Ambivalent Americans*, 19; Evitts, *Matter of Allegiances*, 61–62.

11. Evitts, *Matter of Allegiances*, 99; Baker, *Ambivalent Americans*, 3.

12. Baker, *Ambivalent Americans*, 47; Schmeckebier, *Know Nothing Party*.

13. Carleton Beals, *Brass-Knuckle Crusade: The Great Know-Nothing Conspiracy, 1820–1860* (New York: Hastings House, 1960), 180–181; *Continuity*, 34.

14. Bernard C. Steiner, *The Life of Henry Winter Davis* (Baltimore: John Murphy, 1916), 44; Evitts, *Matter of Allegiances*, 99.

15. Evitts, *Matter of Allegiances*, 93; Richard R. Duncan, "The Era of the Civil War," in *Md. History*, 326–327.

16. Mayor's Communication, 2 December 1854, BCA, RG 16, ser. 1, no. 636; Message of the Mayor, 16 June 1854, ibid., no. 634; *Ordinances and Resolutions of the Mayor and City Council of Baltimore*, 1854, pp. 57–58.

17. Preamble and Resolution in Relation to the Baltimore and Susquehanna Rail Road Company, 5 March 1855, BCA, RG 16, ser. 1, no. 649; *Sun*, 30 December 1854.

18. Resolution of Bond and Agreement, 14 November 1855, BCA, RG 16, ser. 1, no. 721; *Balto Nation*, 201.

19. Petition, n.d., 1855, BCA, RG 16, ser. 1, no. 278(A).

20. *Ordinances and Resolutions of Mayor and City Council*, 1855, pp. 2–9.

21. Water Board Resolution, 29 March 1855, BCA, RG 16, ser. 1, no. 89.

22. Report of Joint Committee on Police and Jail, 24/25 May 1855, ibid., no. 535.

23. An Ordinance for the Support and Encouragement of Volunteer Corps of the City of Baltimore, 3/5 April 1855, ibid., no. 791.

24. Police Bill, 27/28 February 1855, ibid., no. 795; Supplement to an Ordinance no. 28 of Revised Ordinances of 1850, ibid., no. 796.

25. Tracy Matthew Melton, *Hanging Henry Gambrill: The Violent Career of Baltimore's Plug Uglies, 1854–1860* (Baltimore: Maryland Historical Society, 2005), 57.

26. Ibid., 84–85; Evitts, *Matter of Allegiances*, 97.

27. *Sun*, 6 October 1856.

28. Ibid., 9 October 1856.

29. Schmeckebier, *Know Nothing Party*, 37; Evitts, *Matter of Allegiances*, 97–98; *Sun*, 9 October 1856.

30. Melton, *Hanging Henry Gambrill*, 147; Towers, *Urban South*, 119–120; Matthew Page Andrews, "History of Baltimore from 1850 to the Close of the Civil War," in *Balto. Hist.*, 156–160.

31. *Sun*, 9 October 1856.

32. See Frank Towers, "Violence as a Tool of Party Dominance: Election Riots and the Baltimore Know-Nothings, 1854–1860," *MHM* 93 (Spring 1998): 14.

33. *Sun*, 27 October 1856.

34. Schmeckebier, *Know Nothing Party*, 39.

35. *Sun*, 5 November 1856.

36. Ibid., 5, 6 November 1856; Melton, *Hanging Henry Gambrill*, 104–105.

37. *Sun*, 5, 6 November 1856.

38. Ibid., 7 November 1856; Evitts, *Matter of Allegiances*, 98; Schmeckebier, *Know Nothing Party*, 39.

39. *Sun*, 11 November 1856.

40. Ibid., 20 November 1856.

41. *Proceedings of the First Branch of the City Council*, 5 December 1854, p. 261.

42. Ibid., 13 February 1855, pp. 410–411; *Sun*, 21 December 1854.

43. *Proceedings of First Branch*, 2 March 1855, p. 463.

44. *Ordinances of Mayor and City Council*, Passed during the Regular Session of 1857 and the Special Session of 1856, pp. 7–8.

45. Ibid., 12–14; An Ordinance to Establish a Police for the City of Baltimore, 10/22 December 1856, BCA, RG 16, ser. 1, no. 966; *Ordinances of Mayor and City Council*, 1856, p. 17; *Sun*, 11, 23 December 1856.

46. de Francis Folsom, *Our Police: A History of the Baltimore Force from the First Watchman to the Latest Appointee* (Baltimore: J. M. Beers, 1888), 28–29; Evitts, *Matter of Allegiances*, 112–113; Baker, *Ambivalent Americans*, 133; Melton, *Hanging Henry Gambrill*, 125, 149–150.

47. *Sun*, 14 October 1857; Melton, *Hanging Henry Gambrill*, 151–152.

48. Schmeckebier, *Know Nothing Party*, 73; *Sun*, 2, 3 February 1859.

49. Schmeckebier, *Know Nothing Party*, 74.

50. Ibid., 76–77; Evitts, *Matter of Allegiances*, 103.

51. Schmeckebier, *Know Nothing Party*, 83–84.

52. Evitts, *Matter of Allegiances*, 103; Melton, *Hanging Henry Gambrill*, 160.

53. Evitts, *Matter of Allegiances*, 103–104; *Sun*, 1 November 1857.

54. *Sun*, 5, 6 November 1857.

55. US Congress, House of Representatives, "Maryland Contested Election—Third Congressional District," 35th Congress, 1st Session, Miscellaneous Documents, no. 68. p. 20.

56. Ibid.

57. Ibid., 33.

58. Ibid., 29, 32, 289–290.

59. James Q. Wilson, *Varieties of Police Behavior* (New York: Atheneum Books, 1971).

60. Amy S. Greenberg, *Cause for Alarm: The Volunteer Fire Company in the Nineteenth-Century City* (Princeton, N.J.: Princeton University Press, 1998), 139–140; *Sun*, 19 January, 8 September 1858.

61. *Sun*, 22 May, 27 July, 31 August 1858; Clarence H. Forrest, *Official History of the Fire*

Department of the History of Baltimore with Biographies and Portraits of Eminent Citizens of Baltimore (Baltimore: Clarence Forrest, 1898), 84–87.

553

Notes to Pages 217–229

62. Message from the Mayor, 16 November 1858, BCA, RG 16, ser. 1, no. 379; *Ordinances of Mayor and City Council*, Sessions of 1858 and 1859, pp. 8–13.

CHAPTER 18. AMERICAN PARTY RECKONING

1. *Baltimore Sun*, 22 September 1858; Laurence Frederick Schmeckebier, *History of the Know Nothing Party in Maryland* (Baltimore: Johns Hopkins University Press, 1899), 97.

2. Henry Elliot Shepherd (ed.), *History of Baltimore, Maryland, from Its Founding as a Town to the Current Year* (Baltimore: S. B. Nelson, 1893), 108, 970–971.

3. *Sun*, 28 September 1858.

4. Ibid., 14 October 1858.

5. Ibid., 14, 15 October 1858; Schmeckebier, *Know Nothing Party*, 97–98.

6. *Journal of the Proceedings of the First Branch of the City Council*, at the Sessions of 1858 and 1859, pp. 6–8, 434.

7. Tracy Matthew Melton, *Hanging Henry Gambrill: The Violent Career of Baltimore's Plug Uglies, 1854–1860* (Baltimore: Maryland Historical Society, 2005), 4–6.

8. *Sun*, 8 November 1858; Melton, *Hanging Henry Gambrill*, 232.

9. Swann had appealed to the General Assembly for a constitutional convention that would consider reorganization of the criminal courts "investing the Mayor of this city with enlarged powers with offenses of a flagrant character against the public peace." Baltimore's Know-Nothings vigorously supported a referendum on a constitutional convention; the rest of Maryland's electorate voted it down. *Proceedings of First Branch*, 1858, pp. 346–348; Schmeckebier, *Know Nothing Party*, 96.

10. *Proceedings of First Branch*, 1858, pp. 353–354.

11. Petition of Wm. G. Thomas & Others in Reference to Street Passenger Railway, 2 January 1859, BCA, RG 16, ser. 1, no. 300; Petition of Samuel J. Spicer and Others in Favor of Laying Down the Passenger Railway, 21 February 1859, ibid., no. 299; *Sun*, 18 January 1859.

12. Mayor's Message, 22 March 1859, BCA, RG 16, ser. 1, no. 3, reprinted in *Sun*, 23 March 1859.

13. Ibid.

14. Ibid.

15. *Sun*, 23 March 1859.

16. Melton, *Hanging Henry Gambrill*, 314–315. It was rumored that Travers and his associates had actually received $100,000 from Brock.

17. *Sun*, 17 June 1859.

18. Melton, *Hanging Henry Gambrill*, 314.

19. *Sun*, 17 June 1859.

20. Ibid., 5, 22 November 1859.

21. William J. Evitts, *A Matter of Allegiances: Maryland from 1850 to 1861* (Baltimore: Johns Hopkins University Press, 1974), 128–129.

22. *Majority Report of the Committee on Corporations to the House of Delegates in Relation to the Baltimore City Passenger Railway*, 28 February 1860, pp. 9, 120–121.

23. Ibid., 106.

24. Melton, *Hanging Henry Gambrill*, 289, 408–409.

25. Jacob W. Miller to Steptoe B. Taylor, 27 September 1859, BCA, RG 32, ser. 1, no. 59A.

26. *Sun*, 5, 6, 27 August 1857.

27. Ibid., 3 November 1858.

28. Ibid., 17 August 1859; Schmeckebier, *Know Nothing Party*, 99–100.

29. *Sun*, 20, 21 September 1859.

30. House of Delegates of the State of Maryland, *Baltimore Contested Election, Papers in the Contested Election Case* (Annapolis: B. H. Richardson, 1860), 24.

31. Ibid., 46–47.

32. Ibid., 36–37.

33. Evitts, *Matter of Allegiances*, 132.

34. Session Laws, 1860, *AM*, 588, chap. 7, pp. 8–18.

35. Ibid., 588, chap. 9, pp. 21–22.

36. Evitts, *Matter of Allegiances*, 132; Frank Towers, *The Urban South and the Coming of the Civil War* (Charlottesville: University of Virginia Press, 2004), 156–157; Resolution in Relation to the Police Appointments, 21/23 February 1860, BCA, RG 16, ser. 1, no. 1304.

37. Edwin G. Burrows and Mike Wallace, *Gotham: A History of New York City to 1898* (New York: Oxford University Press, 1999), 838–839.

38. Communication from the Mayor Nominating Commissioners of the New City Hall Building, 6 September 1860, BCA, RG 16, ser. 1, no. 588; Communication from His Honor the Mayor Inviting the Councils to Participate in the Dedication of Druid Hill Park, 28 September 1860, ibid., no. 547.

39. Schmeckebier, *Know Nothing Party*, 112–113; *Sun*, 11 October 1860

CHAPTER 19. BALTIMORE IN THE DIVIDED NATION

1. Eugene H. Rosenboom, "Baltimore as a National Nomination City," *MHM* 67 (Fall 1972): 215–217.

2. Michael F. Holt, *The Rise and Fall of the American Whig Party* (New York: Oxford University Press, 1999), 961, 971–978; Richard R. Duncan, "The Era of the Civil War," in *Md. Hist.*, 318.

3. Dorothy Dix Greeman, "The Democratic Convention of 1860: Prelude to Secession," *MHM* 67 (Fall 1972): 232, 235; Charles W. Mitchell, "The Madness of Disunion: The Baltimore Conventions of 1860," *MHM* 92 (Summer 1997): 192; Charles W. Mitchell, "Maryland's Presidential Election of 1860," *MHM* 109 (Fall 2014): 311–312.

4. Greeman, "Democratic Convention of 1860," 245, 249, 252.

5. David Walter Curl, "The Baltimore Convention of the Constitutional Union Party," *MHM* 67 (Fall 1972): 255–256; *Baltimore Sun*, 10 May 1860; Mitchell, "Madness of Disunion," 193.

6. *Sun*, 10 May 1860; Murat Halstead, *Caucuses of 1860: A History of the National Political Conventions* (Columbus, Ohio: Follett Foster and Company, 1860), 109.

7. Halstead, *Caucuses of 1860*, 113; Curl, "Baltimore Convention," 265.

8. Halstead, *Caucuses of 1860*, 109, 119.

9. Curl, "Baltimore Convention," 272.

10. John Pendleton Kennedy, *The Border States: Their Power and Duty in the Present Disordered Condition of the Country* (Philadelphia: J. B. Lippincott, 1861), 14–15, 37.

11. Ibid., 37–39.

12. Ibid., 6.

13. Ibid., 35, 27, 40–41.

14. See Frank Towers, "Violence as a Tool of Party Dominance: Election Riots and the Baltimore Know-Nothings, 1854–1860," *MHM* 93 (Spring 1998): 5.

15. Curtis M. Jacobs, *Speech of Col. Curtis M. Jacobs, on the Free Colored Population of Maryland, Delivered before the House of Delegates on the 17th of February, 1860* (Annapolis: Elihu S. Riley, 1860), 7, 10, 12.

16. Leroy Graham, *Baltimore: The Nineteenth Century Black Capital* (Lanham, Md.: University Press of America, 1983), 155.

17. *Sun*, 13 November 1860.

18. Ibid., 16 November 1860.

19. Ibid.

20. Ibid., 3 December 1860; George William Brown, *Baltimore and the Nineteenth of April, 1861: A Study of the War* (Baltimore: N. Murray, 1887), 36.

21. *Sun*, 27 November 1860.

22. George L. P. Radcliffe, *Governor Thomas H. Hicks of Maryland and the Civil War* (Baltimore: Lord Baltimore Press, 1901), 22.

23. Quoted in Bernard C. Steiner, "Severn Teackle Wallis," *Sewanee Review* 15 (January 1907): 66.

24. *Sun*, 9 January 1861.

25. Ibid., 8 January 1861.

26. Ibid., 27 February 1861.

27. David Stashower, *The Peril of the Hour: The Secret Plot to Murder Lincoln before the Civil War* (New York: Minotaur Books, 2013), 4.

28. *Sun*, 19 April 1861.

29. Matthew Page Andrews, "Passage of the Sixth Massachusetts Regiment through Baltimore," *MHM* 14 (March 1919): 66–67; Scott Sumpter Sheads and Daniel Carroll Toomey, *Baltimore during the Civil War* (Linthicum, Md.: Toomey Press, 1997), 15.

30. Tracy Matthew Melton, "The Lost Lives of George Konig Sr. & Jr., a Father-Son Tale of Old Fell's Point," *MHM* 101 (Fall 2006): 345–346.

31 Andrews, "Passage of Sixth Massachusetts," 67–68, 175; Sheads and Toomey, *Baltimore during Civil War*, 15–16; Jonathan W. White, "Forty-seven Eyewitness Accounts of the Pratt Street Riot and Its Aftermath," *MHM* 106 (Spring 2011): 77.

32. Brown, *Baltimore and Nineteenth of April*, 49–51; Wilbur Coyle, "Mayors of Baltimore: George P. Kane," *Municipal Journal* 7. no. 9 (9 May 1919): 2–3. Coyle appends Kane's report to his mayoral biography.

33. Frank Towers, *The Urban South and the Coming of the Civil War* (Charlottesville: University of Virginia Press, 2004), 159.

34. White, "Forty-seven Eyewitness Accounts," 77.

35. Charles B. Clark, "Baltimore and the Attack on the Sixth Massachusetts Regiment, April 19, 1861," *MHM* 56 (March 1961): 39–71; George Radcliffe, *Governor Thomas H. Hicks and the Civil War* (Baltimore: Johns Hopkins University Press, 1901), 54–55.

36. Brown, *Baltimore and Nineteenth of April*, 52; Radcliffe, *Thomas H. Hicks*, 56–57.

37. Quoted in Brown, *Baltimore and Nineteenth of April*, 62.

38. Ibid., 64; Frank Towers, "Secession in an Urban Context: Municipal Reform and the Coming of the Civil War in Baltimore," in Jessica Elfenbein, John R. Breihan, and Thomas Hollowak (eds.), *From Mobtown to Charm City: New Perspectives on Baltimore's Past* (Baltimore: Maryland Historical Society, 2002), 113.

39. Charles McHenry Howard, "Baltimore and the Crisis of 1861," *MHM* 41 (December 1946): 259; *Sun*, 22 April 1861; Petition of F. W. Bald Praying to Be Reimbursed for Goods Taken by Violence, 3 July 1861, BCA, RG 16, ser. 1, no. 507; Petition of W. Harris, 24 May 1861, ibid., no. 511; Petition of Conrad Shumaker, 1 May 1861, ibid., no. 526; Petition of Pattison and Woolford, 18 July 1861, ibid., no. 528; Petition of O. H. Cromwell for Damages Sustained on the 21 and 22 of April 1861, ibid., no. 546; Clark, "Baltimore and Attack on Sixth Massachusetts," 268–269.

40. Brown, *Baltimore and Nineteenth of April*, 66.

41. Lawrence M. Denton, *A Southern Star for Maryland: Maryland and the Secession Crisis* (Baltimore: Publishing Concepts, 1995), 77.

42. Charles Branch Clark, "Politics in Maryland during the Civil War," *MHM* 36 (September 1941): 249, 260–261.

43. Towers, "Secession in Urban Context," 93–96.

44. *Continuity*, 53–54; Barbara Jeanne Fields. *Slavery and Freedom on the Middle Ground: Maryland during the Nineteenth Century* (New Haven, Conn.: Yale University Press, 1985), 97–98.

45. *Sun*, 25 April 1861.

46. Radcliffe, *Thomas H. Hicks*, 72–73; Denton, *Southern Star*, 94.

47. Radcliffe, *Thomas H. Hicks*, 86–87, 95.

48. Sheads and Toomey, *Baltimore during Civil War*, 29–30; *Official Records*, 1st ser., 1:29–32.

49. Sheads and Toomey, *Baltimore during Civil War*, 33; *Official Records*, 1st ser., 1, pt. 9, pp. 638–639.

50. *Official Records*, 1st ser., 2, pt. 9, pp. 639–641; *Chronicles*, 612.

51. *Official Records*, 2nd ser., 1:574–585, 586n.

52. Ibid., 1st ser., vol. 2, p. 138; *Sun*, 28 June 1861.

53. Quoted in Charles B. Clark, "Suppression and Control of Maryland: A Study of Federal-State Relations during Civil Conflict," *MHM* 54 (September 1959): 248.

54. *Official Records*, 2nd ser., 1:667–675; Sheads and Toomey, *Baltimore during the Civil War*, 42–44; Duncan, "Era of Civil War," 352.

55. *Official Records*, 1st ser., 2:156.

56. Brown, *Baltimore and Nineteenth of April*, 97–98.

57. *Sun*, 28 June, 2 July 1861.

58. *Sun*, 14 September 1861; Brown, *Baltimore and Nineteenth of April*, 104–105; Mayor, 22 January 1862, BCA, RG 16, ser. 1, no. 406.

59. Brown, *Baltimore and Nineteenth of April*, 106.

60. Mayor, 22 January 1862.

61. *Sun*, 28 June, 18 July 1861; Provost Marshal to Mayor and City Council, 5 February 1862, BCA, RG 16, ser. 1, no. 440.

62. Jacob Frey, *Reminiscences of Baltimore* (Baltimore: Maryland Book Concern, 1893), 127, 130; Duncan, "Era of Civil War," 349.

CHAPTER 20. CITY AT WAR

1. Charles B. Clark, "Politics in Maryland during the Civil War," *MHM* 36 (September 1941): 383, 387–388.

2. Gerald S. Henig, "Henry Winter Davis and the Speakership Contest of 1859–1860," *MHM* 68 (Spring 1973): 2.

3. Ibid., 15–17; Bernard C. Steiner, *Life of Henry Winter Davis* (Baltimore: John Murphy Company, 1916), 144–145.

4. *Baltimore Sun*, 28 June 1853, 6, 25 May 1861. In Baltimore's Third Congressional District, Unionist Cornelius Leary ran against William P. Preston, a states' rights candidate. Leary won by a narrow margin. See Clark, "Politics in Maryland," 383.

5. *Congressional Globe*, 37th Congress, 1st Session, pp. 196–200.

6. Clark, "Politics in Maryland," 178–181.

7. Ibid., 184; *Official Records*, 2nd ser., 2:790; Charles B. Clark, "The Civil War," in Morris L. Radoff (ed.), *The Old Line State: A History of Maryland* (Annapolis: Hall of Records Commission, 1971), 85, 91.

8. *Sun*, 9, 10 October 1861.

9. *Continuity*, 64–65, 70–71. Harry Newman suggests that a nervous Governor Hicks asked General Banks to instruct his troops to patrol polling places to protect Unionist voters. See Harry Wright Newman, *Maryland and the Confederacy: An Objective Narrative of Maryland's Participation in the War between the States* (Annapolis: Harry Wright Newman, 1976), 60.

10. *Sun*, 29 July 1862.

11. *Chronicles*, 626–627. The Middle Department was a military district created by the War Department in 1862 to oversee US troops in the Middle Atlantic states, with headquarters in Baltimore.

12. *Sun*, 29 July 1862. Governor Bradford alluded to the second branch's resistance in his oration in Monument Square. He assured the crowd that they would soon have a "municipal legislature both branches of which will be unquestionably loyal."

13. Scott Sumpter Sheads and Daniel Carroll Toomey, *Baltimore during the Civil War* (Linthicum, Md.: Toomey Press, 1997), 129, 175–177, 187–200.

14. William Starr Myers, *The Maryland Constitution of 1864*, Johns Hopkins University Studies in Historical and Political Science, ser. 19, nos. 8–9 (Baltimore: Johns Hopkins University Press, 1901), 11.

15. Ibid., 15.

16. *Sun*, 29 June, 1 July 1863; Matthew Page Andrews, "History of Baltimore from 1850 to the Close of the Civil War," in *Balto Hist.*, 1:194.

17. Myers, *Maryland Constitution*, 20–21.

18. Ibid., 18–23.

19. Ibid., 32.

20. Ibid., 14–15; *Continuity*, 85–86.

21. Myers, *Maryland Constitution*, 37–38.

22. *Continuity*, 104.

23. Barbara Jeanne Fields, *Slavery and Freedom on the Middle Ground* (New Haven, Conn.: Yale University Press, 1985), 123–125.

24. Lt. Colonel Don Piatt, Chief of Staff, Middle Department, to Mayor Chapman, 21 July 1863, BCA, RG 16, ser. 1, no. 62; Charles L. Wagandt, "Redemption or Reaction? Maryland in the Post-Civil War Years," in Richard O. Curry (ed.), *Radicalism, Racism, and Party Realignment: The Border States during Reconstruction* (Baltimore: Johns Hopkins University Press, 1969), 150.

25. Richard R. Duncan, "The Era of the Civil War," in *Md. Hist.*, 370.

26. *A Biographical Sketch of Hon: A. Leo Knott, with a Relation of Some Political Transactions in Maryland, 1861–1867, Being the History of the Redemption of a State* (Baltimore: S. B. Nelson, 1898), 12.

27. Myers, *Maryland Constitution*, 34–35, 39.

28. Ibid., 43–44.

29. Ibid., 47.

30. Ibid., 53–55.

31. Ibid., 56.

32. Ibid., 41.

33. *AM*, 666:14.

34. Myers, *Maryland Constitution*, 60–61.

35. "The Constitution of the State of Maryland, 1864," *AM*, 666:24.

36. Ibid., 43; Myers, *Maryland Constitution*, 69–70.

37. *Baltimore American*, 4 November 1864; William Starr Myers, *The Self-Reconstruction of Maryland, 1864–1867*, Johns Hopkins University Studies in Historical and Political Science, ser. 27, nos. 1–2 (Baltimore: Johns Hopkins University Press, 1909), 31.

38. Myers, *Maryland Constitution*, 88–89; *Sun*, 11 July 1865; *A. Leo Knott*, 46–47.

39. Myers, *Maryland Constitution*, 76.

40. *Continuity*, 84, 87, 98, 103, 152.

41. Ibid., 110.

42. Duncan, "Era of Civil War," 382.

43. *Sun*, 7 November 1860, 9, 10 November 1864.

44. Myers, *Self-Reconstruction*, 23–24.

45. Ibid., 32, 38, 47.

CHAPTER 21. DEMOCRATIC RESURRECTION

1. Aloysius Leo Knott, *A Biographical Sketch of Hon. A. Leo Knott, with a Relation of Some Political Transactions in Maryland, 1861–1867* (Baltimore: S. B. Nelson, 1898), 65–67; *Baltimore Sun*, 11 October 1860.

2. Richard R. Duncan, "The Era of the Civil War," in *Md. Hist.*, 387; *Sun*, 29 October 1866.

3. *A. Leo Knott*, 66–67.

4. Ibid., 49–50.

5. William Starr Myers, *The Self-Reconstruction of Maryland, 1864–1867,* Johns Hopkins University Studies in Historical and Political Science, ser. 27, nos. 1–2 (Baltimore: Johns Hopkins University Press, 1909), 50–52.

6. Ibid., 70–71; *A. Leo Knott,* 75.

7. *A. Leo Knott,* 82.

8. Ibid., 70–71.

9. A. Leo Knott reported that 700 US infantry troops arrived at Fort McHenry just before the election. He speculated that they were present to intervene on behalf of the incumbent Republicans if any outbreak occurred on election day. It is just as reasonable to suppose that they were sent to ensure the fair election that Baltimore's Democrats had been promised by General Canby—especially since the troops took no action when Democrats flocked to the polls. Ibid., 82.

10. *Sun,* 8 November 1866.

11. Ibid.

12. *Continuity,* 164, 179; Matthew Page Andrews, "History of Baltimore from 1850 to the Close of the Civil War," in *Balto Hist.,* 209; John B. Lambert, "Reconstruction to World War I," in Morris L. Radoff (ed.), *The Old Line State: A History of Maryland* (Annapolis: Maryland Hall of Records Commission, 1971), 107.

13. *A. Leo Knott,* 106–107; Myers, *Self-Reconstruction,* 91–92.

14. Myers, *Self-Reconstruction,* 80–81; *Sun,* 4 January 1867.

15. *Continuity,* 17; *Baltimore News,* 9 August 1901.

16. Myers, *Self-Reconstruction,* 98, 99n.

17. Ibid., 99–101; Henry E. Shepard, *The History of Baltimore from Its Founding to the Current Year, 1729 to 1895* (Baltimore: S. B Nelson, 1895), 567. Democrats in the General Assembly were also concerned that the statute calling for new elections in Baltimore would not withstand a legal challenge.

18. Myers, *Self-Reconstruction,* 103–109.

19. "Proceedings and Debates of the 1867 Constitutional Convention," *AM* 74:156–157, 440.

20. See, for example, "Mayor's Message," in *Ordinances of the Mayor and City Council of Baltimore,* Sessions of 1864 and 1865, appendix, pp. 20–28; Communication Board of Finance Commissioners in Relation to Dividend Stock of Balto. & Ohio Rail Road Com., BCA, RG 16, ser. 1, no. 374; Communication Sharretts B&O RR, 22 May 1865, ibid., no. 375; Letter from Thos. Cromer, Director in B&O RR, 19 May 1865, ibid., no. 376; Communication from the Mayor, ibid., no. 377.

21.See, for example, Petition of the Firemen of the City Fire Department for Increase in Pay, 11 January 1866, BCA, RG 16, ser. 1, no. 855; Petition of the Baltimore Lamplighters Praying Increase of Salary, n.d., January 1866, ibid., no. 938.

22. See, for example, Resolution Requesting the Directors in the B&O RR Co. to Enquire into Certain Difficulties &c., 2 January 1866, BCA, RG 16, ser. 1, no. 1780; Resolution in Relation to the Strike of the Machinists on the B&O RR, 8/12 February 1866, ibid., no. 1781.

23. Resolution of Inquiry to the Directors on the Part of the City in the B&O RR, 15 March / 15 May 1865, ibid., no. 723.

24. *Sun,* 10 June 1858, 17 March 1862, 18 April 1865; Resolution for the [Sale of] the City's Interest in the Northern Central Railway, 2 February / 16 June 1865, BCA, RG 16, ser. 1, no. 848.

25. Message from the Mayor Vetoing the Ordinance Granting Permission to the Philadelphia, Wilmington, and Baltimore Railroad to Put Double Tracks on Boston Street, 26 April 1866, ibid., no. 269.

26. *Sun,* 22 January 1867.

27. See, for example, Petition of John [?] & 116 others, a Remonstrance against Renumbering the Houses, 13 December 1866, BCA, RG 16, ser. 1, no. 692; Remonstrance against Renumbering the Houses, Dinsmore & Kyle and 21 Firms and Business Men, 4 January 1867, ibid., [no number]; Petition in Favor of Renumbering the Houses on the Decimal Plan from Thomas

Matthews & Sons and Others, 8 February 1867, ibid., no. 706; Petition of Otto Wilkins and 32 Others against Renumbering the Houses of the City, 11 February 1867, ibid., no. 722; Petition in Favor of Renumbering the Houses on the Decimal Plan from Henry Tyson and Others, 8 February 1867, ibid., no. 672; Petition in Favor of Renumbering the Houses on the Decimal Plan, 7 February 1867, ibid., no. 276.

28. Report of the Standing Committee on Police & Jail in Relation to Renumbering Houses in the City with an Ordinance, 11 February 1867, BCA, RG 16, ser. 1, no. 1304; Minority Report of the Joint Standing Committee on Police & Jail in Relation to the Renumbering of Houses in the City, 8 February 1867, ibid., no. 63.

29. *Sun*, 19 October 1867.

30. *The City Hall, Baltimore, History of Construction and Dedication* (Baltimore: Mayor and City Council, 1876), 16–27; Communication from the Mayor in Regard to Water Rights on the Gunpowder River, 19 February 1866, BCA, RG 16, ser. 1, [no number].

31. *Sun*, 19 October 1867.

32. Ibid., 13 January 1864, 8 September 1865, 19 January 1866; *City Hall*, 29–36.

33. *City Hall*, 38; *Sun*, 19 October 1867.

34. *Sun*, 19 October 1867.

35. Ibid., 8, 20 November 1867; *City Hall*, 53–55.

36. *Sun*, 16 June 1868.

37. Ibid., 23 July, 5 August 1868; *City Hall*, 56–57.

38. *Sun*, 8 September 1869.

39. Ibid., 16 September 1869; The Reply of the Building Committee of the New City Hall to the Report of the Joint Special Committee of the City Council, 15 September 1869, BCA, RG 16, ser. 1, no. 429.

40. *Sun*, 28 September 1869.

41. Ibid., 30 September, 1, 19 October 1869.

42. Veto Message of the Mayor Relative to the Appointment of a New Building Committee for the New City Hall, 11 October 1869, BCA, RG 16, ser. 1, no. 425.

43. Ibid.

44. *Sun*, 25, 29 October, 2, 4 November 1869.

45. Ibid., 10 April 1875.

CHAPTER 22. EX-SLAVES, EX-CONFEDERATES, AND THE NEW REGIME

1. *Balto Nation*, 191; Barbara Jeanne Fields, *Slavery and Freedom on the Middle Ground: Maryland during the Nineteenth Century* (New Haven, Conn.: Yale University Press, 1985), 62.

2. Eleanor Bruchey, "The Industrialization of Maryland, 1860–1914," in *Md. Hist.*, 436–437; M. Rosewin Sweeney, " 'Sonny' Mahon and Baltimore's Irish Machine: Ethnic Politics in a Semi-Southern Setting" (MA thesis, Johns Hopkins University, 1979), 3; William Lloyd Fox, "Social and Cultural Developments from the Civil War to 1920," in *Md. Hist.*, 503; Campbell J. Gibson and Emily Lennon, "Historical Census Statistics on the Foreign-Born Population of the United States" (US Bureau of the Census, Population Division Working Paper no. 29, Washington, D.C., February 1999), table 22.

3. Richard Paul Fuke, *Imperfect Equality: African Americans and the Confines of White Racial Attitudes in Post-Emancipation Maryland* (New York: Fordham University Press, 1999), 117–124; Invitation from Friends' Association in Aid of Freedmen, 2 February 1865, BCA, RG 16, ser. 1, no. 412.

4. Fields, *Slavery and Freedom*, 201–202.

5. Fuke, *Imperfect Equality*, 132–135.

6. Ibid., 135–136; Linda Shopes, "Fells Point: Community and Conflict in a Working-Class Neighborhood," in Elizabeth Fee, Linda Shopes, and Linda Zeidman (eds.), *The Baltimore Book: New Views of Local History* (Philadelphia: Temple University Press, 1991), 128–129; Bet-

tye C. Thomas, "The Nineteenth Century Black Operated Shipyard, 1866–1884: Reflections upon Its Inception and Ownership," *Journal of Negro History* 59 (January 1974): 1–12; *Baltimore American*, 27 January 1891.

7. *Md. Negro*, 13, 17, 63.

8. William George Paul, "The Shadow of Equality: The Negro in Baltimore, 1864–1911" (PhD diss., University of Wisconsin, 1972), 3; "Judge Lynch's Court: Mob Justice in Maryland during the Age of Jim Crow, 1860s–1930s," Maryland State Archives, slavery.msa.maryland.gov/html /casestudies/judge_lynch.html.

9. W. A. Low, "The Freedmen's Bureau and Civil Rights in Maryland," *Journal of Negro History* 37 (July 1952): 228–232.

10. W. A. Low, "The Freedmen's Bureau and Education in Maryland," *MHM* 47 (March 1952): 32.

11. Report of the Joint Standing Committee on Education on the Petition of the President & Managers of the Baltimore Association for the Moral & Educational Improvement of Colored People, 25/30 May 1865, BCA, RG 16, ser. 1, no. 605.

12. Ibid.; Low, "Freedmen's Bureau," 34–36; Fuke, *Imperfect Equality*, 89–90; *Md. Negro*, 64; *Baltimore Sun*, 24 November 1866.

13. Petition of the Baltimore Association for the Moral and Educational Improvement of Colored People of the Colored People Asking an Appropriation of $20,000 for Schools in Baltimore City, 22 January 1867, BCA, RG 16, ser. 1, no. 510.

14. Communication from School Commissioners in Regard to Schools for Colored Children, 20 October 1867, ibid., no. 1132.

15. *Baltimore American*, 10, 24 June 1868.

16. *Sun*, 31 October 1867.

17. Ibid., 25 January, 14 May 1866; *Md. Negro*, 15–16; Communication from City Counsellor to First Branch of City Council, 11 September 1865, BCA, RG 16, ser. 1, no. 403.

18. The provision for reducing representation in Congress was never enforced.

19. *Continuity*, 162.

20. *Baltimore American*, 20 May 1870; *Sun*, 20 May 1870.

21. *Sun*, 5 November 1870.

22. Ibid., 9 November 1870.

23. Ibid., 27 March 1879, quoted in Dennis P. Halpin, *"For My Race against All Parties": Building a Radical African American Activist Foundation in Baltimore, 1870s–1885* (Baltimore: Baltimore City Historical Society, 2014), 6.

24. Halpin, *For My Race*, 8; Bettye Collier-Thomas, "Harvey Johnson and the Mutual United Brotherhood of Liberty, 1885–1919," in Kenneth L. Kusmer (ed.), *Black Communities and Urban Development in America: From Reconstruction to the Great Migration, 1877–1917* (New York: Garland Publishing, 1991), 4:214–225; Larry S. Gibson, *Young Thurgood: The Making of a Supreme Court Justice* (Amherst, N.Y.: Prometheus Books, 2012), 133.

25. *Age* quoted in Halpin, *For My Race*, 2–3, 14–16.

26. Pastor John H. Williams and Committee of the Board of Stewards of Chatsworth Methodist Church to Maj. Gen. Lew Wallace, 26 April 1865, BCA, RG 16, ser. 1, no. 24; Communication from the Mayor and Answer from Genl. Wallace in Relation to Rebel Sympathizers, 1 May 1865, ibid., no. 25; Communication from Col. Woolley in Relation to Mr. Bullock and Others, n.d., ibid., no. 28; Resolution in Relation to Certain Malcontents, 20 April 1865, ibid., no. 903.

27. Communication from the 11th and 12th Wards in Relation to Returned Rebels &c., 2 May 1865, ibid., no. 452.

28. J. Thomas, *History of Baltimore City and County* (Philadelphia: Lewis H. Everts, 1881), 397–398.

29. Based on election returns in the *Sun*, 12 October 1854.

30. *Biographical Cyclopedia of Representative Men of Maryland and the District of Columbia*

(Baltimore: National Biographical Publishing Company, 1879), 159, 486 TM 27; Mary Anne Dunn, "The Life of Isaac Freeman Rasin: Democratic Leader of Baltimore from 1870 to 1907 (MA thesis, Catholic University of America, 1948), 3.

31. *Maryland*, 385; Carl Bode, *Maryland: A Bicentennial History* (New York: W. W. Norton, 1978), 136; Dunn, "Isaac Freeman Rasin," 8; *Sun*, 6 November 1867.

32. Dunn, "Isaac Freeman Rasin," 22; *Sun*, 9 March 1907.

33. *Sun*, 25 September 1867. In addition to its patronage resources, Rasin's office gave him the opportunity to enhance his influence through his authority to issue a variety of state licenses, such as auction licenses. In 1871, he collected almost $300,000 in state license fees—about $5.5 million in current dollars. Ibid., 3 January 1871, 1 May 1873.

34. Dunn, "Isaac Freeman Rasin, 11.

35. *Sun*, 1, 8 October 1922.

36. Sweeney, " 'Sonny' Mahon," 7. It took some time for Mahon to abandon his street-fighting habits. In 1896, when he was a member of the city council's second branch, he was arrested for stabbing another man in a dispute over a promissory note. The victim later refused to press charges, and Mahon was released. See *Sun*, 11, 17 November 1896,

37. *Sun*, 5, 6 June, 24 October 1871.

38. Ibid., 26 October 1871.

39. A Petition from the Residents and Property-Owners on Republican St. Asking That the Name of That Street Be Changed to Carrollton Avenue, 7 May 1874, BCA, RG 16, ser. 1, no. 709.

40. *Sun*, 24 November 1858.

41. Ibid., 9 January 1863.

42. Jones Falls, 18 September 1871, BCA, RG 16, ser. 1, no. 2048.

43. Comm. from the Mayor, 4 September 1871, ibid., no. 2083; *Message of F. C. Latrobe, Mayor, to the First and Second Branches of the City Council of Baltimore* (Baltimore: John Cox, 1876), 53.

44. Comm. from Mayor, 4 September 1871.

45. Ibid.; *Sun*, 17 June 1850, 22 January 1867, 27 January 1874; Joel A. Tarr, *The Search for the Ultimate Sink: Urban Pollution in Historical Perspective* (Akron, Ohio: University of Akron Press, 1996), 296.

46. Comm. from Mayor, 4 September 1871.

47. See Stephen Halliday, *The Great Stink of London: Sir Joseph Bazalgette and the Cleansing of the Victorian Capital* (Thrupp, Stroud, U.K.: Sutton Publishing, 1999).

48. Tarr, *Search for Ultimate Sink*, 12, 134.

49. Communication fr Health Com, 21 May 1872, BCA, RG 16, ser. 2, no. 1020.

50. Ibid.

51. Communication from Chas. P. Kahler, Esq. Civil Engineer about Improvement of the Basin, 23 September 1872, ibid., no. 1021.

52. *Sun*, 22 January, 19 February 1867, 25 August 1869, 24 January 1871.

53. Report of the Joint Special Committee on the Basin with Resolution Annexed, 20/21 October 1872, BCA, RG 16, ser. 1, no. 1271.

54. Report of the Joint Special Committee on the Introduction of the Waters of the Gunpowder River for a Speedy Additional Supply of Water for the City of Baltimore, 12/13 December 1872, ibid., no. 1269; *Sun*, 3 September 1872.

55. Resolution of Enquiry in Relation to the Temporary Water Supply, 25 September 1873, BCA, RG 16, ser. 1, no. 1273; Resolution in Relation to the Permanent Supply of Water from the Gunpowder etc., n.d., ibid., no. 1274.

56. Resolution of Enquiry, 7 April 1874, ibid., no. 1584; Com. from the Mayor, 22 April 1874, ibid., no. 894.

57. Letter Bernard Carter, 4 May 1874, ibid., no. 1117.

58. *Bldg Balto*, 165; *Sun*, 22 November 1877.

59. City Council Committee Report, 27 July 1875, BCA, RG 16, ser. 1, no. 1253.

60. *Sun*, 27 January, 16 March 1875; Resolution Requiring Milo W. Locke to Prepare a Model of His Plan for Improving the Condition of the Basin, 3 May 1875, BCA, RG 16, ser. 1, no. 1451; Resolution to Cut off Sewers from the Basin, 9/22 January 1875, ibid., no. 1454.

61. Alan D. Anderson, *The Origin and Resolution of an Urban Crisis: Baltimore 1890–1930* (Baltimore: Johns Hopkins University Press, 1977), 69. On the Jones Falls Improvement project, see Gerald Michael Macdonald, "Politics and Public Works: Baltimore before Progressivism" (PhD diss., Johns Hopkins University, 1985), 154–174.

62. Charles C. Euchner, "The Politics of Urban Expansion: Baltimore and the Sewerage Question, 1859–1905," *MHM* 86 (Fall 1991): 276.

63. *Sun*, 6 January 1875; Resolution Requesting the Health Commr. to Grant Permits to Night Men to Dump Night Soil, 26/31 May 1875, BCA, RG 16, ser. 1, no. 1268.

64. Communication fr. R. Ritowsky Patentee of Non-Explosive Excavation, 27 January 1875, BCA, RG 16, ser. 1, no. 393; The Odorless Excavating Apparatus Co., *The Odorless Excavating Apparatus for Emptying Vaults, Sinks, Cesspools, Sewers, Cellars, Wells, and Excavations in the Daytime without Offense* (Baltimore: John Murphy, 1875), 7–14.

65. *Sun*, 26 January 1875; Com from Health Commr, 2 June 1875, BCA, RG 16, ser. 1, no. 1162.

66. An Ordinance to Make Provision for an Intercepting Sewer to Divert Sewage from the Waters of the Harbor of Baltimore, 14 March 1877, BCA, RG 16, ser. 1 no. 1869.

67. Comm from Board of Health, 2 January 1873, ibid., no. 603.

68. Communication from City Solicitor, 24 May 1873, ibid., no. [6??]; *Sun*, 21 May 1873; *Ordinances and Resolutions of the Mayor and City Council of Baltimore*, 1880, pp. 139–141.

CHAPTER 23. THE RING

1. Resolution to Place Gas Lamps in Ashland Square, 19/20 May 1873, BCA, RG 16, no. 1467; Resolution in Favor of the Wells and McComas Monument, ibid., no. 1468; Resolution in Favor of 12th of September, ibid., no. 1469.

2. Report of the Joint Standing Committee on Highways with an Ordinance to Provide for Condemning & Opening a Street 66 Feet Wide from Cross Street at Belt Street Southerly & Southeasterly to Connect with the North End of Jackson Street as Opened and Paved, n.d., 1880, ibid., no.1334.

3. John R. Lambert, *Arthur Pue Gorman* (Baton Rouge: Louisiana State University Press, 1953), 31–32, 34.

4. *Md. Polit.*, 21, 36–37.

5. Lambert, *Arthur Pue Gorman*, 33–34.

6. *Md. Polit.*, 22, 308.

7. Lambert, *Arthur Pue Gorman*, 36.

8. Ibid., 60–63.

9. James B. Crooks, "Maryland Progressivism," in *Md. Hist.*, 592–593; *Maryland*, 386; Suzanne Ellery Greene, *Baltimore: An Illustrated History* (Woodland Hills, Calif.: Windsor Publications, 1980), 170.

10. *Baltimore Sun*, 21, 22 February, 24 October, 8, 10 November 1872.

11. Ibid., 16 September 1869, 4 November 1912.

12. See, for example, *Society Visiting List or "Blue Book" for the Season of 1897* (Baltimore: Guggenheimer, Weil and Company, 1896), 152.

13. *Sun*, 5 November 1873; *Maryland*, 388.

14. *Sun*, 16, 22 October 1875.

15. Ibid., 28 October 1875.

16. *Md. Polit.*, 38, 42–43.

17. Lambert, *Arthur Pue Gorman*, 37–38; Paul Winchester, *Men of Maryland since the Civil War: and Sketches of U.S. Senator Arthur Pue Gorman and Successors and Their Connections with Public Affairs* (Baltimore: Maryland County Press Syndicate, 1923), 1:26.

18. S. Z. Ammen, "History of Baltimore, 1875–1895," in *Balto Hist.*, 1:243–244; *Md. Negro*, 42–43.

19. *Md. Polit.*, 44–48; *Sun*, 22, 23 July 1875.

20. *Sun*, 3 November, 1 December 1875, 16 February 1876.

21. Mary Anne Dunn, "The Life of Isaac Freeman Rasin: Democratic Leader of Baltimore from 1870 to 1907" (MA thesis, Catholic University of America, 1948), 30.

22. Ammen, "History of Baltimore," 247; *AM*, 199:357–360.

23. Philip S. Foner, *The Great Labor Uprising of 1877* (New York: Monad Press, 1977), 34; Clifton K. Yearley, "The Baltimore and Ohio Railroad Strike of 1877," *MHM* 51 (September 1956): 192–193.

24. Foner, *Great Labor Uprising*, 34–35; *Sun*, 17 July 1877.

25. Foner, *Great Labor Uprising*, 38–39; Robert V. Bruce, *1877: Year of Violence* (Indianapolis: Bobbs Merrill, 1959), 81–85.

26. Sylvia Gillett, "Camden Yards and the Strike of 1877," in Elizabeth Fee, Linda Shopes, and Linda Zeidman (eds.), *The Baltimore Book: New Views of Local History* (Philadelphia: Temple University Press, 1991), 1–14; *Bldg Balto*, 194–197.

27. Foner, *Great Labor Uprising*, 46–47; Bruce, *1877*, 105–108; Edward Hungerford, *The Story of the Baltimore and Ohio Railroad* (New York: G. P. Putnam's Sons, 1928), 2:141–143; Gillett, "Camden Yards," 7–9.

28. Foner, *Great Labor Uprising*, 48–49; Bruce, *1877*, 112.

29. *Md. Polit.*, 61–62; Ammen, "History of Baltimore," 249.

30. *Sun*, 22 June 1877.

31. Ammen, "History of Baltimore," 248; An Ordinance to Establish a Harbor Commission, 23 February / 14 March 1876, BCA, RG 16, ser. 1, no. 2173; *Ordinances and Resolutions of the City Council*, 1876, 22–23.

32. *Md. Polit.*, 60.

33. Veto Message from His Honor the Mayor, 18 April 1878, BCA, RG 16, ser. 1, no. 1279; Communication from the Mayor, n.d., ibid., no. 1290; Mayor to City Council, 31 January 1878, ibid., no. 1354.

34. *Md. Polit.*, 79; Ammen, "History of Baltimore," 252.

35. *Md. Polit.*, 83.

36. Ibid., 98–99; *Maryland*, 398; Ammen, "History of Baltimore," 258; Dunn, "Isaac Freeman Rasin," 41–42, 44.

37. By 1883, Bonaparte was in contention for a Republican nomination to the state senate. He received unusually extensive coverage in the *Baltimore Sun*. See *Sun*, 25 September, 19 October 1883.

38. Ammen, "History of Baltimore," 260–261.

39. *Md. Polit.*, 125.

40. *Sun*, 14 December 1873, 9 March, 22 April 1877, 6 May 1902; *The Early Eighties: Sidelights on the Baltimore of Forty Years Ago* (Baltimore: Mercantile Trust & Deposit Company, 1924), 4.

41. "Obituary: Mr. J. Frank Morrison," *National Electric Light Bulletin* 10 (July 1916): 545; Tracy Matthew Melton, "Power Networks: The Political and Professional Career of Baltimore Boss J. Frank Morrison," *MHM* 99 (Winter 2004): 459–461, 466; J. F. Morrison to City Council, 14 January 1878, BCA, RG 16, ser. 1, [no number].

42. *Sun*, 11 June 1884; Dunn, "Isaac Freeman Rasin," 37.

43. *Md. Polit.*, 125, 131; M. Rosewin Sweeney, " 'Sonny' Mahon and Baltimore's Irish Machine: Ethnic Politics in a Semi-Southern Setting" (MA thesis, Johns Hopkins University, 1979), 8–9; *Sun*, 9 May 1885.

44. Peter H. Argersinger, "From Party Tickets to Secret Ballots: The Evolution of the Electoral Process in Maryland during the Gilded Age," *MHM* 82 (Fall 1987): 226–227; Ammen, "History of Baltimore," 269.

45. Winchester, *Men of Maryland*, 49.

46. Joseph L. Arnold, "Suburban Growth and Municipal Annexation in Baltimore, 1745–1918," *MHM* 73 (June 1978): 114–117; Report of the Joint Standing Committee on Ways and Means, n.d., 1889, BCA, RG 16, ser. 1, no. 568.

47. Argersinger, "Party Tickets to Secret Ballots," 226.

CHAPTER 24. FIN DE SIÈCLE

1. [Untitled document], n.d., 1888, BCA, RG 16, ser. 1, no. 943; *Bldg Balto*, 203; *Baltimore Sun*, 19 November 1885.

2. Resolution Asking for the Appointment of a Committee to Investigate the Inroads of the Chinese in Balto., 28 January 1889, BCA, RG 16, ser. 1, no. 786.

3. US Census Bureau, *Twelfth Census of the United States, Taken in the Year 1900* (Washington, D.C.: US Census Bureau, 1901), 567; US Census Bureau, "Population of the 100 Largest Cities in the United States: 1790 to 1990" (Population Division, Working Paper no. 27, Washington, D.C., June 1998), table 12.

4. Dieter Cunz, *The Maryland Germans: A History* (Princeton, N.J.: Princeton University Press, 1948), 320–321.

5. Isaac M. Fein, *The Making of an American Jewish Community: The History of Baltimore Jewry from 1773 to 1920* (Philadelphia: Jewish Publication Society of America, 1971), 17.

6. Recommendation by German Am. Dem., 25 January 1888, BCA, RG 9, ser. 2, no. 138; James B. Crooks, *Politics and Progress: The Rise of Urban Progressivism in Baltimore, 1895 to 1911* (Baton Rouge: Louisiana State University Press, 1968), 7. The Turnverein was a gymnastic society with a history of liberal or radical political activism in Germany. Its American offspring concentrated on athletics and socializing.

7. *Bldg Balto*, 181–183; Cunz, *Maryland Germans*, 330–331; Fein, *American Jewish Community*, 28–130.

8. See, for example, Contract of Baltimore General Dispensary, 21 October 1884, BCA, RG 32, no. 263; Baltimore Medical College Dispensary Contract, 9 May 1884, ibid., no. 264; Contract between Mayor and City Council of Baltimore and Eastern Dispensary, 19 June 1884, ibid., no. 265; College of Physicians and Surgeons for 1884, 21 October 1884, ibid., no. 266; Contract with the Home of the Friendless, 1 September 1884, ibid., no. 267.

9. George W. Howard, *The Monumental City: Its Past History and Present Resources*, (Baltimore: J. D. Ehlers & Co., 1873), 44.

10. Unnumbered document filed in BCA with RG 9, ser. 2, no. 1894.

11. *The Ordinances and Resolutions of the Mayor and City Council of Baltimore*, Passed at the Annual Session of 1877, Ordinance no. 14, pp. 11–12; *Sun*, 26 June 1886; Brush's report quoted in ibid., 11 January 1893; ibid., 9 March 1898.

12. Charles Hirschfeld, *Baltimore, 1870–1900: Studies in Social History* (Baltimore: Johns Hopkins University Press, 1941), 36; Communication from the Mayor, 21 March 1887, BCA, RG 16, ser. 1, no. 414.

13. Hirschfeld, *Baltimore*, 34–35.

14. Quoted in ibid., 35–36.

15. Eleanor Bruchey, "The Industrialization of Maryland, 1860–1914," in *Md. Hist.*, 415–417, 420–421; Philip Kahn, Jr., *A Stitch in Time: The Four Seasons of Baltimore's Needle Trades* (Baltimore: Maryland Historical Society, 1989), 33–34.

16. Bruchey, "Industrialization of Maryland," 422–423.

17. James Crooks, "The Baltimore Fire and Baltimore Reform," *MHM* 65 (1970): 11. See also Bruchey, "Industrialization of Maryland," 406–407; Russell Baker, "The Biggest Baltimore Loser of All Time," *New York Times Magazine*, 21 October 1973.

18. Bruchey, "Industrialization of Maryland," 402–403; Hirschfeld, *Baltimore*, 45, 53; *Bldg Balto*, 239.

19. *Bldg Balto*, 241; Hirschfeld, *Baltimore*, 79–80.

20. *The Mayor's Message and Reports of the City Officers for the Year 1888* (Baltimore: John Cox, 1890), 8.

21. *Maryland*, 382–383; Edward Hungerford, *The Story of the Baltimore and Ohio Railroad, 1827–1927* (New York: G. P. Putnam, 1928), 2:216–218.

22. Bruchey, "Industrialization of Maryland," 445–446; Hirschfeld, *Baltimore*, 65–70; *Bldg Balto*, 206.

23. H. E. Shepherd (ed.), *History of Baltimore, Maryland from Its Founding to the Current Year, 1729–1898* (Baltimore: S. B. Nelson, 1898), 238.

24. Communication from the Mayor, 26 October 1886, BCA, RG 16, ser. 1, no. 925.

25. In 1882, the General Assembly approved legislation that reduced the B&O's interest payments. Earnings on the "sinking fund" held by the city register were to be applied to the railroad's payment of interest. Communication from City Counsellor, 8 March 1888, ibid., no. 710.

26. Communication from President B&O RRoad, 27 February 1888, BCA, RG 9, ser. 2, no. 106.

27. Ibid.

28. *Sun*, 28 February 1888.

29. Ibid., 9, 12 March 1888; Communication from the City Counsellor, 8 March 1888; Report of the J. S. Com of Ways & Means upon an Ordinance Approved on 27th Day of December 1853 without Recommendation, BCA, RG 16, ser. 1, no. 734.

30. *Sun*, 1 January 1890.

31. *Baltimore American*, 3 January 1891.

32. Ibid., 17 March 1891; Testimony, Western Md RR Commission, n.d., 1893, BCA, RG 32, ser. 1, no. 151; Testimony of Mr. William Keyser before the Western Maryland Rail Road Commission, 18 January 1893, ibid., no. 157.

33. *Report of the Commission to Investigate the Western Maryland Railroad Company*, 15 May 1893, pp. 34–36; *Sun*, 2 May 1868.

CHAPTER 25. POLITICAL ECONOMY

1. Campbell J. Gibson and Emily Lennon, "Historical Statistics on the Foreign-Born Population of the United States: 1850–1990" (US Bureau of the Census, Population Division Working Paper no. 29, Washington, D.C., February 1999), table 22. In 1890, the average proportion of foreign-born population in the country's 10 largest cities was 32.2 percent—more than twice that for Baltimore.

2. *Baltimore Sun*, 29 September 1903.

3. Martin Shefter, "The Emergence of the Political Machine: An Alternative View," in Willis Hawley et al. (eds.), *Theoretical Perspectives on Urban Politics* (Englewood Cliffs, N.J.: Prentice-Hall, 1976), 29–35; Steven P. Erie, *Rainbow's End: Irish-Americans and the Dilemmas of Urban Machine Politics, 1840–1985* (Berkeley: University of California Press, 1988), 38, 86–87.

4. *Md. Polit.*, 165; S. Z. Ammen, "History of Baltimore," in *Balto Hist.*, 1:268, 273; *Sun*, 28 October 1889.

5. Peter H. Argersinger, "From Party Tickets to Secret Ballots: The Evolution of the Electoral Process in Maryland during the Gilded Age," *MHM* 82 (Fall 1987): 230.

6. *Md. Polit.*, 100.

7. Ibid., 187–188; Ammen, "History of Baltimore," 282.

8. *Md. Polit.*, 100–101; *New York Times*, 24 February 1894.

9. John R. Lambert, *Arthur Pue Gorman* (Baton Rouge: Louisiana State University Press, 1953), 199, 227–228; *Md. Polit.*, 196.

10. *Md. Polit.*, 193.

11. Ibid., 205; Ammen, "History of Baltimore," 287–288; *Sun*, 6 November 1895.

12. *Md. Polit.*, 210–212.

13. Ibid., 217.

14. *Sun*, 26 February 1896.

15. James B. Crooks, *Politics and Progress: The Rise of Urban Progressivism in Baltimore, 1895–1911* (Baton Rouge: Louisiana State University Press, 1968), 87–88.

16. *Sun*, 18 June 1896.

17. John M. Powell, "History of Baltimore, 1870–1912," in *Balto Hist.*, 301; *Sun*, 6, 8 January 1897.

18. Powell, "History of Baltimore," 295.

19. *Sun*, 11 August 1897.

20. Ibid., 28 May 1897, 6 September 1908, 2 May 1915, 23 April 1950.

21. Ibid., 23 April 1891, 18 January 1925, 25 April 1929, 5 March 1946.

22. Ibid., 24 August 1897.

23. Ibid., 24, 25 August, 3 September 1897.

24. Powell, "History of Baltimore," 302–303; *Md. Polit.*, 218; Crooks, *Politics and Progress*, 92.

25. Powell, "History of Baltimore," 305–306; *Balto Financ.*, 36.

26. Lambert, *Arthur Pue Gorman*, 265.

27. John J. Mahon, " 'Politics Is My Business and I Make It Pay': Continuation of the Autobiography of a Baltimore Boss," *Sun*, 15 October 1922.

28. Lambert, *Arthur Pue Gorman*, 292; Powell, "History of Baltimore," 301.

29. M. Rosewin Sweeney, " 'Sonny' Mahon and Baltimore's Irish Machine: Ethnic Politics in a Semi-Southern Setting" (MA thesis, Johns Hopkins University, 1979), 14–15.

30. Powell, "History of Baltimore," 303.

31. *Md. Polit.*, 243–244; Crooks, *Politics and Progress*, 98; Sweeney, " 'Sonny' Mahon," 19.

32. *Md. Polit.*, 244–245; Powell, *History of Baltimore*, 315.

33. *Md. Polit.*, 245; *Baltimore American*, 3 May 1899; *New York Times*, 3 May 1899.

34. *Md. Negro*, 105; Crooks, *Politics and Progress*, 54.

35. *Md. Negro*, 105; H. L. Mencken, *Newspaper Days, 1899–1906* (Baltimore: Johns Hopkins University Press, 1996 [1941]).

36. Lambert, *Arthur Pue Gorman*, 289–290; William George Paul, "The Shadow of Equality: The Negro in Baltimore, 1864–1911" (PhD diss., University of Wisconsin, 1972), 272.

37. *Sun*, 1 May 1901.

38. *Md. Polit.*, 248, 290–291; Suzanne Ellery Greene, *Baltimore: An Illustrated History* (Woodland, Calif.: Windsor Publications, 1980), 174; An Ordinance to Provide for the Creation of an Examination Board for the Fire Department, 18 September 1899, BCA, RG 16, ser. 1, no. 948; *Annual Message of Hon. Thomas G. Hayes, Mayor, to the City Council of Baltimore, September 17th, 1900* (Baltimore: William J. C. Dulany, 1900), 3–4, 64–65.

39. Mencken, *Newspaper Days*, 41–42. Mayor's Message to the City Council for the Year 1900, BCA, RG 16, ser. 1, no. 856.

40. Letters Received by Commr of Health Bosley in Reference to a Hospital for Infectious Diseases, 2 December 1901, BCA, RG 16, ser. 1, no. 466.

41. *Sun*, 17 January, 11 February, 6 March 1902, 10 August 1908. A hospital for patients with infectious diseases would finally be built just east of the Bay View Asylum, years after Hayes left office

42. H. L. Mencken, *Happy Days* (Baltimore: Johns Hopkins Press, 1996 [1936]), 70.

43. Charles C. Euchner, "The Politics of Urban Expansion: Baltimore and the Sewerage Question," *MHM* 86 (Fall 1991): 270–271; Mencken, *Happy Days*, 70; Terry Teachout, *The Skeptic: A Life of H. L. Mencken* (New York: Harper Collins, 2002), 30.

44. Euchner, "Politics of Urban Expansion," 282; Mencken, *Newspaper Days*, 45.

45. *Sun*, 12,15, 29 March 1901; *Baltimore American*, 22 March 1901.

46. Mayor's Communication to Council Submitting a Proposed Ordinance for the Construction of a Sewerage System for Balto. City, 2 September 1902, BCA, RG 16, ser. 1, no. 730; Mayor's

Communication to Council Submitting City Solicitor Whyte's Opinion as to the Construction of a Sewerage System in Balto City, 22 September 1902, ibid., no. 731.

47. *Md. Polit.*, 248; Powell, "History of Baltimore," 329; *Baltimore American*, 16, 19 April, 8 May 1901.

48. *Sun*, 30 March 1894, 4 January, 19 February 1895, 21 September 1897; *Baltimore American*, 7 June 1899. The General Assembly settled the question of sewage disposal. Its 1901 act authorizing the city to borrow up to $12 million for a sewer system required that the system would not, "under any circumstances, permit crude sewerage from the City of Baltimore to empty into the Chesapeake Bay or its tributaries." See *AM*, 215:59.

49. Board of Public Improvements to City Council, 25 October 1902, BCA, RG 16, ser. 1, no. 729.

CHAPTER 26. FIRE, SMOKE, AND SEGREGATION

1. *Baltimore Sun*, 26 October 1903.

2. *Md. Polit.*, 294–295; *Maryland*, 407.

3. *Md. Polit.*, 300; *Sun*, 18 September 1910.

4. *Md. Polit.*, 306–308.

5. John M. Powell, "History of Baltimore," in *Balto Hist.*, 343–348; *Bldg Balto*, 246–247; J. Albert Cassedy, *The Firemen's Record* (Baltimore: Firemen's Relief Association, 1921), 94.

6. Peter B. Peterson, *The Great Baltimore Fire* (Baltimore: Maryland Historical Society, 2004), 176–177; Powell, "History of Baltimore," 351; *Sun*, 19 March 1904.

7. *AM*, 209:145–160, 620–629; Mayor McLane to Second Branch of City Council, 14 January 1904, BCA, RG 16, ser. 1, no. 769.

8. *AM*, 209:148.

9. James B. Crooks, "The Baltimore Fire and Baltimore Reform," *MHM* 100 (Winter 2005): 442; *Bldg Balto*, 247–248; Hamilton Owens, *Baltimore on the Chesapeake* (Garden City, N.Y.: Doubleday, Doran and Co., 1941), 309; *Report of the Burnt District Commission to His Honor the Mayor September 16, 1906* (Baltimore: William J. C. Delany, 1906), 38.

10. Christine Meisner Rosen, "Business, Democracy, and Progressive Reform in the Redevelopment of Baltimore after the Great Fire of 1904," *Business History Review* 63 (Summer 1989): 298–299.

11. *New York Times*, 31 May 1904.

12. *Md. Polit.*, 339–332; Powell, "History of Baltimore," 377.

13. Mayor Veto of Ordinance Authorizing the Burnt District Commission to Straighten & Preserve a Building Line on Baltimore St., 18 June 1904, BCA, RG 16, ser. 1, no. 737.

14. Henry Hind to Mayor Timanus, 23 November and 6 December 1905; to C. J. Bonaparte, 24 November 1905; to Bernard Carter, 24 November 1905; to C. C. McGill, 24 November 1905; and to R. M. Venable, 24 November 1905, BCA, Timanus Administrative Files, folder 41.

15. *Report of the Burnt District Commission*, 28–29; *Sun*, 13 March 1905, 26 October 1907.

16. *Sun*, 25 November 1904; James B. Crooks, *Politics and Progress: The Rise of Urban Progressivism in Baltimore, 1895 to 1911* (Baton Rouge: Louisiana State University Press, 1968), 145–146.

17. Mayor's Appointees on the Commission to Encourage Manufacturing Plants to Locate Here, 5 June 1905, BCA, RG 16, ser. 1, no. 710.

18. A Resolution Declaring It to Be the Policy of the Mayor and City Council of Baltimore for the City to Own and Control Any Railroad Tracks Which May Be Constructed in the New Dock District . . . , 27 November 1905, BCA, RG 16, ser. 1, no. 1065.

19. By some accounts, several deaths resulted from pneumonia contracted while fighting the fire. *Sun*, 7 February 2004.

20. Ibid., 1, 9 September 1906.

21. Grand Jury Report, May Term, 1908, Timanus Files, folder 278. The police-to-civilian ratios are calculated from data on p. 29 of this report.

22. *Sun*, 12 March 1907.

23. *Md. Polit.*, 346.

24. *Baltimore Afro-American*, 16 March 1907.

25. *Md. Negro*, 115.

26. Ibid., 122–125; *Md. Polit.*, 335–336; Crooks, *Politics and Progress*, 62–63; Matthew A. Crenson, "Roots: Baltimore's Long March to the Era of Civil Rights," in Richardson Dilworth (ed.), *The City in American Political Development* (New York: Routledge, 2009), 210–211; S. Z. Ammen, "History of Baltimore, 1870–1895," in *Balto Hist.*, 1:252; *Sun*, 8 November 1905.

27. *Sun*, 3 April 1911.

28. Ibid., 2, 24 March 1907.

29. Ibid., 4 May 1907.

30. Ibid., 22, 28 April 1903.

31. Ibid., 4 November 1909; *Md. Negro*, 130; Powell, "History of Baltimore," 390.

32. *Md. Negro*, 131–132.

33. *Afro-American*, 30 October 1909.

34. *Sun*, 14, 26 September 1910.

35. Ibid., 10 October 1910.

36. Ibid., 27 September 1910.

37. Ibid., 25 October 1910.

38. Edgar Allan Poe to Mayor Mahool, 17 December 1910, BCA, Mahool Administrative Files, RG 9, ser. 14, folder 366(5).

39. Garrett Power, "Apartheid Baltimore Style: The Residential Segregation Ordinances of 1910-1913," *Maryland Law Journal* 42 (1983): 303–305; Samuel West to Mayor Mahool, 6 April 1911, Mahool Files, folder 475.

40. Power, "Apartheid Baltimore Style," 306, 313.

41. *Buchanan v. Warley*, 245 US 60 (1917).

42. *Md. Negro*, 136–137; Crooks, *Politics and Progress*, 147.

43. Janet E. Kemp, *Housing Conditions in Baltimore: Report of a Special Committee of the Association for the Improvement of the Condition of the Poor and the Charity Organization Society* (New York: Arno Press, 1974 [1907]), 16.

44. *Sun*, 1 November 1910.

45. *Afro-American Ledger*, 1 October 1910; Gretchen Boger, "The Meaning of Neighborhood in the Modern City: Baltimore's Residential Segregation Ordinances, 1911–1913," *Journal of Urban History* 35 (January 2009): 244–245.

46. Antero Pietila, *Not in My Neighborhood: How Bigotry Shaped a Great American City* (Chicago: Ivan R. Dee, 2010), 35–36.

47. Boger, "Meaning of Neighborhood," 237–239. See also Carl H. Nightingale, "The Transnational Contexts of Early Twentieth-Century American Urban Segregation," *Journal of Social History* 39 (Spring 2006): 676–679.

48. William Cabell Bruce, *The Negro Problem* (Baltimore: John Murphy, 1891), 13, 22–23.

49. Harvey Johnson, "The Question of Race: A Reply to W. Cabell Bruce, Esq." [1891], African American Perspectives: Pamphlets from the Daniel W. Murray Collection, Library of Congress, Washington, D.C.

50. Edgar Allan Poe to J. Barry Mahool, 17 December 1910, Mahool Files, folder 361.

CHAPTER 27. METROPOLITAN MORALITY

1. *Baltimore Municipal Journal*, 16 March 1917.

2. Antero Pietila, *Not in My Neighborhood: How Bigotry Shaped a Great American City* (Chicago: Ivan R. Dee, 2010), 36, 52–53; *Bldg Balto*, 275–276.

3. *AM*, Biographical Series, SC 3520-1703; *Baltimore Sun*, 15 September 1892.

4. *Sun*, 31 March, 1 April 1911.

5. Ibid., 28 February, 1 March 1911.

6. Ibid., 28 March, 1 April 1911.

7. Ibid., 5 April, 11 November 1911.

8. Ibid., 17 February 1912; M. Rosewin Sweeney, "'Sonny' Mahon and Baltimore's Irish Machine: Ethnic Politics in a Semi-Southern Setting" (MA thesis, Johns Hopkins University, 1979), 31–32.

9. *Sun*, 12 March 1910, 4 March 1911.

10. Ibid., 13, 15, 18 March 1911.

11. Ibid., 11 July 1912, 30 April, 1 May 1913.

12. Maryland House of Delegates, Bill no. 770, 21 March 1912, BCA, Preston Administrative Files, folder 53(5); *Baltimore News*, 24 September 1913.

13. Preston to George A. Frick, 24 February 1912, Preston Files, folder 53(5).

14. Ibid.; *Municipal Journal*, 31 January 1913; Preston to A. S. Goldsborough, 22 September 1915, Preston Files, folder 24(3).

15. *Sun*, 15 August 1915.

16. William McCallister to Preston, 15 March 1913; George A. Frick to Preston, 18 April 1913; Report of the Committee of the Roland Park Civic League regarding the Proposed Borough Bill, n.d.; and Resolution Passed Unanimously at the Regular Meeting of the [Homestead Improvement] Association, 13 October 1913, Preston Files, folder 53.

17. James B. Crooks, "Maryland Progressivism," in *Md. Hist.*, 637.

18. *Sun*, 8 February 1912; City-Wide Congress, "Report of the Committee on the Relation of City and Suburbs," 24 May 1913, Preston Files, folder 53A; DeCourcy Thom to Preston, 20 December 1911, 22 December 1911, and 4 April 1914, ibid., folder 53(7); Mayor James H. Preston, "Fair Play for Baltimore City," n.d., ibid., folder 53(5). The mayor's planned itinerary would take him from Oakland in Garrett County to Salisbury on the Eastern Shore, from October 18 to November 1, 1913; it appears under the title "Subject to Change of Date," ibid., folder 53A.

19. *Sun*, 5, 8 October 1913.

20. Ibid., 9 February 1912.

21. Ibid., 7, 17 October, 23 November, 17 December 1913, 9 January 1914.

22. Ibid., 19 January, 6 April 1914.

23. Joseph L. Arnold, "Suburban Growth and Municipal Annexation in Baltimore, 1745–1918," *MHM* 73 (June 1978): 120.

24. Peter H. Odegard, *Pressure Politics: The Story of the Anti-Saloon League* (New York: Columbia University Press, 1928), 110.

25. Anderson to Preston, 23 January 1912, Preston Files, folder 53.

26. Anderson to Preston, 26 February and 1 March 1912; Preston to Rev. Oscar Lee Owens, 4 March 1912; Preston to J. Harry Smith, 4 March 1912; and Preston to Rev. Gustav A. Briegler, 11 March 1912, ibid.; *Sun*, 26 February, 5 March 1912.

27. F. W. Paap to Mayor and City Council, 3 July 1913, BCA, RG 16, ser. 1, no. 768; E. and G. Scherer to Mayor and City Council, 25 September 1911, ibid., no. 165; George F. Schadel to Mayor and City Council, 24 June 1911, ibid., no. 166.

28. J. Frank Supplee to the First Branch of the City Council of Baltimore, 15 May 1914, ibid., no. 393; Resolution Adopted at a Union Meeting of the Churches of Hampden and Woodberry, 7 June 1914, ibid., no. 349; Luke W. White, President, Sunday Amateur Baseball Association, 1 June 1914, ibid., no. 398; J. Custis Handy to J. Harry Preston, 9 June 1914, Preston Files, folder 21J.

29. Department of Law to Dr. George Keller (Second Branch), 6 June 1914, BCA, RG 16, ser. 1, no. 385.

30. A. S. Goldsborough to Mayor Preston, n.d., Preston Files, folder 21J; Mayor Preston to A. S. Goldsborough, n.d., ibid.

31. Mayor to City Council, 11 June 1914, ibid.

32. Jayme Rae Hill, "From the Brothel to the Block: Politics and Prostitution in Baltimore during the Progressive Era" (MA thesis, University of Maryland Baltimore County, 2008), 42; Donald Hooker, "Pioneer Experiences," *Social Hygiene* 5 (October 1919). The commission extended its investigation to Anne Arundel and Baltimore counties, Cumberland, and Frederick.

33. Society for the Suppression of Vice in Baltimore City, "The Abolition of Red-Light Districts in Baltimore," 1916, p. 3, Enoch Pratt Free Library, Maryland Room, Baltimore; Lauren R. Silberman, *Wicked Baltimore: Charm City Sin and Scandal* (Charleston, S.C.: History Press, 2011), 107.

34. Hill, "From Brothel to Block," 39.

35. Ibid., 42.

36. Pamela Susan Haag, "Commerce in Souls: Vice, Virtue, and Women's Wage Work in Baltimore, 1900–1915," *MHM* 86 (Fall 1991): 296.

37. Maryland Commission on Vice, *Report* (Annapolis: Maryland State Government), 1:2.

38. *Sun*, 28 February 1912; Society for Suppression of Vice, "Abolition of Red-Light Districts," 9.

39. Commission on Vice, *Report*, 1:346, 350.

40. *Sun*, 5 December 1917.

41. Ibid.

CHAPTER 28. WORLD WAR AND MUNICIPAL CONQUEST

1. Secretary Baker to Mayor Preston, 10 August 1917, BCA, Preston Administrative Files, folder 59D(3); Preston to Baker, 13 August 1917, ibid.; Dr. Franklin Martin to Preston, 25 January 1918, ibid., folder 59E(3); "The Responsibility of Civil Communities for Venereal Diseases in the Army," ibid.

2. *Bldg Balto*, 299.

3. Preston to William Howard Taft, 21 June 1915, Preston Files, folder 59(1); Preston to Rufus M. Gibbs et al., 26 November 1915, ibid., folder 59(2); Preston to S. S. Menken, 3 March 1917, ibid., folder 59A(4).

4. Preston to S. Davies Warfield, 3 April 1917, ibid., folder 59B(1); *Baltimore Sun*, 2 April 1917.

5. To the Citizens of Baltimore, n.d., Preston Files, folder 59B(1).

6. Dieter Cunz, *The Maryland Germans: A History* (Princeton, N.J.: Princeton University Press, 1948), 320–324, 395–401.

7. Preston to W. H. Maltbie, 7 June 1916, Preston Files, folder 60(1); *Sun*, 30 March 1914, 24 October 1915, 17 September 1916.

8. *Sun*, 7 May 1915.

9. *Towson New Era*, 12 June 1915.

10. *Sun*, 16 June, 24, 26 September 1915.

11. P. Nicole King, "Baltimore: Seeing the Connections of Research, Teaching, and Service Justice," *Journal of Urban History* 40 (May 2014): 431.

12. Joseph L. Arnold, "Metropolitan Growth and Suburban Annexation," *MHM* 73 (Summer 1978): 121.

13. *Sun*, 30 December 1915.

14. Ibid., 26 November 1915.

15. Anti-Annexation Association to Dr. B. H. Smith, 14 December 1915, Preston Files, folder 68(1); Anti-Annexation Association to Charles Hackett, January 1916, ibid.

16. City-Wide Congress, "Report of Committee on Enlarging the Boundaries of Baltimore City," 20 May 1915, ibid.; A. S. Goldsborough to William J. Ogden, 20 May 1915, ibid., folder 68(2); Preston to A. R. L. Dohme, 21 May 1915, ibid.; A. H. Hecht to Preston, 29 May 1915, ibid.

17. *Sun*, 10 February 1916.

18. Ibid., 18 March 1916.

19. Ibid., 19, 23, 24 March 1916.

20. Ibid., 23 February, 4 March 1916.

21. Ibid., 24 March 1916; Preston to John J. Mahon, 23 March 1916, Preston Files, folder 91A(1).

22. *Sun*, 25, 26 March 1916.

23. Arnold, "Metropolitan Growth," 121; *Sun*, 27, 31 March, 1 April 1916.

24. *Sun*, 1 April 1916.

25. Ibid., 2 April 1916.

26. Ibid., 1 April 1916.

27. Ibid., 5, 14, 30 April 1916.

28. W. W. Davis to Preston, 20 March 1917, Preston Files, folder 68C(3).

29. Eugene H. Beer to Preston, 27 August 1917, ibid., folder 68C(5).

30. *Sun*, 30 May 1916.

31. M. Rosewin Sweeney, " 'Sonny' Mahon and Baltimore's Irish Machine: Ethnic Politics in a Semi-Southern Setting" (MA thesis, Johns Hopkins University, 1979), 22; *Sun*, 20 October 1912.

32. *Sun*, 5 January, 7 April 1915.

33. Ibid., 18 September 1915; Joseph L. Arnold, "The Last of the Good Old Days: Politics in Baltimore, 1920 to 1950," *MHM* 71 (Fall 1976): 444.

34. *Sun*, 30 August 1917.

35. Ibid., 31 August 1917; *Baltimore American*, 24 August 1917.

36. *Sun*, 31 August 1917.

37. Preston to Van Lear Black, 18 September 1917, Preston Files, folder 68C(4). Black was board chairman of the A. S. Abell Company, publisher of the *Baltimore Sun*.

38. *Sun*, 21, 27 September, 2 October 1917.

39. Statement for State Central Committee for Baltimore City, [21 September 1917], Preston Files, folder 68C(5).

40. "Historical Attitudes of the Counties to Baltimore City and Reasons for a Change in This Attitude," n.d., ibid.

41. Lana Stein, *St. Louis Politics: The Triumph of Tradition* (St. Louis: Missouri Historical Society Press, 2002), 250; *St. Louis Post-Dispatch*, 21 August 2013.

42. Horace Edgar Flack, "The Government of the City of Baltimore and Its Relationship to the State Government," in Frederick P. Stieff (ed.), *The Government of a Great American City* (Baltimore: H. G. Roebuck, 1935), 21, 24–25.

43. Preston's handwritten bill of indictment seems to have been a partial outline for an article that appeared in the *Baltimore News*, 1 October 1917, offering a critique of the state's treatment of its largest city—whose residents were largely excluded from the state's judgeships and patronage appointments, whose harbor was the state's most valuable asset, and whose taxes covered the bulk of state expenditures.

44. *Sun*, 13 September, 7 November 1917.

45. Ibid., 2 February, 22, 30 March 1918.

46. *Municipal Journal*, 4 October 1918.

47. *Sun*, 8 March 1918.

CHAPTER 29. CIVIL SERVICE AND PROHIBITION

1. See "Baltimore's Battle Plans" in chapter 28.

2. *Baltimore Sun*, 21 October, 2 November 1917.

3. Ibid., 26 October 1918.

4. Ibid.; Walter L. Clark, "City Service Commission," in Frederick P. Stieff (ed.), *The Government of a Great American City* (Baltimore: H. G. Roebuck, 1935), 252–256.

5. *Sun*, 6 November 1918; Joseph L. Arnold, "The Last of the Good Old Days: Politics in Baltimore, 1920–1950," *MHM* 71 (Fall 1976): 444; Mahon quoted in *Sun*, 22 October 1922.

6. *Sun*, 6 November 1918.

7. Preston to Thomas Hastings, 3 April 1919, BCA, Preston Administrative Files, folder 63E(1);

Antero Pietila, *Not in My Neighborhood: How Bigotry Shaped a Great American City* (Chicago: Ivan R. Dee, 2010), 50–52. For Preston's justification of the St. Paul Street project, see James H. Preston, "Greater Baltimore—A City Beautiful and Useful," *Baltimore Municipal Journal*, 22 November 1918.

8. *Sun*, 1 October 1918.

9. Ibid., 29 October 1911.

10. Ibid., 13 April, 1, 3 May 1919.

11. Ibid., 13 April 1919.

12. *Baltimore American*, 4 April 1919.

13. *Sun*, 1 May 1919.

14. Ibid.

15. Ibid., 7 May 1919, 13 October 1953.

16. Ibid., 7 May 1919.

17. Ibid., 30 April 1919.

18. *Baltimore Afro-American*, 1 July 1911, 31 January 1918, 28 March 1919.

19. *Sun*, 22 April 1922.

20. *Municipal Journal*, 9 May 1919.

21. *Sun*, 21 May 1919.

22. *Baltimore American*, 16, 18, 29, 31 October 1920; *Sun*, 3 November 1920.

23. *Sun*, 3 November 1920.

24. Report of the Committee Appointed by the Mayor to Consider an Amendment to the City Charter with Reference to the Legislative Department of City Government, 12 April 1922, BCA, RG 16, ser. 1, no. 17.

25. *Sun*, 21 June 1921, 27, 29 June 1922.

26. *Baltimore American*, 5 March 1920.

27. Evan Andrew Rea, "The Prohibition Era in Baltimore" (MA thesis, University of Maryland Baltimore County, 2005), 52; *Sun*, 2 September 1925.

28. See "Prelude to Prohibition" in chapter 27; Thomas R. Pegram, "Temperance Politics and Regional Political Culture: The Anti-Saloon League in Maryland and the South, 1907–1915," *Journal of Southern History* 63 (February 1997): 57–58, 83–84, 86.

29. Rea, "Prohibition Era in Baltimore," 24; *Sun*, 18 March 1916.

30. Michael Thomas Walsh, "Wet and Dry in the 'Land of Pleasant Living': Baltimore, Maryland, and the Policy of National Prohibition, 1913–1933" (PhD diss., University of Maryland Baltimore County, 2012), 82–83.

31. Ibid., 93, 102.

32. Rea, "Prohibition Era in Baltimore," 47.

33. George Liebman (ed.), *Prohibition in Maryland: A Collection of Documents* (Baltimore: Calvert Institute for Policy Research, 2011), 6. Ritchie's statement was delivered as part of his second inaugural address in January 1924.

34. Walsh, "Wet and Dry," 190.

35. Ibid., 83; *Maryland*, 468–469.

36. Walsh, "Wet and Dry," 313–314; David E. Kyvig, *Repealing National Prohibition*, 2nd ed. (Kent, Ohio: Kent State University Press, 2000), 39–46.

37. Kyvig, *Repealing National Prohibition*, 46–49; Walsh, "Wet and Dry," 316.

38. *Sun*, 6 December 1933.

39. Ibid., 16 August 1934, 14 July 1942.

40. Liebman, *Prohibition in Maryland*, 26–40.

41. William Cabell Bruce, *The Negro Problem* (Baltimore: John Murphy, 1891). See also "Living Apart" in chapter 26.

42. Walsh, "Wet and Dry," 298.

43. Ibid., 302.

44. Ibid., 305–306.

CHAPTER 30. BOOM TO BUST

1. Edwin Rothman, "Factional Machine-Politics: William Curran and the Baltimore City Democratic Party Organization, 1929–1946" (PhD diss., Johns Hopkins University, 1949), 61; Dorothy M. Brown, "Baltimore between the Wars," in *Md. Hist.*, 675.

2. *Baltimore Sun*, 1 October 1909.

3. Ibid., 17 March 1923; Suzanne Ellery Greene, *Baltimore: An Illustrated History* (Woodland Hills, Calif.: Windsor Publications, 1980), 190.

4. *Sun*, 20 December 1910, 21 December 1911.

5. The commission's membership included William Maltbie, who had once headed Baltimore's independent Bureau of Economy and Efficiency.

6. *Municipal Journal*, 26 May 1924; *Sun*, 27 May, 29 June, 1 September 1923, 16 February, 24, 27 August, 18 September 1924.

7. *Sun*, 10, 12 July 1925.

8. Ibid., 14, 16 July 1925.

9. Articles of Consolidation, n.d., BCA, Preston Administrative Files, RG 9, ser. 17, folder A18-6.

10. *Sun*, 10 August 1924; Theodore Merselles to Howard Jackson, 15 August 1924, BCA, Jackson Administrative Files, RG 9, ser. 17, folder R10(2).

11. Industrial Bureau, Board of Trade, "Baltimore's Industrial Progress in 1923, for Release," Jan. 1, 1924, Jackson Files, folder A18-6.

12. Quoted in Brown, "Maryland between the Wars," 697–698.

13. Eleanor Bruchey, "The Industrialization of Maryland, 1860–1914," in *Md. Hist.*, 421; *Bldg Balto*, 259–261.

14. *Sun*, 23 July 1925; Edward Bieretz to Mayor Jackson, 22 July 1925, Jackson Files, folder B30-219(1); Mayor Jackson to Edward Bieretz, 27 July 1925, ibid.

15. Mayor Jackson to Edward Bieretz, 11 August 1925, Jackson Files, folder B30-219(1); Special Committee on Strike in City Work, 10 August 1925, ibid; *Sun*, 27 August 1925.

16. *Sun*, 7 August 1925. See, for example, Bieretz's early demand that the commission appoint an "impartial" stenographer to keep a word-for-word record of its proceedings. Proceedings of the Current Wage Arbitration Committee, Held in the Mayor's Reception Room, Friday, October 9 [1925], Jackson Files, folder B30-219(4).

17. Executive Session of the Current Wage Arbitration Committee Held in the Mayor's Office, Friday, January 14, 1927, Jackson Files, folder B30-219(4); Opinion by the City Solicitor to the Current Wage Arbitration Committee, 6 November 1925, ibid; *Sun*, 2 November 1926.

18. *Sun*, 20 January 1927.

19. Brown, "Maryland between the Wars," 684–685; Rothman, "Factional Machine-Politics," 37–38.

20. Shannon Lee Parsley, "Presidential Politics and the Building of the Roosevelt Coalition in Baltimore City, 1924–1936" (MA thesis, University of Maryland Baltimore County, 2001), 84–86; *Sun*, 7 April, 1, 4 May 1927; Brown, "Maryland between the Wars," 685.

21. Parsley, "Presidential Politics," 23–27.

22. Marc V. Levine, "Standing Political Decisions and Critical Realignment: The Pattern of Maryland Politics, 1872–1948," *Journal of Politics* 78 (May 1976): 306n, 312–314.

23. Ibid., 314.

24. Quoted in Rothman, "Factional Machine-Politics," 55. After 1923, the First Ward became part of the First District.

25. Jo Ann E. Argersinger, *Toward a New Deal in Baltimore: People and Government in the Great Depression* (Chapel Hill: University of North Carolina Press, 1988), 7.

26. Rothman, "Factional Machine-Politics," 81–82; *Baltimore Observer*, 22 January 1929.

27. Rothman, "Factional Machine-Politics," 14.

28. *Sun*, 18 May 1919, 7 March, 26 April 1924, 17 October, 24 December 1926.

29. Ibid., 8, 25 February, 2 October, 11 December 1928.

30. Ibid., 7 June 1929; Form Letter, 17 June 1929, BCA, Broening Administrative Files, RG 9, ser. 8, folder B1-208(1).

31. H. G. Crosby to Broening, 22 June 1929, Broening Files, folder B1-208(1); William L. Coff to Broening, 5 July 1929, ibid., folder B1-208(2); Gladys Carroll to Broening, 6 July 1929, ibid.; Helen K. Elphinstone to Broening, 27 June 1929, ibid.; *Sun*, 23 November 1928, 23 April 1929.

32. *Sun*, 26 June, 10, 18 July 1929; [Rev.] Luke Schmucker to Broening, 10 July 1929, Broening Files, folder B1-208(2).

33. James Clarke Murray to Broening, 16 July 1929, Broening Files, folder B1-208(2); *Sun*, 18 July 1929.

34. *Sun*, 7 August 1931.

35. Ibid., 17 December 1928.

36. Ibid., 26 January 1929.

37. Ibid., 10 May, 14 December 1929; Frederick Law Olmsted to Robert W. Williams, 2 December 1929, Broening Files, folder D1-427(2).

38. Mrs. Arthur Bibbens (Federation of Republican Women) to Broening, 23 October 1929; James T. Klima (Young Men's Bohemian Democratic Club) to Broening, 13 October 1929; and G. Frank Young (Old Town Merchants and Manufacturers Association), 31 May and 12 June 1929, Broening Files, folder D1-427(1).

39. *Sun*, 17 December 1929, 29 December 1935.

40. Ibid., 1 April 1939, 16 November 1941; Sen. John H. Bouse to Robert Garrett (Chair, Public Improvement Commission), 17 March 1928, Broening Files, folder R10-3(5); Park Heights Improvement Association to Broening, 14 September 1928, ibid., folder R10-3(4).

41. Baltimore Building Trades Alliance to Baltimore Federation of Labor, 13 November 1929; Henry F. Broening, President, Baltimore Federation of Labor, to Broening, 14 November 1929; Broening to Henry F. Broening, 22 November 1929; and Senator E. Milton Altfelt to Broening et al., 22 January 1931, Broening Files, folder D1-427(3).

CHAPTER 31. RELIEF, REPEAL, NEW DEAL

1. Jo Ann E. Argersinger, *Toward a New Deal in Baltimore: People and Government in the Great Depression* (Chapel Hill: University of North Carolina Press, 1988), 1–2; Dorothy M. Brown, "Baltimore between the Wars," in *Md. Hist.*, 697–698.

2. Argersinger, *New Deal in Baltimore*, 3; Brown, "Baltimore between the Wars," 702.

3. Commissioner of Labor and Statistics, press release, 17 March 1930, BCA, Broening Administrative Files, folder N2-24(2); "What Baltimore Is Doing to Meet the Unemployment Crisis," ibid.

4. Nathan L. Smith, Highways Engineer, Department of Public Works, to George J. Clautice, Executive Secretary, Baltimore Association of Commerce, 16 December 1930, ibid., folder N2-24(1); Brown, "Maryland between the Wars," 731; *Sun*, 17 February 1931.

5. Citizens Emergency Relief Committee, 9 March 1931, Broening Files, folder N2-24(1); Broening to W. Frank Roberts, 16 March 1931, ibid.

6. W. Frank Roberts to Broening, 14 February 1931, ibid.

7. Argersinger, *New Deal in Baltimore*, 27; Broening to Chairman of House Judiciary Committee, 1 February 1930, Broening Files, folder G1-585; Ellen M. Holloway to Broening, 15 June 1929, ibid.; *Sun*, 4 March 1931.

8. Edwin Rothman, "Factional Machine-Politics: William Curran and the Baltimore City Democratic Party Organization, 1929–1946" (PhD diss., Johns Hopkins University, 1949), 86, 88.

9. Ibid., 90, 94.

10. Ibid., 89.

11. Argersinger, *New Deal in Baltimore*, 7, 27–28; Charles M. Kimberly, "The Depression in Maryland: The Failure of Voluntarism," *MHM* 70 (Summer 1975): 198; *Sun*, 20, 22 July 1932; John R. Elly to Jackson, 22 July 1932; Commission on Governmental Efficiency and Economy, "Financial Status of the Municipal Corporation of Baltimore," 30 December 1931; Gideon Numsen Stieff to Jackson, 20 July 1932; and Commission on Governmental Efficiency and Economy, "Report on the Financial Situation Facing the City of Baltimore during the Year 1932," 24 March 1932, BCA, Jackson Administrative Files, RG 9, ser. 19, folder B1-38(3).

12. Argersinger, *New Deal in Baltimore*, 29. Many unemployed men drifted into Baltimore from rural Maryland, and elimination of relief funds in the city might induce them to drift back. Ibid., 119.

13. Rothman, "Factional Machine-Politics," 94–95.

14. Argersinger, *New Deal in Baltimore*, 30ff.; *Sun*, 21 June 1933.

15. Sharon Perlman Krefetz, *Welfare Policy Making and City Politics* (New York: Praeger, 1976), 156–157.

16. *Sun*, 22 March 1933; Michael Thomas Walsh, "Wet and Dry in the 'Land of Pleasant Living': Baltimore, Maryland, and the Policy of National Prohibition, 1913–1933" (PhD diss., University of Maryland Baltimore County, 2012), 370–371.

17. Brown, "Maryland between the Wars," 744, 744n.

18. William W. Bremer, " 'Along the American Way': The New Deal's Work Relief Programs for the Unemployed," *Journal of Politics* 62 (December 1975): 636–652.

19. Argersinger, *New Deal in Baltimore*, 46, 98–99.

20. Ibid., 46; Samuel G. Freedman, *The Inheritance: How Three Families and the American Political Majority Moved from Left to Right* (New York: Simon and Schuster, 1996), 89–90.

21. Argersinger, *New Deal in Baltimore*, 186; Brown, "Maryland between the Wars," 764–765; Rothman, "Factional Machine-Politics," 101.

22. Quoted in Rothman, "Factional Machine-Politics," 107.

23. Ibid., 109, 113.

24. Harry W. Kirwin, *The Inevitable Success: Herbert R. O'Conor* (Westminster, Md.: Newman Press, 1962), 202–203.

25. Rothman, "Factional Machine-Politics," 128–129; *Sun*, 5 February 1939.

26. Argersinger, *New Deal in Baltimore*, 201.

27. Bruce M. Stave, *The New Deal and the Last Hurrah: Pittsburgh Machine Politics* (Pittsburgh: University of Pittsburgh Press, 1970), 9–10, 23; Roger Biles, *Memphis in the Great Depression* (Knoxville: University of Tennessee Press, 1986), 82–83; Lyle W. Dorsett, "Kansas City and the New Deal," in John Braeman, Robert H. Bremner, and David Brody (eds.), *The New Deal: The State and Local Levels* (Columbus: Ohio State University Press, 1975), 2:408–409; Andrew J. Badger, "The New Deal and the Localities," in Rhodri Jeffreys-Jones and Bruce Collins (eds.), *The Growth of Federal Power in American History* (DeKalb: Northern Illinois University Press, 1983), 102–115.

28. Rothman, "Factional Machine-Politics," 115.

29. Frank Friedel, *Franklin D. Roosevelt: A Rendezvous with Destiny* (Boston: Little, Brown, 1990), 244–245, 520–521.

30. A 1934 study sponsored by the Baltimore Urban League estimated that 400 black social clubs operated within the city's black community, as well as more than 20 fraternal organizations and a variety of recreational and social welfare groups, such as the black YMCA. There were also numerous Democratic and Republican neighborhood clubs and women's organizations, such as a black chapter of American University Women. The study found 71 black neighborhood clubs with a collective membership of over 5,000. Average Sunday attendance at the city's black Protestant churches was 87,097, and there were four predominantly black Roman Catholic churches with a total membership of 9,000. See Andor D. Skotnes, "The Black

Freedom Movement and the Workers Movement in Baltimore, 1930–1939" (PhD diss., Rutgers University, 1991), 51–52, 78.

31. Verda Welcome, *My Life and Times* (Englewood Cliffs, N.J.: Henry House, 1991), 44, 192; Marion Orr, *Black Social Capital: School Reform in Baltimore, 1986–1998* (Lawrence: University of Kansas Press, 1999), 49; Arthur M. Bragg, Josiah F. Henry, Jr., and Edward C. Ridgely to Jackson, n.d., Jackson Files, RG 9, ser. 20, folder A16.

32. Orr, *Black Social Capital*, 48.

33. Skotnes, "Black Freedom Movement," 193, 197; Denton L. Watson, *Lion in the Lobby: Clarence Mitchell, Jr.'s Struggle for the Passage of Civil Rights Laws* (New York: William Morrow, 1990), 89.

34. Genna Rae McNeil, "Youth Initiative in the African American Struggle for Racial Justice and Constitutional Rights: The City-Wide Young People's Forum of Baltimore, 1931–1941," in John Hope Franklin and Genna Rae McNeil (eds.), *African Americans and the Living Constitution* (Washington, D.C.: Smithsonian Institution Press, 1995), 65–66; Skotnes, "Black Freedom Movement," 221–224.

35. Larry Gibson, *Young Thurgood: The Making of a Supreme Court Justice* (Amherst, N.Y.: Prometheus Books, 2012), 159–161.

36. Skotnes, "Black Freedom Movement," 228.

37. Ibid., 229–230, 235; Gibson, *Young Thurgood*, 162–164.

38. Gibson, *Young Thurgood*, 165.

39. Ibid., 233.

40. Quoted in David Taft Terry, " 'Tramping for Justice': Dismantling Jim Crow in Baltimore, 1942–1954" (PhD diss., Howard University, 2002), 73; Gibson, *Young Thurgood*, 254–256.

41. W. Edward Orser, "Neither Separate Nor Equal: Foreshadowing *Brown* in Baltimore County, 1935–1937," *MHM* 92 (Spring 1997): 5–35. Orser (pp. 22–23) quotes from Thurgood Marshall, "Draft Statement of Baltimore County Case," presented 10 September 1937, NAACP Papers, Library of Congress, Washington, D.C.

42. Terry, "Tramping for Justice," 71; George H. Callcott, *Maryland and America, 1940 to 1980* (Baltimore: Johns Hopkins University Press, 1985), 147; Juan Williams, *Thurgood Marshall: American Revolutionary* (New York: Times Books, 1998), 73, 76–77; Hayward Farrar, *The Baltimore* Afro-American, *1892–1950* (Westport, Conn.: Greenwood Press, 1998), 180–181.

43. Watson, *Lion in the Lobby*, 99.

CHAPTER 32. DEMOCRATIC HARMONY, REPUBLICAN VICTORY

1. Edwin Rothman, "Factional Machine-Politics: William Curran and the Baltimore City Democratic Organization, 1929–1946" (PhD diss., Johns Hopkins University, 1949), 138–139.

2. *Baltimore Sun*, 30 August 1940.

3. Roulhac Anderson to Jackson, 4 September 1940; Carl O. Long to Jackson, 31 August 1940; John M. Whitmore to Jackson, 30 August 1940; and Jackson to W. T. Saunders, 3 September 1940, BCA, Jackson Administrative Files, RG 9, ser. 20, folder G1-1630.

4. *Sun*, 31 October 1940.

5. Ibid., 6 November 1940.

6. Jackson to Roosevelt, 26 May, 7 July, and 19 October 1941, Jackson Files, folder G1-2634.

7. *Sun*, 28 May, 20, 21, 26 October 1941.

8. Rothman, "Factional Machine-Politics," 142–149; *Sun*, 11 January 1942.

9. *Sun*, 30 August, 5 September 1941.

10. Rothman, "Factional Machine-Politics," 147–148; Harry W. Kirwin, *The Inevitable Success: A Biography of Herbert R. O'Conor* (Westminster, Md.: Newman Press, 1962), 353–354.

11. Rothman, "Factional Machine-Politics," 153; *Sun*, 5 May 1943.

12. *Sun*, 1, 5 May 1943.

13. Rothman, "Factional Machine-Politics," 155–157.

14. George H. Callcott, *Maryland and America, 1940 to 1980* (Baltimore: Johns Hopkins University Press, 1985), 133.

15. *Sun*, 8 January 1944.

16. Ibid., 6 June 1943.

17. McKeldin to Hamilton F. Atkinson, Police Commissioner, 26 June 1943, BCA, McKeldin Administrative Files, folder T20.

18. *Sun*, 2, 5, 10, 20 February, 12 March 1942.

19. *Baltimore Afro-American*, 14 February 1942.

20. Ibid., 2 May 1942; Kirwan, *Inevitable Success*, 298–299.

21. *Sun*, 25 September 1942; *Afro-American*, 2 October 1942; David Taft Terry, "Tramping for Justice: Dismantling Jim Crow in Baltimore, 1942–1954" (PhD diss., Howard University, 2002), 91–92.

22. Terry, "Tramping for Justice," 102–103; *Sun*, 24 March 1943.

23. Terry, "Tramping for Justice," 104–105.

24. Ibid., 121; *Afro-American*, 15 May 1943.

25. Kenneth Durr, "When Southern Politics Came North: The Roots of White Working-Class Conservatism in Baltimore, 1940–1964," *Labor History* 37 (Summer 1996): 311–312; Kenneth D. Durr, *Behind the Backlash: White Working-Class Politics in Baltimore, 1940–1980* (Chapel Hill: University of North Carolina Press, 2003), 64.

26. *Sun*, 24 March 1943.

27. Ibid., 3 April 1943; Baltimore Housing Authority, "Low Rent Housing Survey, 1941," table IIA, McKeldin Files, RG 9, ser. 22, folder G1-38(2); Cleveland R. Bealmear, Chairman, Housing Authority of Baltimore City, "Post-War Housing Program for Baltimore, General Statement," January 1944, ibid.

28. *Sun*, 3, 10 April 1943.

29. Ibid., 21, 23, 24 April 1943.

30. Ibid., 28 April, 10, 11 June 1943; Statement of Mayor McKeldin, 9 June 1943, McKeldin Files, folder G1-48(1).

31. *Sun*, 29 June, 6, 9 July 1943; Oliver C. Winston, Director, Region III, to Thomas J. S. Waxter, President, Citizens Planning and Housing Association, 2 July 1943, McKeldin Files, folder G1-48(3). A coalition of labor leaders and local clergy, both black and white, was prepared to send a delegation to the White House to overcome local indecision about the location of black housing. They had scheduled a meeting with Roosevelt aide Stephen Early. A meeting with the head of the PHA induced them to abandon their White House appointment. See *Sun*, 10 July 1943.

32. *Sun*, 13 July 1943.

33. Ibid., 14 July 1943; *Afro-American*, 24 July 1943. A more detailed presentation of McKeldin's nonposition on housing for black workers appears in Statement of Mayor McKeldin, 9 June 1943, McKeldin Files, folder G1-48(1).

34. *Sun*, 21, 27 July, 6 August 1943; Mayor McKeldin to Members of the Baltimore City Council, 23 July 1943, McKeldin Files, folder G1-48(4). The legislation had been drafted by three attorneys representing groups opposed to use of the Herring Run site. One of them was William Curran.

35. *Sun*, 6 August 1943.

36. Herbert Emmerich to McKeldin, n.d., McKeldin Files, folder G1-48(5); McKeldin to Oliver C. Winston, Regional Director, Federal Public Housing Authority, 23 July 1943, ibid.

37. Emmerich to McKeldin, n.d.; McKeldin to Emmerich, 11 August 1943; and McKeldin to R. L. Cochran (Acting Commissioner), National Housing Authority, 16 August 1943, ibid.

38. *Sun*, 11, 17 August, 1 September 1943.

39. Ibid., 1 September 1943.

40. Ibid., 1, 5, 13 October 1943.

41. Ibid., 25 October 1943.

42. Thomas J. Sugrue, "All Politics Is Local: The Persistence of Localism in Twentieth-Century America," in Meg Jacobs, William J. Novak, and Julian E. Zelizer (eds.), *The Democratic Experiment: New Directions in American Political History* (Princeton, N.J.: Princeton University Press, 2003), 309.

43. *Sun*, 25 July 1943, 18 February 1945.

44. Ibid., 31 January, 9, 10 February 1945.

45. Ibid., 23 April, 11 June 1944; Simon Sobeloff, City Solicitor, to McKeldin, 17 January 1944, McKeldin Files, folder G1-38(3); McKeldin to Bancroft Hill, President, Baltimore Transit Company, 26 April 1944, ibid., folder G1-38(1).

46. Statement made by Gen. Schley, n.d., McKeldin Files, folder A4(1); Robert Bonnell, Chairman, Baltimore Aviation Commission, to McKeldin, 9 May 1946, ibid.; Baltimore City Aviation Commission, "Master Plan Report, Proposed City Airport, Friendship Church Site," 21 June 1946, ibid., folder A4(3).

47. *Sun*, 3 April 1945.

48. Ibid.; *Afro-American*, 20 January 1945.

49. *Sun*, 20 April 1944.

50. Ibid., 11 February, 12 June 1946.

51. Callcott, *Maryland and America*, 134.

CHAPTER 33. D'ALESANDRO AND HIS DEMOCRATS

1. Edwin Rothman, "Factional Machine-Politics: William Curran and the Baltimore City Democratic Party Organization, 1929–1946" (PhD diss., Johns Hopkins University, 1949), 159.

2. *Baltimore Sun*, 2 September 1946.

3. Ibid., 22 February, 5 March 1947.

4. Ibid., 14 March 1947.

5. Ibid., 2 April, 7 May 1947.

6. Kenneth D. Durr, *Behind the Backlash: White Working-Class Politics in Baltimore, 1940–1980* (Chapel Hill: University of North Carolina Press, 2003), 20, 54–56.

7. *Sun*, 10 December 1947.

8. Ibid., 20 December 1947, 3, 4 January 1948.

9. Ibid., 10, 25 February, 30 May 1948, 2, 6 April 1949.

10. Ibid., 12 September 1947.

11. Ibid., 9 January 1948.

12. Ibid., 6 July, 22 August, 17 September 1947, 5 November 1948.

13. Ibid., 7 August 1948; ibid., 27 August 1947.

14. Ibid., 30 September 1948.

15. Ibid., 28 August, 27 November 1948; John Kronau et al. to D'Alesandro, 26 November 1948, BCA, D'Alesandro Administrative Files, folder 196(2). Trucking interests still felt sidelined. Baltimore's Industrial Traffic Managers Association complained that it was denied the opportunity to testify before the port committee. It sought "improved approaches to the piers by both rail and roadways" and submitted a report to the Baltimore Association of Commerce emphasizing the need for improved trucking facilities. See *Sun*, 26 February 1949.

16. *Sun*, 26 September 1949; *Bldg Balto*, 353.

17. *Sun*, 13 March 1950.

18. Ibid., 27 August, 24 October 1950.

19. Ibid., 26 June 1950, 26 February 1952.

20. George H. Callcott, *Maryland and America, 1940 to 1980* (Baltimore: Johns Hopkins University Press, 1985), 86.

21. *Maryland*, 558–559; *Sun*, 18 November 1947, 22 October 1949, 27 March 1950, 19 August 1951.

22. *Sun*, 5 February, 25, 27 March 1953.

23. Callcott, *Maryland and America*, 200.

24. W. Edward Orser, *Blockbusting in Baltimore: The Edmondson Village Story* (Lexington: University Press of Kentucky, 1994), 1; Matthew A. Crenson, "Roots: Baltimore's Long March to the Era of Civil Rights," in Richardson Dilworth (ed.), *The City in American Political Development* (New York: Routledge, 2009), 213.

25. *Sun*, 28 May, 12 June 1951.

26. Lillie Mae Jackson to D'Alesandro, 19 January 1948, D'Alessandro Files, folder 156; Lillie Mae Jackson to D'Alesandro, 24 July 1948, ibid., folder 97.

27. Robert Garrett to D'Alesandro, 27 January 1948, ibid., folder 97.

28. Ibid.

29. D'Alesandro to Garrett, 29 January 1948, ibid.

30. *Sun*, 10 July 1951; ibid., 5 June 1950.

31. Ibid., 24, 30 January, 23, 24, 26 February 1951.

32. Ibid., 25 March 1951.

33. Ibid., 28 March 1951.

34. Ibid., 5, 11, 15 April 1951.

35. Ibid., 10 May, 25 June 1951.

36. Department of Finance, Central Payroll Bureau, "Comparative Statement Re Negro Employment, 1946 vs. 1948," 14 June 1948, D'Alesandro Files, folder 156.

37. *Baltimore Afro-American*, 24 November 1951; *Sun*, 14 August 1952. A further complication for Local 825 was its simultaneous dispute with the national Teamsters Union, which ordered the dismissal of the local's officers and seizure of its assets because it had threatened to declare its independence from the Teamsters. See *Sun*, 16, 18 February 1952.

38. *Sun*, 3, 6 January 1953.

39. Durr, *Behind the Backlash*, 79; Board of Estimates Minutes, 31 December 1952, D'Alesandro Files.

40. *Sun*, 12 November 1952, 2, 3, 6, 7, 17 January 1953; Board of Estimates Minutes, 5, 6, 14 January 1953, D'Alesandro Files, folder 301.

41. *Sun*, 25 January 1951, 8, 23 January, 2 February 1952.

42. Howell C. Baum, *Brown in Baltimore: School Desegregation and the Limits of Liberalism* (Ithaca, N.Y.: Cornell University Press, 2010), 69–70; Elinor Pancoast and Others, *Report of a Study on Desegregation in the Baltimore City Schools* (Baltimore: Maryland Commission on Interracial Problems and the Baltimore Commission on Human Relations, 1956), 30; David Taft Terry, "Tramping for Justice: Dismantling Jim Crow in Baltimore" (PhD diss., Howard University, 2002), 336–340.

43. "Segregation," *Sun*, 14 September 1954.

44. "Integration at Southern Stirs Unrest," ibid., 2 October 1954; "19 Groups O.K. School Board Firmness on Desegregation," ibid., 3 October 1954; "Unrest Is Laid to Agitators' 'Cruel' Calls," ibid., 4 October 1954; "Pickets Use NAAWP Technique," *Afro-American*, 9 October 1954; "Judge Favors Mixed Schools," ibid., 16 October 1954.

45. Pancoast et al., *Study on Desegregation*, 69; Baum, *Brown in Baltimore*, 84–86.

46. Robert L. Crain, *The Politics of School Desegregation* (Chicago: Aldine Publishing Company, 1968), 72.

47. Quoted in Durr, *Behind the Backlash*, 96.

48. Pancoast et al., *Study on Desegregation*, 39.

49. Ibid., 31. See also Crain, *Politics of School Desegregation*, 75, 82.

50. Callcott, *Maryland and America*, 151. D'Alesandro quoted in Terry, "Tramping for Justice," 333.

51. Pancoast et al., *Study on Desegregation*, 28; Odell Smith, "Preparation for End of Segregation Is Praised," *Afro-American*, 7 September 1954; Baum, *Brown in Baltimore*, 54–57, 68–69.

52. Callcott, *Maryland and America*, 152.

53. Durr, *Behind the Backlash*, 15–16.

54. C. Fraser Smith, *Here Lies Jim Crow: Civil Rights in Maryland* (Baltimore: Johns Hopkins University Press, 2008), 182.

55. *Sun*, 2, 14, 15, 29 June 1954.

56. W. Theodore Durr, "The Conscience of a City: A History of the Citizens' Planning and Housing Association and Efforts to Improve Housing for the Poor in Baltimore, Maryland, 1937–1954" (PhD diss., Johns Hopkins University, 1972), 377–378, 399, 401–402.

57. Ibid., 315.

58. *Sun*, 5 April 1953.

59. Clarence Miles, Chairman, Greater Baltimore Committee, to D'Alesandro, 27 January 1956, D'Alesandro Files, folder 43; *Sun*, 7 January 1955, 29 August 1956; Commission on Governmental Efficiency and Economy, "Civic Center Performance Spotlights Faulty Planning Practice," August 1957, no. 514; "Proposed Loan for Civic Center and Civic Center Projects," June 1958, no. 541; and Civic Center Authority to Board of Estimates, 7 February 1956, D'Alesandro Files, folder 43.

60. Urban Renewal Subcommittee, "Report to the Greater Baltimore Committee," 15 November 1955, D'Alesandro Files, RG 9, ser. 23, folder 83(1).

61. *Sun*, 23 September 1956, 1 January 1957.

62. Ibid., 14 July, 23 August 1957.

63. Callcott, *Maryland and America*, 87; "New Heart for Baltimore," *Architectural Forum*, June 1958, pp. 88–92; Baltimore Urban Renewal and Housing Agency, "Review of Charles Center Proposal: A Report to Mayor Thomas D'Alesandro, Jr.," 30 July 1958, p. 6., D'Alesandro Files, folder 39.

64. Martin Millspaugh (ed.), *Baltimore's Charles Center: A Case Study of Downtown Renewal* (New York: Urban Land Institute, 1964), 9.

65. Ibid., 14–15; Speech by Mayor Thomas D'Alesandro, Jr., at Meeting Sponsored by the Greater Baltimore Committee on the Report of the Urban Renewal Study Board on Monday, October 29, 1956, D'Alesandro Files, folder 339(4).

66. Speech by Mayor D'Alesandro.

67. "Charles Center–Inner Harbor Management, Inc., Fact Sheet," Martin Millspaugh Archive, Johns Hopkins University, Milton S. Eisenhower Library, Special Collections, box 9, folder 13, "Baltimore's Inner Harbor: A History of Ideas, 1969," ibid., folder 14; David A. Wallace, "An Insider's Story of the Inner Harbor," *Planning*, September 1979, pp. 20–24

CHAPTER 34. I'M ALL RIGHT, JACK

1. *Baltimore Sun*, 8 May 1953, 3, 9, 19 November 1954.

2. Ibid., 29 June 1954.

3. Ibid., 10 August 1957; *Schaefer*, 42.

4. *Sun*, 1 October 1957.

5. Ibid., 30 October 1958.

6. Ibid., 5, 6 November 1958.

7. Ibid., 21 December 1958, 19 January, 27 February, 1, 5 March 1959.

8. Ibid., 3 April 1959.

9. *Schaefer*, 40–41.

10. *Sun*, 9 April 1959.

11. Ibid., 30 April, 1 May 1959.

12. Ibid., 1–4, 10 May 1959.

13. Ibid., 4 May, 3 July, 25 September 1960.

14. For release PMs of Tuesday, Feb. 16, 1960, BCA, RG 9, ser. 24, folder 60(2). "PMs" refers to evening newspapers.

15. Planning Council, Greater Baltimore Committee, "Housing Code Enforcement: A Report to Mayor J. Harold Grady," February 1961, ibid., folder 97; Marjorie Teitelbaum, President, Baltimore League of Women Voters, to Mayor Grady, ibid., folder 246(1); Frances H. Morten, Executive Director, Citizen's Planning and Housing Agency, to Mayor Grady, 19 May 1960, ibid.; *Sun*, 21 July 1961.

16. *Sun*, 6 May 1961.

17. Ibid., 27 June 1961.

18. Ibid., 7 December 1962.

19. Statement by Mayor Philip Goodman, 26 January 1963, BCA, RG 9, ser. 24, folder 115.

20. *Sun*, 19 August 1962.

21. *Schaefer*, 56; *Sun*, 13 March 1962.

22. *Sun*, 12 December 1962, 6 March 1963.

23. Ibid., 18 January, 11, 13 February, 6 March 1963.

24. Ibid., 14, 25, 28, 29 March, 5 April 1963.

25. Ibid., 8 April 1963; ibid., 21 March, 15 April 1963. In Baltimore, the Democratic Party's straight-ticket voters are known as "muldoons."

26. Ibid., 8, 9 May 1963.

27. Ibid., 18 November 1949, 12 June, 28 December 1953, 9, 24 February 1954, 2 February 1955, 16 October 1962.

28. David Barton, Chairman, City Planning Commission, to Mayor McKeldin, 16 December 1965, BCA, RG 9, ser. 25, folder 84(3); News release from the Office of Mayor Theodore R. McKeldin, 18 September 1966, ibid., folder 84(2).

29. Expressway Design Advisory Committee to McKeldin, 10 February 1965, BCA, McKeldin Administrative Files, folder 163; McKeldin to Walter Sondheim, 27 May 1964, ibid.

30. *Sun*, 23 July, 22 August 1963.

31. Ibid., 7, 27 September 1963.

32. Ibid., 5 October, 31 December 1963, 8 January 1964.

33. Ibid., 29 November 1964.

34. Statement by Mayor McKeldin, "Coordination of Baltimore's Interstate Expressway Program," 4 February 1965, McKeldin Files, folder 164(2).

35. George Fallon to McKeldin, 5 March 1965, ibid.

36. Thomas Ward to Abel Wolman et al., 1 February 1965, ibid.

37. Robert Levi and Albert Hutzler to McKeldin, 17 March 1967, ibid., folder 183(1); Report to the Honorable Theodore R. McKeldin, Mayor of Baltimore City, from the Special Mass Transit Committee of the Committee for Downtown and the Greater Baltimore Committee, ibid.

38. Statement of Mayor Theodore R. McKeldin, *for immediate release*, 25 May 1965, McKeldin Files, folder 164(1).

39. Eugene M. Feinblatt to McKeldin, 29 June 1965; Philip Darling to Joseph Allen, 5 August 1965; and R. L. Steiner to Joseph Allen, 6 August 1965, ibid.

40. *Sun*, 13 April 1965, 18 March 1983.

CHAPTER 35. SLOW-MOTION RACE RIOT

1. *Baltimore Sun*, 5, 18 June 1963.

2. Ibid., 11, 13, 20 June 1963; McKeldin to Rev. Marion Bascom, 14 June 1963, BCA, McKeldin Administrative Files, RG 9, ser. 25, folder 206(2).

3. *Sun*, 29 July, 11 August 1963.

4. Ibid., 12 October 1963.

5. Ibid., 22 October 1963, 22, 25 February 1964; *Baltimore Afro-American*, 26 October 1963; C. Fraser Smith, *Here Lies Jim Crow: Civil Rights in Maryland* (Baltimore: Johns Hopkins University Press, 2008), 231–232.

6. *Sun*, 21 January, 8 May, 25 November 1964, 14, 21 November 1965, 18 January, 6 February, 16 November 1966, 26 September 1967.

7. Shriver to McKeldin, September 6, 1965, McKeldin Files, folder 107(1).

8. Meeting on Comprehensive Plan for Attacking Poverty in the City of Baltimore—"Briefing Session," 13 March 1964, McKeldin Files, folder 207; Peter Bachrach and Morton S. Baratz, *Power and Poverty: Theory and Practice* (New York: Oxford University Press, 1970), 162–163; Health and Welfare Council of the Baltimore Area, Inc., "A Letter to Ourselves," 21 July 1961, University of Baltimore, Langsdale Library, Special Collections, '68 Collection.

9. *Sun*, 8 March, 11 August, 6 December 1964; George H. Callcott, *Maryland and America, 1940 to 1980* (Baltimore: Johns Hopkins University Press, 1985), 204.

10. *Sun*, 12, 18 December 1964.

11. Ibid., 18 December 1962, 13 June 1963; Statement by Mayor Goodman, 26 January 1963, BCA, Grady-Goodman Administrative Files, RG 9, ser. 24, folder 115; Bachrach and Baratz, *Power and Poverty*, 82–83.

12. *Sun*, 30 June 1965.

13. *Afro-American*, 22 May 1965.

14. McKeldin to Rep. Carlton Sickles et al., 8 October 1965, McKeldin Files, folder 107(1); *Frederick News*, 10 February 1966.

15. James Griffin to McKeldin, 4 January 1965, McKeldin Files, folder 107(3).

16. Walter Carter and John Roemer, III, to McKeldin, 9 August 1965, ibid., folder 107(6); Statement of Mr. Morton Macht, 27 August 1965, ibid.

17. Statement of the Community Action Commission to the Board of Estimates, 19 October 1965, ibid., folder 107(2); *Sun*, 10 December 1965.

18. *Sun*, 9 December 1965.

19. Ibid., 30 November 1965.

20. Ibid., 8, 9 December 1965.

21. Ibid., 10 December 1965; *Afro-American*, 25 December 1965.

22. *Sun*, 22 December 1965, 8 March 1966.

23. Ibid., 17, 18, 22 January 1966.

24. Ibid., 15 April 1966.

25. Ibid., 27 April 1966.

26. Louis C. Goldberg, "CORE in Trouble: A Social History of the Organizational Dilemmas of the Congress of Racial Equality Target City Project in Baltimore (1965–1967)" (PhD diss., Johns Hopkins University, 1970), 2, 20.

27. For example, Frank L. Williams, President, Interdenominational Ministerial Alliance, to McKeldin, 7 May 1966; Rev. Thomas M. Downing to McKeldin, 3 May 1966; Charles H. Butler to McKeldin, 19 April 1966; and Lillian L. Isbell to McKeldin, [n.d.] May 1966, McKeldin Files, folder 126.

28. McKeldin to Mrs. Lillian Isbell, 1 June 1966, ibid.

29. *Sun*, 17, 21 April 1966.

30. Ibid., 22 June 1966.

31. Goldberg, "CORE in Trouble," 85.

32. "Discussion Guide for Meeting with Community Leaders," McKeldin Files, folder 126; Statement of Mayor Theodore McKeldin, for release at 10:30 a.m., Friday, June 3, 1966, ibid.

33. *Sun*, 3, 5 June 1966.

34. Bachrach and Baratz, *Power and Poverty*, 71.

35. Goldberg, "CORE in Trouble," 9–11, 22, 26, 31.

36. Ibid., 33–39.

37. *Afro-American*, 14 May 1966.

38. Goldberg, "CORE in Trouble," 62–64; *Sun*, 3, 7 May 1966; Barbara Mills and Sampson

Green (CORE Housing Committee) and H. Wharton Smith (Public Accommodations Committee) to McKeldin, 8 May 1966, McKeldin Files, folder 126.

39. McKeldin to Barbara Mills, 11 May 1966, ibid.

40. *Sun*, 20, 21, 25 May, 4 June 1966; *Afro-American*, 4 June 1966.

41. Goldberg, "CORE in Trouble," 110–111, 114.

42. Ibid., 104–105, 123; *Sun*, 31 May 1966.

43. Goldberg, "CORE in Trouble," 129, 133–134.

44. *Sun*, 2, 5 July 1966.

45. Statement by Mayor Theodore R. McKeldin, for Delivery, Annual Convention of the Congress of Racial Equality, July 1, 1966, [delivered on July 3], McKeldin Files, folder 126; *Sun*, 4 July 1966.

46. McKeldin to McKissick 28 September 1966, McKeldin Files, folder 126; McKissick to McKeldin, 4 October 1966, ibid.

47. *Sun*, 6 October 1966.

48. Ibid., 20 July 1966.

49. Ibid., 2 February, 10 April 1967.

50. Ibid., 7 February 1967.

51. Ibid., 16 February 1967.

52. Bachrach and Baratz, *Power and Poverty*, 84.

53. *Sun*, 29 June 1967.

CHAPTER 36. RACIAL BREAKDOWN

1. *Baltimore Sun*, 26 June 1967.

2. Ibid., 2, 22 July 1967; *Baltimore Afro-American*, 8 July 1967; Pollack's press release in *Sun*, 23 July 1967.

3. *Sun*, 3 September 1967.

4. Ibid., 18 September 1967; ibid., 8 September 1967.

5. Ibid., 8 November, 6, 10 December 1967.

6. *Afro-American*, 9 December 1967.

7. *Sun*, 11, 14 January, 9 February, 5 March 1968.

8. Ibid., 10, 26 February, 30 March 1968.

9. See the opening discussion in chapter 7.

10. Raymond Mohl, "Stop the Road: Freeway Revolts in American Cities," *Journal of Urban History* 30 (July 2004): 689.

11. "Analysis of Freeway Proposal" (statement by Herbert M. Brune, Jr. to Harbor Crossing–Freeway Committee, October 11, 1944; as supplemented by statement of October 13, 1944), University of Baltimore, Langsdale Library, Special Collections, Movement Against Destruction (MAD) Collection, ser. 7, http:/ubalt.libguides.com/mad; Mencken quoted in James Dilts, "A Brief History of Baltimore's Transportation Planning," typescript, n.d., 1977, ibid; *Sun*, 22 January 1945.

12. Andrew Giguere, "And Never the Twain Shall Meet" (MA thesis, Ohio University, 2008), 90–92.

13. Michael P. McCarthy, "Baltimore's Highway Wars Revisited," *MHM* 93 (Summer 1998): 140; Mohl, "Stop the Road," 690.

14. Giguere, "Never the Twain," 93, 99–100.

15. Ibid., 103; *Sun*, 31 January 1962.

16. Mohl, "Stop the Road," 698. On disagreements among city leaders, see Giguere, "Never the Twain," 101–109.

17. Dilts, "Brief History," 3.

18. Mark Reutter, "Expressway Paper," typescript, p. 27, n.d., MAD Collection, ser. 7, box A7; Giguere, "Never the Twain," 145.

19. Mark H. Rose and Raymond A. Mohl, *Interstate: Highway Politics and Policy since 1939* (Knoxville: University of Tennessee Press, 2012), 125. Congress later extended this deadline.

20. Mohl, "Stop the Road," 692.

21. Robert Gioielli, *Environmental Activism and the Urban Crisis* (Philadelphia: Temple University Press, 2014), 77.

22. James Bailey, "How S.O.M. Took on the Baltimore Road Gang," *Architectural Forum*, March 1969, pp. 41–42; Giguere, "Never the Twain," 147–148.

23. Sidney Wong, "Architects and Planners in the Middle of a Road War: The Urban Design Concept Team in Baltimore, 1966–71," *Journal of Planning History* 12 (2012): 185.

24. Mohl, "Stop the Road," 680–681.

25. *Sun*, 28 April, 1 August 1967.

26. Quoted in Giguere, "Never the Twain," 149.

27. Gioielli, *Environmental Activism*, 77, 87.

28. Ibid., 81; Louise Campbell, "In Baltimore, New Options Are Opened and New Alliances Formed," *City* 2 (September/October 1968): 30–34.

29. Quoted in Gioielli, *Environmental Activism*, 75; "Position Statement," Relocation Action Movement, 16 January 1968, MAD Collection, ser. 7.

30. Quoted in Gioielli, *Environmental Activism*, 81; "Position Paper of the Harlem Park Neighborhood Council on the East-West Expressway," n.d., MAD Collection, ser. 7, box A7.

31. Community Information Office, Urban Design Concept Associates, n.d., MAD Collection, ser. 7, box A7; Bailey, "S.O.M. Took on the Road Gang," 43; Giguere, "Never the Twain," 110.

32. Emily Lieb, "White Man's Lane: Hollowing out the Highway Ghetto in Baltimore," in Jessica Elfinbein, Thomas Hollowak, and Elizabeth Nix (eds.), *Baltimore '68: Riots and Rebirth in an American City* (Philadelphia: Temple University Press, 2011), 63; Peter B. Levy, "The Dream Deferred: The Assassination of Martin Luther King, Jr., and the Holy Week Uprisings of 1968," in Elfinbein et al., *Baltimore '68*, 6–8.

33. *Baltimore Evening Sun*, 1 March 1968.

34. *Sun*, 11 February 1968.

35. "How Baltimore Fends off Riots," *Reader's Digest*, March 1968, pp.109–113.

36. Robert H. Osborne, "Report on Baltimore City Civil Disorder: Relief and Support Activities," 15 June 1968, pp. 3–4, BCA, D'Alesandro Administrative Files, folder 479(2).

37. Ibid., 11–15.

38. *Sun*, 25 November 1967.

39. Ibid., 23 March 1968.

40. Police Department, City of Baltimore, "1968 Riots," 13 April 1968, pp. 8, 12–13, 15, 18, Middle Atlantic Region, American Friends Service Committee, University of Baltimore, Langsdale Library, Special Collections, Baltimore '68; Jane Motz, "Report of Civil Disorders in Baltimore, April, 1968," n.d., ibid.

41. Police Department, "1968 Riots," 23.

42. Ibid., 16–19; Motz, "Civil Disorders in Baltimore," 8.

43. Motz, "Civil Disorders in Baltimore," 6.

44. *Sun*, 10 April 1968; Police Department, "1968 Riots," 44; Motz, "Civil Disorders in Baltimore," 14–18.

45. Quoted in *Schaefer*, 59.

46. *Sun*, 19 April, 9 May, 8 June 1968.

47. Reuben Jacobson to Commissioner Pomerleau, 11 July 1968, D'Alesandro Files, folder 38(3); Thomas Ward to Mayor D'Alesandro, 9 April 1968, ibid.

48. A transcript of Agnew's remarks appears in the *Sun*, 12 April 1968. As evidence that racial radicals had engineered the riot, Agnew cited reports that Stokely Carmichael had visited Baltimore shortly before the riot to confer with black militants. Carmichael did visit Baltimore

for about four hours, but on April 3—the day before the assassination of Martin Luther King.
The editor of the *Afro-American*, who had spent time with Carmichael on that day, denied that
he had met any militants; he had spent the afternoon with a female friend.

49. Eleanor N. Lewis to Mayor D'Alesandro, 10 May 1968, D'Alesandro Files, folder 38(3);
Sen. Verda Welcome to Mayor D'Alesandro, 19 April 1968, ibid.; NASW Letter to Maryland
Public Officials and Statement for Press Release, n.d., ibid., folder 479(1).

50. *Sun*, 13 April 1968.

51. Kenneth D. Durr, *Behind the Backlash: White Working-Class Politics in Baltimore, 1940–1980* (Chapel Hill: University of North Carolina Press, 2003), 144.

52. *Sun*, 6 December 1967, 23, 25, 30 June, 3, 7 July, 1, 6 October, 6, 8 December 1968.

53. Ibid., 4 August 1968; Giguere, "Never the Twain," 164.

54. *Sun*, 23 August 1968; Reutter, "Expressway Paper," 30.

55. Giguere, "Never the Twain," 151–155. The Fort McHenry Tunnel proposed by the team was
preceded by the Harbor Tunnel opened in 1957, connecting industrial Fairfield on the west with
industrial Canton on the east. It served as the harbor crossing for Baltimore's suburban Beltway
and did little to relieve traffic congestion in the city. Critics had noted this shortcoming when
the tunnel was still in the planning stage.

56. *Sun*, 25 September 1968; Reutter, "Expressway Paper," 30–32; Bailey, "S.O.M. Took on the
Road Gang," 44.

57. Giguere, "Never the Twain," 158; Wong, "Architects and Planners," 188; *Sun*, 22 December
1968.

58. Giguere, "Never the Twain," 157–158.

59. Ibid., 158; Reutter, "Expressway Paper," 34.

60. *Sun*, 13 October 1968; Matthew Crenson, *Survey of Organized Citizen Participation in Baltimore* (Baltimore: Urban Observatory, 1970), 140–141; "Renewing Rosemont Condemnation
Corridor," June 1970, D'Alesandro Files, folder 654(1).

61. *Sun*, 29 December 1968, 29 March 1976; [Baltimore] Department of Housing and Community Development and Urban Design Concept Associates, "Proposed Actions for Renewing
the Rosemont Condemnation Corridor," June 1970, D'Alesandro Files, folder 654(1).

62. Jan D. Bishop to D'Alesandro, 5 March 1969; Florence R. Bahr to D'Alesandro, 7 April
1969; and Virginia S. Park to D'Alesandro, 7 April 1969, D'Alesandro Files, folder 655(2).

63. Matthew A. Crenson, *Neighborhood Politics* (Cambridge, Mass.: Harvard University
Press, 1983), 244–245.

64. *Sun*, 23 May 1969.

65. Resident quoted in Crenson, *Neighborhood Politics*, 245; *Sun*, 22 February 1987; Neil
Friedman, "City Hall," *Baltimore Magazine*, November 1971, p. 18.

66. *Sun*, 26, 27 March 1969.

67. Ibid., 7 September, 8, 9, 24 October 1969, 25 March, 27 June 1970.

68. Ibid., 21 April 1971.

69. *Afro-American*, 9 March 1968; *Schaefer*, 63.

CHAPTER 37. BALTIMORE'S BEST

1. *Schaefer*, 43.

2. Ibid., 66–68; *Baltimore Sun*, 28 May 1967.

3. *Sun*, 15 May, 11 July 1971.

4. *Baltimore Afro-American*, 10 July 1971.

5. *Sun*, 23 June 1971.

6. G. James Fleming, *Baltimore's Failure to Elect a Black Mayor in 1971* (Washington, D.C.:
Joint Center for Political Studies, March 1972), 1:1.

7. Ibid., 4, 6.

8. Quoted in ibid., 8–9; *Sun*, 14, 15 September 1971.

9. *Sun*, 14 September 1971.

10. *Schaefer*, 80; Fleming, *Baltimore's Failure*, 5.

11. *Sun*, 6 October, 28 November 1971.

12. Mark K. Joseph to Robert Gilka and enclosure, 21 December 1972, BCA, William Donald Schaefer Mayoral Papers, box 33, Baltimore Industrial Development folder; Data on the Development of the Baltimore Industrial Development Corporation," n.d., ibid.; *Sun*, 20 April 1980.

13. *Sun*, 26 March 1972; *Schaefer*, 79.

14. Mark K. Joseph to Robert Hillman, Michael Kelly, Quentin Lawson, James Smith, "Monthly Outlines," 22 February 1972, Schaefer Papers, box 29, Cabinet Briefings folder.

15. *Schaefer*, 120.

16. *Sun*, 11 May 1911.

17. "Mayor's Cabinet," 14 March 1972, Schaefer Papers, box 29, Cabinet Briefings folder; "Functioning of the Mayor's Cabinet," n.d., ibid.; *Sun*, 15 March 1972. Creation of the cabinet was coupled with Schaefer's takeover of the Expenditure Control Committee, formed under Mayor D'Alesandro III but run by the outspoken city comptroller, Hyman Pressman. Pressman would continue as a member of the committee, but the city auditor—one of the comptroller's subordinates—would no longer serve on it. The mayor's new development coordinator and labor commissioner were added to the panel. Unnamed city hall sources claimed that reorganization of the committee was "a direct result of the deteriorating relationship between Mr. Schaefer and Mr. Pressman." *Sun*, 15 March 1972.

18. Special Tuesday Cabinet, 15 June 1976, Schaefer Papers, box 329.

19. Second Level Personnel Meeting, n.d., ibid., Maxi-Mini Cabinet folder; Second Level Personnel Agenda, 6 September 1973, ibid.; Richard Cole to Members of the Mayor's Cabinet, Executive "Swap," 10 September 1980, ibid., box 278, Cabinet Meetings folder.

20. First Meeting of the Mayor's Executive Cabinet, 2 February 1975, ibid., box 500, Memos/Personal/City Depts, Dec, 1975 and 1976 folder. The Maxi-Mini Cabinet seems to have been reborn in 1981 as the "Junior Executive Cabinet." See Submitted by the Mayor, "Jr. Executive Cabinet," n.d., ibid., box 730, Junior Executive Cabinet folder.

21. Joseph M. Coale to William Donald Schaefer, "Special Cabinet Meeting Format," 24 April 1976, ibid., box 500, Special Meeting Cabinet folder.

22. *Sun*, 3 February 1974.

23. Ibid., 18 May 1974.

24. Mayor Schaefer to As Listed, Mayor's Cabinet, Schaefer Papers, box 415, (Dept.) Discussion Cabinet (M.O.) folder; General Interest Cabinet Minutes, 10 July 1984, ibid.

25. Douglas S. Tawney, "Report from the Mayor's Cabinet Meeting," 1 June 1976, Schaefer Papers, box 329, Mayor's Cabinet and Special Cabinet folder.

26. Purchase of Service Proposal—Multi-Service Centers—and Addendum, 24 June 1974, ibid., box 29, Multi-Service Center folder.

27. Theodore J. Lowi, "Machine Politics—Old and New," *Public Interest*, no. 9 (Fall 1967): 89. On dispersion of the urban multitude, see also Matthew A. Crenson, "Urban Bureaucracy in Urban Politics: Notes toward a Developmental Theory," in J. David Greenstone (ed.), *Public Values and Private Power in American Politics* (Chicago: University of Chicago Press, 1982), 214–225.

28. *Schaefer*, 161.

29. Statement by Mayor William Donald Schaefer, Advertising Club of Baltimore, 25 October 1972, Schaefer Papers, box 52, Approachways to the City folder.

30. Sandy Hillman to All Media, "The 1974 Baltimore City Fair," ibid., box 111, Baltimore City Fair folder.

31. WBAL-TV, Editorial #57, 6 October 1972; Natalie Levy to Mayor Schaefer, 2 October 1972; and M. J. Brodie to Mayor Schaefer, "Citizens' Comments on Tape at City Fair," 26 September 1974, ibid., box 111, City Fair, 1972 folder.

32. Mayor's Statement to Department Heads, n.d., ibid., box 329, Maxi-Mini Cabinet inc. Mayor's Talks, 1973–74 folder.

33. *Sun*, 22 January, 18 December 1976, 4 August 1977.

34. Mark Joseph to As Listed, 5 February 1973, Schaefer Papers, box 329, Mayor's Cabinet, 12/72–12/73 folder.

35. Maxi-Mini Cabinet, 3 January 1974, ibid., Maxi-Mini Cabinet folder; Mayor's Office, "Human Resources Unit Bulletin," February–June 1977, ibid., box 255, Human Resources "Little Things Mean a Lot" folder.

36. *Sun*, 5, 30 May 1976, 18 April 1977.

37. *Schaefer*, 216.

CHAPTER 38. DRIVING THE CITY

1. Thomas P. Perkins III to Mayor Schaefer, 16 November 1971, BCA, William Donald Schaefer Mayoral Papers, box 117, East/West Expressway folder.

2. *Baltimore Sun*, 26 January 1972.

3. Douglas H. Haeuber, *The Baltimore Expressway Controversy: A Study of the Political Decision-Making Process* (Baltimore: Center for Metropolitan Planning and Research, Johns Hopkins University, 15 May 1974), 23–24; Charles L. Benton, "Report to the People: Highway Financing 1973–1978," 25 January 1972, p. 10, Schaefer Papers, box 64, Expressway Hearings, 1/25 & 1/27 (releases) folder.

4. Benton, "Report to the People," 9.

5. Citizens Planning and Housing Association, "Testimony of CPHA for the Baltimore City Council Regarding the Financing Plan for the Interstate System," for release 21 June 1973, University of Baltimore, Langsdale Library, Special Collections, Movement Against Destruction (MAD), ser. 6, Citizen, Community, and Organizational Statements folder, www.ubalt.libguides.com/MAD. The CPHA estimated that indirect costs of the expressway would add about 14 cents to the city's property tax rate.

6. Hugo O. Liem (Commissioner of Transit and Traffic) to Robert C. Embry, Jr., 11 March 1974, Schaefer Papers, box 117, East/West Expressway folder; *Sun*, 6 March 1974.

7. The Harbor Tunnel, completed in 1957, linked industrial Fairfield, west of the harbor, to industrial Canton, but ran some distance south and east of the city. It functioned primarily as a link in suburban Baltimore's beltway. See also "On the Road Again " in chapter 36.

8. *Baltimore Evening Sun*, 6 August 1971.

9. *Sun*, 5 April 1972, 11 February 1975; Haeuber, *Baltimore Expressway Controversy*, 59.

10. *Sun*, 11 February 1975.

11. Robert Gioielli, *Environmental Activism and the Urban Crisis* (Philadelphia: Temple University Press, 2014), 94–95.

12. Quoted in Matthew Crenson, *Neighborhood Politics* (Cambridge, Mass.: Harvard University Press, 1983), 243; Kenneth D. Durr, *Behind the Backlash: White Working-Class Politics in Baltimore, 1940–1980* (Chapel Hill: University of North Carolina Press, 2003), 156.

13. Haeuber, *Baltimore Expressway Controversy*, 61–62; Gioielli, *Environmental Activism*, 101.

14. *Sun*, 15, 16 December 1972.

15. Ibid., 19 January 1973, 30 June, 1 October 1975, 5 March 1977.

16. Ibid., 7, 8 December 1979, 6 May 1980.

17. Statement by Mayor William Donald Schaefer, the Advertising Club of Baltimore, 25 October 1972, Schaefer Papers, box 52, Approachways to the City folder; *Sun*, 12 September 1976.

18. Howell C. Baum, *Brown in Baltimore: School Desegregation and the Limits of Liberalism* (Ithaca, N.Y.: Cornell University Press, 2010), 217.

19. Ibid., 75–79.

20. *Sun*, 22 November 1966, 13 June 1973; *Adams v. Richardson*, 480 F. 2nd 1159, 156 US App. DC 267 (1972).

21. Baum, *Brown in Baltimore*, 151–152.

22. *Sun*, 24 June 1971.

23. James Zeller to Charles Benton, 11 July 1974, Schaefer Papers, box 305, Desegregation Material folder; Patterson to Board of Estimates, 14 August 1974, ibid., box 280, Desegregation folder. Patterson later submitted a significantly smaller request to the board of estimates in which he estimated the costs of desegregation at about $1.6 million.

24. *Sun*, 16, 24 March 1974; Baum, *Brown in Baltimore*, 126–128.

25. Durr, *Behind the Backlash*, 167.

26. *Sun*, 24, 25 May 1974. Schaefer had treated an African American school board member in a similar fashion when he failed to inform her that she was being replaced.

27. Ibid., 9 June 1974; Concerns of Black Citizens of Baltimore City, n.d., Schaefer Papers, box 325, Black Relations folder.

28. *Sun*, 11 July 1974.

29. Ibid., 12 May, 1 June 1975.

30. Ibid., 19 February, 26 June 1975.

31. Ibid., 15 September 1975.

32. Motion for the Appointment of an Administrative Law Judge, 5 May 1975, Schaefer Papers, box 280, Desegregation folder.

33. Statement by Mayor William Donald Schaefer Announcing Baltimore City Suit against the U.S. Department of Health, Education, and Welfare, 8 January 1977, ibid., Desegregation, Office of Civil Rights; Complaint for Declaratory Relief and for Preliminary and Permanent Injunction, ibid.; Baum, *Brown in Baltimore*, 195–201.

34. Marion Orr, *Black Social Capital: The Politics of School Reform in Baltimore, 1986–1998* (Lawrence: University Press of Kansas, 1999), 57–58.

35. *Schaefer*, 137.

36. Donald Norris, ""If We Build It, They Will Come! Tourism-Based Economic Development in Baltimore," in Dennis Judd (ed.), *The Infrastructure of Play: Building the Tourist City* (Armonk, N.Y.: M. E. Sharpe, 2003), 128; *Sun*, 12 July 1976.

37. Eugene Feinblatt to M. J. Brodie, 26 September 1977, Schaefer Papers, box 33, Inner Harbor, General folder; Zanvyl Krieger to Schaefer, 30 March 1977, ibid.

38. *Sun*, 1, 8 November 1978.

39. Ibid., 11 July 1979.

40. Orr, *Black Social Capital*, 58; Hal Reidl, "Don Schaefer's Town," *New Republic*, 25 November 1981, p. 27.

41. *Daily Record* (Maryland), 26 November 1976.

42. *San Francisco Sunday Examiner and Chronicle*, 22 August 1976; *New York Times*, 8 August 1976; *Wall Street Journal*, 10 February 1978.

43. Fred Kline, "Baltimore: The Hidden City," *National Geographic*, February 1975, pp. 188–213. Fitzgerald quoted (by Kline) from a letter to his friend and sometime secretary Laura Guthrie in 1935.

CHAPTER 39. TURNING POINT

1. *Baltimore Sun*, 25 November 1977, 15 July 1978, 28 May 1979.

2. Ibid., 17 December 1982.

3. *Baltimore Afro-American*, 7 October 1978; David O. Hash to Gloria DeBarry, 19 December 1984; Councilman Timothy D. Murphy to Bernard L. Berkowitz, 19 September 1984; and Berkowitz to Murphy, 2 October 1984, BCA, William Donald Schaefer Mayoral Papers, box 246, Beth. Steel Shipyard folder.

4. Berkowitz to Murphy, 2 October 1984; *Sun*, 22 September 1984.

5. Richard Swirnow to Mayor, 14 December 1984, Schaefer Papers, box 247, Beth. Steel

Shipyard folder; Malcolm Berman to Mayor, 15 December 1984, ibid.; *Sun*, 5 February 1986, 14 October 1987.

6. *Sun*, 24 July, 20 August, 14 September 1983; *Schaefer*, 223.

7. "A Perspective: The Black Community's Role in Baltimore City Politics (1960–1980)," fact sheet, Schaefer Papers, box 325, Black Relations folder.

8. COPE '83, "Objective: to Elect Black City Wide Officials," 31 July 1980, ibid.

9. *Sun*, 20 September 1982, 5 May 1983, 7 January 2005.

10. Ibid., 15 September 1983.

11. *Afro-American*, 19 October 1985.

12. *Daily Record* (Maryland), 26 November 1976.

13. Jon C. Teaford, *The Rough Road to Renaissance: Urban Revitalization in America, 1940–1985* (Baltimore: Johns Hopkins University Press, 1990), 160.

14. *Sun*, 13 April 1980; Fred Durr, "The Corporate Branch of Baltimore City's Government" (paper presented before the Baltimore City Council Policy and Planning Committee, 19 October 1981), 35.

15. *Sun*, 14 April 1980.

16. Ibid., 20 April 1980; Durr, "Corporate Branch."

17. *Sun*, 20 April 1980.

18. C. Fraser Smith, *Sun*, 13, 15 April 1980.

19. Ibid., 15, 16 April 1980.

20. Ibid., 15 April 1980.

21. Ibid., 18 April 1980; *Sun*, 21, 23 May 1982.

22. Smith, *Sun*, 13 April 1980.

23. *Sun*, 25 May 1982.

24. Ibid., 17 August 1982.

25. Burns became president of the city council when Walter Orlinsky was convicted of fraud and extortion for accepting money from companies seeking contracts to haul sludge from the city's sewer system. *Sun*, 23 October 1982.

26. Ibid., 15 September 1984; Richard Ben Cramer, "Can the Best Mayor Win?" *Esquire*, October 1984, p. 60.

27. Marc Levine, "Downtown Redevelopment as an Urban Growth Strategy: A Critical Appraisal of the Baltimore Renaissance," *Journal of Urban Affairs* 9 (June 1987): 103–123.

28. Bernard L. Berkowitz, "Rejoinder to Downtown Development as a Growth Strategy," *Journal of Urban Affairs* 9 (June 1987): 125–132.

29. Donald F. Norris, "If We Build It, They Will Come! Tourism-Based Economic Development in Baltimore," in Dennis R. Judd (ed.), *The Infrastructure of Play: Building the Tourist City* (Armonk, N.Y.: M. E. Sharpe, 2003), 140–142.

30. Peter L. Szanton, "Baltimore 2000" (report to the Morris Goldseker Foundation, 1986), 10, 12, 14–15.

31. *Schaefer*, 251, 262.

32. *Sun*, 8 February 1987.

33. *Washington Post*, 5 January, 22 June 1987.

34. *Afro-American*, 7 February 1987.

35. *Sun*, 25 November 1986, 8, 16 April, 5 July 1987.

36. Ibid., 3 June 1987.

37. Ibid., 4, 27, 29 March, 22 August 1987.

38. Ibid., 16 September 1987.

39. Ibid., 8 March 1987.

AFTERWORD: NOT YET HISTORY

1. *New York Times*, 10 May 2015.

2. Census Scope, "United States, Segregation: Dissimilarity Indices," www.censuscope.org; John R. Logan and Brian Stults, "The Persistence of Segregation in the Metropolis: New Findings from the 2010 Census," 24 March 2011, www.s4.brown.edu/us2010.

3. Alan Berube and Brad McDearman, "Good Fortune, Dire Poverty, and Inequality in Baltimore: An American Story," *The Avenue: Rethinking Urban America* (blog), 11 May 2015, www .brookings.edu/blogs/the-avenue/posts/2015/05/11-poverty-inequality-baltimore-berube -mcdearman; David Rusk, *Baltimore Unbound: A Strategy for Regional Renewal* (Baltimore: Abell Foundation, 1995)

4. Berube and McDearman, "Good Fortune, Dire Poverty"; *Washington Post*, 8 May 2015. In the economists' study, Baltimore was treated as a county because it is an independent municipality, not part of any county.

5. *Washington Post Wonkblog*, 7 May 2015.

6. *Baltimore Sun*, 23 March, 9 December 1987.

7. Marion Orr, *Black Social Capital: School Reform in Baltimore, 1986–1998* (Lawrence: University of Kansas Press, 1999), 123–125, 133.

8. *Sun*, 3 July 1988.

9. Ibid., 12, 16 December 1987, 8, 18 August, 14 September, 14 December 1988.

10. Ibid., 10, 15, 16 March, 30 May 1989, 1 August 1991.

11. Orr, *Black Social Capital*, 178–179.

12. *Sun*, 24 December 1990.

13. David Simon, "Crisis in BLUE," *Sun*, 6–9 February 1994.

14. *Baltimore Afro-American*, 1 December 1999.

15. *Detroit News*, 13 February 2000.

16. *Afro-American*, 10 June 1995; *Sun*, 30 March 1995.

17. Marion Orr, "The Struggle for Black Empowerment in Baltimore," in Rufus P. Browning, Dale Rogers Marshall, and David H. Tabb (eds.), *Racial Politics in American Cities*, 3rd ed. (New York: Addison Wesley Educational Publishers, 2003), 268–269.

18. Ibid., 269–270; *Sun*, 3 September 1999.

19. Orr, "Struggle for Black Empowerment," 269; *Sun*, 11 February 1997, 30 March 1998, 17 September, 21 December 1999.

20. See, for example, Bernard E. Harcourt, *Illusion of Order: The False Promise of Broken Windows Policing* (Cambridge, Mass.: Harvard University Press, 2001); Tanya Erzen, "Turnstile Jumpers and Broken Windows: Policing Disorder in New York City," in Andrea McArle and Tanya Erzen (eds.), *Zero Tolerance: Quality of Life and the New Police Brutality in New York City* (New York: New York University Press, 2001), 19–49.

21. Orlando Patterson, "The Real Problem with America's Inner Cities," *New York Times*, 9 May 2015.

22. Ta-Nehisi Coates, *Between the World and Me* (New York: Spiegel and Grau, 2015).

23. *Sun*, 5 June 2015.

24. Ibid., 11 March 2016.

THE PRINCIPAL SOURCES FOR THIS TEXT lie in the Baltimore City Archives, which contain a rich collection of town and municipal records. For political historians and political scientists, the most useful sections of the archives are the papers of the city council (Record Group 16) and the records of the city's mayors (Record Group 9).

Baltimore has given birth to dozens of newspapers, most of which lived only briefly. Some of the more durable are searchable online. The *Baltimore Sun* is especially useful because of its continuous publication from 1837 to the present. The *Baltimore Afro-American Ledger*, later the *Afro-American*, reports on the city's black community from 1892 to the present. William Goddard's *Maryland Journal and Baltimore Advertiser* (1773–1797) provides coverage of the revolutionary era, though plainly partisan. *Niles' Weekly Register* (1812–1837) was a national news magazine, published in Baltimore, that devoted particular attention to the city. The *Federal Gazette and Baltimore Daily Advertiser* (1795–1825) covers the era of the early Republic, and the *Baltimore Gazette and Daily Advertiser* (1826–1838) is useful for the age of the Jacksonians. Under varying titles, the *Baltimore Patriot* persisted from 1813 to 1859.

A variety of books and articles offer general treatments of Baltimore's political history; some of these proved essential for this book. J. Thomas Scharf's *Chronicles of Baltimore* (1874) and Thomas Griffith's *Annals of Baltimore* (1833) are obviously outdated, but they provide useful year-by-year summaries of local events in the eighteenth and nineteenth centuries. Scharf's *History of Baltimore City and County* (1881) is thematically organized and includes brief biographies of locally prominent persons, all of them white men. Wilbur Coyle's *First Records of Baltimore Town and Jones Town* (1905) preserves documents from earliest Baltimore, some of which are no longer preserved in the city's archives.

Sherry Olson's *Baltimore: The Building of an American City* (2nd ed., 1997) is a comprehensive account of the city's physical development, written by an urban geographer. Clayton Coleman Hall was the editor of

Baltimore: Its History and Its People (1912), a collection of essays organized chronologically, dealing with successive periods in the city's history.

Several histories of Maryland devote considerable attention to developments in Baltimore. In *Maryland: A History, 1632–1974* (1974), Richard Walsh and William Lloyd Fox brought together almost a dozen knowledgeable authors who contributed long, detailed essays on different periods and topics in the state's history. By far the most comprehensive history of Maryland is Robert J. Brugger's *Maryland: A Middle Temperament, 1634–1980* (1988), which devotes considerable attention to developments in Baltimore.

Books and dissertations provide extensive coverage of the run-up to the Revolution and the war itself. Though published 75 years ago, Charles Barker's *The Background of the Revolution in Maryland* (1940) remains essential. Ronald Hoffman's *A Spirit of Dissension: Economics, Politics, and the Revolution in Maryland* (1973) offers a perspective on revolutionary ferment in Maryland and Baltimore that takes account of both economic and ideological impulses toward independence. The most valuable study of the Revolution in Baltimore is Paul Kent Walker's "The Baltimore Community and the American Revolution" (PhD diss., University of North Carolina, 1973). In *The Mechanics of Baltimore* (1983), Charles Steffen presents an analysis of the Revolution as an episode of class politics. Philip Crowl's "Baltimore During and After the Revolution" (PhD diss., Johns Hopkins University, 1943) is helpful for understanding the Revolution's consequences for the city. The papers of the Purviance family, whose members played a significant role in orchestrating Baltimore's role in the Revolution, are in the library of the Maryland Historical Society.

On the early economic development of Baltimore Town, Pearle Blood's journal article "Factors in the Economic Development of Baltimore, Maryland" (*Economic Geography*, 1937) provides an overview. Jack Usher Mowll's "The Economic Development of Eighteenth Century Baltimore" (PhD diss., Johns Hopkins University, 1954) is a more extensive consideration of the subject, and David W. Livingood's *The Philadelphia-Baltimore Trade Rivalry, 1780–1860* (1947) traces the city's competition with its northern neighbor. Dennis Rankin Clark's "Baltimore, 1729–1829: The Genesis of a Community" (PhD diss., Catholic University, 1976) offers a more extensive overview of the period.

The contributions in Aubrey Land, Lois Green, and Edward Papenfuse's *Law, Society, and Politics in Early Maryland* (1977) include several valuable essays about Baltimore. Frank Cassell's "The Structure of Baltimore Politics in the Age of Jefferson, 1795–1812" is especially useful for its discussion of the city's affairs during the early Republic. Cassell's biography of Samuel Smith, *Merchant Congressman in the Young Republic* (1971), is a good treatment not only of Smith but of the city that produced him. Gary Lawrence Browne's *Baltimore in the Nation, 1789–1861* (1980) is an essential source that examines the intertwining of the city's politics and economy during the early Republic and up to the Civil War. Though it concentrates on the state, L. Marx Renzulli's *Maryland: The Federalist Years* (1972) also provides much useful material about Baltimore during the period.

The War of 1812 is a focal point for Baltimore history and its historians. The popular best-seller is *The Dawn's Early Light* (1972), by native Baltimorean Walter Lord. Cassell's biography of Samuel Smith devotes much of its attention to the war. *The Battle for Baltimore* (1997), by Joseph A. Whitehorn, provides a detailed account of the British attack and Baltimore's defense. Though published more than 100 years ago, William M. Marine's *The British Invasion of Maryland, 1812–1815* (1913) remains useful. The authoritative source on Baltimore's role as a port for privateers is Jerome R. Garitee's *The Republic's Private Navy* (1977). A perceptive analysis of the riot that followed the Madison administration's declaration of war is Paul Gilje's "The Baltimore Riots of 1812 and the Breakdown of the Anglo-American Riot Tradition" (*Journal of Social History*, 1980). The papers of Samuel Smith and his family are at the Library of Congress and available on microfilm through interlibrary loan. The bulk of the collection concerns family affairs, but a few pieces of correspondence deal with Smith's military role in the War of 1812.

By 1810, Baltimore was home to the largest population of free African Americans in the United States. Race and slavery, though seldom discussed in public, have been abiding concerns of the city's historians. Christopher Phillips's *Freedom's Port: The African American Community of Baltimore, 1790–1860* (1997) is a basic source on both free and enslaved black Baltimoreans. Ralph Clayton's *Slavery, Slaveholding, and the Free Black Population of Antebellum Baltimore* (1993) recognizes the different degrees of slavery in Baltimore, some of which verged on freedom. Leroy Graham's *Baltimore: The Nineteenth Century Black Capital* (1982) offers a fascinating account of the city's distinctive black community and the responses of white Baltimoreans to black aspirations. T. Stephen Whitman's *The Price of Freedom: Slavery and Manumission in Baltimore and Early National Maryland* (1997) details the processes by which the city and the state reduced their dependence on the peculiar institution. Barbara Jeanne Fields traces the evolution and disappearance of slavery in Maryland, and the aftermath for the state's free blacks, in *Slavery and Freedom on the Middle Ground: Maryland during the Nineteenth Century* (1985). T. Steven Whitman's *Challenging Slavery in the Chesapeake: Black and White Resistance to Human Bondage, 1775–1865* (2007) covers a long time and lots of territory—Maryland, Virginia, and Delaware.

Several of these studies of slavery and race also discuss the influential African Colonization Society based in Baltimore. Other works deal more exclusively with the movement. Robert Goodloe Harper's letter to Elias B. Caldwell, secretary of the American Colonization Society, printed as a pamphlet in 1818 by Baltimore publisher R. J. Matchett, served as the movement's guiding manifesto. The Maryland Historical Society holds the records of the Maryland State Colonization Society and the John H. B. Latrobe Family Papers, which include many items related to Latrobe's efforts on behalf of colonization. Eugene S. Van Sickle's "A Transnational Vision: John H. B. Latrobe and Maryland's Colonization Movement" (PhD diss., University of West Virginia, 2005) examines in detail Latrobe's labors in promoting colonization. Richard Hall's *On Afric's Shore: A History of Maryland in Liberia, 1834–1857* (2003) is a massive and detailed account of the experience of the colonists and organizers of Maryland's African outpost. Penelope Campbell offers a more compact treatment of the same subject in *Maryland in Africa: The Maryland State Colonization Society,*

1831–1837 (1971). For the colonization movement beyond Maryland, see Eric Burin, *Slavery and the Peculiar Solution* (2005), and P. J. Staudenreis, *The African Colonization Movement, 1816–1865* (1961).

Most antebellum Baltimoreans were convinced that the city's economic prospects rode on the B&O. James Dilts has written an authoritative and readable account of the B&O's beginnings, which ended more than a quarter century after their start. *The Great Road: The Building of the Baltimore and Ohio, the Nation's First Railroad, 1828–1853* (1993) covers the obstacles—physical, financial, and political—that the railroad had to overcome to span the territory from Pratt Street to the Ohio River. Edward Hungerford's two-volume history, *The Story of the Baltimore and Ohio Railroad* (1928), carries the story forward from triumph to bankruptcy and beyond, but tends to play down the rough patches such as the railroad's use of overvalued "railroad notes" to finance its construction and its increasingly predatory relationship with Baltimore. John F. Stover's *History of the Baltimore and Ohio Railroad* (1987) brings the story to a close with the B&O's absorption into CSX.

While the B&O was still struggling toward Harper's Ferry, Baltimore was solidifying its reputation as Mobtown. The Bank Riot of 1835 was just one of many upheavals of the Jacksonian era, but Robert E. Shalhope's *The Baltimore Bank Riot* (2009) emphasizes its ideological distinctiveness. In *American Mobbing, 1828–1861* (1998), David Grimsted discusses the riot's place in the civil disorders of the era and the succession of outbreaks that followed, including many precipitated by the followers of local fire companies and one by a nun who had escaped her convent. During the 1850s, the Know-Nothings' party would make collective violence a routine feature of local politics. William Evitts recounts its riotous rule in *A Matter of Allegiances: Maryland from 1854 to 1861* (1974). Jean Baker adds to his retelling in *Ambivalent Americans: The Know-Nothing Party in Maryland* (1977). But perhaps the most vivid close-up of Know-Nothing Baltimore is Tracy Matthew Melton's *Hanging Henry Gambrill: The Violent Career of Baltimore's Plug Uglies, 1854–1860* (2005). Frank Towers's *The Urban South and the Coming of the Civil War* (2004) situates Baltimore's Know-Nothings among others in the region.

When the Civil War came, Baltimore was where the killing began. Mayor George William Brown offered his version of what happened in *Baltimore and the Nineteenth of April, 1861* (1881), when a Massachusetts regiment headed for the defense of Washington was attacked on Pratt Street by a Baltimore mob. John Pendleton Kennedy's pamphlet *The Border States: Their Power and Their Duty in the Current Disordered Condition of the Country* (1861) is a notable expression of Baltimoreans' desperate effort to talk their way around the irrepressible conflict tearing apart their country and their city. Frank Towers's "Secession in an Urban Context: Municipal Reform and the Coming of the Civil War in Baltimore" is a politically astute analysis of local politics on the eve of the conflict; it appears in *From Mobtown to Charm City: New Perspectives on Baltimore's Past* (2002), edited by Jessica Elfenbein, John Breihan, and Thomas Hollowak.

Scott Sumpter Sheads and Daniel Carroll Toomey recount the city's experience of the war in *Baltimore during the Civil War* (1997). Jean Baker's *The Politics of Continu-*

ity: Maryland Political Parties from 1858 to 1870 (1973) is essential for understanding the transition from the era of the Know-Nothings and ethnics to the era of unionists and secessionists, and then to the politics of Republicans and Democrats. In a book and a series of essays published between 1941 and 1971, Charles Branch Clark devoted himself to the study of Baltimore politics during the war. One of his later efforts was "The Civil War," in *The Old Line State: A History of Maryland* (1971), edited by Morris Radoff. Richard R. Duncan's "The Era of the Civil War" is a helpful contribution to Walsh and Fox's *Maryland* (1974).

In addition to Baker's *Politics of Continuity*, several studies address the political recovery of Maryland and Baltimore after the Civil War. William Starr Myers's *The Maryland Constitution of 1864* (1901), published in the Johns Hopkins University Studies in Historical and Political Science series, explores the state's short-lived fundamental law that restricted and reshaped the electorate. Myers's *The Self-Reconstruction of Maryland, 1864–1867* (1909), published in the same series, covers the overthrow of wartime political restrictions and replacement of the 1864 constitution by the 1867 edition. Another important study of the postwar period is Charles L. Wagandt's "Redemption or Reaction? Maryland in the Post Civil War Years," in *Radicalism, Racism, and Party Realignment* (1969), edited by Richard O. Curry.

The political status of African Americans after emancipation was a fraught subject in postbellum Baltimore. William Paul Fuke traces these tensions in *Imperfect Equality: African Americans and the Confines of White Racial Attitudes in Post-Emancipation Maryland* (1999). Margaret Law Callcott covers some of the same ground in *The Negro in Maryland Politics, 1870–1912* (1969). William George Paul's "The Shadow of Equality: The Negro in Baltimore, 1864–1911" (PhD diss., University of Wisconsin, 1972) is one of a handful of studies to focus on postwar race relations in the city rather than the state. Bettye Collier Thomas discusses the emergence and political struggles of Maryland's first civil rights organization in "Harvey Johnson and the Mutual United Brotherhood of Liberty, 1885–1919," in *Black Communities and Urban Development in America* (1991), edited by Kenneth Kusmer.

Eleanor Bruchey offers a valuable account of an important phase in Baltimore's economic development during the Gilded Age in "The Industrialization of Maryland, 1860–1914," in Walsh and Fox's *Maryland* (1974). Jacob Hollander's *The Financial History of Baltimore* (1899) surveys municipal taxation, finance, and expenditure for the entire nineteenth century. Industrialization contributed to the emergence of an urban proletariat, which became violently visible in the railroad strike of 1877. Baltimore kicked off the strife with yet another riot. Philip Foner covers the national disorder in *The Great Labor Uprising of 1877* (1977). Robert V. Bruce has more to say about Baltimore's role in *1877: Year of Violence* (1959).

On nineteenth-century politics, *Sun* columnist Frank Kent provided an insider's perspective in *The Story of Maryland Politics* (1911). On the rise and decline of Baltimore's Democratic boss, Mary Anne Dunn presented a rare overview in "The Life of Isaac Freeman Rasin" (MA thesis, Catholic University of America, 1948). M. Rosewin Sweeney did the same for Rasin's chief lieutenant in " 'Sonny' Mahon and Baltimore's Irish Machine" (MA thesis, Johns Hopkins University, 1979).

In John R. Lambert's biography *Arthur Pue Gorman* (1953), readers meet Rasin's partner in "the Ring." S. Z. Ammen's "History of Baltimore, 1875–1895," in Hall's *Baltimore* (1912), is an overview of the period by a Confederate veteran who lived through all of it.

James B. Crooks presents a comprehensive account of Baltimore's reformers and their efforts to oust the bosses in *Politics and Progress: The Rise of Urban Progressivism in Baltimore, 1895 to 1911* (1968), and Eric Goldman offers a profile of one of the leading reformers in *Charles J. Bonaparte, Patrician Reformer: His Earlier Career* (1943). John M. Powell's "History of Baltimore, 1870–1912," in Hall's *Baltimore* (1912), recounts the reformers' struggles for electoral reform, their new city charter, and the early campaign for female suffrage and a nonpartisan civil service, along with the Republican electoral sweep of 1895 that seemed to bring all of these objectives within reach.

The fire that destroyed much of downtown Baltimore in 1904 opened the way for progressive reform and business-backed economic development. The conflagration itself receives thorough treatment in Peter B. Peterson's *The Great Baltimore Fire* (2004). Its exploitation by progressives and boosters is the chief concern in Christine Meisner Rosen's "Business, Democracy, and Progressive Reform in the Redevelopment of Baltimore after the Great Fire of 1904" (*Business History Review*, 1989). James B. Crooks concentrates on similar developments in "The Baltimore Fire and Baltimore Reform" (*Maryland Historical Magazine*, 2005). Alan D. Anderson sees the fire as one episode that paved the way for upgrading the city's aging infrastructure, in *The Origin and Resolution of an Urban Crisis: Baltimore, 1890–1930* (1977).

Another dimension of progressive reform — the battle against urban vice — is treated in Jayme Rae Hill's "From the Brothel to the Block: Politics and Prostitution in Baltimore during the Progressive Era" (MA thesis, University of Maryland Baltimore County, 2008). A more lengthy treatment of the subject is Lauren Silberman's *Wicked Baltimore: Charm City Sin and Scandal* (2011). Pamela Haag focuses on the vulnerability of the female labor force in "Commerce in Souls: Vice, Virtue, and Women's Wage Work in Baltimore, 1900–1915" (*Maryland Historical Magazine*, 1991).

The campaign against vice raged alongside an even fiercer assault on intemperance. Evan Andrew Rea documents Baltimore's lukewarm reception of Prohibition in "The Prohibition Era In Baltimore" (MA thesis, University of Maryland Baltimore County, 2005). Michael Thomas Walsh extends the scope of inquiry beyond Baltimore to Maryland in "Wet and Dry in the 'Land of Pleasant Living': Baltimore, Maryland, and the Policy of National Prohibition, 1913–1933" (PhD diss., University of Maryland Baltimore County, 2012). Thomas R. Pegram sets Maryland's temperance movement against the background of the American South in "Temperance Politics and Regional Political Culture: The Anti-Saloon League in Maryland and the South, 1907–1915" (*Journal of Southern History*, 1997).

In Baltimore, progressivism was yoked to racism. The city's most overtly racist policy was a residential segregation law first passed in 1910. Garrett Power deals with the impetus, evolution, and enactment of the segregationist policy in "Apartheid

Baltimore Style: The Residential Segregation Ordinances of 1910–1913" (*Maryland Law Review*, 1983). Gretchen Boger examines the social context that lay behind the law in "The Meaning of Neighborhood in the Modern City: Baltimore's Residential Segregation Ordinances, 1911–1913" (*Journal of Urban History*, 2009). Antero Pietela, in his book *Not in My Neighborhood: How Bigotry Shaped a Great American City* (2010), places the ordinance near the root of modern segregation in Baltimore.

A bleak assessment of the city's domination by Annapolis is given by Horace Edgar Flack in "The Government of the City of Baltimore and Its Relationship to the State Government," in *The Government of a Great American City* (1935), edited by Frederick P. Stieff. State government was notably obstructive in Baltimore's last successful annexation of suburban territory in 1918. Joseph L. Arnold examined this change in the city boundaries and all the previous expansions in "Suburban Growth and Municipal Annexation in Baltimore, 1745–1918" (*Maryland Historical Magazine*, 1978). Arnold also wrote a superb summary of city politics in the years that followed: "The Last of the Good Old Days: Politics in Baltimore, 1920- 1950" (*Maryland Historical Magazine*, 1976).

The interwar years are covered in Dorothy Brown's essay "Baltimore between the Wars," in Walsh and Fox's *Maryland* (1974). Edwin Rothman follows the career of a key political actor and the organization he helped to disrupt in "Factional Machine-Politics: William Curran and the Baltimore City Democratic Party Organization, 1929–1946" (PhD diss., Johns Hopkins University, 1949). Shannon Lee Parsley discusses the reorientation of the party in "Presidential Politics and the Building of the Roosevelt Coalition in Baltimore City, 1924–1936" (MA thesis, University of Maryland Baltimore County, 2001), and Jo Ann Argersinger's *Toward a New Deal in Baltimore: People and Government in the Great Depression* (1988) is an unrivaled account of economic crisis and recovery in the city.

In Baltimore, the Depression produced racial protest as well as support for the New Deal. Genna Rae McNeil writes about the crucial role played by the NAACP's Youth Forum in "Youth Initiative in the African American Struggle for Racial Justice and Constitutional Rights: The City-Wide Young People's Forum of Baltimore, 1931–1941." She and John Hope Franklin edited *African Americans and the Living Constitution* (1995), in which her essay appears. Andor Skotnes links black activism to the local labor movement in "The Black Freedom Movement and the Workers Movement in Baltimore, 1930–1939" (PhD diss., Rutgers University, 1991). Larry Gibson's *Young Thurgood: The Making of a Supreme Court Justice* (2012) is a well-told story of the young attorney's participation in the "Buy Where You Can Work" campaign and his subsequent program of litigation to achieve equal rights for Maryland's African Americans. David Taft Terry extends the narrative of racial injustice and protest through World War II and up to the *Brown* decision in " 'Tramping for Justice': Dismantling Jim Crow in Baltimore, 1942–1954" (PhD diss., Howard University, 2002).

George H. Callcott's *Maryland and America, 1940–1980* (1985) is not just a summary of what happened during those 40 years but an analysis of the state's "four cultures," one of which inhabits Baltimore. Baltimore's racial struggles, population loss, economic decline, and urban renewal account for well over one-fourth of this wide-ranging study. Other writers concentrate on just one of these topics. Martin Millspaugh's edited collection *Baltimore's Charles Center: A Case Study of Downtown Renewal* (1964) deals with the centerpiece of the city's campaign to rejuvenate its central business district. David A. Wallace focuses on Baltimore's signature project to renew its waterfront in "An Insider's Story of the Inner Harbor" (*Planning*, 1979). Renewal of the city's housing stock is the subject of W. Theodore Durr's "The Conscience of a City: A History of the Citizens Planning and Housing Association and Efforts to Improve Housing for the Poor in Baltimore, Maryland, 1937–1954" (PhD diss., Johns Hopkins University, 1972).

Though the city's school board acted promptly to comply with court-mandated school integration, it did not succeed in resolving the issue. Howell Baum's *Brown in Baltimore: School Desegregation and the Limits of Liberalism* (2010) is an insightful treatment of the city's largely unsuccessful efforts to achieve racial balance in the schools and to fend off federal sanctions. In *The Politics of School Desegregation* (1969), Robert L. Crain includes a chapter on Baltimore that demonstrates how sharply the city's response to the *Brown* decision differed from the reactions of the other cities in Crain's study. Marion Orr reviews Mayor Kurt Schmoke's school improvement initiatives in *Black Social Capital: The Politics of School Reform in Baltimore, 1986–1998* (1999).

Racial tensions were not confined to schools. C. Fraser Smith documents other eruptions of the race issue in *Here Lies Jim Crow: Civil Rights in Maryland* (2008). Baltimore's poverty program is the chief subject of *Power and Poverty: Theory and Practice* (1970), by Peter Bachrach and Morton Baratz, but the book also addresses the city's attempts to subdue the issue of race. Louis C. Goldberg recounts similar efforts in "CORE in Trouble: A Social History of the Organizational Dilemmas of the Congress of Racial Equality Target City Project in Baltimore, 1965–1967" (PhD diss., Johns Hopkins University, 1970). Kenneth Durr executes a rare (and successful) portrayal of Baltimore whites who were confronted with black demands in *Behind the Backlash: White Working-Class Politics in Baltimore, 1940–1980* (2003).

Along with most other cities, Baltimore finally had a race riot in 1968. Peter B. Levy follows its course in "The Dream Deferred: The Assassination of Martin Luther King, Jr., and the Holy Week Uprisings of 1968." Emily Lieb traces the intrusion of the race issue into Baltimore's highway projects in "White Man's Lane: Hollowing out the Highway Ghetto in Baltimore." Both essays appear in *Baltimore '68: Riot and Rebirth in an American City* (2011), edited by Jessica Elfinbein, Thomas Hollowak, and Betsy Nix.

Baltimore's expressway program was controversial quite apart from its impact on African American residents. One of the most thorough accounts of the road war is Andrew Giguere's "And Never the Twain Shall Meet" (MA thesis, Ohio University, 2008). Battles between architects and highway engineers figure prominently in James Bailey's "How S.O.M. Took on the Baltimore Road Gang" (*Architectural Forum*, 1969) and Sidney Wong's "Architects and Planners in the Middle of a Road War: The Urban Design Concept Team in Baltimore, 1966–71" (*Journal of Planning History*, 2012). Raymond Mohl situates Baltimore's highway fight in the national uprising against urban expressways in "Stop the Road: Freeway Revolts in American Cities" (*Journal of Urban History*, 2004).

William Donald Schaefer: A Political Biography (1999), by C. Fraser Smith, is essential for understanding Baltimore's "renaissance." The reality of the renaissance has been a subject of debate. Marc Levine and Bernard L. Berkowitz, Schaefer's development coordinator, debate its success in Levine's "Downtown Redevelopment as an Urban Growth Strategy" (*Journal of Urban Affairs*, 1987). Two city foundations have sponsored critical assessments of the city's status. Peter L. Szanton's "Baltimore 2000" (report for the Morris Goldseker Foundation, 1988) introduced a phrase that entered local discourse—"the rot beneath the glitter," a suggestion that Mayor Schaefer's triumphs of urban redevelopment were only skin-deep. David Rusk's *Baltimore Unbound: A Strategy for Regional Renewal* (sponsored by the Abell Foundation, 1995), raised the possibility that the city might be too far gone to recover and might drag its suburbs down as it collapsed.

Page numbers in *italics* refer to illustrations.